THE TALENTED MISS HIGHSMITH

ALSO BY JOAN SCHENKAR

Truly Wilde: The Unsettling Story of Dolly Wilde, Oscar's Unusual Niece

Signs of Life: Six Comedies of Menace

THE TALENTED
MISS HIGHSMITH

THE SECRET LIFE AND SERIOUS ART
OF PATRICIA HIGHSMITH

Joan Schenkar

ST. MARTIN'S PRESS ✸ NEW YORK

FRONTISPIECE: Patricia Highsmith, portrait by Ruth Bernhard, 1948 (Collection Ruth Bernhard)

www.stmartins.com

Design by Kelly Too

LIBRARY OF CONGRESS CATALOGING-IN-PUBLICATION DATA

Schenkar, Joan.
  The talented Miss Highsmith : the secret life and serious art of Patricia Highsmith / Joan Schenkar.—1st ed.
      p.   cm.
  Includes bibliographical references.
  ISBN 978-0-312-30375-4
  1. Highsmith, Patricia, 1921–1995. 2. Authors, American—20th century—Biography.
3. Bisexuals—United States—Biography. I. Title.
  PS3558.I366Z87 2009
  813'.54—dc22
  [B]

                                                                        2009018363

For my mother

MARLENE VON NEUMANN SCHENKAR

With love and gratitude

· CONTENTS ·

There may be the girl waiting, the kiss in the dark, the whispered word of promise, the sun in the park or the swans on the lake, the job for me and the job for him and for him, the flag waving bold and free forever, and over and over again the handsome boy meeting lovely girl and all the lovely love pursued and captured. It might all be for the best. . . . but I don't see it that way. I never will. I just don't see it that way.

—PATRICIA HIGHSMITH, 1942

It is terrible to have the life of another person attached to one's own like a bomb which one holds in one's hands, unable to get rid of it without committing a crime.

—MARCEL PROUST, *THE CAPTIVE & THE FUGITIVE*

· A NOTE ON BIOGRAPHY ·

She wasn't nice.

She was rarely polite.

And no one who knew her well would have called her a generous woman.

What Patricia Highsmith was—apart from an outsider artist of exceptional gifts—is something like the negative of an old photograph, with all the black parts white and all the white ones black. Lady Diana Cooper said the same thing about Evelyn Waugh.

"I don't see it that way. I never will. I just don't see it that way," Pat Highsmith wrote in 1942 at twenty-one, as plainly as she could. Plain speech was her usual style, and what she didn't see was the way other people pictured the world. So in the acid bath of her detail-saturated prose she developed her own image of an alternate earth—Highsmith Country. A territory so psychologically threatening that even her most devoted readers hope never to recognize themselves in its pages.

Her slow literary crawl over the surface of things produced one iconic character, the talented Mr. Ripley, and hundreds of raspingly acute portraits of quietly transgressive acts. The toxic brilliance of their trail goes on glowing long after their author—as cruel to her characters as Henry James was to his—has dispatched her perpetrators to their nasty fictional ends.

Miss Highsmith's own end was a model of clarity. She drove a last, devoted visitor from her hospital room—"You should go, you should go, don't stay, don't stay," she repeated until the woman left—and then died unobserved.[1] Everything human was alien to her.

Colliding with American popular culture like one of those speeding trains on which her sublimely indifferent characters carry out so many of their (and her) casual executions, Pat Highsmith—an accomplished, original, immensely alluring twenty-nine-year-old with murder on her mind—saw her first novel, *Strangers on a Train* (1950), made into a feature film by Alfred Hitchcock in 1951. That book posed what was to become the quintessential Highsmith situation: two men bound together psychologically by the stalker-like fixation of one upon the other, a fixation that always involved a disturbing, implicitly homoerotic fantasy. Nothing, it turns out, could have been more American.

Her second, pseudonymous work, *The Price of Salt* (1952), was so marked by her secret obsessions that writing it felt like a birthing. "Oh god," she enthused, "how this story emerges from my own bones!"[2] In it, she mixed images reminiscent of Grimm's fairy tales and *Lolita* (three years *before* Nabokov published his masterpiece) with a luminous halo of incest and a little light pedophilia to bring to an eager and (mildly) misled public the novel they read as the first popular narrative of successful lesbian love. *The Price of Salt* sold hundreds of thousands of copies and made Patricia Highsmith uneasy all her life.

And that was only the beginning of her career.

There is an avalanche of available information about Patricia Highsmith, and the most useful part of it—if certain necessary correctives are applied—is furnished by Highsmith herself. Fascinated by concealment in general (snails were her favorite mollusc) and silent about her own complicated life in particular ("I don't answer personal questions about myself or other people"), she nevertheless repeated the fatal flaw that hobbled every one of her "criminal-heroes" except Tom Ripley: she ratted herself out every chance she got. Her pitiless self-exposures in her notebooks and diaries—slightly compromised by the ice-cold glances she darted towards posterity while making them—have preserved for us what is probably the longest perp walk in American literary history.

Doggedly, religiously, and in eight thousand pages of work she showed to no one, she set down her states of mind, the color of her current lover's hair, the quality of a past relationship, the cost of a Paris hotel breakfast, the number of rejections she received from publishers, the fees, the fears, the falsehoods— as well as thousands of pages of notes for stories, novels, poems, and critical articles.

She told what she knew (but by no means *everything* she knew),[3] and she told it in a far more direct and forthcoming voice than the low, flat, compellingly psychotic murmur she tended to use for her fictions. She makes it easy for us to be ravished by her romances, sullied by her prejudices, shocked by her crimes of the heart, appalled by the corrosive expression of her hatreds. But her long testimony in the witness stand of her notebooks, and in the jury box and judge's chair of her diaries, is far more revealing than anything anyone else has written or said about her.

In her teens and in her twenties Pat read obsessively, using books, she said, as a "drug."[4] But "being influenced" to her meant reading the writers who confirmed her own instincts. Inspired by Dostoyevsky (but not in ways that are usually ascribed to her: half her attraction to his work was his struggle with Christianity, which, she wrote, "was more exciting, dangerous, and horrifying than any murder story he ever invented"),[5] she was also compelled by the cruder psychocategories of Karl Menninger and Richard von Krafft-Ebing. And she found some of her strongest validation in the work of male homosexual novelists.*

It was Proust, after all, who wrote that neurosis gives plot to life, and Pat's own plot, like that of most of her characters, was founded on repetition. She did the same things over and over again. For variation, she tried to do them all at once.

In her fictions, in her facts, and in her affections, Patricia Highsmith, like all obsessive artists, circled around the same coordinates, the same grievances, the same inspirations. Each of her love affairs has its elements of identity with each of her other love affairs. (She dedicated the manuscript version of *Strangers on a Train* to "all the Virginias" because she had slept with several women named Virginia, then slyly changed the paperback dedication to "all the Virginians.") All of her novels have their similar themes. No writer has ever savored the pains or suffered the pleasures of repetition more than she did.

Nothing in this operating principle makes Highsmith a very good subject for traditional, chronological biography. A time line drawn from her orphan-with-parents childhood in Fort Worth, Texas, to her highly public

---

* Of the expatriate American writer Julien Green, whose roots were also Southern and whose religious and sexual preoccupations were as guilty as hers, Pat wrote: "I feel a rare friendship with J. Green. . . . I recognize my own thoughts [in his]." In *The Counterfeiters* of André Gide she saw her own transgressive fascination with the young—along with new ways to represent it. Oscar Wilde's mannered dialogues and capsizing paradoxes were little mirrors for the girl who thought the "words 'average' and 'normal' . . . the most ridiculous of the English language." Henry James gave her the opportunity of a lifetime: she turned his central premise in *The Ambassadors* upside down (the only way she could imagine it) and smuggled it into *The Talented Mr. Ripley*. And in Marcel Proust's resplendent monologues and shimmering sense-memories (she understood just enough of Proust to quote him appropriately) Pat found the explanation for her love life.

and well-attended funeral in Tegna, Switzerland, cannot begin to account for the perversities which hover so persistently at the borders of her writing, or the dazzling doubles act lodged at the dead center of her artistic life. Emotional memory was what lit up Pat's work and darkened her days, and emotional memory rarely wears a watch or walks a straight line.

The "truth" of Pat's life—the deeply eccentric swings and swerves and reversals that make her mind almost mappable and her work always recognizable—is misrepresented by the long lines of dates and hours, the crisp lists of appointments and appearances, the solid sense of case histories completed, that make chronological biography such conventional reading—and such conventional comfort, too. Except in her aspirations, Pat Highsmith was never a conventional woman—and never, *ever* a conventional writer.

Pat used her own lists of dates and data defensively, as imaginary train tracks on which she could run her valiant Little Engine of Ambition and Accomplishment towards a brighter future: a future in which—for she always tried to be a practical woman—she had long since ceased to believe. Chronology was one of her favorite forms of "misdirection."* She employed it to beguile herself into doing the one thing she continued to value: pulling herself "forward" with her work. And so she went on recording the hours, the days, and the years of her life—and measuring, weighing, and counting up everything else.

But Time—that cruel professor whose students never leave the classroom alive—didn't have much to teach Pat Highsmith. Neither her writing nor her approach to living ever "developed" or "matured." (Oscar Wilde said that only mediocrities develop.) She was what she was from the start: fixing her implacable hatred of her stepfather at three and a half years, her sense of her sexuality at six, and the "betrayal" that altered her life at twelve. Her imagination was similarly marked. "The Heroine," the story she wrote at twenty about a disturbed young helper who sets the family house on fire so she can "rescue" the children in her care, was so fully developed (and so good) that she came to regard it as the "curse" which overshadowed her work for the next ten years.

Virginia Woolf, whose novel *The Waves* Pat once hoped to imitate, called biography "a bastard, an impure art," and reckoned that the best way to write a life "would be to separate the two kinds of truths": the "husk" (the facts), and the "atom" (the inner life of the subject). There should be, Woolf thought, a list

---

* Pat often recorded events days and weeks after they had passed, pretending in her diaries and cahiers that her entries were "current." They weren't. She forged her chronologies to give order to her life, altering the record of her life and the purport of her writing by doing so.

of the "facts" set down "in order" and then there should be the "life," written as "fiction."[6] Between Pat Highsmith's conviction that dark forces in her "blood" were directing her life (and that even darker forces in her subconscious were shaping her art), and her attempts to control those forces by list making, diagramming, and compulsive counting, she managed to live out Virginia Woolf's two kinds of "truth" every day.

In life *or* art, Highsmith Country always required plotting. It was a rare Highsmith letter that didn't arrive with a map, or a list, or with several intricate calculations involving numbers punctuating its text. And both Pat and her fictional doubles had their own special fun with graphic design: they drew and painted, devised buildings and books, collected art (and counterfeited it, too), and ordered their lives with lists. Although her mind always worked by intense and repetitive associations, Pat's eyes and her images inched over ordinary surfaces and wrapped themselves around architectural shapes and volumes. In many of her novels, she built the "strong" houses she yearned for in life—and then took the fictional trouble to furnish them. She liked to run her attention over the gear, tackle, and trim of different kinds of work, and some of her objections to women came from her fascination with tools and trades. "It is difficult for me to understand women because they have no jobs," she wrote.[7]

But more than almost anything else, she loved to draw up and pore over maps, charts, plans, lists, and diagrams—and the history of her imagination cannot be told without them.

And so, inspired by both Virginia Woolf and Patricia Highsmith, I have tried to put Pat's solid specifics—what Virginia Woolf would have called her "husk"—into the appendices of *The Talented Miss Highsmith*. Here you will find "Just the Facts," the first fully annotated chronology of her life and work. Its pages of dates, places, and times are Pat's "cover story." Here, too, is "Patricia Highsmith's New York," a map/list/chart/diagram on which the addresses of her New York life are cross-referenced with the coordinates of her New York fictions. Mapping the ways Pat's real life coincided with her imaginary one produced the blueprint of a heart that never really left its home: Pat went right on murdering her fictional victims and lodging her fictional murderers at every single New York City address where she or her lovers had once lived.

Other diagrams important to Pat are also in the appendices: a chilling chart she made in 1945 that ranks and compares her girlfriends; an astrological calculation drawn up by a close friend in 1973; a plan of the house in which she spent the six most important years of her life; a storyboard she created for a Fawcett comic book Superhero during the 1940s when she was the most consistently employed female scriptwriter in the Golden Age of American Comics.

The appendices make Pat's designs for living—her dates and her data, her charts and her plans, the "husk" of her existence—instantly available for reference. And they free up the rest of the book to tell how she *really* lived her life.

Obsession, and the repeated themes and metaphors and intense relations that organize it, is a much better way to think about the overheated connections between Patricia Highsmith's living and her writing, and between her writing and her life. "No use looking for one's self in a static condition, surrounded by the things, attitudes, people one thinks of. . . . The living self," she wrote, "is always in flux."[8] Her "living self" *was* in flux—and repeating it was how she channelled the flow.

"Obsessions are the only things that matter," she wrote. "Perversion interests me most and is my guiding darkness."[9] And as the material of her obsessions migrates from one of the forms she mined so diligently to another; as it is added into her writer's notebooks, multiplied by her diaries, and divides itself throughout her fictions, the twists, the turns, and the abrupt and shocking changes of this essential stuff of her imagination give a fascinating and unprecedented moving picture—more like a film than a document—of the mind of a writer at work.

For much of her life, Patricia Highsmith was an improbably tough woman (and not just tough, but "Texas tough," says her legendary American editor Larry Ashmead) with an impossibly sore center. Early and late, the hopes of many friends and lovers foundered on that adamantine shell of hers. What they saw beneath it, if they even *got* beneath it, was usually more than they could handle. But Pat could handle it, and she handled it with fortitude.

Although nearly every letter she wrote was topped and tailed with racking complaints about the "people, places and things" (a favorite category in her writer's notebooks) that seemed to be conspiring expressly against *her;* although she vacillated between deep trances of desire and the even deeper desire to rip her trances to ribbons; although she was preoccupied with personal, psychological problems as richly detailed as those exhibited by Dostoyevsky's "half-mad" postulants pacing the icy streets of St. Petersburg; nevertheless Pat Highsmith managed to get on very well with her business of writing six, seven, and eight pages a day. "Just now I am working on ONE play . . . also on a novel, of which I've written 160 pages in a month, a normal rate—40 pages per week, but it takes a bit out of one."[10]

"My obsession with duality saves me from a great many other obsessions," she observed with her customary practicality.[11] And she always knew *why* she was writing: "Every artist is in business for his health."[12]

Pat developed a method—it was deceptively simple—which allowed her to shut out the world and get on with her work: "I stand up from my desk and try to pretend I am not me."[13] In the notebook to which she would add the name of the woman she had just fallen in love with to a list of the places she had just visited (as though her new love were a destination all its own), Pat observed:

"There isn't any constant personality for the writer, the face, with which he meets his old friends or strangers. He is always part of his characters, or he is simply in a good or bad mood, one day and another."[14]

Her mother, Mary, thought acting should have been Pat's real vocation. It wasn't a compliment. Pat thought exactly the same thing of Mother Mary—but without the vocation. "She wants attention like an actress," Pat noted when Mary, languishing in a nursing home in Texas, was costing her a little extra in adult diapers.[15] Mother and daughter knew each other too well for courtesy and loved each other too much for comfort.

Never an easy woman to live with, Patricia Highsmith gave me the same hard time she gave to anyone who tried to enter her life with the intention of getting too close or learning too much. Perhaps my time with her was a little harder because I know some of the people Pat knew,* live in some of the places she lived in, and belong to several of the groups (four of them, if you're counting as compulsively as Pat always counted) she spent the last part of her life reviling with such gusto.

Still, I'd read her fictions before investigating her facts, so I thought I understood what I was in for: years of intensely interesting, often excruciating work focused on a woman who seemed to be the sole curator of a Museum of Twentieth-Century American Maladies.[16] Nothing I found—or found out—during the past seven years has altered this first impression.

There may be many reasons to set down the life of Mary Patricia Highsmith, but this one is mine: to try to catch (and in catching, to try to think about)[17] the constant shifting of identities—from the writer at the desk to the woman who got up from it; from the intensely divided personality to the symbolic steps it took to relieve itself of its burdens—that created the consistency, the fierce peculiarity, and the weird, gravelled originality of her work.

In doing so, I have had to innovate the form of her biography in order not to violate the substance of her life. Obsession—the obsessions that governed

---

* A single example: One of my play agents now deceased—a brilliant, elderly, dignified woman when I knew her in the 1980s—had been, unknown to me, a lover of Patricia Highsmith four decades before she became my agent. And one sunny afternoon in the Swiss Literary Archives in Bern, I opened a Highsmith diary at random and found the richly explicit physical details of their torrid love affair. It's a description I still look forward to forgetting.

her life and inspired her writing—will be the organizing principle of this work.

Several pseudonyms for people close to Patricia Highsmith have been used throughout this book. Although their names have been altered, their testimonies are presented exactly as they were given to me. In the delicate balance of competing truths that biography is always on the verge of upsetting, both the living and the dead deserve a little protection from each other. A pseudonym— the kind of small forgery Pat herself gleefully committed when she wanted to cover her tracks *and* speak her mind—allows these crucial witnesses to tell their stories for the first time.

In her only formal attempt to explain the way she worked, *Plotting and Writing Suspense Fiction* (1965), Pat wrote that she liked to start her novels with a "slow, even tranquil beginning . . . in which the reader becomes thoroughly acquainted with the hero-criminal and the people around him." And that's how I'll begin her story. But the fact that she could reverse herself in her very next sentence—"But there is no law about this, and in *The Blunderer* I started out with a sharp bang"—is exactly what *The Talented Miss Highsmith* is all about.

—Joan Schenkar
Paris
Bern
Greenwich Village

· 1 ·

HOW TO BEGIN

PART I

No writer would ever betray his secret life, it would be like standing naked in public.

—**Patricia Highsmith**, 1940

What was difficult was you never saw her alone, in her normal routine, because the moment you were there, she was a different person.

—**Barbara Roett**, in conversation with the author

AN ORDINARY DAY*

On 16 November 1973, a damp, coldish breaking day in the tiny French village of Moncourt, France, Patricia Highsmith, a fifty-two-year-old American writer living an apparently quiet life beside a branch of the Loing Canal,

---

* Previously unseen and unpublished material from friends, family, lovers, photographers, and filmmakers allows us to join Patricia Highsmith in this chapter in both the physical act of writing and in language which reflects some of the secrets of her style: her coroner's eye for detail, her hyperconsciousness of the ways human activity can be enumerated, and the high optical refractions she was able to scan into her mostly plain prose.

At twenty, while Pat was still passionate about other people's writing—and still mixing her metaphors the way a novice bartender might mix her liquors—she dreamt of doing the same thing: "If we were permitted one quarter hour in Shakespeare's study in 1605, how we should watch his every movement, how hungrily we should notice the lift of his head, the touch of his hand on the edge of his paper . . . the angle of his back as he writes. . . . How little we know of history. Time is a column of carbon monoxide fraying into oblivion at its far end like the tail of an old rope" (Cahier 6, 12/12/41).

lit up another Gauloise *jaune,* tightened her grip on her favorite Parker fountain pen, hunched her shoulders over her rolltop desk—her oddly jointed
arms and enormous hands were long enough to reach the back of the roll
while she was still seated—and jotted down in her writer's notebook a short
list of helpful activites which "small children" might do "around the
house."

It's a casual little list, the kind of list Pat liked to make when she was emptying out the back pockets of her mind, and it has the tossed-off quality of an
afterthought. But as any careful reader of Highsmith knows, the time to pay
special attention to her is when she seems to be lounging, negligent, or (God
forbid) mildly relaxed. There is a beast crouched in every "unconcerned" corner of her writing mind, and sure enough, it springs out at us in her list's discomfiting title. "Little Crimes for Little Tots," she called it. And then for good
measure she added a subtitle: "Things around the house—which small children can do . . ."

Pat had recently filled in another little list—it was for the comics historian Jerry Bails back in the United States—with some diversionary information
about her work on the crime-busting comic book adventures of Black Terror
and Sergeant Bill King, so perhaps she was still counting up the ways in which
small children could be slyly associated with crime.[1] In her last writer's journal,
penned from the same perch in semisuburban France, she had also spared a few
thoughts for children. One of them was a simple calculation. She reckoned that
"one blow in anger [would] kill, probably, a child from aged two to eight" and
that "Those over eight would take two blows to kill." The murderer she imagined completing this deed was none other than herself; the circumstance driving her to it was a simple one:

"One situation—maybe one alone—could drive me to murder: family life,
togetherness."[2]

So, difficult as it might be to imagine Pat Highsmith dipping her pen into
child's play, her private writings tell us that she sometimes liked to run her
mind over the more outré problems of dealing with the young. And not only
because her feelings for them wavered between a clinical interest in their upbringing (she made constant inquiries about the children of friends) and a
violent rejection of their actual presence (she couldn't bear the *sounds* children made when they were enjoying themselves).

Like her feisty maternal grandmother, Willie Mae Stewart Coates, who used
to send suggestions for improving the United States to President Franklin Del-
ano Roosevelt (and got handwritten answers *back* from the White House),[3] Pat
kept a drawerful of unconventional ideas for social engineering just itching to
be implemented. Her notebooks are enlivened by large plans for small people,

most of them modelled on some harsh outcropping of her own rocky past. Each one adds a new terror to the study of child development.

One of her plans for youth—just a sample—seems to be a barely suppressed rehearsal of the wrench in 1927 in her own childhood when she was taken from her grandmother's care in the family-owned boardinghouse in Fort Worth, Texas, all the way across the United States to her mother's new marriage in a cramped apartment in the upper reaches of the West Side of Manhattan. Pat's idea for child improvement (it migrated from a serious entry in her 1966 notebook to the mind of the mentally unstable protagonist in her 1977 novel, *Edith's Diary*) was to send very young children to live in places far across the world—"Orphanages could be exploited for willing recruits!" she enthused, alight with her own special brand of practicality—so that they could serve their country as "junior members of the Peace Corps."[4]

Like a tissue culture excised from the skin of her thoughts, her odd, offhand little list of 16 November 1973 (written in her house in a village so small that a visit to the post office lumbered her with unwanted attention) turns out to be a useful entrée into the mind, the matter, and the mise-en-scène of the talented Miss Highsmith. Amongst its other revelations, the list makes recommendations for people (small ones) whose lives parallel her own: people who are fragile enough to be confined to their homes, free enough to be without apparent parental supervision, and angry enough to be preoccupied with murder.

Here is her list.

16/11/73   Little Crimes for Little Tots.
Things around the house—which small children can do, such as:

1) Tying string across top of stairs so adults will trip.
2) Replacing roller skate on stairs, once mother has removed it.
3) Setting careful fires, so that someone else will get the blame if possible.
4) Rearranging pills in medicine cabinets; sleeping pills into aspirin bottle. Pink laxative pills into antibiotic bottle which is kept in fridge.
5) Rat powder or flea powder into flour jar in kitchen.
6) Saw through supports of attic trap door, so that anyone walking on closed trap will fall through to stairs.
7) In summer: fix magnifying glass to focus on dry leaves, or preferably oily rags somewhere. Fire may be attributed to spontaneous combustion.
8) Investigate anti-mildew products in gardening shed. Colorless poison added to gin bottle.

A small thing but very much her own, this piece of ephemera, like almost everything Pat turned her hand to, has murder on its mind, centers itself around a house and its close environs, mentions a mother in a cameo role, and is highly practical in a thoroughly subversive way.

Written in the flat, dragging, uninflected style of her middle years, it leaves no particular sense that she meant it as a joke, but she must have . . . mustn't she? The *real* beast in Highsmith's writing has always been the double-headed dragon of ambiguity. And the dragon often appears with its second head tucked under its foreclaw, and its cue cards—the ones it should be flashing at us to help us with our responses—concealed somewhere beneath its scales. Is Pat serious? Or is she something else?

She is serious and she is *also* something else.

All her life, Pat Highsmith was drawn to list making. She loved lists and she loved them all the more because nothing could be less representative of her chaotic, raging interior than a nice, organizing little list. Like much of what she wrote, this particular list makes use of the materials at hand: no need, children, to look farther than Mother's medicine cabinet or Father's garden shed for the means to murder your parents. Many children in Highsmith fictions, if they are physically able, murder a family member. In 1975 she would devote an entire collection of short stories, *The Animal-Lover's Book of Beastly Murder,* to pets who dispatch their abusive human "parents" straight to Hell.

Nor did Pat herself usually look farther than her immediate environment for props to implement her artistic motives. (And when she did, she got into artistic trouble.) Everything around her was there to be used—and methodically so—even in murder. She fed the odd bits of her gardens, her love life, the carpenter ants in her attic, her old manuscripts, her understanding of the street plan of New York and the transvestite bars of Berlin, into the furnace of her imagination—and then let the fires do their work.

Perhaps suggestion number 3 in "Little Crimes for Little Tots," "the setting of careful fires, so that someone else will get the blame if possible," is the most disturbing, implying, as it does, both the double vision which produced her most interesting fiction (a single crime, but the culpability floats between two characters, as in her novel *The Blunderer*) and the kind of premeditation that might get those "Little Tots" sent straight up the river to the "Big House."

"Deadpan" was Pat's most available mode of expression, and her deadpan style here ("Style does not interest me in the least," she feinted in 1944)[5] blows smoke rings of doubt around her intentions. And because her own childhood was the only childhood which ever truly interested her, there is one final smoke ring that rises mockingly above the rest: which child murdering whose parents was this list really made for?

Could her list's imagined victims have something to do with the complicated parentage of little Patsy Plangman (who had one more parent than she wanted, one less parent than she needed), born on the birthdays of both Edgar Allan Poe and his devilish character-with-a-doppelgänger, William Wilson?* That's the little Patsy Plangman who grew up to be *no* one's "patsy" and who, as Patricia Highsmith, presented herself and her best characters as orphans with parents and adults with double lives. Like her life, Pat's work— even to its smallest element—is full of interesting suggestions.

What was it, for instance, that brought Pat Highsmith, a writer with considerable successes behind and before her—but now, midway on her life's journey, in dark woods, with the right road lost (Pat was reading Dante in Italian just now)—to set up her Fortress of Solitude in an obscure suburban village in France?

There is a good Highsmith story coiled behind this question, as well as a crucial Highsmith history. To find them, we shall have to go back to her desk in Moncourt. Questions concerning Highsmith's life are usually best answered in the vicinity of one of her desks.

As a child, Pat lay seething with resentment on couch-beds in living rooms of too-small apartments in Manhattan and Queens listening to the raised voices of her mother and stepfather. As an adult, she demanded and secured a series of fiercely defended private spaces which allowed her imagination to intensify its own interests. It was in houses (they were never quite the homes she'd hoped for) where she finally arranged the privacy she needed more than she needed anything else. And the most important physical feature of that privacy was always, *always* a room with a desk.

Here in the village of Moncourt, Pat and her desk are tucked up under the eaves in the second-floor bedroom of her house (first-floor in France), an hour's train ride from Paris. Although she sits in front of the scrolled rolltop like a snail in front of its shell, her posture is deceptive; she is not unshelled. The house itself is in a *hameau,* a tiny hamlet within the village of Moncourt, entirely encircled by a protective stone wall. It is two months and three days before her fifty-third birthday.

Eleven months ago, she began a poem: "I live on thin air / And thin ice." Still, here in this house, as in every other place she has ever lived, she has made sure that there are at least two layers of solid material (house walls and a stone wall, in this case) between her and the rest of the world. When she is alone and writing—that is, when she is at her most dangerous—Patricia Highsmith likes to play it safe.

---

* The other figure born on 19 January—Pat later named him as her favorite historical character—was the Confederacy's great hero: General Robert E. Lee.

The desk she is sitting at provides a kind of catalogue of her working habits. Sheaves of printed stationery, filched during her literary sojourns at Europe's better hotels (her publishers pay for these trips), are stacked in its cubbyholes. Matchbooks, acquired by the same means, are secreted in its drawers. There are scraps of paper left over from the two and a half manuscript drafts she types of each of her works (for neatness, she says, not because she needs to revise);[6] she often reuses them for her vast correspondence, cutting them carefully in half if a half sheet is all she needs. Even the rinsed-out receptacle holding her pencils once had another life as a jam jar. Nothing is wasted in her household.

A Gauloise *jaune* smoulders away in a half-filled ashtray beside her. A glass of cheap scotch is within easy reach. Somewhere in the room there is a forgotten tumbler of milk and a cup of cooling coffee. Two bottles of Valstar beer, both empty, are on the floor under the desk.

At twenty, when she was a junior at Barnard College living at home in New York City—and just as liable to falling through the crust of the world as she is now—Pat first wrote about thin ice:

> We live on the thin ice of unexplained phenomena. Suppose our food suddenly did not digest in our stomachs. Suppose it lay like a lump of dough inside us and poisoned us.[7]

Food has disturbed her on and off since she was an adolescent. She wrote to her professor friend Alex Szogyi (he was also a food writer) that food was her bête noire—and she has come to attach many confusions to the act of eating. France, the culinary center of the Western world, means nothing to her: "I don't even like the food," she writes from Fontainebleau.[8] She thinks America's "Nixon" problem is gastric: "the USA [is] suffering a prolonged attack of acid stomach, an irrepressible urge to throw up."[9] She herself often has the urge to throw up. Her idea of an attractive name for a cookbook is "Desperate Measures."[10] For a long time now, liquids have been her most important nourishment.

At this moment, she has put down her pen and begun to type on the coffee-colored Olympia Portable Deluxe typewriter that has accompanied her on all her restless travels since 1956.[11] Its hard-shell carrying case is pasted over with shipping labels from European countries. The Olympia—a ripple of Leni Riefenstahl runs through its brand name—occupies a major portion of the desktop.

Her typing style is distinctive: brutal, dogged, and unhurried. She uses only four or five fingers to strike the keys, she strikes them hard, and she strikes from above, like someone attacking the keyboard of a musical instrument. Her fingers appear to limp a little, and their rhythm is syncopated. She could be playing a harpsichord. She has always *wanted* to play the harpsichord. Instead, she will give a harpsichord and the lessons for playing it to her favorite character, the talented Mr. Ripley. And, as an afterthought, to Ripley's wife, the *belle,* blank Heloise.

The single bed with the striped bedspread, the one she sleeps in when she sleeps alone (which she mostly does these days), is in this small room as well, at a right angle to her desk. A chocolate-point Siamese cat is curled up on it. A radio, a box of tissues, and a bottle of Vicks Vapo-Rub are on a simple stand beside the bed. An old bluish Persian carpet, frayed here and there, is on the floor. There is a roof window just above her eye level—an old-fashioned *tabatière*—which opens onto the courtyard.

As usual, her desk faces a wall.

It is 5:22 in the morning.

As she bends her head over her typewriter, the exposed nape of her neck, usually concealed with a scarf or a turtleneck sweater—"I have no neck," she remarked flatly to an interviewer—shows signs of a dowager's bulge. Her shoulder-length hair, still coiffed in the classic pageboy she went to Barnard with in 1938, falls forward over her face. "Coiffed" is not quite the word for it; Highsmith harbors a lifelong "dislike of being groomed" by professionals, calling it "a curious way to regain morale—having *other* people administer" to you. She pushes her pageboy back with her thumbs—first one side, then the other— and tosses her head slightly in the characteristic gesture that settles her hair. In grooming, as in everything else, Patricia Highsmith prefers to do it herself.

The marmoreal beauty of her youth, abundantly attested to by friends, lovers, family, employers, photographers, and, in a pinch, by the writer herself, is almost gone. Years of drinking, depression, and inadequately extinguished internal fires have ravaged it. The difference between the youthful, coruscatingly seductive Pat Highsmith of her early photographs and the almost-fifty-three-year-old writer who sits typing in front of us now is striking; she looks like another person.

Still, she is capable of radiating the kind of magnetism that draws attention in a room, with her bowed-down head and her piercing dark-eyed glance darting up and out from under the fringe of hair—assessing you, says one young friend, "with the shrewdness of a homicide cop for evidence of wrong-doing."[12] Her eyes are pouched like an owl's (a constant comparison among journalists—they know she likes owls); the oval of her face is disturbed by dewlaps; the skin is shirred and ruched. She looks dissipated, but alert. The fires are banked, but they could break out at any moment.

Like a description she gives of Mr. Ripley, she is "on the edge of [her] chair, if [she] is sitting at all."[13] Except when she's at her desk.

Her arms (they appear to be turned out a little at the elbows even in her long-sleeved shirt) are busy with the peculiar, pistonlike motion of her typing. Home movies reveal that they are genetic copies of the capable arms of her grandmother Willie Mae Coates. Her hands—many of the Coates side of the family have these hands—are enormous: square, powerful, and as large as her head. They are gnarled and nicked from her woodworking and her gardening. "Worker's hands," says one friend.[14] "Butcher's hands, strangler's hands," ventures a neighbor.[15] Her thumbs are extraordinary: huge curved digits, bent out naturally at what appear to be unnatural angles to the rest of her fingers.[16]

As she types, her bottom lip relaxes out over her chin in what her friend, the acidulous memoirist Barbara Skelton, will later call a "rather louche" overhang.[17] Pat is not conscious of this lapse in controlling her lip, something she has felt compelled to do ever since a prospective lover described her mouth as "passionate." Her writing at this hour is the result of an extended bout of insomnia—she suffers from it more and more—and she is just now finishing up the six or seven or eight pages which are her usual day's work.

Outside, just beyond the door in the stone wall at the end of her garden, the Loing Canal, a commercial waterway connected in some mysterious way with the river Seine, flows steadily on. The Loing, broad enough for barges but narrow enough for neighborliness, flows through her imagination as well. It is in this body of water where she will have Tom Ripley deposit some of his most incriminating bodies of evidence. Again, nothing that she can make use of is overlooked.

A practical woman when it comes to necessary transactions, Pat has been unusually adept at getting a handsome return on her social investments. At every move and remove, and with a minimum expenditure of effort, she manages to gather around her a little society of helpful, admiring, understanding people, recruited for the purpose of providing that increasingly well-known writer Patricia Highsmith with just enough human contact (and enough help with the shopping, the sewing, the moving, the gardening, the house painting, etc.) to continue her work in relative comfort.

And as she moves and then moves again (Moncourt is her fourth house in France in two and a half years, all of them near Fontainebleau and friends in the Île-de-France), she goes on making more friends and more acquaintances, telling each of them less about her inner life and less about her past. And she continues to keep in touch with many of these friends, past and present, by a steady stream of letters and postcards filled with the most mundane details of her daily life and with invitations to come and stay; invitations, her correspondents quickly learn, best honored in the breach. Pat likes to invite people to visit, but is not often pleased to see them arrive. Her correspondence—always the preferred method of contact—is enormous.

If Pat is a recluse, she is the most *social* recluse in literary history.

Pat's to-ing and fro-ing—her moves and removes have been quite as extreme and various as her moods—has been going on for some thirty years now. In her lifelong quest for perfect silence and eternal peace (conditions which are always overturned by her unquiet self and its need for "madness and irregularity . . . which," she writes, "is also necessary to me and necessary to my creation"),[18] Pat has been a restless self-exile from New York, from Pennsylvania, from America, from Italy, from England—from everywhere, really.

Through it all, she has remained an extraordinarily productive creator. The hardworking "Little Engine That Could"* is what she most resembles. And that is how she thinks of herself: as someone who gets the job done against the odds.

"Address to younger writers, who think older writers like me are so famous and so different. We are no different at all, we are just the same as other writers, only we work harder."[19]

Her little train of daily accomplishments, freighted with book themes, articles, short-story beginnings, observations, descriptions—an idea a minute, in fact—chugs steadily between the twin terminals of her self-regard and her depressions, and keeps her very busy filling up its cars. And *still* she is afraid of not doing enough. Punctuating every interview she gives to the press with complaints about how her valuable time is slipping away, she usually manages to suggest that the most horrible waste of time is the interview she is giving *right now*. Even when she was in college, in the year she wished she could see Shakespeare "in his study," Pat was terrified of "losing" time: "Six months to fill this notebook? Good heavens, can I be burning out!? Have I shot my bolt!?"[20]

How the Texas-born, New York–reared Mary Patricia Highsmith ended up in a *hameau* in suburban France (a country whose language she generally refuses to speak), calculating the number of blows it would take to kill small children and—her version of fair-mindedness—counting the ways in which

---

* From the 1930 American's children's classic *The Little Engine That Could* by the pseudonymous Watty Piper (a "house-name" used by Platt & Munk Publishers), illustrated by Lois Lenski. The Little Blue Engine (characterized as a female) pulls a trainload of Christmas toys over an impassable mountain by repeating to herself the uplifting phrase "I *think* I can, I *think* I can, I *think* I can." Read by every schoolchild in America and still in print today, *The Little Engine That Could* is among the best self-help books ever written.

tiny tots could murder adults, has as much to do with the rupture of a cross-Channel love affair as it does with the ordinary propensities of her imagination. So let us move periods (we'll go back eight years) and change venues (to England), to visit Pat at a time when her hope, if not her mood, was higher, and when she was still full of feelings for the central figure in her life. Which, as it happens, is not the woman with whom she says she is in love.

· 2 ·

HOW TO BEGIN

PART 2

It is late April, still the cruellest month, in 1965. And it is London, still "swinging"—but not for everyone.

London is certainly not swinging for Patricia Highsmith, the attractive, fiercely ambitious, and, in Europe at least, seriously regarded forty-four-year-old American "suspense" writer whose alabaster skin and almond eyes have only just begun to show the signs of her drinking and her disappointments. She has driven down to North London—she has some business with the BBC[1]—from her rural residence in Suffolk, Bridge Cottage in Earl Soham, having passed the winter holidays of 1964–65 in her usual festive spirits.

"The holidays here exhaust one, creeping through closed windows like a poisonous gas," Pat writes from Suffolk, sounding just like a Highsmith character. Never one to greet the New Year with anything like enthusiasm ("Happy New Year . . . I *hate* the phrase"),[2] she complains steadily of the English weather, the English temperament, and the "dreary" English pubs with their "dangerous dart-games."[3] She is—this has only darkened her mood—deep in the dying stages of an English love affair.

The object of Pat's affections is a vibrantly attractive, classically cultured, solidly married Londoner—we'll call her Caroline Besterman*—and she is the most profound attachment of Pat's adult life. Pat's first meeting with Caroline in London in the summer of 1962 left her love-struck as never before. The honeymoon the two women managed to steal in France that autumn set the seal on their love affair. Pat flew over to Paris from New York to scoop Caroline shyly off the boat train from London and spend a delerious long week

---

* Caroline Besterman is a pseudonym.

with her in a hotel in the Sixth arrondissement, a week Pat described in scorching terms. "She . . . melts into my arms as if she were smelted by Vulcan expressly for that purpose. I can make love happily to her all night long."[4]

Some of this love affair was conducted in public. Pat, whose late-life neighbors in Switzerland saw her shudder away from the touch of other people, even to the extent of refusing formal handshakes, felt free enough on the streets of Paris in late 1962 to embrace Caroline Besterman so passionately that her own earring flew off and rolled out of sight down the Boulevard St-Germain.[5]

" 'Can I kiss you in some doorway?,' " Pat asked, deferentially.

" 'Never mind the doorway,' " said Caroline.[6]

When they could bear to leave their bed, the two women dined and drank à la française, paid a visit to Baudelaire's tomb and Notre Dame, went to the ceremonies for the Prix Goncourt (Pat was a little surprised to see a woman win),[7] and met several times with Pat's French translator, Jean Rosenthal, who gave her clear advice about French publishing houses. Pat, trying to hide her new relationship from Rosenthal and his wife, travelled with Caroline out to a small studio in St. Cloud where they saw a soundless preview of *Le Meurtrier,* Claude Autant-Lara's film of Pat's novel *The Blunderer.* Caroline found the lead actor, Maurice Ronet, "very attractive" and Pat thought the film "very intense, quite faithful to the book."[8] Their long week together was a rare combination of business, culture, and pleasure.

On her way back to the States, the enraptured Pat made a quick stop in London, where Caroline booked her a room at Oscar Wilde's last London hotel, the Cadogan. Pat paid a secret visit to Caroline's marital home, kissed her "in several rooms, though not in every one of them!" and celebrated by playing songs from the cast album of *Pal Joey* before taking a taxi to the airport. Pat was followed as far as the gate by Caroline—and accompanied onto the plane by the bottle of Gordon's gin she kept in the large woven Mexican bag she always carried with her: her *bolsa.*[9]

Back in her house in New Hope, Pennsylvania, in November, Pat finds that all terms are inadequate to her feelings. And that all feelings are inadequate to her situation:

> Beauty, perfection, completion—all achieved and seen. Death is the next territory, one step to the left. I don't want to see any more, to feel or experience any more. . . . Pleasure has already killed me, transformed and translated me. . . . I am the drunken bee wandered into your household. You may with courage eject me through the window; or by accident step on me. Be assured, I'll feel no pain.[10]

Love, as usual, makes Pat think of death, of murder. And thoughts of death, also as usual, force her into a decision.

"But there is no use in making any further effort to live without her. I cannot. And in all my 41 years, I have never said or written this about anyone else before."[11]

So, although Pat was correcting the proofs of her much-rewritten novel *The Two Faces of January,* and had been hoping "to do a short story & make a beginning on paper of the prison novel [*The Prisoner,* later *The Glass Cell*]" she'd been imagining since September of 1962, she "cleared [her] complicated decks,"[12] left her possessions and her rented house in New Hope, where she'd been living since 1960, and, in early 1963, crossed the wine-dark seas and settled in Earl Soham in Suffolk (after moving from Paris to Positano into the house she'd rented the summer before, and thence to Aldeburgh; despite her reference to Emily Dickinson's "drunken bee," the "beeline" was never part of Pat Highsmith's approach to travel) in what had been two country cottages, now "knocked together" as one dwelling: Bridge Cottage.

The double structure of Bridge Cottage suits Pat's psychology just as much as the ambiguities of this love affair with Caroline Besterman, someone else's wife, suit her temperament.

As her feelings for Caroline sink into familiar acrimony (Pat has a fetching habit of falling for women because they are married, then berating them for being attached to their husbands), Pat spends the Suffolk winter of 1964–65 holed up in her "brick-floored" study; freezing, brooding, and trying hard to understand her new country.[13] "England is brilliant at describing its own shortcomings, very slow at doing anything about them."[14] She is also making "Notes on Suspense" for a book she is writing for a Boston publisher.

"Suspense writers, present and future: Remember you are in good company. Dostoyevsky, Wilkie Collins, Henry James, Edgar Allan Poe . . . there are hacks in every kind of literary field. . . . Aim at being a genius."[15]

She saws wood to warm herself instead of firing up her stoves—"I become more Scrooge-like with age," she confesses[16]—and she does not take her mother's practical advice about the excellent insulating properties of old newspapers.[17]

"I see little of my friend [Caroline Besterman] . . . ," Pat writes to her college chum in New York, Kingsley Skattebol, in January of 1965. "It is hard to bear when I sit alone in the country 98% of the time."[18] Kingsley is one of Pat's oldest friends, but she has never been told that Pat and Caroline Besterman are lovers, and she will not learn this interesting fact until after Pat's death.[19] Pat likes to partition her confidences, imagine herself as emotionally neglected (a satisfying habit since childhood), and calculate the percentages of her un-happiness.

Actually, Pat is having a much better time in Earl Soham than she lets on. She has made fast friends with her obliging neighbor, the writer Ronald Blythe, who is working on his soon-to-be-acclaimed book about Suffolk, *Akenfield,* when he first meets her. Ronald Blythe invites Pat into his circle of artistic and literary males. Amongst them is James Hamilton-Paterson, future author of *Gerontius* and *Cooking with Fernet-Branca*. Hamilton-Paterson once walked out of a room after Pat had erupted in a "brief burst of tears."[20] "I don't blame him," wrote Pat, who would certainly have done the same thing herself; "give him my love."[21]

Ronald Blythe and Pat see each other regularly; he, "cycling to Earl Soham to have supper with her, or she, coming to see me in her Volkswagen." They go on day trips together to scout out old churches and unfamiliar pubs, they cook for each other (Pat always "left stuff on her plate, smoked between courses, and didn't much like food"), and—dedicated writers both—they communicate by letter between visits, even though they live only four miles apart.

"She was a great ranter," Ronald Blythe says. And there is certainly "a great deal" of ranting about Caroline Besterman in Pat's early letters to him, while her conversation was "full of hatred for her mother and wild goings on." But Pat never ranted at Blythe or even quarrelled with him—perhaps because he never challenged her. "She had beautiful manners," he thinks, "lovely manners . . . and I got used to her excessive language."[22]

But there are sharp drops into strangeness in their friendship. Cycling home from a visit to Pat, Ronald Blythe—then a warden of his village church, now a canon of the cathedral—was once "overcome by a kind of terrible dark-ness. I felt quite ill, as though I'd been in the presence of something awful. . . . And then the next time we saw each other she said that, well, some things about her, I wasn't to worry about them. *She knew* [what I'd been feeling]. . . . It never happened again[,] but I had just felt awful in her presence."[23]

And on "one or two occasions," Pat breached the boundaries of their friend-ship with "a faint, physical exploration . . . Her attitude was a kind of trespass on my body, rather like a man examining me. . . . I couldn't understand it really, [but] it was of no importance whatsoever."* They were never, says Dr. Blythe, lovers in any conventional sense; this was something else. Some-thing, quite possibly, to do with Pat's rather clinical interest in the male anat-omy and in what she once identified as "the thrill of domination."[24]

---

* Ronald Blythe was "surprised" to see himself featured in a BBC documentary about Pa-tricia Highsmith as one of her "lovers." The idea, he says, is "ridiculous."

Ordinarily, though, Pat is "very close and affectionate and warm and touching. [Our] relationship was almost entirely about writing. . . . We didn't have anyone near we could talk to about writing [and so] we talked by the hour about our work. . . . I took all my friends to see her."[25]

The Suffolk solitude Pat complains of in her letters (and describes self-pityingly in her notebooks, her cahiers) is far more populous and social than she cares to admit. And so, as she chats for hours on end about her work to her fellow writer Ronald Blythe, she is also inserting into her little handbook-in-progress for suspense writers, *Plotting and Writing Suspense Fiction* (1965), this resonant antipathy:

"I cannot think of anything worse or more dangerous than to discuss my work with another writer. It would give me an uncomfortably naked feeling."

Like most writers, what Pat really likes to set down in her notebooks are the things that disturb her, the daily and historic irritations rasping away at her nerves. Because of this, her meticulous self-archiving—at the end of her life, there will be eight thousand pages of notebooks and diaries—can be deceptive. The areas of Pat's life which do not bother her often go unrecorded.

Taking Patricia Highsmith at her "word" will always be a complicated business.

Just now, Pat has come to London to stay for a few days with Barbara Ker-Seymer—the impeccably well-connected, once-bohemian portrait photographer and close friend of most of London's twenties and thirties Café Society—and Ker-Seymer's lover, the enterprising Barbara Roett.

The Barbaras live together in a charming crescent street in Islington with a house on one side of the crescent's curve and a studio *en face*. They prefer to have Pat stay with them because, as Barbara Roett says, "if she were only visiting us, it was hell." When Pat came to London "it was for a binge, [she liked] to chat and tirade around the house until quite late . . . whereas we wanted to go to bed at a reasonable time."[26] It was much easier to give Pat keys of her own.

"Quarrelling with Pat," says Barbara Roett, "would be like quarrelling with a dog with rabies. You could get bitten. But it wasn't the fear of being bitten, it was the fear of knowing better. . . . When I understood her . . . I felt a compassion for her. I thought she was isolated from love in a simple way: Love your parents."[27]

On the other side of London, in a leafy part of Kensington, in a lovely old house with steps that curve like a castle staircase from the walk in its front yard to the top of the house's final floor, lives another friend of Pat Highsmith.

Let us call her Camilla Butterfield.* Camilla Butterfield's house is filled with books and comfortable corners, woodcuts are on the walls, and out in back there is a fragrant, well-tended garden whose green shade gives a slightly aquarium cast to the ground floor.

Pat has just lunched at Mrs. Butterfield's, leaving her white English Volkswagen parked in the drive while she goes off to do her business at the BBC. She intends to return, pick the car up, and head back to the two Barbaras' house in Islington, where she will once again spend the night.

Suddenly the telephone rings at Mrs. Butterfield's house, and it proves to be an unsettling call. It is Pat's mother, Mary Coates Highsmith—always well provided with the coordinates of Pat's friends and lovers—and she has arrived in London from the United States with rather less warning than the Blitz. In a distinctively deep Southern voice, unplaceable, says Mrs. Butterfield, as to social class, and very upset, Mary Highsmith begins to relate a sorry tale.

It seems that Mary, who flew from Texas without a hotel reservation, had directed her taxi driver to take her to the Cavendish Hotel. When "the driver finished laughing," he told Mary that the Cavendish was nothing more than a hole in the ground; it had just been pulled down.[28] Worse, Mary's luggage had been misplaced when she transferred planes in New York City and her traveller's checks had been lost or stolen at the venerable Hotel Earle in Greenwich Village.[29] So Mary Highsmith was stranded on her first day in London with no money, no luggage, no idea of where her daughter might be, and no place to stay. It was "a bad beginning for the poor woman" and the herald of worse to come.[30]

Mary had the presence of mind to ask the taxi man to drive around and find her a hotel, which he did. Mrs. Butterfield thinks it was "something in Bloomsbury." On the telephone, says Mrs. Butterfield, Mary had:

> announced herself as "Mrs. Highsmith"—of course one doesn't do that—and begun this long, terrific series of complaints in a deep Southern voice. All about Pat and everything else. She was neglected, she said, and Pat knew she was coming. Well, I don't know that Pat *did* know she was coming. So I told her that Pat was at the BBC and that . . . I would give Pat the message immediately when she came back.[31]

Pat returned from the BBC to pick up her car at about four o'clock, "or even a bit later, drinks time." Camilla Butterfield, privy to Pat's version of the

---

* Camilla Butterfield is a pseudonym.

tangled emotional relations between the Highsmith mother and daughter, opened the door and greeted Pat jauntily. "Brace yourself," she announced; "the Deep South has arrived.

"And Pat fainted away right on the doorstep.

"It was incredible and it was more than a faint. Her legs just gave way. She just crumpled into a heap on top of herself, like a doll, so to speak.

"I've never seen anything like it."[32]

Pat recovered herself quickly, and, despite the fact that she was driving back to Islington, Mrs. Butterfield poured her a large drink, then gave her Mary's message and the telephone number. But Pat didn't ring her mother. She drove straight back to North London.

Camilla Butterfield discovered subsequently that Pat and Mary "were in touch, and so I invited them to tea. It was brave of me, but I was curious."[33]

When Mrs. Butterfield's husband came back to Kensington from work at about six o'clock on the afternoon of the tea party, he found his wife in "a state of shock. After Pat and Mary Highsmith had gone, the air quivered," says Mrs. Butterfield, "and I just sat on. My husband came in—he had no idea anyone had been in the house—and he said to me: 'You look as though you've been through an earthquake.'

" 'Take me out to dinner,' I said, 'I have.' "[34]

Camilla Butterfield recollects that she sat motionless for about twenty minutes after Mary and Pat left her house, so the tea party couldn't have lasted very long, perhaps an hour and a half. But it was, Mrs. Butterfield thought, "quite long enough." She remembers that the "atmospheric pressure" of the room was "incredible." It was "as though some disturbance in the air had passed through the house and torn everything apart." She felt as though she'd "been in a thunderstorm.

"Well, of course, Pat and Mary were mutually antagonistic, but they were also both *very* rattled. It was chaos, just chaos. Everywhere things were put down out of place. I had made quite a nice formal tea party for them—I had gone to quite a lot of trouble—and when they'd finished, when they'd *gone*, there was a teacup *here* and a saucer over *there*. And a bit of sandwich *there*, a tea strainer *here*, and an olive in a *plant,* and the ashtray . . . Well, it was chaos. After that I think they went straight back to Suffolk and there were dreadful scenes there."[35]

There were indeed dreadful scenes between Pat and her mother, Mary, at Bridge Cottage in Suffolk; so dreadful that Pat had to call in Dr. Auld, the local physician, to sedate them both. Pat reported that Mary had threatened her with a coat hanger—and each woman said things the other never forgot.

Four years earlier, Mary Highsmith had written to her daughter: "I believe you would gladly put me in Dachau if it were possible without a minute's thought."[36] And Pat told her cousin Dan that during Mary's visit to Bridge Cottage in Suffolk she had locked up her writing "at night, out of instinct" because she was certain her mother meant to destroy it.[37]

Patricia Highsmith and her mother, Mary Coates Highsmith—let us take the kind of shortcut that only an introduction permits—were each other's deepest experience of love. This was a rich recipe for hell on earth for both women. "I adored my mother, and could see no wrong in her, until I was near 17," Pat said at forty-six.[38] This version of love would later be measured only by the violence of Pat's rejection of it—and by her violent rejection of Mary.

Art is always the issue of a "tangled bank" and its making is an infinitely complicated matter, but Patricia Highsmith's earth-cracking reversal of feeling for her mother was almost certainly a crucial source for the upside-down view of the world she created in her work—as well as an inspiring pattern for the inverted way she lived most of her affections. Because of it, in spite of it, her retreats in life and her advances in art often appear to adhere to strict dictionary definitions of the word "perverse."

Mary and Pat had what the French call *un amour fusionnel*. Neither woman could distinguish herself from the other in her deepest feelings. And so Pat's lifelong horror at her mother's "failed career" and "irrational behavior" were her worst fears for herself made flesh. And Mary's long-lived anguish at Pat's "disloyalties" and attachments to other women was the rage of someone who felt she was losing her love of self, losing the love that *belonged* to her self. Their profound emotional competitiveness—it would surface from time to time like the flash of a fin above water signalling danger to limbs dangling below—was that of Terrible Twins, Alter Egos, Substitute Siblings locked in a struggle for each other's—and for yet one more woman's—love.*

In later life, when thrown together, Pat and Mary (as Mrs. Butterfield's husband, who experienced only the aftershocks of a disturbing tea party, quickly guessed) made the earth tremble—and not in the conventional way. Chasms of unsatiated pain and need opened in each of them and they devoured each other: first, in love—according to both of them, they had years of only slightly clouded affections, and their early, affectionate letters are the hard copy of these softer feelings—and then in a lifetime of rage and recrimination. There is no mediating a relationship like this, and all their attempts to do so fell into

---

* That of Willie Mae Stewart Coates, Pat's grandmother and Mary's mother.

horrible failure. They could not bear each other's company and they could not leave each other alone.

From the fastness of her care home in Texas, in July of 1972, Mary wrote to Pat in France that she looked like "Dracula" in her photographs, that her books were "forgotten" in America, that no single bookseller in Fort Worth (Mary's current point of reference) knew Pat's name.[39] What Pat wrote to Mary has been mostly lost, but what she wrote *about* her was awful enough: Mary was an inert vegetable, a useless tube, a devouring cloaca with Pat's money being shoveled in at one end (very little of it was, as a matter of fact) and shit coming out the other.[40]

Earlier still, when Mary was sexually viable, Pat wrote her into a slightly more elevated role. Mary was Pat's Bitch from Hell: the paradigmatic femme fatale who haunted all Pat's works and whose shadow Pat stalked in so many of her own sexual affairs, night dreams, and fantasies.

Pat kept a file whose documents, she truly hoped, would prove to the world that her mother was mad. She labelled the file "FOR DOCTOR OR PSYCHIATRIST ONLY."[41] If Mary were mad, Pat's thinking went, then she herself must be sane. Pat also thought—this is more complicated—that Mary "would not have become semi-insane, if I had not existed."[42]

Sanity was a central preoccupation of Patricia Highsmith, who, in certain solid ways, knew herself very well indeed. She *worked hard* at sanity and was mostly successful at it. Her icy, invigilator's eye scanned her own behavior and monitored her own thoughts regularly and often, the way a searchlight sweeps a prison yard for escaping convicts. "I think I have some schizoid tendencies, which must Be Watched," she wrote grimly.[43] And then again: "I fear the madness in me, quite near the surface."[44]

Whenever a destructive feeling tunnelled its way out of confinement and fled howling out into the night, Pat swivelled her lamp, surveyed the terrain around her prison, and froze the miscreant in its tracks. Not, of course, before it had done some impressive damage—usually during the dinner hour. Meals were often a problem for Pat, and she made them a problem for the people she ate with, too. One of her funniest legacies (at this distance from her table, at least) is the long list of her thoroughly harrowed dinner partners.

"How one slides in and conforms easily *within a limited sense of course* to 'normalcy,'"[45] Pat noted with her customary detached interest in 1939. But she would hear nothing except that her mother was crazy.

Mary, a considerable force in her own right, felt the same way about her daughter. "Pat is SICK," Mary wrote to one of Pat's lovers.[46] Their moods were tied and twinned.

Relations like this one are not for sissies. Unfortunately, each woman, though capable of iron-willed action, was also constitutionally quite timid and given to replacing an analysis of her family situation with Vesuvian eruptions of anger and name-calling. So there was no bridge back. It was everybody's fault and it was nobody's fault. "We are in a vicious circle," Pat wrote in a moment of clarity, "of which each of us forms one half. Each the cause and the result. And we can't change the course."[47]

Across their self-made chasm the two women howled brokenheartedly at each other—it was always the howl of love betrayed, the curdled milk of mother-daughter misapprehension—and for very nearly half a century Pat Highsmith's relationship with her mother, Mary, was the *real* love that dared not speak its name.

> [C]ould I possibly be in love with my own mother? Perhaps in some incredible way I am. And it is the recalcitrance in all of us that shows in my ingratitude for my mother's over-zealous effort to please me, and to do things for me. It is the old story of things being too simple—and out of our refusal to throw our love to the easiest and most deserving and most logical object.[48]

Without understanding this fundamental dynamic—that some version of love was, not at the bottom exactly (there *is* no bottom to Pat Highsmith's bag of literary tricks), but somewhere in the forefront of her approach to the world ("My excess baggage—no pun—I'm in no mood for joking—is the eternal love I cannot turn loose of," Pat wrote at forty-one)[49]—there is no understanding Mary Patricia Highsmith. Which, of course, is not quite the "real" name—for even in death, Pat's fascination with sleight of hand seems to have pulled one more stunned bunny from her overstuffed identity hat—of Her High Darkness, Patricia Highsmith: author of some of the twentieth century's most dangerous fictions.*

Highsmith's work, at its best, is highly unusual. At its *very* best (six or seven of the novels and a double handful of the short stories), it is like nothing that surrounds it in time and space. It is far stranger (she was very strange), far more

---

* Pat had good reason to think that her last name, Highsmith, wasn't a legal one. On 16 November 1994, two and a half months before her death, she was still writing to a Swiss lawyer (Dr. Barbara Simone) about her long-pending Swiss citizenship and "in regard to legalizing my name Highsmith," characteristically adding: "I hope I shall not get a large bill for this, or for the name legalization."

obsessive and original and hallucinatory, than anything else in its immediate literary landscape. It splays across genres, interrogates genders, provides as thorough an anatomy of guilt as can be found in contemporary literature, and attacks its readers right where they live. And—an oddly convincing proof of its staying power—quite a bit of it is as flat as Kansas and clumsily phrased to boot.

In very nearly everything she wrote, good intentions corrupt naturally and automatically, guilt often afflicts the innocent and not the culpable, and life is a suffocating trap from which even an escape artist like the talented Mr. Ripley cannot find a graceful exit. Although she never tried to achieve its style, High Art was always Highsmith's inspiration. What makes her own work so undefinably odd is that most of her murdering, mutilating, muggish characters are inspired by it as well.

There is often a bit of blood in the corner of a smile—and a recommendation to read Henry James; a knife turning restlessly in someone's hand at the mildest moment—and a preference for the poems of Auden; a lunch punctured by a horrible suspicion—and a man weeping at the grave of Keats.

"I don't think my books should be in prison libraries," Pat Highsmith wrote circumspectly in 1966. They probably shouldn't be in bedroom libraries, either; no Highsmith fiction qualifies as a book before bedtime. Her work belongs way down at the bottom of the Sandman's bag where all the bad dreams are kept. While quite literally preserving her own life, her writing quite figuratively endangers ours. It's a hard job, but only Patricia Highsmith could manage it in exactly this way.

Highsmith was an amazingly fecund creator. She had, she wrote in a grating and characteristically unpleasant comparison, "ideas as often as rats have orgasms" and they came to her in many forms. Aside from her scores of published works, she left 250 unpublished manuscripts of varying length, thirty-eight writer's notebooks (or "cahiers," as she rather grandly called them, using a term from a language she couldn't really speak), and at least eighteen diaries. She drew, she sketched, she made sculpture. She hand-crafted furniture and carved out little statues. Her notebooks and diaries are punctuated with charts, symbols, line drawings, and thumbnail sketches. She pasted up her own Christmas and birthday cards and decorated the covers of all fourteen of her fat press books with cutouts and lettering of her own devising. At the end of her life, she tried oil-painting lessons, but quarrelled with her teacher. The teacher said that Pat had her own way of doing things.

"I dabble in all the arts," Pat wrote in a 1961 quatrain, "And make a mess of each. / I'm a person of many parts, / With a goal beyond my reach.[50]

She couldn't *not* make art—but she often preferred to practice it as a craft:

i.e., the kind of art that comes out of daily life and goes back into it as something useful. She made her own mailbox in Fontainebleau,[51] and she rifled dumps for odd objects to incorporate into indoor mobiles and outdoor assemblages.[52] She insisted that furniture making and digging a garden gave her as much pleasure as writing.

But it was the writing that was essential to her. She lived to write and she literally wrote, as we shall see, for her life. There is no imagining her life without her work. You have to see it to believe it (the preceding chapter is a faithful portrayal of Pat at her desk), and you have to believe it to understand its life-sustaining importance to her.

After one or two unpublished starts—*The Click of the Shutting* and *The Dove Descending* are the interesting ones—Highsmith simply leapt full blown into the set of styles and modalities which she would continue to employ until she aged and iced and became too removed from her sources—and too ill—to do her best work. Or any work at all. And if she couldn't do her work, there was really not much reason to go on. Her last writer's notebook, Cahier 38, titled and prepared by her for use when she was dying of two competing diseases, is very eloquently blank.

"There is no depression for a writer but a return to the Self",[53] Pat wrote in 1960 (and again, in slightly altered form, in *Ripley Under Ground* in 1970), neatly separating her "Self" from her work. And no writer has more successfully concealed the ways in which her art and her life transfused each other's material than the talented Miss Highsmith. The Patricia Highsmith who did the writing and the Pat Highsmith who lived the life, like Terrible Twins arising from the vapors of her youthful obsession with both sides of her complicated parentage ("Deep in my heart stands a silver sword with two edges," she declared at twenty-four),[54] stalked each other for more than fifty years, forging out of their deep and necessary doubling a very profitable partnership.

In thirty volumes of horrific novels and uncannily unpleasant short stories, and in eight thousand obsessively notated pages of notebooks and diaries, the two Highsmiths rehearsed the same primary wounds and repeated the same compulsive themes, passing them back and forth with a dexterous flick of the writer's wrist and (as Henry James once said of an expatriate American life *he* was writing) a slight rotation of aspects.[55] Only illness and the last big move of her life to Switzerland were able to dissolve Highsmith's long-enduring doubles act.

Doubled, too, were the problems of her nationality. Pat was as American as rattlesnake venom—and never more so than in her valiant attempts to master in exile that uniquely American vocation (Benjamin Franklin invented it for *Poor Richard's Almanack*, Scott Fitzgerald adapted it for *The Great Gatsby*) of self-help. Many of the obsessive little lists and charts she devoted herself to making are all about strenuous self-improvement and serious self-betterment. As hard (almost) on herself as she was on everyone else, Pat would list and compare what she considered to be her own failing traits or the failing traits of others; she would contrast these traits with her goals or with her romantic ideals; and she would resolve to do much, much better.

At the end of one riveting chart plotted out in 1945 when she was twenty-four—it rates her women lovers by category and character trait—she writes:

> I lack sympathy, am impatient with that which attracted me. Unconscious masochism, I am resolved to do better as well as change my *type* radically.[56]

And then she adds, typically: "From the two most advantageous, I fled, was false."[57]

Gary Fisketjon, Pat's editor at Atlantic Monthly Press and Knopf in New York, who met her infrequently, drank with her socially, and found her "terrific company," felt that Pat was like a "child of 10 or 11" who has been told she had to "grow up on her own." "Keeping lists like that," he thinks, "is the way a child figures out how to live in an alien world."[58]

Larry Ashmead, the legendary American editor who supervised her novels at Doubleday, Simon & Schuster, and Lippincott, caught Pat in a distinctly performative mood one night in the late 1960s when he telephoned her in London and invited her to dinner.

"And she said to me, 'Remember, no romance.' I recall that very clearly. She was very gruff. And I said: 'Of *course* not, we're just meeting for the first time.'

"She was very talkative at dinner and she was drinking, which was par for the course. . . . She had bought this house in France and she wanted to take her [pet] snails there, and she couldn't take them because there's a gastronomic law: no transportation of live snails into France. But she was slowly smuggling them in. Every time she went, she would put some under her breasts and take them in that way. And, as I was eating my steak tartare, she was telling me this story and I wanted to say something about the state of her breasts. But I thought that would be too 'romantic,' so I didn't."*[59]

Otto Penzler, who published seven of Pat's books under his Mysterious

---

* This was Pat being theatrical; as one of her former lovers sensibly pointed out (and as nude photographs confirm), Pat's breasts were too small to conceal anything. Her usual method of snail smuggling was cottage cheese cartons.

Press imprimatur in Manhattan during the 1980s and remains "a great fan" of her work, had a series of exchanges with her which were so dire that he concluded it must be her character that was preventing her books from selling in the United States.

"She was a horrible human being. I think people somehow feel it. They don't know why they know it, but they don't like Pat. . . . Who wants to identify with a character in a Highsmith story? . . . [T]hese are mean-spirited people, they have no humanity, no spirit of shared experience, they're otherworldly in a way."[60]

Otto Penzler is correct. Highsmith Country *is* another world. And Patricia Highsmith was its only begettor.

In 1967, when Pat's American agent, Patricia Schartle (later Patricia Schartle Myrer), reported that the reason editors said her paperbacks weren't selling in the States was that they were "too subtle" and that there was "no one likeable in the book," Pat's response was: "Perhaps it is because I don't like anyone. My last books may be about animals."[61] One of them—*The Animal-Lover's Book of Beastly Murder* (1975)—was.

A libertarian *au fond* (but a libertarian who preferred countries where there was an established "peasant class" and who was regularly enraged by the "liberties" other people were entitled to), Pat believed with all her heart that people ought to pull themselves up by their bootstraps and "stand on their own two feet." Just as she had always done, just as her enterprising family had always done. She had the Calvinist worldview and tried her best to refuse the theology that went with it. Count Alexis de Tocqueville, whose *Democracy in America* she read in preparation for writing *The Talented Mr. Ripley* one long, hot summer in western Massachusetts, noted similar leanings in the citizens of North America during his travels across that continent in 1835. He thought—correctly, it turns out—that such traits would lead to isolationism.

But it was her lifelong lovers' quarrel with her "mother-country" (that's what she called it) and the lifelong self-exile that quarrel produced which were the most significant signs of Pat Highsmith's Americanism. American artists, flinging bitter indictments of their native land over their shoulders, have always refugeed to Europe for cultural development, political shelter, and artistic support. The youthful Pat shared this pleasant dream of a self-liberating European continent. It's a dream usually entertained by Romantics in love with displacement and the favorable rate of currency exchange whose imaginations have been colonized by European novels long before their actual selves have had to rub up against the realities of European life.

At twenty-six Pat wrote:

"My most persistent obsession—that America is fatally (from my point, an artist's point of view) off the road of the true reality, that the Europeans have it precisely."[62]

But Pat Highsmith does not slip comfortably into *any* convenient categories, and her European expatriatism was unlike that of any other American artist: it did not contribute to her "development."

Although her fictions include many serious critiques of the American society she left behind, her unusual way of living—the constant moves (early on, she began the compulsive, roving patterns that were to govern the rest of her life; her mother said she was "born restless"), the protections her solitudes and her obsessions required, the insularities of her own nature—encouraged her to archive, conserve, and concentrate the social maladies and personal biases she brought with her when she first arrived in Europe. Many of these maladies festered away untreated in the high-security cell of her long exile, and her later life was disfigured by open, ugly expressions of the racial and ethnic prejudices which found their first form in her high school notebooks. For the most part, her fictional work—the work she allowed to be published— escaped the infection.

Principally, it was anti-Semitism that clawed her, although it is difficult to label as an anti-Semite someone who threatened to leave her entire fortune to the Intifada. (Palestinians are Semites too.) "Jew-hater" is really the proper term for what Patricia Highsmith was. When she wasn't calling the Holocaust "Holocaust, Inc.," she was referring to it as the "semicaust"—apparently because it had destroyed only half of world Jewry. And she was none too fond of Blacks, Italians, Portuguese, Latinos, Catholics, Koreans, East Indians, "Red Indians," small, dark children, or, if you look closely at her work (we will), Arabs, either.

Naturally, given the deep divisions and strange attractors in her nature, Pat's Jew-hating came partnered with quite a bit of what might be mistaken for its opposite. She had serious love affairs and long, close friendships with many Jews. Jews were her principal employers, her frequent publishers, and they numbered amongst her most consistent supporters. None of this was accidental.

In 1942, the year she graduated from Barnard College, Fate (apparently disguised as a Borscht Belt comedian) made Pat the editorial assistant to a certain Mr. Ben-Zion Goldberg at FFF Publications in Manhattan, a publishing company that provided topical articles to the Jewish press. And so, in her first long-term paying job, Pat Highsmith, scribbling anti-Semitisms in her notebook, also found herself scribbling away on such subjects as Jewish homemaking, Jewish art, and Jewish culture for *The Jewish Family Year Book*—an employment she entirely neglected to mention in the article "My First Job" she wrote for *The Oldie* magazine in 1993.[63]

Pat seemed to admire Hannah Arendt—she cited Arendt's residency in Tegna for having made that region "famous"[64]—but she read Arendt's *Anti-Semitism: Part One of the Origins of Totalitarianism* in conjunction with Adolf Hitler's *Mein Kampf* as though the two works were of equal argument. In the same high school notebook in which she used a repellent epithet for her Jewish classmates, she also recorded her pleasure in a growing friendship with Judy Tuvim—the precocious, fifteen-year-old Jewish Proustian who grew up to become the brilliant, Oscar-winning comic actress Judy Holliday. (This is the place to put a persistent biographical rumor to rest: Pat Highsmith and Judy Holliday were never lovers. It was Judy's best friend Pat was after.)

Judy's mother, Helen Tuvim, offered Pat free piano lessons at the Henry Street Settlement House on Manhattan's Lower East Side. Pat, fiercely disparaging Mrs. Tuvim and her family in her notebook (it was the generous quantities of food served in the Tuvim household—such a *Jewish* trait—that drew the semi-anorectic teenager's scalding commentary),[65] gladly took up the offer of instruction. Pat Highsmith was constitutionally incapable of single-mindedness. She also played the piano rather badly.

In fact, Pat's rapid rotation of "selves"—those advances and retreats of the extreme emotional states that composed her character—often appear to be guided by Newton's third law of motion. A student of the classics in her youth, employing a little high Greek at the end of her life (her lone late-life tattoo, hidden under the watchband she wore on her left wrist, was made up of her initials in Greek),[66] and deeply involved in her own bodily functions, Pat Highsmith would probably prefer to invoke Galen's theory of an imbalance of "humours" or Richard Burton's "atrabiliousness" (an excess of black bile) to explain her vascillations.

Every strong, positive reaction Pat had seemed to force her into a devastating withdrawal. Psychologically, she veered between attraction and revulsion, self-hatred and self-aggrandizement. Not to mention her simultaneous consciousness (and hypergraphic diary and cahier notations) of all her emotional, spiritual, and physical states at once.

It was an exhausting way to live—like seeing double all the time—and Pat began to feel that all her good work came out of having "enough sleep." Sleep affected her, she said, like the "resurrection of Christ";[67] her attachment to it was sacramental and she "honor[ed] sleep as the highest goddess. She is the source sometimes, she is the fuel always, like love and the sun and food."[68]

In *The Price of Salt,* written before she was thirty, Highsmith makes cool, blond, about-to-be-middle-aged Carol tell her teenage lover, Therese, that "all adults have secrets." In her own midlife, however, Pat rather liked to leave the lid of her personal Pandora's box slightly raised. If you knew how to read her indirectly dropped clues—a few people did—you were often rewarded with some very interesting views. And sometimes, just like the rest of us, she liked to drop little tidbits about herself and her opinions—but never the same tidbits and often not the same opinions—by tailoring her conversation to the milieu, the political leanings, the degree of closeness, and the sexual tastes of her specific and very separate audiences.

Still, in a lifetime of half-revealed mysteries, there was one secret so important that Pat Highsmith kept it entirely to herself. It was a secret that had to do with her work life and she hid it where people often hide the things they are ashamed of: right out there in plain sight, just like Edgar Allan Poe's purloined letter.

For at least seven years—long before and after she was a published writer and far more seriously than has been previously assumed—Patricia Highsmith wrote scripts and scenarios for America's most successful publishing industry: comic book companies. She created dialogue and story lines for dozens of desperate Alter Egos trailing their Superior Selves and Secret Identities through violently threatening terrains and luridly colored fantasies.

If this motif—the threatening terrain, the lurid fantasy, the desperate pursuit of Alter Egos by each other—sounds familiar, it should: it is the central obsession of practically every novel Patricia Highsmith ever wrote, from *Strangers on a Train* to *Ripley Under Water*. But she worked on that obsession in the comics *before* she worked it into her fictions, and, covering her tracks, she obfuscated the comics' titles she wrote for. "Comics like *Superman* and *Batman*," she sometimes replied when interviewers asked, leaving the impression that "to pay the rent" she'd trifled—ever so briefly in the year after graduating from college—with the lives of those two respectable Superheroes.[69]

Superman and *Batman* made good copy, but the truth was much stranger and seven years longer than the little misdirection she gave to the press, and Pat Highsmith—a woman who kept every single artifact associated with her writing for a posterity she fully expected to have—*removed all traces of her lengthy comics career from her own archives*. Almost all traces, that is.

With the (super)heroic aid of many of the great comics creators and historians of the Golden Age of American Comics, I have been able to exemplify Pat's long career in the comics, one of only two art forms native to the United States (the other, for the record, is jazz). We can now add "Black Terror," "Pyroman," "Fighting Yank," "The Destroyer," "Sergeant Bill King," "Jap Buster Johnson," "The Human Torch," "Crisco and Jasper," "Real Life Comics," "Spy Smasher," "Captain Midnight," "Golden Arrow," and a panoply of other comics titles, writers, and artists as well as Dostoyevsky, Proust, Kafka, Gide, Wilde, Willa Cather, Julien Green, Graham Greene, and Edgar Allan Poe to the universe of Pat Highsmith's influences.

Always keen on advancement, Pat tried to write for the high-paying, widely distributed *Wonder Woman* comic book, but was shut out of the job.[70] This was in 1947, just one year before she began to imagine her lesbian novel, *The Price of Salt*. Wonder Woman, daughter of Amazon Queen Hippolyta and still the heroine of her own comic book, has a favorite exclamation: "Suffering Sappho!" She lives on the forbidden-to-males Paradise Island with a happy *coepheroi* of lithe young Amazons, and she arrived in America in 1942, in the form of her Alter Ego, Lieutenant Diana Prince, to help the Allies fight World War II. The thought of what Patricia Highsmith, in her most sexually active period (the 1940s were feverish for Pat) and in the right mood, might have made of *Wonder Woman*'s bondage-obsessed plots and nubile young Amazons can only be inscribed on the short list of popular culture's lingering regrets.

On the subject of love-and-money—the subject of love *of* money—Pat was impossible. The richer she got, the poorer she felt and the more costive she became. She knew, of course, what she was doing—"My poverty has become a disease, unfortunately one of the mind"[71]—and her description of the island of Majorca in 1958 illustrates how she often tried to understand a new experience; she measured it entirely in currency: "Deya, Majorca. 60 pesetas to the dollar. 10 to post a letter airmail to USA. Six for a packet of cigarettes. 45 for a good meal. 50 for table bottle of good (RIOJA) wine."[72]

On the subject of love of women, Pat was merely incredible. She appeared to dislike women and said so. Her notebooks are full of disapproving judgements of women as humans and intoxicated statements about them as inspirational love objects. It was an extraordinary position for a lesbian to maintain, but then, the extraordinary was Highsmith's Saturday Night Special.

At a precocious twenty, she wrote this about love:

I often wonder if it is love I want or the thrill of domination—not thrill exactly but satisfaction. Because this is often more enjoyable than the love itself; though I cannot imagine a domination without love, nor a love without domination.[73]

But she also wrote this:

Every move I make on earth is in some way for women. I adore them! I need them as I need music, as I need drawings. I would give up anything visible to the eye for them, but this is not saying much. I would give up music for them: that is saying much.[74]

The emotional experience Pat most often left out of her published fictions was requited love—but her private writings and her life were filled with it. Few writers have been more inspired by love than Patricia Highsmith. She lived for love, she died a thousand symbolic deaths for love, and she killed for love—over and over and over again in her novels.

Her own problem with love was proximity. She could live *for* love, but she couldn't live *with* it. And she really couldn't bear anything that wasn't writing for very long.

Here is Pat at twenty-seven, yearning for her society lover, "Ginnie" Kent Catherwood, one of the several "Virginias" she would take into her bed:

My green and red goddess, my jade and garnet, my moss and holly-berry, my sea and sun, my marrow and my blood, my stop and go baby, I adore you, I worship you, I kiss you, I cherish you, I defend you, I defy you ever not to love me, I caress your nipples with my tongue.[75]

Although she liked to imagine her favorite lovers as goddesses or mon-archs, Pat's behavior in love was usually that of a regicide. She approached the queens of her heart with a crown in one hand and a headsman's axe in the other. The love affair with Virginia Catherwood which provoked the luscious paragraph above (a paragraph written as their affair was in its final stages of alcohol and accusation) lasted only a turbulent year, but it continued to gener-ate images for Pat's work for decades. Emotional memory was Pat Highsmith's personal mausoleum, but it was also her best inspiration for making art.

Touchingly certain that the women she slept with were telling her the truth when they said she was the best lover they'd ever had (she set that phrase down in a cahier or diary whenever she heard it, and she seems to have heard it a lot),[76] Pat continued to lie to every one of her girlfriends, usu-ally by omitting information they would have considered vital to love's un-derstandings.

She carried on multiple affairs involving various degrees of physicality during many of the "committed" love relationships she had, taking care that none of her myriad women friends—or either of her serious male attachments—would ever learn the truth of her fluctuating feelings or the facts about her sexual adventuring.

Pat thought about love the way she thought about murder: as an emo-tional urgency between two people, one of whom dies in the act. Love had the driving force of a faith for her—"A sexual love can become a religion, and serve as well"[77]—and she always managed to find Satan at the center of it. "The lover (in love) suffers complete upset of all principles. To the man in love, all axioms, and all truths, may be askew."[78]

One reason her work is so often characterized as "amoral" is that the moral disorder that love created in her life always made its way into her novels. But even though crime was always on her mind (like Edgar Wallace's enigmatic detector, JG Reeder, she saw evil everywhere), and even though murder was her absolute necessity, Pat's self-hating, self-torturing "hero-criminals" make her—if indeed they make her anything at all—much more of a "punishment novelist" than a "crime novelist."

A party girl in her Manhattan youth despite her extreme shyness, and very attractive to men as well as seductive to women, Pat had a preference for bowling over both halves of a female couple (another kind of doubling) and extending her charms to their extracurricular lovers as well. In middle age, she began to operate directly on families—including, as it happens, her own. One or two rebelliously feminist ideas came to her while she was forcing herself to sleep with Marc Brandel, the English novelist she was trying to persuade herself to marry. ("I do not feel . . . that going to bed with him will ever be anything to anticipate with unbridled delight." "Oh, the unfairness of this sexual business to women!")[79]

In the context of her usual thoughts about women, Pat's "feminist" notions couldn't be funnier.

Surprisingly—she is often surprising—Pat Highsmith sang in a church choir as late as the age of thirty-seven, joking that the "only trouble is I can be heard when I sing."[80] Joking aside, she makes many references to God—and many more references to Jesus—throughout her cahiers and diaries. Kingsley Skattebol, her oldest friend from school, thinks Pat wasn't a "God-fearing person, but a God-reverencing one" and that "she attributed to God the custody of her unconscious."[81]

Pat's strong Southern Calvinist family background and stern moral underpinnings have eluded the notice of previous biographers. Her family's religious history included prominent preachers, interesting apostasies, and a tradition of opposed and opposing religious communities. Much like her overlooked work in the comics, her involvement with religious tenets was another critical part of a life concealed in plain sight. It was responsible for her lifelong preoccupation with Jesus Christ and, to a large extent, for the Big Chill at the center of her work: the one she defined so aptly as "the presence of the absence of guilt."[82]

God was a long argument Pat seemed to be having with herself, and it was an argument she eventually lost. "If I happen to think that I can be a happier person for believing in God, then I shall believe," she wrote pugnaciously in June of 1940, at an age when most college students are flirting with atheism. (Even her religiosity had a practical side.) By 1947, she was more serious about God and more regular about noting her attendance at His services. "Today yes, no church. I miss it. If I don't go to God for a couple of hours (on Sundays), I like to listen to holy music or words."[83] At twenty-eight, she was still proclaiming God's central importance:

A certain calm is essential in order to live, relief from anxiety. I myself can never have this without belief in the power of God which is greater than man and all the power in the universe.[84]

Twenty years later, having given up on church, Pat, still thinking about what it meant to be a "religious person," provided a perfect description of herself. "It is not in the nature of truly religious people to join anything," she wrote in an inadvertently revealing little essay, "Between Jane Austen and Philby," in 1968. "The religious person is ascetic and lives alone. . . . Anyway, if one has enough sense of guilt, it is not necessary to belong to a church."[85] No one could explain Highsmith more clearly than Patricia Highsmith—especially if she thought she was writing about someone *other* than Patricia Highsmith.

Of course, Pat had her mother's Christian Science to combat (evil, Mary Baker Eddy wrote, is only a form of ignorance), and she did so with frequent and convoluted disquisitions on Jesus, with whom, just like her early idol Dostoyevsky, she tended to identify. Later on, a kind of ensorcelled and ecstatic union with a long list of female lovers was her closest approach to religious communion—and much of the inspiration for her writing. ("With the complete opening of the heart in love of another person, there is surely an opening directly to God.")[86]

The last person to share a house with her shortly before her death (he was on his way to a monastery and taking care of Pat Highsmith was his six-month preparation for monastic life) thought she was seeking some kind of spiritual life, but couldn't face the "cage" of religion. Religion was one of the two subjects he had to stop discussing with her.

But I am getting ahead of her story.

All through the 1970s, at her house in the hamlet of Moncourt (the house she loved the best and the one she kept the longest), Pat had a near neighbor, a Czechoslovakian émigré who occasionally did odd jobs for her. Monsieur Knet was exactly the kind of self-made man Pat liked to trade small talk with. He used to return home from his night job in the early-morning hours and note the lighted roof window in Pat's upstairs bedroom—the only light visible at that hour in the *hameau*—and the sound of her venerable Olympia portable typewriter clickety-clacking across the courtyard.

And that is how Monsieur Knet remembered Patricia to me: a sharply syncopated sound in the night, a rectangle of eery illumination, a woman sitting at her desk, writing, he said, "frightful things dripping with blood."

But then he remembered one more thing: "But if she so much as scratched her finger, there would be a *terrible* drama."[87]

Typing away in the attic of her favorite of all the temporary houses she hopes to make permanent, the top of her head framed by the high, lighted window in her writing room so that she appears to her neighbor as a mostly missing portrait nailed up to the night sky, Patricia Highsmith steadily pilots her old German typewriter into the early hours of a cool French dawn. . . . It's as good an introduction as any to the life of this profoundly complicated writer who, despite all her restless travels, made her most rewarding journeys seated at her desk in what she called an "appointment kept on the edge of a chair."[88]

It scarcely needs saying that "the edge of a chair" is where people usually perch when they expect to receive bad news.

Patricia Highsmith's news *is* disturbing—perhaps it was even more disturbing for her than it is for her readers—and she always went to the ends of her nerves to get it. But there is nothing like taking that journey with her (nothing like it in the *world*, in fact) for illuminating the resemblances between what your imagination has been concealing from you and the pitiless exposures of her dark and dangerous art.

And here that journey must continue.

I wish you a *bon voyage*.

3

A SIMPLE ACT OF FORGERY

PART I

"One usually pays more dearly for the false than for the true, mademoiselle," Lucien said.

—**"The Great Cardhouse"**

It was a phony though. That was why Tom preferred it.
—*The Boy Who Followed Ripley*

Honesty, for me, is usually the worst policy imaginable.
—**Patricia Highsmith**, 1960

In the simple act of forgery—by no means her first or her last—committed in her thirty-fourth writer's notebook in the spring of 1978, Patricia Highsmith pretended that it was April, that she was in London, and that she was making sketchy notes on an interview she had just completed with "one of the very few journalists I've ever liked!"

Well, the first part was true enough.

Pat *had* been in North London on 4 April, recuperating from her official duties at the Berlin Film Festival, alarming her friends with her behavior, and entertaining impolite thoughts about a journalist. Not the amiable young man she says she has just spoken to, but the intrusive woman who called to ask her opinion on the "man who [had just] knifed the Poussin in the National Gallery."[1]

Disobliging behavior to members of the press—her little exercise in home-
land defense—is nothing new for Pat Highsmith, who usually prefers to secure her borders *before* she is invited to explore them by pushy journalists. On
the long list of loathing she gleefully compiled during her thirty-five years of
self-exile from the United States, "circling vultures" (her term for members of
the press who want to write her biography) vies for pride of place with Women
Who Remind Her of Her Mother. "Journalists," she wrote scornfully. "I prefer
prostitutes, who sell only their bodies, not their minds."[2] Every lengthy interview she has ever given to a journalist—and despite her reputation for reclu-
siveness, she has given many—has been marked by evasion, misdirection,
and what could politely be construed as a distinct economy with the truth.

Of course, there are regular exceptions to Pat's personal hate parade. She is
pleased to have articles by the journalists and authors she respects (like Francis Wyndham, Noëlle Loriot, Julian Symons, and Josyane Savigneau) form
the public perception of her work. And women who behave like her mother,
Mary (not to mention Mother Mary herself), have been the bliss and bale of
her life as a lover.

But here she is in the scented spring of 1978 writing that she's in London, in
April, in conversation with a journalist she likes, when in fact it's May, and she's
back in her house in suburban France; alone with her disturbing emotions
(love again, the feeling she most often confuses with murder or self-extinction)
and enclosed in her customary habitat: a cone of watchful darkness.

What's more, she is poised on the edge of some very characteristic trouble
with her new friend, the likeable journalist. It's the kind of trouble that only
an imagination as concentrated, as detailed, and as eccentric as Patricia Highsmith's can produce.

Why Pat was forging entries in her notebooks, and what the slow roiling of
her emotions was about to provide for a hapless member of the press, are important keys to the imagination of an author whose own character is as difficult to "undo" as the famous set of double-nested Bramah locks which forced
the great Harry Houdini—an artist only sightly more obsessed with escape
than Patricia Highsmith—into an unbecoming act of forgery himself.*

On 22 March, thirteen days before her trip to London, Pat began a fortnight's stay in Berlin as a jury member of the 1978 Berlin Film Festival. In what
might have reminded her of her own partitioned imagination, the ten-foot-
high depression-gray Berlin Wall, fancifully garnished with barbed wire, still

---

* Harry Houdini's celebrated "escape" from handcuffs secured by a double-nested Bramah
lock at the London Hippodrome in 1904 seems to have been the result of a setup between
the *Daily Mirror*'s owner, Alfred Charles Harmsworth, and Houdini himself. Harmsworth,
incidentally, was a relation of one of Pat Highsmith's young lovers.

divided this city on whose kinkier qualities the fifty-seven-year-old Pat had been taking desultory notes since August of 1976. Because she cast the net of her obsessions over everything she looked at, the Berlin of Pat's cahier seems to be the setting for a Highsmith novel: it teams with people in disguise, violent inexplicable acts, and sudden odd affinities.

A "sturdy macho girl" in a lesbian bar pokes Pat in the ribs, declares she's "not too soft," then smashes her glass of vodka on the floor. Pat rather admires this gesture. She has been frequenting gay, lesbian, and transvestite bars like the Ax-Bax, Romy Haag, and Pour Ellen to save her "heart from the boring bourgeois" she is "otherwise surrounded by" at the film festival. She receives these small aggressions from her barmate as friendly overtures. Possibly she is influenced by the fact that the sturdy girl has already paid for her vodka.

A few snapshots from Pat's infrequent visits to Germany (this was her fourth) live on in her archives. In two or three of them, she is grinning and appears to be almost at ease. She *is* almost at ease—or in some vague relationship to that condition—and this anomaly is due to the presence of the other figures in the photos: a troupe of transvestites who have dolled themselves up for the camera in sequins, feathers, and more makeup than most people manage to apply in a year. Pat feels right at home with them.

"No wonder Berliners liked disguises!" she writes in the book that she will set partially in Berlin, *The Boy Who Followed Ripley.* "One could feel free, and in a sense like *oneself* in a disguise."[3]

In public (private is another matter), Pat still tends to wear beautifully starched and ironed clothing—shirts, vests, and pants—which she still mail-orders from Brooks Brothers in the United States. She slips her feet into men's black loafers whenever she can and accessorizes her "look" with what could be mistaken for her own version of transvestism: a scarf, a necklace, a bracelet, even a trace of lipstick.

In a photograph taken in the early 1940s in New York City by her friend the great photographer Ruth Bernhard, Pat looks attractively and impenetrably thoughtful. In other photographs from the same era by another friend, Rolf Tietgens, she seems to be provocatively and abstractedly *garçonne.* Interpreted in her twenties in very different ways by two photographers who were competing for her attentions, Pat still manages not to give away a great deal.

Photographs of Patricia Highsmith at fifty-seven, however, are more likely to arrest than to attract. Her posture, as always, is braced against embarrassment, but her face seems to be involved in a furious rebellion against her oxford collars and her preppy, perfectly turned-back cuffs. Her eyes are heavily pouched now, the parabola of the jaw is swollen, and the provocative pout of her mouth in adolescence has given way to the pendulous lower lip of middle age. The ivory of her skin is creased, stained, and lined by her heavy drinking and smoking and—even worse for her complexion—by the violent ideas which have worked their way through her imagination. A thicket of bangs provides the cover through which she still looks up and out at the world with a remarkably sharp regard.

At twenty, as Gabrielle Chanel famously said, you have the face you were born with. At fifty, you have the face you have earned.

In Paris restaurants, where French waiters are uncomfortably good at reading gender code, Pat is sometimes directed to the men's lavatory.

"Now, matter of fact, I am addressed as M'sieur so often it is quite disconcerting. Granted long hair doesn't do much to make one look more feminine these days, I should think a touch of lipstick and a necklace would. No. I am halted from going into ladies' rooms. 'Not that door M'sieur!' It's enough to drive one mad."[4]

Pat thought that waiters stopped her "because I have big feet and skinny thighs."[5] She had to think something.

Certainly, there is room to speculate about who the "real" cross-dresser is in those photographs of Pat and her merry band of transvestites from the Fatherland. For the moment, it is enough to remember that Pat's letters to her mother were filled with lists of clothing as specifically described as the costumes in her novels.

"People," Pat notes, ever-hopeful on her nights out in Berlin that a quick change means a new life, "carry two changes of clothing for the evening." She likes "the unreality of the city . . . ," its "end of the world quality," the fact that it is "artifically maintained and is in danger of being abandoned." Berlin in 1978 is definitely Highsmith Country.

But Pat was not writing her Berlin notes when she was in Berlin. She wrote up her notes—they continued to be the skeleton of every fiction she devised—when she was back at her house in Moncourt, after her short detour through London. She was weeks away from what she appeared to be writing about with such immediacy.

"A pity," she writes, confessing to her forgery like the good Dostoyevskyan she is, that "I didn't keep a diary all those thirteen days."

For the past forty years, chronological notation has been Patricia Highsmith's lifeline; the increasingly fraying strand she follows compulsively through the unchronological labyrinth she has made of her life. She began taking notes on herself, her ideas, and her surroundings at the age of fifteen or sixteen (she says twelve, but those notes are lost) when she was living with her family in Manhattan and acknowledging her unconventional emotions and the even more unconventional ways she found to accommodate them. Her obsessive intelligence quickly codified the note taking into two categories: her writer's notebooks, to which she gives the slightly elevated term "cahiers" and which she uses as a seedbed for her fictions; and her personal "diaries," the "journals" to which she confides the often extreme details of her intimate life.

The cahiers never vary, either in shape or form: they are always Columbia University or New York University notebooks (or notebooks identical in size to these) with firm boards, wire rolls to bind them, and lined pages. And, starting with Cahier 26, they always begin with a front-cover list of the places she has travelled to and they always end with an inside-the-back-cover list of the book titles she is considering. They are further divided into rigidly subtitled and heavily cultivated creative territories: "People and Places," "Keime" (German for "germs," a fertile term she lifted from Henry James), daily notes, favorite quotes, lengthy ideas for longer fictions, as well as "Notes on an Ever-Present Subject": the rubric for her persistent musings on her own and everyone else's homosexuality. Pat conscientiously maintained these categories in all her cahiers throughout her entire writing life.

Sometimes Pat rehearses the motives for her prolixity in the cahiers, and sometimes she simply tries to deduce her motives from her actions. "But there must be a certain core of self-respect in a person who continuously keeps a diary. Maybe he doesn't intend to look back, but someone else might, even if the diary is in code."[6]

Code is the word for it. From her very first entries, Pat flogged herself into double duty by keeping her notebooks and diaries in five languages: serviceable English (or, rather, good American) in the main, but also ungainly French, bad Italian, awkward German, and a sprinkling of more or less strangled Spanish. ("I am so ambitious that I must telescope 2 separate ambitions—writing a diary and learning a language.")[7] Regularly, she mixes up which materials should go in which book (notebook or diary)—and then apologizes with the guilt of someone who feels her impulses to be so unruly that she just *has* to corral them into the proper category.

Days, months, and years after she has filled up the pages of her cahiers and diaries, she continues to insert marginal comments, underlinings, and exclamation points. These remarkings and rereadings—from the vantage point of a self-critical present or an embittered future—ensure that Pat's longest and most crucial conversations are always with herself: "This doesn't get any point across. And furthermore it's *weak!*"[8]

Occasionally, Pat the Part-Time Librarian takes up the pen and starts to cross-reference the material in the notebooks with the material in her diaries.[9] She doesn't want future readers of any of these confessional works to miss a trick or overlook an implication. And because she's practical about what her imagination produces, and also because waste of any kind makes her angry, she likes to remind herself that there is yet plenty of useful material for fiction to be mined from these little life-books.

Still, any writer who keeps eight thousand pages of notebooks and diaries in five languages—four of which she has never mastered—and, what's more, keeps them in a hand as difficult to decipher as a physician's scrawl on a prescription pad, really does raise the question of just how much she wants people to know about what is *in* this mountain of pages she left behind. Pat's family in Fort Worth used to labor over the "hieroglyphics" in her letters home, and even then, said her cousin Dan Walton Coates, they "couldn't ever tell if she was saying that she was coming home on the seventeenth or leaving on the seventeenth!"[10]

Moreover, because Pat is committed to the principle that nothing is as it seems to be, and because she cannot allow herself to vacate her lifelong habit of keeping the chronological time (even when she is interrupting the chronological clock), she does just what her fictional characters do when *their* "real" relations to the exterior world start to crumble.

She fakes it. She forges the dates and the places—long after she has lived through the times and the experiences—to make it appear that she has not turned her detailed, daily-kept notations into records which are more like memoirs than like chronicles. Gore Vidal, Pat's fellow expatriate and occasional correspondent, makes a lucid distinction: a memoir, he writes, is "how one remembers one's own life."[11] Memory is not history.

For now, it is useful to note that a writer—especially a writer like Patricia Highsmith who is working in what she swears to you is her most explicit manner—can't always be taken at her word.

What has been engaging Pat about Berlin—aside from the link with her own shadowy Germanic paternal origins and the possibility of lucrative film and television contracts there[12]—is what interests her about everything: "the element of disguise," the possibility of impersonation, of transformation, of forgery. But forgery, like the other shortcuts to transformation (murder, robbery, theft of identity, etc.) which occupy her imagination, has always been her favorite crime and strongest principle.* Nestling just under the surface of

---

* The urge to transform is as American as it is Ovidian. It was America's first statesman and inventor, Benjamin Franklin, whose obsession with transformation from poverty to wealth produced *Poor Richard's Almanack*: the self-help manual designed to instruct Americans in the useful art of reinventing themselves. And it was Franklin's quick-change compatriots— the rebellious English colonists in Massachusetts whose forged identities as "Indians" allowed them to dump tea belonging to the East India Company into Boston Harbor and spark the American Revolution—who transformed themselves into the first American citizens.

her second Ripley novel, *Ripley Under Ground* (1970), is a convincing aesthetic argument in favor of forged art (Ripley prefers Bernard Tufts's forged Derwatt painting to any original) and impersonated lives (Ripley himself impersonates the long-dead artist Derwatt). "I am afraid to say how much I like it," Pat wrote when she finished the manuscript.[13] One of her inspirations for the forgery business at the center of this book (Derwatt Ltd.) was the Dutch artist Hans van Meegeren's successful counterfeiting of several Vermeer paintings during the late 1930s and early 1940s. Amongst van Meegeren's happy customers was Hitler's deputy, Herman Göring. Pat liked van Meegeren's style.

For a long time, Pat has been thinking about what she calls her "4th Ripley"— *The Boy Who Followed Ripley*—a novel which will once again depend on forgery, the counterfeiting of identity, and even on the appearance of a youthful "copy" of Tom Ripley himself: sixteen-year-old Frank Pierson. By 1978, the year Pat is getting ready to finish this novel by slipping Ripley into a frilly party frock and designer heels and handing him a large handbag, forgery is as reflexive a reaction for her as it is for her characters.

Very soon now, Pat will start generating dozens of false names and fake identities—not one of which is meant for life in a Highsmith novel or short story. She creates these characters all through the 1980s and early 1990s in Switzerland, encourages them to write letters of "political opinion," and then mails their urgent messages off (signature and handwriting disguised) to newspapers, journals, politicians, and state officials. It's the same old Highsmith hand doing what it does best: counterfeiting identity. But in this case, Pat counterfeits with a purpose. She wants her forgeries to express her unrelenting hatred of the State of Israel.

Over the years, Pat managed to ventriloquize letters for at least thirty-eight "politically concerned" characters. "Edgar S. Sallich" from Locarno, "Isabel Little," "Maria L. Leone," "Janet Tamagni," "Eddie Stefano," "Elaine Dutweiler," and "Phyllis Cutler" were among her most prolific pseudonyms, but Pat kept all her mouthpieces reasonably busy. Still, no one who reads the heat-seeking little missives these characters produced—and no one who counts up the myriad false names Pat needed to produce them—could ever imagine that her motives in this matter were entirely (or even predominantly) "political."[14]

Pat's arrival in Berlin on 22 March 1978 for the Berlin Film Festival was slightly shadowed by the fact that she failed to recognize Christa Maerker, the helpful friend who had come to pick her up at the airport. Pat and Christa, a German journalist and filmmaker, were introduced to each other on Pat's last trip to Berlin. They got on "incredibly well and laughed through the evening," then continued their friendship by correspondence when Pat went back to France. Christa was so impressed by Pat that she recommended her for the Berlin Film Festival jury; and the festival director "was thrilled" by the idea.[15]

But when Christa met Pat at the Berlin airport and tried to hug her, Pat, without a flicker of recognition, "became like a piece of wood," leaned down, and whispered in her ear: "Please help me, I want to meet Christa Maerker." "Still in a state of awe" about Pat's work, Christa refused to believe Pat was drunk. But she noticed that when they reached the hotel Pat's only request was for a bottle of scotch.[16]

Thirteen tumultuous days later when the festival was over, Pat had filched from her hotel room a blue and white bath mat embossed with two words and a date—"Hotel Palace . . . 1973." The mat was meant to be a souvenir of a newly kindled Berlin romance, but thirty years on it looks more like a symbol of the rituals she was using to control her anxieties: rigorous washing, the replacement of feelings with objects, and a compulsion to number her desires.[17]

Although Pat is only a working rumor in her native United States, she has been invited to this festival because of her European celebrity. Despite paralyzing shyness, she accepted the invitation because she is both professional about her work and alert to its perquisites, which sometimes include expenses-paid junkets to good hotels (like this one) in cities (like Berlin) where a writer (like herself) can gather useful material for a new novel.

When the festival showings begin, Pat finds that she is busier than she wants to be, trying to keep up with the (rather relaxed) twenty-three-film viewing schedule. She asks her translator friend, Anne Morneweg, to accompany her to the German-language films so she won't miss any of the dialogue.

Predictably, Pat is unhappy at the festival—looking, as she has always looked in public, "uncomfortable with the proceedings," *any* proceedings. David Streiff, the director of the Locarno Film Festival, spotted Pat sitting "alone in a restaurant—a cheap and uncomfortable beer place right between the Zoo Palast and the Aeroflot offices. She impressed me strongly, through the strength and solitude she expressed—or better: the visible will to be left alone which she transmitted to everybody around."[18]

Pat has reasons for her discomfort. She is being obliged to watch scenes of a sexual nature on film, while her usual preference is to cover her eyes during film sex and keep them open for film violence. When her irrepressible friend the seventy-five-year-old performance artist Lil Picard wrote to her from New York to praise some erotic films, Pat's reponse was characteristic: "I don't think I would enjoy these sex films. I have never seen any and have no curiosity about them. Maybe something is the matter with me. Of course a lot is the matter with me. But I have never enjoyed on the screen watching people petting or making love."[19]

Worse, even, than having to watch sex on film was Pat's selection as president of the Berlin Film Festival jury. It was a terrible idea.

Short on famous figures for the job of jury president, the festival elevated Pat to the office over her own objections—or so she wrote. She "tried to push [the honor off] on "Angelopoulos or Sergio Leone, but [had no] success." She was modest enough to know that her film experience was insufficient to the occasion and canny enough to realize that even a "presidency" was too democratic an office for her to enjoy. She said later that her "simplest suggestions were thwarted," but working with—or even in—a group of people was well outside Pat's capacities. Very soon, the other jurors were unhappier with her presidency than she was. The reports filtering out from the committee meetings were not good: "She was usually half asleep, she never took notes, she never participated, she never took over the discussions, and [she even tried to change] the format by appointing someone else." The director of the festival was forced to conclude, politely and privately: "We made a tremendous mistake."[20]

And then, all of a sudden, just as it does in a Highsmith novel, something completely different broke into Pat's Berlin experience. Something—as the writer and critic Susannah Clapp said about another feature of Pat's fiction—that seemed to make its appearance from "another world."[21]

Imagine—let's have some fun with this—that an otherwise idle little devil, engaged by Hell's Upper Management to plant crippling suspicions into the minds of working writers, has applied itself directly to the Problem of Patricia Highsmith. Perhaps this junior demon is something like the diminutive black figure with the harrowing laugh whose antic presence creates such havoc in Pat's early satire, *The Straightforward Lie*. Or perhaps it resembles the small, dark creature of her anxieties—the "Yuma baby"—which featured in her only attempt to write a "ghost" story: the brilliantly creepy "The Empty Birdhouse" (aka "The Yuma Baby," written in September of 1966), a story prompted by Caroline Besterman's admiration for the supernatural tales of M. R. James.[22]

And let us further imagine that Hell's concentration on Pat Highsmith has produced something like the deranged little details of a typical Highsmith anecdote; the very elements which obsess her in her cahiers and diaries. "The chance meeting," "the slightly tainted exchange of favors," "the semisuppressed confession," "the poison pen letter"—all of which, in their confusion of bad motive and good intention, could easily have been imported from anything Patricia Highsmith ever wrote.

In fact, this is exactly what happened to Pat at the Berlin Film Festival of

1978—without, perhaps, the active participation of Hell's Executive Commit-tee. And the complication of events that produced this tangle of woe demon-strates just how closely Pat's life could resemble her work—and just how responsible she was for that resemblance.

Sometime during her thirteen-day residence at the film festival, Pat Highsmith was "stopped in the street" by a stranger, a young Highsmith fan named Christopher Petit. (He was also a friend of David Streiff.) He was and is an English writer and journalist and he had, he says, been "watching her for several days." "My behavior with her," says Chris Petit, "was kind of unchar-acteristic. [Accosting her on the street] is not something I normally would have done."

Chris Petit is not the first or last Highsmith fan to find himself behaving "uncharacteristically" in Pat's presence. Both Pat's work and life exerted a sub-lunary pull on friends, fans, and lovers, who, against their better judgment, sometimes caught themselves acting just like characters in a Highsmith novel.

Pat's lover in 1960–61, Marijane Meaker, was so driven by jealousy of a ri-val that she had to be talked out of committing a mail fraud that would have redirected all Pat's mail to her own apartment for inspection. Undeterred, Meaker busily steamed open Pat's letters when they lived together in Pennsyl-vania and took some secret peeks at Pat's cahiers. Ellen Blumenthal Hill, Pat's longtime partner in the kind of bad behavior obsessive love can inspire, found Pat's diaries irresistible reading (until, that is, she read what Pat wrote about her); and Pat had to lock her teenage journals away from Mother Mary's prying eyes.

Marion Aboudaram, Pat's current lover in Paris, first introduced herself to Pat with a straightforward lie. She said she had an assignment to interview Pat for *Cosmopolitan* magazine. But Marion had no assignment. "*Cosmo* didn't ask me," she says. "I decided it was a way to meet her."[23]

A young friend of Pat—the kind of friend who painted Pat's kitchen for free and went out to Moncourt to turn over the engine of Pat's "awful metallic blue Simca" so the battery wouldn't die when Pat was away (Pat managed to find many such friends)—was given a key to Pat's house so she could use it in Pat's absence. One time, when Pat was gone, the young woman opened the door to a photographer who was obsessed by Pat's work, and the photographer took se-cret pictures of Pat's personal possessions and of all the rooms in her house.[24]

(Because the existence of these photographs is a violation of privacy, and because I took information from them for this book, I can now add my own name to the list of people inspired to behave badly by Patricia Highsmith.)

A fervid fan of Pat's novels in Paris, "an orphan of 21 who lives with his aunt" (he strongly identified with all the orphaned males in Pat's work), was allowed to meet Pat in 1969. He immediately drove her mad: "He is so neurotic himself, it makes me feel almost normal," she wrote to Lil Picard. "He gushes at me, praises me, until I want to scream."[25] Still, this fan, who knew all about cats, was allowed to select a seal-point Siamese kitten for Pat, and he and his aunt sometimes looked after Pat's cats on her trips away. One night—the circumstances were complicated and involved a fight with her current lover, Jacqui—Pat ended up sleeping in the aunt's bed, where, for once, Pat herself was on the receiving end of an unwelcome sexual advance.[26]

The list of aberrant activities by people under the sway of Patricia Highsmith—one way or another—is long and varied. Although on a good day her personal appeal was considerable, Pat did not have the kind of celebrity or, by now, the sort of looks which usually magnetize such antics. What the antics expose is the power of Pat's work "to breed about her the world she created in her novels."[27] Pat conferred what all powerful writers confer upon their "friends and acquaintances: the vocabulary to describe life in [her] terms."[28] The related irony—that readers of Highsmith's prose then imposed their Highsmith-inflected lives back upon *her*—caused Pat no end of trouble.

But she wasn't troubled by her new acquaintance in Berlin, the journalist Christopher Petit. Quite the opposite.

In one of those numerical calculations she could never quite resist, Pat immediately reckoned that Petit had to be "about 28" years old. Her numbers were good: he was *exactly* twenty-eight, and he turned out to be the film critic for the London publication *Time Out*. In the kind of unlikely coincidence usually found in a Highsmith work, Chris Petit's own first film would be produced by Wim Wenders, the man who had just directed *The American Friend,* a film adaptation of two of Highsmith's Ripley books: *Ripley's Game* and *Ripley Under Ground.* ("He mingled two books for *American Friend,*" Pat said tartly of Wenders's adaptation.)[29]

Like the chance encounters in her stories, Highsmith's meeting with this young journalist was familiar in its ordinariness. But it was also the kind of meeting with which she liked to ignite the spiralling paranoias of her murdering "hero-criminals."

Compliments were offered by Chris Petit. Miss Highsmith was "one of the two or three authors who mattered to him." A favor was asked: he'd like to do an interview with her for *Time Out*. Perhaps, because Pat was canny about such things and intent on receiving good value for her investments, there was a little probing of mutual intentions on Pat's part before the interview was actually granted. But she did grant an interview to Christopher Petit—and rather easily, too. She would be in London briefly, she told him, after the festival ended. He could see her there.

Pat was usually eager for publicity—her letters to editors are full of helpful suggestions for *her* kind of public relations, the kind that don't get too close and ruin a writer's workday—and she kept tabs on everything her publishers and agents did and didn't do for her. But, like the title of one of her short stories, this encounter with the young journalist produced "nothing that meets the eye"—for now. For now, it was just one of those serendipitous meetings between hopeful youth and middle-aged achievement that punctuate the career of every successful writer.

So Pat gave Chris Petit a number where she could be reached in North London (it was at the two Barbaras' studio in Islington), and that was that. It was a leisurely beginning to a complicated episode—just the way she said she liked to start her novels.

"I am inclined to write books with slow, even tranquil beginnings, in which the reader becomes thoroughly acquainted with the hero-criminal and the people around him."[30]

Meanwhile, the film festival was in full swing and so were Pat's most volatile feelings. Like Colette—whose work Pat once "defended" against an "attack" by the illustrious French writer Nathalie Sarraute during a Paris luncheon (Sarraute had maintained that Colette was too "feminine" for her; the much-younger Highsmith gathered the courage to disagree)[31]—Pat was still capable of the premonitory strike, of writing her own life before it happened. In the plots she has been notating for her "4th Ripley," Tom is deeply and ambiguously attached to an attractively wealthy teenage boy. And Pat Highsmith, at fifty-seven years of age in the city of Berlin, has just been "bowled . . . over . . . knocked . . . mentally on the floor" by a twenty-five-year-old girl: an up-and-comer on Berlin's avant-garde art circuit who enjoys slipping into male drag.

Tabea Blumenschein was the star of experimental director Ulrike Ottinger's new film, *Madame X,* and she had been Ottinger's live-in lover for the last seven years. Pat's feelings for Tabea, kindled on a previous trip to Berlin, flared up now at the festival, although Pat was still involved in her three-year-long relationship with the French novelist and translator Marion Aboudaram.

Tabea—deploying equal amounts of makeup and flair—liked to get herself up as both a louche boy and a flamboyant woman. As a boy, she was dark and sneering, with a disreputable mustache and an ear loop. Dressed as a woman, she was a glamorously assertive blonde whose S&M accoutrements were part of her impersonation.

An enthusiastic participant in the sexual, social, and artistic experiments with which Berlin's (and New York's and Paris's and London's) art world amused itself in the late 1970s ("T. spoke often of the Berlin discos, the one-night-stands," Pat wrote),[32] Tabea was also an eclectic maker of art: she designed costumes, she painted and drew, she acted in films. Without her makeup—there is a pale photograph of her with an unadorned face, plump and puppyish and blinking into the sun—Tabea seems hardly to exist. Her face paint, her disco nights, and her elaborate rotations of dress and disguise and transformation were all raw materials for her fresh identities. It was half performance art, half character armor, and wholly fun for a twenty-five-year-old caught up in Berlin nightlife. If, that is, you didn't think too deeply about what those impostures might be concealing.

Pat always thought deeply about impostures and concealment, but for a woman like her—a woman in late middle age, profoundly repetitive in her habits, writing characters who were themselves obsessed with transformation—Tabea's quick-change artistry and avant-garde glamour arrived as a *coup de foudre*.

"Pat," says Tabea Blumenschein,

> never had friends like me. Her women friends were always dressed the same, she never saw anyone change costume and appearance like me. She was excited by my changing of my appearance, she was always asking what I was wearing in letters.[33]

Pat's courting habits, always a little unusual, were, with Tabea, strongly marked by her fetishes. As though she couldn't quite distinguish between herself and Tabea (whose behavior in Berlin in the 1970s resembled Pat's behavior in Manhattan in the 1940s), Pat often doubled the presents she bought for Tabea, purchasing one item for the young woman and a twin item for herself.

Amongst her gifts to Tabea were a "flick knife," a wristwatch with a black face and no numerals, an odd mirror, and striped shirts that she insisted on calling "sailor clothes." (They both liked sailors: Pat was first attracted to Tabea because she appeared as a sailor in a campy sailor film by Ulrike Ottinger, and Tabea, in the present day, still paints jaunty pictures of sailors.) Pat bought a mysterious object for which she paid "3 pounds liquid" and which she described to a perplexed Christopher Petit as a "Filthy Paperclip." This object, mailed out to both Pat and Tabea with the label "Toy Airplane" on it, might have been an erotic toy, but Pat's reference to it was so coy that its purpose was entirely obscured.

Despite her dislike of sex on film, Pat had always warmed to dirty jokes, filthy limericks (she was the author of many an unprintable verse), and vulgar descriptions. She liked to refer to the third French village she lived in, Montmachoux, as "Mount-my-shoe," thus neatly connecting her distaste for the habits of dogs to a slur on her surroundings, and she always found verbal and visual jokes involving human sexual parts and bathroom habits hilarious. She happily described to friends a joke photograph she kept of a woman with one naked breast caught in a washing machine mangle (the photograph is excruciating to look at), captioned: "You think you've got problems?"

In the book she's writing now, her "4th Ripley," Pat imagines Tom Ripley toying with the idea of acquiring the ultimate dirty joke: an inflatable doll wife and an inflatable doll mistress. Ripley, whose sexual instincts are perhaps most clearly expressed by his later bedtime readings of *Christopher and His Kind* by Christopher Isherwood and Richard Ellmann's biography of Oscar Wilde (Pat's own bedtime reading), decides what Pat herself might have decided under the circumstances: that the rubber sex dolls are as threatening to him as "real" women are. "It would take all the breath out of a man" to blow those dolls up, Ripley thinks.[34]

In her most recently published work, *Edith's Diary* (1977), Pat made Edith's son Cliffie, a character so unattractive that readers can feel the motives she had in creating him (Cliffie was suggested by a boy of whom Pat was both jealous and scornful; a boy she later compared to the cannibal Jeffrey Dahmer), fantasize about creating a doppelgänger of the woman who obsesses him. But what will he use? "The problem of the materials threw him off."[35] Pat's male characters can rarely be bothered to have sex of any kind.

During her thirteen days in Berlin, Pat's courting habits followed the rules of revulsion as closely as they obeyed the laws of attraction. Her most inspired idea for a romantic outing with a woman thirty-two years her junior was to take Tabea Blumenschein to a place made memorable by the courting rituals of another species—the crocodile pen at the Berlin zoo.*

"I shall remember the zoo, with its crocodiles, and Tabea leaning on a rail, on the left, gazing down into their heated pond. She remarked that they had wounded each other by their biting. True. The blood was visible."[36]

Blood was usually "visible" when the talented Miss Highsmith fell in love. But from the onset of every love affair she was convinced that the blood would be her own. When Pat was Tabea's age, she was phrasing love as something that would empty the blood from her body.

"Tonight I want to rid myself forever of love, tear it out of me as I would a tick sucking my blood."[37]

Pat burned, suffered, and died in love—and so, if they returned her feel-

---

* She gives Tom Ripley exactly the same adventure with young Frank Pierson in *The Boy Who Followed Ripley*.

ings, did the women who loved her. Lynn Roth—her affair of a few separated weeks in 1953 and 1954—was someone whose pervasive influence she would compare to Tabea's. For now, the battered veteran of many love wars, Pat was confining herself to liquids and modest hopes: "To laugh and have a beer with [Tabea]—that seems all I want in life just now."

So she drinks floods of beer and visits the aquarium with Tabea ("her favorite," Pat says), as well as those attractively bleeding crocodiles in their hot-water bath. Berlin's distinctively double nature—two cities with opposing, "entirely artificial" governments, and it's worth your life to breach the Wall that separates them—is newly attractive to Pat. And Berlin's S&M nightlife, and the gratuitous sexual transformations of the artists who assist in it, cannot help but appeal to a writer who declared at the age of twenty: "We love either to dominate or to be mastered ourselves. . . . there is no love without some element of hate," "nor a love without domination."[38]

Unchanged in her inclinations since she first voiced those opinions, and an old if still somewhat naïve hand in these matters by now, Pat assessed Tabea as a girl who "need[s] a boss." Tabea herself says: "I felt I couldn't live in Berlin alone. . . . I was so young. . . . I couldn't live [alone] like Pat was living."[39]

No one could live "like Pat was living" for long, not even Pat herself. Falling in love with Tabea was a catastrophe for her. Pat's lover Marion Aboudaram witnessed the damage when Pat finally returned to Moncourt from Berlin and London:

Pat's eyes were completely closed, she was trembling, she had drunk so much. All the time I gave her vitamins. All she did was drink milk and beer and eat oranges. Tabea and I both had blue-gray eyes and when she looked at mine, she almost swooned.[40]

On 11 April, Pat wrote a plain little poem to Tabea to show just where this love was leading her. Pat was feeling the "strange impulse or desire"

To throw myself into the nearest
Body of deep water,
And drown.
I am not trying to prove
Anything to anybody.
This isn't blackmail.
I'd do it with a smile.[41]

Although she adored boats, fantasized many times about being a sailor, and ended the lives of several of her characters in "deep water," Pat had always feared dying in water. "[T]he thought of drowning is very unpleasant to me," she told a British journalist in 1987. Naturally, she hid this true fact from her interviewer (Duncan Fallowell) in a haze of misdirection; telling him that her health was "excellent" and that her only illness had been "five cases of the flu." This, after a life of racking hypochondria, serious blood diseases (chronic anemia and clotting deficiencies), grave arterial maladies (Buerger's disease), terrible problems with her teeth, and a very recent (1986) operation for lung cancer. She also left out the alcoholism, the anorexia, and the depression.[42]

It's 4 April, now, the morning of her interview with Chris Petit, the young journalist she met in Berlin. Pat left the film festival three days ago to go directly to London, bypassing her house in Moncourt. She writes that she is still "spinning" from the experience of spending time with Tabea Blumenschein. In London, Pat is staying once again at the Islington home of Barbara Ker-Seymer, the highly regarded avant-garde photographer of the 1920s and 1930s (when the avant-garde was still en avant), and Ker-Seymer's companion, Barbara Roett. The two Barbaras met Pat in the 1960s at the Cagnes-sur-Mer home of Annie Duveen, a lesbian relation of the art authority Sir Joseph Duveen. Annie Duveen, Barbara Roett says, "was terrified of Pat and didn't know why she was being swooped down on": Pat could be as unsettling a houseguest as she was a hostess. But the Barbaras are as aware of Pat's eccentricities as they are sympathetic to the volatility of her current state—which has yet to involve (as did the last "crush" Pat brought to their house, the young journalist Madeleine Harmsworth) reservoir-sized applications of alcohol, faked telephone calls, and the slamming of interior doors.[43]

Chris Petit arrived in Islington to the crescent street where the Barbaras lived "early in the morning"—it was 11:00 A.M.—to find Pat already (or still) drinking beer. Right away they discovered a shared taste: "we both smoked the same untipped French cigarettes and she was impressed because I had some Boyars."

But Chris "found her sufficiently intimidating to make questions almost impossible to ask," and Pat gave him a "rotten interview." The talk was, he says, "of no consequence" except at the very end when Pat unexpectedly answered a question he put to her about her authorship of The Price of Salt, the pseudonymous "lesbian" novel she had never publicly claimed.

Pat had always been anxious about being identified with The Price of Salt, and she "stewed"—her word—terribly before and after publishing it. (See "Les Girls: Part 1.") By now, she regularly denigrated the book, attacked her mother for revealing her as the author (Mary Highsmith had spilled the beans to her minister in Texas), and only with the greatest reluctance allowed it to be brought out under her own name in England in 1990. She had had some nervous exchanges in 1985 with Alain Oulman, her editor at Calmann-Lévy in Paris, about the security of her nom de plume Claire Morgan, fearful that her authorship of the work had been leaked in France. (It hadn't, but the critics found "a Highsmith touch" in the book.)[44] When Bloomsbury finally republished *Salt* in London in 1990 with the name "Patricia Highsmith" on the front cover, they altered the title of the novel to *Carol*. Some part of *The Price of Salt* always seemed to be in disguise.

The likely reason for Pat's anxiety about the novel is the one she admitted to when she was writing it. She couldn't bear the exposure. She also couldn't resist the temptation of creating the work as a double forgery: in the novel she is both pseudonymous (she published under the name of Claire Morgan) and eponymous (she created the character of Therese from her own experience).

The Price of Salt, written in the richly figured language of pursuit, betrayal, and murder, trails elements of crime fiction but is most redolent of fairy tale. Its line of force, in Susannah Clapp's felicitous phrase, is "a detection of the heart,"[45] and its central criminal act—homosexual love—is the only one the outlaw heroines get away with.

Salt's beginnings in the toy section of a department store are filled with crude salesgirls who surround the precocious, artistic Therese like "a pack of wolves"[46]—a phrase Pat used in her notebook to describe her fellow coworkers at Bloomingdale's department store during her cameo appearance there as a salesgirl in December of 1948. (See "Les Girls: Part 1.") In a reimagining of what had actually happened to her, Pat makes one of the "wolves" steal the "bloody bag of meat" young Therese is saving for her dinner. (Pat's contempt for working-class women is palpable in this book.) Therese is dressed ritually like a "doll" in a hand-stitched bloodred dress by a gnomelike coworker who tries to mother her. Later on, Therese is redressed in a snow-white gown—again she looks like a "doll"—by another mother: her soon-to-be-disappointed prospective mother-in-law. Therese is symbolically wounded (a cut on her leg which she staunches with Kotex) just before meeting Carol, the older Ice Queen, who steals her heart, spirits her away to a kind of castle in the suburbs, feeds her a milky potion (in which Therese can taste blood and bone), asks her three important questions, and then grooms her for a long connubial voyage across the United States in a car.

Therese is courted by several men and another woman, undergoes serious tests of moral courage, and is awarded every single thing her heart desires— including Carol, the Ice Queen, who gives up her daughter for Therese. (And how Pat must have enjoyed writing *that*.) Therese's final reward is Pat's own American Dream, slightly transmuted: a really good chance at becoming a famous stage designer and a large apartment on Madison Avenue with her much older lover.

Because *The Price of Salt* is a Highsmith fairy tale, there are a few irregularities. The two heroines prefer each other to any of their attendant males (or females). The seesaw of their love balances itself on dominance and submission and teeters, refreshingly, back and forth between the two women. The power to say no (always stronger in Highsmith novels than the power to say yes) is slyly applied like an unexpected thumb to a grocer's scale. Blood is in the corner of every smile, and sexual consummations are spied upon, recorded, and offered up as legal threats. The beautiful Carol keeps a gun in the glove box of her automobile. The odor of mother-daughter incest is everywhere.

Carol and Therese's cross-country motor flight from a shadowy male pursuer is the centerpiece of *The Price of Salt*—just as the months-long motor trip of Vladimir Nabokov's brilliant hallucination, *Lolita,* is the spine which compresses the nerves of that novel—and their drive begins, as does Humbert's with his Lo, as an unacknowledged and incestuous honeymoon. Throughout the book, Carol and Therese enact a parody of mother-daughter relations which, in its quieter way, is almost as unsettling as Humbert and Lolita's awful caricature of father-daughter love.

The Price of Salt is far less conventional in its distribution of justice than Nabokov's tour de force. Nabokov's characters all get what the mid-1950s thought they "deserved" for their behavior—an early and agonizing death, mostly, and no profit from their transgressive pleasures. (Only the reader is allowed to profit from Nabokov's gorgeous prose.)

But *The Price of Salt,* published three years before *Lolita* appeared, is a homosexual love story with an almost happy ending and not, as Pat wrote in the 1990 preface to the edition bearing her name, what the literary code of the time required: a novel with an ending in which the characters "pay for their deviation by cutting their wrists, drowning themselves in a swimming pool, or by switching to heterosexuality."[47] And its pseudonymous, eponymous author actually *fell in love* with the character of Carol and with Carol's relationship to Therese as she was writing about them—a far more subtle and artistic response than falling in love with Mrs. E. R. Senn, the well-dressed bourgeoise whose chance meeting with Pat was the "germ" of *The Price of Salt*.[48] (See "Les Girls:" Part 1.)*

But on this spring morning in 1978, says Christopher Petit, Pat "did admit to me at the end that she had written *The Price of Salt*." And then she made "me promise for about 15 minutes that I wouldn't mention it in the interview or attribute it to her."

Chris Petit thinks Pat made this unusual declaration "because I'd plied her with cigarettes" and "laid it on" about her work. A year or two ago, he'd managed to get hold of a xeroxed copy of her *Plotting and Writing Suspense Fiction*—"It's not easy to find," Pat responded, grasping the fact that only a real Highsmith fan would go to that length to read her work—and Petit brought to the interview an American first edition of *Strangers on a Train* for her to sign.

"And that basically was the end of that," says Mr. Petit, except for "some [of her] pretty wacky political views. . . . Until the question of the dictionary came up."

They were talking about Berlin and Petit remarked that "visiting East Berlin is less of a cultural shock" than going to London.[49] Always happy to identify a flaw in any country she'd left behind (Pat had moved from England to France ten years before), Pat thought "that was the funniest remark I'd heard in a week. The people in London streets *do* look scruffy, shabby, unwashed even. . . . Even Regent Street begins to look like Oxford Street."[50]

Chris, who had met Tabea through the film circles he frequented, mentioned that he was going back to Berlin shortly. And then it was Pat's turn to pose a question: "In that case," she said, "perhaps you can do me a favor."

Enthralled with the idea of herself as mentor (she continued to cherish some unsettling ideas about the education of the young), Pat wanted to improve her friend Tabea Blumenschein's English vocabulary by purchasing a "German-English, English-German dictionary from Foyles, Schoeffler-Weis"[51]—as she described the tome two weeks later in a letter to Chris Petit's editor at *Time Out,* a letter which suggested that her new friend, the engaging Mr. Petit, was perhaps an imposter and almost certainly a thief—and she

---

* The publication of *Women's Barracks* by Tereska Torres in 1950 (Fawcett) opened the door to lesbian pulp fiction with its sales of four million copies, although Tereska Torres was and is a serious novelist, and *Women's Barracks,* like *The Price of Salt,* is by no means a "pulp novel." It was Torres's husband, the writer Meyer Levin—as Torres revealed to me in an interview published in the fifty-fifth-anniversary edition of *Women's Barracks* in 2005—who rewrote her novel in English (Torres wrote it in French) to include both the narrator's anti-lesbian attitude and the invented "male friend" whose faintly prurient "introduction" frames the book.

wanted Chris to take the dictionary to Berlin and deliver it to Tabea. It was "quite clear" to Chris that Pat was "too mean to pay the postage."

It was a very large dictionary.

"I . . . had to not take half my luggage in order to take this dictionary. It was an extremely heavy dictionary. Extremely heavy . . . And it was pretty clear at the end of the interview that she'd very nicely signed my book but this was the price I was going to have to pay."[52]

So Chris Petit "lugged" the dictionary to Berlin and saw the producer he was supposed to see. And during the meeting, the subject of the dictionary came up somehow, and—that little Highsmithian coincidence again—the producer, who had worked with Wim Wenders on his Highsmith film, *The American Friend,* said: "Oh I'm seeing Tabea next week and you can leave the dictionary with me." And that's what Chris Petit did, putting an end to the matter. Or so he thought. Then he "went back to London and forgot all about it."

Until, that is, a call came from his editor at *Time Out.* The editor, says Chris Petit, got directly to the point.

"He'd had this strange letter from Highsmith, accusing me of being an impersonator, an imposter . . . Because I told her that I'd promised to deliver the dictionary for her and it had never turned up [at Tabea's] . . . She was, she said, confused as to whether I'd had anything to do with *Time Out* or whether I'd made that up. . . . God knows what lengths she was going to go to."

But as a close and admiring reader of Highsmith for many years, Chris Petit thought he did know what lengths Pat was going to go with her bland, insinuating little letter to his editor about "Christopher Pettit [*sic*], who interviewed me (with tape) Tuesday April 4 . . . and seemed happy to do me this favour. The problem is, the dictionary has not arrived. Forgive me for being puzzled. . . . My London friends were unable to find him in the book."[53]

Still, Petit has been puzzling "for years" about that parenthetical phrase "(with tape)." "I always thought that was the most damning aside," he says, "the implication being that the interview was probably bogus but I had been prepared to trick myself up with a tape recorder to fool her into believing I was a journalist."[54]

Writing an accusatory letter to an editor after an interview is an unusual thing to do, even for a writer like Pat whose short stories and novels drip with poison pens.* (But she did it again when David Streitfeld interviewed her for

---

* In October of 1977, Pat, rightfully enraged, sent a letter to the editor of the *Evening Standard* in London which had printed an article by Sam White ("That Lady from Texas," 30 September 1977) mistaking Pat's age and tastes while insinuating her sexual preference: "Markedly masculine in appearance, she is something of a man-hater, a kind of female

The Washington Post. See: "The Cake That Was Shaped Like a Coffin: Part 1.")[55] Petit thinks there was a "certain glee, perhaps even malice, at the thought of causing trouble. I think it's pretty clear she thought I had run off with, dumped, or lost the dictionary and hadn't owned up. I remember the editor at the time thinking the letter odd.

"I don't suppose he'd had another like it.

"And the source of [her] confusion," says Petit, "can actually be found in *Strangers on a Train*."[56]

When Pat signed Chris Petit's first edition of *Strangers on a Train* at their little tête-à-tête in Islington, she made what was for her an unlikely error. Despite his giving her the correct spelling, and despite her own careful orthography, she misspelled Petit's name, adding an extra *t* to make it "Pettit." (Perhaps it was a likely error after all: doubling was one of Pat's deeper instincts.) That was how she wrote his name in her notebook; that was how she spelled it in the agitated letters she sent to her London friends and in the letter she sent to the editor of *Time Out* about his employee, the newly criminalized Mr. Petit. Or rather, Mr. Petit's newly criminalized double, "Mr. Pettit."

Pat's methods of inquiry, under her normal operating modes (suspicion and doubt), were circumlocuitous at best. If she could help it, she never approached anything directly. Chris Petit wondered why she didn't simply call *Time Out* magazine. "It was pretty easy to establish that I worked there." Instead, "she had all her English friends scouring the phone book under the wrong spelling when they could have looked me up on the *Time Out* masthead. If she hadn't spelt my name wrong she could have saved herself a lot of trouble!"

Six days after this little rent in the fabric of their relations occurred, the matter had been set to rights and Pat was convinced that Christopher Petit wasn't an imposter. Everything was calm again in Highsmith Country. "I think she kind of lost interest when she discovered there was no dark mystery to the fate of the dictionary," says Chris Petit.[57]

"Anyway all is cleared up now," Pat writes cheerily to Petit,[58] thanking him for his call to her in France which explained the source of her confusion: her own bad spelling and Tabea's failure to keep her appointment with the producer who was holding the dictionary for her. And she invites Chris Petit to give her a ring when she's next in London. (He did so and had an unnerving beer with Pat and Tabea; Pat had forgotten he was coming, and she and Tabea were "resting" together in bed in television director Julian Jebb's borrowed flat.) And then,

---

chauvinist." White had (less rightfully) also incurred the wrath of Nancy Mitford, who satirized him as Amyas Mockbar in her final novel, *Don't Tell Alfred*.

palpably playing with fire, Pat and Chris start exchanging letters about the possibility of his optioning a certain novel of hers for film; a novel whose title could easily be the rubric for their recent, racking relations: *The Tremor of Forgery*.

In her subsequent letters to Petit, Pat, as she usually was with young professionals, was chatty, forthcoming, supportive, and determined to get her money's worth out of the exchange. Remarking that Tabea had counted up his numerous film reviews, Pat cannily promoted one of her young protégées to another one:

> I wonder if your strenuous film-viewing activities will get you to the Edinburgh Festival? I hope so, as *Madame X* is being shown there, and Tabea Blumenschein and her partner Ulrike Ottinger are invited . . . I hope Time-Out can give it a mention, at least.[59]

And so the surface ripples closed gently over the deep waters of Pat's suspicions. But for six anxious days, Patricia Highsmith, awash in her overwhelming feelings for a much younger woman, nervous because she'd admitted her authorship of *The Price of Salt*, gamely attempting to keep her life in line by a small but significant act of forgery in her cahier, and occupied with what she automatically assumed were the criminal pursuits of her new friend, the young journalist Chris Petit, snapped right back to her default emotional position; the position which had long since determined her vision of how she confronted the world:

As an island of honesty in a sea of swindlers.

As a woman who always expected to be cheated.

As a writer who believed that everyone had something to hide.

Pat gave Therese in *The Price of Salt* and Howard Ingham in *The Tremor of Forgery* the suspicion on which this operating principle was founded: "All adults have secrets." And all her murderers and escape artists live out its most extreme version. At moments of intolerable stress, they evacuate their identities, split off into Alter Egos, and re-create their personalities accordingly.

Here is David Kelsey, the romantic psychopath with the double identity in *This Sweet Sickness*, Pat's 1962 novel about the *other* love that dare not speak its name, summing himself up: "Call me Bill," David said.[60]

And Tom Ripley, in *The Boy Who Followed Ripley*, costumed and made up as a woman and about to rescue a boy for whom he has an obvious attraction: "Don't call me Tom."[61]

And the affectless Ray Garrett, in *Those Who Walk Away*, hiding from himself and plagiarizing Sartre: "I'm not Ray Garrett tonight. I haven't been for days. . . . Perhaps identity, like hell, was merely other people."[62]

In Highsmith Country, everyone—including the author—is a forger.

4

A SIMPLE ACT OF FORGERY

PART 2

Sixteen years before her spring break in the bars at the Berlin Film Festival with Tabea Blumenschein, Pat made another kind of pilgrimage to another European country—and it produced another act of forgery. She was still the official resident of a house on Sugan Road in New Hope, Pennsylvania (see "Les Girls: Part 8"), still travelling restlessly between countries, and still a month or so away from having her lifeline permanently crossed by a meeting with Caroline Besterman in London. Now she was in Paris to pay homage to the writer— himself a connoisseur of forgery and counterfeit—whose books she'd been reading since she was seventeen years old.

On 12 July 1962 Pat emerged from a lengthy ride on the Paris metro and entered a large gate set in a stone wall so long she couldn't see the end of it. She kept her eyes on her size 9½ shoes as they walked her up and over the hilly streets, "cobbled with huge, irregular stones," of France's largest literary gathering ground: the Père Lachaise Cemetery in "the 20th Arrondissement of eastern Paris."

"These stones," she imagined with the kind of satisfaction that only thoughts of death could bring her, "must make a grim, loud noise when metal wheels of carts, carrying bodies, go over them!"[1]

It wasn't only Pat Highsmith who had to watch her feet on the cobblestones of Père Lachaise. Every writer who makes the pilgrimage there—and every writer does; Père Lachaise is the Dead Letter Office of Literary Aspirations— ends up with her eyes on the ground and "not," as Pat carefully noted in her cahier, "on the names on the vaults and tombs." Part of the secret pleasure in wandering the streets of this city of the dead is the perpendicularity of the visitor's position in relation to that of the defunct writers she is visiting; and no one strolling the cemetery wants to stumble on a stone and fall upon a grave. Pat, who would kill quite a few of her characters with nasty fictional falls, understood very well how the smallest irregularity in a rock could make the difference between life and death.

Paris is hot and bright this July day, perfect weather for cemetery walking. Fleecy clouds are chasing each other across an enormous expanse of Cézanne-blue sky, but Pat, who has a goal in mind, is not much interested in the atmosphere. She is carrying her *bolsa,* one of those large woven bags she brought back from her five months in Mexico in the early 1940s and never threw away. In it, she packs a three-by-five-inch spiral "travelling" notebook, along with something to drink and something to smoke. These are the props of her creative life and she is never without them: a notebook, a fountain pen, a lit cigarette, a bottle—and her tenebrous imagination.

Because the only thing Pat likes more than a good list is a good map, she is very much at home here. The moment she walked through the gate, she was handed—without charge; this was 1962—a map of the cemetery. And she needs it: Père Lachaise is the largest burial ground in Paris. It has its own "real roads," its own prominently posted dead celebrity lists, and the map Pat is looking at shows the neat segments into which the cemetery's 105-acre plot is partitioned. But as she walks past the graves of Bizet, Balzac, and Alfred de Musset (and bypasses entirely the graves of Chopin, Sarah Bernhardt, and Isadora Duncan), "the only name which interested" her on the map was "Oscar Wilde's." She finally "reached [his grave] after nearly a mile of walking among time-darkened rectangular vaults."

"I came upon Oscar's [monument]—a large nearly square rectangle of granite with a large Egyptian figure in headdress, flying horizontally. Only his name on the front in large letters. On the back is engraved his birth and death dates, his achievements at school, data of the Newdigate Poetry prize at the age of 24, and then those great and most fitting lines."

To an outsider artist—an outsider *everything*—like Pat Highsmith, the lines inscribed on Oscar's marble headstone (from his poem "The Ballad of Reading Gaol") seem to be written for her alone. "And alien tears will fill for him pity's long-broken urn. . . . his mourners will be outcast men."

"My eyes fill with tears," she writes, and then corrects herself in her notebook: "(filled)." She doesn't want her future readers to think she is composing these words as she weeps at Oscar's grave. Nor she does she want them to feel she is conjugating the tense of her experience to harmonize the chronology of her notebook—something she has done many times before and will do many times again. This moment is too important, too *authentic,* to counterfeit. (But, still, she never takes her eyes off her audience.)

"Such tears," she writes, meaning her own, "are brief and deep, like a stab wound," and her mind flashes to her own fear of obscurity as she "remember[s] well the various accounts of [Oscar's] lonely, pauper's funeral to which nearly nobody came." Pat needn't have worried. Her memorial service in Switzerland will have a full house and a German television crew to record it.

And then—perhaps it's an early appearance by the little fiend from Satan's Inner Circle who visited her in the preceding chapter—something rather odd happens; something which cuts another key to the complicated lock guarding the Highsmith imagination. The hypervigilant Pat misses a detail, mistakes a date, fastens on a wrong impression, and then creates a counterfeit description from her string of errors. It's the kind of mistake she will make more and more as her imagination, never really at home in Europe, is distanced by decades from the only place and time she ever knew well: New York City in the 1940s and 1950s. This is the modus operandi she will apply to Christopher Petit in May of 1978 when she misspells the young journalist's last name and then— improvising madly—turns him into a felon and a forger.

Although her tears for Oscar's fate are deeply felt, Pat has always cast a cold eye on life and death. And so, as she weeps, she can't stop herself from criticizing Oscar's funerary architecture. This is a most inappropriate monument, she thinks, for the tomb of a writer whose meditations on forgery and counterfeit, seductive portrayal of criminals, and long, unlovely martyrdom for homosexuality have moved her since she was a teenager. But Pat's critique of Oscar's grave rests squarely on the error she has just made; the result of a faulty application of the talent she is widely supposed to have mastered: close observation of detail.

Pat's mistake is to imagine that the sculpture surmounting Oscar's grave, Jacob Epstein's famous funerary monument of a winged Egyptian erected in the belle epoque, in 1909, is an art deco construction of the "mid-Twenties." What's more, she judges "the Egyptian motif not at all appropriate" for Oscar Wilde. Thus, as well as getting the sculpture's style and epoch all wrong, she fails to understand the suitability of a pharaonic figure for the tomb of a writer whose delusions of grandeur were as outsized as those of Ozymandias; a writer who composed his own Egyptian-influenced poem called "The Sphinx" and who gave the sobriquet "Sphinx" to one of his dearest friends, Ada Leverson, grandmother of Francis Wyndham, the author and critic who will shortly give Pat's work its first and most intelligent written introduction in England.

And—was it her famous reluctance to see or speak in public anything that had to do with sex?—Pat also managed to miss the winged Egyptian's most salient feature: the mutilation of its marble genitalia. Jacob Epstein, the sculptor, had been criticized before for his "undue attention" to the sexual characteristics of his statues, and the prominent genitalia of this one had been hacked away by industrious lycée students in the half century since the monument was put in place. When Janet Flanner made her own pilgrimage to Père Lachaise in the early 1920s to place a single black iris on Oscar's tomb, Epstein's statue had already been emasculated.[2] Even today, almost five decades after Pat's visit, the winged Egyptian is still without its principal part.

And so Pat Highsmith—inspired observer of minute detail, serious fan of all things Wildean, compulsive collector of dates and times in her cahiers—mistook every single thing she saw at the tomb of Oscar Wilde: the style, the substance, the suitability, the context, even the epoch.

But at the graveside, the wheel of Pat's imagination was already spinning her errors of understanding into fictional gold. Because she didn't like what she had just misidentified as the *"Art Deco* Egyptian motif" of Oscar's art nouveau Egyptian monument, she began to search her mind for a suitable replacement, for the kind of tomb *she* might have created for the King of Counterfeit.

And inspiration came to her.

Oscar's funerary monument, Pat decided, "should have been a Greek boy."

· 5 ·

LA MAMMA

PART I

I am married to my mother.
I shall never wed another.
—**Patricia Highsmith**, 1940

Momma Mia, what is mine on earth?
Tell me, of all things, that I pass by.
What must I wrest, and what is mine by birth,
And of all mothers here, whose child am I?
—**Patricia Highsmith**, 1941

Have a great desire to write sometime of a young girl putting her mother
(guardian, aunt) to bed, agreeing to all her proposals . . . nicely pouring her
cup of warm milk, promising never to speak to her young man again, and
then, with a smile, the girl plunges the scissors into her mother's bosom, and
turns them.

—**Patricia Highsmith**, 1942

Pat's owl's eye for detail—however she used it—was matched only by her proof-
reader's instinct for orthography and punctuation. There are just a handful of
uncorrected errors in her manuscript files, which, says Anna von Planta, her
editor at Diogenes Verlag, in a phrase Pat would have loved, are "so massive
that when spread out they are 150 feet in length."[1] Pat liked to look at language in its simplest form before she fell asleep, so every night she read her

dictionary for half an hour. ("As a novelist, I can say . . . the dictionary is the most entertaining book I have ever read.")[2] And she kept endless lists of words and phrases in four or five languages and queried her publishers relentlessly about misprints and wrong facts.[3] "It is hard to believe so many errors could occur in such few lines," she reproved the staff at *Who's Who*.[4] "This minuscule erratum will probably catch the eye of only one out of every three hundred and sixty-five Ellery Queen Magazine readers," she wrote to *Ellery Queen's Mystery Magazine*.[5]

Her editor at William Heinemann in London, Janice Robertson, says that Pat's submitted manuscripts were so "clean" that they rarely required correction.[6]

But in the first few hundred of the thousands of pages of plain prose and careful grammar that Patricia Highsmith plied in her thirty-eight journals and eighteen diaries, there are two words she continued to capitalize unnecessarily and more frequently than any others. "Martini" is one of those words and "Mother" is the other one, and she capitalized them both with intention. Certainly, her "Mother" and her "Martinis" (as well as her Manhattans, her ryes, her scotches, and her beers) marked her life, branded her work, and deeply affected her development.

By the time she moved to her last house in Switzerland at the end of the 1980s, Patricia Highsmith had refined her martini consumption right down to its essential ingredient: a bottle of alcohol (beer and gin or vodka for the mornings, scotch for the remains of the day) whose rations she carefully measured out for herself by drawing a line across the label.[7] Every day, she drank down to that mark, and then, rigorous as always when in the grip of a "plan," she stopped cold. But she was never able to draw a careful line across her mother, or to make a "plan" that would measure out Mary Highsmith's painful loving into doses an achingly resentful daughter could tolerate.

In the end, her mother proved to be a more potent brew than her martinis, and twenty years before Pat Highsmith's death, it was not the alcohol she felt she had to give up for good—it was her mother, Mary Coates Highsmith. ("The warmth of brandy," Pat had written in 1949, "is very like that of mother love.")[8]

The trouble with Mary Coates Highsmith was not, as her only child, Patricia, continued to insist, that she wasn't a "rational" woman. The trouble with Mary Highsmith was that she was more like a character in a book or a play than she was like anything else.

"Mary," said her Texas grandnephew Dan, "was always an eccentric. You'd recognize Mary in a roomful of people; she just had a way about her. She was squirrelly as a tree full of owls and more fun than anyone you'd ever run into. Mary had a sharp, sharp wit—there's no comparison with Pat." She "wasn't a drinker per se" but she was the life of every party, was *ready* for every party "with the most outlandish costumes and the funniest stories you ever heard." She loved to be "the center of attention and she made sure that happened."

"Mary was the only woman I knew that smoked cigarettes with a cigarette holder. Hell, it depended on where you were going; she might have a twelve-inch cigarette holder for large occasions, and then for smaller occasions, she might have one that was three inches. She had an assortment of them. And Mary had the most beautiful hands, being an artist, and she had long fingers . . . a very artistic hand."

"What I remember most was the way Mary used her hands in conversation. It was so graceful, it was just beautiful, and you put a twelve-inch cigarette holder in that hand and she makes a sweeping gesture, and it's Auntie Mame."[9]

Auntie Mame is the flamboyant character Patrick Dennis raised up to the level of literature in his 1955 bestselling novel, *Auntie Mame*. And Auntie Mame would have been an obvious comparison for an adoring nephew to make to his theatrical and glamorous Aunt Mary—especially because his aunt Mary seemed to share so many of Auntie Mame's traits.

In the postscript to a chatty, good-natured, bossy letter to her daughter, Patricia (ten-, twenty-, thirty-page single-spaced typewritten letters were *nothing* to the Highsmith women when they had something to say to each other), Mary Highsmith displayed the same weakness for attractive, youthful protégés that marked both the fictional Auntie Mame and the real Pat Highsmith in middle age.

But, unlike her daughter's much-younger, late-life protégées (who were mostly her lovers and whose memories of Pat—with one exception—are decidedly mixed), Mary Highsmith's young friend, whom she called her "adopted boy," went on to a spectacular career of his own and says that his relations with Mary were entirely pleasurable. Like her grandnephew Dan, he, too, saw Mary as a kind of Auntie Mame.

Mary's letter to Pat in January of 1965 introduces him:

My adopted boy (by mutual wishes) whom I call Romano . . . is opening on B[road]way in Baker St[reet]—the musical. . . . He's about 22 & handsome as a Greek god. Calls me Mamma mia. He said he was of English extraction. I said remember there was a Roman invasion. He's tall, slim, and dark with the most beautiful black hair & handsome

face. He's as yet unspoiled, sweet and modest. I sent him a congratulation telegram last night.[10]

Tommy Tune, the real name of the tall, dark, handsome young Texan Mary
called "Romano," grew up to be one of the American theater's most accomplished stars. An actor, dancer, singer, choreographer, and director, Tune is the
only artist in American stage history to win four of his nine Tony Awards—the
Oscars of American theater—in four different categories. If nothing else, Mary
Highsmith had a good eye for developing artists.

Or perhaps, as Tommy Tune put it, "She just liked the way I looked."

In the summer of 1965, Tommy Tune was a stagestruck young performer
working in a little theater in the Hill Country of Texas, "part of the performing
troupe and also choreographing." The theater was called the Point Summer
Theatre and it was under the aegis of the Hill Country Arts Foundation. It was
the kind of regional theater from whose stage hordes of young theatrical hope-
fuls issue forth to take the metropolis of New York by storm, ending, usually,
by taking shelter from the storm themselves in the only performing jobs they
can get: as members of Manhattan's charmingly untrained chorus of restaurant
workers. But Tommy Tune was that one-in-a-million talent who succeeds in
New York—and he did so in the musical for which Mary Highsmith sent him
her "congratulation telegram."[11]

The Point Summer Theatre was on the banks of the Guadalupe River, and
Tommy Tune remembers that "you could open the back doors of the upstage
and . . . see the river passing by." The arts foundation running it had "an art
class and I would pose for the art class to make extra money. And Mary was
painting in the art class. She was quite a good painter . . . and on breaks we
would go and have a Coke."

"I just thought Mary was so glamorous. She represented something you
just didn't find in the Hill Country. She was cosmopolitan in a way, and she
was artistic. She'd make great sweeping gestures with her hands and I seem to
remember her hair being red, almost Lucille Ball red. And she was an eccentric and of course I gravitated right to her. She was like Auntie Mame and she
called me 'Romano Romano.' And that sounded *so good* because in Texas we
didn't know anything about Italy except spaghetti.

"She was an opening for me; she opened a little bit of my tight fabric so
that I might peer through."[12]

Tommy Tune can still visualize Mary's handwriting—"sort of European . . .
very legible, and it's larger than we are taught and it's on a slant"—so he and
Mary must have corresponded for a while after he left for the bright lights and
the big city. "It was an impressionistic relationship," he says, "artist and model,

Auntie Mame and young Patrick," and because of Patricia Highsmith and because of Mary herself, he "often wondered what happened to Mary and what
happened to the paintings she did." When I told him that Mary lived to be
ninety-five, he was delighted: "Oh she *would* be one of those! She *would* be one
of those!"[13]

And there was something else Tommy Tune remembered about Mary
Highsmith, something about which he was emphatic:

"She was so proud of her daughter, so proud of her. She just was so proud
of her, not one inkling led me to believe that there were problems. She was SO
PROUD."[14]

Even though Mary seemed to friends and family like an Auntie Mame, the
American type she resembled most closely was the semitragic Southern Belle,
dramatized on stage by Tennessee Williams and represented in art and life by
Scott Fitzgerald's wife, Zelda Sayre. Zelda Sayre Fitzgerald came from a social
background that was several notches above Mary Highsmith's, but she was
Mary's near contemporary, and like Mary she was an Alabama girl, a talented
painter, and a witty, attractive, erratic, misunderstood "eccentric." (Zelda
had wanted to name her only daughter, born in the same year as Pat, Patricia.)

Mary's face was longer and more vulpine than Zelda's, but her photographed
image has Zelda's up-to-the-minute style and Zelda's put-on self-confidence.
And Mary's pose, just like Zelda's, conceals a history of wasted love and desperately thwarted ambitions.

Patricia Highsmith was, as she liked to say, "born out of wedlock" but still "le-
gitimate"; making her debut on 19 January 1921, at three thirty in the morning, several months after the physical separation—and nine days following
the legal divorce—of her twenty-five-year-old mother, Mary Coates Plangman,
from her thirty-seven-year-old father, Jay Bernard Plangman, in the oil-rich,
railroad-crossed city of Fort Worth, Texas.[15]

Even her birth was the result of a dispute. Jay B, as her father was called,
much in love with his new wife, Mary, said he wanted to establish them both
as commercial artists in Manhattan before starting a family.[16] Mary's grand-
nephew Dan Walton Coates had a slightly different interpretation of Plangman's motives: "He thought with Mary's ability and his selling they could
make some good money."[17] Mary and Jay B Plangman were already living in
New York, "just getting started in the art field," when Mary's pregnancy became apparent.[18] Plangman pressed Mary to have an abortion.

Mary, who had been struck by a display *picture* of the darkly good-looking
young Plangman in a "photographer's window" in Fort Worth and then

"sought (somehow) his acquaintance"[19]—a tendency to confuse art and life that her only child would inherit[20]—reluctantly agreed to terminate her pregnancy. When the turpentine she swallowed ("suggested by a friend") didn't work, Mary decided to keep the pregnancy and get rid of Jay B so she "could have the [child] in peace."[21] Returning to New York from a three-week separation from her husband in Alabama, Mary announced that she wanted a divorce. The Plangmans went back to Fort Worth because, as Jay B primly wrote his daughter fifty years later, "Mary had no grounds for a divorce in New York."[22]

Fort Worth, to which Pat Highsmith and her mother, Mary, were to return many times in the course of their checkered careers, is thirty miles from Dallas, Texas. At the time of Pat's birth in 1921, Dallas was the cultural and industrial center of northeast Texas. With the establishment of the eleventh branch of the Federal Reserve Bank in Dallas in 1911, it had also become the financial center. Fort Worth was not yet the lively cultural municipality it is today; it was considered to be a second-class city, "a 'cow-town' where the West begins and culture ends," as one prosperous Dallas resident put it. Leaving Manhattan and going home to her mother's boardinghouse in Fort Worth must have felt a lot like failure to the career-minded Mary Coates.

From start to finish—photograph to divorce court—the union of Mary Coates and Jay Bernard Plangman lasted little more than a year and a half.

And so, despite her mother's paint-thinner cocktail, Mary Patricia Plangman was born in her grandmother's boardinghouse (no one ever called it her grandfather's boardinghouse) in Fort Worth, at 603 West Daggett Avenue, a couple of blocks from the railroad tracks and just across the street from the Judson Boot Company and a printing business whose employees sometimes took their meals at Willie Mae's table.[23] The child came into a marriage dissolving in a cloud of acrimony and a sea of roiled feelings, and she bore if not the scent then certainly the burden of Mary's turpentine tipple. Mother Mary liked to tell the turpentine story to Pat's friends and lovers, in Pat's presence and to Pat's mortification. And Pat, insisting that she "didn't mind one bit," liked to repeat—to Mary's detriment and for the benefit of interviewers—the way in which Mary always introduced the story: "It's funny you adore the smell of turpentine, Pat, because . . ."[24]

Nevertheless, the great love of Pat Highsmith's life—and, certainly, her greatest hate—was her artistic, stylish, erratic, critical, and very frustrated mother, Mary Highsmith. No one affected Pat more strongly than Mary did, and the reverse was also true. Until the moment she stopped communicating with her mother about twenty years before her own death (Pat actually disinherited *herself* in a letter to Mary) no one's opinion mattered more to Pat than Mary's.

A critical letter from her mother—Mary and Pat wrote to each other with the venom and energy of disappointed lovers—was enough to do what perpetual motion, heavy drinking, racking love affairs, and financial and professional setbacks could *never* do; it stopped the formidable engine that was Patricia Highsmith's writing. Sometimes, Pat said, it stopped it for days. Only noise from neighbors—Pat was sound-phobic and instantly converted all sound to "noise"—had anywhere near as disastrous an effect on Pat's work habits as the maternal criticism. And this was criticism from a mother who loved her daughter passionately and said so, critically, at every opportunity.

Dan Walton Coates thought it was "easier to be Mary's friend or other relation than to be her daughter." Don Coates, Dan's younger brother and the Coates family historian, remembers that "Aunt Mary was a very talented artist," very "career-minded," and not at all the "gushing type" of mother. But he wonders if "Pat ever thought that it was Aunt Mary who actually educated Pat as to what a woman could do." (Yes and no is the answer to that question.) It was Mary's hard work that put Pat through Barnard College—and gave her an allowance, too—at a time when a college education was still considered a privilege for a young woman in America.[25]

Everyone in the Coates family was abundantly aware that Mary and Pat's relationship was "not a good one." Still, like Tommy Tune, Dan Walton Coates was unequivocal: "Mary was very, very proud of Pat.

"[But] I'll tell you, Mary could be and was critical, and she would and did write some very hateful things [to Pat]. . . . And my father would say, Mary, why in the hell do you want to say something like that? It's hurtful and it doesn't do any good. And Mary would say: 'Well, that's the way I felt. And Pat ought to know it.'

"Those two," said Dan Walton Coates, "would burn each other up in the mail."[26]

Sulphur and brimstone are amongst the mildest of the odors that cling to many of the later, surviving letters the Highsmith women wrote to each other: the typewriters on which they were written should have been reduced to smoking slag and quivering springs. These epistles—as successful as smart bombs, as twinned as photographic negatives and their developed prints, and almost as painful as their authors' actual physical meetings—kept the home fires of their bondage burning brightly.

In a carefully controlled letter to Mary (very much foreshortened below), written on 12 April 1966, a year after Camilla Butterfield's stormy tea party in Kensington and the violent "incident" at Pat's Suffolk cottage, and simmering with every resentment it denies (including the inevitable Highsmith touch: a little prophecy of mutual death in the last paragraph), Pat states her case against her mother—her cases, actually. And she delivers a very good idea of what, by now, was the motor that drove these two women to run each other over every single time they met.

"It is a terrible thing," Pat writes to Mary, "if you think I have resentment toward you, and I shall try once more to explain why I haven't." And then Pat continues with a long list of burning resentments which trace back to her central complaint—the circumstances of her birth and her mother's remarriage ("You had one divorce, but you might have had four or five.")—and then works forward again to a long-cherished grudge:

> [T]o expect a child with such an odd parental history as mine to be like "other people" is a bit mistaken on your part. When I was fourteen, you said to me, "Why don't you straighten up and fly right." . . . And if you were concerned with me at fourteen, [you should] have taken me to a child psychiatrist, instead of . . . leaving me . . . to feel somehow inferior, or at any rate as if I were not meeting your approval.
>
> The reason I become upset after more than forty-eight hours with you is quite simple, and also has nothing to do with resentment.

And Pat goes on, resentfully, with another long list of Mary's "sniping remarks" and "illogical" behavior at Bridge Cottage a year earlier, finishing with a description of how Mary always makes her feel: "I am in a state of mind best described as shattered. I feel helpless, baffled, even inarticulate.

"I do not accuse you of it, but it may be you that resent me. . . .

"I hope very much I have made it clear that I have no resentment, not even for the broken promise when I was twelve, which marked a turning point in my life. [Mary, bent on divorcing Pat's stepfather, Stanley, and joining Pat in Texas, sent Pat to Fort Worth for a year, but reconciled with Stanley instead.] If you would get rid of your guilt, it would make things better . . . because we may both die tomorrow—just by slipping in the bathtub, for instance—and I wanted to say all this to you before it is too late."[27]

And Pat signed this letter "With much love, PAT."

Mary seems to have retained something of her sense of humor—like Pat's, it was interested in bodily functions—during that disastrous Bridge Cottage visit. As a souvenir, she sent her nephew Dan Coates in Texas ninety-four sheets of "Jeyes hygienic toilet paper," including an advertising flyer for Jeyes on which she wrote jauntily: "That this T.P. is absolutely inadequate has been proven by me beyond the shadow of a doubt!!!"[28]

As late as 1977, Pat was still preoccupied with dramatizing Mary's visit to Bridge Cottage. In a letter to her cousin Dan, who with his wife, Florine, had assumed all the responsibilities for Mary's later, erratic progress, Pat wrote from Moncourt:

> You are saving me from ruining the end of my life, for which I can't thank you enough, nor can money even pay for it. If I lived anywhere near my mother, I shouldn't be able to work, and even in Suffolk, 1965, I locked up my work at night, out of instinct, lest she destroy it.[29]

Mary's visits to Pat in Europe always seemed to produce some kind of "earthquake." Six years earlier, in September of 1959, Mary had travelled to New York from Texas to fly with Pat to Paris, where Pat "had a book coming out" with her French publisher, Calmann-Lévy. While Pat was upstairs in their hotel, Mary ran into two French journalists in the lobby who had come to interview Pat. In Pat's version of this encounter—Pat was still burning with indignation nearly two decades later—Mary, "for five minutes or more[,] had tried to convince them that she was me. They took a snap of her to please her. If you, or I, were ever to bring this anecdote up, my mother would first deny that it ever happened; then . . . she would say that she was only joking. . . . I think a psychiatrist would put another meaning to it."[30]

A psychiatrist would also put the kind of meaning Pat is talking about to a similar confusion of identity—this time the confusion was Pat's—displayed in a letter Pat wrote to her father, Jay B Plangman, when she was fifty-one years old. Pat was asking for Jay B's help in putting her in "touch with any lawyer in Fort Worth who might be able to handle this problem. The problem is I would like to separate myself from my mother, my mother from me."[31]

On Pat and Mary's 1959 trip to Europe together (during which Mary was trying to shake off the effects of a serious depression), mother and daughter travelled pleasantly enough to London and Paris. Then Doris, a woman with whom Pat had recently lived in Palisades, New York, joined them in Paris, precipitating an explosion which cut short Mary's travel with her daughter and sent her off to Rome alone. Mary's post-trip letter to Pat (the merest fragment of which is printed below) is the aggressive passion to Pat's passive aggression.

> [Y]ou said at your place after all the early day bickering of Stanley [Pat's stepfather] and me could I not understand why you would never

marry—*that* was not the reason. . . . The only reason you have never married is because you are wholly without loyalties. You are not even loyal to *yourself.* . . . You have wholly excluded LOVE from your emotions as deliberately as you would turn a tap. . . .

If I were a second-rate whore I might stand higher in your esteem. I say second-rate because that is what your friend is. . . .

I believe you would gladly put me in Dachau if it were possible without out a minute's loss of sleep. . . .

Yes, I think you are sicker in the mind than I ever was. I *never* changed personality . . . NOT SO YOU.[32]

A forty-four-year-old daughter who collapses into unconsciousness on a friend's doorstep when she hears that her mother is in town on a visit, and then hides her writing "out of instinct" because she is afraid her mother will destroy it, and a sixty-six-year-old mother who thinks her daughter treats her worse than a "second-rate whore" and would put her in "Dachau without a minute's loss of sleep," have both taken up residence in what Jean Genet called "the universe of the irremediable." Each one is striking out at the other because she feels attacked in her very core; both use the beard of marriage to cover up Pat's lesbianism, which they both feel is awful. Pat wanted Mary to admit that she alone was responsible for the dreadful "abnormality" of her daughter's sexuality; Mary refused to do so. Mary and Pat continued to drive each other crazy with accusations.

Camilla Butterfield, whose tea party Pat and Mary had so fatally upset, took Pat's "side" in the long, sad case of *Highsmith v. Highsmith.* "Having had one experience of Mary Highsmith," says Camilla Butterfield, "I certainly didn't want another." She describes Mary as "very feminine" and "scatty; a type, an American type . . . really quite mad or *driven* mad by the presence of her daughter."[33] Marijane Meaker, who lived with Pat for six months in Bucks County, Pennsylvania, in 1960–61, shared Mrs. Butterfield's assessment of Mary Highsmith. But she added: "Pat . . . loved her mother very much and her mother was . . . jealous of all Pat's lovers. They had a very seductive relationship. Her mother was very powerful."[34]

Mrs. Butterfield's dramatic picture of the mad tea party she hosted for the Highsmith women is a portrait of the terrible effect *two* people can have upon each other. It was the collision (and collusion) of mother and daughter that so disturbed the "atmosphere" of Camilla Butterfield's house, not Mary's demeanor by itself. Twenty years later, in May of 1985, Pat wrote in a cahier: "My mother would not have become semi-insane, if I had not existed."[35] She could easily have reversed the subjects of her sentence.

The intricate relations of this alarming mother-and-daughter duo had an amply archived past and went on to a well-documented future. The careful curators preserving its history were none other than Pat and Mary Highsmith themselves.

Like jailhouse lawyers, Pat and Mary did fervid research on each other's faults and *faiblesses,* kept lists of witnesses (lists, apparently, were in the blood),* and retained each other's letters (scribbled over with corrective explanations) to support their endless grievances. They wrote to each other's friends, complaining and justifying. Mary wrote to Pat's lovers, and Pat wrote to her stepfather (Mary's second husband, Stanley Highsmith), to Mary's closest woman friend (the fashion illustrator Jeva Cralick), and to Mary's doctors—one of whom, Pat noted grimly, was called Dr. Ripley.[36]

The Coateses, the Stewarts (Mary's mother's family), and even the Plangman family were caught up in their fierce struggle. Third cousins (Millie Alford, who had another role to play in Pat's life, was amongst them) were enlisted in the battle. The heavens above were regularly appealed to for assistance, and far too many false oaths were sworn on either side. The imaginary courthouse for the Highsmith women's untried lawsuit against each other always had its doors flung open wide, and both of them cried out for the justice they both passionately felt they had been denied.

But *what* justice—and denied by *whom*?

Mary Highsmith, writing as she usually did from her House of Perpetual Trouble to her Daughter of Deepest Shame, still managed to have herself a pretty good time. Saying exactly what she felt came as easily to her as it came awkwardly to her daughter—and Mary never bothered to hold back an opinion.

But in one of her most excoriating letters to Pat, Mary suddenly intermits the name-calling—both Mary and Pat were subject to these constant volte-faces—with these words:

"When you were born, I was the happiest person imagineable [*sic*]. I was going to give you freedom, a free rein to do the things you wanted to do. Something I was NEVER allowed."[37]

This is anguish unadorned: the cri de coeur of a mother who projects her childhood fantasies of liberation on her daughter, and then, because no parental hope ever goes unpunished, lives to watch her bright dreams of fulfillment dissolve in a life-and-death struggle between her and her only child.

Of course, the hostilities of mother and daughter were intermitted—they

---

* On both sides. Jay B Plangman is quoted at his retirement dinner in Fort Worth as having told his art students that they should "memorize eight new things a day."

had to be, given the complexity of their feelings—with great, painful bouts of caring, sympathy, and worry for each other's welfare. When the two women weren't accusing each other of something (and even when they were), they were intensely involved in each other's lives. In ways that made the mother experience life as a mirthless joke and the daughter insist that existence was a meaningless jest, Mary and Patricia Highsmith were fatally alike.

Mary's chatty letter introducing Tommy Tune to Pat (written only four months before she and Pat had collided at Camilla Butterfield's tea party) was, allowing for differences in style, exactly the kind of letter Pat herself loved to send out to her hundreds of correspondents every year. Mary uses her sentences as a broom to sweep up all the external details of her life. When she isn't in a depression (Pat, too, was often depressed), Mary, just like Pat, is always infernally busy. In this letter, she's readying two drawings for an exhibition at the Houston Museum, exchanging some Levi's for Pat (who would wear only Levi-Strauss 501 jeans sent from Texas), painting her cement side porch, covering the fruit trees against a frost, puttying the windows, setting out bulbs in the garden beds which she has outlined with stones, and espousing a "CAUSE—that of saving the Majestic Theatre."[38]

While Mary is working her socks off, her husband, Stanley ["I have relieved him of everything around the place in order for him to have his precious time"]; is "fast becoming a problem." Mary wants to ask Pat's "advice on how to help Stanley," who "fritters away his [retirement] time," reading in "PREPARATION" for becoming the writer he has always wanted to be.

"Well, you and I know that [preparation] can go on forever. . . . My heart bleeds for him to have some sort of satisfaction and feeling of achievement. But how can he in the manner he's chosen?"[39]

The complicity in this appeal from one "artist" to another is unmistakable. Mary knows how her complaints about Stanley will please Pat, who has "disliked" (the mild verb Pat generally uses for the boiling, seething, twitching hatred for Stanley Highsmith she spent her childhood repressing) her stepfather since she was introduced to him at the age of three and a half. And then Mary begins to fret that Pat, in her freezing cottage in Suffolk, "can't do your best work and be cold. Do you use only one door in exiting? Do you realize how wonderful newspaper is for insulation?" And she goes on for several hundred words about how Pat can warm up her house and then rattles on for another few hundred words about their mutual interest in the genealogy of their maternal family line: the Stewarts.[40]

Mary and Pat's Troubles (long enough and bitter enough to be capitalized) began with the sleight of hand that reshuffled the cards of Pat Highsmith's parentage. It was, on the face of it, a reshuffling that made Pat's birth possible and allowed Mary to sustain her child and give her a future. But the whole business left little Patsy, as she was called in childhood, feeling cheated of just about everything.

Pat lost her father before she was born, and she lost him completely. Mary refused (and even Pat thought her refusal admirable) to take any money from Jay B Plangman for their daughter, and Plangman seems to have dealt himself—or perhaps he was dealt—out of the family deck, never making a recorded attempt to see his only child while she was living with Willie Mae in Fort Worth and Mary was out earning a living.

But Pat, for the first few years of her life, also lost a mother: figuratively, because of the circumstances of their housing, and then actually, because Mary travelled far and wide to get work, and then remarried. Although Pat frequently blamed the loss of her father on her mother, it was the repeated loss of her mother, Mary, that threw Patricia Highsmith into a persistent mourning for her life.

· 6 ·

LA MAMMA

PART 2

When Mary Coates—twenty-five years old, pregnant, separated from her husband, set on divorcing and continuing a career in fashion illustration—stepped back over the threshold of the Coates family boardinghouse in Fort Worth, Texas, she surrendered much of her maternal authority. Her departure for Chicago to look for a job three weeks after she gave birth to her baby girl transferred whatever was left of that power.[1] Mary's infant came under the jurisdiction of the woman who, as Mary wrote plaintively, had "tried her sorely," curbed her socially ("In high school I finally quit having dates [she] was so hard on me about them"), and made her feel a parental disapproval so strong that Mary swore "no daughter of mine would suffer that."[2]

This commanding figure, still dominating Mary well into middle age, was the diminutive, nearsighted, Alabama-born doctor's daughter whose double first name bridged both genders, whose Southern Calvinist heritage was founded on Puritan rock—her great-grandson Don says that "her back never touched a chair's back"—and whose rule over the Coates family was absolute: Mary's mother and Pat's grandmother, the invincible Willie Mae Stewart Coates.

"Grandma," says Willie Mae's great-grandson Don, "was a tiny little thing.

"If you saw Grandma in a car sitting in a passenger seat, the only thing you saw above the doorline was her head. And Grandpa was just as tall as he could be."

Don's elder brother Dan remembered: "Willie Mae was the cutest, toughest little 'toot' who ever lived. Mary came by her strong personality from Willie Mae."

In home movies of the Coates family shot in Texas in the 1930s and 1940s, it is the self-possessed Willie Mae who draws the spectator's gaze, just as Mary and Pat do when they're being filmed or photographed with other people. Mary Highsmith, in a typical family film shot at her Hastings-on-Hudson house in New York State, has put a stalk of celery in her hair, and her mugging and manifestations for the camera manage to crowd nearly everyone else out of the frame. Pat, the reverse *médaille* of this regiment of camera-ready women, makes herself as starched, as stiff, and as still as possible whenever she is caught on film. Her visual grammar is that of the reluctant star of a hostage video.[3]

In photographs, Willie Mae and Mary resemble each other closely; Mary is the elongated, modish, nervous, flirtatious version of her mother. Pat, with her cat-shaped eyes, oval visage, and black hair, looks like no one in the Coates or Stewart (Willie Mae's maiden name) family. Of the three generations of women, it is Willie Mae who moves with the kind of definition and authority that allowed her to make such an impression—such a *different* impression—on the lives of both Mary and Patricia Highsmith.*

Willie Mae Stewart Coates was born in Alabama in September of 1866. Much of the personal power she always seemed to possess came from the Calvinist line in her heritage, stretching backwards for generations. Her long family history of religious devotion and involvement in social justice was marked by the spiritual rebellions and odd, intense pieties that would trouble her granddaughter Patricia all her life.

In the careful genealogy worked out in 1954 by the biographer of Pat's relation,[†] Confederate general A. P. Stewart (later president of the University of Misssippi at Oxford), the Stewart family to which Willie Mae Coates belonged was firmly established as being of Scots-Irish origin. The American

---

* The Coates and Stewart families' bloodlines were the family histories Pat Highsmith researched most fully. She continued to link many of her own traits to them, even when she had taken to calling herself a "kraut." Her inquiries into her father Jay B Plangman's German Lutheran heritage were minimal; limited, more or less, to asking her father and his brother, Walter Plangman, if there was any "red Indian blood" in the family because they were all, Pat included, so very dark. Jay B assured Pat that the dark complexion came from his mother Minna Hartman's family, direct from his grandmother Liena, who, with her two sisters, was part of the vast emigration of Germans to the United States in the 1850s. The three Hartman sisters became, Jay B wrote to his daughter, "servants in well-to-do homes in Galveston." The Plangmans, Gesina and Herman, were also emigrants from Germany, and their son Herman Plangman married Minna Hartman and fathered Jay Bernard Plangman. Jay B's brother Walter remembered that one of his grandmothers had taught him German before he learned English. He recollected this as he was answering yet another question from his uneasy niece Patricia about her German grandmother: "She definitely had no Indian Blood," Walter wrote.

† He was assisted by Samuel Smith Stewart, the genealogist of the Stewart family, who sent all his research to Pat.

branch of the Stewart clan associated itself with the tonier "Baltimore Stew-arts," and Willie Mae's grandfather, William Stewart, was second-generation Scots-Irish. He traced his origins, Pat was pleased to note, to Ninion Stewart, younger son of James I of Scotland and brother of James II.[4]

William Stewart, whose maternal grandfather was a Presbyterian minis-ter, moved from his birthplace in Delaware to Tennessee, where he became the postmaster of Winchester and the treasurer of Franklin County: a lead-ing citizen and a public official. The records of the Winchester, Tennessee, Masonic Lodge No. 158 show that he was a Presbyterian and a "man of un-doubted piety"[5] whose reverence took a curiously physical turn: his "frequent and protracted kneeling in the act of prayer" are said to have worn holes in his bedroom carpet.[6] He married Elizabeth Decherd (now spelled Deckerd), and Elizabeth, a serious convert to Methodism, bore sixteen children and died in 1847, a "bright ornament of the Methodist Church." She, too, was in-tensely devout: "a truly praying woman."

The Stewart children were raised in the Presbyterian church, although two of the Stewart sons became well-known Methodist preachers. These conversions to (and promulgations of) Methodism in a devotedly Presbyte-rian family were as shocking a heresy in their day as an open profession of Communism would have been in the McCarthy era.[7] Pat's grandmother Willie Mae, who followed the family's Methodist line, joined the St. Mark's Methodist Church in Fort Worth.[8] Affirming her faith, Willie Mae named one of her sons after the early Methodist spiritual leader John Wesley, whose principles of social justice later surfaced in peculiarly twisted forms in the musings of Willie Mae's novelist granddaughter. Underscoring the family's religious bent, Willie Mae's grandparents William and Elizabeth Stewart had spent eleven years in the "strict Presbyterian community" of Rogersville, Tennessee (even though Elizabeth was a Methodist), a community founded by the grandparents of the legendary American frontiersman Davy Crock-ett. Their eighth child, Oscar Wilkinson Stewart, Willie Mae's father, was first a schoolmaster and then a doctor who served out his Civil War duties as a surgeon.[9]

Unlike the Coates family into which his granddaughter Willie Mae would marry, William Stewart disapproved of the institution of slavery and never owned slaves himself. But the Stewarts' nine sons all served in the Confeder-ate army and all of them were Masons.

This is straightforward enough as a family history—even with the family emphasis on radiant piety, and with what must have been troubling family divisions on the subjects of religion and slave owning. But then, slowly, some-thing almost as interesting as the Presbyterian/Methodist split starts to work its way though successive generations of the Stewart family. Sets of brothers and sisters begin to marry other sets of sisters and brothers—as though the Stewart family were gradually developing double vision. The pious William Stewart, married to the saintly Elizabeth Decherd, had a brother, Charles Stewart. Charles Stewart married his brother's wife's sister, Ellen Decherd. Then two of William and Elizabeth Stewart's sons, Oscar Wilkinson and Leonidas, married the Pope sisters, Mary Ann Pope and Martha Clarissa Pope. And then two of Oscar Wilkinson Stewart's daughters, Martha and Willie Mae, married the Coates boys, Andrew Jackson Coates and Daniel Hokes Coates.

Pat Highsmith, who in later life entertained a mystical belief in the inherited properties of "blood," would have known just what to say about all this doubling up and religious division in her family. She would have said that double trouble was in her blood from the moment she was conceived—and she would have blamed her mother, Mary, for it, too.

Daniel Hokes Coates, Willie Mae's husband, was the son of Gideon Coats, the man who founded Coats' Bend, Alabama. Coats' Bend was the Coates family's Big Historical Moment, one they never forgot. Like any Founding Father, Gideon Coates got his land from the Native Americans, the Cherokees: five thousand acres of it. Although the Coateses' founding of this township and the Coates family's Confederate war history figured largely in Pat's imagination,* the Coates she lived with, her grandfather Daniel Coates, made little impression on her. In the current generation of Coateses', only Willie Mae, Mother Mary, and her cousin Dan were "real" for Pat. Still, almost all the Coates males were named for Willie Mae's husband, Daniel Hokes Coates, and for Willie Mae's father, Oscar Wilkinson Stewart. Willie Mae's great-grandson Don Coates explains the family's richly confusing tendency to double its nomenclature:

> My great-grandfather was Dan'l Hokes Coates (Willie Mae's husband). My grandfather was Dan Oscar Coates—the Oscar comes from the Stewarts [Willie Mae's father, Oscar Wilkinson Stewart]. My father was Dan Oscar Coates. My brother [was] Dan Walton Coates—Walton was the name of my mother's father. My nephew is Dan Oscar Coates and his . . . son is Dan Oscar Coates, making him Dan IV. My name is Don Oscar Coates. And then to keep it interesting we had a dog named Dan. No

* Like Oscar Wilkinson Stewart, Daniel Hokes Coates's three brothers fought in the War Between the States, taking their personal slaves with them and dying in battle. A mostly unreconstructed Rebel, Pat visited Civil War battlefields in states of high emotion and repeatedly named Robert E. Lee, commander of the Rebel army, as her favorite historical figure.

middle name. So around our house you could call for Dan and get my
father, brother, nephew, and dog. . . .

And by the way, I was usually called Dan when addressed.[10]

Mary Coates repeated the family custom (it was another way of reproducing herself) when she gave her own first name to her only child. "Mary" was a
name Pat Highsmith refused to live or die with, but she used it in her most
revealing early short story, "The Legend of the Convent of St. Fotheringay,"
and in many stories thereafter.

Some instinct for strict propriety, upright appearance, and the desire not to
be confused with criminals—Pat sustained this odd combination of urges all
her life—caused the Coats family, sometime after Coats' Bend was incorpo-
rated, to add an *e* to their last name. It seems, says Don Coates, that in Alabama
"there were some men named Coats who were horse thieves and in those days
[that was] the worst thing you could be. They hung you right on the spot. The
family changed the name to Coates so that everyone in the South would know
they weren't connected with the kind of people who would steal horses."[11]

Coats' Bend, Alabama, was the site of the original of the many "houses of
fiction" that figured in Pat Highsmith's life and work: the white, fourteen-
room "Coats' Mansion" built in 1842 by Pat's slave-owning great-grandfather
Gideon Coats in the best mortise-and-tenon tradition of fine carpentry, without the use of a single nail. Willie Mae, whose boardinghouse in Fort Worth
was a working-class version of the plantation-style "mansion," embroidered a
picture of the Coats' Mansion for her Fort Worth wall, and her son Edward
did the same thing for his wall.[12] Pat kept a photograph of the Coats' Mansion
in one of her albums, referred to it regularly in her letters, and built it and re-
built it in various ways in her novels. And in all her domiciles, she managed to
reproduce something of the mansion's plantation ethos, inveigling some of her
poorer neighbors into genial servitude and persuading wealthier friends and
family members to run errands and do chores for her. Even at her most financially reduced, when she was just out of college and living in a one-room studio
in Manhattan, Pat always had a weekly "maid" in to help with the cleaning.

In her mind, Pat settled quite comfortably into what Gore Vidal likes to
call "Margaret Mitchell Country." She was quick to cite *Gone with the Wind* as
her favorite novel, insisting that it was "a true novel of the South." (In that irresistible book, loyal, happy slaves serve their romantically unhappy masters
until the Marauding Northerners come to Lay Waste to Our Southern Way of
Life. And that's when Scarlett O'Hara, a feminist *avant la lettre*, decides to act
now and think about the consequences "tomorrow.") In 1977, Pat added to
her preference for *Gone with the Wind* the opinion that her great-grandfather

Gideon Coats's "110 body-slaves" (she *loved* the phrase "body-slaves") were "not unhappy."[13] The dreams and values of the Old South were still working their Mason-Dixon Line magic in Pat's imagination, fifty years after she'd heard them told to her in her grandmother's kitchen.

Willie Mae and Dan Coates and their five children travelled to Fort Worth, Texas, from Coats' Bend, Alabama, in 1904, mostly, says their great-grandson Don, because Dan Coates's sister Dolly was given the Coats' Mansion as well as the family cotton gin and grist mill, and Dan and Willie Mae didn't want to "carry the rest of the family financially." When the Coateses went west, they travelled in style. Family legend has it that Willie Mae and Daniel "had all their possessions . . . the crystal and china and silver and all of that packed into bales of cotton and they rented a [railway car] and put all of those bales of cotton with the crystal and the china and the silver in the train car with all their furniture and then they rented another railway car for the family itself."[14]

It's like a fairy tale, and it probably *was* a fairy tale: the entire family travelling from Alabama to Texas in a private railway car with everything they owned wrapped up in snowy bales of cotton. But it was the trains themselves (along with the strict timetables that governed them) and not the billowing cotton bales that would catch the imagination of the family's writing granddaughter.*

Somewhere on that cross-country journey, despite the private railway car and the wrapped-in-cotton furniture, Willie Mae and her family seem to have gotten a lot poorer. By the time they fetched up in Fort Worth, a modest boardinghouse was all they could afford, and Daniel Coates went to work driving a wagon to deliver the local newspaper, the *Fort Worth Star-Telegram,* in downtown Fort Worth.[15] But the life the Coates family constructed in Fort Worth was a demotic version of the plantation life they'd left behind. There was, first, the Main House on West Daggett Avenue in which boarders were housed and fed by Willie Mae and at which factory workers sometimes took their meals. Pat, deploring the downward transmission of the Coateses, always referred to the boarders as "gentlemen," but, said Dan Walton Coates, they were "just steady working people," people

> who did factory-type work, single males with the exception of one couple who lived downstairs, the Syleses, and he did a lot of maintenance work for my grandma on the place. She probably swapped part of the work for rent. People who stayed there were not transients. They

---

* Standard time wasn't actually "standardized" or strictly enforced until the great train lines were laid across whole continents in the nineteenth century: in order to catch a train, you had to know the exact time it was leaving. It's a sidelight on the imagination of Pat Highsmith, who, preoccupied with time herself, ran so many trains through her novels.

had fairly good jobs. There was a man there that repaired violins. They were long-termers. Willie Mae ran the show.[16]

And then there was the shack-filled alley behind the house, called, in the locution of the times, "Negro Alley" or "Nigger Alley," or "Red Alley" because of the color of the shack roofs. There were back-shacks like these all over Fort Worth, rented out to blacks who worked in the yards and houses of Fort Worth whites. The workers would otherwise have had to travel long distances from far-away communities to get to their yard jobs in Fort Worth. So they slept out in back of main houses in little rented shacks.[17]

Dan Walton Coates remembered staying at his great-grandmother's boardinghouse one night when "there was a hell of a racket [in Negro Alley] . . . music going and loud talking." Willie Mae jumped out of bed in the middle of the night, her hair still in curlers, grabbed a robe, and told young Dan that they were going out back.

"And there was a fellow [living] out there, he was big as a mountain and his name was House. . . . We walked back there and that place was full and everybody was outside having a big party in a little common ground area. And I'm not but about seven or eight years old and Grandma walked right through the middle of that thing and found House and told him [in the accepted parlance of the day] that the party was over: 'You get these niggers back where they belong and I don't want to hear another word out here!' And he said 'Oh yes, Mrs. Coates,' and with that, we turned around and went back to the house and it got quiet as a jug."

Don Coates believes that the "House" of this incident, whose last name was also Coates, was an emancipated slave who had been trained to work in the Coats' Mansion in Alabama, where he would have been given the Coates family surname and called "House" by his mother, a common custom with "house slaves." House Coates was probably Daniel Hokes Coates's personal slave when Daniel was a child during the Civil War—all the Coates children had slaves of their own—and he came with the Coates family on their mythical cotton-swathed journey from Alabama. The family would have felt responsible for him, Don says, and wouldn't have left him behind in Alabama if he didn't want to stay there. House Coates was set up out back in one of the little shacks, just as, in pre–Civil War circumstances, he would have been set up in the old slave quarters behind the Coats' Mansion in Coats' Bend.[18]

And so Pat Highsmith, who wrote to her stepfather in 1970 that "[m]y character was essentially made before I was six,"[19] had, until she was taken to Manhattan by her mother at the age of six, a model for living that was much closer to antebellum Alabama than it was to anything else. Born in Texas, Pat grew up, as her antic Alabama-born friend Eugene Walter reminded her, with "Alabama genes."[20]

But if her links with Alabama were inborn and enculturated, the signs and symbols of Pat's home state of Texas seem to suit her just as well. Texas is known as the "Lone Star State"; there was never a loner star than Patricia Highsmith. Yellow, Pat's favorite color, is reminiscent of the famous Yellow Rose of Texas. The reptile most often associated with Texas, the rattlesnake, has been depicted on banners in America since 1775—all of them inscribed with some version of the phrase "Don't Tread on Me," a motto Pat could comfortably have embossed on her business cards. The state of Texas would always have a great deal to do with *all* the states Patricia Highsmith found herself in.

Mary Coates Highsmith was Willie Mae's youngest child. She was preceded in the Coates family by four favored brothers, and she complained to her daughter that Willie Mae "went to her grave never letting me know that I had made the grade."[21] But Mary kept trying, plaintively, to get her mother's attention by "doing things" for her. She gave Willie Mae "trips to NY on three different occasions. . . . None of my brothers did it *ever*." For which Willie Mae "could never bring herself to genuinely thank me, but that was HER block and she was stuck with it 'til her death."[22] And Pat, pitiless in her observations of her mother in later life, found Mary's repeated attempts to make a good impression on Willie Mae painfully hard to think about.

"Now my poor mother is even ashamed to return to Texas for a visit because she needs a new bag, hasn't a winter coat, & because they are all swimming in money there. This fills me with more tragic emotion than I realize consciously & accounts for much of my depression lately."[23]

Subtly, and by degrees, little Patsy Plangman, taught to read by her grandmother (no memory could be more important for a writer, and Pat refers to it often, changing her stories of how and when it happened), and raised up for most of her first six years in a household dominated by Willie Mae, seems to have become more like a sibling to her mother than a daughter. Mary's and Pat's later behaviors, their letters to each other and notes to themselves, and their lengthy arguments, were often driven by what looks very much like sibling competition.

Mary to Pat:

"She [Willie Mae] treated you [Pat] differently than she did me. It was as if she was not the same person. . . . But my father wasn't like that—he told her I was better than all the boys put together."[24]

Pat to herself:

"Anyway, she [Mary] is safe in her insanity, safe in being on home ground, Texas; safe in having a nephew, one of the family, dancing attendance. . . . I must not forget that my grandmother (her mother) remarked, 'Mary is insane,' when my mother was 44."[25]

Pat and Mary would quarrel, with the jealousy going every which way, about the "possession" of their mutual friends, and Mary warned Pat when she was in high school not to write to her fashion illustrator chums, Marjorie Thompson and Jeva Cralick.[26] Then Pat upset Mary by taking over Mary's friendship with Jean David (known as "Jeannot"), the young French cartoonist from Marseille who was Mary's foreign pen pal and who had stayed with the Highsmiths in Manhattan when Pat was still a teenager.[27] Although Jean David signed himself "Jeannot" in his letters to both Mary and Pat, and although Mary and Pat each had her own pages in his family photo albums, Jeannot kept many more photos of Pat than he kept of Mary. (See illustrations.)

Like a jealous sibling, Pat sometimes cautioned her lovers and friends not to get too close to her mother. She loved to tell tales on Mary to her grandmother, and, siblinglike, Mary found out about the stories and berated Pat:

"Then I learned to my horror you flatly lied about me to Mamma to the effect that I was jealous of you being at Yaddo. . . . God how that information shook me."[28]

Pat said that jealousy was the emotion she hated the most—"No, I shall never be jealous, only die of jealousy"[29]—but her complicated, divided childhood was wreathed in it.

Willie Mae Coates's ideas about family responsibility were strong ones. Seven years before Pat was born, Willie Mae, a "reading" woman with phenomenal energy, "a big library," and a strong interest in public affairs (the heritage of her strict Presbyterian/Methodist upbringing), took charge of Mary's nephew and Pat's first cousin, Dan Coates, father of Dan Walton and Don Coates and the son of her own dead son Daniel. Young Dan's mother had been "a bride, a widow, and a mother" within ten months and then died suddenly when Dan was three.[30] And young Dan, said his eldest son, Dan Walton, "identified with Pat a great deal because [he] felt like an orphan and Pat felt like she was an orphan too."[31] In their lifelong correspondence, Dan and Pat always addressed each other as siblings: "sis Pat" and "brother Dan." And Mary, too, said Dan Walton Coates, "was more a sister to my father than an aunt" because they were both raised by Willie Mae.[32]

Given this unusual history—the magnet-grandmother to whom the loose family filings returned to have their relations reordered—it is not so remarkable that adoptions, actual and figurative, are a recurrent theme in much of Pat Highsmith's work, beginning with her first, unfinished novel, *The Click of the Shutting,* and continuing on through her posthumous novel, *Small g.* But as in Pat's own family (and as in the fictions of Colette, whom Pat admired), many of the "orphans" who appear in her novels are also well provided with parents.[33]

On Dan Coates's eightieth birthday (that's the Dan who was raised with Pat in Willie Mae's boardinghouse) he told his family a story about Willie Mae, a story which still impressed him greatly although it had occurred more than seventy years before. One day, Dan said, Willie Mae was in her kitchen, and Dan, just a little boy at the time, came up behind her, put an arm around her waist, and patted her affectionately on the upper leg. And Willie Mae turned around to him and said very firmly: "Young man, don't you *ever* touch me *in that way again!*" Dan never did.

Dan's son Don says that physical and verbal manifestations of affection were never part of the Coates family lexicon, although love was offered in every other way. "Aunt Mary didn't know how to touch Pat or use the words. It was the whole Victorian sort of thing . . . and Grandma was definitely a Victorian. . . . That was how [Mary] was raised. [Physical expression] just wasn't there because they just didn't know how to do it."[34]

But Willie Mae was far more lenient with her granddaughter, Pat, than she had ever been with her daughter, Mary, and almost all Pat's memories of her grandmother are exalted and idealized. A born hero-worshipper, Pat filled in the generation that separated her from Willie Mae with a version of heroic grandmotherhood so unassailable that she could never write about it. Although Pat said that it was "much easier to create from positive, affectionate emotions than from negative and hateful ones,"[35] she rarely did so, and in a sentence whose meaning is almost as confused as the intentions which provoked it, she seems to have excluded the possibility of ever writing about Willie Mae: "If I ever write about my grandmother, it will have to be very good or not at all."[36]

And then there is this circumstance to think about. Little Patsy Plangman was a particularly androgynous child. Photographs of her from the age of one upward are ambiguously gendered: she could be a girly boy or a boyish girl. Mary kept Patsy's infant hair short and fashionable, and at three she looks like a little flapper, with her hair in a bowl cut. By the age of twelve, Pat's own preference was for boys' clothes, and she had already adopted a style: dressing herself in a cap and knickers like Jackie Coogan in *The Kid,* a film she might have seen with Willie Mae, who, twenty years later, was still faithfully taking her great-grandsons every single Saturday to the double-featured Westerns and comedies at the Hollywood and the Palace theaters in downtown Fort Worth.[37] There is a photograph of Pat in her cap and knickers, unsettlingly boyish and looking out from the frame with a boy's audacious stare; she's ready with a challenge and spoiling for a fight.

In a vignette Pat tailored for the "suspense market," the "market" in whose category she always stirred so restively, she remembered herself at the age of four "racing barefoot in my dropseat overalls down the hall to pick up the *Fort Worth Star-Telegram* from the front porch, and racing back to the kitchen to read aloud to my Scots grandmother. This was my first adventure story, strung out with all the suspense of installments."[38]

Patsy is reading at four all right—part of the point of her anecdote is to show that off—and she is reading "suspense," too, and to her beloved grandmother. But the newspaper story she is reading would have been ripped out of the hands of any four-year-old today: the gothic, gruesome Floyd Collins saga, a true-life horror story that began when a Kentucky hillbilly was trapped by a rockslide in a cavern near his home at the end of January 1925. It took two dreadful weeks to dig the expiring Collins out—and every moment of his death agony was reported on in installments by the popular press.

Yes, Patsy is reading, but she is also running in bare feet and dropseat overalls to pick up the newspaper. And overalls (not to mention bare feet) were not a general feature of the wardrobes of proper little girls in 1925. The fact that Patsy was more like a proper little boy than a proper little girl is the nugget of information concealed in this well-polished reminiscence. Despite her later and always-doomed attempts to live and love like a good bourgeoise, Pat never could change her nature. She was most at home in the gay bars of Greenwich Village in the 1940s and 1950s and in the lesbian boîtes of Paris and Berlin in the 1970s, where she could appear—with some purpose at last—in the semidrag she wore all her adult life: the starched and ironed oxford shirts, the Levi-Strauss 501 jeans, the men's loafers, the handsome cravats, the trim little vests. Grandmother Willie Mae, a woman whose preference for sons was undoubtedly reawakened by her granddaughter's androgyny, never had a word of criticism to say to Pat about the way she dressed.

At the age of sixty-six, Mary Highsmith was still complaining that she hadn't been given roller skates as a child when all her brothers got them, and that her mother Willie Mae's reproving "look" left her "sweating blood."[39] Pat always had Willie Mae to compare her mother to, and her mother always came up short. And it is likely that Willie Mae's partiality for boys laid the foundation for Pat's own later preference for the "active and positive" qualities of men instead of for the "negative and passive" gender with which she so inconveniently continued to fall in love. And so Pat's attentions and affections continued to be split by the circumstances of her birth—circumstances which tightened the passionate lines of tension between mother and daughter and blurred the boundaries between love and hate.

In this house of trespassed borders and reordered relations one clear principle flew like a flag: Willie Mae Stewart Coates was the head of the family.

LA MAMMA

Patsy Plangman was three and a half years old in 1924 when she met Stanley Highsmith. She took one look at her mild-mannered stepfather-to-be and turned him into her first criminal: the man who robbed her of language. As creative in her aversions as she was in her attractions, the infant Pat imagined Stanley to be a kind of fairy-tale ogre (she was holding a book of fairy tales when she met him) pointing "a long, crooked, hairy forefinger" at her and instantly stealing away her pleasure.

Stanley, to be sure, had come to take Pat's mother away—"Marriage," says a character in one of the stories Pat started to write as a teenager, "is a thief in the night"[1]—and Pat's family life was already confusingly involved with substitutions, subtractions, and adoptions. Her birth father was defined only by his absence; her grandmother was more like her mother; her mother was like an adored older sister; and her live-in male cousin, orphaned and taken in by her grandmother, was her "brother Dan." And Pat, before the age of six (or so she wrote to Stanley Highsmith in one of three novella-length letters she attacked him with during May and June of 1970), was already entertaining unconventional feelings about her gender and her sexuality. Gender and sexuality must have seemed to the little girl to be as movable and changeable as all the other counters in her life.

In his photographs, Stanley Highsmith resembles Pat's biological father, Jay B Plangman. Like her daughter, Mary Highsmith was attracted to "types": both her husbands had dark hair and a mustache, both wore glasses, and both were commercial illustrators. Dan Walton Coates, whose assessing Coates eye had been sharpened by drawing lessons given to him by both his aunt Mary and his cousin Pat, saw at least one difference between Mary's two husbands.

Dan thought Stanley was a good fellow, but he felt there was definitely something "fishy" about Jay B Plangman.

"He was a dark, swarthy-looking kind of fellow, very quiet when he was around us. Instinctively I never liked him, and he had a 'don't trust me' look about him and he had a bit of an evil look about him. And I have nothing in the way of experience with him that would make me feel that way, but that's the way I felt about him."[2]

In her whole diary and cahier life, the secret written life she tried to keep for herself while alive but intended, somewhat ambivalently, for publication after death, Pat was to make only four direct notes about her biological father, Jay B Plangman. Three of these notes belie the vigorous defenses of Jay B she always mounted in letters to her mother and stepfather. Two of her references to Jay B were made on a single trip to Fort Worth in 1938.

At seventeen, in February of 1938, after completing the last term of her senior year at Julia Richman High School in New York City, Pat decided to visit her grandmother Willie Mae in Fort Worth, in the house on West Daggett Avenue she still called "home." She booked a steamer ticket from New York to the port of Galveston, Texas, writing in her journal that she had "the greatest expectations of this trip." She left, as usual, a tangle of flirtations with her female classmates behind her ("I like M. Wolf—I like anyone with a brain. . . . I am very sorry I must leave B[abs] B[aer] and J[udy] T[uvim]," etc., etc.) along with the obsessive habit of frequently recording her own scanty weight. At five feet six and a half inches, Pat weighed as little as 103 pounds and never more than 110. Years later, in 1969, she cut out from the London *Sunday Times* (and pasted in the back of her Cahier 30) an article about "Slimming Sickness" describing how certain "types" of young girls—those who "tend to be obsessional, meticulous and compulsive"—can't stop dieting. The article named the condition as "anorexia nervosa," and Pat wrote across it: "I had all these symptoms aged 15–19." "These symptoms" included "the presence of downy hair over normally hairless parts of the body," "cold blue extremities," and "low basal metabolic rate."[3] Pat, who always also suffered from (female) hormone deficiencies, had another of anorexia nervosa's symptoms, too: dysmenorrhea—very infrequent menses until her periods ceased. There were whole years during which she didn't menstruate more than two or three times in twelve months.

Pat took with her on this boat trip the copy of Adolf Hitler's *Mein Kampf* that she'd bought in New York in early January, as well as *Sir Roger de Coverley,* a book of essays taken from the eighteenth-century journal *The Spectator,* edited by Addison and Steele. She was intent on justifying her high school English teacher's remark that she had "the best vocabulary in the class."[4] Ambitious as always, she determined that her "studies must not go up in smoke" on board, and read throughout the voyage.[5] She watched the lights of Miami from the deck, viewed a bad movie in the theater, and met Ernst Hauser, a German traveller and journalist. Later, Hauser became a friend Pat would share with the writer Mary McCarthy; now, he was just a "nuisance."

After the boat docked in Galveston, Pat made the journey to Fort Worth, where she remarked censoriously that her grandmother's house, with "brother Dan's" wife Florine and baby (Dan Walton) visiting, was "looking more neglected." She began her furious habits of reading again—Proust, Hitler, Addison and Steele—and decided that she "must go deeper into Xian [Christian] Science." And, on her third day in Fort Worth, she got in touch with her father, "J.B." "My father will never simply sit & talk," she noted disappointedly of their meeting. In March, she travelled the thirty miles to Dallas, where she was "drink[ing] secretly from excitement" and judging that her penmanship was developing "for the first time." (It didn't develop much.)

Sometime later in March, after a "happy day, quite alone" in Fort Worth, Pat made a note: "B. shows me pornographic pictures (to my mingled disgust & fascination & shame for him)."[6] Pat set this incident down in a list of other occurrences—a long-awaited letter from a high school crush, a decision to go to Barnard "au lieu de N.Y.U.," and the feeling that this was an "Ecstatic day!"—and gave it no more weight than she gave to anything else that was happening to her.[7] But she wrote a very ambivalent B, a B that might have something like a J attached to it. In which case, the person who showed her the pornographic pictures would have been her father, J. B. Plangman.

Or maybe not. Maybe her ambivalent B stood for the "completely disso-lute" young man she'd also met during this time in Texas. It was a brief meet-ing when "I was 17" and he was "a very spoiled boy who was very much like Bruno [the psychopath in Strangers on a Train]. . . . He was an adopted boy in a wealthy family and completely worthless, and he was the sort of genesis of Bruno."[8] One of the geneses of Bruno, anyway, and he made an indelible im-pression on Pat.

Burying crucial information such as who showed her the "pornographic pictures"—or conveying this information ambiguously—was a technique Pat was later to use in her novels. Her employment of long lists of lightly de-scribed objects, equalized or neutralized by being in lists and carried forward across the pages by connective participles, leads (as did this entry in her ca-hier) to the kind of accumulation of detail which suspends or obliterates the reader's ability to compare the importance of one detail with any other. In a list, even in a numbered list, there tends to be no foreground and no background. Everything is flat and judgment is suspended.

But in 1970, when she was barraging her bewildered stepfather, Stanley, with her raging, heartbroken, historical reasons for cutting off her relations with Mother Mary (and mounting a strong defense of her biological father as a secondary assault), Pat added to one letter a disturbing incident she'd left out of the sparse notes she made on her father at seventeen. It was, apparently, part of the "real" content of the relations between Pat and Jay B on that visit to Fort Worth in 1938, and it shows just how much Pat could exclude from her diaries when she wanted to:

"And now to my father. There were some lingering kisses when I was seventeen in Texas, not exactly paternal. This is all I meant. I do not want to make a big thing out of it. The word incestuous is a strong one."[9]

At thirty, staying in the German countryside and stimulated by reading "Theodor Reik's psychoanalytic biography," Pat made a note to herself:

I think I should make a serious effort at psychoanalysing my relationship with my father. Something certainly tremendous is there. And I have buried it under total neutrality of attitude, under ten feet of cold ashes, dull as a roadbed. Psychoanalyse *him*, of course, as well.[10]

And that's as far as Patricia Highsmith—painfully alert observer of acutely abnormal psychological states—ever got in assessing what was "buried" under her "total neutrality of attitude" towards her biological father, Jay Bernard Plangman. With Stanley Highsmith, however, all too available and in the same living quarters, her critical analyses never stopped.

Dan Walton Coates thought that Stanley was "good to Pat" but that he "was a very easily dominated man and Mary was THE dominator."[11]

Like Jay B and Mary, Stanley earned his living as a commercial artist. He was more advanced in his profession than Pat ever cared to admit. In a radio interview in 1987 in New York, Pat, dripping scorn, indicated that Stanley did drawings for the "yellow pages," the telephone book. But Stanley worked longest for Bell Laboratories making "very complicated drawings, exploded views of helicopters, mechanical-type drawings."[12] And because he didn't like bossing people around—Pat said dismissively that he lacked "push"—he refused an important managerial position at Bell Helicopter a few years before his retirement.[13] Mary married him on 14 June 1924, and Pat's new stepfather, brought up by his mother and five years younger than Mary, came into the Coates family with a crippling secret of his own: he was illegitimate and ashamed of it.

Pat's first memory of Stanley was that of being cheated. She allowed this memory to substitute for the real resentment (being cheated of her mother) underlying all her feelings for Stanley.

From first acquaintance I had never liked my step-father. I was about four when I met him, and I had already been reading for more than a year. I remember it was a book of fairy tales I had that day.

"What's that word?" said my step-father indicating with a long, crooked, hairy forefinger the most magical phrase I knew.

"Open *See*-same!" I cried.

"Sess-a-mi!" replied my step-father with didactic peremptoriness.

"Sess-a-mi," I echoed weakly.

My step-father smiled indulgently down upon me, his red heavy lips tight together and spread wide below his black moustache. And I knew he was right, and I hated him because he was right like grown-up people always were, and because he had forever destroyed my enchanting "Open See-same," and because now the new word would have no meaning to me, had destroyed my picture, had become strange, un-friendly and unknown.[14]

The precociously alert, preschool Patsy took immediate offense; the adult artist Pat never forgot the insult. She wrote her painful, feeling description of meeting Stanley Highsmith seventeen years after that meeting took place, when she was twenty-one years old and keenly sensing the confinements of her family. During the infrequent separations that characterized her mother's marriage to Stanley (Stanley moved out twice for brief periods, once when Pat was sixteen and once when she was nineteen),[15] Pat argued as hard as she could that Stanley was draining Mary's creativity and that Mary should leave him. Mary agreed with Pat, but kept the marriage together.

Later, after Stanley died, when Mary Highsmith was asked by her grand-nephew Don what she'd done with Stanley's ashes, she replied puckishly: "I flushed them," and refused to add another word. Mary also said she wanted her own ashes scattered from a plane while it played a recording of "Hey Look Me Over" from a loudspeaker.[16]

Whether or not she deposited her second husband's remains in her toilet bowl and pulled the chain, Mary gave Stanley a rather expensive funeral when he died of an aneurysm brought on by treatment for Parkinson's disease in 1970. It was one more thing for Mary and Pat to quarrel about. That, and the fact that Pat wanted to "correct" Stanley's obituary, which listed her as his "daughter" even though he'd adopted her at her own suggestion. "I feel,"

Mary wrote to Pat and not for the first time, "that anyone who reads your correction will think you are sick."[17]

But it was when Mary and Stanley, having put together "six hundred dollars,"[18] travelled back from New York (where they'd gone to earn the money) to pluck the six-year-old Pat from Fort Worth and her grandmother Willie Mae's watchful care that Pat began consciously to have "evil thoughts" about the "murder of my step-father." Pat fixed her murderous fantasies as starting "when I was eight or less."[19] Thirty years later, she ascribed her unusual self-possession—her classmates at Barnard College noticed it, labelling her "Pat the ultra" in their college yearbook—to her efforts at repressing a strong urge to murder her stepfather.

"I learned to live with a grievous and murderous hatred very early on. And learned to stifle also my more positive emotions. In adolescence therefore I was oddly in command of myself, more so than most people—judging from case histories of more average or ordinary (whatever that is) people that I read about. It is strange. Some adolescents explode at nineteen or twenty and get into trouble. Others—well—"[20]

From "gloomy, masculine, functional" Trieste, in January of 1953, searching for an apartment with her lover Ellen Hill, a sociologist who was working to settle displaced persons (and living with one, too: Pat Highsmith), Pat received a long, depressed letter from Mother Mary, who was as unanchored as her daughter. Mary and Stanley had been shuttling back and forth between Miami (Pat calls it "that crap town") and Orlando, Florida, while Pat had been unhappily trailing Ellen from one European capital to another. Mary had a "small fashion job she already anticipates losing" and was contemplating a trip to Texas for "emotional help."[21] Pat, miserable about her writing and her love life, was waiting for Harper & Brothers to reply to yet another version of her much-rewritten novel *The Two Faces of January*. (Her editor, Joan Kahn, would reject it regretfully for the second time as "not worthy of Pat.")[22]

By Valentine's Day, Pat was feeling "like a 3rd rate writer": she was in debt to Ellen for $250 and her "work [was] at a standstill because Ellen cannot bear the [sound of] typing."[23] Ellen and Pat had just returned from Venice, where Pat had busied herself with the kind of social climbing and social criticism she was always condemning in Mother Mary:

Called Peggy Guggenheim for 6:30 cocktails at Harry's [Bar]. With 3 dogs & a fairy is how she appeared. . . . I began talking with Mary Oliver [the English writer] & friend Jody in Harry's [Bar]—a red headed horror of an international tramp. Jane Bowles' friends' types. Both queer, in pants. Peggy nervous but very amicable.[24]

In this critical mood and responding in her diary to Mary's depressed letter, Pat identified so strongly with Mary that she made what she called her "poor mother's pain" her own; managing, nevertheless, to criticize her poor mother's choices.

"*Death of a Salesman* story all over again, the merciless rules of the game they unfortunately chose to play so many years ago—yet without the vicious push that game demands to make it pay after so many years."[25]

Still, Pat couldn't help but entertain a small hope amongst all her unhappy speculations. It was another version of the feeling she'd formed for Stanley Highsmith the moment he made the mistake of correcting her pronunciation all those years ago.

"I should really not be surprised if one of them should commit suicide for the insurance," Pat wrote about her parents.

And then, brightening a little, she added: "[I]t would have to be Stanley, I believe."[26]

· 8 ·

LA MAMMA

PART 4

"Childhood is the only reality," said André Breton, who was a psychiatrist long before he was a Surrealist. When it came to the sourcing of her own wounds and grievances, Pat Highsmith would have agreed with him.

There is scarcely a nervous condition, a night terror, or a broken relationship Pat suffered as an adult that she did not directly relate to her childhood. In her late-life copy of *The Prisoner of Childhood* (1979), Alice Miller's classic text on narcissistic disturbances in gifted children, Pat bracketed passages that pertained to her own history. Then, as if marking Dr. Miller's book weren't enough, she made a short list of notes numbered with the book pages she'd written on—it was a kind of concordance—to ensure that her early life would be doubly linked to Alice Miller's conclusions: "p. 47 (best for me)," "p. 57: In 1971 wrote the 3 letters elucidating and calling it quits," etc., etc.*

Alice Miller's theories about gifted children were useful explanations for someone like Pat, who always thought of her child-self as both gifted *and* deprived. Miller believed that the way to recover the child's "authentic self" was to learn to blame the parent—a nostrum Pat had already applied with great enthusiasm and little success for much of her life. In 1960, as Miller was developing her theories, the English pediatrician and analyst D. W. Winnicott published his famous paper on the subject of double lives, "Ego Distortion in Terms of True and False Self." In it, Winnicott observed that a child's "false

---

* Mistaking the date, Pat refers here to the three letters she wrote to her stepfather in 1970 justifying a break with her mother.

self" emerged in households where the child was raised to be so responsive to the parent's narcissistic demands that she cannot separate her own needs and wants from those of the parent. Winnicott's other observation—it is one Pat would have vigorously endorsed—was that the mother hates the child long before the child hates the mother.

Pat Highsmith never read Dr. Winnicott. But much of her fiction and most of her life gave a local habitation and a name to what Winnicott supposed about the divided self: that the "false self" covers the "true self" in order to protect it. And that the two selves, true and false, are yoked together by a violent psychology.

Despite her brief late-life attention to Alice Miller, Pat's interpretations of the years and fears that formed her were unvaryingly, if unwittingly, Freudian. Naturally, she hated Freudians—she gave a lover terrible trouble over her friendship with a prominent Freudian[1]—but on the worst days of her life she usually thought about consulting one. When she was very young, nine and ten years old, she found a resemblance to her own imaginative life in the "abnormal" case histories of *The Human Mind* (1930) by Karl Augustus Menninger (1893–1990), an American popularizer of Freudian analysis who advocated treating psychiatry as a science.* *The Human Mind* gave young Patsy Highsmith "case models" with which to compare her own shifting psychological states, states to which the hypervigilant child was always hyperalert. And Menninger's embrace of the "abnormal" in the preface to his bestselling book must have been especially appealing to a girl whose every childhood memory shows how far from "normal" she always felt.

"The adjuration to be 'normal' seems shockingly repellent to me," Dr. Menninger wrote.

"I think it is ignorance that makes people think of abnormality only with horror and allows them to remain undismayed at the proximity of the 'normal' to average and mediocre. For surely anyone who achieves anything is, a priori, abnormal."[2]

Many of Pat's short fictions are phrased in the matter-of-fact American manner Menninger used to write up his psychological studies. This case history from *The Human Mind*—it is one of many examples—could almost be mistaken for the plain-style opening of a Highsmith short story:

* Menninger, with his father and later his brother, founded the Menninger Clinic in Topeka, Kansas, and the clinic's enlightened practices and sophisticated public relations did much to legitimize and Americanize Freudian theories of psychiatry in the United States.

The Manhaters:
Mary's parents had done everything they could to break up a crush between her and her pal Nell but in spite of tears and lectures and threats and scoldings Mary and Nell were steadfast.[3]

Patsy Highsmith spent two years in grade schools on the Upper West Side of Manhattan. Fresh from Texas, with a Southern accent a steak knife couldn't cut, she was six years old when Mother Mary walked her to her first Manhattan grade school, a "four or five story red brick building trimmed with grey cement" on what she remembered as West Ninety-ninth Street. (The Highsmiths were living on West 103rd Street.) Patsy tested two years above her age for reading, but the school forgot to check her arithmetic, and in her advanced class she "developed a traumatic fear of mathematics from which I have never recovered." Her fear didn't stop her from being obsessed with numbers.

But back in Fort Worth, Willie Mae was pulling the family strings. When she learned that Patsy had emerged from her first day in a Manhattan public school "walking hand in hand down the steps of the school with a little black boy," she insisted that her granddaughter be taken out of the school. Pat wrote that she'd clung to the little boy because she was used to playing with black children in Willie Mae's "alley" and "we could at least understand what the other was saying . . . what else is the Southern accent but the African accent?" Mary Highsmith bent to Willie Mae's will: she put Patsy in a "private" school on Riverside Drive "around 103rd Street" for about a year. Pat's chief memory of this school was of throwing up in the toilet every Friday afternoon because Friday was the day they had kidneys for lunch.

"Later," Pat wrote, "my grandmother came to her senses, I am glad to say, and I was back in an ordinary school, with blacks, within a year."[4]

Willie Mae was still running the show.

Pat's memories of all her schools in New York City throb with resentment. She explained her feelings about Julia Richman High School, the school at 317 East Sixty-seventh Street she'd attended for four years (its motto, "Knowledge Is Power," was chiseled over the front door) by referring to the noise, the neopenal architecture, and the overcrowding—but she seems, finally, to have blamed her unhappiness on the ethnic mix that is part of New York life. "We were sixty percent Italian, maybe thirty percent Jewish, and there was a handful of Irish, German and Polish." When she was fifteen, the Italians began dropping out and this "led to a preponderance of Jews."

"[F]rom 1934 until 1938 (when I graduated from high school) we often had to sit two at a seat and desk, because the Jews fleeing Hitler had begun to arrive en masse in Manhattan. I always had to share my seat, though some girls plumper than me had their seats to themselves."[5] (Pat went on to rail against overweight people—irrationally—all her life.)

Sharing—even (or especially) with young Jewish refugees or with the daughters of Jewish doctors and dentists from the Upper West Side who were getting better grades than she was—never brought out the best in Pat.

In February of 1929, Mary and Stanley Highsmith gave up their apartment in Upper Manhattan and travelled with their eight-year-old daughter back to Fort Worth, Texas, where Patsy was enrolled in the old Sixth Ward grade school near Willie Mae's boardinghouse. Eleven months later, Patsy, Stanley, and Mary were back in New York again. These to-ings and fro-ings between the boardinghouse in Texas and apartments in New York—the product of financial, psychological, and marital crises—were a frequent and unhappy feature of Pat's childhood. This time, the Highsmiths moved to the farthest reaches of Astoria in the western part of the borough of Queens, gateway to Long Island. Queens, then as now (with exceptions like the solidly middle-class enclave of Forest Hills), was the working-class stepsister of the more or less glamorous Manhattan. Manhattan mythologized itself. Queens was just a decent, inexpensive place to live.

Between 1930 and 1933 the Highsmiths lived first at 1919 Twenty-first Road in Astoria, near the East River, and then in an apartment on Twenty-eighth Street in the 2200 block, a few streets away. Patsy was enrolled as a fourth-grader at Public School 122 on Ditmars Boulevard on 10 February 1930. During her three years there, her grades for conduct were better than her term course grades (three As and five Bs for her courses, straight As for conduct); and her tenseness about time and numbers was already evident: she was never late for school. But she was frequently absent: thirteen times in one term, six, five, and four times in others. She was tall and skinny for a fifth-grader (57½ inches and 80¼ pounds), and her vision was twenty-twenty.[6] It was at P.S. 122 that Patsy had the first of the vivid views of single men in empty spaces that would inspire and guide her at odd moments in her life. She called this one a "vision of freedom."

Patsy was in the P.S. 122 building, "six feet from the floor, clinging to a wooden pole some twelve feet long which was used to pull down the windows from the top."[7] She'd been given the assignment by her teacher to shinny up the pole and open the window, but she was using it as an opportunity to make the class laugh—a rare attempt at being class clown. It was ten o'clock in the morning and she was looking down from the second- or third-story window of a classroom when she saw

> a solitary figure, a man, walking briskly along the pavement with a briefcase under his arm. The sun was shining through the trees that bordered the otherwise empty residential streets in Astoria. . . . The man was hatless, I remember, wearing a dark suit, and he seemed to be in a hurry. I now realize he was probably a salesman, perhaps late for an appointment, but to me he symbolized freedom-at-ten-in-the-morning . . . answerable to nobody as to how he spent his time. The image made an indelible impression on me. . . . I felt that was what I wanted too.[8]

Nothing could better symbolize the American Dream than a salesman in a hurry with a briefcase under his arm—except perhaps that traditionally free safe haven of all American dreamers, the municipal branch library. Patsy had already begun to borrow books from her local branch, the Queensborough Public Library in Astoria, and it was there that she "plunged at once into the psychology section, took books out, and often sat reading books which were not meant to be borrowed."[9]

Sixty years later, Pat wrote to Karl Menninger to let him know why reading case studies in *The Human Mind* had meant so much to her when she was a child living in Astoria: "To me they were real, of course, consequently more stimulating to my imagination than fairy tales or fiction would have been."[10] Practical even in her early thinking, Pat *used* abnormal psychology to stimulate her imagination just as she would use it when she began to write. "I can't think," she said at the end of her life, "of anything more apt to set the imagination stirring, drifting, creating, than the idea—the fact—that anyone you walk past on the pavement anywhere may be a sadist, a compulsive thief, or even a murderer."[11]

An imagination that muddles its creative cocktails with sadists, murderers, and compulsive thieves, has probably been helped along the way by something more than an unsuccessfully blended family, a tense psychological heritage, or even one of Satan's little sidekicks looking for trouble. Pat's years in Astoria add a faintly delinquent note to the brine and brimstone mixture in which she had begun to marinate her fantasies, but the innocent corruptions of reading forbidden psychology texts in the Queensborough Public Library weren't enough to make Highsmith Country. It took an entire village to raise a Patricia Highsmith. Or, rather, it took the atmosphere of an unusual neighborhood in Queens, New York, to help form Highsmith's imagination.

"The Kite," one of many Highsmith short stories about children, is about an unhappy little boy named Walter. Walter's nine-year-old sister, with whom he loved to build kites, has suddenly died of double pneumonia. "The Kite," published in 1981 in Pat's collection of stories *The Black House,* might have been written at any time. It is full of the delights of building something (the instructions for kite making are quite complete), and it seems to be set in an amber era much earlier than the one in which it appeared. Walter's family eats fried ham, baked apple, and garlic bread. He lives in a town where he can ride a bike, climb a cemetery fence, and build and fly a kite. He is the age Pat was when she lived in Queens, and he, too, has parents who argue incessantly with each other.

Secretly, Walter makes an enormous kite on which he writes his dead sister's name. When he reels it into the sky, the kite, which has a mind of its own, takes him up with it. The aerial view delights him until a "rescue" helicopter punctures the kite and Walter has one of those nasty, skull-cracking falls with which Pat Highsmith liked to kill her idealists. It's a simple story, crudely written. Everything about it is obvious except Walter's delight in the flight—and the actual flight itself.

The story becomes interesting when its "reality" pulls apart—which it does with something like the rasping sound Pat's laughter is said to have made in France in the 1970s. (Janine Hérisson, Pat's neighbor in the Île-de-France for fifteen years, said—chillingly because she was chilled by it—that "Patricia never laughed for pleasure. It was more like something breaking than laughter.")[12] In "The Kite," Pat breaks herself out of a dull description of a comic book–like town by flinging her story up into the sky, where "clouds somersaulted over each other like fleecy sheep" and "cars moved like ladybirds in two directions." Walter, in flight in midair, lives "in a more beautiful atmosphere," dreams of going to Acapulco with his dead sister, and becomes a poet, composing some lines as he glides. And that's when the helicopter's attempt to "rescue" Walter ends by killing him. Despite the boy's screams— "Keep clear!" and "Leave me alone!" (phrases like those used by Pat Highsmith on her deathbed)—the rescuers inadvertently pierce both Walter's kite and his fantasy, and he drops, dead, into the reality of a tree.

Whatever else the story does, it makes a powerful case for leaving children alone with their fantasies—and for how much better the world looks when you can see it from above, from the elevation only a map can show. For that's the view that Walter has, high up in his kite, soaring away from his arguing parents and closer to the beauty of his beloved dead sister. The painful reality of earth, the physical details of which always occupied Pat Highsmith so intensely, is as distanced from him as the coordinates on a map. In "The Kite," it is the map's-eye view that makes Walter so happy. But in the author's life, the map's-eye view shows something quite different from the conditions for happiness. When she was Walter's age, Pat Highsmith was living on a municipal stage set whose purlieus seem to be a lot like the mise-en-scènes of her future novels.

So let's take a look at a map of Astoria, Queens, as it would have been in the palmy days of 1931 when ten-year-old Patsy Highsmith, her mind alive with case studies in abnormal psychology and the lightly suppressed desire to murder her stepfather, was skipping the three or four blocks from the family apartment down to the East River nearly every afternoon—Pat said she was "ebullient" only when out of doors[13]—to play in one of her very favorite places in the neighborhood: the fifty urban acres of Astoria Park.

The two apartments in the Ditmars Boulevard school district where the Highsmiths lived in the early 1930s are close enough to each other to form the apex of an imaginary scalene triangle. The short leg of the triangle ends in the East River (the river that separates Queens from the island of Manhattan) at Wards Island (where the largest mental hospital in the world has been built), while the long leg of the triangle stops farther north in the river at Rikers Island (where the biggest prison in New York State has just been contructed). Lapping the shores of Astoria Park are the dangerous drowning waters of Hell Gate: a narrow channel in the East River which contains some of the deepest water in all New York Harbor. Hell Gate is spanned by the longest railway arch bridge in the United States, Hell Gate Bridge. The bridge carries the trains from Canada and the United States over the river which churns and roils perilously at the very edge of Patsy's playground.

The fantastic new skyscrapers of Manhattan (the Empire State Building was completed in 1931, the Chrysler Building in 1930) are mere vertical brackets in the corner of the forbidding landscape created by the Wards Island mental hospital. More than four thousand inmates are kept in this asylum (in an era when the insane are still "criminalized"), and it dominates the view from Astoria Park. From the northwest tip of Astoria Park (Hell Gate Bridge Park is another name for Patsy's playground), it is just possible to catch a glimpse of a much smaller island called North Brother Island. It is here where the talented cook named Mary Mallon—latterly known as "Typhoid Mary"—is still alive and in residence: quarantined for life after having served up enough typhoid bacillus with her superb cuisine to kill several dozen New Yorkers.

Could anything be plainer than this map? In Astoria, Queens, during her ninth, tenth, and eleventh years, little Patsy Highsmith, already inclined towards thoughts of murder and melancholy, was separated from Manhattan and the Bronx by an atmosphere of Crime (the insane inmates of Wards Island who were treated like criminals) and Punishment (the criminals on Rikers Island who were certainly being punished), while a vision of Hell was just at her feet (Hell Gate) and over her head (Hell Gate Bridge). It's worth repeating (although Pat didn't repeat it herself) that the compass points of the Highsmith neighborhood in Astoria, Queens—Crime, Punishment, Railroads, and Hell—are also the plotting points of that other interesting neighborhood Pat grew up to inhabit: Highsmith Country.

Hell Gate and the Ditmars Boulevard neighborhood worked their magic on Patsy, and later on, Pat Highsmith attempted to unpack them in fictions. When she was twenty-five, Pat took character notes "for an atmospheric piece with realistic dialogue [about a girl who has a] childhood in Astoria [and about] the strange power Hellgate Bridge" exerts on her. Letitia, the girl, is a character on whom Pat cast the darkest suspicions she had about her own psychology and future.

"Essentially, the development of a *schizophrene*, who is optimistic, tending to the extrovert, as she scampers around the Hellgate Bridge Park at the age of ten. In her is a tolerance for all, low and high: history is being made. Things are taking *form*. . . .

"She has made the only compromise possible for her with the world: she has withdrawn into herself. At the age of thirty."[14]

Pat slipped a reference to Hell Gate into one of Charles Bruno's attempts to elude the pursuing detective Gerard in *Strangers on a Train*, and after she moved to Europe, she wrote to Jeva Cralick, Mother Mary's friend, for drawings and descriptions of her old Ditmars Boulevard neighborhood. She was hoping to use it in a novel. And Jeva Cralick sent back detailed maps, charts of streets, the racial compositions of neighborhoods—just the kind of information Pat loved best. But Cralick also added an artist's warning about the danger of using details you haven't gathered for yourself. "You have been away too long from these shores to really have the feel of things—you'd have to stay here for a long time to get the drift."[15]

Along with *The Human Mind*—it was on her parents' bookshelf—Patsy read an anatomical textbook used by Mary and Stanley for their illustration work: George Bridgeman's *The Human Machine*. Both books made their impressions on the girl, but it was *The Human Mind* that stayed and stayed.

Always happy to think of herself as neglected, Pat said she used to return to an empty apartment from P.S. 122, sit down in the big green armchair in the living room, and read through the plain prose Menninger used for the cases he'd culled from his own practice and from other, less reliable sources. But Mother Mary was a freelance fashion illustrator whose most frequent employer, *Women's Wear Daily*, kept her working mostly at home. Perhaps young Patsy just *felt* she was home alone.

It was in Queens, too, where Pat joined a girl gang, another faintly delinquent experience she remembered with great pleasure in the last decade of her life. It was the "activity" of the gang—"they mostly ran around and had meetings, a lot of physical movement"[16]—that Pat liked: the same active life she was later to admire so much in men. Her gang memories undoubtedly colored the wonderful review she gave to *Meg* (1950), a first novel by an ex–ballet dancer who also happened to be the adventurous granddaughter of a U.S. president. The ex-dancer's name was Theodora Roosevelt Keogh and she lived in Paris with her artist husband Tom Keogh, resolutely refusing to give her publisher, Roger Straus, permission to trade on her illustrious name. A favorite of her formidable aunt, Alice Roosevelt Longworth, Theodora shunned *The Paris Review* crowd (they ignored her work as well, as they ignored the work of most women writers),[17] and went on to write novels of such piercing sensual perception—a marriage of Colette and L. P. Hartley—that composer and diarist Ned Rorem remembers her from 1950s Paris as "our best American writer—certainly our best female writer."[18]

Pat wrote her review of Keogh's novel *Meg* for *The Saturday Review* in April of 1950. It was Pat's first published piece of criticism—one of the few reviews she would ever write about a work authored by a woman—and it is probably the most favorable review she ever published. The novel about which Pat was so untypically excited is a wayward work, with just the kind of heroine who would appeal to Pat: a preadolescent, androgynous prep school girl from the Upper East Side of Manhattan who carries a knife, dreams of being suckled by lions, blackmails her lesbian history teacher, runs with a wild gang of boys from the docks, and has a distinctly undaughterly relationship with the father of one of her friends. In the last sentence of her critique of *Meg,* Pat left no doubt about how much of herself she saw in Theodora Keogh's young heroine.

"Such an admirable personage is she with her banged-up knees, her dirty sweaters, her proud vision of the universe that, remembering one's own childhood, one wishes one had kept more of Meg intact."[19]

While she was still living in Queens in the early 1930s, Patsy's reading of Menninger was augmented by the conventional tropes of a bookish American childhood: *Bob Son of Battle, Dracula,* the Sherlock Holmes stories, and *Little Women,* along with generous helpings of Robert Louis Stevenson and Jack London. She also read the somewhat less conventional *Sesame and Lilies*—perhaps it had been assigned her by a hopeful educator at P.S. 122—a book of lectures for schoolchildren about aesthetics by the arch-aesthete himself, John Ruskin. Her enthusiasm for Edgar Allan Poe, who shared her January birthdate and her future interest in alcohol and pubescent girls, and for Herman Melville's *Moby-Dick,* which gave a form to her fantasy of sailing the high seas in homosocial company, came a little later. But it was Menninger whom Pat never stopped mentioning to the press, and she was thrilled to get a letter from the old man in 1989. Flattered by Pat's reference to *The Human Mind* in a *Vogue* magazine interview, Karl Menninger wrote Pat in his unadorned way to say that he'd met, but didn't like, Truman Capote, and that he was "going to get some of your books and read them."[20]

Karl Menninger was Patricia Highsmith's first Freudian.

The most unusual feature of Patricia Highsmith's unusual childhood is the fact that nearly every story about it comes directly from Pat Highsmith herself. In her memory books, no fond friends or foul neighbors or feisty family members have been allowed to contribute an impression or dredge up an anecdote. Each vignette from her upbringing has been shaped and colored by Pat's own assumptions and interpretations, and is transmitted in her own peculiar style in her diaries, her cahiers, her articles, and her interviews. And in her novels and short stories, like any good practitioner of the art, Pat puts many of her own inferences in her characters' mouths and pretends to pluck many more of them from her characters' minds.

Pat's editing of her early life—perhaps it was really only her isolation from other people's attitudes—gave her a claustral as well as a *usable* view of childhood. She often produced an early memory to explain a recurring unhappiness or to justify a returning depression or a lingering anomie. At twenty, she wrote: "I cannot remember as much of my childhood as I should like, or even remember myself a few years back. I hope to do better when I am older."[21] As she aged, her memories of things past were triggered by her present emotional states. And so it seems just as important to understand *when* in the life of her emotions Pat remembered something as it is to understand her very specific memories. Understanding the occasion as well as the content of her memories gives us two ways of thinking about Patricia Highsmith instead of one—and Pat Highsmith was always at least two people at once.

For such a fiercely private woman, so intolerant of personal exposure, Pat was uncommonly ready to dig up the dark familial roots from which she felt all her "deformities" had sprung. What she didn't record plainly in her journals for posterity, she published outright in articles or books or told to disconcerted journalists. *Plotting and Writing Suspense Fiction,* the self-help book for writers it took her only a month to finish, is filled with personal, emotionally charged vignettes disguised in back-of-the-matchbook prose as little recipes for successful suspense writing. But the real "suspense" delivered by this book lies in just which secret about her private life Patricia Highsmith will reveal next.

There are the personal revelations, like this one:

My grandmother died some years ago. I was very fond of her, and she had most of the job of raising me until I was six, as my mother was busy with her work. There was little or no resemblance between me and my grandmother, though of course she gave me some of the bones and blood that I have, and our hands were a little alike. Not long ago, I happened to glance at a nearly worn-out shoe of mine which had taken the shape of my foot and there I saw the shape, or expression of my grandmother's foot, as I remembered it. [And it was then that] I shed the first real tears for my grandmother, realized her death for the first time, her long life, her absence now, and I realized also my own death to come.[22]

And there are the professional revelations, which were also personal. This innocuous statement was linked by lines of fire to Pat's childhood: "Good short stories are made from the writer's emotions alone."[23]

Pat's early memories and feelings often blazed up during her adult battles with her parents (she remembered that she had "learned to live with a grievous and murderous hatred very early on" in 1970, when she was particularly enraged with Mother Mary and preparing herself for another break),[24] and she put these "writer's emotions" to creatively transformed use in her short stories—especially in the short stories she wrote about children.

In "The Legend of the Convent of St. Fotheringay," a story Pat wrote at Barnard College and published in the *Barnard Quarterly* in the spring of 1941, a baby boy is found and adopted by a convent of nuns. The nuns name him Mary and conceal his gender by raising and dressing him as a girl.

Pat wrote the story "for relaxation" in a period when she could "[c]laim no amorous attachments" and "[c]annot interest myself in *The Ambassadors*."[25] "St. Fotheringay" is set in a world much like the female-dominated one in which Pat grew up: "there was not one masculine organism on the grounds outside of possible insect life." Fotheringay, it is helpful to remember, is the name of the castle in Scotland in which one queen (Elizabeth I of England) imprisoned and then executed another one (Mary Queen of Scots). And Pat's first six years were spent in a boardinghouse in Fort Worth in which her mother, Mary, was subject to her Scots-Irish grandmother Willie Mae's iron rule of law.

Pat illustrated "The Legend of the Convent of St. Fotheringay" with little cartoons of the boy called Mary (her own first name as well as her mother's), and she drew him to look exactly like herself. The boy, who feels he is on his way to becoming a great and famous genius, blackmails his way out of the convent by threatening to blow it up—and then, the jocular narrator's voice intimates, he dynamites it anyway and covers up his crime. "St. Fotheringay" is an excellent origin story for the complicated childhood loyalties and rages—both gender and familial—by which Pat felt confined and confused as a child. Whether or not she meant it to directly represent her life is a secret she probably preferred to keep from herself.

In "The Terrapin" (1962), a boy with some of Pat's childhood feelings is constantly degraded and humiliated by his commercial-artist mother. She makes him a mirror of her desires and dresses him up as a much younger child. When his mother cooks alive the terrapin he'd hoped to keep as a pet, he stabs her to death in her bedroom with the same knife she used to dismember the terrapin. In *Plotting and Writing Suspense Fiction,* Pat tells us that "The Terrapin" required "two germs" (the helpful term for inspirational spark she lifted from Henry James) to come alive. The first "germ"—a story she heard about a commercial artist who made terrible use of her ten-year-old son, turning him into a "tortured neurotic"—was activated by a second "germ": her reading of a "horrifying recipe for cooking a terrapin stew. . . .

"The method of killing the terrapin was to boil it alive. The word killing was not used and did not have to be. . . . Readers who find that thrillers are beginning to pall may may like to skim sections in cookbooks that have to do with our feathered and shelled friends; a housewife has got to have a heart of stone to read these recipes, much less carry them out."[26]

Pat paired her recounting of "The Terrapins"' provenience with the casual revelation that her own mother was a "commercial artist (though not like this mother)."[27] She wrote this parenthetical disclaimer at a time when she was thinking of Mary, once again, as a mother who was *exactly* like the mother in "The Terrapin."

In "Hamsters vs. Websters," little Larry Webster watches interestedly as his furry pets turn into feral killers and rip his father into bleeding pieces. In "Harry: A Ferret," fifteen-year-old Roland thinks of his ferret as "his secret weapon, better than a gun," and allows him to tear out the throat of an old family retainer. (Pat had read Saki, and Saki's own famous ferret story, "Sredni Vashtar," was a favorite of William Burroughs, whose disgust with life often resembles Pat's own disgust at its most disgusted.) In "Those Awful Dawns" (1972)—Pat called it "my beaten baby story"[28]—the negligence of the parents and the physical battery of the children are almost too well imagined. Although the story portrays the parents as indifferent to the point of depravity, and although its real point is an attack on Catholicism's birth-control ban, the narrative leaves a nasty glow of qualified pleasure around the abuse of the children. It lingers like its less violent (but equally ambivalent) analogue in another tale much admired by Pat: the smile of the Cheshire Cat in *Alice in Wonderland.*

In "A Mighty Nice Man," another story Pat wrote at Barnard College, it is the little girl and her all-too-willing mother, as the German critic Paul Ingendaay noted, who are most conscious of "the conditions of sexual transaction" and not the "nice man" pressing to take the little girl for a "ride."[29] In "The Mightiest Mornings" (1945), the corrupting condition is provided by a *rumor* of sexual relations between the adult newcomer Bentley (so close to Ripley in name) and Freya, a ten-year-old outcast girl. Bentley's guilt, contracted like a disease from the small-town whispers about his behavior, suggests that his intentions towards the child are less than honorable. But it is the gossip that forces Bentley into exile.

Pat did once tell a Swiss neighbor in the Ticino—this would have been sometime in the 1980s when Virginia Woolf's story of being stood on a wall and "interfered with" by her half brothers was still the subject of literary conversation—that she had a blurred recollection of sexual "interference" from her early Fort Worth years. "She thought she had been lifted up on the kitchen sink by two travelling salesmen when she was a child" and perhaps touched in some way. "Pat didn't have a clear memory of this," says her neighbor.[30]

Pat, so sensitive to spatial and physical encroachments that any touch at all would have seemed like an aggression, left no other reference to this "memory," so it is impossible to know whether this was a memory of something that actually happened, or a memory of something Pat *felt* had happened (bad enough), or if, on the particular day she decided to remember it, Pat simply needed another origin story for her harrowed feelings.

One of those harrowed feelings was Pat's own marked interest in young girls. Not the twenty-somethings who attracted her at the end of her amatory life, but the eight- and ten-year-olds who caught her attention at the beginning of it. It is probably because she acknowledged these feelings (about which she did nothing but dream) that Pat wanted to bring her own childhood "case"—*all* the cases of her uncomfortable childhood—to the public. She managed, finally, to publish most of them, and we can add to the importance of noting just *when* Pat Highsmith remembered her memories the necessity of figuring out just how she *used* them.

Still, in her recollections of her early life, nothing comes through more clearly than Pat's feeling that she was cursed at birth. Cursed, even, by being born. Amongst American fiction writers, only Edgar Allan Poe approaches her developed sense of personal doom.

"Before the age of six and frequently afterward," Pat had a "dream, or vision" of what it meant to be born.[31] She presented this recurrent "dream, or vision" to the world in an article written, unaccountably, for *Vogue* magazine in 1968.[32] True to her lifelong ability to experience most normal feelings in reverse ("It is always so easy for me to see the world upside down," she wrote),[33] Pat's dream of birth is like anyone else's vision of death, of Last Judgment. In this "dream, or vision," Pat is surrounded by seven doctors and nurses—they are more like a tribunal than a medical team—all of whom are regarding her tiny body, laid out on a table in an atmosphere of "murk and gloom," with a mixture of the "horror" and "pity" which Aristotle thought were the proper responses to classical tragedy. The doctors and nurses nod in "solemn agreement over some unspeakable defect in me." Their "irrevocable pronouncement is worse than death because I am fated to live."[34]

Pat offered more dark early memories in an article she sent to *Granta* in March of 1990: "Some Christmases—Mine or Anybody's." The article is a lengthy recital of some of her worst Christmases (her only Christmas pleasure seems to have been the many church services she attended on many Christmas Eves), and it includes her deep identification with a Christ whom she imagines to be inviting crucifixion with calculated acts of passive aggression. ("I believe that Jesus, who wished to fulfill what he saw as his destiny, turned the other cheek because he knew that . . . would hasten events. . . . Mildness did not soothe his taunters, it was fat in the fire. Jesus was in a hurry.")[35] Pat was five years from her own death when she summoned up these Christmases—and much less happy than she'd hoped to be in the last house of her life in Tegna, Switzerland.

"The first Christmas, or Christmas tree that I remember is the one when I was four. My mother reports that I peeked around or between sliding doors which separated my grandparents' living-room from the room we called the parlour, where the tree always was. She says I was silent, looking serious or apprehensive, as well I might, as my stepfather had in the last months come on the scene, and it seemed to me that he and my mother were often quarrelling, though maybe this impression was half-wrong."[36]

Pat followed this anxious description of infant demeanor with a full list of dishes from the traditional Christmas dinner (preceded by the traditional spoken grace) prepared by her grandmother Willie Mae for the family in the house on West Daggett Avenue in Fort Worth. The menu, a Southern Christmas dinner menu, is worth reprinting. It's replete with the kind of comfort food Pat hankered for (and couldn't get) in all the countries of her European exile: roast turkey and corn bread, sweet potatoes with walnuts and marshmallows, and home-cranked vanilla ice cream. But what Pat's memory lingered on most lovingly was the large quantity of alcohol Willie Mae put into her Christmas fruitcake.[37] This was 1925. Prohibition—the United States' great experiment in trying to keep alcohol out of the hands of its citizens—wasn't repealed until Pat's twelfth year, 1933. (And even after Prohibition was voted down nationally, Texas remained a technically "dry" state.) Willie Mae's famous fruitcake, soaked in rum for many months, was, strictly speaking, contraband material. Even in childhood, Pat's eye was attracted to life's little irregularities.

At nineteen, Pat remembered an alarming childhood affliction. It was a regularly appearing "hallucinatory 'mouse'" or "grey blob that darted diagonally across the upper left hand corner of my vision." It "bothered" her from the ages of five to seven and appeared whenever she was "reading or looking at anything intently."[38] If her dating is correct, the hallucination came to her during a time of unusual stress in an already stressful childhood: the two bridging years which comprised her last offical year in Fort Worth and her first school year in New York City (from 1926 to 1928). The picture she paints of herself is of a frightened, guilty, secretive child—unable to confide in the "other people" she can't quite bring herself to call "family."

> This [the "mouse"] I should not have minded myself, had not other people remarked my start of terror and surprise whenever it happened. I was ashamed to tell them, of course, about my "mouse." But the imagined figure was so lifelike, I was never able to control my shock. During these years the mouse appeared four and five times a week. At the age of seven I was given a brindle cat for my birthday. Shortly after that the mouse stopped appearing. I have never seen it since. Of course this has nothing to do with the cat, although it might if the cat had been hallucinatory too.[39]

At twenty-seven, the Drama Queen who regularly seized Pat's pen when she was feeling sorry for herself seized it again. Pat remembered another childhood feeling when she was mourning her lost lover Ginnie Catherwood in March of 1948, and she wrote it into her cahier just after a passage which compares her thwarted love for Ginnie to "a towering, white, straight and strong thing, an elephant's gigantic tusk, Pharos of my existence."[40] And so, not for the first time, Pat managed to echo Sigmund Freud as she moved, lugubriously, from the phallic to the Attic, seeing herself as

> an alert, anxious faced child over whom hangs already the grey-black spirit of doom, of foreordained unhappiness . . . which would have made its elders beat their breasts like the Greek tragedians. So much promised! So young to bear so cruel a fate! . . . O pity! O pause and shed a tear! O Thermopylae! Even you were not defeated without a chance to fight![41]

And it was only when she appeared on a British television show in 1982 that she decided to share with the world that at "nine or ten," "I had a feeling that I would die when I fell asleep and I was afraid of that." Many a night, Pat reported to what must have been her disconcerted viewers, she would lie awake until two in the morning with the fear of death around her. Her remedy for this night terror was to sniff water up her nose in the hopes that it would keep her awake.[42] It is not surprising that she grew up to be mortally afraid of drowning—or that she drowned so many of the characters in her fictions. Anxiety was Pat's second self from an early age, and from an early age she was good at making use of it.

In a letter in 1968, Pat managed to diverge from her long list of aggrieved childhood memories. From Montmachoux, France, living in a house bracketed by the houses of noisy Portuguese families who were giving her a foretaste of hell, she wrote to her cousin Dan in Texas about the one and "only happy thing" in the year she'd spent with Willie Mae in Fort Worth when she was twelve. In her one good memory of this crucial year, Pat and Dan, ten years older than Pat, are like two fraternity boys horsing around in a locker room shower: "[Y]ou and me drying dishes in the kitchen, and afterwards, snapping moist dishtowels at each other, then tossing a football on the front lawn."[43]

Pat's cahiers—she expected that her college friend Kingsley would edit and publish them one day and stuck a note to Kingsley in her nineteenth cahier to "have some taste, have at least the taste I have in 1950 in weeding out what is already written, and recently written"[44]—are full of what Pat called "comfortable personal outgushings." (Her diaries, on the other hand, she called "exercise books in languages I do not know." She toyed with burning them or giving them to the Lesbian Herstory Archives in Brooklyn—but Kingsley's disapproval put a stop to the donation.)[45] But even in the cahiers, there is only one early memory Pat recalled with pleasure; a memory that came back to her in "every comfortable and happy moment" of her life.

She described it when she was twenty-four years old and whirling through the bedrooms, barrooms, and dining rooms of Manhattan.

The setting was once again Willie Mae's house on West Daggett Avenue in Fort Worth. Pat remembered it as "plain and ramshackle, showing a hint of poverty . . . here and there." (Ordinarily, Pat avoided references to the working-class setting and worn appurtenances of Willie Mae's boardinghouse.) The household "could always make room for one more, could always provide food for one more mouth, and generously, and love for one more heart." Pat's memory was compounded "of all the five senses' reports," but it needed a sixth sense, she thought, to clarify why it always made her so happy.

"I remember myself before the age of six, sitting in my beloved overalls before a gas stove in Gramma's living room, reading the evening *Press* or the morning *Star-Telegram,* reading the serials in them, now and again holding the paper close to my nose for it would be still fragrant, almost warm, from the inky press. I recall the sound of the thin old door, wainscotted at the bottom, as my cousin Dan entered, chaffing his hands."[46]

The last witnesses who might have lightened the dark landscapes of Pat's early memories (she began a youthful poem with the image that she was "born under a sickly star") with other, more pleasant recollections were her cousin Dan ("brother Dan" to Pat) and her mother, Mary. Mother Mary would have had a lot to say—and she did manage to say most of it in letters which contradict Pat's accounts. Brother Dan would have been factual, fair, and diplomatic just as he was in August of 1975 when, trying to balance the needs of the two seasoned combatants who were his aunt Mary and his "sis Pat," he recorded in his "golden voice"* a touching narrative on tape with which he hoped to awaken Pat to the knowledge that Mother Mary—alone, aging, and increasingly disoriented in Fort Worth with only her cat and her little dog Zsa Zsa (dead of smoke inhalation when her house burned down that same year) for company—was in desperate need of medical attention and custodial care.[47]

Pat was living in Moncourt in the summer of 1975 when Dan sent her the cassette tape on which he'd recorded his impression of Mary's failing condition, and for an entire year Pat ignored it, simply refused to listen to it, and then finally summoned up the excuse in a letter to Dan that it was her friend Marion Aboudaram—she saw Marion every weekend—who had a cassette recorder, not she.[48] In 1963 and 1964, Pat used to wait "three weeks until I replied to [Mother's] letters, by which time my sense of disturbance had died down." By 1968, she was "on quite good terms with my mother, thank God. I suppose for three years now." In May and June of 1970, she was, again, writing her stepfather lengthy letters filled with fulsome reasons for cutting off communication with her mother. But her real avoidance of Mary started only after her stepfather, Stanley, died in September of 1970.

Because Pat had spent so much of her childhood and adolescence hoping (and worse) for the death of Stanley Highsmith or for his divorce from her

---

* In Texas, Dan Oscar Coates, rodeo entrepreneur, cattleman, and wrestling announcer, was renowned as "the man with the Golden Voice," and he was much better known in the West than his novelist cousin. Dan's speaking voice, like Pat's, was beautiful: compellingly deep and dramatic. Dan Oscar Coates was posthumously inducted into the Texas Rodeo Cowboy Hall of Fame.

mother, her decision to break with Mother Mary only *after* Stanley was gone is telling. (After Stanley's death, Pat asked to examine his autopsy report; Mary found the request perfectly normal and sent the report off to Pat in France.) Mary—increasingly forgetful and eccentric, without a husband to help anchor the triangulated family relationship to which Pat had become so accustomed— was something Pat just couldn't face alone. And so she avoided Mary *and* her problems, even on tape.

Dan Coates died of Parkinson's disease three years after Pat, on 15 March 1998, at the age of eighty-seven. Mary had faded away seven years earlier, more or less undone by an undiagnosed form of senile dementia, on 12 March 1991, at the age of ninety-five. (In letters, Pat was often hazy about Mary's birth date, writing that Mary was born in 1896. Mary was born in 1895.)[49] So the rather touchy history of Pat's relations with the adults who brought her up and her rather slippery view of those relations have to be told just the way Pat liked to tell them: in her own version. There are no primary witnesses left alive to balance her telling. But beneath Pat's stories of falling familial fortunes and failed personal relations, of the "good" grandmother and the "bad" mother, of the absent but "respectable" father and the present but "weak and creatively draining" stepfather, another, more subtle, family drama was playing itself out.

Pat spent her life insisting that her mother's quarrelsome, intermittently troubled marriage to Stanley Highsmith had made her childhood "a little hell." In promoting this view, she forgot, as she also forgot when she was toting up the bitter failures of her own love affairs, to acknowledge the brighter side of the conditions she'd lived with. Parents who are idyllically in love with each other are often *exclusively* in love: they don't have much emotional time for their children. And children who are blessed with happy childhoods almost never grow up to become famous writers.

· 9 ·

GREEK GAMES

Although Pat thought classes without boys were classes without "any sense of humor,"[1] Julia Richman High School,* the eight-thousand-student-strong, penitential-looking secondary school for girls on Manhattan's Upper East Side where she was a student from 1934 to 1938, managed to provide her with plenty of entertainment. Her divided affections and perpetual crushes leapt from girl to girl so quickly that she found it difficult to keep track of their movements. But keep track of them she did, and, assembled from the cryptic notes she began keeping at fifteen, here is a small sampling of what more or less constitutes Patricia Highsmith's High School Book of Love.

"Mickey . . . I hate her & she pleases me very much," although "I thought I loved J." ("J" is Judy Tuvim, who grew up to become the Tony- and Oscar-winning actress and comedienne Judy Holliday.) But it was Judy's girlfriend, Babs, to whom Pat was more attracted and to whom she wrote secret summer letters from Fort Worth. Still, Pat loved triangles and felt that "[w]ith B[abs] and J[udy] T[uvim] it is something stronger. We are like each other."[2] Besides, "J.S." still had a serious place in her heart along with the first of her several "Virginias" and "Brillhart," a married socialite from Texas.[3]

Pat's relations with her girl schoolmates were so complicated that her smart high school friends—and Judy Tuvim was the smartest (Pat noted sourly that Judy got a 97 in English while she got only an 85)—had to conduct themselves like teenage Prousts to explain her behavior.

"Everything Judy said came true; that Va. [Virginia] was not good enough

* Named after Julia Richman (1855–1912), the descendant of a long line of Prague rabbis and the first woman district school superintendent in New York City.

for me—that I should spoil myself—that I should go back to her. Judy has much woman in her. The masculinity is only an exaggeration. *Das glaube ich.*"[4]

By the age of seventeen, Pat was reminding herself that she already had a lot to remember—and still there were so many girls to choose from. "Affair [of the heart] with B.Z. beginning in October '35. B. or C. or H. or E. or A.?"[5] Whenever she saw "M.G. [Mickey Goldfarb]" her feeling for "Judy goes to thin air"[6] and she was pleased to "find it surprisingly easy to forget Helen."[7]

In the same notebook entry in which she mentioned her "43 in geometry" and her "resolve to apply Christian Science (Mother Mary's spiritual practice)," Pat also recorded her central *chagrin d'amour*: the betrayal in love by the first and longest love of her life. "M[other] will never leave S[tanley] and never know real happiness. I know we could be happy us two."[8]

Meanwhile she had only recently stopped writing in her notebook the initials "ILE." They stood for "I Love Eliane"—a classmate she had yearned after for three years and with whom she parted over a misunderstanding about dental fillings. Eliane had complimented Pat's teeth, and Pat, humiliated, felt she'd opened her mouth too wide. Pat's teeth remained sore subjects and painful objects for her all her life and she never learned to accept a compliment gracefully. But she quickly replaced ILE with "ILH" (I Love Helen) in her notebook; apparently "Helen" was *not* so "easy to forget" after all.[9]

"Sept. 9 Judy keeps breaking dates. . . . I tell Judy I am jealous of Mickey. . . . Sept. 21 Judy & Adolph [Green]* come at 5:00. . . . I am uncomfortable that she knows I was with Mickey. . . . Sept. 26 I tell [Mickey] I shall never forget her. . . . I am tired, depressed, disturbed. Lunch with J. Strauss. She says I build marble pedestals of ones I like."

"I observe the pickings at Barnard."[10]

Pat's most accurate judgment of her behavior during her high school years was probably the one she gave to Judy Tuvim: "I tell Judy I lie always."[11] It's a nice variation on that oldest of logical paradoxes: " 'All Cretans are liars,' said the Cretan."

When Pat went looking for higher education, she let her fear of crowds— as well as her fear of being "crowded out"—be her guide. At least, that's how she explained herself in an undated essay she wrote in midlife, "A Try at Freedom." She never thought of leaving Manhattan to go to college, so she began her search with New York University, the institution closest to the Highsmith

---

* With Betty Comden and Judy Tuvim (Holliday), Adolph Green founded the Revuers sketch comedy group which played the Village Vanguard in Greenwich Village regularly. (Leonard Bernstein was the pianist.) Betty Comden and Adolph Green, the longest-collaborating team in American musical theater, went on to write the lyrics for some of Broadway's most celebrated musical comedies.

apartment in Greenwich Village. There, she found what she'd already found at Julia Richman High School: that, like Fiorello La Guardia, the half-Catholic, half-Jewish mayor of New York from 1934 to 1945, and like New York City itself, the majority of the student body was divided between Catholics and Jews.

Here for the first time in three years I saw the brothers of the [Jewish and Italian] girls I had been going to high school with, and I couldn't face it. Already I knew that the rare Protestant or the Nothing could count on the Catholics and the Jews for a social ostracism. . . . There were never enough Protestants to throw a party. . . . [T]he student body of N.Y.U. looked twenty-five years old to me. . . . everyone seemed to weigh two hundred pounds and to be covered with hair, and I knew what it was to be bumped by one of them while walking in a hall or climbing a stairway.[12]

In 1988, she gave an equally visceral explanation to a journalist interviewing her for *The New York Times:* "About NYU. Having come from Julia Richman (crowded, girls) I was terrified at Large Figures at NYU. . . . I weighed 10 pounds less than I do now, and frankly did not relish the idea of tangling with big people going up a stairway."[13]

And so Pat chose to go to "Barnard College of Columbia University" in the upper reaches of Broadway. Like Julia Richman High School, Barnard was for women only, it was part of the Ivy League, and it had been turning out distinguished women graduates since its founding in 1889.

What Pat would make of Barnard, however, was something else: "Here was a taste of the freedom I craved."[14]

"Grief fills the world. Pluto, the God of Hades, has carried Persephone off in his chariot: but no one is as grief-stricken as Demeter, the mother of the Goddess [Persephone]. After searching for her daughter in vain, Demeter, in great anguish, throws herself before the altar."

This isn't a descriptive paragraph lifted from the painful history of Pat and Mary Highsmith—although it could easily be mistaken for the Attic version of their grief-streaked relations. It's a quotation from the program for a Barnard College annual event, the Greek Games of 1939. The theme of Barnard's 1939 Greek Games was "The Return of Persephone," and college sophomore Patricia Highsmith was competing, appropriately enough, as a hurdler: a girl athlete who jumps over fences.[15] The next year, 1940, she was back in the Greek Games jumping over fences again.

On her 1937 application form to Barnard, Pat wrote that the two subjects which interested her most were "English" and "German." She wanted to be a novelist, she said, because that was the work she was best "fitted for," and she was quick to cite secondary interests in "drama" and "journalism."[16] When she was accepted at Barnard, she was accepted "with conditions" (much as she would be accepted at Yaddo in 1948: categorizing Highsmith would always be difficult), meaning that Barnard had some reservations about taking her— probably because the B– average she earned at Julia Richman High School gave the college admission's committee pause. (Although Pat's New York State Regents exams were a decent 88 percent, her overall grade average was 79.6 percent.)[17] Pat's school marks were never as fancy as her self-presentations, and her grades at Barnard weren't high enough to admit her to the national university honors society, Phi Beta Kappa.

For someone so resistant to group behavior, Pat Highsmith had a lot of schooling. And it wasn't the kind of schooling that matched her parents' precarious income, either. Pat's education was provided by a mother hell-bent on her child's upward mobility; a precious-only-child-who's-going-to-make-me-proud kind of education. Although Julia Richman High School was a city-supported institution, it had high standards and rigorous classes. It also had a dress code. Barnard College, the "women's division" of the all-male Columbia University, was a private school, Mary Highsmith's earnings paid for it, and Pat wasn't required to work her way through college or to get a job during the school holidays. Mary gave her daughter an allowance (intermittently and briefly suspended for bad behavior) until she graduated.

During Pat's first two years at Barnard, Mary, Stanley, and Pat were living in a one-bedroom apartment at One Bank Street: a massive yellow brick apartment house in Greenwich Village constructed on the site of the brownstone where novelist Willa Cather had lived with her companion, the editor Edith Lewis, from 1913 to 1927. Cather, just like Pat, detested noise and rented the apartment above her own to ensure the silence she required for her work. At the end of 1939, the Highsmiths briefly rented an apartment at 35 Morton Street, also in Greenwich Village, and then in 1940, when Pat was a junior at Barnard, the family moved to another one-bedroom apartment (Pat slept in the front room) in what Pat called a "humble, reasonably tidy" four-story red-brick building at 48 Grove Street.*[18] The Highsmith apartment was directly across the street from 45 Grove Street: the Federal-style manor house where

---

* A previous biography has incorrectly placed the Highsmith family apartment on Grove Street in the building where Marie's Crisis Café is located. The Highsmith apartment was (and still is) across the street and one block to the west of Marie's Crisis Café.

the poet Hart Crane had lived in the early 1920s, where Djuna Barnes would sojourn on her return from Europe with the actual heroine of her novel *Nightwood*, and where the actor John Wilkes Booth and his fellow conspirators are said to have successfully plotted the assassination of Abraham Lincoln eighty years before.

Pat, whose engagement with history was erratic but whose unreconstructed Rebel soul lived on as a romantic legacy from her Confederate heritage (one of the three places where she is known to have shed public tears was the battlefield where two of her maternal grandfather's brothers lost their lives), would have been delighted by the association of the manor house across the street with the Confederate cause—if she'd known about it.

In 1919, on the Highsmiths' side of Grove Street, the south side, the great anarchist Emma Goldman, released from one of her imprisonments in the United States, was living at number 36—from which address the U.S. government chose to deport her to the Soviet Union. In the Highsmiths' same apartment building, when Pat was living there, was another well-known radical, Sidney Hook. Hook was then New York's leading Marxist theorist (literary critic Alfred Kazin called him "the most devastating logician the world would ever see").[19] Forty years after she left 48 Grove Street, Pat suddenly remembered that Sidney Hook had lived there when she did—and made a note about him in her cahier.[20]

Farther east on Grove Street, towards Seventh Avenue on the north side of the street, the place of death of the political pamphleteer and agitator Tom Paine was marked by a plaque on the façade of Marie's Crisis Café, still one of the oldest piano bars in Greenwich Village and a place Pat used to frequent. Next to Marie's Crisis is the building where the murder that inspired the film *On the Waterfront* was committed in 1947. Every block in Greenwich Village has a rich history of rebellion against practically everything—and Grove Street was no exception. Pat put Edith Howland, of her 1977 novel *Edith's Diary*, in an apartment on Grove Street and gave her an affinity for Tom Paine's most obvious phrases, then used the street again for the residence of the handsome, wealthy, oddly matched couple, Jack and Natalia Sutherland, at the center of her New York novel, *Found in the Street*. (See "Patricia Highsmith's New York.")

Pat's four years at Barnard were marked by a taste for the classics—Latin, French, German, English, and Greek (at P.S. 122 in Astoria, she'd refused to learn French before Latin because that was the "order observed in English schools"); an attachment to the works of Sir Thomas Browne (*Religio Medici* was her favorite, and she made Guy Haines read it in *Strangers on a Train*) and the novels of Graham Greene; a D grade in her Logic course; and a freshman year election to the editorial board of the Barnard College literary magazine in which she would publish nine stories and which, as a senior, she would edit.

Alice Gershon (Lassally), a student editor with Pat on the *Barnard Quarterly*, had some dramatic tales to tell about her old classmate.

Pat always had an aura about her, there was something special. It wasn't just from the students, it was from the faculty. . . . Pat was very tied in with her mother. She hated her or loved her. I knew that but I don't know how I knew that.[21] [Author's note: Every one of Pat's living classmates says this about Pat and Mary; usually adding, as Mrs. Lassally did, that Pat always gave the impression of being "raised by women." Helen Kandel (Hyman), another classmate, thought Pat had grown up "in a house without men."][22] But I knew there was something special. . . . She was a very attractive girl. When I saw pictures of her later on, I couldn't believe them. Was that a disease? But she was *seething*—one felt that—and she looked tremendously sophisticated to me. . . . My vision of her is with a cigarette hanging out of the corner of her mouth. And the camel hair coat, the high white collar and I think she wore an ascot. I mean, she was very stylish.[23]

Helen Kandel (Hyman) also remembered Pat for her dress:

My image of Pat is wearing riding clothes and starched white shirts. I remember those starched white shirts of Pat's. I remember nothing about how anybody else dressed—including myself—but I remember those starched white shirts. She would stand in the library reading at a kind of a lectern instead of sitting down as we all did. She was something of a loner, but she had a little group around her.[24]

Alice Gershon recalled sitting near Pat in their freshman Hygiene class. The class always featured a sex lecture by the school doctor, "a darling, jolly little woman" named Dr. Alsop, who was the live-in lover of their playwriting professor, Minor Latham, a famously prejudiced and inspiring woman. Latham, says Helen Kandel, who was Latham's advisee, "wore suits and ties and was very gruff."[25] Alice Gershon remembers Dr. Alsop's freshman Hygiene lectures as "adorable and very nonthreatening."

There was always a legend that in freshman Hygiene the most sophisticated girl in the class would pass out. And lo and behold one of them did at that freshman class. But Pat sat next to me in that class and she put the

collar of her camel's hair coat way up and sunk into it. I thought: Is she
going to be the sophisticated one who passes out? I wasn't sure if she
was full of disdain or full of fear or what in the world was going on.

I told this to my friend Midge [Kurtz], who got to know Pat pretty
well. . . . Midge used to go down to the Village and see Pat some, while
we were in school . . . and Midge laughed and said Pat was having an
affair with Leadbelly. That's what Midge told me, that Pat told her she
was having an affair with Leadbelly. I'm sure she was experimental, I
wouldn't be surprised. But it amazed me at the time.[26]

"Leadbelly" was the performing name of Huddie Ledbetter, the black,
Southern convicted murderer and folk and blues singer—his signature song,
"Goodnight Irene," was made famous by the Weavers in 1950—whose murderous past and several jail terms (the last one was served at Rikers Island in
1940 within view of the Highsmith family apartments in Queens) mingled
with his arresting artistry to provide him with a dangerously attractive aura
in liberal New York. During Pat's time at Barnard College, and until his death
in 1949, Leadbelly was performing his huge repertoire of songs in many
Greenwich Village cafés.

If Pat really did tell this story about herself—and there's no reason to assume she didn't; it's not the kind of story Barnard girls were making up about
each other in 1940—then she was behaving like any self-mythologizing English major: polishing her reputation as a college sophisticate with tales of an
outré relationship which she would have been quite incapable—because of
her feelings about race *and* gender—of entering into. It's also a story which
might have helped dissemble her sexuality to her "straight" classmates. Mary
Highsmith, no small-time self-mythologizer herself, always said that Pat had
missed her true calling as an "actress." Mary would have been shocked but
not surprised by this overheated little tale from her daughter's college days.

Rita Rohner (Semel), editor of the *Barnard Quarterly* when Pat was associate
editor, had another kind of story to tell about Pat.

She was unlike anybody I'd ever met before. Those were quite innocent
days. And she was a very sophisticated young woman who lived with
her mother in Greenwich Village and I realized dimly, I'm trying to
think of how to put this because I don't want to color it with hindsight,
I think I realized that she was . . . we didn't even have the word for it.

It was obvious even then. Her talent. I saw only the stories she published [in the *Barnard Quarterly:* nine of Pat's stories were published,
including "Quiet Night" (rewritten in 1966 as "The Cries of Love"), "A

Mighty Nice Man," "The Legend of the Convent of St. Fotheringay," and "Silver Horn of Plenty"]. I think people thought of her as a loner; I don't recall her having any friends, now that I think about it. I did go to dinner at her house one night, down on Grove Street. It was very peculiar. If I thought anything, I would have thought the apartment was bohemian. Her mother wasn't there and I thought her mother was going to be there. And as I recall we sort of foraged around for something to eat. . . . I was offered wine, which was not done, and I had a glass and I felt very daring about it. . . . It wasn't a family dinner and I got away as soon as I could. . . . I realized long years later that she was, in today's phrase, "coming on to me.". . .

She was very needy and her abrupt manner covered that up. In fact, most people really didn't get along with her.

Her face just flashed into my mind, kind of hawklike, almost Indian, very angular. And she dressed up, but she wore very, very tailored clothes. And very simple and she had this black hair. . . .

She [was] bound and determined to be a success at college. She was ambitious and hardworking [and] when she was successful, I wasn't surprised. But I wouldn't have wanted her life.[27]

Pat's college career (a more useful term might be Pat's "behavior at college"), like her four years in high school, threads its way through this book. For now, it is enough to say that although she favored and was favored by her literature and short-story-writing teacher, the theatrical and supportive Miss Ethel Sturtevant (in the "minute" devoted to her at a faculty meeting at Barnard after her death, Sturtevant was eulogized as having "a magical voice," "the airs of a beauty," and the adoration of her students, to whom she gave "unremitting attention"),[28] Pat took notes which recorded her contempt for her favorite teacher's long service to Barnard as "only" an assistant professor and for Ethel Sturtevant's depressed powerlessness in the face of the academic hierarchy. Pat wouldn't be caught dead in such a situation herself.

While she was still at Barnard, Pat, always ready to improve, allowed herself to be stimulated by "even the dullest people. Being amusing for them is like practising the piano when you are sure no one is listening. You can be freer, attempt bolder things, and often succeed."[29]

Pat liked to rehearse her social graces with people who didn't intimidate her, just as she liked to practice certain states of mind and emotions for her novels. One of the attitudes she was rehearsing at Barnard was her politics, which shifted as frequently and as theatrically as her affections; at first showing brief signs of egalitarianism, even of Communism. Inspired by the

Spanish Civil War, she joined the Young Communist League, persuaded her reluctant parents to attend a birthday celebration for Lenin in Madison Square Garden, and wrote a play that was criticized as "too communist" by her drama professor, Minor Latham.[30] As late as 1947, she seems to have been vaguely acquainted with the notorious Communist Party organizer and spy Josef Peters, who telephoned her—"surprisingly," she wrote in her diary—under his pseudonym of Alex Goldfarb. Pat's German friend Rolf Tietgens was convinced that it was Goldfarb's "words [which] had sent him" to an alien internment camp in El Paso, Texas.[31]

Although the injustices in Spain attracted Pat to the Young Communist League, it was the cloak-and-dagger "activities" of American Communism that held her interest. "This business of dodging and bulldozing the authorities has limitless opportunities for clever remarks!"[32] Eventually she decided that the high life, the high culture, and the high crowd of *Time, Life,* and *Fortune* magazines were closer to her ambitions (though farther from her tastes), and Communist—or, more accurately, communitarian—ideas would appear in her notebooks only when they represented the kind of social ideals embodied by the life of Jesus Christ.[33]

Like many of her fellow Americans, Pat gave lip service to the disadvantaged. In actual fact, she preferred the society, if not the close company, of "winners." (The home church of capitalism has always counted poverty as a sin.) Pat wanted only what she thought of as "the best" for herself, and she sought the same thing in her friendships and her loves. Many of her relationships had social and professional implications, and it was the letters from her more prominent friends which Pat tended to keep. Kingsley Skattebol (Kate Kingsley as she was then), Pat's oldest platonic friend from Barnard College—a worshipful college freshman to Pat's superior college junior—said that finding out Pat had destroyed the hundreds of letters she'd written to her over the half century of their friendship was more painful than learning that Pat had cut her out of her will.[34]

At twenty, between her junior and senior years at Barnard and still doing more theorizing about writing than actual writing, Pat was describing the characters she thought were inside her—and what she was going to do with them.

"I am four people: the Jewish intellectual, the success, the failure, and the Fascist-snob. These shall be my novel characters."[35]

Three months later, in December of 1941, she made up an image that pleased her so much she marked it with a vertical line in the margin of her cahier:

"God knows love, in this room with us now, is not kisses or embraces or touches. Not even a glance or a feeling. Love is a monster between us, each of us caught in a fist."[36]

Pat would harvest the image for *The Price of Salt* in 1950, but in the novel she turned its meaning to a commentary on the world: "the whole world was ready to be their enemy, and suddenly what [Therese] and Carol had together seemed no longer love . . . but a monster between them, with each of them caught in a fist."[37]

On the evening in Grove Street when she imagined love to be a "monster," Pat "passed" what she called her "first suicide moment."[38] Love and death would always be in the room with her, but it wasn't love the college senior wanted to die for. What made her want to kill herself was something more exasperating than love. Pat couldn't, on this particular evening, find the right form on paper for her feelings. "[O]ne stands confronted with work, empty sheets of paper all about, and inside one's head, shame and confusion, inside a maelström that will not subside, fragments that will not hang together. . . . This was a great emotion."[39]

The idea of dying immediately whetted Pat's sense of competition: "Life is a matter of self-denial at the right moments. . . . My solace is in thinking: what are other people doing now? And if they are playing, I feel better, because I want always to be doing something a little more difficult, a little more demanding."[40]

Pat's competitive edge would find its sharpest expression in her cahiers and diaries; they were what she really meant by "doing something a little more difficult" than what her classmates were doing. She began keeping her cahiers the month she entered Barnard and she started the diaries when she was twenty. The journals gave her an opportunity to continually renew her vows for the only lasting "marriage" she ever made: the union that joined her intense rushes of feeling with her compelling need to commit them to paper. The fact that she repeated those vows dressed more like a groom than a bride and that she usually did so in a counterfeit "male voice" ("I am a strong man, like Chaucer, like Shakespeare, like Joe Louis")[41] was merely one of the ways her obsessions colored her work. But Pat's journals were the real harvest of her years at Barnard College: the physical proof of a professional approach to writing.

Thirty-seven notebooks of identical size and similar organization followed her first cahier (see "A Simple Act of Forgery: Part 1"), and all of them were standard-issue Barnard College or Columbia University notebooks, 7 by 8½ inches with rolled wire binders. By the time she finished college, she had also filled nine cahiers and four diaries.

Pat was already taking notes when she was at Julia Richman High School—bitingly candid comments on her classmates, her moods, and her ideas—and she was writing stories, too. There was a forgotten first story written when she was fourteen. And, before high school, there was a (mercifully) lost blank-verse poem in the style of Tennyson's *Idylls of the King*. Then there was "Crime Begins," the short story she wrote at sixteen about a sixteen-year-old girl who steals a book and gets away with it. It was the result, she explained thirty-six years later, of her "desperate" need to take out a history book from the library at Julia Richman High School. There were only three copies of the book, 150 girls were after it, and Pat, "strongly tempted to steal it," wrote the story instead.[42] Pat was subject to many such temptations.

In 1935, the ambitious fourteen-year-old already had the instinct to put her private feelings in print in the magazine *Woman's World*. She published (and was paid twenty-five dollars for) a series of letters she'd written to Stanley and Mary Highsmith two years before, when she was a yearning twelve-year-old packed away to a sleepover camp near West Point, New York, for a month of summer. The camp provided her with some early material: her attention was caught by her female tennis instructor and by the camp rituals of girls swimming naked and counsellors and campers exchanging clothes. By the fall of 1937, Pat was displaying feelings of another kind, publishing her short story "Primroses Are Pink" in the *Bluebird,* the Julia Richman High School literary magazine. "Primroses Are Pink" is a tale of class pretensions and the instabilities introduced into a marital relationship by a work of art.

In a 1968 article written for *Vogue* magazine (it ranges from Jane Austen to Kim Philby), Pat typed out the first sentence of the first story she ever wrote, the lost story written when she was fourteen: "He prepared to go to sleep, removed his shoes and set them parallel, toe outward, beside his bed." More like a map locator than the beginning of a fiction, this sentence gave her, she said, "a sense of order, seeing the shoes neatly beside the bed in my imagination." Pat blamed her need for order on her turbulent family circumstances, but she was silent on the origin of another important need: the need to embody her feelings in a male character.

Very little of Pat's juvenilia, apart from what she published in school magazines, survived her childhood. But from the care she took in setting up her 1938 cahier—dividing it into separate categories, belatedly inserting dates—it is clear she was thinking professionally. Later on, she copied her 1935–38 high school journals into her ninth cahier—and her cahiers became more important to her than any manuscript. She preserved them as evidence of the life of her mind, and she reread, reworked, reused, and responded to them in a dialogue with herself that went on for decades. They are the record and, in many cases, the origin of her creative impulses.

The cahier that launched her life as a writer in her first term at Barnard College, Cahier 1, did so with a rare kind of ecstasy: the evocation of a young girl in the act of creation rising wraithlike off its first page. At not quite eighteen, Pat was not yet as adept as she would become about nailing her journal notes to dates and times. But a few pages into this cahier she was already being compulsive about another kind of numbering: the kind that measured her competitive drive against a clock:

> The only time I feel that I am cheating time, is when I walk a block, or read or write a sentence, or solve a problem while I hear a clock striking the hour. Then time stands still for a few seconds and one can start off again with a slight advantage.[43]

"[E]ternally ashamed of [her] backwardness in mathematics," given to repeating that "[t]he arts and literature are not enough to live by," and that "without mathematics," you can't really be "civilized,"[44] Pat was obsessed by numbers. Her letters, cahiers, and diaries bristle with figures—financial calculations, numbered lines of tasks, addresses, miles, kilometers, times, dates, body temperatures, red blood cell counts, her IQ (121 in her midteens), etc., etc. Early in her college career, Pat was also making numbered lists of the relative virtues of different religions. She delved into Hinduism (while still under the protection of her mother's Christian Science), but—ever ambitious and still computing her chances—decided that she couldn't possibly get ahead in the Western world with *that* philosophy.[45]

Henry David Thoreau, calculating every nail in his cabin on Walden Pond (and going home regularly to lunch with his mother), was no match for Patricia Highsmith in the compulsive counting department.

Pat's numbering and tallying went on to the very end of her life. During an interview for *Publishers Weekly* in 1992, she surveyed the land beyond her Swiss property with a baleful eye—local developers had designs on it—and then treated what must have been her suprised interviewer to the fruits of her survey:

"They've got easily 14 little houses going up there. That means 28 adults, 28 cars, and something like 56 children, and an underground garage. It's going to be hell."[46]

But Pat doesn't begin her first cahier by counting anything. She begins it with a lyrical vision of a "phantom-like girl dancing to a Tschaikowski waltz," in "selfless-spontaneity" as if "the music had been growing within her and ripening through the years." It is Pat's coming out as a writer, and she joins the "phantom-like girl's" dance and Tchaikovsky's music to a kind of tribute to Marcel Proust, whose initials are prominently entered and lightly crossed out on the page. It's as though the youthful Pat were inviting those representatives of the high arts, Tchaikovsky and Proust, to lend inspiration to her maiden effort.

A more prosaic explanation for this fancy footwork from an ambitious and self-regarding seventeen-year-old might be this one: Pat had recently been given the first volume of Proust's *A la recherche du temps perdu* by Judy Tuvim and Babs Baer, who had been her most envied, most precocious, and most attractive schoolmates at Julia Richman High School—and she simply couldn't resist the opportunity to show off her newly acquired cultural credential.

Three years after she started this notebook, Pat was inscribing her first diary: "And here is my diary, containing the body."[47] She wasn't kidding. Although she tried to keep her cahiers for notes on writing and her diaries for life notes and sexual encounters, she couldn't quite keep these divisions separate, and her cahiers and diaries—especially the cahiers—are always begging and borrowing materials from each other. And Pat was always reminding herself in marginal notes that they were doing so.

But this first notebook, in the partitioned format she would keep all her life, was a nice beginning for the young writer. She would continue as she began, using visions of women and cross-dressed narrative voices to convey the complex mechanism of her fantasies.

Pat had always been fascinated by the image or the presence of a young girl—even when she herself was still a young girl. On her first trip to Italy in high summer of 1949, sitting in a restaurant in Florence, "a graceful hospitable city . . . where more beauty is gathered in less space than anywhere else in the world,"[48] she made candid notes on the subject of her feelings for young girls. Then she crossed them out.

"On regarding a beautiful young girl in a Florence restaurant. Finally, it gets to be the pleasure of the adoration, the fascination one exerts over the young. No longer can we say, it is to *give* pleasure that is our greatest pleasure. We have become the self-cognisant satyrs."[49]

Pat yearned after youth and idealized her own past (when she wasn't complaining about it) all her life. While she was at Barnard, she was already nostalgic for her early adolescence, momentarily forgetting her bitter descriptions of her childhood as an "endless hell on earth."[50] Later, she dotted her cahiers with notes for backward-looking works she would never write, like this one: "A novel of America's sadness and longing for the remembered childhood neighborhood, for the tranquil past in a Civil War photograph."[51] And she rejoiced in her first trip to Europe because it made her feel "young" again: "for the first time at twenty-eight . . . it widens one's interests again, makes one diverse as at seventeen. This closing up! I hate it. It grows on one slowly from nineteen onward, as S. Johnson said."[52]

Withal, it's hard to imagine that the girl doing the dancing on the first page of Pat's 1938 cahier might actually be Pat herself. Her self-consciousness was such that she rarely permitted herself spontaneous expressions in public. But of course Pat *did* think of herself as the dancing girl: a young artist, filled with inspiration, performing alone on the dance floor with the tacit support of her two fairy godfathers, Proust and Tschaikovsky.

Caroline Besterman, deeply schooled in the languages and literatures of France and Germany, doesn't believe Pat had a good understanding of the works of Marcel Proust.

"When Pat talked about Proust . . . I'd just change the subject because I didn't understand her understanding. Of course he's not an easy writer and you'd have to know more than she did about France and French society and the placement of adverbs and the faubourg. . . . She just didn't understand."[53]

There is no evidence that Pat's reading of Proust ever amounted to more than the sum of her college girl remarks about his work ("I can never make a character unless I take him from actual life—with as little changes as possible . . . even Proust had a germ of reality for his characters. And why not?").[54] Or that she ever got beyond her repeated reworking of Proust's observation that nothing is more pleasurable than falling back into the arms of someone who is bad for us.[55]

Although Pat's array of styles and subjects couldn't be more different from Proust's exquisite deconstructions of the phantoms of the faubourg, her best long fictions—like demented, demotic chips off the Proustian block—share a serious approach with Proust: the capillarial crawl of a hypervigilant consciousness over a detailed psychological territory, every word of whose narrative is conveyed in a voice cloaked (but not necessarily concealed) by another (but not exactly opposite) gender.

One of the things Pat did with her adolescent energy in college was walking. She often walked herself into exhaustion so she could sleep, and it was these long walks in New York that filled her cahiers with observations—and helped inspire the writing of one of her better college short stories. "Quiet Night," published in the fall edition of the 1939 *Barnard Quarterly* (and rewritten with a more explicitly savage ending as "The Cries of Love" in 1966 when her relations with Caroline Besterman were breaking down), came from one of Pat's rambles in Manhattan's most genteel and only private park, Gramercy Park, on East Twentieth Street. Pat went there to observe the elderly ladies sitting on the benches, but part of her pleasure must have come from her trespassing.

Gramercy Park is surrounded by a high cast-iron fence to which the use of a gate key by a local property owner is the only legal means of entry.

"Quiet Night"—the story nicely tries to marry love and loathing—puts two old women, Hattie and Alice, together as roommates in a residence hotel. One night, Hattie takes a scissors and deliberately makes slashing cuts in Alice's favorite sweater. When Alice finds it and accuses her, Hattie dissolves into the first inappropriate fit of laughter to appear in a Highsmith fiction. In the 1939 version of the story, Alice poises herself to cut off Hattie's long braid—her only glory—as she sleeps. But she fails to do so. (By 1966, Pat was embittered enough to rewrite the story and make Alice cut off Hattie's braid.) "Quiet Night," published posthumously in its earliest version in 2002, shows only Alice's desire to wreak damage: "Her revenge had to be something that would last, that would hurt, something that Hattie must endure and that she, Alice, could enjoy." The work's maturity lies in its affirmation of how united the two women are in the impurity of their feelings.

All through her college years, Pat's eyes were creatively filled by what she saw on the streets of Greenwich Village, on the Upper West Side of Manhattan near Columbia University, and on the Upper East Side near the East River. She spent hours riding the metropolitan underground trains between these neighborhoods; the same trains also took her back and forth between rendezvous with her many girl friends (see "Social Studies: Part 1"). Pat's earliest cahiers are descriptive feasts mixing the contents of subway cars after midnight, the courting habits of adolescents lurking in doorways, and the marginal life of people working along the docks.

> One meets terrifying characters on the subway at one thirty in the morning. The pasty couple hanging one on either side of the Exit doorway, chewing gum, and moon-eyed, plotting their next assignation; the pale fairy in the beige jacket and grey flannels, with the holes in both heels of his socks, smoking, and looking into everyone's eyes; the prostitute with a mass of yellow curls all over her head like a poodle dog; . . . the lonely sailor desperate now for a girl. . . . This is sordid. But it is the bill of fare for New York, my daily scene after a certain hour of the night. It is the same in love and out of love.[56]

Pat was more than a walker and a rider in the city. She was someone in whom the visual sense was preternaturally developed; someone stimulated to excitation by what she saw. She stalked with her eyes as well as with her imagination, and she often attracted what she was looking for. The streets of New

York performed for her, and occasionally something that she saw kicked over the concealing rocks of her own early sexual history.

During one mid-September walk in 1940, wrapped in a gray coat—perhaps it was the trench coat her Barnard classmates remember her wearing in college— Pat's eye caught something going on between "two little girls sitting on the threshold of a door with their feet on the sidewalk."

> The older was touching the other in some way so that when they saw me pass they drew back and pulled their dresses over their knees. They looked at me then a little embarrassed and I waited a few feet away to watch them a moment. I knew in that moment that something had occurred that they would remember possibly all their lives. Something that would flash into their minds at strange times during childhood and adolescence, that would make them wince and close their teeth in shame—and perhaps when they were older make them smile. . . . I know all this, of course, because the same thing has happened to me.[57]

In 1941, when Pat was a junior at Barnard, F. O. Matthiesen, the brilliant, left-leaning, closeted literary scholar at Harvard University, published his revolutionary study of American literature, *American Renaissance: Art and Expression in the Age of Emerson and Whitman.* He and the other scholars in the expanding field of American Studies were beginning to claim a local habitation and a name for American writing and thought. The universities were suddenly alive with the idea of American literature, which until now had always been treated as a parenthesis in the larger sentence of English literature. But Pat, reading American literature (Mother Mary had already accused her of being as egotistical as Theodore Dreiser), had eyes only for European culture and was impervious to the enticements of Greenwich Village—which was undergoing its gaudiest creative flowering since 1914, the year Mabel Dodge's influential salon at 23 Fifth Avenue closed its doors. New York was now welcoming some of the world's most creative people: National Socialism and the Second World War had already forced many of the best European cultural thinkers and artists to refugee to the United States. These brilliant emigrants (amongst them Claude Lévi-Strauss, Erich Fromm, and Hannah Arendt) were finding teaching jobs at the University in Exile at the New School for Social Research on West Twelfth Street, seeking out patrons amongst the bohemian rich (Peggy Guggenheim, who herself had just escaped from France in 1941, was under constant siege), and meeting their fellow Europeans and American counterparts in Greenwich Village cafés and bars and bookstores.

But Pat and Mother Mary, bent on fleeing their bohemian neighborhood, were, in Pat's senior year at Barnard, looking for apartments on the Upper East Side of Manhattan. It was their idea of "quality." When they finally found an apartment on East Fifty-seventh Street, Pat was thrilled.

"Saw our future apartment: 345 E. 57th St. Only drawback is the view over yards to homebacks. . . . The fireplace isn't real either, but the neighborhood! And the house!"[58]

Even when she was in college, Patricia Highsmith always wanted to be someplace else.

10

ALTER EGO

PART I

What, they're all Jewish, Superheroes. Superman, you don't think he's Jewish? Coming over from the old country, changing his name like that. Clark Kent, only a Jew would pick a name like that for himself.
            —**Michael Chabon**, *The Amazing Adventures of Kavalier & Klay*

Before Patricia Highsmith wrote "Strangers on a Train" for Alfred Hitchcock, she wrote "Jap Buster Johnson" for me.
                              —**Vince Fago**, editor, Timely comics[1]

During the three spring months of 1940 when Pat, nineteen years old and still a live-at-home sophomore at Barnard College, was rereading the Dostoyevsky novel she'd relished at thirteen (*Crime and Punishment*), refreshing herself with André Gide's seducible adolescents in *The Counterfeiters,* criticizing Henry James's *The Ambassadors* as "overconfident," casting a competitive eye on the works of Malraux, Nietzsche, Hardy, Mansfield, Dickens, Molière, Goethe, and Dreiser, and deciding that because of her books she had "the whole world" at hand, "[e]ven with all my *greed*,"[2] she was also writing this interesting little sentence in her cahier:

"My father is a cartoon of me."[3]

Besides teaching high school art in Texas for many years, the shadowy J. B. Plangman—more like a family ghost than a biological father—eked out a living by drawing cartoons for the *Fort Worth Star-Telegram*. Something about Jay B's cartooning seems to have influenced his only child's entry into the world of comic books. One clue to the connection is how quiet Pat kept about both subjects—her father *and* the comics; promising herself to "make a serious effort at psychoanalysing my relationship with my father" but instead burying J. B. Plangman "under 6 feet of dull roadbed." Six feet under was only slightly deeper than she buried the truth about her seven years' employment as a scriptwriter for comic books during the Golden Age of American Comics.

Still, in early 1940s Manhattan, if you had to pick an apprenticeship with pay for a young writer whose attractions to secrecy, shame, and hero-worship were as all-consuming as Pat Highsmith's, you couldn't do better than to choose a job in the comic book business. Comic books were not only at the center of America's most successful publishing industry, they were also, if you were hoping to be a serious writer, the source of some highly embarrassing employment. And the entire comics milieu—authors, illustrators, publishers, and the improbable characters they were creating—was alive with the same collection of crooks and cons, artists with secret identities and heroes with Alter Egos, with which the talented Miss Highsmith would later populate so much of her fiction.

Decades after she'd stopped writing for the comics, when she was relatively rich and famous and living in Europe, Pat used to respond to the question all authors dread to hear—"And where do get your ideas from, Miss Highsmith?"—by saying that her ideas often came to her "out of thin air." In the year Pat graduated from Barnard College, 1942, one of the *airs du temps* blowing through New York City was the secret and often illegal excitements surrounding America's newest art form, the comic book.

Like millions of American teenagers in the early 1940s, Everett Raymond Kinstler, a polite, good-looking boy with a talent for drawing portraits, was crazy for comic books. Everett was an honors student at the High School of Music and Art in New York City, where his teachers did their best to discourage his taste for popular culture. "That's not really art," they reminded him in a slightly elevated version of the lesson parents all over the country were trying to drill into the skulls of their comics-addicted children.

But Everett's ambitions extended beyond just reading the garish little picture books whose narratives-in-dialogue ballooned above their heroes' heads, so, shortly before his sixteenth birthday in August of 1943, he answered an ad—it would have been something like the ad for a "writer/research" job that an attractive, desperate-for-work English major from Barnard College had successfully answered six months earlier[4]—for "apprentice inker" at an outfit called Cinema Comics at 10 West Forty-fifth Street in Manhattan. Cinema was one of the many companies producing comic books for the Sangor-Pines comics shop (others were Better, Standard, Cinema, Michel, America's Best, and Exciting) and Cinema's office was in the Sangor-Pines headquarters. All of the Cinema comic books were written, lettered, and illustrated (but not lithographed or printed) in the office at West Forty-fifth Street.[5]

"Nowadays," says Ray Kinstler, the name under which Everett Raymond Kinstler grew up to become one of America's most prominent portrait painters, "people are impressed that I did *Zorro* and *The Hawkman* and *The Shadow*, but in the 30's and 40's . . ." And here Kinstler repeats what every comics artist, writer, and historian of the Golden Age of American Comics (1938–1954) told me: comic book creators were looked down on as lowly laborers in a deeply disreputable business.

Just how comic books were generally regarded is made clear in this excerpt from an editorial in the *Chicago Daily News* published on 8 May 1940:

> Badly drawn, badly written, badly printed—a strain on the young eyes and nervous systems—the effects of these pulp-paper nightmares is that of a violent stimulant. Their crude blacks and reds spoil a child's natural sense of color; their hypodermic injections of sex and murder make the child impatient with better, though quieter, stories.[6]

Quality fiction writers were almost as dismissive of the comics as exasperated parents and crusading journalists. In her witty roman à clef about the New York publishing world of the 1940s, *The Locusts Have No King* (1948), Dawn Powell makes her reticent, scholarly, Greenwich Village–dwelling protagonist transform a vulgar magazine called *HAW* into a commercial success by commissioning artists from the comics ("Al Capp or Caniff") to illustrate plots from classic novels.[7] For Powell, a brilliant social satirist (Gore Vidal called her the "American Thackeray"), "comics" was a code word for ethical and aesthetic decay.

Still, young Everett Kinstler was thrilled when he got that job at Cinema Comics. He was hired by the respected Sangor-Pines editor Richard E. Hughes, the same editor who had hired the attractive Barnard College graduate the previous winter. Mr. Hughes was married to Ned Pines's daughter (Ned Pines was half owner of the company), and Ned Pines was married to Ben Sangor's daughter (Ben Sangor owned the other half of the company). The comics were nothing if not tribal.

"Hughes," says Kinstler, had "a habit of smoking his pipe at the office, a very rubbery lower lip, and the kind of face I like to paint because it had character." Hughes hired Everett to help ink in comic book "pencils," the draft drawings made by the "pencillers," at "fifteen dollars a week, five days a week, a half day on Saturday." It was big money for a teenager in an era when "lunch was twenty-five cents." By the end of the year, Everett was earning thirty dollars a week.[8]

When Everett started work, one of "the main comics at Cinema was *Fighting Yank*," a Superhero with a blue-blooded, eighteenth-century Alter Ego and a bland, socially leveraged, Anglo-Saxon name: Bruce Carter III. Whenever Bruce Carter III was in trouble, "a mighty figure would appear out of America's past [wearing, with unfortunate effect, a hat like a portobello mushroom]." It was Bruce Carter I, the Fighting Yank himself: Bruce III's Revolutionary War hero "ancestor" and Alter Ego.[9]

One of *Fighting Yank*'s writers—she was typing away in the writers' bullpen the day Everett was hired—was the twenty-two-year-old Barnard girl Richard Hughes had hired the previous December. She had been taken on to replace a comics writer who was on his way to becoming a distinguished theater and film critic. The writer's name was Stanley Kauffmann. The Barnard girl was Patricia Highsmith.[10]

Sixty years later, Ray Kinstler had a specific, portrait painter's memory of Pat:

Physically, Pat was deceptive; she had a bony figure, a little bit like Katharine Hepburn, and she must have looked taller than she really was. She had *cheekbones*. [And Kinstler describes the precise points of Pat's dark pageboy falling below her ears, the way her hair was loosely parted and lay flat across the top of her head, and her habit of chain-smoking in the office.] She was a type. A lanky, scrubbed type. An American college girl type. I could have pictured her at Smith College.

Patricia reminded me of Spencer Tracy's remark about Kate Hepburn in a film. Someone had called Hepburn "kinda skinny" and Tracy came back with "Yeah, but what there is is cheerce" [choice].

Sixteen-year-old Everett "had a teenager, heavy crush on Patricia. . . . I would have done anything for her. In the beginning it was Miss Highsmith this and Miss Highsmith that. 'Oh, Miss Highsmith, could I do this for you or could I get that for you?' Later on it was Patricia or Pat. And I think she tolerated me good-naturedly."

And Kinstler remembers just how Pat's assignments at Sangor-Pines were determined: they were the result of an exchange between the writer and her editor, Richard E. Hughes.

Hughes would commission a script: 'Here's an idea for *The Fighting Yank*, Patricia. I want one dealing with Nazis and submarines.' Or Hughes would say: 'Here's a three-page insert on the WACS or the WAVES.' And Pat would have to come up with a synopsis or a scenario [and eventually] come back with a script. Hughes was a very nice man, very gentle, supportive and understanding, and he would do some minor editing on the script. And the script would then be turned over to the artists in the bullpen who would balloon it with six or eight panels to a page, usually six. The opening page would sometimes be doubled out into a splash page [the illustrated title page which introduces comic book stories]. Sometimes the squares would be broken up into vignettes.[11]

One afternoon, Pat, usually so taciturn at the office, managed to express the desire to drink a Coca-Cola at her desk. Young Everett gallantly offered to bring her the soft drink "from the luncheonette downstairs. She gave me a nickel and I returned with a Pepsi-Cola." Deeply pleased with his resourcefulness, Everett proudly "told Patricia the Pepsi-Cola was the same price as the Coke but had a few more ounces."

Pat's response struck the boy like a blow.

"When you get older, Everett," Pat said in a coolly measured phrase he never forgot, "you will buy for quality, not quantity."[12]

Pat's remark about "quality" had a painful history behind it and an ambitious future in front of it.

For six nervous months after she graduated from Barnard College in June of 1942, and for some years thereafter, Patricia Highsmith failed to be hired by every one of the "quality" magazines to which, like any enterprising literature major, she'd applied for work. Despite impressive recommendations from highly placed professionals like Rosalind Constable (the cultural eyes and ears of the powerful American publisher Henry Luce), *Harper's Bazaar, Vogue, The New Yorker, Mademoiselle, Good Housekeeping, Time,* and *Fortune* had all refused to take Pat on after meeting her.

This was the period when magazines were the motor of Manhattan's literary and social life, publishing and promoting everything that was new. It was also the era when pulp publishing companies and their upscale relations, the "quality" magazine and book publishers, were beginning to encroach on each other's territories. Quality book publisher Harper & Brothers (later Harper & Row), in an elegantly bracketed promotion of a so-called pulp genre, assigned its senior editor Joan Kahn to oversee the Harper Novel of Suspense, the imprimatur under which all of Patricia Highsmith's Harper novels, beginning with

Strangers on a Train, would be brought out.[13] Marc Jaffe, from 1948 onwards an editor at the New American Library (itself busily engaged in revolutionizing the paperback novel) says that Harper Novels of Suspense were considered a "literary" category and that he always thought of Highsmith as a "classy mystery writer" whose work belonged in a category "with Josephine Tey, who was, perhaps, a tad more literary."[14] Even Pat's contemporaries had trouble trying to "place" her writing.

Cross-propagation, conflation, and confusion of "low" and "high" literary genres and categories were rampant in New York publishing—especially because pulp publishers often printed the kind of writing that the more respectable publishers turned down. *Weird Tales,* an outré pulp magazine of fantasy and horror (and the principal publisher of that master of the macabre, H. P. Lovecraft), gave America's greatest playwright, Tennessee Williams, his first public exposure when it published his youthful short story "The Vengeance of Nitocris" in 1928. *Black Mask Magazine,* founded in 1920, was a showcase for "hard-boiled" crime fictions which early on launched both Dashiell Hammett and Raymond Chandler and printed established writers like Edna Ferber, Cecil Day-Lewis (writing as Nicholas Blake),[15] Elizabeth Sanxay Holding, Eric Ambler, Graham Greene, Edgar Wallace, Alberto Moravia, Agatha Christie, and the prolific and reclusive Cornell Woolrich, whose story "Murder After Death" Pat would single out in her thinly veiled artistic autobiography, *Plotting and Writing Suspense Fiction.*

These same authors also appeared in *Ellery Queen's Mystery Magazine,* begun in 1941 as a "high-class" pulp venture by two cousins writing under the name "Ellery Queen." *Ellery Queen's Mystery Magazine* subsequently took over *Black Mask Magazine,* obscuring the fact that one of *Black Mask*'s founders was the "Sage of Baltimore," the caustic American social critic H. L. Mencken, who once defined American Puritanism as "the haunting fear that someone, somewhere might be happy" and wrote a sentence Pat Highsmith would have been happy to endorse at any time in her life: "I have always lived in the wrong country."[16]

Beginning in the 1950s, to Pat's barely suppressed embarrassment, *Ellery Queen's Mystery Magazine* would become the most frequent publisher of her short fictions.[17] One of her worst stories ("The Perfect Alibi," the first Highsmith story to be published in *EQMM,* in 1957) and one of her best stories ("The Terrapin," published in 1961) would appear in *EQMM.** The editors at *Ellery Queen's* liked to mix their contributors: in the August 1960 edition

---

* Pat would both suffer artistically and profit financially from the "crime" and suspense" categories into which her unruly work was regularly corralled.

of *EQMM,* Pat's tale of yet another nerveless psychopath with a taste for symbolic trophies, "The Thrill Seeker," was printed alongside "The Club," a story by the great American poet Muriel Rukeyser.[18]

At the time Pat graduated from Barnard, popular publishing giants Condé Nast (*Vogue, Mademoiselle, Vanity Fair*), Henry Luce (*Time, Life, Fortune*), and William Randolph Hearst (*Harper's Bazaar, Cosmopolitan, Town & Country*) were beginning to hire fiction and poetry editors for many of the fashion, style, and news magazines under their vast New York umbrellas. And these editors were giving national exposure to the writers they published. Meanwhile, small literary and political journals—like *Partisan Review*—were exercising a disproportionate influence on the American intellectual conversation.

With a subscriber base that never exceeded fifteen thousand, *Partisan Review,* begun in 1934 by William Phillips and Philip Rahv (who liked to refer to the USA as "the United States of Amnesia"), published serious, anti-Stalinist literary writers, many of them from Jewish immigrant families and most of them defenders of high modernism: Lionel Trilling, Clement Greenberg, Lionel Abel, Delmore Schwartz, Elizabeth Hardwick, Saul Bellow, Norman Mailer, Daniel Bell, Meyer Schapiro, Dwight Macdonald, Alfred Kazin, Arthur Koestler, Mary McCarthy, Edmund Wilson, et al.

Earnestly preparing for her literary close-up, Pat was subscribing to *Partisan Review* in the 1940s: "The *Partisan Review* has arrived and I am very proud of it," she enthused in 1943.[19] But she was unequipped for its fierce intellectual arguments and could never write the kind of fiction *PR* liked to publish. Still, Pat read *PR* avidly, and her introduction to the work of Saul Bellow, a novelist whose writing makes profound use of what used to be called "the modern Jewish experience," probably dates from her discovery of his stories in *PR.* (It was Bellow's uncanny ability to reimagine the New York she'd lived in, to bring the alienated European emigrant experience to bear upon it, and to vividly dramatize his moral concerns that caused Pat to write an article for a German paper in 1987 naming Saul Bellow as her "favorite" author and *Mr. Sammler's Planet* as his best book. Pat wouldn't have disagreed with the harsh fictional views Bellow took of the women in his life, either.)[20]

In 1950, still hoping to be introduced to "the *Partisan Review* crowd" by her new friend, the novelist Arthur Koestler, Pat was pleased to hear that Koestler had mentioned her name to Philip Rahv.[21] But what Pat really wanted when she got out of college was something closer to the conventional center of New York power: a staff job at *The New Yorker* or, at least, an assistant's position at *Mademoiselle.*

William Shawn of *The New Yorker* turned Pat down for a job in June of 1942 after scanning four issues of the *Barnard Quarterly* containing her stories, reading some "on spec" pieces she'd done for the magazine's "Talk of the Town" feature, and giving her reason to hope for work as a "girl reporter." Four months after Pat talked to Shawn, a reader at *The New Yorker* compounded the insult by rejecting as "sordid" her unsolicited story "These Sad Pillars," about a man and a woman who scribble notes to each other on subway posts.[22] In 1958, Pat was still finding *The New Yorker* "so forbidding" that she was "afraid even to telephone them for . . . information" on how to submit an idea for a cover drawing, so she diffidently wrote to ask her editor at Harper & Brothers, Joan Kahn, to do it for her.[23]

Vogue joined the chorus of disapproval by refusing to give the newly graduated Pat a position after a particularly disastrous interview. *Harper's Bazaar* asked to see "several short stories" and then didn't take them.[24] *Mademoiselle,* where Carson McCullers's sister Rita was the fiction editor, invited Pat for a meeting some months later, praised her "references & accomplishments," put her in their "active file," but never called her back.[25] There were just too many smart English majors with "references & accomplishments" jostling for jobs in wartime Manhattan, and something about Pat—could they have guessed what she was *thinking*?—put the magazine editors off.

It was the *Vogue* rejection that did the most damage. ("I'm horribly worried about *Vogue*. Rosalind told me *not* to write.")[26] Pat's well-connected friend the arts journalist Rosalind Constable—Pat was desperate to please her—had taken the trouble to recommend Pat personally to the ladies at *Vogue*, and Pat showed up for her interview in June of 1942, bright eyed and bushy tailed, but also, apparently, disheveled and *décoiffée*.

What wayward impulse, it is useful to ask, could have brought a young woman as ambitious and self-conscious as Patricia Highsmith to an interview at *Vogue* magazine in such a disorderly state? Something, perhaps, about not wanting to conform to the impeccably *female* image *Vogue* was showcasing in page after page of its perfectly styled fashion photographs?

Pat's mother, after all, was a fashion illustrator who had worked on and off for years for *Women's Wear Daily* (and had done a cover illustration for *Collier's* magazine in 1936).[27] From her earliest days Pat was absorbing the grammar of women's fashions from Mary—although no one would ever accuse Pat Highsmith of dressing like a girl. (Caroline Besterman says that even in a skirt she looked "rather like a sailor.")[28] Pat grew up listening to the shop talk of Mary's fashion illustrator friends Jeva Cralick and Marjorie Thompson, and Pat and "Cralick," as she was always called, had an affectionate correspondence that went on for decades. Pat and Mary, too, wrote to each other in letters that feature descriptions of clothing, and Pat's sole surviving letter from childhood (to her grandmother Willie Mae) includes an extended phrase about her favorite tennis shoes.[29]

It was probably the size of Pat's feet—all the Coates family had big hands and big feet, and Pat's hands and feet were enormous—that provoked her lifelong fascination with shoes. By the end of her life she was slipping those big feet into size 9½ loafers, and her lamb's-wool-lined moccasins from L.L. Bean, preserved in her archives, really do look like gunboats. Shoes were among Pat's initial artistic inspirations: the first line of the first story she ever wrote began with a pair of shoes beside a bed (see "Greek Games").[30]

Pat's emotional memory continued to be stimulated by footwear as she got older. In 1942 she remembered a boy from her Astoria childhood because she had given him her "new tennis shoes, much too masculine, I discovered, even for me to play in unselfconsciously." When the boy died shortly afterward, Pat wondered guiltily: would they "put my shoes into the coffin with him?"[31] Her first published novel, *Strangers on a Train* (1950), introduces its two fatal Alter Egos to each other by having Guy "accidentally touch the outstretched foot of [Bruno,] the young man asleep[,]" with his own.[32] And Guy's pointless confession of murder to the oafish, unheeding Owen Markman at the novel's end is perfectly symbolized by Markman's "big scuffed brown shoes. . . . Suddenly their flaccid, shameless, massive stupidity seemed the essence of all human stupidity . . . and before he knew how or why, [Guy] had kicked, viciously, the side of Owen's shoe."[33]

Shoes brought death sharply into Pat's mind once again when, years after her beloved grandmother Willie Mae's demise, one of her own shoes made her remember that Willie Mae's feet were shaped like her own feet, and only then, Pat wrote, had she been able to "shed the first real tears for my grandmother."[34] And in Munich, in 1951, the sense-memory of her ex-lover Virginia Catherwood's shoes pierced her heart with quite another feeling: "O Ginnie, your little black suede shoes, sitting in the hall side by side, so small in the hall, sexy beautiful shoes that made my heart jump and my lips smile . . . and I could have made love to you in a minute."[35]

Twenty years later, shoes were still fascinating her. Pat, staying with Barbara Ker-Seymer and Barbara Roett in Islington, was taken to dinner with her hosts at Simpson's-in-the-Strand in early November of 1972 by the Barbaras' two other houseguests, France Burke, daughter of the literary philosopher Kenneth Burke, and her lover, "Sam." Sam, who sat next to Pat at dinner, says that aside from "worrying" about the huge joints of meat that were arriving at their table with alarming frequency and orating obsessively about some family silver she was intent on extracting from an aunt, Pat's principal topic of conversation was shoes.

Sam was wearing a pair of Gucci loafers that were too narrow for her feet, and "Pat was VERY involved with this and she took the whole thing very seriously." Pat liked Gucci loafers too, but suggested that Sam buy them in men's sizes because only "the men's sizes were wide enough." Pat was "quietly peculiar, worrying about silver and shoes," but about the shoes, she was "quite earnest and very precise," sizing up Sam's foot with practiced accuracy and giving her an exact men's size equivalent.[36]

Fashion footwear evidently did a lot for Pat—she even said that one of her first reasons for liking Switzerland was that only the Swiss made the kind of shoes that fit her feet[37]—but shoes weren't the sole reason Pat was interested in fashion. Fashion, after all, was the glamorous province of beautiful women.

In New York, Pat loved to socialize with women in the world of *la mode*. She had a twenty-year, deeply attached friendship (ruined forever by their house-owning venture together in Samois-sur-Seine in the late 1960s) with Mme Elizabeth Lyne, the much older designer and painter who created dress lines for Hattie Carnegie. The painter, writer, and performance artist Lil Picard, Pat's friend for three decades and older than Pat by twenty years, began as a fashion designer and fashion editor in Berlin, made jewelry in Manhattan, and had her own milliner's studio—the Custom Hat Box—in Bloomingdale's department store, where Pat was to set crucial scenes for *The Price of Salt*.

Pat went on to have affairs with a bevy of attractive dress models—blondes of course—and her novels show that she was familiar with the art of dressmaking. In *The Price of Salt* and in her posthumously published novel, *Small g*—during whose writing she frequently consulted her dress-designer neighbor in Tegna, Julia Diener-Diethelm[38]—Pat gives detailed accounts of how fashion and fashions are created. Two of the older women characters in *The Price of Salt* present its young heroine, Therese, with handmade dresses, and elaborate rituals surround Therese's fittings for these garments. One of the central relationships in *Small g* owes something to Pat's careful observation in Manhattan in 1961 of the "old witch with the button shop on Madison Avenue [who tyrannized] over the younger, more sensitive, more beautiful redheaded girl—who did escape."[39]

In her cahiers, as early as 1940, Pat was giving proper dress, and the concealing/revealing/role-playing purposes of it, close attention in both fact and fiction. She always remarked when a jacket or a pair of slacks was "well cut," when a dress draped nicely over a woman's shapely torso, or when an attractive girl who was pretending to be seductively rich had a visible hole in the sole of her shoe.[40]

On one of her trips "home" to Texas—she was still in her teens—Pat made friends with a married couple in El Paso, a city on the Texas-Mexican border just across the Rio Grande from Ciudad Juárez. The woman, Eddy, was a very masculine horse-trainer, and the man, Ruthie, was an exceedingly effeminate dress designer. They were both homosexual and had married each other, Pat wrote approvingly, for cover. (Eddy and Ruthie's behavior in gay bars was so outrageous that their marriage was "urgently advisable.") Even better, Eddy and Ruthie had married in order to wear each other's clothes. Pat was enthralled.

"Eddy [the woman] wore beautifully cut jackets with silk shorts and foulard ties. Ruthie [the man] wore open collar sport shirts and loud tweed jackets and also beautifully cut English slacks. . . . Each would have liked the other's body for his own to put clothes on. . . . [T]hey were . . . finding the greatest pleasure in the world in buying clothes for each other—which neither wore—and which soon were taken back and worn by each respectively—which was what they'd wanted after all."[41]

Three years before her death, Pat was still thinking about clothes. In an article about Venice written for *The Oldie* in July of 1992, she lingered lovingly over the wares of her favorite Venetian "haberdashery," where she liked to buy shirts of unusual colors that were still hanging in her wardrobe: a yellow shirt (yellow, the color of warning signs, was Pat's favorite hue) and a porter's yellow and black striped jacket with yellow metal buttons which, Pat reported with the satisfaction of someone who has spent her money wisely, "has worn like iron."[42]

Pat's own clothing always had a ritually gendered aspect—and left open the question of which gender, too. But her most consistent gift to the women she cared about (including her mother and her editor at Heinemann in London, Janice Robertson) couldn't have been more feminine: she liked to present them with handbags. Pat gave Janice Robertson a Hermès bag when Robertson left Heinemann in 1972—and, says Janice Robertson, Pat was the only author to remember her with a going-away gift.*[43]

It wasn't until 1983, when Pat made a list for her Swiss publisher Diogenes of "Twenty Things I Like," that she publicly announced her penchant for wearing old clothes. "Old clothes" was number 9 on her preference list, followed by "Sneakers" at number 10. "Kafka's writing" was number 20.[44]

During different periods in her life, Pat's costumes really *were* costumes:

---

* Pat's fashion sense became markedly eccentric when she was required to dress like a "girl." After finishing her novel *A Dog's Ransom* in 1971, Pat went to visit her friend Trudi Gill, a painter who was also the wife of the American ambassador to Panama, in Vienna. Pat took her "one Yves St-Laurent dress"—which must have caused quite a stir at the three "embassy functions" to which she wore it in the chill Austrian November. The dress was "bright orange cotton."

composed expressions of the gender wars she waged within herself and represented in her dress. Her boy's shirts, men's trousers, collegiate loafers, tailored jackets, smart vests—as well as the little beaded necklaces and bracelets, the jaunty ascots, the occasional skirt, and the light lipsticks she sometimes applied—kept her suspended between the possibilities she'd acknowledged so "brilliantly" at the age of twelve: "I am a walking perpetual example of . . . a boy in a girl's body."[45] At twenty-seven, she was phrasing her dilemma a little more philosophically: "The most beautiful word is 'transcend.' By all the laws that are Platonic, I am a man and love women."[46]

The term "transgender" hadn't yet been invented. If it had been, Pat wouldn't have used it.

At Barnard College, Pat's riding breeches, hacking jackets, and signature trench and polo coats (she pawned the polo coat and her green Harris Tweed riding jacket, "in which I spent the proudest, happiest hours of my life," in an "ignominious" moment in December of 1942 when she ran out of cash)[47] made her memorable; attracting her classmates' wary admiration and lending a cultivated air of sophistication to her appearance. From her trips to Mexico, she brought back white waiter's jackets—they suited her very well, says a lover[48]— and the giant woven purses, *bolsas,* which she carried everywhere and filled with her necessaries: her cigarettes, her writer's notebooks, her Parker fountain pens (later on, it was Esterbrook pump pens with stainless-steel nibs), and the inevitable little bottle of something with a high alcohol proof.

After she moved to Europe, Pat continued to send for clothes from the United States, ordering her vests and white oxford shirts with the turn-back cuffs shipped from the boys' department of Brooks Brothers in Manhattan, where she had a charge account, and making sure that her Levi's and belts came directly from Texas. And she carried her *bolsas* from Mexico to Europe with her. In Tegna, her attentive occasional next-door neighbor Bert Diener, who drove her to the hospital in Locarno for blood treatments during her final illness, remembered how Pat always carried her *bolsa* and just what she kept in the "big woven bag: something to read, something to write with, and a little something to drink."[49]

Pat's distinctive "look" is still a subject of conversation for her former lovers. When Caroline Besterman first met Pat in 1962, she was struck by Pat's good looks *and* her fashion sense. Pat, says Besterman, was "fantastically, arrestingly good-looking." Although Pat "was awkward in company [and] handled cigarettes very badly—she looked as though she were mending roads with them, stubbing out her Gauloises most ungracefully—I found her [privately] quite graceful."

Caroline remembers Pat as

very exotic, the kind of person to whom you would immediately be drawn in a room. And she was still very much in control of her look, always well dressed, her hair was well cut. . . . Until the later years, Pat always had a certain style, *comme les garçons*. . . . The first time I met her, she was in a yellow sailcloth skirt and tight top and she did look rather like a sailor. There was a dash to her. . . . She always liked to change her clothes and get nicely ready for supper. She always had beads and a bracelet, her things were well cut and elegant.[50]

Pat kept her loyal friend Kingsley; her mother, Mary; and several other members of the Coates family on the hop for four decades, mailing the items she urgently required from the United States: the shirts, the vests, the leather belts, the bolo ties and tie slides, the inevitable Levi's and loafers, the "bedclothes," and those special pens and notebooks which are always part of a writer's "outfit." One of the many requests Pat sent to Mary from France—this one came from Samois-sur-Seine in 1969—shows just how pernickety she could be about her dress:

"I wouldn't mind a Western shirt. I was not mad about the last pattern you sent: I prefer a stripe, or a solid dark blue, for instance. . . . I think I take neck 14 (inches), therefore size fourteen.

". . . The last (brownish-tan) western shirt you sent is a good fit: I have just checked its size: 14; and 32 (sleeve). . . . I have plenty of bedding thanks to you. The only thing else I can think of—is a pen, of a decent variety with a point that is not a ball point but a real point."[51]

And Pat paid close attention to how she dressed her favorite characters, too, especially when she was dressing them up to kill someone. In *The Talented Mr. Ripley*, Tom Ripley, attired without permission in Dickie Greenleaf's expensive clothes, is caught by Dickie in Dickie's own bedroom in Mongibello just as Tom has finished miming the murder of Dickie's "girlfriend," Marge Sherwood, in a mirror. After he murders Dickie and Dickie's friend Freddie, and installs himself in a palazzo apartment on the Grand Canal in Venice with Dickie's money, Tom likes to spend whole

evenings looking at his clothes—his clothes and Dickie's—and feeling Dickie's rings between his palms and running his fingers over the antelope suitcase he had bought at Gucci's. . . . He loved possessions, not masses of them, but a select few. . . . They gave a man self-respect. Not ostentation but quality, and the love that cherished the quality. Possessions reminded him that he existed. . . . It was as simple as that.[52]

In later Ripley novels, Tom shares Pat's taste for well-pressed Levi's, pyjamas with bottoms, and handsome bathrobes from the better men's shops.

But the desire for conventional success that sent the young, fashion-conscious Barnard graduate to *Vogue* magazine for an interview in June of 1942 was apparently overtaken by an equal and opposite reaction, something like an undertow in her ambition. And so the girl who was so particular about her clothes, the girl who had already filled hundreds of pages of cahiers and diaries with her reflections on dress and appearance—on the way *she* looked at the world, on the way the world looked at *her,* on the way the world would *one day look upon her*—managed to show up for her appointment at *Vogue,* New York's principal style and fashion magazine, with a stained and wrinkled blouse, bad hair, and, in the formal 1940s, a head unadorned by a hat.

Pat's messy presentation at her *Vogue* interview is especially suspicious because she was such a sedulous wielder of the steam iron. Like her mother, Mary, who used to go to Pat's apartment on East Fifty-sixth Street to talk to Pat and when "[t]here would be no satisfactory contact" ended up frustratedly "ironing [Pat's clothes] until time to go,"[53] Pat ironed for satisfaction and she ironed for inspiration. She ironed because pressing freshly washed materials flat and sharpening their creases to a knife-edged perfection gave a little order to the conflicting emotions she dealt with every day.

"She ironed everything herself, she wouldn't let me take anything to the cleaners," says Marijane Meaker of her short cohabitation with Pat in Pennsylvania in 1960.[54] And Caroline Besterman confirms that Pat went right on ironing through the 1960s in England at Bridge Cottage: "She ironed a lot, she loved ironing, she found it soothing."[55] Pat used to tell journalists that she got "ideas" for her work at the ironing board—although no Highsmith character was ever dispatched with a blow from a red-hot steam iron.

It was an obviously exasperated Rosalind Constable who telephoned Pat on 17 June 1942 at her parents' apartment to deliver the bad news from the *Vogue* interview: "They said you looked like you'd just got out of bed."[56] Rosalind made it clear that Pat should have had more sense than to show up "looking as [she] did." Humiliated because she'd embarrassed Rosalind, Pat set the whole incident down defensively in her diary, dealing with it as she always dealt with rejection: "Well, I *did* wash my hair just before going in. . . . There'll come a time when I shall be bigger than *Vogue* and I can thank my lucky star I escaped their corruptive influences."[57]

Pat never said so, but the serial rejections she suffered at *Harper's Bazaar* for her story submissions in the 1940s must have been as painful to her as the rejection from *Vogue*. The forward-looking *Harper's* was setting an enviable literary tone for New York. Under, first, George Davis's and then Mary Louise Aswell's more or less unbridled fiction editorship, *Harper's* was publishing Truman Capote, Jean Cocteau, and Salvador Dalí as well as Carson McCullers, W. H. Auden, Gypsy Rose Lee, and most of the other former inhabitants of George Davis's roisterous, rented, boardinghouse-to-the-arts on Middagh Street in Brooklyn.[58]

Daniel Bell, the eminent sociologist whose widely influential book, *The End of Ideology* (1960), gave a name to the tenor of political debate in 1950s America (Edith of *Edith's Diary* reads Daniel Bell, so Pat read him as well: her characters always read what she read), says that before William Shawn became its editor *The New Yorker* was "quite hostile to new fiction, so writers who ordinarily would have been published in *The New Yorker* went to *Harper's*."[59] When Mary Louise Aswell took over as fiction editor, *Harper's* published Pat's own superb story "The Heroine," written while she was at Barnard and rejected by her fellow student editors at the *Barnard Quarterly* as too "upsetting" to publish. The *Harper's* publication of "The Heroine" attracted some interest from the publisher Knopf, which Pat failed—was it insecurity? lack of finished material?—to follow up on.[60] But that was later, in August of 1945.[61] This was now. Now, Pat was on the outside looking in.

Editor and literary critic Pearl Kazin, Daniel Bell's wife, former lover of Dylan Thomas, and sister of critic Alfred Kazin (Pat, always interested in surveying the competition, read Kazin's book about American literature's golden age, *On Native Grounds*, and failed to find it brilliant),[62] worked at *Harper's* before she became the chief copy editor at *The New Yorker*. She says that she, too, had a hand in editing Pat at *Harper's Bazaar*. In 2003, Pearl Kazin managed, from her sickbed, to deliver a trenchant summary of the impression Patricia Highsmith had made on her in the 1940s in New York City.

"Terrible," said Pearl Kazin. Just "terrible."[63]

And Daniel Bell gives an idea of how absent from the American literary landscape Pat has always been: "In all the years that Pearl and I were married [since 1960] she never mentioned Highsmith."[64] Robert Gottlieb, who had been Pat's editor at Knopf for *A Dog's Ransom* and *Ripley's Game* (he found her style "pebbly"), says the same thing: "She seemed to have no presence in New York."[65] Her last American editor, Gary Fisketjon at Atlantic Monthly Press and Knopf, agrees: "I never heard of her growing up; she wasn't even remotely in the lexicon."[66] Norman Mailer, two years younger than Pat and, along with Truman Capote, one of the New York publishing sensations of 1948 with his war novel *The Naked and the Dead*, had a similar response.

"Remind me, Joan," said Norman Mailer, "what was Highsmith? A high-class detective novelist?"[67]

Pat's humiliation at not securing a job after she graduated from Barnard—even before she left college she had been anxiously seeking a good position—was intense. She said to herself that she really "didn't want to see anyone" from Barnard until she had some decent employment. Perhaps her failure to be elected to the honorary academic society, Phi Beta Kappa, had something to do with her humiliation. "Went to school this P.M. and got the shock of my life: *D in Logic*. My first D of course. Phi Beta Kappa—forever goodby! It upset me terribly more than I had believed it would."[68]

For decades after she left Barnard, Pat made shamed references to that D in Logic, which had not, after all, killed her chances for a Phi Beta Kappa key: her grades at Barnard were already quite a bit lower than what Phi Beta Kappa required for membership. But a D in Logic (part of her yearlong philosophy course) was another unwelcome point of resemblance to Mother Mary. Pat was always criticizing Mary for being "illogical."

Shame for not finding a job was certainly the reason Pat quietly skipped her college graduation, slipping into the *Barnard Quarterly* offices the day before the ceremony, 31 May 1942, and "bringing home my weight in manila envelopes, stationery, etc," but avoiding her classmates. "Saw no one, tho' today was S[enior] picnic & tomorrow graduation!"[69]

She got herself excused from the graduation ceremony by writing a false letter saying that she had a job interview at a New Jersey newspaper on graduation day. Pleased with her alibi and even more pleased to be hoodwinking the administration, she wrote in her diary: "Barnard sent me the mark sheet & blanks for diploma by mail, apparently on the strength of my beautiful letter yesterday to [Columbia University president] N.M. Butler."[70]

But Pat wasn't so pleased about missing a graduation lunch at Schrafft's with her circle of intimate classmates, Babs and Peter (a girl) and Helen, at least two of whom, as a matter of course, she'd slept with. And she wasn't happy at all about not appearing at her graduation. "I had to convince myself that I didn't want to go."[71] In the week after graduation, she consoled herself by trying to write like the expatriate American novelist Kay Boyle, whose work she was reading with great attention. Kay Boyle, Pat wrote in her diary in yet another of her attempts at impersonation, "has the style I feel I should naturally continue."[72]

After she left Barnard, aside from a little temping work, Pat was forced to accept the only job offer she got: an offer for work researching and writing factual pieces at FFF Publications. She considered this respectable job degrading, and as the work was petering out, she hastened to answer Richard Hughes's ad for a "writer-researcher" at Sangor-Pines—a job *everyone* considered degrading. Ever after, Pat would tell prying journalists (if she mentioned the subject at all) that she hadn't "realized" she was applying to a comic book company for work.[73]

Pat's sharp history of failure in the New York job market, where "quality" was both a requirement for success and the reward you received for *being* a success, made it especially important for the ambitious young writer, living on the fringes of her older friends' well-remunerated lives, to keep up a good front. It was the counterweight to what she referred to, always, as her "maimed" nature, a nature that needed "crutches."[74] "I never fall asleep at night," she wrote, "without writhing in agony at least twice, remembering something which I imagine *horrid* that I have done that day, or the day before.[75] Pierced by insecurities about her family background, Pat brought forth analyses as harsh as punishments whenever she encountered her blood relatives in Fort Worth or in New York; analyses which reinforced her sense of being a "loser" in a wide world of "winners."

"Marriages, in all of my grandmother's children, have been to people beneath them, intellectually and culturally, as if the entire family, through want of education or money or both had been permeated with the disease of inferiority."[76]

Success, expecially in the postwar boom years, always seemed to Pat to be everywhere but in the Highsmith house. Her Deep Southern background, alive with the family mythology of a glorious but defeated Confederacy and a long-gone Southern Way of Life, as well as her birth in what was then considered to be a second-class Texas cow town, couldn't have helped. (In 1906, the American philosopher-psychologist William James defined success, at that time a more or less Northern notion, as "our national disease"—and memorably called it a "bitch-goddess." "Bitch-goddess" is a good description of how Pat liked to think of her lovers.) In the winter of 1948, surveying the sullied New York snow in the backyard of her apartment building on East Fifty-sixth Street and immersing herself in critical works about Kafka all weekend, Pat felt she was being swiftly driven "from neurosis to psychosis" by the thought of failure:

"In every direction I turn and move, I am met by failure or a wall impenetrable. The only success I can recall recently is a successful batch of hardened fudge."[77]

She wasn't kidding.

After attending a Broadway performance of Arthur Miller's *Death of a Salesman* in November of 1950, Pat, for the rest of her life, would compare her mother Mary's perpetually collapsing career as a fashion illustrator to the situation of Willy Loman, the "hero" of Miller's tragedy, undone by his passive faith in the American Dream. Pat's private response to Willy Loman's downfall was completely consistent with her own ambitions and entirely *in*consistent with the meaning of *Death of a Saleman*. "I find I have no sympathy," Pat wrote in her diary on 17 November 1950, "for the individual whose spirit has not led him to seek higher goals, in the first place, at a much younger age."[78]

Pat was seeking "higher goals," and at a "younger age," too, while she labored away at the comics. During this time Mary Louise Aswell—she and Pat would keep up with each other through lesbian circles when Mrs. Aswell retired with her lover Agnes Sims to New Mexico—sent Pat another rejection letter from *Harper's Bazaar* which summed up Pat's ironic relationship to "quality." It was the kind of encouraging letter—Mrs. Aswell genuinely admired Pat's writing and was one of her recommenders to the artists' colony, Yaddo, in 1948—which usually has the opposite effect on its recipient, implying that while Pat's toe might be on the literary ladder, her heel was still firmly fixed to the waiting room floor. "Your writing," wrote Mary Louise Aswell, "has considerable quality, & while this story is not for us, would you let us see some more of your work?"[79]

One of the ways Pat kept her front up and her goals high was to conceal the extent of her participation in the comics trade. She also took the trouble to conceal the nature and even the fact of her first postcollege job, at FFF Publications. Pat had been taken on at FFF Publications to work with the author, newspaper columnist, and editor Ben-Zion Goldberg—already a household name among readers of Yiddish journals in America. Goldberg, the son of a rabbi from Vilnius, had travelled the world reporting and writing on Jewish matters. In 1931, he published a book about sex in religion called *The Sacred Fire* (1931), and by the mid-1940s he was chairman of the Committee of Jewish Scientists, Writers, and Artists of the United States. (Albert Einstein was the president of that committee.) Goldberg wrote for many papers and journals in both English and Yiddish in Canada and the United States (including *The New Republic*), and he was active in antifascist organizations. In 1946, he spent six months in Russia meeting with Soviet writers and Jewish political committees.[80]

Ben-Zion Goldberg hired Pat as his editorial assistant at FFF Publications in the last week of June 1942, when she was at the end of her job-hunting rope. (She would eke out the finish of her employment with Goldberg with some temping work at *Modern Baby* magazine.)[81] He chose her over two hundred other applicants, but Pat was not pleased to be joining the only "club" that would admit her: a publishing company run by Jews who hired her to do research on Jewish history and provide articles to the national Jewish press. The Jewish press was FFF Publications' primary market. "It's a lousy, journalistic . . . job," she wrote in her diary, "and I'm frankly bored & ashamed of it. Why couldn't it be on the scarabs of Tutankhamen? Why not the history of the Dalai Lamas? . . . Why not the story of the philosopher's stone?"[82] Pat was afraid Goldberg would "try to Jew me down to eighteen [dollars] a week" and wrote of him contemptuously: "He seems to be of some repute—somewhere."[83] But Goldberg hired Pat at twenty dollars a week, and ten days later he gave her a raise.

So, just her luck, not only was Pat Highsmith—busily scribbling anti-Semitisms in her notebook—researching and providing material for a large part of the North American Jewish press, she had also managed to get herself hired by the son-in-law of the world's most famous Jewish writer. Ben-Zion Goldberg had been the tutor of the renowned Yiddish fabulist Sholem Aleichem's youngest daughter, and he married her in 1917.* Now Goldberg was Pat's boss: the only person in New York, apparently, who wanted to hire her. The situation was alive with all the convergent ironies of a good Jewish joke. Not for the talented Miss Highsmith, however, who had never heard of Sholem Aleichem.

But then Pat did some research on Goldberg (while she was doing some research *for* him), and discovered that he'd been arrested for shouting "Scab!" at a political demonstration. She decided this was a pretty good character recommendation, that she "liked Goldberg personally," and that his "methods are sound."[84] And then Pat and Mother Mary started studying Spanish together and going to more galleries, and Pat's evening life sparkled and scintillated with more sexual and social possibilities. So she settled down to working for Goldberg with something resembling goodwill.

Pat and Goldberg stayed friendly for years (see "Alter Ego: Part 4"), and it was Goldberg to whom she first showed her early attempts at long fiction writing. And when Pat was twenty-six, it was Goldberg who pointed out to her—she said she'd never realized it before—that her perennial "theme" was the relationship between two "ill-matched" men.[85] When she first gave him her work to read, he said: "There's something in your writing that intrigues me—a rhythm . . . an occasional new form. . . . But it's inclined to be rocky. Uneven."[86]

But rather than tell the world that she'd written the "household section for The Jewish Family Year Book" in 1942, and had worked for the well-known

---

* Sholem Aleichem (real name: Sholem Rabinowitz), 1859–1916, the Ukrainian Jewish writer and popular humorist, was a prodigious author of works in Yiddish. The musical comedy *Fiddler on the Roof* is based on his collection of stories about Tevye the Milkman.

Yiddish journalist Ben-Zion Goldberg for six months,[87] Pat published an article in *The Oldie* magazine in 1993 ("My First Job")," describing as her "first job" one of the "filler" jobs she'd taken *after* her employment with Goldberg and FFF Publications ended: a "fortnight's" stint as a street pollster for the Arrid Deodorant Company.[88] For this polling job, the constitutionally shy Pat was required to stand in front of Saks, Macy's, and Bloomingdale's department stores and try out advertising slogans on passers-by.

Fifty years on, Pat still remembered the accosting phrases she'd had to repeat to strangers in her disguise as a pollster: "Arrid is the most efficient deodorant in the world today." "Arrid is the fastest selling underarm deodorant in America and the world."[89] She added, making a feeble joke, that she hoped that publishing these phrases so much later didn't mean she was *still* advertising Arrid.[90] But Pat knew very well she wasn't advertising anything. In 1993, when she published the article in *The Oldie*—it was late in her life and her anti-Israeli stance had become a propulsive obsession—Pat was hiding the fact that her "first real job" in Manhattan had been a job compiling research for the Jewish press.

Pat used her nineteen-dollar-a-week salary pitching deodorant to move, briefly, to a bed-sitting room in a "respectable house in the East Sixties" (the adjective "respectable" made all the difference to class-conscious Pat) "from [w]here I could walk to my parents' apartment in East Fifty-seventh Street [also proximate to a "good address"] where I often had dinner which was economical and cheering." But cheap and cheerful wasn't what Pat was looking for, and one of the ways she dissembled her financial condition was to rent an apartment in the *vicinity* of a "quality" neigborhood: the Upper East Side.

Because the stuff of Pat's hopes and dreams always found its way into her work, the fragile, tentative dream of happiness she put together at the end of the 1940s for the two lesbian lovers Carol and Therese in *The Price of Salt* depends partially upon Carol securing an apartment on Madison Avenue (an Upper East Side address) and inviting Therese to share it. In the 1940s, Madison Avenue, with its sedate buildings and elegant shops, was well on the way to becoming the ultraexpensive thoroughfare of symbolic achievement and carbon monoxide gas that it is today. Madison Avenue must have seemed like Heaven's Own Boulevard to the young writer whose birth in her grandmother's boardinghouse in Fort Worth, Texas, was "mid-wived" by one of the upstairs' boarders,[91] and whose first six years there were spent close enough to railyard crossings to hear the lonesome freight trains whistling down the tracks.

Pat's next New York home, a studio apartment at 353 East Fifty-sixth Street, into which she moved in early 1943 and kept, on and off, until 1960 (subletting it briefly to Truman Capote and lengthily and contentiously to the designer Eveline Phimister, lover of her friend the photographer Ruth Bernhard),[92] was just around the block from her parents' apartment on East Fifty-seventh Street. She bought furniture for the apartment, painted the walls and bookshelves a greenish blue, and Mary Highsmith came over to help with the painting. While mother and daughter were wielding their paintbrushes, Mary, with her usual disconcerting prescience in anything that concerned her daughter, told Pat that she shouldn't become like Allela Cornell (the young painter who was about to become Pat's lover), crying every evening, wanting to be "beautiful," and doing nothing about it. Mary uttered the word "lesbian" about Allela and Pat was unnerved.[93] Pat hung up one of her friend Ruth Bernhard's exquisite photographs—an arm made of wood, cradling the head of a doll[94]—but Kingsley Skattebol says that the apartment's "chief attraction was the trompe l'oeil fireplace Pat had cleverly painted on one wall."[95] Pat couldn't afford an apartment with a fireplace, so she made one for herself.

Although the painter Buffie Johnson (see "Social Studies: Part 1") described Pat's neighborhood as "posh enough,"[96] this new apartment fell quite a bit short of "posh." It did have an unobstructed view out the back window, but it was on the first floor, the backyard was full of the washing of Irish tenants, and there was a fire escape with a ladder just outside her window that provided easy access to her living room.

Still, Vince Fago, Pat's editor at Timely comics, remembered her apartment (in one of those careful calibrations that social life in Manhattan always requires) just as Pat would have wanted him to: as being "near Sutton Place."[97] Sutton Place is the exclusive, expensive enclave of private houses, terraced gardens, and luxury apartment buildings clustered between Fifty-seventh and Fifty-ninth streets, one block east of First Avenue. It was colonized in 1920, when America's first theatrical agent, the legendary lesbian Elisabeth "Bessie" Marbury,* and her like-minded lady friends Elsie de Wolfe, Anne Morgan (J. P. Morgan's daughter), and Anne Vanderbilt began buying up the town houses next to the Burns Brothers coal yard and opening up their new homes to society. Sutton Place has been one of New York's best addresses for the better part of a century.†

Pat's social weakness was the one she always criticized in Mother Mary:

* Bessie Marbury, an outsized (in every way) personality and a mainstay of the Democratic Party, invented the profession of theatrical agent in America, saved Oscar Wilde's royalties for him while he was in prison, produced Cole Porter's first musical, and also backed a Broadway play in which Pat's future lover, Kathryn Hamill Cohen, appeared.
† In *A Suspension of Mercy* (1965), Pat introduces her murdering fantasist, Sydney Bartleby, to his well-to-do young wife at a party on Sutton Place.

the desire to appear before the world surrounded by "the best." At 353 East Fifty-sixth Street she would have been a couple of blocks from it. And despite her constant complaints about her mother, Pat didn't seem to want to live very far from her. With the Highsmiths installed on East Fifty-seventh Street, around the corner from Mary was as far away as Pat ever got.

In October of 1947, after Mary and Stanley had moved up the Hudson River to the fancy house they couldn't afford in Hastings-on-Hudson (Mary, just as intent as her daughter on the American Dream, was thrilled to have a live-in Filipino "houseboy"), Pat admitted in her cahier just how much having a family meant to her work.

"What the young artist loses when he moves away from home may easily outweigh his gained independence. He loses an all important psychological security and framework, which has to do with his state of mind, the all important self. The artist is forever a child in some respects. . . . Ergo, to write with the free declarations of childhood it is essential sometimes to be in the shadow of the parents' wings."[98]

So perhaps the detail Pat recorded so casually in her diary on 16 December 1945 has greater significance than the short sentence she allotted to it. Pat wrote that the plot of *Strangers on a Train* came to her while she was out for a walk in Hastings-on-Hudson with her parents, Mary and Stanley Highsmith.

On the night of 18 October 1944, Pat was sitting up with a book in bed in her studio apartment, holding the cup of hot milk she always liked to drink before she fell asleep. Two years earlier, she'd described her bedtime drink in a notebook in tropes she would later import to *The Price of Salt,* making Carol serve Therese a similar cup of milk in similar circumstances.

"Hot milk. How wonderful on autumn idle days, lovely with silent books. I hold a finger-burning cup of it in my hands. It tastes organic, of blood and hair, meat and bone. It is alive as an embryo, sucked from a womb."[99]

Pat would go on drinking milk, sometimes by the liter, for most of the rest of her life.[100] She wouldn't have denied the Freudian explanation for her taste, either: the one that begins with the theory that because Mother Mary had left Fort Worth three weeks after Pat was born to look for work in Chicago, she wouldn't have been able to nurse her infant daughter for very long.

Alone with her book and her ritual tipple in her first real apartment, with its three-quarter couch-bed, "plus a real kitchen, plus a bath with tub and shower,"[101] Pat came close to sounding like Walt Whitman. In a long passage in her cahier, she managed to merge with her surroundings, her country, her kind—with everything, in fact, except her own gender. "The sudden feeling tonight, coming to me with a pleasurable start, the kinship, brotherhood, I have with all the lighted homes all over America, stretching behind me four thousand miles westward."[102]

This feeling of peace and reconciliation on an autumn night in the middle of the Second World War wouldn't last. It was, anyway, a far cry from Pat's "normal" feelings of being out of place everywhere—and a *very* far cry from the artistic theme she would pursue in every single work of fiction she ever wrote.

"What keeps recurring to me as a fundamental of the novel is the individual out of place in this century."[103]

Alienation has been the house specialty of writers since Cervantes, but nothing could have been more alienating to Pat's ambitions than her current work as a comic book scriptwriter. The idea that comics were at the center of the American Zeitgeist wouldn't occur to anyone for several decades—and it never did occur to Patricia Highsmith. But when Pat declared that the novel had to be about an "individual out of place in this century" she had already been writing works about displaced individuals for quite a while: comic book Superheroes whose traits were so alien to their epoch that they required earthbound Alter Egos for ballast (see "Alter Ego: Part 2"). And Pat's other writing, the "serious" writing she did at night after work, was stealthily borrowing from her "pulp" scenarios, as though the comic book work were the secret Alter Ego of her serious stories.

Pat—who complained about everything—complained that she was bored writing for comics, but boredom, as she took the trouble to explain some years later, was a state her imagination positively thrived on: "Whenever I become intolerably bored, I produce another story, in my head."[104]

In December of 1944, writing hard for the comics and grumbling about it, working on the novel she'd been thinking about for two years, *The Click of the Shutting,* making notes for short stories at night, entertaining more love possibilities than she could possibly handle (a Virginia or two, the socialite Natica Waterbury, an Anne and an Ann, the model Chloe, et al.) and feeling abysmally poor, Pat still kept her eyes on the prize. She framed her desire for the "best" in life in metaphors saturated by the war and couched in the language of the enemy. (Her diary note is in bad German.)

"When I work (write), I must have the best, the best cigarettes, a clean shirt, because I am a soldier, who fights, but in this case the enemy is terrible and brave, and sometimes I don't win."[105]

In August of 1949, on her first trip to London, already planning to seduce her English publisher Dennis Cohen's brilliant, beautiful showgirl-turned-psychiatrist wife, Kathryn Hamill Cohen, Pat was still holding fast to her conviction of "quality."

"I shall have the best, in the long run. Not a house with children, not even a permanent thing (what is permanent in life and in art? What ever is permanent except one's own heartbeat?) but the best will always be attracted to me. For this, I do, most sincerely, thank God."[106]

In June of 1952, from Florence, Pat wrote to Kingsley in New York to explain why she'd gone back to Europe. The subject of "the best"—never far from Pat's mind—came up again in the letter. The fact that Mary and Stanley Highsmith had left New York State was one of the interesting reasons Pat gave for leaving the United States,[107] but her old obsession with quality was her strongest theme.

"I did *not* come away with a bitter hatred of American commercialism or bad taste, or any usual complaint. . . . I cannot imagine going on forever not returning to America. But I can imagine living mostly in Europe the rest of my life. . . . [T]o have a good time in America costs a lot. It is the opposite in Europe. . . . [T]o have an elegant good time, with beautiful surroundings, is cheap."[108]

In 1955, three years after her letter to Kingsley about the "elegant good time" she was having in Europe, Pat was back in the United States making her credo of "quality" the central obsession of the character who was to become, crudely speaking, her own fictional Alter Ego: Tom Ripley. (Pat was *never* "the woman who was Ripley," but she did give Ripley many of the traits she wished she had, as well as quite a few of her obsessive little habits.) Like Pat, Ripley began as a flunker of job interviews and a failure at self-respect. Like Pat, Ripley found his "quality" of life in Europe.

"The best" is Tom Ripley's reward for the murder and impersonation of *his* Alter Ego, Dickie Greenleaf, but it is also Ripley's goal. *"Il meglio, il meglio!"*— "The best, the best!"—Tom cries out at the end of *The Talented Mr. Ripley* when the taxi driver asks him what kind of hotel he wants to go to.[109] Tom means what he says to the taxi driver: he wants *only* the best. And Pat meant what she said about "quality" that day at Sangor-Pines to young Everett Ray Kinstler.

Pat's offhand comment to Kinstler when he brought her a Pepsi instead of a Coke, he remembers, "was said in an amusing way. Not that it hit me like that; I was devastated."[110] Perhaps the love-struck sixteen-year-old—his talent was for "telling stories" in portraits, and he was already perceptive about reading character in a face—had caught the operating principle underlying Pat's response: a deadly serious decision to have "the best" of everything and an unwavering determination to reject those who did not. Pat would continue to wield this principle as both a sword and a shield for the rest of her life.

Years later, when he returned from his tour of duty in World War II, Ray Kinstler happened to come across Pat in a crowded café in Greenwich Village.

"I used to frequent the Village then and sometime in the late 1940s I saw her, recognized her in a café. Of course, I was older—and there's a big difference between being sixteen and being twenty-two.

"She was sitting at a table . . . smoking and drinking. I did a double take, but I don't think she spotted me.

"It seemed to me—I don't want to use the word 'seedy'—but it looked to me like she'd changed a lot. Maybe I'd just grown up, but . . . my recollection was, she just, uh, she just didn't look as attractive, and that's not a negative. I was just more grown up . . . and I saw something in her that didn't appeal to me. Something about her pushed me back."

"Just imagine," said Ray Kinstler, casting his mind back sixty years to the twenty-two-year-old Pat Highsmith waiting upstairs in the Sangor-Pines comics shop on West Forty-fifth Street for his lovelorn younger self to bring her the wrong soft drink. "Just imagine if I'd gotten that Coca-Cola for her what would have happened."

It only took him a second to come up with the right answer.

"Nothing."[111]

11

ALTER EGO

PART 2

Pat once told a lover that life "didn't make any sense without a crime in it."[1] Writing for the crime-themed, criminally inclined comic book industry of the 1940s—the only long-term "job" she ever had—must have seemed to her like compounding a felony.

Pat stopped her typing in the office, said a co-worker at Sangor-Pines, only long enough to have a cup of coffee or light up a cigarette.[2] Coffee and cigarettes were the twin stimulants of her working days, and all her life she remained an enthusiastic coffee drinker. After she moved to Europe, her letters to her professor friend Alex Szogyi in New York were wreathed in nostalgic reminiscences of staying up all night and talking, their conversations fueled by cup after cup of strong coffee.

Pat linked her earliest memories of coffee with her experience of suspense, mystery, and "story." She remembered with unusual pleasure the Sunday nights of her childhood in Queens when she sat in the kitchen with Mary and Stanley at nine o'clock to hear the weekly broadcast of the half-hour Sherlock Holmes* serial during which "Sherlock and Watson were always stirring G[eorge] Washington Coffee before beginning their fascinating story."[3] And as she listened to Holmes and Watson advertise their American coffee sponsors, she had a cup of that same coffee with them. And she ate a bowl of Jell-O, too, "which Jack Benny had been advertising an hour before on the radio."[4] At eleven or twelve, Pat Highsmith was still susceptible to advertising.

---

* "Everyone already knows, instinctively," writes Graham Robb in *Strangers: Homosexual Love in the Nineteenth Century,* "that Holmes is homosexual. . . . Without the tense, suppressed passion that binds him to his biographer, Holmes is merely a man with an interesting hobby" (pp.260–61).

But coffee was not the only liquid Pat grew up to drink enthusiastically, and during her year at Sangor-Pines her heavy alcohol intake and subsequent nighttime roistering began to affect her work. (See "Social Studies: Part 1.") Lending support to her claim that justice didn't exist—or that if it did, the world wasn't much interested in it—Pat never suffered from hangovers. She awoke in the morning, says a still-awed lover, fresh as a daisy and ready to write after drinking the liquor-cabinet equivalent of a small pond. Only sleep deprivation interfered with her ferocious will to create.

Sometime in the late 1960s or early 1970s, when Pat's London friends Barbara Ker-Seymer and Barbara Roett were worried enough about her drinking to suspect cirrhosis of the liver, they determined to do something about it. Barbara Roett took charge of the formalities.

"I had an ex-lover, a doctor, Geoffrey [Dove], and I said to Pat, 'Come, I want you to go to Geoffrey, he's going to look at your liver.' I wanted to frighten her. At that time I didn't know her well enough[;] I really didn't understand her nature. And so I took her to Geoffrey and we had the results the next day. And to my horror, Geoffrey rang and said, 'There's nothing at all the matter with Pat's liver!'[5]

Coffee, scientists now tell us gravely, helps to protect the livers of heavy drinkers from cirrhosis. So perhaps it was Pat's instinct for self-preservation—just as well developed as her instinct for self-destruction—that had kept her drinking coffee with pleasure and purpose since she was "11 and 12 years old."[6]

For most of the 1940s Pat smoked Camel cigarettes. (Her doctors told her that her late-life lung cancer had nothing to do with her smoking.) After she came back to New York in the fall of 1949 from her first trip to Europe, she refused to smoke anything but French Gauloise *jaune* or German cigarettes. And in 1963 in England, reliably perverse in a foreign country, Pat had a short fling with American cigarettes again, finding that her brand choices in Suffolk were limited. There was only one tobacconist in Aldeburgh who carried American cigarettes, and those were Philip Morrises.[7] But in the 1940s she was still inhaling Camels by the carton. And in midtown Manhattan, where many of the comics shops and comic book publishers were located, there was plenty of advertising around to remind her to stick with her brand.

The celebrated Camel cigarette sign in Times Square, mounted on the side of the Claridge Hotel on Broadway between Forty-third and Forty-fourth streets, did not escape the attention of the writer who, ten years later, would say she remembered the name "Ripley" from a sign advertising male attire on the Henry Hudson Parkway. (This is rather like James M. Cain's claim that the origin of *Double Indemnity* was a lingerie ad.) Every morning on her way to Sangor-Pines from her East Fifty-sixth Street apartment, Pat passed near enough to the Camel sign (a several-stories-high male head, repainted as a soldier after America entered the war, with a cigarette in his hand and "real" smoke billowing out of his mouth) to see it smoking. The sign, erected in 1941 by the R. J. Reynolds Tobacco Company, was one of the more creative displays in the neon-saturated Times Square, and the Camel Man, a superheroic smoker if ever there was one, continued to blow his enormous white smoke rings skyward every four seconds until 1966.

Although the comics company on Forty-fifth Street where Pat started out as a scriptwriter was usually known as Sangor-Pines, it produced comic books for so many publishers that it was often called by the names of the comics companies it packaged: Michel Publications, Cinema Comics, Nedor, Better, Standard Publications, etc. Like everything else that had to do with the comics, Sangor-Pines operated under a multitude of shifting identities.

Bob Oksner, cartoonist and art director at Sangor-Pines in the 1940s, remembers seeing Pat at work on her scripts in the Sangor-Pines writers' bullpen.[8] But the writers' room had other occupants as well; Pat was never alone there.

Pat's desk in the seventh-floor Sangor-Pines office was flanked by four other desks, small ones just big enough to set a typewriter on. They were placed about "six to eight feet apart," and four other writers were seated at them. Three of the writers were men, a Miss Taub worked somewhere else in the office, and, briefly, another woman scriptwriter also named Patricia (Patricia Cher) sat next to Pat. And so for a short time in an industry and an office where women were almost never employed, there were two women named Patricia sitting side by side, typing out scenarios for the comics.[9] Coincidentally, doubling was also the theme of the comics stories Pat Highsmith was working on in the office—and the subject of the novel (*The Click of the Shutting*) she was taking notes for at home.

Later on, space in the writers' bullpen got tight and Pat was moved around the floor. For a while she shared a corner with Dan Gordon, an illustrator and writer whom she regarded as an "intelligent artist." (Her editor at Timely comics, Vince Fago, thought Gordon was a "genius.") Dan Gordon drank. "One can see it in his face," Pat noted, confident in her judgement, and she flirted with him at work. He made her "feel like a 16 year old girl with Clark Gable," and the remark about Gable means something: *Gone with the Wind* (1939) was still her favorite movie.[10]

In 1943, Gerald Albert, the twenty-six-year-old son of a smart lawyer-turned-pulp publisher who sold his wartime paper allotment to Ben Sangor, got himself a job writing comics for Sangor-Pines a few months after Richard

Hughes hired Pat. Albert thinks his job may have been part of the paper-supplying deal his father made with Ben Sangor. However it transpired, Gerry Albert found himself sitting in the writers' bullpen at Sangor-Pines two seats away from a "tall, dark, serious, attractive, rather remote young woman [with] good features"—like everyone else who met her at this time, Albert emphasizes how "good-looking" she was—named Patricia Highsmith.

Gerald Albert was not the only scriptwriter to find Pat attractive. Leo Isaacs, a freelance writer for Sangor-Pines, fell "passionately" in love with Pat and besieged her with more or less unwelcome sonnets.[11] Pat, interested in a clinical way in his emotions (but not in responding to them), took appraising notes on poor Mr. Isaacs's psychology.

Gerald Albert, who later became a psychotherapist (his leading questions in the office to Pat—"You seem sad"—annoyed her), says he somehow formed the impression that Pat "was a homosexual." He never heard a word about it at the office, but thinks his feeling may have been prompted by Pat's rather severe style of dress, or by the "semimasculine disdain for the feminine" which seemed to emanate from her.[12]

"But," says Dr. Albert, "what I remember most is her ability to produce an enormous amount of material."[13]

The four other Sangor shop writers would come to the office, get their individual assignments from Richard Hughes—the assignments would be for different kinds of stories—and try to bat ideas around with each other, spinning out the time while they tested out their "gimmicks" or their story lines on themselves and on their typewriters. But Pat would come in and start typing—"Just like a machine," says Gerald Albert, and he said it several times—the moment she arrived at the office. And she wouldn't quit until it was time to leave. "As a producer of comics, she was a huge producer. And she was constantly producing stuff that was useful."[14]

Pat stayed with the Sangor-Pines comics shop as a full-time writer for "a year." And then she spent the next six years and more as a freelance comic book scriptwriter, sending back material from wherever she was in the world. And wherever she was and whatever else she was writing, Pat was also, as a rule, working on something for the comics. In June of 1949, resentfully crammed into the tourist class of an ocean liner on her first trip to Europe, Pat wrote scripts for Timely comics all the way across the Atlantic.[15] Coming back from that same trip in October of 1949, this time in steerage on a freighter where only Italian was spoken, Pat, writing hard on *The Argument of Tantalus* (the manuscript title for *The Price of Salt*), was also typing away on comics material for the Fawcett company.[16]

In Italy, in Mexico, in the South of France, in Germany, on trains and slow boats, Pat did the comics fillers, the scenarios, and the odd text story. The long lead time between the writing and the publication of most comic books made scripting for the comics a good job for a restless traveller like Pat Highsmith. She could write her scripts and scenarios and submit them in advance because the Superhero stories she was writing—the ones that had their own titles—were quarterlies, published only four times a year. *America's Best Comics* anthologized many of the stories Pat wrote, and it, too, was a quarterly until 1947.[17] Pat worked on a variety of titles and stories for different companies, and she wrote in all the comics genres: "silly animal" comics, historical comics, "indeterminate comics material," and romance comics (like *Betty the Nurse*)—which she predictably loathed. But the preponderance of stories she wrote were stories for Superheroes. Superheroes with Alter Egos.

During the year Pat worked at Sangor-Pines, the shop's most prominent Superheroes were Black Terror and Fighting Yank. But because the Golden Age of American Comics was shining most brightly for young men, Gerry Albert, sitting two desks away from Pat at Sangor-Pines, had no idea that Pat had been given Superhero stories to work on. The few women who found their way into the comics shops of the 1940s (most of them were artists)[18] were usually assigned the kind of ancillary material Pat also wrote: the "indeterminate comics material," the "romance" comics, and the "silly animal" comics. "Silly animals," imported from stop-motion movie cartoons, had three fingers, prominent ears, and the kind of dialogue writers hated to even think about.

Perhaps with her love of reversing things, Pat's work on "silly animal comics" was a prompt for the vengeful, homicidal pets she created for her collection of short stories, *The Animal-Lover's Book of Beastly Murder*—but her real concentration at Sangor-Pines was on Superheroes. (And while she was there, she worked for other comics companies on Superhero titles like *Spy Smasher, Ghost, The Champion,* etc.) Always aiming for "the best," Pat pressed editors all over town for these assignments. Writing for Superheroes, even sublunary ones like the Black Terror, was about as good as you could get in the comics.

The burgeoning comic book industry into which Pat Highsmith stumbled in 1942 was introduced into the United States by the same small crimes she liked to use to start her plots and feed her imagination: plagiarism and forgery. The prototype for the first "modern" comic book, *The Adventures of Mr. Obadiah Oldbuck,* appeared as an illustrated supplement in a New York newspaper in 1842, pirated (some publishing practices never change) from an illustrated book in Switzerland: *L'Histoire de M. Vieux Bois,* by the nineteenth-century Genevan cartoonist Rodolph Töppfer. Töppfer's book was republished in the twentieth century in Zurich by Daniel Keel, cofounder of the Swiss publishing company Diogenes Verlag. Diogenes Verlag became Pat's world representative and primary publisher; Daniel Keel is her literary executor.

In short—and with the kind of coincidence that marked her work—comic books began their artistic life in the same country in which Pat Highsmith ended hers: Switzerland. And Rodolph Töppfer, the progenitor of the comic book, and Patricia Highsmith, the comics' most secretive scriptwriter, were both published by the same Swiss company, Diogenes Verlag.

The fantastic trail cut by early comics publishing through "yellow journalism," "pulp" fiction, and "soft" pornography—as well as its creative intersection with the diaspora of Eastern European Jews (who did much of the publishing, editing, writing, and artwork of early comics) and with gangster-boss Frank Costello's Canadian bootlegging business and pioneering feminist Margaret Sanger's illegal mail-order contraception company—is outside the scope of this book. Perhaps it's enough to know that Margaret Sanger's "Dainty Maid" douche bags travelled in the same delivery trucks as Costello's bootleg liquor—and that these same trucks were also carrying the pulp publications of Harry Donenfeld's Eastern News/Eastern Color, the parent company for the hundreds of Timely comics Pat would later write—to get a sense of just how appropriate the milieu of comics was for the already criminally inclined imagination of young Miss Highsmith.*[19]

By 1939, garishly illustrated comic books were appearing on metal magazine racks, wire lines, and serried wooden shelves in every candy store, newsstand, and corner drugstore in the United States. Bound in wraparound covers and stapled in two places, the little magazines rarely varied in cost or style: ten cents was the cover price, and the format was a sixty-four-page, eight-by-ten-inch magazine—just the right size to fit inside a high school history textbook. The wood-grain paper on which comics were printed was so crudely pulped ("pulp" novels were printed on the same paper and took their name from it) that readers could almost count the tree rings and smell the chainsaw oil.

Gertrude Stein, already a fan of the American newspaper comic strips *Krazy Kat* (Surrealism by another name) and *The Katzenjammer Kids* (an American rip-off of the naughtiest comic strip boys in Germany, *Max und Moritz*), had the strips mailed to her in Paris and then passed them along to her equally enchanted friend, Pablo Picasso. In 1934–35, on her first visit to the United

---

* Not to mention the fact that the comics publishers Pat worked for were also producing pulp novels and magazines with fetching titles like *Spicy Detective Stories, Ranch Romances, Hot Tales,* and (the flirting-with-frontal-nudity) *Pep Stories.*

States in three decades, Stein, beguiled by the look of comic books, called them in her best faux-naïf manner "square books" and said they showed how Americans can "do the best designing and use the best material in the cheapest thing."[20]

At its height, to which it was just beginning to rise when Pat walked into the Sangor-Pines comics shop in December of 1942, the comics industry was the largest publication business in the United States. In 1941, thirty comic book publishers were producing 150 different titles monthly, with sales of fifteen million copies and an estimated readership of sixty million Americans.[21] During the early war years, comics, along with cigarettes and candy bars, were sent by the tankerful to Allied forces overseas.[22] At the end of the 1940s there were close to forty comics publishers in business, selling 300 titles and fifty million comics a month.[23] And by 1953, just as the Golden Age of American Comics was about to turn to brass, one in every three publications bought and sold in the United States was a comic book.[24]

The first comic books were pasted together from comic strips in newspapers, and comics continued as they began. The stories retained the panel form—like frames in a strip of film—which were then ballooned out by letterers with the (mostly) rudimentary dialogue supplied by the writers. U.S. Post Office regulations required that two pages of "text stories" (stories in prose without illustration) had to be squeezed in amongst the illustrated tales in order to qualify the comics for a mass-mailing rate. All writers for the comics, including Pat Highsmith, had to write pseudonymous text stories, and their scenarios for regular comic book stories went mostly uncredited as well. Text stories were printed under "house" pseudonyms: "Sam Brant," "Charles Stoddard," "Tex Mumford," and "Allen Douglass" are amongst them.[25]

Unusually, one of the text stories Pat wrote for the comics was apparently published under her own name. The story is supposed to have appeared in a Standard comic book of the 1940s, and a copy of it is said to still be in existence. Given Pat's perennial Christmas sentiments ("Christmas itself is positively the erupting boil of human guilt")[26] and her lifelong refusal to acknowledge the extent of her comic book work, the way in which her sole signed creation for the comics has been filed could hardly be more fitting. The Standard comic containing this signed Highsmith text story is buried in a warehouse in North Carolina under twenty thousand other uncatalogued comics and one withered pine: a long-dead Christmas tree belonging to the collector of the only comic book in which the name "Patricia Highsmith" was ever printed.[27,28]

Late in life Pat told interviewers, if she told them anything at all, that she'd spent a few months after she got out of college writing comic book stories for characters "like Superman or Batman." In the hierarchy of Superheroes,

Superman was the first *and* the best; the model for the hundreds that followed. Black Terror, however, the character Pat was really writing for, epitomized her worst fear: Black Terror was a very second-rate Superhero.

Only his boy sidekick, Tim Roland, knew that the real name and true identity of the Black Terror, two-fisted nemesis of "Our Fascist Enemies," was Bob Benton, "mild-mannered" neighborhood pharmacist. And only his creator, Pat's meticulous editor at the Sangor-Pines comics shop, Richard E. Hughes (*his* real name was Leo Rosenbaum), understood just how closely Bob Benton and his Alter Ego, the Black Terror, were modeled on the comic book characters of Clark Kent and Superman.[29]

Superman was the creation of two seventeen-year-old carriers of the Zeitgeist from Cleveland, Ohio, Jerry Siegel and Joe Shuster; both of them were children of Jewish emigrants from Eastern Europe. In 1938, six years after they first imagined him, the dogged young duo finally published a story about Superman in a DC comic book. The starkly illustrated myth of the superpowered orphan from another galaxy, the kindly farm family who adopted him, and his mild-mannered second self, Clark Kent, the human shield for Superman's secret identity, quickly inflamed the imaginations of America's children—as well as the business instincts of some of New York's more disreputable publishers.*

"After Superman," says Stan Lee, godfather of the Superhero Spider-Man and the figure from the Golden Age of American Comics most closely associated with Pat's favorite employer, Timely comics (now the world-renowned Marvel Comics), "if artists wanted to be successful, they thought, 'I guess we better give our characters costumes and double identities.'"[30] And if those artists and writers had "ethnic" names, they usually provided themselves with the same cover story they gave to their characters: another identity cloaked by an anglicized surname. (Stan Lee's real name: Stanley Martin Lieber.) In the world of American comics of the 1940s, imitation was the most commercial form of flattery.

Bob Benton/Black Terror was one of a long line of Clark Kent/Superman imitations. Like all copies, he suffers from a deteriorated image; his story is less sharply focused than Superman's. He follows the common Superhero

---

* The story of how Jerry Siegel and Joe Shuster's "Superman" was sold out from under them (for $130) in a transaction almost as pitiful as the deal local Indians made when they traded the island of Manhattan for a fistful of beads and a few dollars—and the subsequent tale of how Siegel and Shuster's Clark Kent/Superman was copied in some form or other by every comics shop in New York—is one of the founding fables in the short, violent, utterly absorbing history of the Golden Age of American Comics.

formula of costume (tights, a cape, an insignia), a series of evil opponents to vanquish, and a boy sidekick to help with the fights. In 1954, in a book called *Seduction of the Innocent,* the well-meaning, socially concerned, progressive psychiatrist Dr. Frederic Wertham*—subsequently much vilified by comic book fans—had a fine time exposing just what another successful Superhero, Batman, was *really* getting up to with his boy sidekick Robin (homosexual relations)—and cataloguing the dangers (violence, racism, and sexism) he thought comic books posed to the psyches of America's children. Black Terror's own special superpower—the result of his Alter Ego's life-changing laboratory accident—is his bullet-repelling superskin. But Black Terror's birth in a pharmacist's lab could never compare to the glorious emigrant myth propelling Superman: an intergalactic journey to Kansas in a transparent capsule launched by his doomed parents from their dying planet Krypton.

Still, as the splash page of a wartime *Black Terror* comic tells us, Black Terror could always be counted upon to fight for his country: he went wherever the "Axis octopus rears its deadly head." Some of the Superheroes who preceded Black Terror did more than that. They went to war against Hitler long before the United States joined the battle—and for the most obvious reason: American Jews were writing and drawing them.†

Like Pat, her mostly youthful confrères in the comics business were underdogs yearning to be top dogs. Like Pat, they had all been schooled in the American Dream. But unlike Pat, many of them had been locked out of the "quality" ends of their chosen professions—for them, it was commercial illustration and advertising—because of ethnic prejudice. Most of Pat's cohorts in the comics, said Al Jaffee, cartoonist and editor at Timely comics, would have "drifted into the comic-book business [because] most of the comic-book publishers were Jewish." Will Eisner, cofounder of the world famous Eisner-Iger comics shop and inspired creator of *The Spirit,* precurser of the graphic novel, agreed: "[T]his business was brand new. It was the bottom of the social ladder. [Those who wanted to get] into the field of illustration found it very easy to come aboard."[31]

---

* Frederic Wertham was the consulting pyschiatrist for Zelda Sayre Fitzgerald at the Phipps Clinic in Baltimore during her incarceration there. He was one of the first psychiatrists to use art therapy for diagnosis and encouraged Zelda in her painting. In gratitude, she gave him eleven watercolors.
† In 1940, nearly two years before the United States entered the war, Superman hauled Hitler and Stalin before a World Court in a DC comic. In February of that same year, Timely comics' Superhero Sub-Mariner tackled Nazi submarines. And in March of 1941, nine months before Pearl Harbor, the most successful Superhero at Timely, Joe Simon and Jack Kirby's Captain America, made his début on a sensational comic book cover by Jack Kirby (real name: Jacob Kurtzberg) on which Captain America knocked Hitler out of the frame with a well-placed punch to the jaw.

Most of these young comics artists and writers were steeped in popular culture: detective magazines, science fiction magazines, fantasy and horror magazines, and crème de la hard-boiled crime fiction magazines like *Black Mask.**
And many of the stories in the magazines they were reading had been infused
by their authors' admiration for the same writers who had illuminated Pat's
youth: Fyodor Dostoyevsky, Friedrich Nietzsche, Søren Kierkegaard, Edgar Allan Poe, Franz Kafka, et al. This dilution of high culture slowly trickled down
into the rough, rich mix that was the American comic book in the 1940s, helping to shape its stories and its artwork, however crudely and simplistically. (Pat
once described her comics work as being like "writing two 'B movies' a day.")[32]
Dostoyevsky and Kafka, Nietzsche and Poe, Rider Haggard and H. G. Wells,
hard-boiled crime fiction, science fiction, pulp romance, and German Expressionist film—anything vividly adrift in the Zeitgeist was vacuumed up and
made use of by the four-color, six-panel world of the comic book.

And there was another crucial source comic book creators were drawing
on: their own ethnic and religious histories. Siegel and Shuster's "Krypton"
names for Superman and his father, Kal-El and Jor-El, are both derived from
the Hebrew nomenclature for "God." And the story of Moses, the Jewish hero
who led his people out of Egypt, and the legend of the sixteenth-century
Golem—the giant, incomplete, servant-being created from the clay of the
Vltava River by the chief rabbi of Prague to protect his community from anti-
Semitic attacks—took on special significance in an era when the very survival
of European Jewry was being threatened. The Golem, especially, had all the
attributes of a Superhero except one: he was a little lacking in initiative.

"You shall obey my commands," [said Rabbi Judah Loew to the Golem,]
"and do all that I may require of you, go through fire, jump into water or
throw yourself down from a high tower."[33]

Will Eisner thought the "Golem was very much the precursor of the

---

* A word about *Black Mask*. *Black Mask* magazine was founded in 1920 by the prominent
critics H. L. Mencken and George Jean Nathan to generate money for their upscale publication, *Smart Set*. *Black Mask* published "hard-boiled" fictions by mostly contemporary writers, many of whom were much better known than Pat, and most of whom went on to
publish with *Ellery Queen's Mystery Magazine* when *Black Mask* was folded into it. (Pat's story
"The Perfect Alibi" appeared in the March 1957 issue of *EQMM* along with stories by Alberto
Moravia and Agatha Christie.) Although *EQMM* was the most consistent publisher of Pat's
short fiction for decades, in later life she didn't care to emphasize her "pulp" connection,
even as a link to other authors. In 1950, Raymond Chandler, who published his first story in
Black Mask, had a terrible time trying to make a film script from *Strangers on a Train* for Alfred Hitchcock. In 1977, in the introduction she wrote to a book about Chandler, "A Galahad in L.A.," Pat deliberately ignored her *EQMM* "pulp" connection to Chandler,
mentioning *Black Mask* only to say that it "paid a penny a word," and alluding only to her
more "respectable" film connection with him.

super-hero" because the Jews "needed someone who could protect us. . . . against an almost invincible force. So [Siegel and Shuster] created an invincible hero."[34] Cartoonist Jules Feiffer, invoking the Eastern European emigrant background of Siegel and Shuster, provided the wittiest variation on Eisner's comment: "It wasn't Krypton that Superman really came from, it was the planet Minsk."[35]

When Pat gave her "criminal-hero" Tom Ripley a charmed and parentless life, a wealthy, socially poised Alter Ego (Dickie Greenleaf), and a guilt-free modus operandi (after he kills Dickie, Tom murders only when necessary), she was doing just what her fellow comic book artists were doing with their Superheroes: allowing her fictional character to finesse situations she herself could only approach in wish fulfillment. And when she reimagined her own psychological split in Ripley's character—endowing him with both her weakest traits (paralyzing self-consciousness and hero-worship) and her wildest dreams (murder and money)—she was turning the material of the "comic book" upside down and making it into something very like a "tragic book."[36] "It is always so easy for me to see the world upside down," Pat wrote in her diary—and everywhere else.[37]

In October of 1954, working on *The Talented Mr. Ripley* and thrilling to the idea of corrupting her readers, Pat said plainly what she was doing.

"What I predicted I would once do, I am doing already in this very book (Tom Ripley), that is, showing the unequivocal triumph of evil over good, and rejoicing in it. I shall make my readers rejoice in it, too."[38]

And then, just as plainly, Pat said *why* she was doing it, giving an account that sounds like Will Eisner's explanation of how people who are trapped by "invincible forces" might feel compelled to escape into "invincible" Alter Egos.

"The *main* reason I write is quite clear to me. My own life, however interesting I try to make it by traveling and so forth, is always boring to me, periodically. Whenever I become intolerably bored, I produce another story, in my head. My story can move fast, as I can't, it can have a reasonable and perhaps perfect solution, as mine can't. A solution that is somehow satisfying, as my personal solution never can be.

"It is not an infatuation with words. It is absolute day dreaming, for day dreaming's sake."[39]

Certainly, the suggestion that any of her novels could have shared a creative inspiration with comic books would have driven the talented Miss H into conniption fits. And the tenor of her response to the hint that Thomas P. Ripley, her boyish (and goyische) "hero-criminal," might owe even a fraction of his identity to the Golem of Prague, the Moses who led the Jews through the desert, or the Superman imagined by two Bar Mitzvah boys from Cleveland, Ohio, is only too easy to imagine.*

But *Crime and Punishment* and *The Ambassadors* were not the only fictions working away in Pat's imagination while she was making up *Strangers on a Train, The Talented Mr. Ripley,* et al. Hundreds, probably thousands of comic book scenarios dramatizing the escape from one identity to another—and the uncomfortably yoked lives of Alter Egos—had already passed through her mind, coloring it, in Emily Brontë's luminous phrase, "like wine through water." The inspiration that made a "hero" of a conscienceless killer like Tom Ripley in 1955, and Alter Egos of the high-minded architect and the sodden, psychopathic spawn of a rich man in *Strangers on a Train* in 1950, was one of the distinguishing marks of Pat's imagination. But that imagination had not only been infused by Dostoyevsky and Poe, Proust and James and André Gide; it had also been marinating for seven long years in the colorful tropes of the American comic book.[40]

Pat Highsmith got her culture "high" and—complaining about working for the comics almost as much as she complained about loving women—she also got her culture "low."

Pat's late nights in the early 1940s (see "Social Studies, Part 1") affected her concentration so seriously that six months after she was hired at Sangor-Pines, Richard Hughes called her on the carpet and taxed her with a lack of "enthusiasm" and "precision" in her comics work. (Pat was writing stories for *Spy Smasher* and *Ghost* comics and hating them both.) Alas, it's true, Pat thought; I'm "hopelessly bored."[41]

So, from her typewriter table in the Sangor-Pines office and, in the evenings, from her desk on East Fifty-sixth Street, Pat, who usually managed not to understand just how subversive her work really was, went right on sending drawings, stories, and even cartoons to *The New Yorker* magazine, which went right on rejecting them.

"The New Yorker, alas, does not like my alcoholic story. 'Too unpleasant a subject—two people who become alcoholics,' says Mrs. Richardson Wood. And that it doesn't move. The N[ew] Y[orker], I thought, made a science of stories that don't move."[42]

The world of quality publishing was Pat's longed-for escape from comics

---

* The American painter Edward Hopper, who shared Pat's fascination with architecture and alienation, labored for fourteen years as an advertising illustrator. His advertising work influenced his American subjects in much the same way that working for the comics—and sourcing her fictional crimes from newspaper articles—colored Pat's.

writing. She would have been vaguely surprised to learn that the Superheroes whose adventures she was pounding out on her typewriter—Whizzer, Pyroman, the Human Torch, the Destroyer, Captain Midnight, Black Terror, Flying Yank, Spy Smasher, Ghost, the Champion—and the war heroes and adventurers she was also writing for—Jap Buster Johnson, Sergeant Bill King, Golden Arrow[43]—were all seeking similar (and similarly illusory) escapes themselves, as they changed their clothes or apostrophized their Alter Egos in order to flee their confining circumstances. (Pat's psychology had always included the refinement of keeping things from itself.) Later, she would offer the same escape to most of her fictional psychopaths, locked up in the double-doored, no-exit cells of their obsessions. That escape, too, was an illusion, but it would borrow more than a little from her "hack writing" about men in tights—and in tight spots.

Many of the comics plots Pat was writing concentrated on men of action who were either chasing or fleeing some aspect of what might be thought of as themselves. They could fly like birds, outrun a speeding train, slither up a skyscraper, change costumes in the blink of an eye, shoot straight, ride fast, or in a pinch drive like hell. Pat would say many times that the reason men and not women were the "heroes" of most of her novels was because men had the capacity for "action." Men, she said, can "do things. . . . men can leave the house."[44] In fact, in the Coates family, it was Pat's grandmother who "did things" by keeping the family boardinghouse together, and it was Pat's mother who left the Plangman "house" and marriage and went on to earn most of the money for the Highsmith establishments as well. But logic was never Pat's strong point.

Always excepting the two female lovers in *The Price of Salt* and Edith Howland of *Edith's Diary,* most of Pat's women characters are as close to comic book caricatures as a serious novelist can write them. They are vengeful bitches like Nickie in *The Cry of the Owl*; instinctual sluts like Melinda in *Deep Water*; blank innocents like Annabelle in *This Sweet Sickness*; nagging wives like Clara in *The Blunderer*; fantasy figures like Elsie in *Found in the Street*; or passive dilettantes like Alicia in *A Suspension of Mercy*. Pat had no problem (except boredom) with the subordinate roles she and her cohorts were creating for the women characters in their comic book stories. Her usual line on the Second Sex was: "It's hard for me to see women (as a whole) standing on their own feet. I still see them as sort of in relationship to a man."[45] Except in the first blush of love, Pat never could imagine a woman with super-powers.

Male characters were a different matter. In the comics Pat was writing for, it was the male Superheroes who are natural-born escape artists. They live in a world of perpetual threat. They spend their time escaping external danger (sometimes their Evil Twins want to kill them; sometimes a Super Criminal is the adversary), eluding the exposure of their feebler Alter Egos, and brooding handsomely in their palaces of secret repose: their Batcaves and their Fortresses of Solitude. Superheroes—in a phrase Pat Highsmith once slipped into a radio interview about the character she called her favorite "hero-criminal," Tom Ripley—"will always get away with it; [they'll] always be age thirty-four, one foot in the grave."[46]

Ripley is Pat's most developed escape artist. In *The Talented Mr. Ripley* he is in perpetual flight from his enfeebled, giggling, sexually incoherent, impoverished Alter Ego (see "Les Girls: Part 5"). Still, he manages to pull off the escape that every comic book Alter Ego dreams of: the artful dodge of never having to settle into a single self. Orphaned like Superman and Batman, provided with his own Fortress of Solitude (Belle Ombre), Ripley becomes more successful (and less interesting) with each new Ripley novel: a character who rarely questions himself, he can fly anywhere in the world at a moment's notice, assume any disguise or age or gender, and subsist on very little sleep. His courage fails him only once: he turns "green" with terror at his own wedding.

Certainly, the artistic use of escape had occurred to Pat long before she went to work as a comic book writer. Escape from a fixed identity was not only the theme of every novel that attracted her, it was her own favorite operating principle. (The first thing she always thought of when she fell in love was . . . leaving town.) Escape as a controlling idea turned up early on in her college short story "The Legend of the Convent of St. Fotheringay"; but it was her much grimmer effort, a story called "Uncertain Treasure," that set the two-man pattern of paranoid pursuit and ambiguous escape which would come to define Highsmith Country.

"Uncertain Treasure" first appeared in print in August of 1943, eight months after Pat started working in the writers' bullpen at Sangor-Pines. The magazine which printed it was a wartime Greenwich Village journal with the uninspiring title of *Home and Food.*[47] (It was later published in another small journal called *The Writer.*) "Uncertain Treasure" was the first fiction Pat would publish outside her high school and college journals, the *Bluebird* and the *Barnard Quarterly,* and her diaries and cahiers show that it was formed, contoured, and colored by her work for the comics.

Home and Food published "Uncertain Treasure" alongside such unpromisingly titled articles as "Dehydration," "Rummage and Sew," "Shoe String Suppers," and "Canning." These were the war years, the national belt was being tightened, and canning, the dehydration of food for preservation, and cheap suppers—suppers on a shoestring—were subjects of real interest. Pat had started to write "Uncertain Treasure" while she was still working for Ben-Zion Goldberg at FFF Publications. One of the employees in Goldberg's office was a cripple, his lurching gait caught Pat's attention, and she built it into the beginning of a story she was calling "Mountain Treasure." But when Pat went to work at Sangor-Pines, she reimagined the story over a period of several months, then finished and published it as "Uncertain Treasure." And because she liked her Sangor-Pines editor Richard Hughes so much, she showed him the story and took his criticism on it.[48]

Richard Hughes's own scripts for the comics have been described as exposing "the Faustian bargain" that lurked "behind the calm façade of the normal American home."[49] Hughes, like Ben-Zion Goldberg before him, was the right reader at the right time for Patricia Highsmith.

The "cripple" of "Uncertain Treasure," Archie, is reading a "*Daily News* comic strip" when he notices the "treasure" of the title, an abandoned "khaki utility bag," on a subway platform. A "smaller man" (he has no other designation) dressed in the crude, bold colors used by comic book illustrators begins to circle the "treasure," making sounds with his shoes like the onomatopoetic sounds Pat read every day in the page mock-ups for her scripts at Sangor-Pines: *"thock-thock."* Archie, afflicted with a speech impediment, a slow mind, and a missing ear (his ear has been replaced with a vivid, visual image: "a daub of white flesh like the opening of a balloon which is tied with a string") makes the first move: he grabs the bag from the subway platform.

The smaller man takes the bag back from Archie: "Thief! . . . Dope!" he says. The dialect Pat used is as simple, as tone-deaf, and as classically paranoid as the dialogue she was writing for the comics. "Wh-what the hell am I doin' bein' chased by a nut. . . . Suppose he don't leave me alone all night! Suppose he don't never leave me alone!"

Everything in the landscape of "Uncertain Treasure" is aggressively visual and garishly colorful. Pat daubed the details in as though she were holding a loaded paintbrush. Her previous fictions had been mostly imagined in black and white; and when they were not, the introduction of color usually meant trouble—as in the class distinctions insinuated into her short story "Primroses Are Pink" by an argument over the color of a painting.*[50]

But "Uncertain Treasure" is not burdened by the subtleties of psychology or the shadings of color charts. It is a purely paranoid pursuit dressed up in primary

---

* "Primroses Are Pink" (it exists in a longer, loopier manuscript copy) dramatizes the fatal instability introduced into a marriage when a husband brings home a monochrome painting of a jockey, sends it away to have the jockey's silks properly colored, and then has a disturbing disagreement with his wife about just what color "primrose" actually is: is it American "primrose pink" or the more properly English "primrose yellow"? (The calibrations of class implied in this story were always on Pat's mind anyway—and yellow was her favorite color.)

colors. Archie follows the smaller man through a noirishly depicted Greenwich Village like "the inescapable, machinelike figure of a nightmare . . . after him, now, not the bag, driven by a crazy desire for revenge." Archie repossesses the bag (the smaller man drops it in terror) and takes it back to his "cube of a room, furnished with a bed that sagged like a hammock" whose walls are covered by "tiny notations, so closely and equidistantly written as to make almost a pattern."

This "cube" is the first of Highsmith's fictional fortresses: the prototype for Guy Haines's solitary rented room in *Strangers on a Train* (where he dreams of Charles Bruno performing superheroic feats); for Tom Ripley's fortress-home Belle Ombre, anxiously patrolled by Ripley; for William Neumeister/David Kelsey's fantasy house in the woods in *This Sweet Sickness;* and for Vic Van Allen's garage-bunker in *Deep Water* with its copulating snails and blood-gorged bedbugs. Archie is the first of Pat's reclusive males to be caught up in the kind of pursuit she would later deploy to such haunting effect in *Strangers on a Train.*

When Archie opens the bag, he finds only a riot of comic book colors: "many columns of glossy blue and gold paper and red and yellow and green and gray and mauve and white papers." They conceal nothing but "penny chocolates and chewing gums" and two dollars in change. The treasure turns out to be valueless; it was the *pursuit* that mattered.

Perhaps it was the profusion of colored candy at the end of this laborious little tale that got it published in a magazine with the word "Food" in its title—although a recommendation by Rolf Tietgens, Pat's new friend and *Home and Food*'s art editor, helped it along. "Uncertain Treasure" has the flatness that is characteristic of much of Highsmith's work—early and late, good and bad. She gives equal treatment to every object in her field of vision, and her overviews are as uninflected as a depression—are, quite likely, the *result* of a depression. As early as 1940 Pat was noting that one of the several Virginias in her life "tells me I don't know when to stop when I write—or what to leave out."[51] In Highsmith Country, everything generally weighs the same, has the same value, and carries the same charge of life—or lack of life. The landscape and characters of "Uncertain Treasure" are no exception.

However it found its way to publication, "Uncertain Treasure"'s criminal intentions and duplicating pursuits, its thick visual impasto and riot of primary colors, were already part of the atmosphere of the Sangor-Pines comics shop. The story reads like both the scenario *and* the brightly colored panels for a comic book—and the Sangor-Pines office, with its "posters of Black Terror on the walls and various characters who could fly in the air,"[52] wouldn't exactly have been unknown territory to the girl writer looking for a paying job in December of 1942. Alive with the idea of male Superheroes and their Alter Egos, staffed by artists and writers barred from the "quality" professions and shielded by their anglicized aliases, the Sangor-Pines office was much closer to the double nature of Pat's own imagination than any of the other professional *milieux* she was trying so hard to enter.

Six days after Richard Hughes hired her at Sangor-Pines, Pat began to expand the character studies she'd started a month and half earlier for *The Click of the Shutting*, her first long fiction: a novel about an artistic, dependent teenage boy, prone to feelings of inferiority and crushes on other boys, who insinuates himself into the household of a rich and spoiled young man.[53] A prototype for Tom Ripley, Gregory was Pat's first foray into the extended imagining of the lives of Alter Egos (she wrote 385 pages before she gave the novel up as half finished). Just as she had with "Uncertain Treasure," she worked on the book while she was writing the adventures of her other Alter Egos; the kind who wore tights and capes at night and square-rimmed glasses and sober suits during the day. (See "Alter Ego: Part 4.")

Pat's first month at Sangor-Pines—the end of December 1942 to January 1943—was spent in writing factual tales: biographical scenarios for true-life comics. Her initial writing assignment from Richard Hughes must have felt like an extension of her work for Ben-Zion Goldberg and the Jewish press; she was asked to research and write a script for *Real Life Comics* about Barney Ross, the Jewish welterweight boxing champion, war hero, and ardent advocate for the Zionist state.[54]

Her second script for *Real Life Comics* was a "Catherine the Great" story.[55] Influenced by her reading of the Russian masters in Constance Garnett's heroically anglicized translations, Pat's dialogue for Catherine's Court belongs more to the Court of St. James's than the palaces of St. Petersburg.[56] Although she gave the Empress Catherine diary-keeping habits like her own and played up her personal bravery, Pat was more at home with the male war hero who was her next assignment: "Hughes made an historical outline of [Eddie] Rickenbacker [the World War I flying ace]—a brilliant outline that I follow now," she wrote in her diary."[57]

As ambitious as she was persevering, Pat was always proposing new ideas for comic book stories, ideas which were sometimes too wayward even for the comics. Her proposal for the life story of the Confederate guerrilla-turned-outlaw Jesse James (a "criminal-hero" from the devastating War Between the States) was too "controversial" for true-life comics. At least that's what the *Real Life Comics* editor said when he rejected her Jesse James scenario.[58] Another of her proposals was too naïve. In May of 1946, she wanted to do something with a Joseph Conrad novel for Sangor-Pines. Richard Hughes's cynical assistant, who was "sure our happy intellects would not be interested in"—he quotes Pat here—"'Conrad's simplicity and unfailing honesty in his writing,'" wrote back to Pat in the spirit of her future novels: "I can't imagine anything more difficult to dramatize. After all, honesty belongs among the negative virtues."[59]

And when Pat, walking up Lexington Avenue and always on the lookout for work, ran into Jack Schiff, the editor of DC comics (known as the "Tiffany" of comic book publishers because it published *Superman*) and "gives him some ideas" for comics stories—those ideas, while they apparently got her hired at DC (DC almost never hired women), didn't get her hired for long.[60] Bob Oksner remembered that Pat, typing away in the bullpen at Sangor-Pines ("she wouldn't let anyone get too close," Oksner said, echoing everyone else), was also doing some work for DC.[61] But Pat usually kept quiet about her attempts to rustle up work at other companies while she was writing for Sangor-Pines—just as she kept quiet about nearly everything that had to do with the comics.

Still, everyone at Sangor-Pines knew that Pat "went home and did serious writing at night,"[62] that she was leading a double life. After a long day typing up Superheroes at the office, she would return to her studio apartment at 353 East Fifty-sixth Street, run herself through a wall of water (either a long bath or a short shower), take a restorative nap, and emerge cleansed, rested, and transformed into her Alter Ego: *Patricia Highsmith: Girl Writer Working on the Great American Novel.* Pat's life during this time might have made an absorbing comic book itself—but it would have been a comic book suitable for reading by adults only. (See "Social Studies: Part 1.")

Always essentially divided, Pat's mind adapted itself easily to her two writing identities. Water would regularly be a transforming and absolving element in her life, and she used her showers and her naps to separate her daylight psychology (the daytime comic book writer) from her nighttime self (the nocturnal author of potentially great books). She knew that her more creative Alter Ego—that part of the double identity she shared with the Superheroes she was writing for—functioned best in the nighttime hours.

"One other major reason for my preferring to write at night (apart from the obvious one of increased quietude & privacy) is that when I am mildly tired the censor and the constraining factors of sharp consciousness, self doubt and criticism are not functioning well."[63]

By 1948, Pat was acknowledging serious separations between "the person I am at night" and "the person I am by day:

Already the great dichotomy between the person I am at night, the person I am by day, even doing my own writing. The nocturnal person is far advanced in thought and imagination. The daytime person still lives and works too much with the world which is not mine. I must get them together and toward the night.[64]

Night and shadow were natural habitats for Pat, just as secrecy and shame were the default postures of her psychology. Even her attraction to nonhuman creatures was an attraction to creatures of the night (cats and owls) and to creatures who carried their coffins on their backs (snails). In 1990, indulging her passion for Broadway musicals, she would listen over and over again to Andrew Lloyd Webber's music from *Phantom of the Opera,* writing in her diary that she was "spellbound" by it.[65] *Phantom*'s signature song, "Music of the Night," sets out in easy images everything Pat thought the night could do for her:

Nighttime sharpens, heightens each sensation
Darkness stirs and wakes imagination.

Pat's friend Kingsley Skattebol recalls that Pat "was very much at home, she was her best self, in shadowy places. She loved going into dingy beer parlours where she could sit and talk and be herself (whatever that was) in the dark."[66]

Pat's night and day identities—each one rooted in opposition—only began to branch into each other later in her writing life. It was when the boundaries between her "day self" and her "night self" were finally breached that her imaginative life started to break down, muting the resonant echoes and flattening the intense flights and drops which, early on, had issued so fluidly from her creatively doubled identities. The slow erosion of her natural psychological partitions may be one of the reasons her later novels (*The Two Faces of January, People Who Knock on the Door, A Suspension of Mercy, Ripley Under Water,* and *Small g*) and some of her themed collections of short stories (*Little Tales of Misogyny, The Animal-Lover's Book of Beastly Murder, Mermaids on the Golf Course*) are more like awkwardly imagined cartoons—or like the cruder comic book plots she was writing in the 1940s—than like the delicate, deeply nuanced renderings of disruption at the heart of her earlier works of fiction.

Kingsley thinks Pat "mortally wounded herself working for the comics. Her style was never the same afterwards."[67] Kingsley is partly right: Pat's work *wasn't* the same after the comics, but it was the *form* of the work that changed, not the style. While the author of "The Heroine" (1940) appears to be a far more sophisticated writer than the comics-influenced creator of "Uncertain Treasure" (1943), it was with this crude little story that Pat ventured into something like her major theme; working and reworking it for much of the rest of her writing life. Pat was a writer who could rarely distinguish what was good or bad about her own work, but who always seemed to find the conditions she needed in order to produce it. And in the 1940s, Pat Highsmith found much of what she needed working for the comics.

Pat must have mentioned her "serious writing" at the Sangor-Pines office, because it is Gerald Albert, sitting two desks away from her, who says that "everyone" there knew about it—although Pat rarely directed a word about anything to anyone at Sangor-Pines, even to the person sitting next to her. Pat was always too busy typing to talk, too busy churning out the material. Typing was money.

A year before she got the job with the Sangor shop, Pat wrote in her diary: "God damn it to hell I want money and that's all I want."[68] Money was the repeated reason she gave herself for continuing to write for the comics—and money was always a deadly serious, not to mention an obsessive, subject for Patricia Highsmith. (By August of 1943, Pat, after asking Richard Hughes for another raise, was earning more money than her stepfather, Stanley: fifty dollars a week.)[69] But the things Pat told herself she was doing and the reasons she gave herself for doing them didn't always match. On her own evidence, money was not the only motive that kept Pat Highsmith working for Sangor-Pines.

When she'd been writing at Sangor-Pines for less than a month, Pat was already giving her editor, Richard Hughes, high marks as a boss. "He is a good writer, and he considers this work most seriously."[70] And she was saying to herself that writing for the comics "does me good, because it makes me write rapidly, with a lot of action, and even with a certain style of sincerity—this is necessary."[71]

The comics did much more than that for Pat, and it was a crucial part of her divided life that her seven-year apprenticeship in the four-color, six-panel-per-page world of the American comic book would be both a secret she kept for (and, in many respects, from) herself and one of her most important entrées into the eerie, alternate universe by which she was to make her reputation.

Of *course* Pat adored Dostoyevsky (but didn't really read him again after her twenties), of *course* she was attracted by the "perversions" of Gide and Proust and Julian Green,* by the analyses of Freud, and by the classifications

---

* But she hadn't read Julien Green's novel *Si j'étais vous,* which a previous biographer thinks is an influence on *The Talented Mr. Ripley.*

of Krafft-Ebing and Karl Menninger. But her cahiers and diaries show that it was only after she went to work at the Sangor-Pines comic shop that her fiction took its sharp turn into the territory of mutually pursuing Alter Egos and obsessed-and-opposed Criminal Others.*

Gerald Albert's impression of Pat as a nonstop worker in the Sangor-Pines shop was right on the money. Pat seems never to have allowed herself a moment's reflection when she was typing up her scripts. It exasperated her—words to that effect punctuate her diaries—to put more mental energy than she needed into what she regarded as strictly commercial work.[72] Like many of the young artists who wrote for this newly popular storytelling genre, Pat thought of the comics as trash, pulp trash, and her work as "hack" work. And it is true that many comic books were badly drawn, even barely drawn, and very crudely written.

Much of the comic book work in the 1940s was assembly-line work, piece-work, a lot like what went on in New York's garment industry. Each worker had his (it *was* mostly his) specialty: the inker, the penciller, the letterer, the colorist, the scriptwriter. And most of the writers, even well-regarded ones like Bill Finger (the writer who cocreated *Batman* and *The Green Lantern*), almost never got their names on the stories they wrote. Sometimes (as in the case of *Batman*'s other creator, the illustrator Bob Kane), even the name of the artist on the story wasn't the name of the artist who drew it: Kane (real name: Robert Kahn) hired artists like the gifted teenage Jerry Robinson to draw *Batman* for him.

In short, comic book work was a job done partially, quickly, anonymously and/or pseudonymously, and strictly for the money. Except, of course, when it wasn't. When it was at its best, it was a whole new art form whose stunningly original creators (Will Eisner, Steve Ditko, Jerry Siegel, Joe Shuster, Jack Kirby, Gil Kane [real name: Eli Katz], Bill Finger, Jerry Robinson, et al.) are revered today, and whose formal parameters are still being explored in graphic novels.

But in the 1940s, as Stan Lee said, comics "were the bottom of the cultural totem pole. . . . No one had any respect for a fella who wrote comic books." At parties, when people found out what Lee did for a living, they avoided him as though he were "infected."[73]

Many comic book illustrators and writers from the 1940s kept quiet about their profession (and still do), and Pat, for whom shame was practically a religious principle and secrecy a profession of the faith, was no exception. So

---

* With one of her discarded titles for *Strangers on a Train,* Pat gave a name to this territory. The name was *The Other* and she thought it "the best yet" for her book.

deep was her desire for silence on the subject that she kept no copies of the work she did for comic books.

A natural-born curator and self-recorder, Pat always collected the details of her life. No item, no artifact, was too small to escape her attention: even the matchbooks she took from bars and the maps she got from gas stations were added to her archives. (See "The Real Romance of Objects: Part 2.") She stashed away stationery and writing implements taken from the hotels she stayed in. She preserved every article written about her work in fourteen large press books. She appears to have kept every piece of paper on which she ever wrote or drew a line.

In an undated folder marked "Incomplete Old Stories," Pat filed a story called "The Last Unmaidenly Voyage of the S.S." on which she scribbled, with perfect justification, a critical phrase: "Shape this tripe up." She never got around to shaping up the "tripe," but she didn't consider throwing the story out, either.

Nor did she toss out a number of equally undeveloped drafts of short stories she'd filed away in a folder marked with her then-agent's name, Margot Johnson. They, too, are far from being ready for publication—but Pat hung on to them all the same. (Eventually she did do some winnowing of the alpine accumulations of her story drafts; what she threw out was the work she thought she couldn't "shape up.")

Pat pasted hundreds of photographs—many of them are of attractive women whom no one but Pat could identify, and all the pictures are unlabelled—into her photograph albums, and she kept those albums up to date. In small "business books" she recorded every penny she earned. During the war years, she made lists of every nickel she ever spent and of exactly what she got for her money—right down to the coffee delivered to her in cardboard containers at the Timely comics office in suite 1401 of the Empire State Building.[74]

Pat felt the necessity—perhaps it was more like a destiny—of hanging on to everything she ever wrote or made. When she gave something away, particularly something she had fashioned with her own hands or offered up with a prematurely full heart, she often regretted the gesture, and sometimes she even tried to get the object back. (See "The Real Romance of Objects: Part 1.")

But Pat systematically erased from her life every single thing that had to do with comics; she threw away every comic script, every proposal for a comic script, and every scenario for a comic book story she ever wrote. There would have been *thousands* of pages of comics work to cull—and she culled every one of them. Nor did she keep any copies.

The sole remnant of her long career in comic books appears on a list of

French phrases she was trying to memorize. It's the kind of obsessive little list she made all her life, and I found it, forgotten by her and tucked away, in a book left with a friend.[75] On the reverse side of this page of French vocabulary is the fragment of a scenario for a story about an even feebler character than Black Terror—a character called Golden Arrow (murdered parents, a miraculous escape from carnage, a crack shot with gilded arrows, and a horse called White Wind) for whom she had already written a few stories. At the top of the page, Pat drew a radiating golden arrow and made a sketch of a *"garçon au parapet"* (she was still practicing her French) as an entry point into the script. The drawing is enhanced by a long line of actions Golden Arrow might perform.

"Spice this up with detail," she reminded herself in the middle of the page—an internal note which she also applied to every single work of fiction she ever wrote.

Pat charted the plot of this comic book scenario just as she later made a chart of her own love life and a kind of chart for the plot of *The Price of Salt;* and it is almost too easy to explain her affinity for diagrams as the natural response of someone who always felt "displaced." Sometimes Pat made a diagram just for the fun of it. On the last page of her first cahier is a chart she drew up when she was eighteen years old, showing how a trumpet should be played in the first, second, and third movements of a piece of music. Her pleasure was wholly in the making of the chart; she had no interest at all in learning to play the trumpet.[76]

On a second list of French phrases folded up with her sketches for *Golden Arrow,* Pat made a few scribbles for *Ghost,* a comics "filler" she was writing for. "Fillers" were stories which comics' publishers ran periodically when they had extra space to fill in an issue. Pat particularly hated writing for *Ghost.* On this page, she calls the comic book panels "boxes," as though she couldn't be bothered to use the professional term "panels." But her imagination, represented by these scraps of work, seems well suited to the medium of the comic book. She tells the stories graphically and she sees the actions in pictures.[77]

What didn't suit Pat—despite that playwriting course with Minor Latham at Barnard College and years of producing silent sentences spoken by comic book characters—was writing good dialogue. Dialogue writing is like perfect pitch; you're either born with the ability or you are not. Pat was not. Her later attempts to write commercial plays, television scripts, imaginary conversations—anything, in fact, to do with the spoken word—are uniformly awful; as unconvincingly tuned to the sounds of human speech and human rhythm as are most of the conversations in her novels.

A quarter of a century or so after she'd made her little chart for Golden

Arrow, in February of 1969, Pat, living in Montmachoux, France, was struggling with an original script for the London theater producer Martin Tickner ("a two-acter, which I call STORIES"). She wrote her friend Lil Picard in New York that she'd "nearly had a nervous breakdown over writing my play. Caused by not knowing what SHOULD go into a play, how to write a play."[78] She had rewritten the script three times in three weeks, from beginning to end; and she would continue to work on it almost through the end of 1969 (including an October working holiday in a villa in the south of Portugal provided by her hopeful producer—of which experience Madeleine Harmsworth, the young lover who accompanied Pat to the villa, said: "I was rather fond of Portugal until then.")[79]

Pat would eventually call this play *When the Sleep Ends* and she wrote the female lead for her friend the English actress Heather Chasen. Chasen says that not only could Pat "not write dialogue . . . she seemed to have no understanding of women at all." Chasen thought the character Pat had written for her was violently unsympathetic, and that "the part was unplayable."[80] The work was never produced.

Pat's best talents were like dedicated bombs: specific to certain targets and not to others. She knew this, but sometimes managed to fool herself into thinking that her secondary talents—her extraordinary gift for hard work and discipline—could overcome the deficit.

In 1946, after four years of writing scripts expressly designed for the panel construction of comic books—each panel a little inked and colored painting of its own—Pat wrote of the short stories she was working on at the same time as her comic book writing: "I think of each story to be written, as a painted picture. I think more clearly in painter's terms."[81] It was another way of acknowledging what the comics were doing for her.

Pat was much better paid for her comics work than her fellow writers toiling away in pulp fiction, pornography, or lower-end "suspense" and "crime" novels.[82] But the shame Pat felt about her comic book writing and about the whole comics milieu of pirated stories, forged identities, false names, and compartmentalized activities makes her persistence in the job much more a matter of like being attracted to like than of poverty being attracted to a good salary.

Sixty-five years later, her lengthy, uneasy, self-embarrassed career as a writer for comic books seems part and parcel of her own internal division and her artistic obsession with doubling; the product of a magnetic attraction of opposites. The talented young woman and the disreputable new graphic narrative form: each one charged with the same affinities, the same embarrassments, and with some of the same uncomfortable secrets.

Still, the money was no small thing. In the 1940s, the novelist Anaïs Nin (whose work Pat first read on a visit to Fort Worth in 1948),[83] intent on generating spicy material for her voluminous diaries, was writing pornography-to-order for a United States senator for two dollars a page. Nin cannily contracted the work out to other writers for one dollar a page, making herself a tidy profit. But Pat Highsmith, even cannier than Anaïs Nin (and lacking both Nin's wealthy husband and Nin's desire to appear bohemian), was taking home between four and eight dollars for every comic book page she wrote.

· 12 ·

ALTER EGO

Like most of the people at work in the comics, Pat Highsmith wasn't working under her real name. Her "real" name—for once, the double-identity joke was on Highsmith—was actually the name she was born with, Mary Patricia Plangman. When the bubble of her "false identity" finally burst, the lateness of the news was almost as shocking to her as the knowledge itself.

It was in November of 1946, while applying for her first passport in a U.S. government office, that Pat learned that her stepfather, Stanley Highsmith, had never actually adopted her. Mother Mary, regally ignoring the legalities of adoption (Pat would have said "as usual"; Mary said she did so with the cooperation of the school authorities), had simply registered the six-year-old Patsy in grade school in New York under the Highsmith name and continued to do so right up through college. And so Pat, like many of her male fictional characters, had to be adopted—and for the second time, too, since grandmother Willie Mae had more or less taken charge of Pat's first six years. The documents securing Pat's legal status in New York State are rife with confusion.

In the first of the two files that comprise the adoption papers of Mary Patricia Highsmith (filed with the Westchester County Surrogate Court in November of 1946), "the deponent" (Mother Mary) states that "her husband and her daughter have lived together for over twenty years and that always the relationship between Mr. Highsmith and Mary [Pat is referred to by her first name in the document] was that of father and daughter. . . . deponent earnestly desires that said relationship become a legal one for all purposes through adoption."[1] The Westchester County clerk did not distinguish, as he/she should have done, between Mary Highsmith (mother) and the new Mary Highsmith-to-be (daughter), Mary Patricia. Thus, although Pat signed the adoption papers with her old name, Mary Patricia Plangman, she and her mother, nominally at least, are treated as a single entity in the deposition. It was a case of the law inadvertently following the life.

In the second of the two papers, Pat attests that "I have always looked upon Stanley Highsmith . . . with daughter-like love and respect and desire now to make him my foster father in the eyes of the law as well [because we have] lived together as one closely-knit family."[2] Pat would blame Mary bitterly for the necessity of this adoption, as she would blame her for most things. Blaming her mother was a convenience of which Pat never failed to take advantage.

Like many people working for the comics—let's imagine Pat back at her desk in the Sangor-Pines bullpen for a moment, cigarette lit, a cup of coffee balanced on the narrow strip of desk next to her typewriter, and Ken Battefield, the "Dickensian-type" artist she liked to chat with at the office,[3] leaning over to give her quiet advice about working for Quality Comics—Pat can both draw and write. She has been sketching, cartooning, and illustrating all her life. It's one of the tastes and talents she inherited from Mother Mary, who, as her daughter would do in later life, paints and draws her own Christmas cards. All through the 1940s, Pat and Mary go to museums and art galleries together, draw together (eying each other's work competitively), and, quarrelling or not, continue to seek each other's company.

"Will be unspeakably glad to see Mother altho' I can't tell her all my problems. She symbolizes all the stability, the femininity, the comfort and warmth of my life. Shall have to take her . . . for champagne cocktails and a long talk Friday."[4]

Pat's cousin Don Coates remembers Pat and Mary in New Hope, Pennsylvania, in 1961 mesmerized by the same dead bird. The bird had fallen to the ground with one of its "little claws stuck up in the air," and Mary and Pat were making drawings of the tiny corpse in impromptu *nature morte* sessions.[5] While they drew, Pat repeated a line from a poem by Dylan Thomas and Mary carefully copied the quotation onto one of her sketches.[6]

Mary's and Pat's letters to each other are full of references to drawing and painting. In her diaries, Pat records sketching trips with her mother to places as far away as the Minots' farm in New Hampshire, where, in August of 1950, they spent a week, got on "well enough," slept on "poor mattresses," and "starve[d] for our eighteen dollars a week." They had been going to New Hampshire together on little vacations for years, and photographs of Pat and Mary in the New England countryside in 1937 show more than either woman cared to tell. Mary is always dressed to the nines—she had been wearing high heels for so long that the backs of her legs hurt if she didn't put them on, even in the country—and Pat is always dressed as Mary's charmingly androgynous sidekick. (There is more than a suggestion of Batman and Robin—or Black Terror and Tiny Tim—in these photographs. See illustrations.)

On this particular trip to New Hampshire, Pat made her usual character notes on the people around her, but it was the farmer's sons who really caught her eye: "One gregarious and jolly, the other taciturn, the unknown." She saw them as paired opposites, and, as Alter Egos often did, they set her to thinking about murder. "Anyway, here are the characters. Who did the murder?"[7] She was hoping to write "a long story in a place just such as this . . . with some mystery and crime in it."[8]

Pat did most of the sketching on this trip, while Mary did most of the canasta playing—which prompted Pat to "list the things I dislike about her."[9] Pat's list neatly summarized some of the traits Pat herself retreated to in middle age ("rigid thought patterns," "self-consciousness," "refusal to face facts").[10] Pat complained that Mary never praised her drawings, and after Mary's death, when a cousin wrote to ask if she could send one of Mary's early paintings to Pat in Switzerland, Pat ignored the offer. Instead, she queried the cousin about what was currently obsessing her: family genealogy.

At twenty-two, Pat's artwork was as discretely partitioned as everything else about her. Born left-handed, she was forced by her grade school teachers to shift her writing implement to her right hand. (But the teachers forgot to make her *draw* with her right hand.) She got low marks for "handwriting" in grade school, and in 1960, in a story that coincides nicely with the absence of her German-American birth father, Pat told a lover that she "taught herself" to write with her right hand by copying out "German phrases."[11] Divided between being an artist and becoming a writer right up until the time she left the Sangor-Pines shop at the end of 1943, Pat kept on drawing with her left hand and writing with her right hand for the rest of her life. She split her talents, just as she split her differences. Just as she split everything.

Pat's divisions went even deeper than her talents. Because her chronic anemia was a constant source of worry, she made careful records of her frequent blood tests and kept up a murmur of anxiety about her low red blood cell count (Mary Highsmith was badly anemic, too) and low blood pressure (for which she was always getting "injections"). Like the rest of her, her blood was subject to partitioning and disguise. Pat had type O blood, the blood type of the "universal donor." The Japanese, perhaps the only people to use blood type for character analysis, regard possessers of O type blood as "warriors." The Americans, always more interested in stress than in character, discovered that people in the O blood group are most prone to developing ulcers. (Pat

suffered severe gastric problems all her life.) For the purposes of blood donation, a person in the O group can receive blood only from another O type, but
an O type can still donate to anyone in the ABO blood groups. O blood, in
other words, can both disguise itself and remain itself; it mimics other blood
types. Right down to her platelets, Pat was capable of doing double duty.

By August of 1943, the month young Everett Kinstler was hired at Sangor-
Pines, Pat had published some drawings as well as her short story "Uncertain
Treasure" in the magazine *Home and Food*.[12] The magazine's art director, Rolf
Tietgens, a stylish, gloomy German émigré photographer, was her new friend,
and his capacity for melancholy was not relieved by having a steady job. In
1967, Pat remembered: "when I could not too well understand it, being
twenty-one and hopeful, [Rolf said] that we are living in the Middle Ages
now."[13] At the time, Pat thought that Rolf, a German alien, really shouldn't be
criticizing the United States.

Pat hoped to buy a radio with the money she would get for "Uncertain
Treasure." The day she learned the story was going be published, 21 June 1943,
she went straight to Rolf's studio to be photographed. It was a commemora-
tive photo session—the triumphant young author on the occasion of her first
serious publication—and the photos would be used in *Home and Food*. Pat disliked them. Perhaps this was also the afternoon during which Rolf took a series of nude photos of Pat, photos whose "positives" she got back from him in
1968 and kept for the rest of her life. Much later, two of Rolf's (clothed) photos
of Pat would be used on the book jackets of two of her Doubleday publications.[14] But on this afternoon, Rolf elevated the posing experience for Pat by
translating and reading out a "poem by Hölderlin, which sound[ed] beautiful"
to her. Pat felt that Rolf loved her "a little," but he hated the new short story
she showed him, "Laval," and she agreed with him. It needed work.[15]

Rolf introduced Pat to his boyfriend, Frank, and Pat imagined that *he,* at
least, was falling for her. Then Pat and Rolf went to dinner alone. They talked
about "the Greeks and art," and Pat wondered how, after such an uplifting
conversation, she could go back and work on such "nonsense" as "Bill King."
Bill King—that's *Sergeant* Bill King—was another comic book character Pat
had been writing stories for, and Pat was quite right: Bill King is of minor interest. But three weeks earlier, she'd been enjoying the sergeant's exploits
enough to comment on them and was even claiming divine inspiration for
her work in her diary: "[S]at in the sun and got from heaven a story for [Sgt.]
Bill King."[16]

Sergeant Bill King's story lines are always clear: he must do more damage
to the German army than an atom bomb. He outwits, outfights, and outma-
neuvers whole squadrons of badly drawn, stereotypically portrayed German

soldiers. In writing for Black Terror, Fighting Yank, Sergeant Bill King, and a host of other war heroes and their diminished doubles, Pat entered into another of the many contradictions that would mark her life. She was a woman who couldn't tolerate visible signs of conflict, but she was writing graphic and violent war propaganda with every "heroic" comic book scenario she filed. And because this was wartime America, most of the stories she wrote were pocked and pitted with vulgar racial stereotypings: "Japs" and "Krauts" were the mildest terms used for enemy Asians and Teutons. Pat objected to the stereotyping of Germans, but not to the caricaturing of Japanese, and her later work for Fawcett Publications on the comic book *Crisco and Jasper* (taken from film shorts that feature stop-motion animation puppets) would run along the same lines. *Crisco and Jasper* stories used a Southern Negro dialect so crude that it made the Uncle Remus tales sound like Virgillian idylls.[17]

However bloody-minded Sergeant Bill King's exploits were, they don't begin to compare to the homicidal adventures of the character Pat would start writing for Timely comics in 1944. That character, Everett Johnson (like Tom Ripley, he hails from Boston), is notorious throughout the U.S. Pacific naval fleet for his nom de guerre: "Jap Buster" Johnson. Jap Buster Johnson is a *real* killer, and his mass murders, like those of Bill King, are sanctioned by the circumstances of war.

In every one of his stories, Jap Buster Johnson, stationed on an American destroyer somewhere in the Pacific, mercilessly slaughters an endless rotation of Japanese soldiers, sailors, and pilots. And he has his reasons. Jap Buster's Best Buddy, his closest pal, his almost–Alter Ego, is Dave Nichols. One fateful day, when a Japanese bomber strafes Everett Johnson's and Nichols's aircraft carrier, Dave dies with his boots on. Vowing vengeance, Everett is transformed into an enhanced self, "Jap Buster Johnson": a war machine who kills the Japanese swiftly, violently, and in their thousands.

And when Jap Buster Johnson takes time off from his daily slaughter to stand on the deck of his destroyer and smoke a reflective pipe—the blood of a thousand bucktoothed, slit-eyed Japanese sailors running a red river underneath his feet—he sees the ghostly image of his Best Buddy Dave's face shimmering out there on the ocean surface just beyond the starboard side of his ship. And that's when Johnson feels he has to say something to Dave, something meaningful. So he looks down into Dave's watery reflection and he dedicates the day's body count to his Best Buddy. "I did it for you Dave old boy," says Jap Buster Johnson, tenderly. "I wish you had been there with me fellow."[18]

Jap Buster "did it" for Dave, all right, but—it can't be said too plainly—he also "did it" for the fictional work of Patricia Highsmith. Those classic authors,

Dostoyevsky, Gide, Proust, Julien Green, et al., hovering, Pat liked to think (and wanted *us* to think) over her artistic life, weren't the only figures in her universe concerned with suggestive relations between men, the double nature of reality, and the instability of identity. It is possible to see, even in characters as crude as Black Terror and Jap Buster Johnson, how the great themes of the Zeitgeist—also, as it happens, the great themes of American literature—slowly trickled downwards and found a form in comic books—comic books for which Patricia Highsmith was writing.

Those "great themes" were not obvious to everyone—or to *anyone,* apparently, judging by the unholy stir a little essay published in *Partisan Review,* the journal Pat was so proudly subscribing to in the 1940s, made when it appeared in 1948. The essay was titled "Come Back to the Raft Ag'in, Huck Honey,"[19] and it was written by one of the Bad Boys of American Criticism, a maverick young scholar named Leslie Fiedler. Fiedler was indeed a bad boy; he was the first person, according to the *Oxford English Dictionary,* to apply the word "postmodern" to literature.

Just as Pat was packing up her kit bag for the Saratoga Springs artists' colony, Yaddo, in June of 1948 for six weeks of public and private drinking, enthusiastic flirtation, and some very serious revisions of the manuscript that would become *Strangers on a Train,* Fiedler's explosive essay (it added an extra line to Mark Twain's masterpiece *Huckleberry Finn,* because Nigger Jim never did say "Come back to the raft ag'in, Huck honey") hit American literary life like a bucket of dirty water gleefully hurled against a windshield by a rebellious teenager.

Fiedler's theory in "Come Back to the Raft Ag'in, Huck Honey"—fully presented in his 1960 book, *Love and Death in the American Novel*—is that American literature was a literature for, by, and about boys; obsessed with death and characterized by the implicitly homosexual pairing of two men (Fiedler noted the frequency of mixed-racial pairings in Twain, Melville, and Cooper) who, hand in hand, "light out for the territory"; that is, anyplace without civilizing females. The American novel, according to Fiedler, was vibrant with sexual anxieties about women, who are always portrayed as "monsters of virtue or bitchery, symbols of the rejection or fear of sexuality."

Fiedler's essay forever readjusted the American view of just what was *really* going on in the novels of Mark Twain, James Fenimore Cooper, Nathaniel Hawthorne, and Herman Melville. (In 1979, on the BBC4 radio interview program *Desert Island Discs,* Pat selected *Moby-Dick,* Herman Melville's brilliant, ham-handed, poetic epic of obsessed pursuit, social Darwinism, and extreme Calvinism, as the only book she'd want to take with her to a desert island.)[20] And Fiedler's essay, if you substitute class for race, and Europe (in the Ripley books) or Central Park (in *The Blunderer*) or the woods of Pennsylvania (in *The Cry of the Owl*) for the "territory," also provided a pretty good *avant-première* of what would go on in the novels of Patricia Highsmith.

Looked at through Leslie Fiedler's lens, Patricia Highsmith has all the minor marks of the archetypal American writer and two of the major marks as well: She is the most unconscious "gay male novelist" since Ernest Hemingway, and she is as gifted an anatomist of male sexual anxiety as Norman Mailer.

Later, Fiedler turned his theoretical attentions to comic books, as did his contemporary, Gershon Legman, the self-taught American sexologist, folklorist, and social critic. Legman, living in the South of France in the 1970s when Pat was occupying the North, was Pat's favorite editor of limericks and dirty jokes. And Pat—one of whose ideas of humor was to collect names from the "Sunday Social columns [of the] NY Times, people getting engaged or married. . . . Barbara Scheetz getting married, e.g., is the low standard I aspire to"[21]—kept at least one of Legman's massive editions of limericks in her personal library and consulted it frequently. She would have been as delighted by Legman's next book, *Rationale of the Dirty Joke* (with a whole section devoted to dirty jokes about Texas), as Legman himself would have been clinically interested in Pat's own favorite dirty joke, "The Japanese Wife Joke." (See "Les Girls: Part 11.")

In his Freud-influenced pamphlet, *Love and Death*, published in 1949— much of it was about the comic books of the 1940s during the period that Pat was writing steadily for the genre—the exuberantly eccentric (and steadfastly homophobic) Gershon Legman saw male homosexuality and misogyny every single place he looked.*

Pat's love life during her year at Sangor-Pines was like her imagination and her work habits: more or less in a hyperkinetic state.

In May of 1943, she fell in love with a dedicated young painter, Allela Cornell: "I love Allela and God within her. . . . she is the best! The best soul I could ever find!"[22] Holding hands with Allela at the movies made Pat want more of her, in the same way, she said, that she wanted "more and more money."[23] Allela was a slim, spiritually inclined, short-haired girl with round, rimless glasses, a plain face, an earnest manner, and larger problems than Pat

---

*In 1949, Legman wrote to Raymond Chandler, soon to be the unhappy script adaptor of *Strangers on a Train* for Alfred Hitchcock, accusing him, as Chandler put it, of "homosexualism" in his novels.

could guess at, although the clues were there in letters Allela sent to Pat: "I am destroyed," she wrote to Pat, "and I don't know why."[24]

Pat didn't like Allela's body and was much more excited by thinking "male" thoughts about Allela than by sleeping with her. "This morning, I thought so much about Allela that I had to go to the bathroom to relieve myself of a big erection. Is this disgusting? Am I a psychopath? Yes, but why not!?"[25] In 1946, three years after Allela and Pat broke up, Allela drank a bottle of nitric acid—her suicide had nothing to do with Pat—and suffered a lingering and painful death. It was especially poignant because Allela had decided she didn't want to die after all. Pat, as always, felt guilty for some callous behavior towards Allela and tried to get Allela's paintings placed in New York galleries. She was unsuccessful in her attempt, but later used Allela's situation as one of the "germs" for her novel *Ripley Under Ground*.

Allela Cornell had the good painter's ability to foretell the future of her human subject in the subject's present pose, and she did an uncannily predictive portrait of Pat in oils. In the painting, Pat is in a red jacket, with her massive hands wrapped around her torso and her thumbs sticking straight up. A trademark furrow folds the space between her brows. On her face is a fixed, mature, intractable expression—not at all the expression of a twenty-two- or twenty-three-year-old girl—of controlled rage and pain: it's the terrible frown Pat was always reminding herself to get rid of; the frown her face just naturally fell into. The painting is like the portrait Picasso did of Gertrude Stein: if it didn't look like Pat when Allela made it, it would look like Pat later on. It did. Pat hung it in every house she ever lived in.

As she always did with a new lover, Pat dreamt of travelling with Allela. Since high school, travelling had been "the most desirable thing on earth" to her.[26] She sent Allela her poems and one of the *Spy Smasher* stories she was writing for Sangor-Pines.[27] (She was also writing *Pyroman* and *Sergeant Bill King* for Sangor-Pines, and *Golden Arrow* for Fawcett.) Their communion was more that of two spiritually inclined artists—"Cornell was an idea, born of an x-ray," Pat wrote—than of a sensual union of the flesh.[28] Inevitably, Pat began to sleep with Allela's other lover, too, an attractive blond woman named Tex whom Pat had noticed riding her bicycle before learning that Tex was involved with Allela. The ensuing jealous scenes made Pat "want to jump out a window."[29]

Pat was also seeing a woman named Ann T., who, like Allela and Pat's co-worker at Sangor-Pines, Leo Isaacs, dedicated some poems to Pat; Pat slipped them into her cahier.[30] She let Leo Isaacs, who was married, kiss her and instantly regretted the liberty: "I allowed too much. It has to stop."[31] Pat's good looks and reckless behavior, and the slow sexual burn she emitted, inspired a lot of poetry and stirred many emotions in the people around her.

Like the proverbial pinball, Pat's feelings occasionally stopped ricochet-
ing around: "Our three lives [Allela's, Tex's, and Pat's] are bound tightly together. We love each other—what will happen now?"[32] The triangle was Pat's
favorite form of loving and she never could sustain it. The relationship with
Allela unraveled after only five months, in September of 1943.

Pat's second favorite form of loving—the tantalizing, torturing, withholding kind—was what she moved towards in her next affair: a mostly unconsummated relationship with a beautiful, married-but-separated thirty-year-old
Hattie Carnegie model, Chloe. Pat first met Chloe at a party at Angelica de
Monocol's, and continued to meet her at the Manhattan art gallery of Julien
Levy, son-in-law of the avant-garde artist and writer Mina Loy. Levy's gallery
on Fifty-seventh and Madison had been a showplace for Modernist works of
art in New York for the last twelve years. Pat thought Julien Levy was a "snake"
and his wife a "piglet." Perhaps this opinion was colored by the fact that Chloe
was staying with the Levys, and Rosalind Constable told Pat that Julien Levy
had a reputation as a "skirt chaser." Pat wooed Chloe with a bottle of Calvert's
whiskey which she was almost prevented from buying. Liquor store owners
still thought Pat was "17 or 18."[33] So did Pat.

Pat and Chloe spent passionate, but unconsummated, Saturday nights
together. Chloe's condition for staying with Pat was kissing but no sex. Pat
was thrilled with this (and then she wasn't), rhapsodizing about the excitements of limited physical contact in her diary. "By God! I remember the days
when I was fifteen or sixteen, when the accidental touch of the hand of a girl
was a whole heaven!"[34] But through her haze of desire, Pat's assessing eye was
still on Chloe: "Like all beautiful women, she prefers talking about herself."[35]
Pat and Chloe listened to Pat's favorite popular songs—a taste that lasted
thoughout Pat's life—at Pat's apartment on East Fifty-sixth Street: "The Last
Time I Saw Paris," "Why Do I Love You," and "Make Believe." Chloe was constantly drunk and wore black underwear. "My god!" thought Pat, as naïve as
any schoolboy, when she first saw Chloe drunk and passed out in her lingerie.[36] When Pat and Chloe finally did make love Pat's comment to herself was
typical: "[T]he earth didn't move."[37]

Chloe was clever and flattering as well as fragile and beautiful. She read
two of Pat's short stories, "Silver Horn of Plenty" and "Uncertain Treasure,"
and told Pat that as a writer she had the same problem as Djuna Barnes: she
didn't know how to end her fictions.[38] Chloe also told Pat that "if she were in
love with a woman, it would be me, but that she preferred men." Since Pat had
just confessed to her friend Rosalind Constable that "there is something perverted in me; I don't love a girl any more, if she loves me more than I love her,"
Chloe's attitude suited her very well.[39]

Almost immediately Pat started to do "good work on the story called *The Three* [which I am] proud of . . . as much as of my *Uncertain Treasure.*"[40] Perhaps "The Three" had something to do with the "three loves" Pat said she had had in the last two years: Rosalind Constable (a beacon of accomplishment in Pat's dark night of professional struggles), Allela Cornell, and Chloe. Or perhaps it was the three people Chloe said she was in love with just then. Chloe's withholding was giving Pat the impetus for her work on "The Three," another story Rolf Tietgens didn't like. "[T]oo peculiar, not clear, not poetic enough," he told Pat. What Pat told herself was that Rolf wasn't always right, that it was time to make use of Leo Isaacs's critical talents (Leo, her fellow comic book writer, was still in love with her), and that she would send the story to *The New Yorker* anyway.[41] In fact, she sent it to *Harper's Bazaar.* It wasn't published.

"I have to work like a man and I need a woman—but one who loves me strongly and quietly," Pat wrote in the creative afterglow of yet another physical rejection from Chloe—and after having to listen to yet another love poem read aloud to her by the besotted Leo Isaacs.[42]

On 12 October 1943, Pat went to East Fifty-seventh Street to have dinner with "the parents" and her cousin Dan Coates, who had been travelling for some time in the East. This was the second time Dan had visited the Highsmiths since August. Mary had to hold the meal back more than an hour for Dan—Pat decided this was evidence that Dan was "destructive" (but she went to a rodeo in Madison Square Garden with him the next day anyway, a rodeo she would carefully describe in *The Click of the Shutting*)—and Mary and Stanley lectured Pat about "my drinking, my friends (and girl friends) etc." "The parents ruin me," she thought. Everyone wondered aloud about what Pat saw in Chloe, whom they thought of as "an unintellectual model." As usual, Pat was at the center of her family's conversation.

At this dinner with Dan, it was Mary, always hoping for a suitable boyfriend, *any* boyfriend, for Pat, who taxed her with rejecting "Leo [Isaacs]'s questions like a man who refuses to give insight into his private life. I answered that I could never love a Jew and that, if he tried to discover anything, I wouldn't see him again."[43] This was plain enough, but it wouldn't have stopped Mary's prodding. The other plain thing—Pat said it to herself and to no one else—was that she didn't think Leo had "the big dream," the ambition that "makes real artists."[44] He was not headed in a direction that would lead to the "best" in life. But Pat didn't say the plainest thing of all, which was that Leo Isaacs was not the right gender for her.

The next evening, 13 October, Ann T. and Chloe met at Pat's apartment. Pat always liked to have her lovers meet each other; the geometry of the triangle never lost its appeal. Chloe left first, and then Ann got drunk in order to sleep with Pat. Pat confessed to Ann, a little inopportunely, that "Chloe fills my whole life," and the day after that, Pat broke up with Ann. (Not, as it turned out, for long.) Pat was still not sleeping with Chloe, but she would always prefer the bird in the bush to the bird in her bed.[45] Besides, Pat was still emotionally involved with Allela Cornell, who gained in imaginative and artistic importance the further she receded from Pat's direct experience. For the rest of her life, Pat would refer to Allela with love, respect, and lingering regret.

Pat had been introduced to Allela Cornell by one of the many other Anns in her life, a woman named Ann McFarland. Allela was living in a loft on Hudson Street with a roommate, the composer David Diamond. David, who went on to become romantically involved with both Carson McCullers and McCullers's husband, Reeves, became friendly with Pat, too. Whenever Pat came to the loft, David and Pat would go around the corner to talk and have lunch at the Jai Alai, a Basque restaurant which was a fixture in Greenwich Village for decades.

"Pat," said David Diamond, "was quite a depressed person—and I think people explain her by pulling out traits like cold and reserved, when in fact it all came from depression." That, and the "loneliness" which outlined her life like an aura, is why Diamond thought Pat valued Allela's "devoted friendship" so much.[46]

"I never connected Pat with the Village," he said. "I always connected her with uptown. She wasn't bohemian at all. People thought she was because she wore men's white shirts. They mistook [her mild form of cross-dressing] for bohemianism. I found her a very warm human being and I loved talking with her about music. I think she was obsessed with music."[47]

Pat and David Diamond shared a fondness for certain composers—Ravel, for instance, whom David had met when he was ten and who told him that he must go to Paris to study with the great teacher Nadia Boulanger. Like very nearly his entire generation of gifted American composers, David Diamond did just that.

"Pat and I would always talk about where musical notes came from. . . . A piece of mine that was very popular in the 1940s—'Round for Street Orchestra'—she wondered where I got the idea for that because it was so popular. She could practically imitate the whole first movement. . . ." And Pat would let me read some short works that were still in manuscript. I thought she was a remarkable writer and that she had great psychological insight.

"I do remember that she was as fascinated by Greta Garbo as I was. And when she found out that I had met Garbo in Hollywood, of course she was always hoping that I could perhaps introduce her to Garbo."[48]

Greta Garbo was a lifelong obsession for Pat, and Pat knew, through lesbian circles in New York and Paris, Garbo's former lover, the flamboyant play-wright Mercedes de Acosta.* De Acosta's romantic hats, stylish slacks, auto-cratic demeanor, and striking Cuban looks made her a standout in the 1920s. (At ten, she had been Dorothy Parker's classmate at a convent school in Man-hattan.) De Acosta, who was always kind to Pat, inviting her for dinner sev-eral times when Pat first arrived in Paris in July of 1949, had the distinction of having slept with, as Alice B. Toklas put it, "three of the most important women of the twentieth century." Two of those women were Marlene Diet-rich and Greta Garbo. (Eva Le Gallienne and Isadora Duncan are candidates for the third.) Pat herself, when young and lovely, sometimes brought out Garbo-like comparisons from her friends, and her admiring English profes-sor, Ethel Sturtevant, once invited her to "[b]e the Greta Garbo of the novel!"[49] Pat tried her best.

After Garbo's death in 1990, Pat wrote an entirely worshipful article about the reclusive star, "My Life with Greta Garbo," published finally in *The Oldie* on 3 April 1992. The piece is aglow with love, admiration, and incomprehen-sion (Pat never met Garbo). And it is as quirky as anything Pat ever put on pa-per, dappled and stippled with all her perverse little interests. It also shows just how much of herself Pat projected into whatever she was working out in her writing at the moment. Pat's work, despite its vaunted "neutrality," was almost always intensely personal.

In this article, Pat fondly remembers stalking Garbo on the streets of Upper East Side Manhattan (Pat was not unique—all New Yorkers did this) while keeping a respectful distance. She recollects almost colliding with Garbo on a corner; the experience "made" her day. And although Pat loved to imagine Garbo alone, so alone, she also liked to imagine the enormous telephone bills—the size of them had a near-pornographic excitement for Pat—that Garbo must be racking up by talking to her many admirers all over the world.

---

* In Paris, where Pat usually saw Mercedes de Acosta, she also met Germaine Beaumont, the novelist and literary critic who had been Colette's protégée (and perhaps something more). Beaumont, who was an intimate friend of Janet Flanner (and saw Flanner regularly at Nata-lie Barney's literary salon), admired Pat's novels and wrote about them. Pat never quite grasped the importance of having someone as discerning as Germaine Beaumont approve her work. On 24 September 1966, the publicist for Calmann-Lévy in Paris had to remind Pat about the "[e]xtremely good article concerning *This Sweet Sickness,* written by Mrs. Ger-maine Beaumont, who is one of your most faithful fans. Since she is herself an excellent writer and a member of the Jury Femina, her appreciation has a great value." Pat had a simi-lar experience with Edouard Roditi. In 1967 she found herself at Roditi's Paris apartment at 8 rue Grégoire-de-Tours. Again, Pat had no idea of who Roditi—polylingual poet, author of many books, and distinguished translator from ten languages—was. She thought he might be an art critic, tried to guess his age, and noticed only that a "diminutive Arab" (Roditi's lover) was monopolizing his bathroom.

By the time Pat wrote her Garbo article, she owned a little drawing that had once been in Garbo's personal collection: a sexually ambiguous study of an older man who is pictured with a much younger person of indeterminate gender. She ruminated on it avidly. "That there is a sexual business between the two figures there is no doubt. The real ambiguity is in the beautiful face of the blond figure, which except for a strong jaw appears female. . . ."[50] Pat wanted to think Garbo bought the drawing because the ambiguous figure looked like Garbo herself. And Pat imagined that she "can never forget—and I can hear this too—Garbo's voice saying, 'I vant to be alone,' in a deep and earnest tone that meant to any hearer, Garbo speaks the truth."[51]

Garbo may have been speaking the truth, but Pat wasn't quoting it. Like almost everyone else, she misquotes Garbo on this particular line. What Garbo actually said was, "I want to be *let* alone." Given Pat's proclivities, her misquotation is perfectly understandable.

In 1977, thirteen or so years before she wrote the piece on Garbo and three or four years after she and her mother cut off their relations, Pat made another interesting allusion to the Swedish actress during a seven-hour interview with the writer and journalist Joan Juliet Buck, who had come to Moncourt to talk to Pat for the *Observer Magazine*. It's a sign of the feelings Pat still harbored for Mother Mary after all those years (and all those tears) that she told Buck that Mary Highsmith was "the double of Greta Garbo."[52] Mary Highsmith had her own Modigliani-like attractiveness, but only a besotted daughter could assert that Mary was a "double" for Greta Garbo's unearthly beauty and paralyzing presence, best summed up by theater critic Kenneth Tynan with the sentence: "What one sees in other women drunk, one sees in Garbo sober."

Drunk or sober, when Pat looked at Mary with her mind's eye, she saw Greta Garbo—or, at least, she sometimes said she did.

For most of the 1940s Pat never stopped falling for women—sometimes for no more than an hour or an evening. She also began to date a few men. The majority of them were young Jewish males by whom she seemed to be both repelled and fascinated. These young men were up-and-comers with names like Jack Berger and Walter Marlowe and Lewis Howard—she particularly liked Jack Berger because he criticized his own milieu as being "sort of Jewy sometimes"—and she speculated on their potential earning power with the calculating enthusiasm of any bourgeoise. (In 1984, she would reprise this enthusiasm in a conversation with Bettina Berch: "You have to marry a man who has quite a bit of money," Pat told Berch with a keen grasp of what marriage meant, "or you turn into a servant.")[53]

When Pat was seeing a lot of Jack Berger in early 1942—("I was practically the only Gentile in the house")—she complained about how his Jewish friends seemed to need to *eat* all the time.[54] And then she criticized everything else about them. It was an interesting point of view for a woman who was to spend so much of her creative and personal life in close—often very close—association with Jews.

"Went to American Institute of Graphic Arts tonight with Berger. I like him a lot. The Jewish mind is analytical, critical, but not sympathetic or creative. I enjoy Jews' company when I am most on the surface of my mind—when I am concerned with superficial things or impersonal things. When I am the other way—they are intolerable to me. Babs B has been intolerable at times."[55]

A couple of months later, Pat was still preoccupied with the subject, but in a different way.

"Walked with M. Wolf over Queensborough Bridge. She talked intelligently, but *too* pro-communist on my tradition question. One has to go to a Jew for decent conversation these days."[56]

One of Mary's complaints against her daughter—that Pat calculated her female friendships according to what they could bring her—might help to explain Pat's always-ambivalent association with Jews. Mary wrote in a letter to one of Pat's lovers that Pat had made friends with the Alsatian-raised Jewish refugee artist Lil Picard because, as Pat told Mary, Lil was "going places."[57]

Pat liked to explore sex intellectually, but not necessarily physically, with the young men she was seeing. In the summer between her junior and senior years in college, one of her young men made a remark about Pat's potential for heterosexual relations that caught her attention: "[He says] that I'm always psychologically unready but often physically ready. What an observant lad."[58]

Later on, Pat would dine with and then try out in bed the occasional young man. "Herbert L. called, we had dinner and he stayed for the night. . . . I *want* to learn to love men."[59] Her attitude towards men was usually that of a canny shopper testing out an unknown product which she strongly suspected was not going to live up to its advertising. She judged these (mostly) nameless encounters solely on the kind of sexual response they produced in her. And it was never enough; it was negligible, in fact. What she was hoping for couldn't happen because she always set the bar too high. She set it at the physical/spiritual communion she attained with women. She would always be disappointed.

"Don't you ever desire a man's body?" asked one of her male candidates plaintively. Pat had been mentally—and very unfavorably—comparing his profusion of "awful" chest hair, "which he thinks to be so beautiful," with her female lover Ginnie's "sweet breasts."[60] The young men never stood a chance, although Pat kept on hoping they would.

While still at Sangor-Pines, Pat continued to be preoccupied by thoughts of religion and spirituality, just as she would be for the rest of her life. She was reading Freud on religion in June of 1943 and finding him "wonderfully interesting."[61] Freud and his disciples would always be a good fit for Pat. (Jean Genet's biographer Edmund White writes that Genet thought Freud was the best friend homosexuals ever had.) A little later, she became interested in a book by Theodor Reik, one of Freud's first pupils, called *The Unknown Murderer* (1932): a study of how to profile unidentified criminals by tracking the clues their unconscious guilt compelled them to leave behind.[62] In her work, Pat returned repeatedly to the effects of unconscious guilt. It was a condition she understood in her bones.

And nothing so clearly reveals her creative reliance on frustrated desires—that classic Freudian explanation for both creation and its achievements—than the idea for a story Pat wrote down in a cahier in early September of 1947. Considering her mostly effaced paternal history, the continued reliance on male "hero-criminals" in her work, and the fact that her own first name was Mary, the meaning of this cloudy little *keime* couldn't be clearer:

> Mary loved and worshiped her father. When he died, she fell ill herself, was in delirium even as he was buried. She was not told of his death. Afterward she ministered still to his needs, bringing him broth and tea, shading the light from the eyes of the figure half asleep, face turned to the wall, on its bed.[63]

For her forty-sixth birthday in 1967, Mary and Stanley Highsmith gave Pat a book by another of Freud's disciples, Erich Fromm. The book, no doubt a pointed present on Mary's part, was called *The Art of Loving*. Seven years later—as though she'd read no psychology in the intervening years, which, probably, she had not—Pat noted that "Erich Fromm states boldly that if a person cannot get from another the love he desires, the person resorts to sadism,"[64] and gave the irritatingly passive and masochistic Edith Howland of *Edith's Diary* a taste for Fromm's Talmud-inflected psychology.[65] But in the summer of 1983, Pat came away from an *avant-première* in London of Hans Geissendörfer's TV film of *Edith's Diary* (*Ediths Tagebuch*) irritated herself to see how the filmmaker had imposed a Freudian interpretation on her novel. She thought Geissendörfer had reduced the complications of Edith's relationship with Cliffie to "a neat Freudian mother-son love relationship" and that the film was "obvious and a bit vulgar."[66] There was nothing, she felt, neat about Edith and Cliffie.

Pat always hated to be classified—especially by others. And she was quite capable of contradicting herself without having *other* people trying to contradict her.

Still, it was Sigmund Freud's interpretations to which Pat usually returned. His bold, artistic analyses attracted her, his misogynies were congruent with her own, and his sense of art as the locus of loss suited her understanding of the act of creation. She had begun to read his work at Barnard, and the only time she seriously rebelled against his schematic approach was when it was applied to her own psychology during her six-month stint in Freudian therapy in 1948–49. And on only one occasion—at the beginning of 1956, in the deep depression that sparked another of her long interior dialogues with herself about God and "the humanistic morale versus Freud"—did she decide, briefly, to favor the "pre-Freudian Joseph Conrad" of *The Outcast of the Islands* over Freud. "The old fashioned, human morality is far more appealing to the writer" than Freud, she wrote.[67] It was the way Grandmother Willie Mae had brought her up—although, with his silver lining of irony, Joseph Conrad is anything but old-fashioned.

But this lapse from Freudian faith was a brief one, and as late as 1988, Pat, a guest on a British television program devoted to the investigation of how to survive the murder of a loved one, gave her only direct response (it was Freudian) to a question about the definition of a murderer. "Frankly," she said, "I'd call them sick if they were murderers, mentally sick."[68] For most of her life, Pat would explain herself to herself, and life to others, in more or less Freudian terms. Her novels do the same thing.

In July of 1943, Pat was paying attention to Mother Mary's faith in Christian Science again, and she did a drawing "while listening to a sermon by a X[Christian] Scientist.[69] She tried her hand at the liturgical form herself, writing "sermons in my cahiers like the one of Jonathan Edwards."[70] The eighteenth-century Calvinist theologian Jonathan Edwards's most famous sermon—it was part of the curriculum of every American junior high school for most of the twentieth century, so it must have been the one Pat was referring to—is "Sinners in the Hands of an Angry God." It begins: "In this verse is threatened the vengeance of God on the wicked unbelieving Israelites."

Pat, turning things upside down as usual, wrote a sermon called "Will the Lesbian's Soul Sleep in Peace?" (she seemed to feel that her own soul might *not* rest in peace) and then dropped in on the artist and art dealer Betty Parsons in the gallery where she worked in order to show her the sermon. Parsons asked

Pat for a copy. Parsons was Rosalind Constable's lover, and Pat was always fascinated by the lovers of women she was attached to.[71] The fact that Betty Parsons was not only an artist herself but a dealer at an important midtown gallery did not escape Pat's attention, and Pat followed Parsons's career as she went on to open her own gallery in 1946, the Betty Parsons Gallery, and become the most influential female gallerist in New York City. Parsons was the first person to exhibit the Abstract Expressionists, and amongst her artists were Jackson Pollock, Barnett Newman, Agnes Martin, Ellsworth Kelly, Robert Rauschenberg, and Pat's friend Buffie Johnson.

Dan Coates's travels in the East had begun late in the summer of 1943, and so it was in August that he dropped in on Mary and Stanley in New York for the first time. During this visit, Pat felt that "mother has no time" (for *her*) and that Dan was "very boring, living completely for the present and the present is little and insignificant."[72] Good-natured, handsome Dan didn't share Pat's dreams of Manhattan triumph and eventual world conquest—but, then, Pat usually disliked her favorite relatives when they came to New York.

When her beloved grandmother Willie Mae showed up in New York in October of 1943, Pat suddenly started to see Willie Mae in another light: "Grandmother makes me nervous. . . . She lives in the past and always talks— every minute, about 'your uncle,' 'my brothers,' 'your aunt'—all people who died 50 years ago."[73] This had something to do with Willie Mae's proximity. Pat preferred her family in their proper places, in a stable "character," and in the relations and the context in which she first knew them. Pat's artistic concentrations were always the opposite of her hopeless yearning for stability.

Relations got worse during Willie Mae's visit to New York, and Pat went so far as to have a disloyal little chat with her mother about her grandmother. The chat, however, was loyal to Mary, and it is the only time on record that Pat took Mary's side against Willie Mae.

"At home a secret is spoken out: we don't like Grandma. She is disagreeable, because she doesn't let anybody tell her anything, she is jealous, talks too much, wants to spend money (!), go out and doesn't show any thoughtfulness towards Mother. It worries me that Mother still tries to understand and change Grandma, to show her where she is wrong, and that mother still is looking for something that has never been. Something must be done, as she intends to come here every summer and this will make Mother old: she drives us all to drink!"[74]

Like mothers, like daughters. These were the same criticisms Pat and Mary Highsmith would hurl at each other—in far more developed and colorful language—for decades; each woman standing in the dock, each woman sitting in the judge's chair. Mary, Pat would insist, had "shattered" her with criticisms, made her shake for days, and twisted her sexually, while Pat's physical and emotional "violence," Stanley Highsmith (standing in for Mary) told Pat, had driven Mary to hysterical vomiting and a consultation with a psychiatrist. (The psychiatrist's name was Dr. Ripley, and he may have been the same Dr. Ripley who "treated" the novelist Mary McCarthy when her first husband committed her to the Harkness Pavilion in New York—and left her there.)

"[S]till looking for something that has never been"—it is Pat's phrase for Mary's attempts to get Willie Mae to pay attention to her—would be a long life's work for both the Highsmith women. Each of them was irretrievably linked to loss; and both of them were linked by their "loss" of each other.

And when Pat, in early November, finally persuaded Chloe to go to Mexico with her, another family fault line was exposed. Mary and Grandmother Willie Mae, still in New York, joined together in their jealousy of Chloe. "Grandma and Mother very curious about my feelings for Chloe," Pat wrote in her diary. "'Why?' [they ask] and 'What does she have?' and 'I would like to learn what strange power this girl has!'"[75]

· 13 ·

ALTER EGO

PART 4

Like all her later travels outside the United States, Pat's trip to Mexico in December of 1943 started out in one direction, took an unexpected turn, and picked up enough emotional baggage and artistic impression to fill several of her future fictions. The purpose of her voyage—to continue to write her novel *The Click of the Shutting* in a setting of exotic exile—was followed by another urge just as basic: the urge to run away. Whenever Pat fell in love, her first thought was to escape with her new lover and her second thought was to escape *from* her new lover. Newly in love with Chloe, Pat was feeling the old, romantic pull of the road again. This time, she managed to persuade her girlfriend to go with her.

Perhaps the $350 Pat had saved up from her comics work*—and from selling her radio and record player to Mary and Stanley—had something to do with Chloe's initial assent to the trip. Richard Hughes agreed to allow Pat to send in comic book scenarios by mail to Sangor-Pines from Mexico, so she was secure in the promise of a little income. But Chloe was ambivalent about going anywhere with Pat, changing her mind, Pat noted acidly, "faster than the Russian frontlines."[1]

There was something premonitory about this Mexican trip. Once Pat had stepped across the border, the needle on her personal compass swung around to point to the country where all her journeys would end: Switzerland. The novel she went to Mexico to work on, *The Click of the Shutting,* took some of its impetus from her writing for comic books (whose progenitor was the Swiss

---

* Worth more than $4,000 in current buying power in the United States according to Department of Labor statistics—and considerably more than that in Mexico in 1943.

graphic artist Rodolph Töpffer); she based one of her two Mexican short stories, "The Car," on the odd relations of a Swiss hotel owner with his American wife in Taxco; and in Mexico City she spent time (reluctantly, because he was pursuing Chloe) with a naughty Swiss bandleader and nightclub owner, Teddy Stauffer, whose jazz band, the Original Teddies, was named after the bear on the coat of arms of Bern, Switzerland. Bern is the Swiss city where all Pat's literary archives are now kept.

Mexico—to which Pat would return several times and for several reasons—shared a border with her home state of Texas. It was also the place where she first began to lay down patterns for her "songlines," those magnetic meridians of travel which all her later, far-flung journeys would follow.

If you couldn't get to Paris in the 1940s (and in 1943 you couldn't; the city had been occupied by the Germans since June of 1940), Mexico would do. Every American (and many a European) who considered herself or himself an artist, a free spirit, a bohemian, or even a fan of D. H. Lawrence was attracted to the idea of Mexico. Katherine Anne Porter and Hart Crane went to Mexico in the 1930s; Tennessee Williams visited a recessive Paul and a receptive Jane Bowles in Acapulco in 1940; Saul Bellow managed to spend his mother's life-insurance money on an extended sojourn in Taxco. And the teenage aesthete Ned Rorem seems to have dropped in on everyone who was anyone South of the Border. In the 1930s and 1940s, Americans were drawn to Mexico by what always draws people who make more art than money to such places: cheap rents, cheap food, abundant liquor, exotic scenery, and the recklessness of behavior that is permissible in a country to which you owe no allegiance. American nationals came in droves, and they usually returned with complaints about the low class and excessive drinking of their fellow expatriates.

Saul Bellow, who lived and travelled in Mexico in 1940, said "Mexico was everything that D. H. Lawrence said it was, and a good deal more besides." He and his wife fetched up in Taxco, the silver-working center of Mexico: a town on a hill with a fantastically mannered cathedral, Santa Pisca. (Sybille Bedford* described Santa Pisca as "shimmering with chromatic tiles" like "a brilliant pastiche of late—very late—Hispano American Baroque.")[2] Taxco was where Pat would spend most of her Mexican time.

Taxco, Bellow said, "had a sizable foreign colony, mostly Americans, but also Japanese, Dutch, and British." None of the people Bellow met there "had a very firm grip on anything at all." The Bellows were able to rent a fine house

* The great German-born English writer Sybille Bedford travelled through Mexico with Esther Murphy Arthur in the early 1950s. Pat knew Esther Murphy Arthur and would meet Sybille Bedford in Rome and Paris. Out of her journey, Bedford produced the best book ever written about travelling in Mexico: *A Visit to Don Otavio* (1953).

and pay two Indian servants to take care of everything "for about ten bucks a week." And the sun "shone so dramatically, so explicitly, you were never allowed to forget death." In Taxco, Bellow found that he was drinking more than usual, much more, he said, than was good for him. He drank with his "American buddies in the zócalo . . . and with hard-drinking professionals who wrote for *Black Mask* and other pulps." Like most American writers with any pretensions to seriousness—like Pat herself at the Sangor-Pines shop—Saul Bellow was ashamed to be "in the low company of the pulp writers."[3]

Sybille Bedford, in Taxco ten years after Bellow on a yearlong odyssey with her companion Esther Murphy Arthur, praised the town's "lovely position" and the "houses sprawling across a slope on four levels, everywhere red-tiled roofs, archways, flowers, prospects." Bedford wrote slyly that Taxco's famous silversmiths were now performing for "the transient and the naïve" and that "the foreigners who live in Taxco take villas and stay a very long time. Some may once have thought of writing a book; a few do paint."[4]

Like Teddy Stauffer, who opened his Casablanca Club with its death-defying pearl divers in 1943 in Acapulco, the entrepreneuring expatriates who came to Mexico catered to what Bedford called the "Americans fast and rich."[5] Pat and Chloe met Teddy Stauffer in Mexico City during a season which often spelled trouble for Pat: the Christmas holiday.

Pat and Chloe arrived by train in San Antonio, Texas, from New York on 14 December 1943. Pat had a bad toothache and suffered, at the Mexican border, the first of what would become her lifelong travel troubles with luggage and typewriters. She was carrying so many books that some of her bags had to be sent back to New York, others of her bags got lost, and her typewriter was detained. The two women turned around, spent the night in Laredo, and crossed into Mexico the next day. They parked themselves at a hotel Betty Parsons had recommended to Pat, the Guardiola (Chloe, already beginning to chafe, found it distasteful and was attacking Pat verbally), and began a frantic round of going out, attracting new people, and drinking too much. Chloe stayed out later than Pat, and Pat let a man take her home and kiss her. ("Since he has got a brain it was not too bad.")[6] By Christmas, Pat and Chloe had been in Mexico City for little more than a week, and their relationship was in tatters; the following year, Pat remembered this Christmas in Mexico as yet another "miserable" Christmas holiday.[7]

Chloe, not much moved by Pat's passion for her and still in love with her husband, went out drinking every night with Teddy Stauffer, who would later succeed in charming many movie stars into his bed. (In 1951, he married the cleverest of them: Hedy Lamarr.) Stauffer's band had played jazz in the style of Benny Goodman at the infamous 1936 Olympic Games in Berlin, and he turned the "Horst Wessel Song" into a "swing" number in Germany—and managed to avoid being jailed for it. The competition was too stiff for Pat. She decided that further relations with Chloe would ruin her work, and she went back to what she'd come to Mexico for in the first place: the idea of writing *The Click of the Shutting.* "My novel still needs a lot of work, of course I think of it all day long."[8]

By 7 January, Pat was high in the Atachi hills of Mexico, alone in picturesque Taxco except for a part-time maid, in what she called "the most beautiful house" in town: La Casa Chiquita, which she rented from the Castillo family. Before she moved into La Casa Chiquita, Pat had taken a room with a balcony and a washing machine in Taxco, bought paper and pencils, and set up a work schedule which called for her to draw in the morning, walk in the afternoon, and write at night. She drank seven cups of coffee a day and yearned for her typewriter, which hadn't yet made it over the border. She began to imagine a future for herself in Mexico—it was the future she would have in Switzerland forty years later—as a rich and famous writer in exile, estranged in a strange land and missing her native country. Pat often went away from places so she could miss them; yearning is a productive emotion for writers.

One of the reasons Pat decided to stay in Taxco was the fact that the town was so full of foreigners that trousers on women were tolerated there, as they were not in other Mexican villages. On the nineteenth of January, Pat's twenty-third birthday, Mother Mary sent her a telegram, saying that their mutual friend Jeva Cralick had a present for her. Mary also sent what Pat called a "terrible" letter, full of criticisms and endearments. "My darling," Mary wrote, and then launched into one of her searing lectures. It was just the taste of home and the touch of emotional battery that Pat had been longing for. (In her diary, Pat was writing: *"Suche jeden Tag nach einem Brief von mother. Warum nicht? Warum?"* "Every day I look for a letter from my mother. Why not? Why?")[9]

Then Mary, as she often did, enclosed money in a missive, and followed that charitable act with several more letters accusing Pat of drinking too much, of not cleaning her house, and of living a "phony life" built on alcohol. Mary's letters upset Pat so much that she couldn't write her novel for a while. When she started work again, she was hoping that her former employer, Ben-Zion Goldberg, would like her book; he had telegrammed her that he was coming to visit. Grandmother Willie Mae weighed in with a letter from Fort Worth to say that she was "praying" for Pat. Pat, according to her diary, was reading and thinking about God every day.

Pat also got a letter from her father; a letter from Richard Hughes (to whom she was sending two of her "best 16 page comic book" synopses); a letter from her inquisitive seatmate at Sangor-Pincs, Gerry Albert; a letter from Allela Cornell; a letter from Chloe saying she'd like to visit in February; and a letter from a man who was in love with Chloe and wanted a report on Chloe's current drinking habits. Lacking neither correspondents nor the will to correspond, Pat answered everyone. And she wrote a letter to her friend the photographer Ruth Bernhard for good measure. Another of Pat's lifelong patterns was being laid down here in her first month in Mexico: a massive and quotidian foreign correspondence.

La Casa Chiquita and its part-time maid cost Pat nearly twice as much as Saul Bellow said he had been paying for his Taxco house and two servants in 1940—Pat's rent was about fifty-four dollars a month—so the inflation of prices that accompanies American expatriatism was already biting into beautiful Taxco. Pat's house was a low adobe affair with a charming pitched roof, handcrafted Mexican tiles framing the lintel, and a cactus garden around the side. Pat did a nice drawing of the house. The native wildlife—*pulgas* (fleas) and ants and little hopping lizards—made free with the door and the open windows. In February, she took in a cat, calling it Frank. In April, the month before she left Taxco, she adopted a kitten. The kitten wouldn't sleep on her bed, perhaps in mute rebellion against the name she gave it: Fragonard.[10]

Very soon, Pat began to set down in her cahier her customarily sharp character notes, longer than the ones she usually wrote, on the expatriate residents of Taxco. She was finding or seeking in her neighbors what she would always find or seek in humans: cracks in their characters, traits and patterns which reinforced her view that human behavior was unreliable, double-natured, and capable of turning on a dime. Pat looked into people for much the same reasons that she read books or fell in love with women: to "recognize" something in them that corresponded to her belief that life was flawed, cleft, and sundered.

And so the "characters" she records in her cahiers often appear to have been alive in her imagination long before she met and described them—rather than the other way around. (The cool eye Pat cast on people would always merge with her imaginative taste for fiasco: despite having at least a normal experience of both, she almost never wrote about "good" people or "happy" circumstances in her notebooks.) But the unusual thing about these Taxco portraits is just how affectionate their ironies are: especially her portrait of "Paul Cook," a budding "hero-criminal." Pat was young, only twenty-three, and as yet relatively unembittered. Nothing would ever be quite so affectionate again.

Although Pat complained constantly of loneliness, continued to yearn for letters from her mother (and felt terrible when she got them), and cursed the food on a daily basis ("Fish again!" "Ohh, if only I could have a carrot, a banana, a piece of celery with no salt! I would be so happy!"),[11] she was deeply engaged by Taxco and by the side trips she took to Acapulco, Jalapa, Cuernavacas, Monterrey, and other places. Her descriptions of her neighbors are as graphic as if they were painted. Oddly, these descriptions were dulled down, made less vivid and plausible and emotional, when she folded them into her Mexican fictions: the two short stories ("In the Plaza"[12] and "The Car"[13]) and the one novel (*A Game for the Living*) written from her direct experience of Mexico. It is only in their original form—a portrait gallery of the people who surrounded her in Taxco in the winter and spring of 1944—that these studies give a picture of Pat's artistic weights and measures, of her intense socializing (despite constant claims of loneliness), and of the exotic environment in which she had chosen to work on her first novel.

Here are a few of Pat's Mexican portraits, printed at length. They are as much a study of the young writer's state of mind as they are likenesses of her subjects.

Margot Castillo and Tonio Castillo—Margot charming, French and Dutch, but before an artist, before a wife, a hard business woman. Tonio, a clerk in Spratling's "persuaded her" they should marry. . . . * For a couple of years they worked hard, building their own business . . . and finally built up to be second to Spratling in design and volume of business.

Tonio is generous, warm, youthful. Twenty-six now. Margot is economical, warm when she wants to be, a garrulous talker, and perhaps thirty-eight or forty-two now. They build a house, in Margot's excellent style . . . but Tonio does not think he will like it. He cannot live without her and can hardly live with her . . . Tonio . . . pays high wages so [the workers] will love him. Margot delights in pointing out to him that they don't.

Margot no longer draws for pleasure, or paints, but concentrates on her business. She wears fuchsia ribbons in her coal black hair, (upswept) and is often bandboxy. Tonio must be rather a cute pet to be

---

* William Spratling, an American architect who settled in Taxco in 1929 and opened a silver shop, designed silver jewelry inspired by pre-Columbian Mexican motifs. He is credited with making Taxco the "silver industry" center of Mexico and is still known as "the Father of Mexican Silver." Pat, who knew Spratling a little, was impressed: *"Was für ein Mann! Interessante Keime,"* she wrote. "What a man! Interesting germs."

seen with in New York restaurants. . . . Margot shows an excess of affection & generosity. Margot is black and white.

The Luzis—Alexander Luzi—Swiss born, linguist, rather ordinary but pine-knotty family. . . . He was engaged to a Mexican woman when Marguerite Re came down on a visit. . . . It was love at first sight. Alex invited her and her friend to stay three days at the Victoria Hotel, the best here, of which he was part owner. ["As a Swiss, he is expert at all tourist rackets."] "Will you marry me?" he asked one night over dinner. "I never got the spoon to my mouth," says Mrs. Luzi. . . . Later, Marguerite found he had a son to support. ["Alex married a Mexican-Arabian girl of low family, five days before their son was born."] . . . If Alex had not been quite the fellow he is, he would have left the little chippie in the trouble she deserved. . . .

. . . Alex wants [Marguerite] to buy property to nail herself down here, selling her car (the symbol of flight) to get the money for it. . . . "I can't stand it much longer. I certainly can't stand it the rest of my life," Marguerite says.

. . . Their arguments are few but interesting: the second major one in five years started when Alex asked for Marguerite's car. . . . "You can pack your things and go," he said. "You can pack yours, and I'll do it for you right now," she said, doing it, and setting the valise outside the door. . . . He has something of the personality of Stanley Laurel, with not all the comedy removed. They have the neatest kitchen in Taxco.

Paul Cook—who talks better than he writes or paints. . . . He was a football player, married at thirty-two, to a Texas woman of good and wealthy family. Divorced last year after 14 years because of jealousy on her part, demands, criticism of his drinking. He has always drunk quite a little and now in Taxco drinks quite a lot. . . . He is the son of a Welsh doctor and an Italian woman. He is 6'3", lanky, blue eyed, and distinguished looking no matter what he does or how he dresses. . . . The *cantina* proprietors adore him, for sincere reasons.

He is paid $150 dollars per month by the U.S. Government to catch dope peddlers. Sometimes he makes a catch. Ostensibly, he is the washed-up American painter going to hell in Taxco. . . . People get attached to [Paul], admire him, even want to be like him. . . . He has done what no other American I know has done, made the Mexicans like him, I mean inspired their friendship. Despite his height, despite his blue eyes, they love him. . . .

Paul came home with me for the first time one night to read my manuscript. He read 11 pages and said it was excellent, told me good reasons why. Then I went to bed and he was to sleep on the porch. Later he joined me in my bed, and while I didn't like it at first, I decided it was not true cameraderie [*sic*] to stand on ceremony. He slept like a log on his side all night, got up first and got breakfast. The next night when I got home at 12:45 A.M. he was in my bed and I *had* to sleep on the porch. He is as undependable as a Negro when he is drunk. Wants to do my portrait. He can make drama, and art, out of nothing.

Miss Jones—hostess at the Victoria. Moles all over her face, and a Chicago accent. Vender-Bearer of delicious imported cheeses which come in excess of the pecan pie that concludes the five peso meal—the best Taxco or even Mexico City affords. She is patient, friendly, and somehow immeasurably sad. . . . Discovered crying in her room because a 26 year old woman's child was so beautiful.

Stanley Coventry—fop, fascist. Britisher, sponger off his aunt, Mrs. Auchinclaus (Samuel). Stanley is a frightful bore, inspiring hatred in Paul Cook. . . . He goes about with a Schnauzer. Has done some good designs, they say, for jewelry. Paints when he needs money, which is seldom. Has lived two years in Tahiti and tells his sexual experiences on short acquaintance. . . . His voice, like many Englishmen's voices, from a distance sounds effete and like a homosexual's. . . . A namby-pamby, pantywaist, generally repulsive character. Looks much like the Prince of Wales, though taller, with the incipient *embonpoint* of a gourmet.

Mrs. Auchinclaus, a dowager widow, blue, alert eyes, constant smoker, quizzes me with an interest as to what I am writing. . . . When she was young, she saw all Europe, made photographs of places of interest and sold them to museums and galleries. She clings to youth and life, as I have seen so many her age and type cling to it.

Pat also cast her assessing eye on the Weltons: he looks like "Carl Sandburg," she like "Julie Haydon"; Colonel Newton, "the West Point graduate" back on a thirty-day leave from the war and married to a "26 year old girl, very sweet, a trifle hebraic"; and the other Newton family, the female half of which "was seen in Chachalaca's bar by half the town one afternoon pulling her dress down and presenting her fifty year old bosom to all who would have a feel," and the husband, Dr. Newton, who "left Taxco [without his wife] owing me ten pesos, Paul about 300, Chachalaca's 180, Arturo's 140." And then there was "Fidel Figueroa," an early, compellingly heterosexual prototype for her hero-criminals, whom Pat put at the center of her short story "In the Plaza." Fidel is "an Indian, who came into town with one peso, and a handsome face, and somewhere underneath it, the energy to climb fast and the ruthlessness."

Murder was usually on Pat's mind when she wrote fiction, and as her fictions took their various forms in Mexico, she began to use murder as a replacement for love—or as a reaction to love. Fifteen years later she would admit to a lover that life didn't make any sense unless there was a crime in it. In early manuscript versions of several of her novels (*A Game for the Living, The Two Faces of January* amongst them), Pat changed the murderer from manuscript to manuscript—sometimes at the suggestion of an editor—as though it didn't really matter to her who did the deed as long as the impulse to kill found expression in the plot.[14] Even in *The Talented Mr. Ripley*, the novel whose initial murder is so iconically linked to its theme, the original murder victim was Dickie's father, Herbert Greenleaf, who, in various versions, is pushed from a cliff by both Dickie and Tom or stabbed and filled with opium so Tom Ripley can "engage . . . in a smuggling operation."[15]

Both Pat's Mexican short stories end in awkward deaths. She has the character who represents Fidel Figueroa killed in "In the Plaza," and she also kills the character who stands in for Marguerite Luzi in her short story "The Car." But in life, Mrs. Luzi lived on in Taxco, and in life Fidel Figueroa enchanted many foreign ladies with his paintings (which sold "faster than he could paint them"), left Mrs. Cadenas, who had pulled him up from poverty and kept and dressed him beautifully—Pat lingers on Fidel's "New York" clothes—and married the "none too prepossessing Mrs. Kitzelman, whose husband made his fortune in barbed wire fences." "They live in the most ornate house in Taxco, decorated by all the best decorators from Mexico City in Mrs. K's execrable taste." Pat took the happy ends in her models' lives and turned them into tragedy (or at least into murder) in her fictions.

Fiction, as Pat was to say decades later in an interview on American radio, was for what she really *wished* would happen.[16]

Pat also took careful notes on the Taxco residents' most serious extracurricular activity: drinking. Taxco was a place where steady drinkers could find plenty of company. Pat did most of her own imbibing at the bar in the Victoria Hotel and in Chachalaca's Bar. In Mexico, she wrote with less embarrassment about drinking than she was ever to do again.

The moon is a tired wheel of chance rolling across the sky, and I am to be found in a bar. Hours and hours I sit watching the business man from Chicago paw a lady who is not his wife, listening to the jaded mariachis grinding out "Jalisco," absorbing greedily a thousand monotonous details that I have seen a thousand times before, absorbing alcohol to feel things I have felt a thousand times before.[17]

In Taxco people do not drink to fill social intervals, or as a ritual between four and six, and do not drink for a mild lift, but for total oblivion.[18]

Alcohol is a virus. . . . One drink leads to another, with an infallibility unequalled anywhere else on the globe. Masculine cameraderie is strong. Wines are comic.[19]

Pat was considering writing a "book or short stories on Taxco, preferably a book,"[20] and her thoughts were a variation on the theme she'd identified at the age of twenty: "What keeps recurring to me as a fundamental of the novel is the individual out of place in this century."[21]

As always, Pat was following the split, the fault line, the fracture in her own psychology to imagine the subject of her future novels. But her musings in Taxco seemed to predict her future life as well, setting out with uncanny prescience her struggles in the next five decades in all those foreign countries where she lived and worked as a resident alien. Pat said she wanted her writing to

show the effects of foreign milieu on Americans. Americans, because Americans, less than French, Germans, far less than the English, do not know whether to assimilate themselves or hold apart. They try to do both, and lose their own souls, their mores, their minds. The Englishman takes a little England along with him, and lives in proud isolation. The Frenchman forgets his European blood and marries. The American sits astride the fence, drinks, and earns the hostility of every native in the foreign country. It is this split personality that makes the American a total failure, that tears him apart.[22]

In between her bouts of tequila drinking, drawing and sketching, taking observant character notes, and imagining new fictions, Pat, full of confidence and despair, worked on the novel at hand, the novel she was never to finish: *The Click of the Shutting.*

In 1965, in an interview for the London *Sunday Times*—the same interview in which she announced that "stories are absolutely essential to me, like poetry: I write a lot of both"—Pat gave an account of her abandoned novel to the writer and critic Francis Wyndham:

> I . . . went to Mexico and started a long Gothic novel which never got finished. It was about two boys of fourteen, one rich and one poor. The poor boy goes and stays in the rich boy's house and falls in love with his mother. I described the house in great detail, and when I realised I'd written hundreds of pages and still hadn't got to the action, I gave it up. It was quite unlike my later books.[23]

On the first day of 1943, a week after she got her job at Sangor-Pines, Pat had taken a New Year's walk to Sutton Place, the expensive Manhattan enclave close to her new apartment on East Fifty-sixth Street. It was a walk she would turn into a little voyage of discovery for Gregory, the main character of her "long Gothic novel," *The Click of the Shutting*. (The title, borrowed from one of Elizabeth Barrett Browning's sonnets, refers to the sound a clasp knife, the kind of knife Pat always carried, makes as it closes.) Although Pat insisted that "[u]nlike Nietzsche, my best thoughts do not come in the fresh air,"[24] some of her best images did, and in her notes for the novel the boy Gregory sees what Pat saw that day on Sutton Place: a lamp enclosed in an iron frame over a colonial doorway, "all grey like an ancient knight's crest. . . . It was then, young as he was at sixteen, that Gregory knew he must have always and only his love of the fantastic and the unreal."[25]

As she walked past Manhattan's elegant mansions, Pat must have repeated to herself many times the phrase with which she began *The Click of the Shutting*: " 'I'll pretend that I live there,' Gregory whispered as he came into the block."[26]

Pat did describe a "house in great detail" in this novel—which, contrary to what she told Francis Wyndham, was so much like her "later books" that most of the themes (including the "big signet ring,"[27] a feature of all Pat's Ripley novels)[28] in most of her later works can be found in *The Click of the Shutting*.[29] The novel's grand house, the house of the Willson family, is the first of many invented houses—a "house of fiction," in Henry James's phrase—to appear in a Highsmith novel. Like all the other houses she would make up, this house was what Patricia Highsmith desperately wanted at twenty-three.

Pat had Edgar Allan Poe at the back of her mind while she was working on *The Click of the Shutting* (she was thinking of "William Wilson," Poe's 1839 tale of paranoid and murderous doubles, when she named the house's proprietary family "Willson"). But despite long, shapely passages and some subtle characterizations, much of her writing approached the ungainly style that made the novelist E. L. Doctorow call Edgar Allan Poe a "genius hack" and "our greatest bad writer."[30]

Besides "great detail," Pat invested the Willson house with its own "character," and her manuscript predates by fifteen years the next American novel to present a house with a personality: Shirley Jackson's elegant psychological ghost story, *The Haunting of Hill House.* The first sentence of Jackson's 1959 work could almost be a summary of the reasons Pat would always give for why she wrote. "No live organism," Shirley Jackson wrote, "can continue for long to exist sanely under conditions of absolute reality.[31]

Pat began to make little notes for *The Click of the Shutting* six weeks before she started work for Richard Hughes at Sangor-Pines. In September of 1942, she'd been imagining the "enormous possibilities" of using adolescents as major characters "in a novel." She was thinking about (but not reading again) André Gide's *The Counterfeiters,* reminding herself of the precocity of his teenagers.[32] A week after Hughes hired her, Pat began extending her notes into the idea of a novel about an artistic teenage boy who spies upon the house and enters the life of another, far wealthier boy.[33]

Pat was, after all, still an adolescent herself (she liked to think of herself as an adolescent boy), and so she imagined Gregory Bullick as a high school student who had some of the characteristics of one of her high school friends. "Let Gregory=B.B. but he will not be the main character because he is a Jew. A perfectionist."[34]

"B.B." was Babs, the close friend of Judy Tuvim (Holliday) and a girl to whom Pat had been attracted. But as Pat, in Taxco, was writing her way through the comic book scenarios she was mailing back to Sangor-Pines in Manhattan, her notes for Gregory show that she was allowing him to split off, to become half of a double nature, to take something from her own psychology and something from what she was writing for Richard Hughes.[35] She gave Gregory some of her tastes, too: sending him to Carnegie Hall to see the cross-dressed Flamenco dancer, Carmen Amaya, by whom both she and Ruth Bernhard had been enthalled.[36]

So Gregory loses his "Jewishness" and his minor status and becomes a major character whose homoerotic attachments and meek outward demeanor are more like Patricia Highsmith's—and more like the Alter Egos she is writing for Sangor-Pines ("Bob Benton: mild-mannered young pharmacist")—than they are like the traits of Dostoyevsky's liverish young antiheroes or Gide's perversely philosophical adolescent geniuses.

An impoverished boy, Gregory is also a talented one, and parasitical in his

attachments to the other, richer boys he worships. He has some of Pat's pro-
tectiveness about his art: he is horribly insulted when a friend of his father's
looks at his drawing of "the wind" and says: "It's nothing." He shares with Pat
the double conviction that he is worthless and that, therefore, the world must
revolve around him. Gregory's narcissism fosters the creation of an Alter Ego
the way a petri dish encourages the growth of bacteria; he's a candidate for the
dark side of the American Dream. "[Gregory] felt he was driven by some terrific energy that would never exhaust itself and that must surely translate itself finally into something magnificent."[37] Like Pat, he "driv[es] himself on
nerve alone" and loves the "destructive" way this makes him feel.[38]

Gregory lives with his alcoholic father, a failed passport photographer, in
a disheveled loft in Pat's old neighborhood in Greenwich Village. Gregory
uses Pat's old subway stop, the Christopher Street station, and, like her, he has
a penchant for good addresses, fine houses, and drinking at Pete's Tavern. He
comes back every day for weeks to spy on the house of the Willson family,
with whose spoiled and destructive son, George, he creates a rivalrous and
Alter Ego–like relationship. Gregory is also a would-be novelist.

When Gregory enters George Willson's house for the first time, George
sees that Gregory is ravished by the house's interior; Gregory seems zombie-
like to George, seems "to be in a perpetual trance. . . . It was like he was dead
and would do anything he was told to do."[39] Gregory is trying to think himself into George Willson's body, trying to be "born directly into heaven without the trouble of a lifetime of living and dying."[40] "Wanting the house was
a strange and unreasonable thing."[41] Wanting George's family was even
stranger: "It was as much the imagined household as the physical house that
he loved."[42]

As though the Willsons have been compelled by the force of Gregory's
feelings, they pack off their son George to a military academy and invite
Gregory to take his place. While Gregory is not the first of Pat's long line of
adopted or semiadopted characters—that distinction goes to the "boy called
Mary" in "The Legend of the Convent of St. Fotheringay"—Gregory is the
first fully developed character who is "adopted," and the first one who tries
to replace his Alter Ego. In The Click of the Shutting, Pat was beginning to test
out some of the abiding themes—replacement, substitution, and forgery—
that would color even the works she devoted to women. Therese in The Price
of Salt is an "orphan" whose absent, neglectful mother is still alive, while
Edith Howland of Edith's Diary has unresponsive parents but a motherly
Aunt Melanie.

Pat's imagination liked to exclude birth families or destroy them, and this
preference found expression even in her most casual lines. One of them was

part of a little limerick she wrote in 1976: "Home presents a dismal picture / Things are gloomy as the tomb."[43] Another is a note she took a couple of years later: "Families are nice to visit but I wouldn't want to live with one."[44]

André Gide, Pat's literary guide to sexualizing adolescents, had already reduced the familial subject to its essentials: *"Familles! Je vous haïs!"*

Early on, Pat was thinking of The Murder in *The Click of the Shutting* as essential: "[c]ommitted on a day when Dominick and Donato [she uses the names of several other paired boys in subplots: Bernard and Charles, Gregory and George, Alex and Paul, etc.] have been laughing too much."[45] In a later version, it is the boys' high school teacher who is murdered. Pat frames this murder in homosexual terms, and the killing is committed, once again, because the boys have been laughing too much:

> Gregory haunts the pistol all the week, the pistol which Alphonse owns. . . . And on the day it happens, the chemistry teacher scolds the two of them for unruliness, and they still laugh too much, and Alphonse, softened by the gentle lapping, licking of Gregory's adulation, pulls the trigger at his broad short back.[46]

In the notes Pat made for the end of *The Click of the Shutting* (she managed 385 pages before abandoning it as unfinishable) she indicated that she wanted Gregory to sketch George's mother, Margaret, then sleep with her, and then, in a scuffle with George, accidentally kill her. Her first idea was that it was Margaret's son, George Willson, who should do the killing.

As befits a recent college graduate whose longest experience of life has been school, Pat's imagination of the high school in *The Click of the Shutting* is the best thing in the novel. Reminiscent of Kafka's confining structures, the school is more vicious, more contemporary, and less randomly organized than Kafka's trackless mental architectures. The deteriorating physical plant— everything is gray and greasy and abandoned—the violent hall monitors, the hungover children, the persistent and cruel torturing of teachers by students and the students' torturing of each other, are both uncomfortably modern and sinisterly Gothic.

Many of Pat's conflicted feelings about women went straight into the male characters of *The Click of the Shutting*. It was a double displacement for her (and a nice play on Gide's idea of *dédoublement,* although her understanding of Gide was limited to his adolescent boys) by which, as she became a boy on the page, she lost both her "female self" and her "real" antipathies for women. (Pat had begun the book by thinking of herself as the boy who would fall in love with George's mother, Margaret.) Her antipathies towards women were much more powerful (and much less subtle) when she wrote about them in the voice of her cahiers, which was, more or less, her own voice. Or, rather, *one* of her voices.

Gregory has odd feelings about girls: "Most of all he hated to bump into the girls' breast. Their soft pressure was to him unclean and a little spooky."[47] Everett, George Willson's uncle, looks down into the "disconcertingly intense face" of his wife, Lydia, and says: "You remind me of Lady Macbeth."[48] And "[a]s he strokes her hair, he thinks: It was an ugly thing he did, touching her . . . a very ugly thing."[49] George Willson plays a nastily misogynist game with his great uncle Alfred called "Lord Twitchbottom and Lady Twot."

Gregory develops a crush on another wealthy male classmate, too, Paul Cotton. "His devotion to Paul was a far worthier thing, for Paul was a fine person." Gregory, as Tom Ripley will do ten years later, impersonates the object of his crush: "Still being Paul, mingling friendliness with unconcern, he descended the rest of the stairs."[50] And, just as Ripley will do, Gregory makes a throat-slitting gesture in front of a mirror with a razor and calls out the name of Paul's girlfriend.[51] Gregory's crush on Paul might have forced *The Click of the Shutting* to follow an even more dangerous direction—but Pat held that particular fire for *The Talented Mr. Ripley*.

Pat worked diligently on *The Click of the Shutting* in Taxco, in between bouts of watching her recent history parade itself before her eyes. Ben-Zion Goldberg, her employer from FFF Publications, did come to visit her in Mexico, just as he'd written he would, and he stayed there mooning around her for quite a while. He told Pat he wanted to share a house with her for "two years." Mother Mary took alarm from afar, calling him an "old goat" in a letter. Goldberg and Pat did some travelling together—to Acapulco, principally, in March—and some flirting too.

In Acapulco, Pat worked on her novel while small lizards ran through her room and across the roof, and a "noisy pig" noisily enjoyed the orange peels she'd thrown away.[52] The heavy concentration of ions in the air excited and energized her; the green sparks she and Goldberg could make by stamping on wet sand and the sparks she saw dancing on the water made her "very happy." Those green sparks found their way into another interesting, unfinished text Pat would set partially in Mexico: *The Dove Descending*.

Ben-Zion Goldberg, according to Pat, was in love with her, and he came to the same conclusion most of Pat's rejected admirers would come to: "Goldberg says that I'm incapable of loving, that I am in love. . . . with myself." On their trip to Acapulco, Goldberg visited her diligently every night at eleven o'clock in her room by the sea to speak about her novel and about their possible relations. And he stayed, talking, until the early hours of the morning.[53]

He was too much of a gentleman to press his case with more than a few "advances"—and Pat was too much of a lesbian to be interested in them.

"His conversation is very inspiring," Pat wrote in her Mexico Diary of their Acapulco trip, "and he tries with much patience to make me really fall in love with him, but that is impossible."[54] Goldberg would later ask her to read a lengthy novel he'd written, so she could show it to her agent, Margot Johnson. Pat didn't find much in the manuscript to interest her.

On 20 March, taking the swaying bus back from Acapulco to Taxco with Goldberg (who accompanied Pat even though it was out of his way), Pat refused to sit with other people because she wanted "to dream" by herself. When the bus stopped in Tierra Colorada, she was suddenly and sharply transfixed by the figure of a child which seemed to materialize out of previous "dreams"— transgressive dreams about young girls. This figure was "a nine year old girl, the most beautiful girl I've seen in Mexico. I wanted to bring her with me. She was asking for some centavos with others. I thought of her until Chispamingo and Iguala."[55]

Just before she left Taxco for the United States, Pat saw Chloe again, "my alcoholic beauty . . . in Mexico City. She, being immune to the subtle . . . effects of this Latin atmosphere, is staying on. Her hands still shake as badly as they did in New York—and for the same thing."[56]

As usual, Pat's interest in herself and in what was directly around her in Mexico precluded interest in anything else. The Second World War didn't wrest much prose from her pen. The few entries she made in her journals about the war seem to have been made in summary, with an eye to her future readers. They run along the lines of the journal entry she made shortly before leaving Barnard:

Bali is now partially occupied, the British are maneuvering at Rangoon, the first American battleship has been sunk, the Bali fleet of Japan smashed and a new Russian army, trained east of the Urals, is ready to go. Today's the anniversary of the Red Army! And tomorrow I have a date for lunch with Rosalind![57]

Unlike the comics Superheroes and war heroes whose scenarios she was still sending to Richard Hughes, and unlike some of her more adventurous Barnard classmates, it never occurred to Pat, once she'd left Barnard and the Sangor-Pines shop, to assist the U.S. war effort or to actually *go* to war. She was already indirectly assisting the armed forces by writing what amounted to war propaganda for the comics, but her most obvious response to the Second World War was to ignore it. Instead of going to war, she went to Mexico with an attractive model—and she worked on her first novel and hoarded up material for her cahiers and diaries.

From Monterrey, in the second week of May 1944, Pat wrote to Kingsley wistfully about her Barnard classmates (and bedmates, although Kingsley wasn't privy to this part of the story)—feeling, suddenly, as though she'd been left out of one of history's great designs. She righted herself with a burst of ironic fantasy and a short shot of false "feminism." (Even in the palmy days of its ascendancy, "feminism" was a word Pat would have used only under water torture.)

"What has become of Babs? Is she in the war? . . . That girl will never know how much I like and admire her, and maybe it's best that way. . . . And what of Helen and Peter? Bumping along in some ambulance in France, I suppose. Or in the Marines. My God, if I wanted to join any of those goddam things, I'd go to Russia, where they give women the honor of being fighter pilots. Better than cleaning out kitchens, no?"[58]

No. Being a fighter pilot *wasn't* better than cleaning out kitchens for someone like Pat Highsmith. She would never have joined the Russian air force because she was (1) too ambivalent to fight for any side but her own, (2) a terrible driver of any vehicle that required steering, (3) terrified of the sight of blood, and (4) actually very enthusiastic about cleaning out almost anything, kitchens included.

In the same letter, Pat said that she was reading Joyce's *Portrait of the Artist as a Young Man* and wondered if it was a bad thing to do "for anyone writing a first novel . . . for the inevitable question appears—what need of more after this?" And she made the first of many requests over many decades for Kingsley to pick up for her personal use some of "the old Columbia spiral notebooks. . . . You know what a stickler I am for uniformity and I'll need one soon."[59]

"Contrary to what you've read and heard," said Pat's cousin Dan Walton Coates, "for someone who didn't like Fort Worth worth a damn, Pat sure as hell surfaced here quite frequently. When things were down for her, it was nice to go home."[60] Texas was both a magnet for Pat's irritations and a mythical harbor where her battered little love boat could anchor and shelter in Grandmother Willie Mae's upright manners and unyielding morals. Because of Willie Mae's rocklike presence, the stability of the home situation in Fort Worth attracted Pat in exactly the same measure as its rigidity oppressed her. One of her notes for a "3rd person" short story, written during her precollege Fort Worth visit of 1938, reads: "Sunday at Grandmother's . . . Stillness, the silence, the noises, the air, heat, the *purpose*. Depression, oppression, con-science."[61] But Pat kept coming back to Willie Mae, and Fort Worth was an interim stop on some of her trips to and from Mexico.

Willie Mae's house on West Daggett Avenue had a den with storage cabi-nets which ran all the way around the room. The doors to these cabinets were made up of unusually tall wooden panels, and Pat, stopping at Willie Mae's on her way back to New York from Taxco, decorated every single one of the panels with paintings. She painted scenes from the Texas countryside into which she set, naturally enough, Texas cattle. And on the ground under the tail of one of those Texas cows, she carefully brushed in a large, fresh pile of cow dung. "That," said her cousin Dan, "was a big subject of conversation."[62]

Back in New York at the end of May, Pat was poring over John Ruskin's work. By the end of September, she was toting up the progress of her love life over the summer of 1944, during which she had enjoyed the reverse of her usual love troubles. One of the multiple affairs Pat began that summer was with the lovely, adventurous, alcoholic blond socialite Natica Waterbury, a woman Pat would keep up with all her life. Natica's early death prompted Pat to dedicate a collection of short stories to her, and Natica's daredevil exploits (she was a pilot) and literary and social interests (she assisted Sylvia Beach at Shakespeare & Company in Paris and was part of the international lesbian daisy chain) commanded Pat's heart and head for quite a while. Still, it all seemed to come to the same thing in the end.

"Loves by the dozen, love affairs by the dozen are all very well. But oh God, when they overlap! If one could merely be clear with one before begin-ning another, all would be well. It is the overlapping, the overlapping, the overlapping, until where one's love heart is, is so thickly padded, nothing can any longer be felt."[63]

ALTER EGO

Vince Fago, a cartoonist of considerable charm and sweetness (rabbits were his signature cartoon animal), was one of Pat's editors at the comics company that was her most regular employer after she came back from Mexico; a company called Timely comics. Timely had offices in New York's most famous landmark, the Empire State Building. During the Second World War, Vince Fago was responsible for hiring Timely's freelance writers, and he would take the occasional walk and have the odd cup of coffee with his freelancer Patricia Highsmith. It was for Vince that Pat wrote the blood-drenched adventures of Jap Buster Johnson and the action-filled exploits of The Destroyer.[1] ("The Destroyer" was a long-running feature story published in many comic books; amongst its other scripters were Otto Binder and Stan Lee.) Pat, always a go-getter, had approached Vince Fago for work in his office.

"She came up and talked to me and I hired her. She did script scenarios, which meant a scene description and dialogue and sounds and captions for each panel. I'd give her eight- to ten-page stories to do at six to eight dollars a page. The money was terrific for anybody. We were rich and didn't know it."[2]

On his eighty-eighth birthday, Vince Fago still remembered Pat Highsmith very well. It was her "beauty," he said, which struck him first; he thought she was "just amazing," a "terrific looker." But Vince was newly and happily married when Pat came to work for him, so he thought he'd introduce Pat to the Timely editor whose post he had taken for the duration of the war, Stan Lee. Lee, now known worldwide as the public face of Marvel Comics (Timely evolved into Marvel) and the godfather of the enduring Superhero Spider-Man, was then a young soldier back in New York on leave from the U.S. Army. Vince Fago took Lee up to Pat's apartment "near Sutton Place," hoping to make a "match" between Pat and Stan Lee. But the future creator of the talented Mr. Ripley was not fated to go out on a date with the future facilitator of Spider-Man. "Stan Lee," said Vince Fago, "was only interested in Stan Lee," and Pat wasn't exactly admitting where her real sexual interests lay.[3] Lee, who invokes his failing memory and "murky mind," remembers only Pat's name from the incident.[4]

Leon Lazarus, an associate editor at Timely for whom Pat wrote some romance comics at the end of the 1940s, remembered Pat as a "quiet, discreet person; a very intelligent woman" who moved in and out of the Timely offices like a ghost, delivering her scripts by laying them on his desk and then disappearing. He also thought he recalled one flattering notice: Eleanor Roosevelt, he said, had mentioned in her long-running newspaper column "My Day" (1935–62) that she was reading *Strangers on a Train* while riding on an actual train—and had liked the novel. And, said Lazarus, "The next thing you know, everybody went out and bought [the] book because Eleanor Roosevelt recommended it."*[5]

Pat had another editor at Timely after the war ended. Her name was Dorothy Roubicek. Will Eisner (whose testimony on this subject has been echoed by his contemporaries) emphasized that no women were really "well known" in the comics business.[6] Roubicek, he said, was one of the few who had made her way into an administrative position. Pat used Dorothy Roubicek's last name—minus the *u*—for one of the Grimm-est fairy-tale characters in *The Price of Salt:* the exhausted, middle-aged emigrée dressmaker whose attempt to reclothe and comfort the young heroine Therese ends in Therese's disgusted rejection. Pat also slipped the name Sinnott into a manuscript: Joe Sinnott was one of the top artists at Timely comics. And in her Suffolk novel, *A Suspension of Mercy,* the television crime serial which her obsessive character Sydney Bartleby is trying to write with a partner (Pat was trying to do the same thing herself in Suffolk) is called "The Whip." The Whip was a 1940s comics Superhero whose costume included a whip, very heavy makeup, and a fake Mexican accent.[7]

Dorothy Roubicek was married to William Woolfolk, dubbed "the Shakespeare of comics" by one of the great rendering artists of the comics, Lou Fine. Woolfolk, a prolific television writer, the author of nineteen books and plays, and the creator of the comic book Superhero Captain Marvel's immortal exclamation, "Holey Moley!" remembered what every man who worked with

* Pat returned the favor, if favor it was (a search of the electronic edition of Eleanor Roosevelt's "My Day" columns couldn't confirm Lazarus's anecdote), in *The Talented Mr. Ripley.* Tom Ripley's best party trick is an impersonation of Mrs. Roosevelt writing her "My Day" column.

Pat remembered: how very "attractive" Patricia Highsmith had been in those days.[8]

"We weren't particularly sophisticated," Woolfolk said of the people making the comics, "but we were all doing everything for the first time, including making money, having children, being comfortable. We were all chaste then about drink, but Pat wasn't. She was very disappointed when she came to dinner and discovered that we didn't have enough alcohol."[9] Pat said the same thing in her diary—and much less politely. By now, a dinner party without enough alcohol to help her through it made Pat furious.

Woolfolk thought Pat was living "with the man who wrote *Rain Before Seven*." That would have been Marc Brandel (real name: Marcus Beresford)—whose name Pat must have offered as both a smokescreen and a hope, for it was during the time she had dinner with Roubicek and Woolfolk that Pat was still trying to talk herself into marrying Marc.[10] (See "Social Studies: Part 2.") Pat liked to say that it was her grandmother Willie Mae who gave her the advice that closed the marriage-door on Marc Brandel. Could Pat bring herself to "wash Marc's socks?" Willie Mae asked Pat in April of 1948. "I replied, no, come to think of it, I don't think I'd like to. . . . So my grandmother advised me not to marry. May I say she was right."[11]

Vince Fago, Pat's usual editor at Timely, met his artist wife, D'Anne, through another colleague at Timely—the eminent American fiction writer, critic, essayist, and editor Elizabeth Hardwick. Hardwick was an editor at Timely Publications then, but not in the comics end of the business: "Why, I never read a comic in my life!" said Hardwick emphatically.[12] Timely put out many kinds of publications, and Elizabeth Hardwick was editing Timely's mystery-story line as well as contributing seriously to the intellectual circle supporting *Partisan Review*. She had no contact at all with the deadline-driven, pieceworking, assembly-line division that Pat was toiling for, although, said Hardwick, she wished she "*had* managed to meet Pat Highsmith."

Elizabeth Hardwick wasn't the only prominent writer to work for a publishing company which also produced comic books. When Sam Rosen, a letterer for many comics companies, went into the army, his fellow artist Pierce Rice says, "there was a little going away luncheon for him. . . . The participants were: Miss Highsmith, then a comics writer, one of the [comics] editors, the guest of honor, and myself."[13]

The editor at that going-away luncheon was Stanley Kauffmann, later a theater critic for *The New York Times* and then, for twenty-five years, the film and theater critic for *The New Republic* magazine. He was the writer Pat had replaced at Cinema Comics when she went to work for Sangor-Pines (See "Alter Ego: Part 1.") Kauffmann was a comics editor at Fawcett when this luncheon took place, and Pierce Rice thought that Kauffmann's memoirs—"which included a chapter on the comics"—made "his connection [to them] more distant than it really was."[14] Many people who went on to distinguished careers outside the comics were unwilling to say they had ever worked in America's newest art form.

Mickey ("I always say never hit a woman when you can kick her") Spillane was one of the exceptions.[15] Spillane was working for Vince Fago at Timely comics when Pat was writing for Vince. Spillane and Pat both wrote stories for the same character—the bloodthirsty Jap Buster Johnson—but never at the same time. Comics' artist Allen Bellman remembers Stan Lee handing him a Mickey Spillane script for *Jap Buster Johnson* in 1942 (a few months before Pat worked on the title), and Vince Fago said that during the war Spillane would come up to the Timely offices in the Empire State Building in his navy uniform to hand in his assignments. Spillane continued to write for the comics for years; he thought it was "a great training ground for writers."[16]

Mickey Spillane had originally written up his perennial character Mike Hammer's exploits as a feature story for comic books called "Mike Danger." No one would publish it. In 1947, Spillane rewrote his comic book story as a pulp novel, *I, the Jury,* transforming Mike Danger into the violent, hard-boiled detective Mike Hammer, whose subsequent adventures made Mickey Spillane the twentieth century's best-selling novelist. It's the kind of joke Hammer himself might have tossed off before plugging yet another double-crossing dame.

Pat didn't think much of Mickey Spillane. "The old-fashioned morality of E[dmond] C[lerihew] Bentley will be remembered when Mickey Spillane is forgotten," she wrote primly in 1953—making the rare admission that she was actually reading something other than the classics.[17] As usual, the notes in her cahier give her away: she was not only reading the elegant English detective writer E. C. Bentley, she was also reading the work of Spillane himself. Bentley's cleverly plotted, finely written works (there were only four detective novels, and he invented the verse form "clerihew") focus on the "breakdown of identity" and the "false alibi"—two crucial themes that ran through everything Pat herself liked to read and write. Pat was eying *all* the competition, and the competition—no matter how much she tried to give the impression—wasn't always Gide or Dostoyevsky.

Vince Fago thought a lot of Pat. "She was a smart cookie. She could adapt herself," he said. Adaptation to the quick reversals required by plot demands and printing deadlines was essential to success in the comics business. Pat was a "professional," Vince said, "meticulous and clean and always met the deadline."[18] It was the same assessment Gerald Albert made of her when she worked at the Sangor-Pines shop. But Vince went a little further. "Working with her was just like working with a man," Vince said. "She was one of the boys."[19]

Pat—turning out scripts and scenarios during the day in a genre dominated by male fantasies and entertaining herself lavishly at home at night with her *own* richly detailed, "male" fanatasies—would have considered Vince Fago's description quite a compliment.

In 1970, twenty-five years after they'd last worked together, Vince wrote to Pat in France asking her to participate in a book featuring the "hundred best comics" he'd ever edited. Pat replied briefly that she was "too busy" to have anything to do with comic books.[20] A few years later, at the end of 1973, the comic book historian Dr. Jerry Bails, who was compiling his second edition of *Who's Who of American Comic Books*, sent Pat a list of questions about her comics work.[21]

Pat always did like to see her name in professional journals. The exception (naturally) was a reference collection entitled *Contemporary Lesbian Writers*, to whose editor in 1992 she sent a registered letter saying that she "did not want to have a biographical essay written about me." Generally, though, Pat added her name to *Who's Who*s and to professional catalogues whenever she was invited to do so.* Professional listings had the advantage of making good ammunition in an argument, and well into her fifth decade, Pat was using this ammunition to assert her worth in quarrels with her parents. "I am not playing the martyr," she wrote in 1970 to her long-suffering stepfather, who was, as always, the proxy for Mother Mary:

> In fact, I often wonder what my mother thinks is so wrong with me. I have not been in prison, I do not take drugs, I have had no car accidents, no broken marriages, no illegitimate children, I earn a good living—I am even in *Who's Who*—the International, published in London. This honour came to me less than a year ago.[22]

In 1978 Pat employed one of her *Who's Who* credentials in a more public way. Gore Vidal's vocal involvement in the controversy between the newly forming Christian Right and male homosexuals in the United States drew Pat into the debate. She wrote a perfectly Highsmithian response to the American singer Anita Bryant's campaign against the influence of homosexuals in

---

* In September of 1977, Pat took notes for a story, "As If Dead," about a man who exaggerates his *Who's Who* listing, then commits suicide "after rereading what he might have been, what he felt he *was*." He is destroyed by his own entry "because it is false . . . and worse, some people believe it and write him congratulations" (Cahier 34, 9/15/77).

public schools: actually "coming out" to Anita Bryant twelve years before she could bear to acknowledge her authorship of *The Price of Salt,* then bolstering herself with her listing in *Who's Who.* "I am an American," Pat began her letter to Bryant coolly. "You have taken on quite a target, however, in the homosexuals. We are not a stupid lot, we are sharp as foxes. . . . Curiously, I wish you good luck—you may need it. . . . For further information on me, see *Who's Who,* the one published in England."[23]

So, although she left out most of the details of her comics career for the *Who's Who of American Comic Books* questionnaire sent to her in Moncourt, France, in 1973 by Jerry Bails—i.e., she omitted Jap Buster Johnson, Pyroman, The Whizzer, Spy Smasher, Captain Midnight, Fighting Yank, The Champion, Ghost, Golden Arrow, The Destroyer, Rangers, Betty Fairfield, Nellie the Nurse, as well as all the biographical stories she wrote for *Real Life Comics*—Pat actually did reply to Bails's questions about her comics work. It was probably the "fill-in-the-list" form of Bails's query that tempted Pat to mark down two or three of the comics titles she'd written for—*The Black Terror, Sergeant Bill King, Crisco and Jasper,* along with some "unidentified comics materials"[24]—and send the entire questionnaire straight back to Jerry Bails.[25]

Pat just couldn't resist the impulse to add her name to another list.

· 15 ·

SOCIAL STUDIES

PART I

No one who knew Patricia Highsmith in the last, claustral years of her life in Switzerland can believe just how social—and even how socially confident—she could seem to be in the 1940s in Manhattan. The Embittered Old Oyster, shut up in a shell of her own devising in suburban Switzerland in the last decade of the twentieth century, was once a Pearl of a Girl in wartime Manhattan: avid for experience, hungry for connections, and going to every single place in New York City where she could find both.

Romanticism was one of Pat's best excuses for her sexual adventuring. In New York in the 1940s, she pursued her constantly upgraded romantic ideals in the beds of (mostly) women who sometimes, though not always, became her primary lovers. Part of her desire to look ever upwards in her sexual affections had to do with her early understanding of New York's stairway to success—and with her shame at how her family couldn't seem to get beyond the first step. "Making it" has always been a double entendre in Manhattan, and whenever Pat felt herself sinking lower on the city's socio-sexual-professional ladder, she did her best to reverse direction: first by self-analysis and then by action.

At twenty-four, in the spring of 1945, Pat drew up a chart for the purpose of comparing, ranking, and categorizing her ten most important love affairs with women to date (see illustration). Her goal was to "do better" in love (this, too, had a double meaning for Pat), and the chart is a chilling record of her attempt to impose this ambition on her wayward affections. The chart is much influenced by the only thing in Proust's work which ever really spoke to Pat: his insistence that you can never change your "type" in love. (Pat's understanding of Proust was eccentric. She thought he made Virginia Woolf seem "too femi-

nine" and once compared his writing unfavorably to that of John Steinbeck.)*[1]
Pat's chart is also, as near as she could make it, a diagram of her ideas about love.
She inserted it into a cahier in April of 1945 shortly after noting that "[d]eep in
my heart stands a silver sword with two edges,"[2] and a little while after kissing
a "twenty-three year old New Zealander I met tonight in a Sixth Avenue Penny
Arcade [whom I didn't] ask . . . up [for] his last night in America."[3]

On her chart, Pat's careful listing of her lovers includes the duration of
each love affair; the age of the lover in relation to Pat (of the ten, all but two are
older); the color of each woman's hair (she definitely prefers blondes); their
physicality ("slim," "sturdy"); their work status; the reason for the breakup
("time," "cruelty," "boredom"); their psychology ("neurotic," "extroverted"); a
rating of each affair on a scale of 100 (no one gets less than an 80); and the
length of time Pat thinks the affair lingered on after it was actually over ("2
years?," "9 months?").

Some lovers' initials on the chart are starred ("End due to my lack of sympathy") or marked with a cross ("End due to her lack of sympathy") or circled
("Bad judgement on my part"). Her "most advantageous" lovers are awarded
a second cross: only three of them got it.

Pat's conclusions are as unnerving as they are revealing: "I lack sympathy,
am impatient with that which attracted me. Unconscious masochism, I am
resolved to do better as well as change my *type* radically. . . . From the two
most advantageous, I fled, was false."[4]

Pat's summer of love in 1944 notwithstanding, the entire decade of the
1940s was one of intense sexual and social activity for her: the kind of intoxi-
cating experience Manhattan can offer to an attractive, talented, seriously
ambitious young woman who is using enough alcohol—more than enough
alcohol—to cover her shyness, fuel her energy, and help her, in a phrase she
used again and again, "try her luck." By Thanksgiving Day of 1949, having
spent the afternoon quietly reading and raking leaves in the sun and open air
of her parents' house in Hastings-on-Hudson, Pat was thinking over her last
ten years in Manhattan.

"[I]f my experience should be shut off now, sexually, emotionally (not intellectually), but mundanely, practically, I feel I should have enough. I have
stretched an hour into eternity."[5]

---

* Nevertheless, Proust's *In Search of Lost Time*—with its narrator-author consumed by love,
loathing, and capillarial investigations of the faubourg's forgeries—shares some fictional
territory with Highsmith's demotic dandies and middle-class sociopaths. And its fifth volume—*The Captive & The Fugitive*—reads like a paradigm for the fluctuations of Pat's love
life: "[I]t is a mistake to speak of a bad choice in love, since as soon as there is a choice it can
only be a bad one."

She also took the trouble, that afternoon, to make up one of the little sanity tests she liked to spring on herself from time to time. This one involved watching herself "lov[ing] my love with all my heart." The fact that she could concentrate on a current lover (or at least concentrate on her *feelings* for that lover) reassured her that her complete absorption thirty minutes before in Herman Melville's novel *Pierre, or The Ambiguities,* "following his vagaries of soul with the most personally involved Fascination," didn't mean that she was going "mad." "For Melville became insane and I shall not," she wrote smugly.[6] The threat of insanity was always buzzing around the corners of Pat Highsmith's ideas about herself.

"People are less sharply divided as men and women," she wrote penetratingly at nineteen, "as they are as people with ambition and people without."[7] Although Pat seemed ready to go anywhere in New York City that might offer an opportunity, she was most at ease in smaller gatherings, and so intimate parties, gallery exhibitions, and drawing classes were the assemblies she frequented most. It was only when she was looking for sexual adventure that she found Manhattan's crowded bars attractive.

It wasn't until 1968, when Pat was living in France, that she discovered the right phrase for her aversion to crowds. "I seem to suffer involuntarily, like an animal, from a sense of overcrowding, or the fact of overcrowding."[8] It was why, she said, she was willing to live in a village of 160 people (it was Montmachoux, then), far from the butcher, the sanitation department, the library, and company in the evenings: "it is worth it to me to have a sense of elbow room."[9]

Space and its encroachments would always be a problem for the writer whose first beds in New York were a succession of living-room couches in her parents' small apartments, and whose invasive mother seemed to her to be everywhere. Mother Mary's powers of simultaneous occupancy were certainly impressive. She corresponded with Pat's friends and lovers about Pat's behavior, filled the *postes restantes* of Europe with letters of advice and boxes of presents for her daughter, and always managed to track Pat down wherever she was. In 1969, when Pat, forty-eight years old and living in Montmachoux, hadn't written to Mary for a few weeks, Mary sent a telegram of admirably compressed panic to their mutual friend in Paris, the cartoonist Jeannot (Jean David): "WORRIED ABOUT PAT ONE MONTH NO LETTER HELP ME . . . MARY."[10]

In 1970, in one of three long letters to her stepfather, Stanley—letters that, in their way, were just as panicked as Mary's 1969 telegram to Jeannot—Pat tried to justify her violent behavior at her parents' home in Texas during a visit she'd paid to them earlier in the year. Her stepfather said she'd behaved like a "mad woman."[11] Pat had wrecked the Highsmith kitchen—thrown milk all over it and shattered a louvered door—and her letter to Stanley cited Mary's pervasive "crowding" of her as the reason for her explosion.

"In the kitchen at Fort Worth, after I'd cleared a few square inches to whip an egg in a bowl . . . that space was instantly filled with something my mother put there. It is as if she sees a clear space anywhere, she has to fill it."[12]

Pat was so sensitive to spatial proprieties that she felt crowded by signs of her own success. When invited to tell how she reacted when she saw her first copies of *Strangers on a Train,* she gave an odd response to her interviewer. The books were delivered to her apartment on East Fifty-sixth Street, she said, in a "cube," a big box. And "My first thought was: these are taking up a lot of space in the world. . . . I didn't feel particularly proud or shy. I thought: *These take up space.*"[13]

Always *en garde* against invasion, Pat made concerted efforts to preserve her sense of self by "avoiding meeting people, encountering them on my walks, greeting even the most pleasant acquaintances by crossing the street when I see them far ahead of me on the sidewalk. . . . Perhaps it is, basically, the eternal hypocrisy in me, of which I've been aware since about thirteen. I may feel, therefore, that I am never quite myself with others. . . .

"What troubles me somewhat is the superimposed problem of being in touch with humanity. Flatly, I do not want it."[14]

She felt the same way about "the afterworld." If the afterworld were an "active" place, with "contact . . . to others living or dead," then, she wrote, she found it not only "improbable," but "definitely untempting."[15] Heaven for Highsmith would have to have a countable population of one.

Because art classes were well within her comfort zone (attention was fixed on the model; the only necessary contact was with the drawing you were making), she started attending drawing classes, sometimes with Allela Cornell, later with her friend Lil Picard. Karl Bissinger, the photographer and political activist who was Pat's sympathetic neighbor on the Upper East Side in the 1940s, was one of the organizers of a rather chic drawing class Pat went to. In this class, Pat said, she often found herself drawing "cartoons."[16]

Karl Bissinger was taking photographs for *Harper's Bazaar* when he first met Pat. By the end of the 1940s, he was the resident photographer for the world's most elegant magazine, Fleur Cowles's star-studded *Flair,* a publication so expensive to put out that it lasted for only twelve issues.* Bissinger knew a lot of people in the wide world of "quality" Pat was anxious to enter.

---

* In a coincidental Manhattan crossing, Fleur Cowles, when she was Fleur Fenton, was responsible for reorganizing *Home and Food,* the little Greenwich Village journal that published Pat's first "professional" story, "Uncertain Treasure."

A photograph Bissinger made for *Flair* magazine has become, *faute de mieux,* one of the iconic images of America's "Golden Years," a term Gore Vidal likes to apply to the period in the 1940s just after the Second World War ended and before the "Korean Adventure" began, when the arts in New York, energized by the influx of brilliant refugees from a ravaged Europe and by enterprising veterans returning from war service, flourished and flowered as never before. Bissinger's photograph, taken in 1949 in the garden of the Café Nicholson on East Fifty-seventh Street (owned by Bissinger's then-partner, Johnny Nicholson), seems to incarnate everything Pat meant when she spoke or dreamt of "the best."

Café Nicholson was a place Pat herself went to, a place, said the painter Buffie Johnson, "where everyone knew everyone else and you knew you were making history." It was the enclave where High Society first crossed with High Bohemia, and Bissinger's alluring photograph captures the spirit of the era. In his photograph, seated around a garden table laughing and talking, are Pat's old friend Buffie Johnson; Buffie's friend the playwright Tennessee Williams (Williams used to stay in the building Buffie Johnson owned, and he broke, said Buffie, every single piece of her good china); the novelist Donald Windham; the ballerina Tanaquil Le Clercq; and the writer Gore Vidal, looking beyond the frame of the photograph. A formally attired black waitress, Virginia Reed, is in the background, serving tray in hand.

Everyone at the table is young and beautiful; everyone at the table looks rich and successful. In fact, Buffie Johnson was the only person there with any real money, and Tennessee Williams, the only one with solid success.

Pat was *never* photographed in circumstances like those in Karl Bissinger's photograph. Judging by her youthful pictures, you wouldn't know she'd ever attended any convocation of humans that numbered more than two or three. (One of her stories is called "One Is a Number You Can't Divide.") She is notably absent from the biographies and cultural histories of the period, and if she shows up in someone's memoir or memory, it is usually as a cameo player in a darkly framed vignette; she's like the Third Murderer in an Elizabethan tragedy. (Pat made this association herself. At Julia Richman High School she chose to write a "good essay on the third murderer in *Macbeth*,"[17] and when she was at Barnard she authored a play called *The Saboteurs,* which "went on after much difficulty" but produced "a pattern of applause" in the audience.)[18]

The vignettes in the few memoirs which feature Pat are little scenes of eccentricity and oddness. She is the woman who brought a tortoise to a party;[19] the woman who produced snails from her handbag and encouraged them to leave sticky trails all over her host's tabletop;[20] the woman who "drifted dark and concerned from one room to another"[21] and then jumped out at her guest from behind a tree;[22] the woman who railed against her mother in a Greenwich Village bar.[23]

Broadly speaking, though, Pat is as absent from the cultural and/or personal histories of mid-twentieth century New York as she was absent from Karl Bissinger's photograph. Her European success must have come as quite a surprise to the people who knew her then.

"She could never have made it here," says Karl Bissinger, who knew all the ropes in New York. "And because she was an exotic in Europe, it worked for her."

Pat's American agent for twenty years, Patricia Schartle (from 1970, after she married, she was known as Patricia Schartle Myrer) agrees with Bissinger. Pat first brought herself to Schartle's attention in 1958, after she had fallen out with her first real agent, Margot Johnson, a supportive woman who was, says Patricia Schartle, twenty years older than Pat and, "like Pat," a "notorious lesbian and a drunk."[24] Schartle was recommended to Pat by a woman who had been Schartle's copy editor when Schartle was editor in chief at the Appleton-Century Publishing Company. By the time Pat met Patricia Schartle, she had travelled extensively and lived in Europe, won two foreign literary awards, and spent a couple of years living with Doris, an advertising copywriter, in the socially exclusive outpost of Snedens Landing (yet another good address) in Palisades, New York, just outside New York City. There, says Schartle, Pat had begun to think of herself as "a sophisticated cosmopolitan who had lived abroad and had great success."

But Pat was not cosmopolitan, writes Schartle, and certainly not cosmopolitan enough to handle herself socially in Snedens Landing, where "the artists [Katharine] Cornell, [Guthrie] McClintock, Nancy Hamilton, The Murphies [Gerald and Sara], Paul Manship, etc. etc., were *really* cosmopolitan. . . . [S]he did not fit in. When Noel Coward and the Lunts visited Cornell she would have been totally out of place. Even after the first success of *Strangers* she knew she would be more interesting if she returned and lived in Europe. It was one of the few things we really talked about. Living abroad saved her."[25]

Pat's social awkwardnesses and confusions were usually most apparent in formal or crowded *milieux*; places where instant recognitions of social and cultural patterns were necessary. Without directions, without a chart or a map or a near-diagrammatic understanding of a social situation, Pat was often lost in a maze. (Most of Manhattan, with its gridiron street design, was an uncomplicated pleasure to Pat, while Greenwich Village, with its atypically winding streets and wayward byways, was one of her favorite venues for fictional crime.)

In the mid-1960s, in London, Caroline Besterman witnessed Pat's discomfort with crowds. "I'm a great football fan and I took Pat to the Arsenal once in Highbury, to a football game there: fifty thousand people. It was hilarious. 'How do they know when to stop?' she asked. . . . What she meant was that play stops when the referee blows the whistle, but she was too [stupefied]—literally—to figure that out. It's a simple game but it has many subtleties. Women didn't go then; it was the maleness of the crowd, I think, that confused her. She couldn't understand it."[26]

Social awkwardness was not the only jarring trait people noticed in Pat as she got older. There was something else, too, something Pat herself often mentioned in her self-appraising way. It was the sense that something was "wrong" with Pat. Or rather, the sense that something was "not right" with her. People close to Pat felt this, made allowances for it, and tried to avoid its consequences. Patricia Schartle writes:

When I first met Highsmith and in the years that followed, I felt great sympathy for her. She was forever ill at ease. Awkward and gauche, she had very little grace, if any. She was hard to like. No I did not like her. But I cared about her. One did not like her because there was a curious cunning about her just when you thought she might be more human.

Caroline Besterman felt something like this, too. Pat, says Caroline, always thought that "people didn't help her," but

I have never seen someone who was so "helped." And she was given so much leeway, everyone gave her leeway—and had it been anyone else they would have been thrown out the door. It wasn't sympathy, exactly, it was some sort of feeling that she must somehow have got something wrong with her. But no, you couldn't do anything, she would be sidetracked onto a branch line that went God knows where. She had no way of saying, "Well, that's that." It was very, very sad, given that she had a very good capacity for being a good friend and having a good time and making fun of everybody and all that kind of thing. And being witty and making a quick little drawing. But it didn't last because nothing was right enough for her. She wanted *more*.[27]

One evening in 1963, when Pat first moved to Suffolk, a friend invited her to have dinner at an old hotel in Aldeburgh. Pat tended to be "very mute" in Aldeburgh, says the friend, because it was full of the "old bourgeoisie. There were writers there, there were artists there, and they were all extremely 'U' " [Nancy Mitford's borrowed term for upper-class characteristics]—and Pat "didn't like that either because she didn't understand it. It frightened her." But the hotel was full of "nice people."[28]

"The owner of [the hotel], an extremely bizarre woman, was a good artist; a very excitable but interesting person, and sharp as anything. We arrived and we were having a drink in the dining hall and another visitor who was a psychiatrist went over to Connie and [nodding in Pat's direction] said: 'You do know you have a psychopath in the hall.' Yes. Just from observation of Pat. Connie told me this because she had always suspected, too, that there was not anything at all right with Pat."

"I remember Pat sitting there with a hard, baffled look on her face. She was lost; these people were all very sure of themselves. A heavy, a really heavy look. Full of hatred."[29]

"The two of them," Caroline Besterman said, referring to what she believed was the root of Pat's problem. "Mary and Pat. Just destroying each other. Like the old nursery rhyme: 'The gingham dog and the calico cat side by side on the mantle sat' . . . and they tore each other to pieces. It was one of those *real* nursery rhymes, you know. Dark. I was always very fond of it."*

Karl Bissinger lived with Johnny Nicholson on East Fifty-eighth Street between First and Second Avenues just a couple of blocks from Pat, and he used to see her on the street "all the time" when she was still working for the comics. They were neighbors in a New Yorkish kind of way, and his recollections of Pat were vivid.

I knew Pat before the war; when the war was coming on. It was her psychosexual presentation that drew me to her: The Troubled Woman. And we were seen, roughly, in the same—let's call it what it was— lesbian set.

The war years in New York were very interesting because the forbidden life—things now are complicated in another way and on the surface—the forbidden life was alive [if you knew where to look for it]. Before the Kinsey Report, they used to say that 2 percent of the world was homosexual, and if that's true, then it's like the Jews: they've had

---

* Caroline Besterman slightly misremembered Eugene Field's poem for children, "The Duel" (the gingham dog and the calico cat sat on a table not a mantle), but she got the sentiment right. The gingham dog and the calico cat "Wallowed this way and tumbled that / Employing every tooth and claw / In the awfullest way you ever saw." The finale: "Next morning where the two had sat / They found no trace of dog or cat . . . / But the truth about the cat and pup / Is this: they ate each other up!"

the biggest influence on everything in the world that any group ever had. . . .

Everyone drank a lot more in the 1940s. Imagine having three martinis before lunch and going back to the office. It can't be done now, but everyone did it then. . . .

One of the things we did, we would get together once a week or so, hire a model, and have a sketch class. . . . Let's call it "Bohemia" for lack of a better word. We all know what that meant in those days. Some of us had money, some of us were on our way somewhere, and some if us were, I guess, shooting up, and I don't know what some of us were doing. Most of the people in the group were what we now call "gay." And among the people who came to the sketch class was Pat Highsmith.

Now Pat, I liked her immediately because she was difficult; and when I say difficult I mean she was the kind of woman—you immediately sensed this as a male—you sensed she didn't like men. She just plain didn't like men. On the other hand, she sensed my empathy for her, the fact that I liked her. She didn't smile easily and she made NO effort to reach out socially as far as I had any idea. She was very reserved and I sort of understood very much that she was what I would call "angry at the world." In those days, I would have called her a "man-hater." But of course, she had a long life, she went abroad, she could have changed, I'm sure there were lots of other sides to her.

It was clear that she would have preferred to be a man—though that's an oversimplification of the complicated emotional thing that she had. I liked the way she cut her hair. She made an effort not to be what we used to call "butch." Underneath that, of course, that was clearly what she was.

The gossip: Pat was supposed to be in love with Babs Simpson.*

When you talk about Americans being aristocrats, Babs Simpson is a wonderful example. [She came from the de Monocol family,] who had a lot of money. A lot of these kids in this drawing class had a lot of money. [Babs] was one of the senior fashion editors who went from *Harper's Bazaar* to *Vogue*. These were the days when the top fashion magazines, almost all of them, had poetry editors and *Harper's* was the

---

* A sentiment entirely unreciprocated by Mrs. Simpson, an elegant fashion editor at *Vogue* whose "set" included the decadent jeweler Fulco di Vedura; Johnny Nicholson, owner of the Café Nicholson; and the decorator and wife of Somerset Maugham, Syrie Maugham. Mrs. Simpson's assistant at *Vogue* recalls her wearing "nothing but black dresses and huge jewels" ("Lady Liberty," *Vogue*, August 2006).

first to publish Truman Capote and I could go down the list of all the neurotics they published. Carson McCullers [for example]—who was out of the same pod as Pat Highsmith. They were two women who probably wouldn't like each other if they knew each other. I don't know that they did know each other, though they probably did.

Carson McCullers and Pat did know each other, and one Sunday afternoon, 27 February 1949 to be precise, Pat and two of the women she was sleeping with, Jeanne and Dione, went to visit Carson McCullers and her family at the McCullerses' house in Nyack, New York, a half hour's drive outside of New York City. Pat's diary notes on the day were succinct: "Carson very hospitable, and we stay for about 4 hours. Reeves (Carson's husband), her mother, and Margerita Smith, her sister." Carson continued, all afternoon, to tell Pat that she had a "very good figure." And Pat continued, all afternoon, to drink Cokes and sherry. No one seems to have disliked anyone, although Pat did allow herself the comment that she'd heard Reeves and Carson had been drinking too much in Paris.[30]

"The reason I remember these small things," says Karl Bissinger,

is because Pat's name kept flashing across the screen of memory as her books came out. I began to follow her as a writer, and I began to read in her writing so much of what I knew instinctively about her: the anger that was deep within her. She really looked at herself through masculine eyes. On the other hand she did know a little something about what was called bisexual men—or men who were meant to be bisexual. . . . It was clear that she adored the looks of those ambiguous males she wrote about.

I'm sure nobody could claim they knew Patricia. . . .

My feeling about Pat is that she was only interested in success. That would make up for a lot of the anger which she probably carried around.[31]

Pat, in her periods of social confidence in the 1940s, during which she was certain of her destiny and her attractiveness, lived in a whirl of social and sexual connections, and continued to assess everyone with a coroner's eye, were always followed by equal and opposite periods of feelings of insufficiency. The flights and drops of her self-regard in her private writings are as regular as the ups and downs of a working seesaw. But Pat's interests and attractions, as they had in high school, still flew everywhere: to "Hilda" and "Mary" and "Jackie" and "Dickie" and "Barbara" and "ABBOTT" (Berenice

Abbott) and "Billie" and "Corinne" and "Virginia." Several Virginias. And then there was "Madeleine Bemelmans," a student at Barnard, ten years older than Pat, who was the wife of the writer, illustrator, and wit Ludwig Bemelmans and the eponym of his enchanting *Madeline* books.* Pat liked Madeleine Bemelmans, was interested by her husband's success, and kept in sporadic touch with her for some years.

During the early 1940s, Pat attended the mostly female parties in the two flats and a hallway that Berenice Abbott shared with her lover, the editor Elizabeth McCausland, on the fourth floor of an old building at 50 Commerce Street in Greenwich Village. (Pat complained that the females at Abbott's parties weren't interesting enough).[32] Abbott, an inventor of photographic apparatuses and one of the world's great photographers, washed her own prints in a big wooden tub in her studio, lamenting, "No matter what I do, these prints won't last more than a hundred years."[33] Mother Mary's suspicions were aroused: "Is she a les [lesbian]?" Mary inelegantly queried Pat about Berenice Abbott. Pat adroitly replied that there were always men at Abbott's parties.

With her women friends, and later with her professional acquaintances, Pat was always concerned with who was "superior" to whom. Her compulsion was to list, rank, classify, and put everyone in their proper place in relation to herself (i.e.: "V[irginia] better than J.S. & also has a brain"). Pat also weighed herself obsessively, recording the results (they ranged from "108½" to "114"), and washed her hands, as she said, "too often." In both high school and college Pat liked to note the failing grades of her classmates, to calculate their suitability for friendship ("She has no contacts that I know of"),[34] to record their (and her) couplings and uncouplings, and to refer to all her connections as "Proustian." What she meant by this was that her relationships were complicated *and* snobbish, but her use of the adjective "Proustian" gives a good idea of just how grandly the adolescent Pat was phrasing her social life.[35]

Later on, she would lend tricky Tom Ripley her ability to size up a room and assess the opportunities in it. Ripley's reaction to anything less than "quality" company was exactly the same as Pat's:

---

* At the height of her brief and uncharacteristically intense "Communist period" in 1941, Pat contemplated Ludwig Bemelmans's work and decided that " 'artists' like Bemelmans will still be allowed to work in the Socialist state, that people, out of sheer need for recreation and diversion, will buy his things. . . . Even though he is not a fine-school artist and though he does not paint or write things with social significance. . . . Now Bemelmans is a poor example because his stuff is really the most socially conscious in the world: Café Society & Hotel Society" (Cahier 5, 24/7/41).

Tom . . . realiz[ed] that he had been rude, was being rude, and that he
ought to pull himself together, because behaving courteously even to
this handful of second-rate antique dealers and bric-a-brac and ashtray
buyers . . . was part of the business of being a gentleman. But they reminded him too much of the people he had said good-bye to in New
York, he thought, and that was why they got under his skin like an itch
and made him want to run. . . . It was the class of people he despised,
and why say that to Marge, who was of the same class?"[36]

Pat's sexual attractions were also subject to elaborate rephrasings. In the
fall semester of her freshman year at Barnard College, when she was trying to
lure Mickey (a girl) away from Judy Tuvim (*tuvim* resembles part of the Hebrew
word for "holiday," hence Judy's stage name, "Holliday"), and fending off, as
well as encouraging, the advances of Ernst Hauser, the journalist she met on
her spring boat trip to Texas, Pat began to fall in love with the first of her several Virginias.[37] Pat always wrote this first Virginia's name as though it were an
abbreviation for the state, "Va.," and Virginia tormented Pat in just the way Pat
preferred: "Va. criticizes me always" and "Phoned Va. who was terrible to me
as always on phone."[38] Virginia was two years older than Pat, and they kissed
but rarely went further than that. The "Proustian" part of Pat's attraction is
that Pat thought this first Virginia looked just like the resident royalty of English literature, Virginia Woolf.

This relationship, as well as Pat's scrutiny of two young girls, "Charlotte
and Emily," at play, helped to inspire a powerfully allusive short story of sexual complicity, "A Mighty Nice Man." Pat finished "A Mighty Nice Man" on
24 August 1939, and it was one of the stories she published in the *Barnard
Quarterly*. It is a testament to her naïveté about her work *and* the world that Pat
thought this story of a very young girl being "groomed" by a molesting male
was an example of the "good popular stuff . . . I shall yet write."[39]

In the 1940s, much of Manhattan was still a place of unlocked doors, open
hospitalities, and relatively inexpensive pleasures. Anatole Broyard captured
its postwar spirit—and the *soul* of that spirit, which was Greenwich Village—in his memoir of the forties, *Kafka Was the Rage*. "New York City had
never been so attractive. The postwar years were like a great smile in its sullen
history. The Village was as close in 1946 as it would ever come to Paris in the
Twenties. Rents were cheap, restaurants were cheap, and it seemed to me that
happiness itself might be cheaply had."[40]

But it was just as she was leaving her teens, six months before the bombing
of Pearl Harbor—the act which would eventually produce the "open Manhat-

tan" Broyard was writing about—that Pat's serious sexual life began. Pat went to a gay party in Greenwich Village, to which she had been invited by an older woman she met in a bar, Mary Sullivan. Pat noticed the photographer Ruth Bernhard at the party but spoke a great deal with Sullivan, watching Mary "fly here and there all evening. The boys adore her!" Finally, Mary and Pat went to Child's Restaurant in Times Square to eat, where they talked until four thirty in the morning. Since they were near Mary's apartment, Pat went there to sleep. Mary politely gave Pat her bed and took the divan for herself. And it was then that the teenage Pat began her sexual career as she meant to continue it—aggressively, suggesting to Mary that the bed was big enough for both of them. As Pat later wrote in her diary in the bad French she reserved for matters of the body, Mary "accepted with alacrity. Quickly. And then well, we barely slept, but what does that matter? She is marvellous. Kind, sweet, understanding."[41]

Mary Sullivan ran what Ruth Bernhard called a "wonderful bookstore at the Waldorf Astoria Hotel," and it was there that Bernhard, beginning her career in New York at her famous father's insistence (Bernhard's father was Lucian Bernhard [real name: Emil Kahn], the German graphic designer known as "the Father of the German Poster," who created the running torchbearer emblem still used for Modern Library publications), met "the little Irish woman, Mary Sullivan," some years before Pat did. This was in the late 1930s, when the same Child's Restaurant in Times Square where Mary Sullivan and Pat went to talk had "tea dancing for girls in the afternoon. The space was always filled, with everyone in snappy clothes, dressed up, even sophisticated. There was a band playing all the best tunes of the era. Everyone danced."[42]

Mary Sullivan introduced Bernhard to Berenice Abbott—who would later say that no one photographed female nudes better than Bernhard—and so perhaps it was Mary who introduced Bernhard to Pat as well. A year or so after meeting Sullivan, Pat developed an intense friendship with Ruth Bernhard that, as all Pat's intense friendships did, briefly broke into a kind of love. But Bernhard, whose photography studio was in the same building as Rolf Tietgens's studio, introduced Pat to Rolf in the summer of 1942—thus giving Pat another chance to feature in her favorite geometrical figure, the triangle. And Pat came to feel that Bernhard was too "unfortunately feminine inside" for her.[43]

In the summer of 1942, Pat and Bernhard went with Rolf Tietgens on a weekend trip to a house on the swampy North Shore of Long Island—where Pat, whose luck with dogs was never good, was bitten on the "rear end" by a local canine. Ruth Bernhard almost fainted in response, and Pat and Bernhard spent a night in the same bed.[44] Later, Bernhard and her sister read Pat's early stories and thought them "wonderful," and Pat and Bernhard went out regularly for coffee, took the subway to Harlem together, and accompanied each other to gallery openings. Pat's lengthy description of an evening spent at the gallery managed by Betty Parsons shows her alertness to social maneuvering— and just how much she was depending on Ruth Bernhard for support.

> I moved about the room, waiting to be spoken to before I should have to speak, and saw Lola, drinking a Martini, and as I had seen her in Saks' lady's room only two hours before. I said loftily, "What again?" And I told her . . . that I had spent the afternoon reading *View* in the library*—(because her lover writes *surréaliste* articles for it) and she said she'd spent hers even better, seeing the Tchelichew [Pavel Tchelitchew] show at the Museum of Modern Art. . . .
>
> Bernhard came in, all aglow with inner fire. . . . [S]everal of my friends knew how often I saw Bernhard, until she had become a part of my own protectorate, to guard against darts of criticism. And regally, we viewed the exhibit, I now much more comfortably drawing back & squinting my eyes as I love to do at art exhibits, Bernhard steadying herself, guarding me with a hand ever on my arm.[45]

In May of 1943, Pat asked Mother Mary if she thought Ruth Bernhard would be a good roommate for her: "I should be able to get along with her well."[46] Mary said it was an "excellent" idea and then asked the same inelegant question she'd asked about Berenice Abbott: "[D]id I think Bernhard was a les?"[47]

Pat knew just how to deflect a question like that. In 1941, when Mary Sullivan was sending Pat gardenias every day under the name of "Mike Thomas" (the name of the host at their first party together), Pat, living at home on Grove Street with Mary and Stanley, put the flowers in her parents' refrigerator with the card still attached, amusing herself by allowing Mother Mary to think that a man named Mike Thomas was courting her.[48] Perhaps she also amused herself with the idea that her first "real lesbian lover" had her own *and* her mother's first name.†

Pat's meeting with Mary Sullivan was her entrée into the big-city world of casual and not-so-casual sexual encounters. With extraordinary confidence for a college girl, Pat was soon going through women like wildfire. A month after they met, in July of 1941, Pat got rid of Mary Sullivan. In fact, she got rid

---

* *View* was the Surrealist art and literary magazine started by Charles Henri Ford in 1940.
† Pat stayed friendly with Mary Sullivan and her longtime companion Rose, writing to one of her Greenwich Village "good eggs," Rachel Kipness, in 1974 that Mary had just died shortly after a disastrously alcoholic visit to Pat's house in Moncourt, France.

of her twice—once in life, and once in the first of the diaries (it had an appropriate superscription: "And here is my diary, containing the body") she'd begun to use for recording her sexual adventures. "But I know in the way of intelligence, fidelity, dependability, and intensity, Mary is superior to Virginia. Perhaps I shall live to regret it—breaking with her. I told Mary what I felt about her. 'But it wasn't enough.' And it wasn't."[49]

"Mary Sullivan was an interesting woman," Ruth Bernhard remembered during the conversations I had with her in her ninety-ninth year. "I never knew anyone that Mary Sullivan had a relationship with. If it was Pat, it was not a bad choice. . . . Pat was a very attractive person, a wonderful-looking woman, and people were drawn to her. She . . . had lots of connections and quite a few little love affairs."[50] Although Ruth Bernhard was "sure" she had taken nude photographs of Pat in the early 1940s, the photograph she best remembered making of Pat has nothing to do with physical exposure. It is as she described it: a "thoughtful," dignified portrait of a young writer thinking about her work and imagining her future. Ruth Bernhard gave a copy of the photograph to Pat—and sixty years after she took it, she gave me permission to publish it here (see frontispiece).

The next phase of Pat's Manhattan social life—the phase that lasted the longest—coincided with the war-inspired exodus from Europe to New York of a great number of interesting and artistic expatriate women. And Pat was ready to meet them: an attractive, intermittently forward, highly talented twenty-year-old; a kind of "club kid" with brains and a master plan (success!), trying her luck and dreaming of artistic immortality. Until she could be famous, however, Pat was settling for seductive friendships. And many people were interested.

In 1991, Pat remembered her longest streak of New York social luck.

"I met Janet [Flanner] whan I was 20 in Manhattan, when I met some 20 interesting people all in a fortnight, many of whom I still know—it's only a matter of their being alive."[51]

In July of 1941, Pat met Buffie Johnson, a wealthy, witty, charming painter with exquisite, if sometimes imperious, manners and highly cultivated tastes. Donald Windham, the handsome young novelist sitting next to Tanaquil LeClercq in Karl Bissinger's Café Nicholson photograph, remembers when Buffie Johnson rented the whole floor of a palazzo on the Grand Canal in Venice and let him stay there, but then wanted him to chaperone a statue back to the United States for her. "Just something small, darling," said Buffie winningly. The statue was five feet tall and heavy as a house, and Windham wisely declined to be its minder.[52]

In 1941, Buffie had recently returned from Paris, where she'd been living in the soprano Mary Garden's famous house at 44 rue du Bac and studying painting with Francisco Pissarro. Buffie would later become known for painting the largest abstract expressionist mural ever to be commissioned in New York, the mural at the old Astor Theatre, but her social persona, her money, and her commitment to Jungian psychology and goddess history tended to overshadow her reputation as a painter.

When she was in Paris, Buffie, who knew everyone and went everywhere, was invited to both Natalie Barney's literary salon and Gertrude Stein's gatherings on the rue de Fleurus. When Buffie went to the rue de Fleurus, Gertrude, as was her custom, immediately relegated her to the "women's corner" of the room with Alice B. Toklas, while she, Gertrude, spoke of important things with the men. Although Alice Toklas was very kind, Buffie was piqued at being ignored by Gertrude, and so, as she was leaving the atelier, she leaned over and surreptitiously pinched Gertrude Stein on her bottom. "It had," Buffie reported, "the consistency of a block of mahogany."[53]

At ninety, Buffie Johnson recalled for me where and how she first met Patricia Highsmith.

"I met her at a party, a party of people I never saw again; people I didn't care to see again. . . . I knew right away that Pat was very intelligent. There was an immediate [she made an intertwining gesture with her fingers to signal "connection"]. She was rather bold in her approach. . . . She wasn't at all sophisticated when I first met her. . . . She wasn't sleeping with just everyone. [Buffie stopped to correct herself.] Well I guess she was sleeping with someone or *someones*."

Buffie knew that "Pat was a student at Columbia" and was quite convinced that Pat was living with her grandmother. She thought Pat had told her that. "I didn't know she *had* a mother." Buffie also thought that Pat was "terrificly attractive and sparkly and energetic." Invited to make a painter's assessment of the likenesses of a number of photographs taken of Pat in her early twenties, Buffie chose a photo of Pat gesturing vigorously over a railing as "the most like." "Not facially," she said, but the gesture, the energy, *that's* what was "like" Pat. She paused over a rather plain photograph of Pat's face: "I forgot about that furrow," she said, pointing to the concentrated knot of problems that had settled between Pat's eyebrows by the time she was twenty. "She looks cross." Pat did look cross in the photograph. But Pat didn't look cross when Buffie first met her: "I would have remembered if she did," Buffie said.

Some years before I spoke with her, Buffie Johnson had dictated in a formal way her memories of meeting Pat—and the memoir fills in some gaps. At that time, in 1941, Buffie owned a "little house on East Fifty-eighth Street" on the Upper East Side, Pat's favorite neighborhood for socializing.

Although I cannot recollect our conversation at the party I was aware from her attention that she wanted to become my friend. When I was about to leave she asked if she could see me again and I said yes. But when I gave her my telephone number I noticed that she didn't write it down. I mentioned this and she laughed, saying, "I'll remember." To my surprise, she did and I was impressed with this trick of memory especially since my own is so abominable.

Although she was far from being sweet, she had an interesting and well-organized mind and indeed she knew what she wanted. More-over, it was not every day that one meets an attractive and intelligent young woman. So, later when she did telephone we got together and would thereafter meet fairly often.[54]

Pat's accounts of her meetings with Buffie and of her own intentions are more intimate. Pat liked Buffie's situation—monied—and she more than liked Buffie herself, wondering if her feelings for Buffie might be deepening. In her cool way, she assessed Buffie's painting. "I was pleasantly surprised. Somewhat derivative—the Cezanne, Dalí—Chirico . . . Renoir School, but some portraits have something too."[55] Pat and Buffie continued to see each other—and Pat continued to meet many other women—for some months. Buffie allowed Pat to stay in her house when she went to California to pre-pare for her first marriage, and she continued to provide Pat with important introductions to people in the world of arts: people like the cult lyricist and wit John La Touche ("horribly, silencingly flip," the intimidated Pat thought), who would write the lyrics for *Cabin in the Sky* and for the songs "Taking a Chance on Love" and "Lazy Afternoon"; "Touche's" quondam wife "Ted-die" ("in cream colored tights, coachman livery . . . with black boots"),[56] a lesbian from a prominent banking and investment family who interested Pat quite a bit; and the painter Fernand Léger ("Simply wonderful," Pat en-thused when Buffie invited her to a Léger cocktail party).[57]

It was probably Buffie who was Pat's introduction to the heiress, art phi-lanthropist, and gallerist Peggy Guggenheim (she had exhibited Buffie's paintings) as well as to a larger professional circle to which Buffie had access and Pat, still just a junior at Barnard College but circulating socially with as-tounding assurance, did not. Forty years later, Buffie was also responsible for Pat's reintroduction to Paul Bowles in Tangier, and Buffie remained a fre-quent subject for the lively correspondence that sprang up between Bowles and Highsmith.

Two weeks after Pat and Buffie met, as Buffie Johnson tells it, "I was invited to a party of a friend whose husband was the editor and chief of *Fortune* magazine. Thinking this might prove fortuitous for my young acquaintance—many people there were highly placed in the hierarchy of Luce Publications—I took Patricia with me and, although they were much older, she immediately busied herself among them. Emerging from a deep conversation with my friend, I looked up and the room had emptied. Without even saying good-night, Patricia had left with the group of editors."

Amongst those editors was Rosalind Constable, the woman who would haunt Pat's diaries, cahiers, and life for the next ten years.

Sybille Bedford, who remembered meeting Pat in the 1940s "in Rome when she was a little bit wild,"[58] knew Rosalind Constable very well. In her dazzling memoir, *Quicksands,* Bedford wrote that Constable was "a bright light of the *Life/Time* establishment, hard-working, hard-playing."[59]

Fourteen years older than Pat, Rosalind Constable was a sophisticated arts journalist from England. She knew and was known by nearly everyone in British and American arts and publishing circles. She had blond "Norwegian"-looking hair, light, cold eyes, a serious intellectual background, and a pro-nounced ability to spot coming trends in all the arts: Rosalind was a "cool-hunter" *avant la lettre.* Long employed at *Fortune,* she was greatly influ-ential in the magazine publishing world that Pat was finding so attractive. Rosalind had the ear of the publishing magnate Henry Luce, who, Daniel Bell says, gave Rosalind one of the most "enviable" jobs in New York. Rosalind was the editor of an in-house newsletter in the Luce corporation called *Rosie's Bugle.* Its purpose was to alert all the other Luce magazine editors to the cul-tural subjects about which they should be writing.[60]

Mary Highsmith—Pat had made the mistake of excitedly pointing out Rosalind to Mary from a Manhattan bus one day—took an instant dislike to Rosalind. And Mary's eye for serious rivals was at least as good as Rosalind's eye for serious art.[61] She continued to blame Rosalind for years for the alien-ation of Pat's affections: "Stanley and I were with you 100%," she wrote painedly to Pat in Europe. "Then you met Rosalind—everything changed. We were no longer your friends . . . you wanted to make us out ignorant, crude and unthinking so you could show people how far you had sprung from your poor and slimy background."[62] Mary's criticisms were rewarded in the way such criticisms are usually rewarded: Pat created a pedestal for Rosa-lind Constable and kept her on it for the next decade.

Pat, more socially aggressive in the 1940s than she would ever be again (sober, that is), telephoned to Rosalind the day after they met and launched a long, complex friendship. The connection was vigorously pursued by Pat and indulgently encouraged by Rosalind. On her first visit, Pat was invited to spend the night in Rosalind's guest bedroom and she did so. Long walks with hands intertwined followed, and Rosalind—this thrilled Pat—called her "Baby," gave her cryptically dedicated books, and introduced her to people prominent in the arts world, including Rosalind's own lover, the gallerist and artist Betty Parsons. "You're a sloppy Joe," Rosalind said to Pat, who never quite came up to Rosalind's expectations of public presentation, "but I think you're an artist!" Pat thought it was a fair exchange.[63] There were lunches in expensive restaurants liberally irrigated with alcohol and much anticipated by Pat. (Rosalind, in the style of the times, drank a lot.) After lunch, Pat sometimes sat on Rosalind's lap. It was the kind of Courtly Love story Pat preferred when she was young: a sensual pursuit of an older woman gauzily masked by an artistic and professional mentoring/mothering. This one had all the intoxications of a love affair that would never be physically consummated.

Pat transferred to Rosalind some of the liens of her bondage to Mother Mary; that boyish and intermittent courtship of her mother of which Pat wrote at twenty: "I'm happy if I can be boss, lighting her cigarettes and dominating as I did yesterday."[64] Pat encouraged her friends to bring back reports of Rosalind—and delighted in the backchat. When Kingsley telephoned Pat with a "wonderful message"—"I have it on reliable authority that Rosalind Constable is your slave!"—Pat gleefully extracted the details from her. Kingsley had been to the Wakefield gallery, where Rosalind's lover Betty Parsons presided, and Parsons had said to Kingsley: " 'Oh, Pat! Yes, Rosalind talks about her constantly! About how brilliant she is. In fact, I'm rather tired of hearing about her, etc.' and how I inspire Rosalind to work so hard."[65]

Pat herself, although notoriously closemouthed in her suburban life in France and Switzerland, was regularly and correctly accused of gossiping in New York, in Snedens Landing, in New Hope, Pennsylvania, and in Earl Soham, Suffolk. Pat couldn't help telling tales on people: she was always somehow involved in making a "case" for herself—and that meant recounting stories of other people's "behavior" towards her. "The reason I like to document things, and to have witnesses—is because I do not like to be falsely accused," she wrote to her stepfather in the middle of a five-page single-spaced torrent of tattling on her mother.[66] Perhaps Pat's childhood habit of coolly and hotly discussing her mother with her grandmother had something to do with her tattling.

Like Buffie Johnson, Rosalind was responsible for Pat's introduction to "quality" and also to some very high-style amusements. Through Rosalind, Pat met sophisticates like Peggy Fears, the former Ziegfeld Follies girl whose film career had fizzled out by the mid-1930s but whose Hollywood connections, incessant partying (she was a close friend of the film actress Louise Brooks: *c'est tout dire*), and pursuit of beautiful women on both coasts was notorious. Pat, announcing that she was "looking for adventure," began to visit Peggy daily in the fall of 1947 and was being far "too enthusiastic" about her for Rosalind's taste. Peggy Fears, in addition to her other attractions, supplied the intermittently insomniac Pat with sleeping pills.[67]

According to her diaries, Pat was always telephoning women at one thirty in the morning—from other women's bedrooms, corner phone booths, bars, almost never from her own apartment—to come by unexpectedly, make love with them if they were willing and she was interested, and then depart. Sometimes Pat's intentions were indirectly expressed, as when she paid an unanticipated visit to the novelist Hortense Calisher. (Decades later, Curtis Harnack, Calisher's husband, would become the executive director of Yaddo, the arts colony to which Pat—at the very last possible moment—left all her worldly goods.) Calisher said that Pat dropped in on her apartment announcing "that she came about a house, but I really wondered if it wasn't about *me*."[68]

Pat talked to every magazine editor, book publisher, and cultural arbiter she could get an appointment with: inviting Betty Parsons to dinner so that Parsons could look at her drawings (Parsons, as Rosalind Constable's lover, provided Pat with another opportunity to be the third arm of yet another triangle); accompanying Buffie Johnson to artist "[Fernand] Léger's madhouse cocktail party," where she met the set and costume designer Stewart Chaney and the architect Frederick Kiesler ("very nice," Pat thought), who in 1942, the year Pat met him, would create and supervise the visionary design of Peggy Guggenheim's gallery, Art of This Century. Pat went, despite her afflicting shyness and contrasting boldness, to whatever she was invited to—to "[s]omething terrific . . . at Rosalind's Thursday night,"[69] to publishing parties, to art lectures, to openings. Wherever there might be people able to help a career or connect a social life, there was this intelligent, magnetically attractive college girl, consumed by the American Dream of the perfect house, the right book contract, the burgeoning bank account, and the series of selves whose perfectability was always just around the corner.

It would have taken a keener eye than the casually admiring or coldly censorious ones turned towards Patricia Highsmith during all those Manhattan evenings to see that her seductive behavior, heavy imbibing, rapid advances, and sharp withdrawals were signals through the flames burning in her psyche. ("Now I feel quite socialized once more," she wrote after a week of frantic activity. "I want to be alone now.")[70] Only Karl Bissinger and the composer David Diamond seemed to notice the skull beneath her skin—and what was going on inside it. And only Buffie Johnson was perceptive enough to talk with Pat about her sexuality.

"Buffie . . . told me she worried about me sexually and in a neat, catchy presentation like a lawyer's two-edged sword, told me she worried if I had ever had an orgasm. . . . She said my tenseness is dynamic and charming now, but later will be a problem. . . . In the course of the afternoon, I assured her, with conviction, of being a confirmed free-lover."[71]

"Peculiar," Pat wrote defensively in her diary, "with all [Mary] Sullivan's experience *she* never had any complaints."[72]

In these heavily monitored times, it is easy to look askance at the young (and the old) Patricia Highsmith for her marathon drinking. More useful to remember—as every single person who approached drinking age in the 1940s told me—is the fact that people in New York in the 1940s drank a great deal more than people drink today. As the writer and editor Dorothy Wheelock Edson said, after explaining how her husband, "a very considerate man, always drove the drunks home" after one of their lively parties at their home on the North Shore of Long Island: "I can't say that I knew Patricia Highsmith was an alcoholic—because everyone was drinking so much in the 1940s you could hardly tell the difference."[73]

But Pat, by her own account, seems to have been drinking even more than the people she drank with, and her drinking raises all the serious questions about the motives and responsibilities of a chronic drinker. Can an alcoholic be held accountable for what she says when she is drunk? Or is alcoholism so distorting a disease that a prejudice expressed by an inveterate drinker is merely the bomb site for the detonation of a rage that cannot be released in any other way?

Because Pat, like her birthday twin and fellow alcoholic, Edgar Allan Poe, suffered all her life from depressive cycles and agitated mental states, there are other questions to be raised. Kay Redfield Jamison, in her invaluable book *Touched with Fire: Manic Depressive Illness and the Artistic Temperament,* has called them "complicated questions about whether the melancholic muse is also a 'thirsty muse.'"[74]

Did the drinking help ease Pat into the subconscious state from which her writing proceeded? And did she use it to relieve her depressions? Or did the alcohol itself increase her depressions, add to her rages, and contribute to the late-life waning of her work? Was she enough like Poe so that we can say—as Poe's biographers have already said of him—that the forces which made Patricia Highsmith write were also the forces which made her drink? The answer to each of these questions is probably a variously qualified yes.

And there is one more thing to be accounted for. In light of Pat's more or less morning-till-night drinking habits (begun in late adolescence and exacerbated in her twenties), did anyone, after a certain point, ever actually see

Patricia Highsmith sober? Some friends even claim to have been unaware that Pat was ever drunk, mostly because they had no basis of sobriety with which to compare her behavior.

Phillip Lloyd Powell, furniture maker, designer, and resident of New Hope, Pennsylvania, for sixty years, was a close friend of Pat's New Hope lover, Daisy Winston. He was "part of a group of people in New Hope" with whom Pat occasionally socialized in the very early 1960s. Although a casual acquaintance, he formed a vivid impression of Pat's relationship to alcohol.

"She was never visibly drunk; she kept a certain level. Her darkness would be exuded. She was surrounded by a black cloud. She WAS a black cloud."[75]

On 10 March 1963 (Pat noted the date and the encounter in her diary), Powell ran into Pat in Rome. They were both on their way to the airport. Pat had been staying in Positano, and she was on her way to London to be with Caroline Besterman, whose confusions over her marriage and her long-distance love affair with Pat had made her ill. Powell continues the story:

At that time in Rome, the airport bus stopped in the train station. It was a beauty, an architectural landmark. You came into the bus station on the train and then the bus took you to the airport. The waiting room had all the amenities, cafeterias, bars, etc. . . .

I was sitting there waiting for my bus to the plane, with my Italian suit on, done up to the hilt because at that time you dressed to travel. And I saw this figure pacing, up and down the corridor, stalking was more the word, in a big ankle-length cloak. This tall dark figure, brooding and stalking up and down. And I realized it was Pat Highsmith. It was such a visual experience; she looked like a character out of a Gorey illustration. And she was very very into herself.

And I went up to her and said, "Hello, I'm Daisy's friend." And she said "Oh I'm in a terrible state. A friend of mine in England, a married friend, a woman, is very ill. And I'm going back to see her and the plane is late." And so we went for a coffee and as we were approaching the bar she said: "I don't think I'll have a coffee, I'll have a grappa." And I go up and I order an espresso and a grappa. And when we were served, the bartender put the coffee in front of me and the grappa in front of her. He knew, without being told, *exactly* who should get the alcohol in that group.[76]

The English actress Heather Chasen, for whom Pat wrote her unproduced play *When the Sleep Ends,* met Pat through Annie Duveen shortly after Pat moved to England in the early 1960s. Like all theater people, Chasen dates her life from the plays she performed in, and she remembers that she was doing *The Severed Head* in London ("I was in it for two years, God help me") when she first met Pat. "If *Severed Head* was on, it must have been '63 or '64."

"I was very fond of Pat . . . and I admired her talent . . . but she was an extremely difficult woman, *extremely* difficult. There was a period of time when I didn't see her for several years when I felt she'd gone too far in her very strange behavior and she really pissed me off. The best relationship I had with Pat was through letters because she wrote wonderful letters and you couldn't really fall out with her in letters."

When asked if she had ever seen Pat intoxicated, Chasen roared with laughter.

> All the time, dear. The proper question would be: did I ever see her sober. She was always the same, she was always topped up with alcohol, but it didn't make any difference in her behavior. I never saw her sober, so I don't know the difference. She was always aggressive and grumpy [and] she was always making passes. When you've had enough to drink, dear, you overcome your shyness. . . . [But] I saw underneath all this sort of grumpy, belligerent behavior and I saw a very vulnerable person and that touched me. . . .
>
> I did a play, *Call Me Jacky,* by Enid Bagnold, and I played opposite Dame Sybil Thorndike. I played Jacky. When Enid lived in Brighton in the war, she couldn't get a cook, so she got her staff from a local lunatic asylum and she got this woman called Jacky who was a homicidal lesbian drunk. And she wrote a play about her. It was a wonderful part to play. They wanted to dress Jacky in a cashmere twin set and pearls, but I dressed her like Pat, and Pat never knew. A maniac, an alcoholic. Perfect. [See illustration.][77]

Chasen visited Pat in France in the late 1960s and 1970s "in several places . . . she didn't stay with me but I stayed with her and that was worse" and had the experience common to most Highsmith guests: she went hungry in a house whose hostess was indifferent, if not positively hostile, to food.

"I remember being absolutely starving and looking in the fridge and all there was was peanut butter and vodka. I hardly saw her eat. . . . When she came here, she ate, because I provided the food. But when I used to say to Pat, "Oh come and let's have lunch," she would say: "I'VE *GOT* TO WATER THE *GARDEN* IF YOU DON'T MIND!" And lunch was never mentioned again and you never got it. . . .

"Someone asked me do they change for dinner in France and I said: 'Yes, Pat used to change from gin to whiskey.'"[78]

Jeanne Moreau, who met Pat in 1974 when she was acting in a Peter Handke play at L'Espace Cardin in Paris, had a somewhat similar experience at Pat's house, although she framed it differently. Moreau and Pat got on very well, and she was invited to visit Pat with Peter Handke at Pat's house in Moncourt. There, Moreau, a famous gourmand, "discovered that [Patricia's] refrigerator was almost empty."

"She explained to me that she was very frugal and didn't know how to cook. I told her that I adored cooking and she proposed that I return and cook a duck because she liked duck very much. So much so that each time I saw her, I arrived with a duck, we feasted, and Patricia's cats feasted with us."[79]

Pat, who liked Jeanne Moreau very much—"I like the way she talks, I like the way she smokes," she told a young friend[80]—made a culinary exception for her. Moreau was too discreet to mention the fact that while Pat's houses were usually empty of food, they were always well stocked with alcohol. In 1975, Jeanne Moreau gave Pat a hazelnut tree for her Moncourt garden: Pat planted it and it continued to flourish.[81] And Moreau visited Pat for lunch in Moncourt and traveled to her last house in Tegna, where Pat's neighbor, Peter Huber, taking no chances, cooked for both of them.

Another of Pat's neighbors in Tegna remembered the time she'd brought "a dear friend and houseguest" who was "quite heavy" to Pat's house.

"Pat was horrible, insulted her with a comment about some people going to the grocery store and buying everything in sight. . . . The next day I telephoned Pat from the office [to confront her] with [her] totally unacceptable behavior. . . . [S]he didn't remember a single thing! She genuinely didn't know what I was talking about. I wondered if she'd been drunk and we couldn't tell. . . . I don't think I ever introduced her to a friend . . . again."[82]

In most of Pat's later-life outbursts, outbursts in which she had no trouble giving her array of prejudices overt and vocal form, alcohol was implicated. Enforcing the importance of drink in Pat's life was the fact that alcohol is a recurring prop—virtually a character—in many of her novels. Like the small flask of gin, vodka, or scotch she always kept in her large Mexican purse, her *bolsa* (Grandmother Willie Mae also carried a flask of her "toddy" on car journeys with her family "in case she got sick"),[83] Pat Highsmith took the idea of drink with her everywhere.

In June of 1943, Pat accompanied Seymour Krim, a fledgling journalist who would later spend much of his career glorifying the Beat writers, to have coffee at the Greenwich Village apartment of Stanley Edgar Hyman and his wife, Shirley Jackson. Hyman, a brilliantly loquacious twenty-four-year-old literary critic, was already a staff writer at *The New Yorker,* while Shirley Jackson was at the beginning of her own career as a writer of near-perfect short stories ("The Lottery") and uncanny novels (*The Haunting of Hill House, We Have Always Lived in the Castle,* et al.) Later in the decade, Jackson's fictions would elegantly explore some of the same psychological states which obsessed Pat. A recurrent character in Jackson's collection of short stories *The Lottery* (1949), Jamie Harris, "the daemon lover," is a trickster figure who was more than a bit of a Ripley himself—six years before Tom Ripley made his literary debut.[84]

On this visit to the Jackson/Hyman household, Pat seems to have been infuriated by the talk, and had undoubtedly tried to calm her insecurities by some presocial drinking at home. Perhaps Stanley Edgar Hyman's wunderkind status at *The New Yorker* (which continued to reject Pat's manuscripts and cartoons) got under her skin. Or maybe it was Hyman's garrulousness (he was famously exuberant and Pat always felt inadequate around intellectuals) that provoked the little French phrase she wrote in her diary about the afternoon's social call: "[T]he Jews disgusting!"[85] Pat did better with Shirley Jackson, who, to be sure, wasn't Jewish. Shirley gave her good advice about the importance of finding a literary agent.

Pat usually preferred to do her socializing uptown, and as soon as she had moved to the Upper East Side, she declared her preference for it and her rejection of all the Village "losers" she had known. Among the people she called upon in her new neighborhood was Fanny Lee Myers (later Fanny Myers Brennan). Pat called Fanny Myers "a girl painter," the same term she used for Buffie Johnson, and at twenty Fanny was already a known artist, with reviews and gallery showings to her credit. Fanny was the daughter of the *Herald Tribune*'s Paris bureau chief, Richard Myers, and the international hostess Alice Lee Herrick Myers, and she was connected through her parents to all the well-known or socially prominent people Pat would meet in New York and Paris, among them, Americans such as Janet Flanner (who had gone to the University of Chicago with both the Myerses) and Esther Murphy Arthur.

After Fanny married Hank Brennan, Pat went to a party the couple hosted for Rosalind Constable in March of 1949. And she remembered that Fanny had been a painting student of Buffie Johnson, "which evokes a host of memories."[86] Fanny was Pat's exact contemporary, and she had the kind of background Pat coveted: graduation from the Spence School and art study in Paris before coming back to New York. Fanny made perfect, minuscule landscapes, captivating worlds on a thumbnail, none of them larger than two or three inches on any side.[87]

Fanny Myers's tiny paintings were the likely source of inspiration for the character of Ripley's friend Cleo in *The Talented Mr. Ripley,* although Pat, who knew Myers only slightly, entirely invented the relationship for Tom in the novel. Cleo comes from the same social background as Myers, and she paints exquisitely tiny paintings just as Myers did—except that Cleo paints them on pieces of ivory. In *The Talented Mr. Ripley,* Ripley spends chaste nights at Cleo's Upper East Side apartment admiring her miniature paintings, drinking heavily of her wine, and sleeping quietly beside her—as a sister might do—on the floor in front of her fireplace. Cleo is the one person with whom Tom can share the good news of his "ambassadorship" to Europe, and she is the recipient of the only kiss—again, it is sisterly—he bestows in the novel. (Kisses in Highsmith novels are not quite as rare as kisses in Henry James's work, but "scant" is a good description of their number.) Cleo is also the only good artist in the novel. Tom, who has both an "eye" and the adopted New Yorker's desire to use it critically, is both disappointed by Dickie Greenleaf's mediocre paintings and disgusted with Marge Sherwood's dilatory attempts at novel writing.

But nothing picked Pat out as a New Yorker more than her classically Manhattan attachment to musical comedy—and to her old classmate Judy Tuvim/Holliday's musical comedy sketch group, the Revuers. Pat followed Judy's career and the careers of two of her collaborators in the Revuers, Betty Comden and Adolph Green, in their shows at the Village Vanguard in Greenwich Village in the 1940s. And she went uptown to see them at the Rainbow Room, bringing Rosalind Constable with her. When Judy Tuvim transformed herself into Judy Holliday and starred as Billie Dawn in Garson Kanin's play *Born Yesterday* (it opened on Broadway on 4 February 1946), Pat went to see the show several times and remembered that "Judy always welcomed me backstage . . . and was very friendly also to whomever I dragged along—my mother or my grandmother, maybe."[88]

When Pat moved to Europe, she brought her mid-century American taste for musical comedy with her, choosing, in April of 1979, as one of her selections for the BBC4 radio interview program *Desert Island Discs* a witty little ditty from the Rodgers and Hart musical *Pal Joey,* "Our Little Den of Iniquity" ("Just two little lovebirds all alone / In a cozy nest . . ."). It was perhaps a tip of the Highsmith hat to her lost but not forgotten love, Caroline Besterman, at whose house in London she had played that same song one amorous afternoon in 1962.

In May of 1988, when Pat was phrasing her anger at the "career failure" of her ex-lover, Tabea Blumenschein, in terms of a fictional murder—she thought about writing a "story reversing gender, so that a woman kills a younger man in whom she once had confidence perhaps as playwright, or actor, or writer"—the

Cole Porter song "Use Your Imagination" (from the 1950 musical comedy *Out of This World*) became her inspiration for imagining the crime.[89] "Cole Porter's Imagination—which I adore, puts me into a higher world, so that visible failure makes me angry. One is of course angry at past misjudgements, mistakes. Consequently, murder sometimes follows."[90]

And one day, in the middle of a short filmed interview for German television about the Geissendörfer film *Die Gläserne Zelle* (*The Glass Cell*) at her house in Moncourt in 1977, Pat, "quite drunk," grabbed the cameraman's white lighting umbrella and began to dance around the room with it, intoning the title song from the musical comedy film *Singin' in the Rain,* in her deep cigarette-and-alcohol-flavored voice. The celebrated lyricists for *Singin' in the Rain* were the very same Betty Comden and Adolph Green who had been Judy Holliday's young partners in the Revuers at the Village Vanguard in Greenwich Village—where Pat had gone to applaud them so many times in the 1940s.

At this unexpected display of high spirits and musical comedy–consciousness from the forbidding Miss Highsmith, the cameraman shooting the television film, Wilfried Reichardt, and the writer doing the interviewing, Christa Maerker, threw their own inhibitions to the wind and happily "joined in" to sing and dance along with Pat.[91]

It must have been quite an international tableau: two filmmakers from Berlin and one soused and happy Texas-American novelist interrupting the shooting of an interview for a German television channel in the novelist's house in suburban France to perform an American musical comedy number whose words they all knew.[92] Pat's early association with Judy Holliday, Betty Comden, and Adolph Green makes the vignette more personal. Betty Comden, the last of the Revuers and, when she spoke with me in 2003, the last surviving member of the celebrated musical comedy team of Comden and Green, remembered very well how Judy Holliday had "mentioned Patricia to me and admired her work."

"We all did," said the legendary Miss Comden.[93]

Although Pat continued to love musical comedy all her life, a middle-of-the-night visit she made to a theatrical milieu in the winter of 1947 opened up another, darker side of the business for her.

On 9 December 1947, on her way back from yet another evening out on the town, Pat casually dropped in on the home of a Broadway producer, an unnamed woman she apparently knew quite well; well enough, anyway, to visit unannounced in the middle of the night. The producer was probably Peggy Fears, whom Pat had been visiting all fall and whose lengthy and contentious divorce from the financier A. C. Blumenthal—"I'm down to my last string of pearls" is how Fears put it in 1938—allowed her to try her hand at independent theatrical production. Pat wrote about this evening as a kind of warning to herself; a warning of what can happen when alcohol affects a talent, flattens a career, and diminishes the sexual appeal on which performing artists count so heavily.

The end of a talent, perhaps a genius. For where does genius show itself more brilliantly in America than in the creation of musical comedy . . . ? I chanced to drop in on the way home at one in the morning on a producer then hard at work with her two writers. . . . All were tight on Rheims champagne. "I've been auditioning hit shows—I BEG your pardon—since 1926, and you two CHILDREN try to tell me how to audition?—I'm very sorry, let's try that number again, Phil." And she sings to his piano playing . . . a few lines from the song's main lyric. . . . What heart, male or female, can this soprano with the cracked face, the exhausted and false eyes, the straggling, not-even-bedroomy hair enflame . . . ?[94]

After the war, Pat's social life in New York tilted more towards the professional and the commercial—she was particularly interested in selling her work to the "money magazines"—and she was careful to note the notables and the notables-in-waiting she met on her evenings out, often writing up her experiences in French or German. Her commercial intentions began to leak into her creative work, and in the days after Christmas of 1947 she was pierced with guilt about this artistic and spiritual "self-betrayal":

Note after writing my first insincere story: it eats at my brain when I turn from it to write my book [*Strangers on a Train*]. I feel my thoughts are soiled and unclear. God forgive me for turning my talents to ugliness and to lies. God forgive me. I shall not do it again. Only this vow permits me to work any longer tonight at all. Best if I were punished by the story's being a complete fiasco. *Miserere mihi. Dirige me, Domine, sempiterne.*[95]

But in May of 1947, Pat had been writing her story "Mrs. Afton, Among Thy Green Braes," and feeling very pleased with it. She hadn't, she said, "worked so hard on a story since 'The Heroine.' "[96] "The Heroine" was the story against which Pat measured all her writing in the 1940s, going so far as to say, while she was working on *The Price of Salt*, that she hoped this book would be "better than 'The Heroine.' O to remove that curse one day!"[97] "Mrs. Afton" is a fine, quiet, disturbing tale, reminiscent of the eerie economies of Shirley Jackson's best short fictions.

Mrs. Afton (an alias) is a well-mannered, middle-aged Southern lady whose detailed report of her imaginary husband gives a consulting psychiatrist a bad afternoon. Because of Mrs. Afton's deception, the psychiatrist must track down Mrs. Afton's real name (it's Miss Gorham), and he is forced into a serious readjustment of his own ideas of "reality": i.e., the knowledge that his psychiatric sense has failed him and that now he must treat "Miss Gorham" for a disease that "Mrs. Afton" did not seem to suffer from. "Mrs. Afton," like so many of Pat's best stories, was published, fifteen years after she wrote it, in *Ellery Queen's Mystery Magazine* in December of 1962.

While she was working on "Mrs. Afton," Pat was invited to a party given by the set designer Oliver Smith in the writer Jane Bowles's apartment on Tenth Street in Greenwich Village. Jane's wealthy lover from Vermont, Helvetia Perkins, was there, as well as the refugee composer Marc Blitzstein ("who had some sort of passion for me," Pat thought),[98] the choreographer Jerry Robbins, and the great theater actress Stella Adler. Forty years later, Pat remembered the evening as "a fabulous party, including Paul [Bowles], John Gielgud, Oliver Smith, Jerome Robbins—everybody notable except me—I felt! . . . I always had a high and awed respect for [Jane's] talent."[99] Pat, who had given some stories to Jane, got, not for the first time, some writerly advice from her: "Don't plan," Jane said to the diagram-obsessed Pat. "It always works better to write first, and then rewrite."[100]

At some point, Pat made a little line drawing of Jane Bowles.[101] Although Pat and Jane would never be more than social acquaintances eying each other appraisingly (Pat said that Jane was amongst the women who were sexually available to her, but that she wasn't "really attractive to me"),[102] they actually had some common lifelines. For one thing, Jane, as Pat wrote appreciatively, "could hold half a bottle of gin in an admirably quiet way."[103] Jane and Pat had both lived in the borough of Queens as children, they had both attended Julia Richman High School (at different times), and they had discussed the idea of going to North Africa together, during the period when Jane was anxiously trying to rejoin her husband, Paul, in Tangier. In 1949, they accompanied each other to the passport office in New York City to register for their passports; Pat remembered the occasion because this was her first passport, although not her first attempt to get one.[104] She also remembered that "at the question 'What is the purpose of your journey (to N. Africa)' Jane said she wanted to write 'To rejoin tribe.' "[105] Although sexually uninterested in Jane, Pat was still alert to the opportunity: "[I]f we go to Africa no doubt something would happen."[106]

Luckily, their African trip never came off. Jane Bowles had phobias about trains, tunnels, bridges, elevators, and making decisions, while Pat's phobias included, but were not confined to, noise, space, cleanliness, and food, as well as making decisions. A journey to the Dark Continent by Patricia Highsmith and Jane Bowles in each other's unmediated company doesn't bear thinking about.

The night after the party at Oliver Smith's, Pat went to a reception at Rosalind Constable's apartment to honor another potentially incongruous duo: Dorothy Parker and Simone de Beauvoir. Pat wangled an invitation for her then-primary lover, the alcoholic, divorced socialite Ginnie Kent Catherwood (see "Les Girls: Part 1")—Pat called Ginnie her "wife, harlot, sweetheart—all in one! Irresistible."[107]—whose marital woes and child custody problems Pat would ruthlessly mine for the character of Carol in *The Price of Salt*. Securing an invitation for Ginnie entailed elaborate explanations to Rosalind by Pat, and after the party, Ginnie, in a rage about something, punched Pat. Pat laughed at Ginnie's flailing fists, just as she often laughed at violence. Everyone Rosalind had invited to the party for Simone de Beauvoir and Dorothy Parker showed up—except the guests of honor themselves. Wisely, they had decided to absent themselves from an evening which seemed to promise, in Dorothy Parker's immortal phrase, "fresh hell."[108]

Ten days later, Pat was at a reception given by a well-connected lesbian couple for "Mrs. Chester Arthur," the brilliant, garrulous, aggressively intellectual Esther Murphy Arthur, whose long-awaited book on Mme de Maintenon, last wife of Louis XIV, never did get written. (Perhaps it was unwritten because of Mme de Maintenon's own caveat: "I shall not write my life. I cannot tell everything, and what I could tell would not be believed.") The English writer and wit Nancy Mitford, who was very fond of Esther Murphy Arthur, once described her to Evelyn Waugh as "a large sandy person like a bedroom cupboard packed full of information, much of it useless, all of it accurate."[109]

Pat knew how brilliant Esther Murphy Arthur was, but she always got restive when Esther spoke. In Paris in the early 1950s, when she was seeing a lot of Esther Murphy Arthur in her "palatial apartment" on the rue de Lille, Pat just had to flee a St-Germain café in the middle of one of Esther's learned discourses. Esther, a daughter of the family that owned the Mark Cross Company, a companion of Sybille Bedford, and a friend of Janet Flanner (author of *The New Yorker*'s fifty-year-long column, "Letter from Paris," whom Pat had met through the lesbian community in New York), was a sister of Gerald Murphy, the American expatriate who "discovered" the Riviera and gave far too many parties for Scott Fitzgerald and Ernest Hemingway. During this reception for Esther Murphy Arthur, Pat also met the sharp-tongued, discreetly homosexual

Bowden Broadwater, a researcher at *The New Yorker.* He was a year older than Pat and newly married to Mary McCarthy, the bright star in *Partisan Review*'s firmament.

Amongst the other gatherings at which Pat was making appearances was Leo Lerman's informal Sunday evening salon at his Lexington Avenue apartment in Manhattan. Perhaps Pat had been introduced into the Lerman milieu by Buffie Johnson, who saw Lerman frequently and whose name was on Lerman's luminary-packed guest list for a party he gave for the couturier Pierre Balmain in 1948. Possibly it was the photographer who had also recently been Pat's lover, "Sheila"—she photographed Leo Lerman—who directed her to Lerman.[110] Perhaps Mme (Elizabeth) Lyne, the Hattie Carnegie designer who also knew Lerman and whose attentions Pat craved so deeply during the 1940s, was her entrée to Lerman's gatherings. Or maybe it was Betty Parsons. By now, Pat, advancing steadily if idiosyncratically in the direction of her dreams, was well connected enough to have been handed several keys to Leo Lerman's salon door.

Leo Lerman, the son of Eastern European Jewish immigrants, wrote for many magazines and papers on the arts; he became a features editor at *Vogue,* then editor in chief of *Vanity Fair,* and finally served as editorial advisor to Condé Nast Publications until his death in 1994. Lerman shared with Pat a Proustian scrutiny of the social circles in which he moved (in his case, High Society and Café Society) and his journals are a treasure trove of 1940s Manhattan observations: "Stella Adler, when Ned Rorem told her that he had been introduced to her five times and she still did not recognize him: 'To me all *goyim* look alike.'"[111] "When Marlene [Dietrich] sits or rather strides a chair and growls 'One for the Road' she is very beautiful in two sexes simultaneously."[112]

At Lerman's Sundays, "[p]eople came for one another [and not for the food or the drink]. . . . Tennessee, Truman, Gore, Mr. Faulkner . . . I remember passing Tilly Losch on the landing, kissing Martha Graham's hand."[113] *Le tout* New York and many of its brilliant war refugees were there: Marlene Dietrich, Eleonora von Mendelssohn, Pearl Kazin, Muriel Draper, Adolph Green and Betty Comden, Lionel and Diana Trilling, Truman Capote, Jane Bowles, John La Touche, Imogene Coca, Carl Van Vechten, Stark Young, Eugene Berman, and Ruth Landshoff-Yorck.

Pat liked to position herself at the outer edge of this inner circle: the view was good, the participants famous or notorious, and the interaction was strictly voluntary. She was both an admiring audience and a resentful one, as this recollection of her salad days shows: "[T]he forties were the days of somewhat snob magazines. . . . All was whimsy, fuzziness, humour—of closed circle sort. Obscure, too. Tinged with Edith Sitwell and Djuna Barnes. . . . I was in my twenties and in awe of them all, because they had literary recognition and all that."[114] In the canny guest list that the twenty-nine-year-old Pat prepared for the launch party for her novel *Strangers on a Train*—the book was published on the ides of March 1950, the party was given at Mme Lyne's apartment, and Mother Mary, miffed at not having received a personal invitation from Mme Lyne, refused to come—both Leo Lerman and Djuna Barnes were invited. Neither of them came. Djuna Barnes pleaded a "sprained back," and Pat thought Leo Lerman didn't show up because he was offended that "I didn't send him an advance copy of my book."[115]

Still, she said she found Lerman's Sundays "very agreeable" indeed. Pat's friend Lil Picard compared the company there "with the one she knew in Berlin before Hitler; intellectuals, free spirits; the first that would disappear."[116]

Pat met both Truman Capote and film actress Luise Rainer in January of 1948 at one of Lerman's Sundays. She also made the acquaintance of yet another of her young male Jewish suitors, Lewis Howard, "a pleasant writer. Really—ideas that we were married—daydreams. I had to tell him everything about me." Pat alternated her romantic dreams of Howard—"I have the constant feeling that Lewis is going to be my husband"[117]—with slightly less romantic reflections: a discussion of contraception with Mother Mary ("I feel so feminine tonight!") and the realization that "Lewis is a Jew, therefore I feel even more that I can't go to him. But we have so much in common."[118] She intermitted these thoughts with some even more characteristic ideas: "I want to change my sex. Is it possible? . . . Twice I tried to sleep with Lewis—masochistic failure. Lewis is an angel of patience [but I have] [n]o pleasure—God—how funny! When all parents have to forbid their children—I hate it!"[119]

Three days after another failed attempt at making love with Lewis (she didn't call it making love), Pat was happy to see Truman Capote again at Leo Lerman's. This was the year that Capote's first novel, *Other Voices, Other Rooms* would be published, with the back cover adorned by the notorious Harold Halma photograph of the young author reclining in resplendent decadence on a Victorian sofa. Truman, three years younger than Pat, and as talented a self-publicist as he promised to be a writer (he'd posed that sulphurous Halma photograph himself when he was only twenty-two), shared an Alabama background with Pat. (Capote's mother's backwoods Alabama name—before she changed it to the more sophisticated Nina—was Lillie Mae, like the Willie Mae of Pat's own Alabama-born grandmother.) Capote was the most prominent of the Alabamians who fetched up in Manhattan in the 1940s. Another of them, Truman's childhood friend from Alabama, Nelle Harper Lee, the future author of *To Kill a Mockingbird*, was also living on the Upper East Side, trying to make her writerly way.

On this Sunday afternoon at Leo Lerman's, Truman sat next to Pat and "held my hand and was very devoted. He wants to see my room."[120] The next day, the first of March, Truman went with Pat to see her studio apartment on East Fifty-sixth Street—he was thinking of renting it as a writing studio so he could finish *The Tree of Night,* and she had been thinking of going to New Orleans—and he liked it. And Pat liked "to go out with little Truman: He is so attentive and so famous! And so sweet!"[121] Pat changed her mind about going to New Orleans, and she eventually changed her mind about Truman (as she did about nearly everyone), but Truman didn't change his opinion of Pat: his biographer Gerald Clarke writes that "Capote's high opinion of her work never wavered."[122] And Donald Windham, who never met Patricia but knew Capote very well, confirms it: "Truman always spoke well of Highsmith's novels to me."[123]

After having dinner with Mother Mary and Rolf Tietgens, Pat and Truman agreed on the apartment rental: he gave her eighty dollars for two months' rent. Decades later, she began to say that she and Capote had a "deal": that he had sublet her apartment in return for recommending her to Yaddo, the artist's colony in Saratoga Springs, New York. Although Capote did send his recommendation letter for Pat to Yaddo the day after the apartment money changed hands, Pat had already been thinking of going to New Orleans; she wanted, anyway, to sublet her apartment; and there is not one word about a "deal" in her diary. Capote had probably suggested Yaddo to Pat as a better idea than New Orleans, and she made the best of a situation that would supply her with both a paying sublettor *and* a recommender to an arts colony. Capote's recommendation to Yaddo was addressed to Elizabeth Ames, Yaddo's imposing director, and it shows, even for a young man given to hyperbole, just how taken he was with Pat.

"She is really enormously gifted, one story of hers shows a talent as fine as any I know. Moreover, she is a charming, thoroughly civilized person, someone I'm quite certain you would like."[124]

It was during this March that Pat, accompanied by Jeanne (one of the several women she was sleeping with while trying to establish a physical relationship with Lewis Howard), went to see what she called "the best play of my life": *A Streetcar Named Desire* by Tennessee Williams. Unlike Williams himself, who reserved his tenderness for Blanche DuBois (the Southern fantasist who depends upon "the kindness of strangers"), Pat didn't announce a character preference. But perhaps one of her reasons for calling it "the best play of my life" was that she recognized something of Mother Mary in Blanche Dubois's rearrangements of reality—"I don't tell the truth. I tell what ought to be the truth,"

Blanche says—and something of herself in the themes of male violence and homosexuality that run under the play.

On the day of the evening she saw *Streetcar*, Pat began "my first snail story," "The Snail-Watcher." "I like it," she noted, pleased with herself.[125]

Over the years, Pat would repeat a couple of origin stories for her first attraction to snails. They are disturbing stories, involving long descriptions of what it was that fascinated her about the molluscs: watching the "mating process" of two living organisms that "can go on for fourteen hours." She found it "relaxing" to watch her snails mate because their copulation had "an aesthetic quality, nothing more bestial in it than necking, really," and she liked to take her snails on trips with her. In Suffolk, in her cottage at Earl Soham in the 1960s, Pat kept three hundred snails as pets, and her longest-lived snail, Hortense (who appears with her real-life, loving snail partner Edgar in *Deep Water*), was, Pat claimed, "the world's most widely travelled snail. She has been to New York and back by jet, and has visited Paris, Rome, and Venice." "It is quite impossible," Pat wrote happily about her snails, "to tell which is the male and which is the female, because their behavior and appearance is exactly the same."

The first of Pat's own origin stories about how she took up with snails is from 1946: she saw, in this version, snails locked in an embrace in a fish store and took six of them home. Her second story is from 1949: Pat, passing the same fish store in Manhattan, saw two snails "kissing"—[l]ittle did I know they were mating"—and brought them home to keep as pets because they "shouldn't be separated." "The mother snail gives [the baby snails] no assistance and never appears to even see them," she wrote in an undated self-interview she composed about her attraction to snails. "But," she went on in what sounds like a pointed reference to her relations with her mother, "I have never found an adult snail damaging a baby snail by crawling over it."[126]

Pat showed this first snail story—in which the intense mating of pet snails generates enough offspring to smother to death the admiring man who has kept them (love kills, even in the sticky world of molluscs)—to her college friend Kingsley, whom she hadn't seen in a long time. Kingsley said it gave her the "only happy day she has had in months" and that she found the snail story "funny." Lil Picard, who began her friendship with Pat by praising her story "The World's Champion Ball-Bouncer" (published in *Woman's Home Companion* in April of 1948), "loved" "The Snail-Watcher," and Pat wrote that she was "so overflowing with happiness if *anybody* loves something from me!"[127]

"The Snail-Watcher" would go on to have a checkered publishing history.

In June of 1948, Pat wrote to Kingsley from Yaddo: "My snail story that I adore, my agent writes is too repellent to show editors. Cannot express how disappointed I am. Have even offered to bowdlerize it."[128] In 1960, "The Snail-Watcher" was finally bought by Pat's friend Jack Matcha, who edited "*Gamma* [magazine] of California." It had, she said, "elicit[ed] 'nays' and 'ughs' from editors" for twelve solid years, and she noted grimly that just after "The Snail-Watcher" appeared in *Gamma,* the magazine was "seized for bankruptcy."[129]

SOCIAL STUDIES

PART 2

Before Pat applied to the artists' colony called Yaddo in March of 1948 to work on *Strangers on a Train,* another art colony, the MacDowell Colony in Peterborough, New Hampshire, had already turned her down. She muttered something about how this proved you had to know people to get in anywhere—it was true for Yaddo, which preferred to select its "guests" from recommendations made by previous colonists—and then she went on to apply to Yaddo using the kind of recommenders (besides Truman Capote) who "knew people": Marguerite Young, the novelist and Greenwich Village resident; Mary Louise Aswell, the literary editor of *Harper's Bazaar*; Rosalind Constable, the cultural eyes of the Luce empire; Ethel Sturtevant, her old literature professor at Barnard College; and Margot Johnson, her literary agent.

Yaddo was an obvious choice for Pat. Many of the writers, composers, and artists she was meeting in New York—and many of those she would later meet—had spent time at Yaddo. Leo Lerman went there with Truman Capote; Marguerite Young was a perennial guest; Marc Blitzstein, David Diamond, Virgil Thompson, Buffie Johnson, Paul Bowles, Carson McCullers, and dozens of others had all worked at their various arts in the main mansion, in the icehouse Tower, or in the fanciful stone-and-shingle West House on Yaddo's four hundred secluded acres.

Yaddo made a little revision to Pat's arrival date, and Mary Highsmith, moving as she always did into any territory Pat was trying to occupy, responded for her daughter in her best white-glove manner while Pat was out of town. "In the interest of my daughter, Patricia, I am taking the liberty of answering your note.[1] Mary's letter affirmed the change in Pat's arrival from 3 May to 10

May and that she would be staying for two months. Finally, the thing was done and Pat was there.

Three weeks into her residency, Pat was praising Yaddo in a letter to Kingsley (and indirectly praising Kingsley) to the skies: "Yaddo is everything you've ever heard about it and lots more. . . . [T]he solitude builds up great electrical charges of gregariousness . . . so that when we do go on a spree we overdo and suffer 48 hour hangovers. . . . [T]he work seems going fine, I am staying on the subject like a tightrope walker, but it is already a little longer than I should like. I have cause to think of you every day certainly, because I've used your plot suggestions to get going on it."[2]

But Pat was less thrilled with her fellow colonists, who were not, as she'd hoped, people who "knew" people: "A singularly dull bunch, no big names—though Marc Brandel is interesting. . . . Chester Himes [the black, gay male novelist installed across the hall from her in West House] tried to kiss me in my room. Did I mention it? Never mind. I read the Bible every morning."[3]

Of the eleven other colonists who were at Yaddo while Pat was there, four of them were men who irritated her by borrowing money and cigarettes from her and "forgetting" to pay her back. Marc Brandel, an attractive six-footer with red-gold hair and a radiating intelligence, was one of the borrowers, but he, at least, balanced his debt by proposing marriage to her four times in six weeks. Another male colonist who was at Yaddo with his artist wife was similarly smitten. But because Pat was sneaking her current lover Jeanne onto the Yaddo premises (and enraging "the board" by going off to Glens Falls for two nights with her), she wasn't bothering much about the women at Yaddo.

When Pat arrived at Yaddo's rural retreat in Saratoga Springs, the colony had already been in operation for twenty-two years. The Corporation of Yaddo was formed in 1900 by Katrina and Spencer Trask, artistically minded, wealthy, philanthropic residents of Brooklyn, New York, who bought the land that became Yaddo with an old Queen Anne *maison de maître* on it for summer living. Eventually, their haunting and melodramatic family history—four children tragically dead and their summerhouse burned to the ground—inspired them to construct four lakes to commemorate the spirits of their dead children and to build a brooding stone mansion on the ashes of the house that had burned down. They added eccentrically designed outbuildings to shelter the bodies and stimulate the work habits of the artists to whom they had decided to consecrate their property.

The main mansion at Yaddo, always described as "Tudor-like," mixes the Gothic and the Medieval with a dash of Victorian fantasy. Several hundred yards away, West House, the turreted building where Pat was billeted in May and June of 1948, is the material of which fantasies are made. The Trasks indulged themselves with elaborate dramatic scenarios (Katrina Trask was crowned "Queen of Yaddo" in one such ceremony), and once the Corporation had been firmly established with Elizabeth Ames at its head, the resident artists did the same thing in their work.

Pat, who lived at home the whole time she was going to Barnard College, had never had a taste of dormitory life. The moment she got to Yaddo she set about transforming Yaddo's Elizabeth Ames into a dormitory mistress: She Who Must Be Disobeyed. Pat was not alone in this behavior. Many colonists, lapsing into early adolescence in the dignified presence of Miss Ames, would stage rebellions against her. The worst rebellion occurred in 1949, the year after Pat was in residence, when the poet Robert Lowell tried to have Miss Ames denounced and fired as a Communist sympathizer.

So, while Pat did her work at Yaddo and did it religiously (in every sense of the word), she also systematically violated the colony's rules. In a spring season of hard-drinking colonists, Pat was a standout. The day after she arrived at Yaddo, she walked with a group of other Yaddo guests into the town of Saratoga Springs (a refreshing two-mile hike if you weren't drunk), quaffed almost as many martinis and Manhattans as she had fingers on both hands, added a skinful of wine to her cocktails, and nearly passed out in the restaurant. She managed to drink Marc Brandel under the table: "Marc soon succumbed, with his carrot hair in his carrot soup."[4] Her hard drinking caught Elizabeth Ames's attention, and Pat thought the drinking and her association with Marc Brandel were the reasons she was turned down for a second residency at Yaddo a year later.[5]

A month into her stay, Pat was mixing Jehovah up with Bacchus—or perhaps just mixing her morning martinis with her morning Bible reading.

"I am drunk every morning almost, at Yaddo. Who knows not what I mean knows not the kingdom of heaven within him. I am the God-intoxicated, the material-intoxicated, the art-intoxicated, yes and the something that would transcend even God-intoxicated!"[6]

Pat drank at Yaddo, she told herself, to harness the creative energy that was coursing through her with a power she found terrifying. Pat always had a handful of reasons for drinking to excess, but this one was at least biologically sound: alcohol is a depressant, and in the healthful countryside, left alone all day to work with a staff-prepared box lunch to sustain her, Pat was electrified by bolts of writing energy she didn't know how to handle. She described herself as being as tense as "a coiled spring"[7] and "happy like a battery chicken": her way of saying that she was poised for greatness and producing like mad.

At the beginning of June, the twenty-four-year-old writer Flannery O'Connor arrived to join the other colonists at Yaddo. Pat identified her as the "[n]ew writer Capote likes very much. Maybe another McCullers, I don't know. . . . I expected from the name a racy colt with reddish hair, a six-gear brain [but she] personifies Iowa [the Iowa Writers' Workshop at the University of Iowa] once removed from Georgia, which she is."[8]

Forty years later, Pat told a young friend who loved Flannery O'Connor's work a story about her time at Yaddo with the deeply religious O'Connor. Nearly every night, she said, she and Chester Himes and other colonists would go out and drink themselves into stupors, and

> Flannery O'Connor would never go with them. One night they went out on another bender, and once again, Flannery refused to come, and they left her on the porch. And there was a tremendous thunder and lightning storm and [when they came back] there was Flannery kneeling on the porch. And Pat said: "*What* are you doing?" And Flannery said: "*Look,* can't you *see* it?!" And she's pointing to some knot in the porch wood. And then she said: "Jesus' face."
>
> And Pat said to me, "That happened. And ever since then I've not liked that woman."[9]

Pat went on drinking heavily and reading her Bible every day—a satisfyingly oppositional regime which she continued more or less without interruption for the rest of her life. On her second day at Yaddo, the day of the evening on which she drank all those martinis and Manhattans, Pat, glancing through *Harper's Bazaar,* came upon an article about the theoretical work the physicist Albert Einstein was doing with electromagnetic energy. It added a few nouns—"electrons," "matter," and "energy" were three of them—to how she was already thinking about God and the Devil, and to how she would write about Guy and Bruno in *Strangers on a Train.* God kept turning up in the poems she was dedicating to women in her cahier, while her Bible's influence was obvious in the many uplifting notes she took: "How beautiful the words of Peter and John—ignorant and poor men—when seized for their preachings of Christ! . . . All sin (R. Niebuhr) comes from man's forgetting that God is the center of the universe."[10]

"N.B. Small wonder the old-timers tell us to go back to moral standards. Not only more security but more happiness follows. Our guilt is not that we have broken away from moral laws, but that we are not voyaging toward anything."[11]

"Guilt" was a word that would always catch Pat's attention, and the carrot-haired Marc Brandel used it publicly nine days into her stay at Yaddo. Two years older than Pat, the English-born, Cambridge-educated Brandel had already published in 1945 the novel for which he would be best known: *Rain*

Before Seven. Brandel's real name was Marcus Beresford, and his attractions included the high, beautiful "Beresford brow" of his aristocratic family.[12] (Pat seems to have been entirely surrounded by pseudonymous males in the 1940s.) Marc made a little speech at dinner about how children rebel against their parents and then are left with the "guilt which produces all our neuroses."[13] Immersed in Dostoyevsky's *House of the Dead* (and certain that Dostoyevsky shared her guilt feelings), Pat had just spent three illicit days with her lover Jeanne and was feeling "a persistent need to be forgiven." But the offers of marriage coming from Marc Brandel were turning her head and her attention to other questions.

"What is so impossible, is that the male face doesn't attract me, isn't *beautiful* to me. Though I can imagine a familiarity with a man, which would . . . allow us to work and make us happy—and certainly sane . . . [t]he question is, whether men alone, their *selves*, don't get *unbearably boring?*"[14]

Meanwhile, Pat's revisions and additions to her manuscript were multiplying. The brilliant premise that had come to her on a walk with Mary and Stanley in Hastings-on-Hudson in 1945—two men exchanging crimes and "getting away with it"—was finding a far more complex and shadowy form in a novel which perverted the Platonic ideal of love and duality, embedded it in a history of coerced murder and mutual seduction, and was as much about the pathology of Superheroes and their Alter Egos as it was about guilt, the spirituality of architecture, and the horrible need to submit to the right, the true confessor.

Six months before she'd arrived at Yaddo—having worked for almost twelve hours on a single scene in the novel that would become *Strangers on a Train*—Pat made a frank confession of just how much the idea of murder meant to her life, and to her book. She'd just killed the character she was calling Tucker and would eventually call Guy Haines. (Later, as she often did, she changed the victim and killed only Guy's Alter Ego, Bruno.) And she was joyous about it. The murder fullfilled her as nothing else could.

"Today is a great day; I have written the murder, the *raison d'être* of the novel. . . . Something happened today, I feel I have grown older, completely adult. . . . I turned back at home, completely satisfied, very happy. I don't want to marry. I have my good friends (most of them European Jews) and girls?—I always have enough."[15]

Dark as her novel was, the infinite gradations of "character" Pat was beginning to counterfeit for her male protagonists allowed her to try for a lighthearted little sub-Wildean epigram, an epigram in which she distilled all the pleasure she felt in choosing art over life: "Acquired tastes are so much more delightful than natural ones."[16]

Strangers on a Train remains Pat's most Dostoyevskyan novel in that its two male protagonists, like the most fully imagined of Dostoyevsky's creations, vacate their "characters" at the drop of a threat, exchange traits as easily as they trade hats, and, like God and the Devil, "dance hand in hand around every single electron,"[17] mingling their identities and flummoxing their detective pursuer (who is also deceiving them) before surrendering to him completely.

Guy Haines, a brilliant young architect and the divine half of the novel's Terrible Twins, is as obsessed with guilt, God, and the effect his behavior is having on the spiritual dimension of the buildings he designs as any of Dostoyevsky's would-be Christian martyrs. (Guy makes an interesting contrast to that other architect to come out of an American novel of the forties: Ayn Rand's man of steel, Howard Roark, who first appeared in Rand's bestselling 1943 novel, *The Fountainhead,* and then returned—this time with Gary Cooper's face—in the 1949 film of the same name.)

Guy's moody purity summons up the devilish Charles Anthony Bruno—the subliterate, alcoholic scion of a wealthy family who is also a psychopathic genius. Bruno appears on Guy's train to Texas with the physical expression of his inner evil growing in the middle of his forehead: a huge boil, a "plague of Job." "All things had opposites close by, every decision a reason against it, every animal an animal that destroys it, the male the female, the positive the negative."[18] The coincidental meeting of these two opposites—during which Bruno has the infernal inspiration that they should exchange crimes—produces a double negative: the infestation of the best by the worst. "A murderer looks like anybody!" is the conclusion forced upon Guy.[19] *After* he has killed.

Unable to get Miriam, his coarse, unfaithful wife in Texas, to agree to a divorce, Guy has fallen in love with the rich, blond New Yorker of Patricia Highsmith's upper-class dreams: Anne Faulkner. Bruno, homoerotically attached to Guy, coerces Guy into committing the companion murder to his murder of Miriam by showering Guy with diagrammatic instructions for the murder of his own hated father. Bruno's character is accoutered with some of the barely disguised signifiers of homosexuality: he is left in possession of Guy's copy of Plato; his father's company makes "AC-DC gadgets"; he travels to Haiti on a yacht called *The Fairy Prince;* he gives Guy purple women's gloves, which Guy wears when he takes his little pistol out of its lavender sack and uses it to murder Bruno's father.

As if these broad suggestions weren't enough, Bruno sullies Guy's new marriage with Anne Faulkner by constant, drunken intrusions into their gleaming, shining white house. And Guy, feeling guilty for Bruno's murder of his wife (but not for his own murder of Bruno's father), allows Bruno's dreams and passions to penetrate his own. Guy's relations with Bruno destroy his marriage, his career, and his life. Bruno is luckier: he merely drowns in deep water.

The cautionary tale of the brilliant Chicago teenagers and quondam lovers, Nathan Leopold and Robert Loeb, who plotted the "perfect Nietzschean murder"—they were the first Americans to be publicized as "thrill-killers"— of young Bobby Franks in Chicago in 1924 (just about the time little Patsy Plangman in Fort Worth, Texas, was hatching her infant fantasies of knocking off her new stepfather), hovers vaguely and uneasily over the plot of *Strangers on a Train* just as it hovered for decades over the lives of many homosexuals in America. Amongst those shadowed by Leopold and Loeb was Pat's host in the late 1940s, Leo Lerman, who said that his mother used to warn him with: "Don't be a Leopold and Loeb."

Perhaps Alfred Hitchcock, who had already filmed a version of the Leopold and Loeb story in his 1948 movie, *Rope* (starring Farley Granger, who would also star in Hitchcock's *Strangers on a Train*), was thinking of the fatal clue that trapped the two boys—Nathan Leopold's horn-rimmed glasses with the special identifying hinge—when he created the most celebrated scene in his 1951 film of *Strangers on a Train*: the murder of Guy's wife, Miriam, by Bruno reflected in Miriam's discarded glasses. But the film's opening shot, which famously follows the shoes of Guy and Bruno as they separately approach Union Station in Washington, D.C., could only have come from the detailed descriptions of shoes in *Strangers on a Train;* descriptions which were amply furnished by the novel's footwear-obsessed young author.

Intricate as the film is (the scriptwriter who was fired from the film, Raymond Chandler, said the plot drove him "crazy"), it doesn't begin to approach the complexities of the novel which inspired it; and the film's plot excludes the novel's most dangerous games. Pat Highsmith's excesses at Yaddo, her *dérèglement de tous les sens,* managed to produce what Arthur Rimbaud wanted his "disordering of all the senses" to lead to: a masterpiece.* And the brilliance of *Strangers on a Train* owes at least as much to Pat's daily Bible reading (the moral complement to her guilt) and to the crude Alter Ego psychologies which glazed the plots of her comic book scenarios as it does to Dostoyevsky, to Gide, to her quondam college hero Graham Greene, or to Leopold and Loeb.[20] (Bruno, a reader of comic books, says: "Guy and I are supermen!"—but he sounds as though he means "Supermen.")[21]

By the twenty-third of June, Pat had completed a first draft of her as yet

---

* Arthur Rimbaud's phrase is: *"Le Poète se fait voyant par un long, immense et raisonné dérèglement de tous les sens."*

untitled book. (Marc Brandel would eventually supply her with the title, *Strangers on a Train,* and Pat, back in New York and freelancing comic book scenarios for the Fawcett company when she finished the novel, wrote an ending—still visible in one or two metaphors in the last chapter—that saw Guy crushed to death under a large rock. The book was saved from this car-toonlike resolution by Pat's agent, Margot Johnson, who insisted that Guy survive his confession. And so Guy's haunting line, "Take me," was how Pat finished her novel.)[22] On the twenty-fourth and again on the twenty-sixth of June, Pat walked the grounds of Yaddo with Marc Brandel, and it was, once more, her attraction to guilt that brought them together: Pat talked to Marc about her mother and her guilt at being homosexual. She thought Marc was "amazingly tolerant."

"And he convinced me I must abolish guilt for these impulses and feelings. (Can't I remember Gide? Must I always try to 'improve' myself?) I returned with quite a different attitude. I think more lightly of myself. I have opened myself a little to the world."[23]

The next morning, however, she was physically imagining her lover Jeanne's kiss on her lips, feeling bad about it, and also yearning for it.

But before Marc left Yaddo, Pat made plans for him to come and visit her in Hastings-on-Hudson even though she was still living, imaginatively and physically, the life of her novel: "I am in love with Jeanne in the way Guy is in love with Anne. . . . I am pleased with the secrecy." After leaving Yaddo, Pat alternated nights with Jeanne and a new girlfriend named Valerie, spent a night with Herbert L. (she'd tried him out before without satisfaction), and then added Marc to her list. "Three people in three nights!" she wrote, im-pressed with herself.

Pat's sojourn in Saratoga Springs not only allowed her to revise and finish a first draft of her novel, it also provided her with a yearned-for "respectability" (a male fiancé), led her indirectly into psychoanalysis, and, at the end of a life not noted for philanthropy, gave her the opportunity to confound everyone's expectations by endowing Yaddo with her comfortable fortune. Her two months at Yaddo—10 May to the first week of July 1948—produced what would now be called a "perfect Highsmith storm": a capsizing set of circumstances inspired by Pat's entirely contradictory impulses. If she'd ever taken the time to analyze what Yaddo had *really* done for her, Pat would have been doubly thrilled.

Back in New York and still working hard on *Strangers on a Train,* Pat allowed Marc to convince her to visit him in Provincetown, Massachusetts, in Sep-tember. There he made the mistake of introducing her to his new acquain-tance, the artist Ann Smith—and Pat immediately added Ann to the list of women with whom she was already sleeping. Once Ann had left Province-town, Pat felt she was "in prison" with Marc and told him she was leaving. "[B]ecause of that I have to sleep with him, and only the fact that it is the last night strengthens me to bear it."

This unpromising beginning for her love affair with Marc Brandel more or less dictated its direction. Pat never slept with just Marc (nor did Marc con-fine his attentions to Pat) during their turbulent time together; she always had other lovers. And whenever she did sleep with him, she resented it. In a letter she sent to her stepfather, Stanley, in 1970 (every letter Pat sent to her stepfather evokes pity and terror for the man, but this letter is especially hair-raising), Pat, counting her blessings, toted up the number of times she'd made love with Marc and—a bonus for poor Stanley—described their sexual encoun-ters as "steel wool in the face, a sensation of being raped in the wrong place—leading to a sensation of having to have, pretty soon, a boewl [sic] movement." [Pat meant "bowel"; it's one of the very few uncorrected misspellings in her archives.]24

"I have never put this into a book," she added to what must have been her stepfather's relief or, more likely, his dawning horror, since her writing career was far from over and she still had time to put "this" into a book. Pat figured that she'd been to bed with Marc Brandel "many times . . . [t]wenty-thirty," and she thought thirty times was *plenty*.25

It was the psychoanalysis, however, that really finished the affair for her.

At the end of September, back from Provincetown and explaining her complicated sex life to Lil Picard, Pat took Lil's summarizing question to heart—"Why do you torture yourself so much?"—and answered it herself. "The $64 question. Answer: Me."26 Two months later, she decided to have the question answered again—this time with the help of a psychiatrist.

By October, Pat, still seeing both Jeanne and Ann Smith and about to add another woman, Dione, to her lovemaking list, had broken off provisionally with Marc.

By the second week in November, temporarily bored with her work on *Strangers on a Train,* Pat began to write a vividly painful, powerful story set in the South: "When the Fleet Was in at Mobile" (published in *London Life,* 3 December 1965, and reprinted in *Eleven,* by Heinemann, in 1970). Unusually, the story is about a woman who tries to get away with murder in order to get away from marriage—and doesn't. A week later, Pat was at a film with Marc Brandel, an aptly chosen film as it turned out. It was Anatole Litvak's stark drama about insanity, *The Snake Pit* (1948), anchored by Olivia de Havilland's luminous performance as Virginia, a newly married woman haunted by childhood feelings of guilt, and slipping into mental illness. *The Snake Pit* is rife with the kind of psychoanalytic notions which Pat would shortly encounter in her new psychiatrist's office.

Pat was so pleased to be back with Marc (who had just had excellent reviews for his latest novel) that she was thanking God, in her own special way, for their reunion. "God is very kind to me: He gave me Marc—a man who is as neurotic as I am, and He showed me Rosalind [Constable]."[27]

At the end of November, Pat found herself a psychiatrist and began what would become a six-month course of analysis. She wanted to be able to marry Marc Brandel and "to regularize herself sexually," as the (and her) thinking went in mid-twentieth-century America. Things didn't exactly work out that way.

It was the composer David Diamond who gave Pat the names of two psychiatrists. The first one, a man, told her it would take two years to bend her in the direction she said she wanted to go: heterosexuality. She didn't continue to see him. The second psychiatrist, Dr. Eva Klein, newly minted in her field at Pat's old alma mater, Columbia University, and married to a psychiatrist herself (but practicing under her maiden name), seemed to be someone Pat could work with. And so, on 30 November 1948, Pat began the first of what would be forty-seven psychoanalytic sessions with Dr. Klein. Pat summarized each session in her diary, and her summaries stealthily trace her resistance to being "bent out of shape" (*her* shape). The one thing Pat didn't resist was Dr. Klein's classic encouragement to lay the responsibility for her troubles at Mother Mary's feet.

Eva Klein, as socially coercive and attached to a heterosexual agenda as most American psychiatrists were in the 1940s, nevertheless had some very intelligent things to say about her new analysand. (Dr. Klein was conducting a more or less conventional Freudian psychoanalysis—with some help from the theories of Karen Horney.) Many of the remarks Klein made, recorded by Pat, have the ring of authenticity about them, and Pat thought so too. The problem was that Pat was too creatively resistant (and had too many other problems—of which alcoholism was only the most salient) for six months of formal and more or less "criminalizing" analysis (homosexuality treated as an illness) to produce either a full picture or a transformative understanding.

Nevertheless, during her six months with Dr. Klein, Pat Highsmith told more of what she felt and knew about herself to another human being (and heard more cogent theories about what she didn't know) than she was ever to do again in her life. Naturally, the experience left her with the same grinding ambivalences that all her deep experiences left her with: an abiding sense of resentment and another tool to use in her work.

The analysis of Patricia Highsmith by Dr. Eva Klein began promisingly.

After the first visit, Pat was bubbly with enthusiasm: "I like her very much—she instantly asked the necessary questions." Pat had talked about "Ginnie [Catherwood]" while barely mentioning Marc—about whom she was suddenly quite uncertain. The analysis was going to cost her fifteen dollars a session, she was going to have two sessions a week, and she was trying hard not to resent having to pay for them. By the second visit, the canny Dr. Klein was recommending that Pat see a male psychiatrist; Pat instantly refused to do so. Their relationship was already starting "to feel like a mother-child relationship" to Pat, who was "already half in love with Dr. Klein."

By 15 December, the day Pat was "let go" from the sales job she'd taken in the toy section of Bloomingdale's department store to help pay for her analysis, Pat was lunching with Mother Mary, finding it "very comfortable, and I told her almost all I learned from Doctor Klein—and she understands." Two days later, Pat was playing her analyst off against her mother: "Why shouldn't I fall in love with her? Didn't she give me more than a mother?" And she was feeling frightened because she was actually thinking "that Mrs. Klein is my mother." By her eighth visit, very "ill, hot and weak" with the chicken pox she thought she'd picked up at Bloomingdale's,[28] Pat lost consciousness on the subway but staggered to her appointment with Dr. Klein anyway, hoping "Mrs. Klein would nurse me. . . . I only wanted to see Mrs. Klein! She is the only person in the world, who gives me the right answers!" Dr. Klein gave her a cognac and sent her on to a general practitioner. Not, however, before speaking about " 'the vagina'—a favorite subject," Pat said.

Pat, sick as only an adult stricken with chicken pox can be, was cared for over Christmas by Mother Mary at the family house in Hastings-on-Hudson. Mary annoyed her feverish daughter by trying out some Christian Science healing techniques when all Pat wanted was an aspirin. In Hastings-on-Hudson, Pat drew and painted, fretted about her inability to sell stories, and cued up her holiday reading to her holiday depression: Graham Greene's *Ministry of Fear* and Tolstoy's *War and Peace*.[29]

During Pat's ninth analytic session in January of the New Year, 1949, Dr. Klein gave her a Rorschach test. Klein said the test showed that Pat had a "raging violence [which was] completely pent-up," a tendency towards "hypochondriacal" behavior, and a "weak Ego." No one could argue with that.

Pat was reading, as analysands do when they decide to outsmart their analysts, current Freudian psychiatric theory: books by Helene Deutsch, lent to her by Dr. Klein, and books by Edmund Bergler, chosen by Pat herself. Helene Deutsch, a pupil and then an assistant of Sigmund Freud in Vienna, was the first pschoanalyst to concern herself exclusively with the psychology of women. Bergler, a Freudian who was not well disposed towards homosexuals (in January of 1948, he published an article called "The Myth of a New National Disease: Homosexuality and the Kinsey Report"),[30] developed a theory that might have been made for Pat Highsmith: the hypothesis that humans are psychologically and emotionally attached to unresolved negative feelings which they have formed, subjectively, in childhood.

Meanwhile, Dr. Klein told David Diamond—who repeated it to Marc Brandel, who repeated it to Pat—of her genuine interest in Pat. (*Any* psychiatrist would have been interested in the young Patricia Highsmith, with her handsome array of twentieth-century maladies and her uncanny ability to inhabit and/or mimic aberrant psychological states.) Delighted, Pat transcribed the compliment: "Marc said that Mrs. Klein had told David that she was very much interested in me, that I was so creative in everything I did, etc."[31]

It was mostly downhill from there. Pat's typewriter broke, she was "sick of penises," and, despite a little of what she liked to refer to as "success" with Marc Brandel in bed, she was sexually unhappy with him. For her twenty-eighth birthday on 19 January, Willie Mae sent her five dollars from Fort Worth, but neither Stanley Highsmith nor Jay B Plangman gave her a present. (Jay B almost never sent his daughter presents and left nothing to her in his will.) Before Pat's tenth psychoanalytic session, Mary Highsmith "took the liberty" of calling Eva Klein. She provided the usual explanations of a defensive parent: she had educated Pat "very well," Pat came from a "good family," etc., etc. The doctor said Mary was rather "excited" and "tearful" and that Mary had told her she should look into Pat's relations with Lil Picard. But, Pat wrote, "Eva stopped her: 'If you really want to help, be a little more compassionate,'" she said to Pat's mother. Dr. Klein concluded that Mary felt guilty about Pat's depressions.

In the fall, Mary, hoping for a marriage with Marc Brandel for her daughter, had made a familiar offer to Pat: "'Oh, if there's a child you can let me raise it.'" Pat's response was: "My blood ran a bit cold. I don't think this is the ideal way to raise a child."[32] It was the way Pat herself had been raised. In Pat's next session with Eva Klein, after she'd told Klein that Marc was allowing her to "sacrifice" herself sexually to him, the doctor suggested that Pat should abstain from sex for "three months." Pat balked at the idea immediately: "That means men and women. . . . But *women* don't make me feel depressed!"[33]

In the middle of all this, during her thirteenth psychiatric session, Pat made an interesting admission. Contrary to what she would write to her long-suffering stepfather twenty-two years later about the "lingering kisses when I was seventeen in Texas, not exactly paternal" that her father Jay B Plangman had apparently forced upon her,[34] Pat seems to have decided with Dr. Klein that whatever happened between her and her birth father happened when she was "16"—and that the incident was responsible for her barely acknowledged "eating disorder": "Therefore my culpability, when I was 16, and the reason, why I wanted to eat so little."

Dr. Klein, scenting victory for the home team, was zealous in pressing her case: " 'I will try to make you want to be kissed by your father,' she said. . . . 'You don't hate men. . . . I will show you that you look for men in your women.' " Klein was making Pat "furious" and that, Pat thought, was "progress." But Pat had also solipsized the good doctor into her ambivalence. "I love and hate her. Want to give her presents and quarrel with her. Want to arrive drunk. And I want to tell her my passionate feelings for her and her progress with me."[35]

Still, the psychoanalysis was doing something for Pat—but it wasn't quite the something that Dr. Klein had in mind. Pat suddenly wanted to "dominate" a woman again (she did so with Ann Smith), and then she spent a night with Dione, giving her experience the correct analytic spin: "[I]n my current stage of 'hurting' a girl. Sadistic reaction from these years—those eons—of masochism."[36]

Pat continued to be "embarrassed" whenever Dr. Klein asked her to "free-associate" with words. By her twenty-first visit, Klein was able to tell Pat: "Your sexual feeling is completely connected with attack." For her twenty-second visit, on 24 February, Pat managed to produce a "castration" dream for Eva Klein. But she promptly asserted her own attitude towards it: "Shame on Eva," she wrote in her diary, "for taking away my fantasies about having a male penis."[37] Pat knew what she liked.

But Dr. Klein also went on telling her what she didn't like: her mother, Mary. So Pat began deducing, dutifully, that "my guilt drives me to girls, overcompensation . . . with Dione and Ann [Smith], Jeanne, I am acting out that with which my mother served me—the loving and leaving pattern, the basic heartlessness & lack of sympathy." She spoke to her doctor about her early years in Texas, "the hated watermelon parties."[38] But Pat, still seeing Marc, was also having pregnancy scares and trying to avoid Marc as much as she could. She had no problem lying to him, she said, but she resented his inquiries and wanted to be free of him.[39]

It was at this point that Pat began to mount an attack on Eva Klein. By the beginning of May she was writing: "More and more I fear she is a cut & dried Freudian. Her hammerblows of propaganda no longer even sink in properly."[40] Dr. Klein didn't help by providing an unfortunate suggestion; unfortunate, in that it was made to someone who hated crowds and yearned to be the sole focus of her psychiatrist's loving attention.

"At this rate—she [Dr. Klein] decides, I must go into group 'therapy,' with three or four married women who are latent homosexuals. (Better latent than never, remarks Ann [Smith]. And also reminds me of the alcoholic who joined the A.A. when he ran out of drinking companions.) They sound deadly—all progressing so nicely. Though they still have homosexual dreams occasionally and all usually have lunch together after their jolly double sessions."[41]

Pat concluded her little summary of group therapy with women by making the decision that would shut the door on her own psychoanalysis.

"Perhaps I shall amuse myself by seducing a couple of them."[42]

By the middle of May, her forty-fifth visit to Dr. Klein, Pat had already delivered the coup de grâce. She had gone back to Dr. Gutheil, the male psychiatrist she had initially rejected, to check up on Eva Klein's credentials. As a deliberate provocation, she reported this to Dr. Klein—and brought about the hoped-for response: "Eva flared up in typically Jewish way after I mentioned seeing Gutheil."[43] (A former lover of Pat says that whenever Pat was finished with someone, she or he suddenly became "Jewish.")

Pat's very last visit to her psychiatrist on 24 May, before she sailed to England to visit her new publisher, Dennis Cohen (and to fall in love with his wife, Kathryn), is best represented by the final note she took on her psychoanalysis: "Bloody angry at having to pay this bill before I leave."[44] And she blamed Dr. Klein's fees for the fact that she couldn't afford to buy a first-class ticket on the *Queen Mary*.

· 17 ·

LES GIRLS

PART I

Sometimes, when the day had gone right for her, or the stars were in their proper alignment, or the world wasn't entirely out of joint, she could eat a peach with such delight that it was an almost sexual experience.

> —**Caroline Besterman**, in conversation with the author

I don't know why I was very fond of Pat, I don't exactly know why. I was under a spell, like a bird before a snake.

> —**Marion Aboudaram**, in conversation with the author

Her sexual life was really almost nonexistent. It's not a good premise for a book.

> —**Barbara Roett**, in conversation with the author

The way your head tipped back when you reached to drop a cigarette's ashes, the way your hair smelled, of Russian leather, at the exact center above your forehead, the way your voice sounded when your head was light against mine and I embraced you . . . oh bed was always the unbelievable, the unimaginable, the best.

> —**Patricia Highsmith**, 1948

In the Christmas season of 1948 the winter weather in Manhattan was freakishly warm; the warmest ever recorded by the New York Weather Bureau. It wasn't until mid-December that the first major snowstorms blanketed the city and quickly turned to municipal slush under a day of heavy rains.[1] Pat Highsmith—perhaps it was the unseasonable heat—was alight with one of her special "holiday feelings." She wanted to close her hands (tightly, she thought later) around the throat of a "blondish and elegant" married woman from New Jersey who had just bewitched her from across a crowded room.[2]

Kathleen Wiggins Senn (Mrs. E. R. Senn), the woman in question, resplendent in a mink coat, appeared one day in early December in the seventh-floor toy department at Bloomingdale's department store on Fifty-ninth Street and Lexington Avenue, where Pat, anxious to pay for her psychoanalysis and awaiting the publication of *Strangers on a Train,* had just taken a sales job for the Christmas rush season.

Blond, statuesque, with an angled, Saxon profile and "intelligent gray eyes,"[3] Mrs. Senn, slapping a pair of gloves suggestively into the palm of one hand, walked slowly and absently up to the doll counter where a mesmerized Pat stood waiting to serve her.[4] In a voice that class-conscious Americans like Pat (or like Scott Fitzgerald, who provided this metaphor in *The Great Gatsby*) would have recognized as being "full of money," Mrs. Senn ordered a doll sent to her house in Ridgewood, New Jersey, for one of her daughters. The enthralled young salesgirl, Miss Highsmith, filled out the receipt—but her Alter Ego, the canny writer Patricia, quickly memorized the client's address.

In a trance of desire, Pat—both parts of her—went straight downstairs to the Bloomingdale's card shop, bought a Christmas card, signed it with the perfect Highsmith nom de plume, and mailed it off at the post office in Bloomingdale's basement to Kathleen Senn's address.

But the signature Pat put on the card wasn't a name. It was her Bloomingdale's employee number.[5]

Kathleen Senn never connected the number or the Christmas card with the attractive, flustered salesgirl who waited on her, and she never replied to it. Later, Pat felt grateful for Mrs. Senn's incomprehension.[6] But when she came to reimagine her meeting with Mrs. Senn for *The Price of Salt,* the novel their meeting catalyzed, Pat supplied the response Mrs. Senn had failed to make. And it is Carol Aird's reply to the love-struck young Therese Belivet's cryptic card in *The Price of Salt* that kindles their burning love affair and all that follows.

To an imagination like Patricia Highsmith's, Kathleen Senn's "routine transaction" in Bloomingdale's—it lasted, Pat wrote, no more than "two or three minutes" and she never met Mrs. Senn again—had all the features of a sexually charged sadomasochistic fantasy.[7] On one side of the Bloomingdale's counter was the young, poor, seemingly subservient salesgirl; on the other side, the older, wealthy, apparently dominant Venus in furs. Money and class were not the least of the elements in Pat's stunned attraction for Kathleen Senn; her obsession at first sight struck her like a lightning bolt or like a religious experience. The woman "seemed to give off light. . . . I felt odd and swimmy in the head, near to fainting, yet at the same time uplifted, as if I had seen a vision."[8]

After her meeting with Mrs. Senn, Pat went directly back to her apartment, wrote up (in what turned out to be both a metaphorical and, later, a real fever) a plot outline for *The Price of Salt*—"it flowed from my pen as from nowhere—beginning, middle and end" in two hours[9]—and then fell ill with a disease most often associated with children: chicken pox. "One of the small, runny-nosed children [in the toy department] must have passed on the germ, but in a way the germ of a book too: fever is stimulating to the imagination."[10]

Like François Truffaut, who said he preferred his films "to give the impression of having been filmed with a temperature of 112," Pat thought "that when you're feverish, in the medical sense, you are much more vibrant."[11] She would always find high temperatures highly inspiring.

Pat's first version of *The Price of Salt*, written into her Cahier 18 as *The Bloomingdale Story* and later titled *The Argument of Tantalus: or THE LIE*, was couched in a voice that was almost her own—"Am so eager to get back to *Tantalus*! Oh, I shall be myself then!"[12]—and employed by a character she said was completely herself: Therese, a creative adolescent, an orphan with a mother, a girl "flung out of space," who "came from my own bones." But this was not the first time Pat had made use of the self-incriminating "I" in a narrative.

The Dove Descending (a title culled from T. S. Eliot's "Little Gidding"), a seventy-eight-page novel she'd begun with a synopsis in 1944 and left unfinished in its narrative form, is told by a thin, dark, passive girl ("Leonora" in the synopsis, "Marcia" in the narrative), "anesthetized with melancholy and a vague sense of regret," who has been adopted by her flamboyantly aggressive Aunt Vivian. (There are almost as many orphans and adoptions in Highsmith fictions as there are murders.) Vivian gives Marcia a "strange feeling of being stalked by something, as a person might feel in a jungle. The unknown enemy was my aunt's silent fury, for I knew no reason for it."[13] So exquisite are the psychological humiliations Aunt Vivian inflicts upon her niece that they become the unintended focus of a narrative meant to concentrate on three male love choices for Marcia. Aunt Vivian's graphic humiliations of Marcia give us an Early Gothic version of Pat's worst relations with Mother Mary.

Pat used a first-person narrator again in her next serious attempt at a lesbian novel, the fifty-nine-page unfinished epistolary narrative *The First Person Novel*.[14] A married woman, Juliette Tallifer Dorn, who has a lesbian lover and a lesbian past (replete with recognizable details from Pat's own love life), sits in a room in an inn eight miles from Munich (one of Pat's favorite writing rooms had been in an inn "in Ambach, near Munich, with a ceiling so low I could not stand up at one end of it," where she had worked on *The Price of Salt*)[15] and thinks through her history of loving women by writing about it for two hours a day to her husband. Pat began this narrative in her twenty-sixth notebook in January of 1961, as the outline for a short story which she called—as she was to call all her unfinished attempts at writing lesbian fiction after *The Price of Salt*—"Girls' Book."[16]

It's a crucial characteristic of her technique as a writer that the sole use Patricia Highsmith ever made of the first-person narrative in her novels was in abandoned drafts of works meant to portray intense relations between women.[17] Two of these works are lesbian love stories, and the first of them was the draft that became *The Price of Salt*. In her 1965 book about writing, *Plotting and Writing Suspense Fiction*, Pat never revealed the subject of her abandoned first-person fictions. She simply called the first-person singular "the most difficult form," adding, "I have bogged down twice in first-person-singular books, so emphatically that I abandoned any idea of writing the books."[18]

The wrenching ambivalence Pat felt while she was writing *The Price of Salt* (after much agonizing, she finally published the work under a pseudonym, Claire Morgan) meant that it was a long time before the manuscript had its publication title. Amongst the evocative names she considered were *The Bloomingdale Story, The Argument of Tantalus, Blasphemy of Laughter* ("from V. Woolf's *The Waves*"),[19] and *Paths of Lightening*.[20] *Carol*, the title Bloomsbury Press gave to *The Price of Salt* in 1990 when Pat finally allowed her name to be attached to the work in Europe, collapses the novel's mysteries into a single interpretation.

Pat used Kathleen Senn's real name in the first version of *The Price of Salt* (she was still calling it *The Bloomingdale Story*)—she couldn't yet surrender the Senn name up to a fictional disguise[21]—and began the book's intensely personal narration in the voice of the adolescent Therese who falls "instantly," ecstatically, and irretrievably in love with an older woman. Pat was twenty-seven at the time, but to the end of her life she approached love like a teenager.

"I see her the same instant she sees me, and instantly, I love her. Instantly, I am terrified, because I know she knows I am terrified and that I love her. Though there are seven girls between us, I know, she knows, she will come to me and have me wait on her."[22]

"I set her age at thirty-five," Pat wrote in her notes about the "older woman" in her novel, "an exciting thirty-five. Already I think how happy her husband must be."[23]

Three months to the day before she started *The Bloomingdale Story,* Pat had nailed her love colors to the mast in a notebook: "I want to look up to someone, I do not wish to be looked up to."[24] With Kathleen Senn, she got what she wished for—and a little more than that. Mrs. Senn was apparently as interested in death as Pat was, but from a different perspective. The self-sufficient daughter of the owner of an airline company in Massachusetts, a champion golfer and flyer of planes before she was married to the wealthy businessman, Edward R. Senn, and a "very gregarious, empathetic, compassionate" woman, Kathleen Senn was also a troubled alcoholic who had been in and out of psychiatric institutions in New York.[25] And sometime during the Halloween holiday of 1951, she walked into the closed garage of her Bergen County house—the house looked something like a castle in a fairy tale[26]—turned on her car ignition, and killed herself with carbon monoxide gas just as *The Price of Salt* was being readied for its 1952 publication. She died as unconscious of the effect she'd had on Pat Highsmith as Pat was unconscious of her real-life model's unhappy end.

And *The Price of Salt,* faithful to its wish-come-true inspiration and its magically fevered creation, is pervaded by a tranced and hypnotized, fairy-tale atmosphere of precarious dangers and pursuits; closer in spirit to the sadistic cruelties of the Brothers Grimm than to the delicate perversions of Charles Perrault—even in its smallest details.

"Therese bit her tongue. . . . Carol's fingers slid down her cigarette and the fire burned her. When she got the cigarette out of her mouth, her lip began to bleed."[27]

When Carol and Therese try to take an amorous shower together, Carol twists Therese's arm, then Therese drags Carol's head "under the stream of water and there was the horrible sound of a foot slipping."[28]

Even Therese's first sexual experience with Carol is vaguely weaponized:

"The arrow seemed to cross an impossibly wide abyss with ease, seemed to arc on and on in space, and not quite to stop. Then she realized that she still clung to Carol, that she trembled violently, and the arrow was herself."[29]

If we consider that *The Price of Salt* is the only novel Patricia Highsmith wrote in which a murder is *not* committed,* then Kathleen Senn's desperate

* Strictly speaking, there is no murder in Pat's 1965 novel, *Those Who Walk Away,* but the suicide of Peggy Garrett, the wife and daughter, respectively, of the two male protagonists (one of whom blames the other for her death), predates the action, pervades the work, and is the motive for the incessant pursuits that drive the plot. The murder is there—and it's not there: a very Highsmithian way of seeing. And at the end of *A Suspension of Mercy,* Sydney Bartleby, the writer who has murdered only in fantasy, finally (and unconvincingly) forces his dead wife's lover to take enough sleeping pills to end his life. It's another Highsmith murder which is there—and not there.

act—without diminishing in any way its real tragedy—comes to seem a little like a central event Pat might first have imagined and then decided to leave out of this novel whose signs of love are so palpably joined to its signals of war and its sense of danger.

It is at such uncanny intersections of life and art that the awful question arises: Whose life, in the brief encounter Patricia Highsmith had with Kathleen Senn, actually influenced whose? And to what end?

Pat finished the first version of *The Price of Salt*—she was now calling it *The Argument of Tantalus*—on 29 June 1950 "at precisely 2:56 PM," with the ending that came most naturally to her: the ending that separated the two women. Her feeling for the book approached the sacramental, and her gratitude at finishing it came in a rush of religious language. "Thanks be to God," she wrote. "Glory be to God, I have finished another book today. In God is all my strength and my inspiration. In God and Jesus' name is all my courage and fortitude."[30]

Pat said later that the title she finally settled on, *The Price of Salt,* had come from something she was thinking of in the Bible. She might have been remembering the price paid by Hagar, Lot's wife, for that last look back at the Sodomites. More likely, though, she was invoking a biblical reference from another work she had once taken to heart—the Gospel text André Gide inserted into *The Counterfeiters,* his novel about the transgressive love of adolescents: " 'If the salt have lost its flavor wherewith shall it be salted?—that is the tragedy with which I am concerned.' "[31]

The Price of Salt allowed Pat to release herself from what was to become her most reliable artistic forgery: the male "voice" of narration and an apparently heterosexual orientation. She never again published another work like it. "How grateful I am at last," she wrote while working on the manuscript in December of 1949, "not . . . to spoil my best thematic material by transposing it to false male-female relationship."[32]

On 30 June 1950, the day after she finished her first version of *The Price of Salt,* Pat, saturated with images from her manuscript and moved by some demiurge of completion, took a train from Pennsylvania Station in Manhattan to Ridgewood, New Jersey, on her way to the address she'd memorized a year and a half before: Kathleen Senn's address, 315 Murray Avenue.[33] It was the beginning of an ineptly comic episode: a "stalking" of the heroine of her own novel.

Early in June, an accidental meeting with a man from Ridgewood, Carl Hazelwood, had revived Pat's interest in the actual Mrs. Senn. Hazelwood was to drive Pat out to Ridgewood on her second "stalking" trip there six months later (when Pat found the house deserted and "something of a fairy tale[,] something of a castle"),[34] and he joined the long list of young men whom Pat—for a moment—thought she might marry. But as Pat wrote in her diary about Mrs. Senn: "Alas, should I see her, my book would be spoilt! I should be inhibited!"[35]

Pat's instinctively canny separation of her art from her life was followed by a "completely irresponsible desire to drift about picking up strangers, especially girls. Born of confidence & money, of course."[36] Pat had been spending uninspiring nights with casual lovers Billie (a woman) and Sylvia as well as with her serious, off-and-on-again "fiancé," Marc Brandel. It was only when she'd finished the first version of *Salt* that she felt secure enough to make the first trip to New Jersey.

Pat carefully preserved her ticket back from that ride, Ridgewood to New York on the Erie Railroad, on her diary page of 30 June 1950. Just as carefully, she recorded her guilty and self-dramatizing impressions from that day.

"Today feeling quite odd—like a murderer in a novel, I boarded the train for Ridgewood, New Jersey. It shook me physically and left me limp."[37]

Pat had to fortify herself with "two ryes" before taking the 92 bus in Ridgewood to Murray Avenue. She asked the driver where to go and then, "to my dismay and horror, I heard the entire bus shouting Murray Ave?—and giving me directions!" Feeling exposed and unbalanced by the attention, she took the wrong bus, and then, still embarrassed by the remarks of the passengers, she got off at the wrong stop. "I overshot my mark." She found herself in a residential area with no sidewalks where "I was a conspicuous figure. I dared not go any further, up the avenue . . . where she [Mrs. Senn] just might have been on the lawn or porch and I might have betrayed myself with halting too abruptly."

Pat wanted only to look, to gaze at the woman whose essence she had been, in the most profound way, living with and re-creating for the past eighteen months while writing *The Price of Salt*. Like any voyeur, she didn't want to be "a conspicuous figure" or even to make contact with the object of her obsession. But her timidity was so pronounced that it overcame her mild intention of creeping a little closer. So she hovered on a nearby street and watched recessively as a "pale aqua automobile [came] out of Murray Avenue, driven by a woman with dark glasses and short blond hair, alone, and I think in a pale blue or aqua dress with short sleeves." But Pat wasn't at all certain the driver was Mrs. Senn—the hair was different—and her identification of the figure was ambiguous. "My heart leapt but not very high."

Later, she wrote "a tragic little poem" about the sighting—"if it was one"— and announced that she was determined to conceal "these stirrings" from "Mr. M[arc] B[randel]," whom she was still trying to persuade herself to marry.[38]

The whole afternoon was a comedy of errors—more like a failed, farcical rehearsal of transgressive desires than a noirish episode of sexual stalking. Pat was, anyway, a great rehearser and assembler of feelings for her writing, and she carefully described and filed away the humiliation she suffered on this stalking trip to New Jersey. Twelve years later she was able to make use of it in a dazzling novel of misfortune, *The Cry of the Owl,* whose mild-mannered peeping Tom, Robert Forester, suffers the horrible consequences of having a girl he spies upon fall deeply in love with him.

Three weeks before she took the trip to Ridgewood, Pat had gone to visit Mother Mary in Hastings-on-Hudson for another rehearsal: she called it steeping "myself in that which I hate, in that rejection, which is what I am about to describe in my book. My mother grows increasingly neurotic—my god! . . . Yet she insists I do not need an analyst."[39] In her private writing, as she did in this passage, Pat often confused herself with her mother. But in her public writing, she tried to do what she never could do in life: make the best use of her worst feelings.

The day after she returned from Ridgewood, 1 July, Pat went back to Hastings-on-Hudson to visit Mary again, and she found that trip to be just as unsatisfactory as her ride to New Jersey had been the day before. "Though mother always asks when I am coming out . . . she wants me really to leave very soon."[40] Mary was collapsing under the intolerable financial pressure of keeping up a good front. Her fancy house and live-in Filipino "houseboy" in Hastings-on-Hudson were far beyond her means, and all her work opportunities were disappearing. Pat knew—Stanley had told her—that Mary was "ashamed she cannot offer a house with leisure, food, servants, etc. and afraid of what the Southern family will think of her. This reaches serious proportions—so great I am worried that mother may lose her mind, even commit suicide."[41]

Pat felt "conscience stricken" and thought about lending her parents a thousand dollars; she was flush from the sale of some stories. But she decided, typically, against becoming her mother's banker because Mary "resents my success, my ability to organize my life."[42]

On 12 October, Pat finished her second version of *The Price of Salt,* got deeply drunk, and found that she had her period for the first time "since May or June"—something she ascribed to completing her book. Off the leash at last, she extended her "drunk" into a long, bad binge.

"I am ashamed of my self-indulgent and destructive behavior—which I cannot seem to control. I can blame fatigue but not entirely. Such a deplorable waste of time and money—and I feel I sink as low morally as any of the [Greenwich] Village wastrels of whom I have heard, have known, all my life, without suspecting I could ever be like them."[43]

Pat had spent the spring and summer of 1950, with only a week or two out in August, almost completely absorbed in her revisions of *The Price of Salt*, the novel she was still calling *Tantalus*. In May and early June, she was boarding in a fairy-tale setting: an old turreted and towered building in Tarrytown, New York, called the Tarrytown Castle, half an hour up the Henry Hudson Parkway from Manhattan. And she was falling "madly in love with my Carol. . . . I want to spend all my time, all my evenings with her."[44] She was having dreams full of "homosexual symbols" and other dreams "filled with self-confidence. A strange new atmosphere as if even the mind dreaming it were not mine."[45]

Back in Manhattan, along with her work came heavy bouts of drinking, waves of shame and fear at the thought of publishing a "lesbian" novel that would wreck her career ("I shall try to persuade Margot [her literary agent] that the book should not be published now"),[46] and behavior as feverish as that of any of her love-struck protagonists. She experienced a "[t]emporary relief from shame" when her agent suggested she publish the novel under a pseudonym—but she was resolved not to tell "the family" about it.[47]

Pat continued to work on the manuscript in Provincetown, in New York, and on Fire Island, where she was a resentful and messy guest at the house of Rosalind Constable and Rosalind's lover, Claude. Rosalind, drinking heavily herself, stumbled across Pat in bed with yet another woman named Anne in what Rosalind called a "house reeking of liquor, fornication, and unmade beds." It was really, Pat thought, the "cataclysmic end" of her ten-year friendship with Rosalind Constable. But there were compensations: before she left the island, Pat began a secret flirtation with her agent Margot Johnson's girlfriend, Kay.

While Pat was in Provincetown, Alfred Hitchcock sent her a telegram asking for a meeting. He was "already shooting [the tennis scenes of *Strangers on a Train*] in Forest Hills." "He seems to be going . . . mad over my book," she wrote in her diary.[48] But Pat didn't rush away from Provincetown to meet the famous director, and she gave no explanation for her behavior.* Perhaps it was shyness; perhaps she was simply focused on her new book and up to her eyes in her always complicated love life. Films, anyway, weren't a form Pat took very seriously in the 1940s. "Movies in America," she wrote, "destroy

---

* Alfred Hitchcock made a teleplay of another Highsmith novel, *This Sweet Sickness*, but Pat never met Hitchcock. And *Vertigo* (1958), the Hitchcock film adapted from the *roman policier D'Entre les morts,* by Boileau and Narcejac (Narcejac corresponded with Pat in the 1970s when she lived in the Île-de-France), has an unlucky hero, Scottie Ferguson, who is present at three deaths (two of them of the "same" woman). The voyeuristic themes and accidental deaths surrounding Ferguson's character are suggestive of those with which Pat enveloped the unlucky Robert Forester in *The Cry of the Owl* (1962).

that fine, seldom even perceived sense of the importance and dignity of one's own life."[49]

Pat wouldn't have known that Farley Granger, the handsome young actor playing Guy Haines in the tennis scenes Hitchcock was now shooting in Forest Hills, Queens, had the same ambiguous sexuality with which she'd haloed the character of Guy Haines in her novel. Nor would Farley Granger have known what Pat Highsmith's sexual tastes were. And that was the underworld of homosexuality in mid-twentieth-century America: so darkly lit, no one could see anyone else's face.

Returning to New York, Pat managed to find yet another woman named Virginia to sleep with and considered, in her practical way, Ann Smith's invitation to come and live with her in Provincetown: "[P]erhaps her youth . . . would tend to make me stronger . . . rather than if I lived with an older person, which is my inclination." All this happened in July.

Pat began August by relaxing: "Idle-idle-idle-idle—and I love it. All my clothes are clean." From New York she went to New Hampshire with Mother Mary to stay as a paying guest with the family of farmers Pat and Mary usually stayed with on their New Hampshire trips, the Minots, and she sketched and read while Mary played interminable games of canasta. Back in New York, Pat spent the night with one of her casual lovers, Jeanne T., once again wishing for her favorite Virginia, Ginnie Catherwood—"wife, harlot, sweetheart—all in one! Irresistible!" Margot Johnson's magazine sale of Pat's chauffeur story, "Where to, Madame?" for $1,150 made her think of reworking *Tantalus* (*The Price of Salt*) and she thought of two more titles for her revision: *The Sun Gazer* and *The Echo*.

And then, Pat had a wisdom tooth extracted. It was "a ghastly experience. . . . I am conscious at the moment of extraction. And gas dreams are the most cataclysmic episodes of my existence."

Pat's taste for dental gas was one of her stranger introductions into the feelings she usually associated with love. She suffered from bad teeth all her life, and it affected the way she thought of herself. As an early adolescent, Pat had stifled her attraction for a girl classmate because she assumed, mistakenly, that the girl was jibing at her decaying teeth. It was Pat's recurrent attempts to repair that decay that led her into "gas dreams." At thirty-two, agonizing once more over her bad teeth in Trieste, she summed up her problem.

"About twice a week I have bad dreams about my bad teeth, always connected with general inferiority, social and otherwise. With better teeth, I should be quite a different personality."[50]

At forty-nine, Pat already had false teeth she could "sleep in and eat corn on the cob" with. At fifty-three, she reported sarcastically to Kingsley: "Just had the remainder of my upper teeth out—isn't that cheerful news?"[51] From late adolescence, Pat had been writing (sometimes in German) about the pain of her frequent tooth extractions, and about the transcendent ecstasy dental gas afforded her. She said the experience of anesthesia—rather like her contemplations of love and murder—allowed her to have "cosmic" feelings.

In December of 1949, shortly after she'd returned to New York from her first trip to Europe (and then went on to New Jersey, Tennessee, Arkansas, Texas, Louisiana, Mississippi, Alabama, and Florida; she was twitchy as a Mexican jumping bean from her European experiences of art and love), Pat made this enthusiastic entry—one of many on the subject—in her nineteenth cahier.

GAS

My sensations under gas are really too compelling for me to ignore any longer . . . a recurrent pattern with cosmic suggestions. They have made me feel I was all consciousness that ever existed, that in this black bowl at whose perimeter the bouncing rabbit, the bouncing rubber ball races, I feel all sensations, wisdom, achievements, potentialities, and the stupendous failure of the stupendous experiment of the Human Race.[52]

Aside from the occasional porcelain filling, some deeply painful tooth extractions in London, and a crown or two that had to be replaced in Europe, most of the serious repair work on Pat's mouth was done in New York. All of the dentists she saw there were Jews, and she continued to seek out her old New York dentists long after she'd moved permanently to Europe, making appointments with them on her short stays in Manhattan and spending more time with her dentists than she did with any other medical practitioners. Her favorite dentist was Dr. Arnold Gottlieb on Fifth Avenue, and he went on treating her teeth and replacing the last of them, finally, with false teeth well into the 1980s.[53] Pat wrote rhapsodically to Kingsley about the "deep curettage" Gottlieb had performed on her and about the upper bridge he'd installed in 1970: "In his way, I think he's an artist."[54] And she continued to take a relishing pleasure in the gas and in her near-technical familiarity with its administration—for whose details she continued to pump the good doctor. Dr. Gottlieb, Pat said to Kingsley, "doesn't mind telling you what he is doing."[55]

Always able to entertain herself with an array of possible identities (another kind of fun), Pat liked to call herself a "kraut"—and to sprinkle her plain American speech with simple German words and phrases: *"Bitte,"* she would say, and *"Danke."*

"This German thing obsessed her," says Caroline Besterman. "She would always break into German phrases, terribly badly. These lapses into German, there wouldn't be an afternoon or a lunch that would pass without German phrases being intruded. Never French, always German. She knew nothing about Germany. This enormous race, intelligent, cultured, which produced without turning a hair instantly a race of maniacs."[56]

But if Pat's affinity for Jewish dentists was yet another example of the subversive Miss Highsmith turning an ordinary exchange upside down—i.e., the "German-identified" Pat being "gassed" by "Jewish dentists" (an idea so offensive that it might actually have appealed to Pat)—she never said so. Still, she was conscious enough of the connection between gas, Germans, and racial superiority (or unconscious enough of it) to make this little note in the section of her cahier that she reserved for her *Keime,* her "germs": *"Little Keime—* The Element of Dental Gas in the German Nationalism and Psyche." Being fascinating comparison of gaseous dreams of mystical absolute with individual, collective, and national dreams of Germans and Germany as the chosen race."[57]

Perhaps Pat's attraction to dental gas was just another instance of her yearning for a spiritual life in the old German Romantic mode—"those "cosmic suggestions" she talked about—or for leaving her troublesome body behind.[58] Or perhaps the appeal of gas was that it produced a more refined "high" than the alcohol she was consuming. Her down-to-earth Texas family—the only people close to her who can bear to use the word "alcoholic"—say that her taste in beer when she was in Texas (Lone Star beer was her choice there) was just as "inexpensive" as her taste in wine: "She would just suck on that grape," said Dan Walton Coates. "Yeah, everybody understood that Pat was alcoholic [but] you damn sure didn't want to stir her up about the alcohol."[59]

Certainly, the "total anesthesia" of the dental gas allowed Pat to enjoy the kind of intoxication she liked best: the kind that relieved her, if only for an hour, from being Patricia Highsmith.

Restless in Manhattan during the summer of 1950, Pat went back to Fire Island from New York. There, she ran into Jane Bowles, "whose uncustomary fit of working" made Pat feel "vaguely guilty." She went for drinks at Duffy's Hotel with the woman Rosalind Constable had found her in bed with—as well as with her agent Margot's girlfriend and with Carson McCullers and Marc Blitzstein. Nobody could have accused Pat of being idle.

From Fire Island she travelled to Provincetown to stay with Ann Smith, her intermittent lover. Pat usually took up with the lovely Ann as a filler between other, more serious affairs, although she much preferred Ann to her current, official "fiancé" Marc Brandel (who had the bad luck to have introduced her to Ann) and said so.[60] Ann's Provincetown house was without "a tub or hot water," and Pat worked steadily on another version of *Tantalus,* "resting only on Sundays [and] pleased with the speed of its going" but "extremely worried about an itch I have developed in the region generally invaded by crabs."[61]

Pat may have spent a sexually reckless few months, drowning her anxieties about *The Price of Salt* in alcohol and dental gas and slipping into beds and bars up and down the eastern seaboard, but in her written references to her body she remained as prim as a prawn.

By the end of October she was drinking so much that she thought about taking "therapeutic measures against alcoholism. Something must be done."[62] Her new friend, Arthur Koestler, who had finished the novel he was working on, was being "very generous" to her professionally, recommending that she have her manuscript typed so that it would come back to her with "a new dignity." And he did, as he had promised, introduce her to the *"Partisan Review* crowd." She met Philip Rahv and William Phillips with Koestler in Greenwich Village at the Brevoort Café one evening in October. Koestler had talked her up so "considerably" that Rahv and Phillips were "ready to read *Strangers"* and give her reviews to do. And then Calmann-Lévy, Koestler's French publisher, bought *Strangers on a Train,* for which, Pat wrote, Koestler "claims credit, though M[argot]J[ohnson] said she'd had requests before." (Calmann-Lévy's director, Jeanne-Étienne Cohen-Séat, thought it was Koestler who introduced Pat's work to his publishing company.)[63]

But nothing penetrated Pat's terrors about *The Price of Salt* for very long. Suffused with shame, she was trying hard to "suspend [her own] judgement of homosexuality until [Koestler] has seen [the manuscript]."[64] And she was in the state of mind that preferred almost anyone's opinion of the novel to her own.[65] "These days are on the brink again. The least thing depresses me to the point of suicide."[66]

In the beginning of November Pat made a numbered list of the crippling feelings that writing *The Price of Salt* had brought her. She was suffering for having created what she knew to be (and denied for the rest of her life) a most unusual novel which drew its resonant qualities from its "close truthfulness" to her life. It was a sad reward for all her hard work and a self-administered punishment for all her self-exposure.

"Shame . . . for what I have done . . . Plus sense of failure, I have not got it done in the time for spring publication, like Koestler. I shall not have gained in reputation and fame, if it is published not under my name. . . . Leading to drunkenness, bad behavior, especially before people I care about, like Lyne. Desire to shame myself, too, feel guilty & hang my head."[67]

One week later, after spending the evening at Café Society on Sheridan Square with Elizabeth Lyne, the elegant émigrée and chief designer for Hattie Carnegie to whose friendship she became so attached in the 1940s and 1950s, Pat began, aggressively, to cross personal lines. She asked Mme Lyne if she could spend the night in her bed. "Come on, Pat, snap out of it," retorted Mme Lyne. "Which crushed me," Pat wrote in her diary."[68] Then Pat went to see *The Bicycle Thief*, and, just as *Death of a Salesman* had done, the film harrowed up her fears of poverty. She thought it was "the most depressing picture I have ever seen. People through poverty having to live like dogs."[69] Pat's violations extended to her diet: she went on a date with Carl Hazelwood, ate a whole plate of snails at the St. Regis Hotel on the sixteenth of November ("How could I!" she wrote) and was drinking so heavily that she had a "blank in memory until around Dec. 5."

And then, sometime in early December, frustrated that Elizabeth Lyne was late for an evening out with her, she crossed the most dangerous line yet: "on impulse" she went straight to her agent, Margot Johnson, and "told her I'd seen Kay G. [Margot Johnson's lover] several times, which being behind M's back, precipitated her breaking with Kay the following Monday."[70]

At Margot's "after the debacle," Pat, without apparent remorse for purloining her agent's girlfriend but telling herself that she could perhaps use another short course of psychoanalysis, began to feel a "terrific but slowly growing lust" for another guest at Margot's apartment, Sonya Cache*—a richly sophisticated Paris-born theatrical and literary agent whose first affair with a woman had been with the writer Josephine Herbst. "Quite by delicious accident," Sonya Cache joined Pat in bed at Margot's that evening (Pat had used Margot's apartment for assignations before), and Pat went lyrically mad for Sonya.

"I had almost forgotten that pleasure beyond all pleasures, that joy beyond all treasures . . . the pleasure of pleasing a woman. . . . And her body, her head and hair in the darkness . . . was suddenly more than Europe, art, Renoir, which she resembled, one of his women, beyond creative satisfaction. . . . She is mysterious in a Russian Jewish way, melancholic, devious by nature in her mind, witty as a fairy."[71]

Sonya Cache had a long-term lover, and Pat was already calculating the

* Sonya Cache is a pseudonym.

odds of their competition: "I believe I shall stack up better than she in a con-test, and it may come to that."[72] Then, "a bit tight," and reminded by love of the pleasures of war, Pat telephoned Sonya's lover and "announced in a loud clear voice that I was in love with [Sonya]." Pat couldn't, mercifully, remem-ber the conversation that followed, and anyway, she was still secretly seeing Kay, Margot Johnson's newly ex-lover. On the afternoon of New Year's Eve, she got "blind drunk" and had a "slight blackout" which made her late to Mme Lyne's and to a party in Yonkers where she met "a curious little girl, at-tractive."[73]

There was no end to Pat's destructiveness at this time—to herself and to the relationships of others—as she waited to see what would become of *The Price of Salt,* the book into which she had poured her most exalted feelings.

As usual, Pat's creativity was stimulated by destruction. She was reworking two short stories, "Baby Spoon" (another trophy-killer story about the attrac-tion between a professor and his psychopathic student expressed in a theft and in a murder) and "Love Is a Terrible Thing" (a story more representative of Pat's own state: she was anxious about not hearing from Kathryn Hamill Co-hen in London [see "Les Girls: Part 2"] and desperately anxious about what would happen with *The Price of Salt*). She was hoping, to no avail, to sell both of her new stories to *The New Yorker.* "Baby Spoon" and "Love Is a Terrible Thing" were eventually published in *Ellery Queen's Mystery Magazine,* and Pat gave no sign that she might have borrowed the title "Love Is a Terrible Thing" from *The Golden Bowl,* the novel by Henry James in which that line is almost an ostinato.

"Love Is a Terrible Thing" was published in 1968 by *EQMM* as "The Birds Poised to Fly." It is yet another revenge-and-substitution story, about a man who is waiting for a love letter (just as Pat was waiting for a letter from Kathryn Hamill Cohen in London) from a woman who doesn't write to him. He breaks into his vacationing neighbor's mailbox, telling himself that his letter might have been misdelivered, and, using his neighbor's name, answers a letter he finds in the mailbox from the neighbor's lovesick female correspondent. He makes a date with the woman in the name of his neighbor, approaches her, apologizes anonymously, and then, leaving her horribly disappointed, walks away weeping for himself. "Love Is a Terrible Thing" is a fair psychological summary of Pat's own behavior at this time.

The chance meeting with Kathleen Senn in Bloomingdale's in December of 1948 set off a series of reactions which were so disturbing for Patricia that she had to balance them out by squeezing them into the perfections offered by art—and by death. (There is no clearer example of the dangers and delights of creation than Pat's own account of how she behaved while writing *The*

Price of Salt.) Thus, the "automatic writing" of the plot of *The Price of Salt* that "flowed" from her pen was neatly counterweighted by the urge to tighten her hands around Kathleen Senn's throat: an urge that was overpowering Pat by the time she'd finished her novel. It brought forth her fullest explanation of how the muscles of her life moved her work, and she wrote it down the day after she'd first gone to New Jersey to spy on Mrs. Senn.

> I am interested in the murderer's psychology, and also in the opposing planes, drives of good and evil (construction and destruction). How by a slight defection one can be made the *other*, and all the power of a strong mind and body be deflected to murder or destruction! It is simply fascinating!
>
> And to do this primarily, again, as entertainment. (Better than Coates did it in *Wisteria Cottage*.)*
>
> How perhaps even love by having its head persistently bruised, can become hate. For the curious thing yesterday is I felt quite close to murder, as I went to see the house of the woman who almost made me love her when I saw her a moment in December, 1948. Murder is a kind of making love, a kind of possessing. (Is it not, attention, for a moment, from the object of one's affections?) To arrest her suddenly, my hands upon her throat (which I should really like to kiss) as if I took a photograph, to make her in an instant cool and rigid as a statue.[74]

Murder was a call that came quite naturally to Patricia Highsmith when she was in the grip of an overwhelming desire. "Murder fills my heart tonight / Like the words of first love," she'd written in 1947, in a love/jealousy poem to Virginia Kent Catherwood.[75] If Pat's brush with Kathleen Senn had been the inspiration for *The Price of Salt,* then Pat's affair with Ginnie Catherwood provided many of the solid marital details of that novel—even down to the phallic recording spike driven into the wall of the motel room through which the pursuing detective gathers evidence to take Carol's child away from her. The same thing had happened to Ginnie Catherwood, and Pat was "worr[ied] that Ginnie may feel Carol's case too similar to her own."[76] That worry didn't stop her from publishing Ginnie's history, however. Publishing personal histories (lightly or largely transformed) was something Pat would do

---

* *Wisteria Cottage,* aka *The Night Before Dying* (1948), is a novel by Robert M. Coates, art critic at *The New Yorker* and presumptive coiner of the phrase "Abstract Expressionism." Pat's reference to Coates is one of her rare admissions to reading popular fiction. She read popular fiction for competitive reasons and was familiar with all the bestsellers, but she preferred, as with her comic book work, to keep the news about her popular reading out of her cahiers.

again and again to her friends, her lovers, and to herself. The persistent "neutrality" and "coolness" of her prose was the mark of the metaphorical flatiron she passed over these histories in order to press them, hotly, into the forms of her fictions.

Pat first met Virginia Tucker Kent Catherwood at a party at the end of 1944 given by Rosalind Constable; Rosalind knew Ginnie and her husband through the publishing circles she frequented. Virginia's husband, the "youthful Main Line socialite and financier" as *Time* magazine called him, Cummins Catherwood, had inherited fifteen million dollars outright in 1929, as well as a basket of trust funds that paid him an income of nearly a million and a half dollars a year through the Depression.[77] By 1941, Cummins Catherwood was backing his cousin in the purchase of a venerable Philadelphia newspaper, the *Philadelphia Public Ledger*—a strictly Republican paper like the conservative *New York Herald Tribune*, the paper Pat had been reading every weekday since she was in high school.[78]

No matter where else Pat's perverse, unusually criminal imagination went on its travels, the Million Dollar American Dream was where it came to rest. She often placed herself, as she would write to Kingsley, at "that mystical point very near the foot of the rainbow where there is always a pot of gold, and presumably happiness ever after."[79] Virginia Kent Catherwood might have been tailor-made for Pat's aspirations.

Virginia Catherwood's's father, Arthur Atwater Kent, was the American Dream incarnate. A Vermonter whose early interest in automobiles led him to invent, amongst other devices, a distributor to facilitate the ignition of the internal combustion engine, he went on to found the largest radio company in the world, Atwater Kent, which manufactured radios of very high quality. When the fashion for small, cheap radios began, Kent refused to compromise on either the quality or the size of his models. Preferring to do things his way or not at all, he closed his company down in 1936. Virginia's mother, with whom Pat would optimistically correspond about her wayward daughter, gave Ginnie Catherwood the kind of upbringing Mother Mary would have loved to have given to Pat (or to herself): finishing school, art study in Paris, and a socialite's wedding.

By June 1946, when Pat and Ginnie Catherwood started their affair, Ginnie had been divorced for five years, had apparently lost the custody of her daughter, and was a serious alcoholic under periodic treatment for addiction. She drank so much that Pat feared for her life—and with good reason. In May of 1947, Ginnie's drinking caused her to temporarily lose her voice and the sensation in her fingers, a terrifying incident that found its way into the characterization of the alcoholic Charles Anthony Bruno in *Strangers on a Train*.

Ginnie—this would have been the jewel in Pat's psychological crown—even had another girlfriend, a photographer named Sheila. All the emotional and social tensions calculated to excite Pat were in place, and Pat, maddened with jealousy by Ginnie's "infidelity," and finding in her madness the oppositions that always enabled her as an artist, wrote: "There is nothing I would not do, murder, destruction, vile sexual practices. I would also, however, read my Bible."[80]

In fact, at the end of her relationship with Ginnie, Pat confined herself to one vile letter to Ginnie about her lover Sheila—and to the obligatory short affair with Sheila herself.[81] (And she did keep on reading her Bible.) But Pat's year with Virginia Kent Catherwood made an indelible impression: as she suffered, her imagination was set drifting, harvesting, and profiting artistically, as it always would do with every turbulent affair she ever had. It was only the calm affairs, like the bucolic relationship she had with "Doris" in Palisades, New York, in 1956–58, that provided Pat with relatively weak artistic results.

With Ginnie, however, the artistic benefits would come later. In early January of 1948, Pat confided to her diary that the seventy pages of manuscript (*Strangers on a Train*) she'd worked on after her affair with Ginnie collapsed were written "as if I'd had a broken leg, when I wrote them,"[82] and she destroyed several of the chapters. But *The Price of Salt* was a different matter: Pat said the novel could not have been imagined without her love affair with Ginnie, and without Ginnie Catherwood it would surely have been a very different book. While Mrs. Senn may have ignited the imaginative fever from which Pat produced her plot, the structure of Carol Aird's life, her problematic divorce and troubles with child custody, the pursuing detective, the nature of her relations with Therese—everything in the work that was exciting to Pat—was loosely taken from the life of Virginia Kent Catherwood.

Pat chose not to portray Ginnie's daughter in *The Price of Salt* (Carol Aird's daughter appears only as a photograph), but the child spent some time with Ginnie and Pat. And one afternoon by a swimming pool, Pat took the time to read to the little girl her own favorite story, one written in 1865 by an English don with the kind of uncomfortable attachment to young girls Pat had already noticed in herself. Later, Pat sent a letter to Kingsley about the story: "My highest ambition is to write a kind of *Alice in Wonderland*. Actually I'd prefer it to scoring another *Crime and Punishment*."[83]

For the rest of her life—especially when writing—Pat Highsmith would bring out the image of Virginia Kent Catherwood whenever she needed it, even though (and probably because) she and Ginnie never spoke again after they separated.[84] "The Still Point of the Turning World," a short story Pat wrote immediately after she and Ginnie broke up in 1947, is a little representation of Pat's own understanding of the strict moral attitudes and physical jealousies she was left with when she lost Ginnie. Embedded in the tale is another origin story for the homosexual twinnings that would run through her writing. Two little boys, toddlers, Philip and Dickie, fall in infant love in a small Manhattan park in Chelsea and are poignantly separated because Mrs. Robinson, Philip's mother, is both disdainful of Dickie's déclassé mother and jealous of her romantic connection with a man who is not her husband. Mrs. Robinson lives in what is meant to be the lovely art deco London Terrace apartments on West Twenty-third Street in Manhattan. Dickie's mother, palpably poor, uses the park to tryst with her lover-to-be, Lance, while her husband is at work and her child plays. Mrs. Robinson, awash in sexual jealousy and class contempt, takes little Philip away from Dickie and withdraws from the park, forever.

Pat said she was technically interested in the shifting perspective she built into "The Still Point of the Turning World," but the story's best feature is its close observation and painful juxtaposition of the romantic and the "real." It is reminiscent of the skillful economies and heart-piercing disappointments of a Shirley Jackson story.

Although Pat didn't think Ginnie Catherwood's drinking habits would allow her to survive ten years beyond the end of their affair, Ginnie did just that. Her irregular trajectory finally brought her to the colorful southwestern United States—to Tucson, Arizona, in fact, where she did not cease to attract interesting women. Ginnie made a last appearance in print (in the press this time, not in a novel) on 29 November 1959, when she was sued for a million dollars by the imposter prince David Mdivani, a man who had awarded himself and his brothers titles when they arrived, impoverished, in America from the Russian state of Georgia. The Mdivani boys were known as "the marrying Mdivanis" for the astonishing number of wealthy women they managed to wed or otherwise strip of their assets. The legal case David Mdivani launched against Ginnie Catherwood was for alienating the affections of his current wife, the great silent film star Mae Murray, "by lavishing her with expensive gifts."

If Mae Murray, who is rumored to have been the inspiration for the demented movie star played by Gloria Swanson in Billy Wilder's 1950 film *Sunset Blvd.*, really did have a liaison with Ginnie Catherwood, then we are left with the entertaining possibility—in whichever alternate, postmodernist afterlife these things are worked out—of a literary love affair between Norma Desmond and Carol Aird. And if Pat had known about Ginnie's relationship with Murray (she didn't know), her trip to London in 1969 to write a feature article for *Queen* magazine about another Billy Wilder film, *The Private Life of Sherlock Holmes,* might have had better consequences than the rather dull piece of journalism it produced.

Ginnie Catherwood, asked to comment on the false prince's lawsuit against her, declared, with a prudence which might have served her better had it been exercised earlier, that she had "nothing to say to anyone."[85]

· 18 ·

LES GIRLS

PART 2

Pat's first trip to the Europe of her imagination—in June of 1949 just after she'd spent all her money on psychoanalysis—was as an engaged woman: she had changed her mind again and decided that marriage to her on-and-off-again fiancé Marc Brandel might just be possible in the distant month of December. She was also travelling as an author whose first novel, the soon-to-be-titled *Strangers on a Train*, had just been accepted by Joan Kahn at Harper & Brothers.* But she still had to earn money, and so, instead of watching Noël Coward dine at the captain's table on the *Queen Mary* (he had settled in several decks above her in luxury class), Pat typed comic book scenarios for Timely comics in her cattle-class cabin all the way across the Atlantic.

By the time the ship docked at Southampton she was ready to forget her engagement to Marc and travel in style to Waterloo Station. Pat's hosts in London were Dennis Cohen, head of Cresset Press, and his wife, the psychoanalyst Kathryn Hamill Cohen, and they picked her up in their Rolls-Royce at Waterloo and drove her to their handsome house at 64 Old Church Street, Chelsea, just off the King's Road. It was a nice change from the D deck and the third-class cabin Pat had just shared with three other women on the *Queen Mary*.

Kathryn Hamill Cohen was an American-born former Ziegfeld girl who had come to London at twenty-four and trained as a geneticist. She was

---

* Joan Kahn (1914–1994) started as a reader at Harper & Brothers in 1946. Cass Canfield quickly offered her an editorship (she chose to be in the crime fiction department), and she began the imprint Harper Novels of Suspense. In latter years, the imprint became Joan Kahn Harper Novels of Suspense and then, simply, A Joan Kahn Book (CWA Olivia Kahn, 13 February 2003).

working as a psychoanalyst at London's St. George's Hospital when she met Pat in March of 1948 at a party at Rosalind Constable's New York apartment. (Pat had asked Rosalind pointedly if the Cohens' address was the "best address" she had to offer in England.) Kathryn was beautiful, intelligent, melancholy, monied, and married: a combination Pat always found irresistible. The fact that Kathryn's husband, Dennis, founder of London's Cresset Press (an imprint of Bantam Books), was interested in Pat's work and would go on to publish *Strangers on a Train, The Blunderer,* and *The Talented Mr. Ripley* practically assured that a seduction was in the offing.

During Pat's fortnight at the Cohens', Kathryn took her on a small cultural tour of London, out to lunch with the actress Peggy Ashcroft, and then to Oxford and Stratford-upon-Avon, where they saw Kathryn's friend Diana Wynyard play Desdemona and then visited her backstage. Pat's appreciation of the actress known as the "Queen of Stratford" was a foregone conclusion: "She is charming, extremely, touchingly attentive to her guests. And how happy I am to spend a few hours with such a beautiful woman."[1]

Back in London, Kathryn brought a geneticist's mind to Pat's hormone deficiencies and a psychoanalyst's perception to her love life, summing both up in a sentence which signalled her own attraction to Pat: "If you were added up, I think you'd have a little more on the male side—from your reactions to men, I mean."[2] Two days after she'd left the Cohen house for the Continent, Pat was in Paris, in the state of rapture that city always produces, and yearning for two women at once: "I need Kathryn, or Ann!" Then, hedging her bets, she added Chloe Sprague to her wish list.[3]

Pat went to Marseille to stay with Mother Mary's friend the cartoonist Jean David ("Jeannot"), who pressed his attentions on her. From Marseille, she wrote to Marc Brandel breaking off their engagement. (Like her previous good-byes to Marc, this one wasn't quite final. When she did say a final good-bye in July of 1950, Pat recorded Marc's "merciless" response: Marc thought she was "the most self-centered person he knew. . . . people didn't exist for me except as opponents of some sort.")[4]

Beginning a vagabondage that would bring her to Venice, Bologna, and Florence, Pat took a bus from Marseille to Genoa, mopping up impressions as she went. In Genoa, she paused long enough to fling into the already littered streets the yellow pyjamas Marc had given her as a love gift.

Two months after she'd left London, sick and solitary in her hotel room in Rome and feeling deeply sorry for herself, Pat took a chance on her feelings and wired Kathryn Cohen in London, asking her if she'd like to come to Italy. Yes, said Kathryn in a telephone call, she'd like to come to Naples. In anticipation of Kathryn's arrival, Pat allowed the fetid smell and filthy streets of the

city to bring her imagination back to *The Argument of Tantalus,* the manuscript that would become *The Price of Salt.* Love would often be a misery for
Pat, but it never began as anything less than an artistic inspiration.

When Kathryn arrived at the beginning of September, the two women
drove to Positano—this was Pat's introduction to the enchanting hill village
that would prove to be a catalyst for *The Talented Mr. Ripley*—and took a
romantic boat trip to Palermo and Capri. Sometime during the twenty days
of their travels they became lovers.

On her third-class boat passage back to New York from Genoa, Pat, enter-
prisingly carrying an accordion she planned to sell in New York, summoned
up an image of Kathryn and began to work in earnest on *The Argument of
Tantalus.* She was hoping, despite her "dissolute three days" in Paris (where
she'd frequented the venerable lesbian bar Le Monocle), and her promiscu-
ous behavior in London (where she'd managed to pick up and sleep with
several women during the short time she stayed with the Cohens), to wring a
"two year relationship" out of her feelings. Now, however, never a woman to
waste anything, Pat was using those feelings to thicken the texture of *The
Price of Salt.*

Kathryn Hamill Cohen and Pat never renewed their relationship. As a
practicing psychoanalyst, Kathryn would have understood very well what
Pat's alluring needs really represented: flares in the night, illuminating the site
of an accident that was just waiting to happen.

Back in New York from this first exhilarating trip to Europe, in long-
distance love with Kathryn and working on the novel that would make the
most "truthful" use of her own biography, Pat was in "a period of greater happiness and contentment than in the past three or four years." Out of her haze
of happiness, she provided a little theory for her behavior.

"I don't think I trust anyone under the sun further than the length of my
arm."[5]

The theory set out, she went on, three months later, to describe its practice:

The entire pattern of my life has been and is, she has rejected me. The
only thing I can say for myself at the age of twenty-nine, that vast age,
is that I can face it. I can meet it head on. . . . In fact, I have learned to
reject first. The important thing is to practise this. That my limping
crutches are not trained to do. . . . Therefore, to one more love, good
by. A dieu. But no—God will not be with you, not you.[6]

Pat was being modest here; she had long since "learned to reject first" and
even to survive being rejected herself. In fact, she spent the 1940s busily

constructing her character as a "lover" around the flights and drops of rejection. By the end of the preceding paragraph, she was even enlisting God to do her rejecting for her. And she went on to embellish her technique.

In 1957, Pat would briefly entertain the idea of writing a "second homosexual novel" using her sequential, parallel, and lateral love affairs as inspiration. (*The Price of Salt* was her first and only overtly "homosexual novel," but, with the exception of *Edith's Diary*, homosexual themes are everywhere in her fictions.) She made notes for this second homosexual novel in her cahier in the section she always reserved for her thoughts on homosexuality: "Notes on an Ever Present Subject."

"The romantic girl, who could never live long with a lover. Show her from seventeen to sixty. She learns to accept the romantic, neurotic character of her love, to know that the girls will come and go. . . . End of story is . . . a table in a sidewalk café of Portofino, awaiting the next experience."[7]

Caroline Besterman, the married Londoner who had thirty years of intimate opportunity—four of them as the most important "love" of Pat's middle life, the only "love" Pat couldn't make use of in fiction—to reflect on who Pat was and why, put it another way.

"I think, you see, there was always a hope that she would take up with somebody new or find a different situation. If she couldn't change her inside she could change her outside. That's a sign of people who tend to be insane."*[8]

Barbara Roett, who observed Pat's behavior in London in the spring of 1971 when they spent a night on the town together, had another kind of story to tell: "Pat looked at the whole evening as though we were two men going to pick up tarts. Not even women!" They ended up at the "famous old lesbian club," the Gateways, just off the King's Road and a fixture in Chelsea since the 1930s.

"Pat's way of trying to attract young women was so strange and so sort of alarming. She would put her foot up on the bench next to them, with her hair coming down over her face, and look at them in a deeply disapproving fashion. Like this. [Barbara glowered.] And the poor girls would be terrified. . . ."

"But when I saw her behavior that night . . . Well, I didn't even KNOW a man who would behave like that with women!"

Pat and Barbara "were invited to a party by two very hospitable girls." Barbara wanted to invite them back to Islington because Pat seemed to be interested in one of the girls. "And Pat said: 'You CAN'T have women like this, you

---

* Pat had a different explanation: "An artist will always drink . . . because he will always think of the woman he saw last week, or the woman who is a hundred or three thousand miles away, with whom he might have been happier, or just as happy. If he did not think of this, he would not be an artist, suffering with imagination" (Cahier 2, 29/3/53).

CAN'T invite women like this to your own home!!' And they were just a bunch of very innocent gay girls who were being very kind and understanding of Pat. So I realized it would not be simple for her to find a partner."*[9]

Ellen Blumenthal Hill, the woman who had the longest, strongest influence on Pat's life (after Mother Mary) and never one to suppress an opinion, spent four years instructing Pat in a succinct sociologist's "analysis" of her "past pattern" in love. Like the good student of psychology she was, Pat took notes. "She says, I fit the person to my wishes, find they don't fit, and proceed to break it off."[10] Proust *and* Procrustes each had a hand in Patricia Highsmith's ideas of love.

The "truth"—whatever it was at the moment—was something Pat usually reserved for those people with whom she was *not* in love. Or for current lovers she wanted to get away from. Or for prospective lovers she was hoping to fend off. She deployed the truth critically, punitively, or protectively, the way she and Mother Mary had always used it with each other. Pat could be very candid indeed—"authentic" is how one observer put it[11]—but her "authenticity" was often tied up with the immediacy of her responses. With her lover Marion Aboudaram, Pat had no difficulty in being candid.

When Pat met the French novelist and translator Marion Aboudaram alone for the first time in 1976, she said to her straightforwardly: "Go away, you're not my type." It was true, says Marion Aboudaram, "I wasn't. I was a bit plump and boyish. Her type was young blondes, very made up. The first time we met, when I was interviewing her, I brought my girlfriend and Pat winked at her. She would have preferred my girlfriend, I think."

Pat, Marion said, wasn't "in love" with her, but Marion persisted, they got together, and Marion Aboudaram's letters to Pat are amongst the most amusing in the Highsmith archives. Pat gave Marion some help with her translation into French from the American of Rita Mae Brown's lesbian novel, *Rubyfruit Jungle,* in August of 1977[12]—as clear an indication of Pat's real interests as her joining a Presbyterian church choir in Palisades, New York, had been in 1958.

Pat's penchant for speaking her mind to Marion could be charming. Once, when Pat was ill, Marion tried to tempt her into eating a bowl of soup, the way one offers nourishment to a recalcitrant child.

"I would hold the spoon in front of her and say, 'One spoon for Poe, one

---

* Pat had a specific memory of this evening, written in a letter to her friend Ronald Blythe from Moncourt, 9–11 April 1971: "I went to the "Gateways" with younger Barbara Roett, on a Monday night when it was swinging. I saw a pretty girl . . . and when she began to speak, it was Cockney, and I had a hard time in all that noise (juke-box) even getting her name. It was G[eorge] B[ernard] S[haw] all over again, and Pygmalion" (Collection Ronald Blythe).

spoon for Shakespeare, one spoon for Agatha Christie.' And when I got to Agatha Christie, Pat refused the soup.

" 'No,' she said. '*Not* Agatha Christie. She sells more books than I do.' "

When Pat and Marion's three-year relationship was interrupted in 1978 by Pat's *coup de foudre* for the twenty-five-year-old blond "made up" German costume-designer-cum-film-actor Tabea Blumenschein (see "A Simple Act of Forgery: Part 1"), Pat delivered the message to Marion brutally, candidly, and with the flair for adolescent theatricality that marked all her love affairs.

"Pat knew I was coming to the house in Moncourt [says Marion Abouda-ram], and she wrote I LOVE TABEA over every mirror she had. In the bathroom, in the bedroom, everywhere. And she wrote it in lipstick and she wrote it to hurt me."

When Tabea cut off the sexual relationship with Pat (after four fraught weeks), Marion proposed that she and Pat might stay together, "and each do what we wanted. Have affairs, etc." And Pat said, again, very truthfully: " 'I want young girls, I want to be with young girls . . .' I was forty then," says Marion, "already too old for Pat, who was fifty-seven."[13]

With Madeleine Harmsworth, a well-connected, "very nice girl, aged 26, like Keats, which always strikes a bit of a dagger in my heart,"[14] who responded to Pat's advances at her house in Samois-sur-Seine the day she came to interview Pat for the *Guardian* and *Queen* magazine in the spring of 1968, the then-forty-seven-year-old Pat was a little less direct than she would later be with Marion. A few months into her affair with Madeleine, Pat began by remarking sharply on the spinach that had lodged between Madeleine's teeth while she ate her lunch—and the fact that Madeleine was picking at it. Then Pat moved purposefully on to comments about Madeleine's habit of talking and chewing her food simultaneously. Soon thereafter, "I asked her to make her remarks louder and clearer at the table next time. I felt she mumbled. I suppose she will not like my saying this."[15] Pat knew what she was doing: "that might be an excuse on my part to wriggle out of a relationship which is quite good for me, as Madeleine's character is very good."[16]

Finally, Pat delivered the coup de grâce. With obvious inspiration, she managed, *while sound asleep next to Madeleine,* to mumble the name of her tantalizingly unavailable former lover, Jacqui, with whom she was still "a bit in love. . . . I always am, with people who are bad for me."[17] Sounding like a satisfied woman, Pat reported that "Madeleine heard [me mumbling Jacqui's name] twice in Portugal, and blew her stack."[18]

The technique varied; the effect did not. The lover was usually pushed away by Pat's "candor."

Still, proximity in love had always made Pat nervous. At twenty-seven, troubled by her homosexuality and just as troubled by the prospect of taking up residence in a heterosexual world, Pat had already decided that Hell was other people.

"Now I am incapable of the smallest decisions, and cannot even envisage my future life, since I am undecided whether I can be happy alone, or whether I *must* spend it with someone—in which latter case I shall have to make radical adjustments, either to male or female.

"A Quandary? Hell."[19]

In August of 1950—Pat was twenty-nine—her ideas of a live-in love affair were more specific and (unintentionally) much funnier.

"Living with somebody. At first in the moments one wants to read on a bed, for instance, every movement of the other is annoying. . . . Get over the terror and the hostility and one lives with another person very well? Question mark."[20]

Two months later, in October of 1950 in New York City, Pat was introduced to the brilliant Austrian Jewish émigré novelist, political activist, and adventurer Arthur Koestler. His dangerous charms,* "completely masculine . . . ways with the ladies," and professional connections greatly appealed to her. He "wants to introduce me to *Partisan Review* crowd," Pat wrote hopefully in her diary, after noting that she "[c]ould have murdered [Marc] Brandel who it seems told Koestler flatly I was a Lesbian, and that half of his book *The Choice* was about me."[21]

She need not have worried; Koestler made "the inevitable pass" at her anyway.[22] But Pat, filled with guilt as usual, and unable, as she said the next day over "seven martinis, a bottle of wine and three gins" to her friend Elizabeth Lyne, to "bear the thought of *The Price of Salt* appearing in print,"[23] was afraid that a double truth (the publication of her lesbian novel *and* Marc Brandel's revelation to Arthur Koestler about her sexuality) would sink her professionally. So she attempted to dissemble her situation with Koestler by going to bed with him. But truth will out, and the truth of Pat's own tastes "outed" her:

"Koestler came back here, we tried to go to bed. A miserable, joyless episode. There is a mood of self torture in me—when it comes to men. . . . And so hostility, masochism, self-hatred, self-abasement . . . Koestler, efficient as always, decides to abandon the sexual with me. He did not know homosexuality was so deeply engrained, he said."[24]

In Pat's highly personalized system of reversals, truth-in-love continued to be an instrument of war: a shield that could ward off a possible relationship

---

* Arthur Koestler's bust was removed from the University of Edinburgh, where his archives are located, when charges of serial rape were laid against him by his latest biographer.

or a weapon that could rupture an existing one. And she stitched this approach to truth into her novels. In a Highsmith novel (*any* Highsmith novel except *The Price of Salt,* where the murder resides only in the metaphors) the clearest, truest expression of feeling arrives with the instrument of death: a strangler's grip in *Deep Water* and *Strangers on a Train*; the point of a knife in *A Game for the Living, The Blunderer,* and *The Cry of the Owl*; the blunt end of a bludgeon in *The Talented Mr. Ripley and The Glass Cell;* the business end of a gun in *Strangers on a Train, The Cry of the Owl, Those Who Walk Away,* and *People Who Knock on the Door;* the bottom of a body of water in *Deep Water, The Talented Mr. Ripley,* and *Strangers on a Train*; and the end of a long, horrible fall in *Edith's Diary, A Suspension of Mercy, This Sweet Sickness, Deep Water,* and *Small g.**

Pat's deployment of truth, in other words, usually resulted in the violent death of *something*—symbolic or actual, a character or a relationship—and it was always just a little more interesting and a lot more available to her in art than it was in life. Still, she continued to rehearse its techniques in both arenas.

In fact, Pat was more likely to "spill" certain truths about herself or her opinions to casual acquaintances than to near neighbors or close friends. It was the people she ran into in cars and bars, railway stations and airports, the "strangers on trains" she met on her many travels, with whom she often felt safe enough to talk. Guy Haines, in *Strangers on a Train,* acts on this impulse with disastrous results: "And, worst of all, he was aware of an impulse to tell Bruno everything, the stranger on the train who would listen, commiserate, and forget."[25] Pat herself had better luck.

And so some of the most vivid punctuation for this book has come from the briefer encounters of Pat's life: a limousine driver who took her to Heathrow Airport; a piano player at the Hotel Normandy in Deauville; a journalist at the Berlin Film Festival of 1978; a young woman in the Gateways, the lesbian bar in London featured in the film *The Killing of Sister George;* the proprietor of Katmandu, the lesbian *club de luxe* in Paris's St-Germain; a French photographer; a German filmmaker; an eloquent refugee from a Displaced Persons' camp who knew Ellen Hill; and two translator neighbors in Fontainebleau who lived near enough to Pat for observation and far enough away to reflect on what they saw.

There were, certainly, some friends and one or two lovers of Pat's who

---

* *Small g* is not quite the sweet-natured book it has seemed to be to many critics. The club-footed dominatrix at the center of *Small g*'s black mischief falls to her death in one of those Highsmith murders which is not quite a murder: the result of a scheme carried out by the merry band of pranksters who despise her.

thought her incapable of telling a lie. "[T]he Pat I knew," Marijane Meaker told me, "was most unguarded, needy, open, accessible, and never tricky." But Pat kept many things from Meaker—she would say what was *on* her mind but not what was *under* it—including the continuing importance of Mother Mary in her life, the extent of her drinking (Marijane discovered it one morning when Pat handed her the wrong glass of juice, the glass filled mostly with vodka that was meant for Pat herself), the names of certain former lovers (and what she was still doing with them), and her past experiences with psychoanalysis.[26]

The people who found Pat frank may have been confusing her famously candid responses-in-the-moment with her deeper fidelity to an operating principle which made deception, evasion, and secrecy, as well as silence, exile, and cunning, her most important emotional and artistic tools.

And they were natural tools, too, for a woman who could remark, as Pat did when falling in love with Ellen Hill in September of 1951, "Oh who am I? Reflections only in the eyes of those who love me."[27] And whose "typical" daydream—set down when she was working on her novel *Deep Water* in June of 1955—took this form:

"Typical day dream—that a total stranger comes to me when I am alone, criticizes me, points out the ideals to which I have not remained loyal, or have failed to meet; leaving me in tears, completely broken in spirit, leaving me with the idea my life is worthless and I had better not have been born."[28]

It's summer in New York City, the last week of June 1953. Pat is thirty-two years old now, with a plethora of short stories and two published novels to her credit (one of them, *The Price of Salt,* is pseudonymous) and another novel, *The Blunderer,* under way. Conventionally enough, Pat has always used metaphors of childbirth to describe how her books get "born": "How much like babies books are to a writer!" she will write of the book she considered "healthier" and "handsomer" than her other books at its "birth," *The Talented Mr. Ripley* (1955). As early as 1948, she was comparing her residency at Yaddo to time spent in a maternity ward ("If I cannot give birth in the supreme hospital of Yaddo, where can I ever?"), and her 1969 novel *The Tremor of Forgery* is eloquent on the "post-natal," post-novel depression of its writer-hero, Howard Ingham.[29]

Pat has just returned to the United States from a second trip to Europe, a trip that lasted two and a half years. Much of that time has been spent in separating from and going back to Ellen Blumenthal Hill, the fiercely intelligent, ferociously controlling sociologist with whom Pat has been in love and hate for all but three months of her European travels. Her affair with Ellen began in early September of 1951 when, seated on a couch in Ellen's apartment in Munich, Germany, Pat suddenly felt something she could recognize.

"I held her hands that felt like Ginnie's, and her body, too, and soon she asked me to come up to bed. Or would I rather go home? I stayed. She is much like Ginnie. Tonight was only wonderful sensation—blotting out everyone who's been between Ginnie and her."[30]

Ellen and Pat are both Capricorns, born under the astrological sign of the goat, one day and six years apart. Ellen is the elder of the two, and her relationship with Pat has considerably extended the meaning of phrases like "getting each other's goat" and "locking horns." It will continue to do so for most of the next forty years.

When Pat and Ellen arrived back in New York from Europe in early May of 1953, their love affair was in a fragile state. But by 22 May, with Ellen safely in the American Southwest, Pat had decided once and for all to settle down with Ellen to a happy future and an apartment in New York. The next night, she ate a hearty steak dinner and slipped into bed with Rolf Tietgens, the gay German photographer who had played a sporadic, intense, and unconsummated role in her emotional life ever since 1943. (See "Alter Ego: Part 2.") Of her "not quite successful" bedding of Rolf, Pat noted in her diary, "In my system of morals I do not feel this in the least unfaithful to Ellen"—and kept silent about it otherwise.[31]

Rolf's main attraction for Pat had always been his homosexuality ("I feel with him as if he is another girl, or a singularly innocent man, which he is in these respects"),[32] the fact that he continued to insist that she was "really a boy" (and more or less photographed her as one),* and her gleeful understanding of the way they complemented each other: "If God puts us together, I will be the man!"[33] There was the additional lure of Rolf's moroseness, his hypochondria, and his Teutonic romanticism, and Pat matched him easily in all these departments. Rolf's last, alcohol-embittered letters to Pat from his dwelling on King Street in New York in 1968 and 1969 are monuments to self-pity and collapsed hopes.

Immured in his squalid apartment in Greenwich Village with "bursting closets," "no studio, no darkroom," no money, and "thousands of pictures and negatives, which climb up the walls here like poison ivy, reminding me of my past,"[34] Rolf Tietgens described himself as the prey of violent robbers and

---

* There are also nude photographs of Pat in which, aside from her small breasts, she always appeared to be androgynous. One of those photographs—the only one showing Pat's full body—has been torn in half at the waist so that her genitalia and lower body are missing. It's an unsettling remnant.

male hustlers—"I am becoming more and more the victim of the young"[35]—and he wrote that he no longer knew who he was.[36]

"When Tietgens died," says his friend and onetime neighbor on Long Island, the former features editor of *Harper's Bazaar* Dorothy Wheelock Edson, "I found out that his lungs, supposedly shot and keeping him from working, were in good shape."[37] Rolf had brought Pat to Dorothy Edson's house in Wheatley Hills, Long Island, in 1943, and it was this meeting with Mrs. Edson that led to Pat's work being recommended for publication in *Harper's Bazaar.* Mrs. Edson, who surmised from the encounter that Pat was "surely a lesbian," was a little surprised to hear from the homosexual Rolf that he had proposed to Pat. At the time, Rolf kept a "fascinating" apartment in a "made-over dairy" in Locust Valley near Mrs. Edson and her husband on Long Island's North Shore. Rolf's bed was adorned with purple blankets, and his white floors were kept shiny by the practical expedient of making his visitors remove their shoes at the door and enter barefoot. Dorothy Wheelock Edson, a good New Hampshirewoman who was also the first ghostwriter for Gypsy Rose Lee's mystery novel, *The G-String Murders,* was so impressed by Tietgens's decorative tastes that at ninety-seven she said she was still sleeping under purple blankets herself.[38]

"He is nice but increasingly melancholic," Pat observed of Rolf Tietgens in July of 1950, implying somehow that this romantic quality made him "[m]y favorite friend."[39] But the quality of his melancholy began to strain Pat as the years passed—"This German *Weltschmerz* and negativity is so hard to deal with!"[40]—and their mostly epistolary friendship ended in New York in 1970 when, as Pat wrote, Tietgens grabbed the front of Pat's coat, "called me, among other things a shit"[41] . . . "and shoved me against wall of his house."[42]

No doubt it was something she said.

In this last week of June 1953, the temperature in Manhattan is ninety-two degrees in the shade, the heat is shimmering up off the sidewalks, and a pneumatic drill is hard at work breaking up the concrete outside Pat's temporary lodging: an apartment she and Ellen Hill are renting (but it's Ellen who is paying) from Dell (Hans Felix Jüdell), the husband of Pat's friend and confidante, Lil Picard.* Lil is the irrepressible émigrée fashion editor, revue artist, film actor (she appeared in a film with Emil Jannings), milliner, jewelry designer, writer, painter, and, well into old age, outrageous performance artist whom

---

* Lil Picard (1899–1994) was a recognized figure in Manhattan's East Village and in European art circles, known in both New York and Berlin for her performance art.

Pat had met "in an elevator at a gay party" in October of 1947."[43] Pat managed to suppress her desire to kiss Lil, but Lil's position as an older married woman "with a husband from whom she seems to keep secrets" enchanted Pat, and she began to visit Lil every day.[44]

Pat and Lil Picard's tempestuous friendship lasted for thirty years; and Lil, an Alsatian Jew who fled Berlin in 1936 and was au courant with every art movement in New York from Abstract Expressionism to Fluxus (and was photographed by, amongst others, Lotte Jacobi and Andy Warhol) became an identifiable figure in New York's avant-garde. Her flamboyant performance pieces and her column in the house journal of the newly developing East Village, the *East Village Other,* assured her notoriety, although not her solvency, and she never allowed her fondness for Pat to get in the way of calling her a "fascist." Lil called Pat a "fascist" very regularly.

Of the novel Pat dedicated to her father, Jay B Plangman, *A Dog's Ransom,* Pat said that she "rather modeled the character of Greta Reynolds after my friend Lil Picard."[45] If so, it is a pallid version of the real Lil. Mother Mary, only four or five years older than Lil, was horrified by Lil's free-wheeling sex life, her opulently unfettered self-expression, her influence on Pat, and—the very last straw—the fact that Pat had once lent Lil some money for an operation.

Flayed by the sound of the drill outside her window and broiled by the "hot as a furnace" summer weather, Pat has been writhing in her coils for the last fortnight, trying to pick up on the Manhattan social and professional life she allowed to slacken in the two and a half years of her European travels.

Three weeks ago, she'd gone to see Truman Capote's play *The Grass Harp* in Sheridan Square and then tried to catch up on both gossip and business by inviting Betty Parsons, now the doyenne of her own influential art gallery, to have lunch at her apartment and look at her drawings. To Pat's distress, Parsons preferred her "bloodless abstracts" to her representational work and told Pat that Carson McCullers had "fallen madly" in love with Kathryn Hamill Cohen, and had lingered in London for three months, begging Kathryn to live with her although "there was no affair."[46] Now, Pat was writing "only to keep from going mad in my old city where all the business people neglect me as if I were officially boycotted."[47]

Extending her mood into fiction, she'd spent the last week of May composing a short story she called "Born Failure."[48] She continued to meet Betty Parsons for meals and drawing classes, saw "that burly fellow" Philip Rahv again at a *Partisan Review* party on Forty-eighth Street, and had dinner with Bobby Isaacson, lover of the poet James Merrill (son of one of the founders of New York's largest stock brokerage company, Merrill Lynch). She noted, without personal comment, the imminent electrocution of the Rosenbergs for spying, but was exercised at the way American libraries were suddenly eliminating "controversial" authors from their shelves; authors like Dashiell Hammett, Howard Fast, and Langston Hughes.[49] She "was on the brink of a depression quite as serious as the 1948–49 winter one" and was doubting both her agent Margot and her relationship with Ellen Hill: "Nothing is ever permanent," she said. But it was really the permanency of her *own* feelings that Pat was doubting.[50]

On the seventeenth of June, Pat went to a cocktail party at James Merrill's apartment at 28 West Tenth Street where she ran into Jane Bowles. "She looks plumper, older, and is otherwise much the same—moderately friendly," Pat thought. Jim Merrill "looked sweet in a lavender shirt of subtle hue. Also Oliver Smith, Johnny Myers, Harry Ford & wife, etc. Tietgens is not invited." Rolf Tietgens hadn't been invited because he'd had an unauthorized fling with Bobby Isaacson in Rome. One month ago, Pat had had her own unauthorized fling: the one-night stand with Tietgens she'd neglected to mention to Ellen Hill.[51] At the party, Pat talked to Terese Hayden, manager of the Theatre de Lys on Christopher Street. Hayden had done an "apparently unsuccessful" screen treatment of *The Price of Salt,* which Pat had received in Florence in June of 1952[52]—with the character of "Carol . . . changed to Carl" and the title of the screen treatment changed to *Winter Journey.*[53] By then Pat, embarrassed anew by her novel, was calling *The Price of Salt* a "stinking book" and marvelled to Kingsley that it had "sold to Bantam for $6500."[54]

On the eighteenth of June, tossing and turning in the unendurable heat, Pat had a nearly "sleepless night" which produced a "curious dream"—made out of the weather and her illicit feelings.* In retrospect, the dream seems almost to be a preparation for the dreadful incident which occurred with Ellen Hill ten days later. In the dream, Pat was with Kathryn Hamill Cohen and a naked girl. Their clear "intention was to burn the girl alive." They put the girl in a wooden bathtub along with a wooden effigy of Pat's grandmother "with arms outstretched," and it was Pat who picked the bathtub up and ignited the papers under it. Pat reminded the weeping Kathryn: "Don't forget, the girl *asked* us to do it to her!" But then a "horror went through" Pat at the "suffering of the girl.

"A moment later, the naked girl simply stood up, stopped her crying, and stepped out of the bathtub unhurt except for singes: the fire had gone out. I

---

* A previous biography has mistakenly set this dream in June of 1952 in Florence. Pat dreamt it in New York in 1953—more horribly, and more appropriately, because it came just a few days before a near catastrophe overtook Ellen Hill.

felt guilty at the thought the girl would report what we had done. . . . Then I awakened.

"I subsequently had the feeling the girl in the tub might have represented myself, because she looked a little like me in the dream, at the end. In that case I had two identities: the victim and the murderer."[55]

Despite the continuing heat, the lingering effects of this "horrid vivid dream," and her daily efforts to break into the new medium of television with a script called "Innocent Witness," Pat was finding the strength to launch a few more professional and personal advances.

On the twenty-fourth of June, Pat went to lunch with a man "I like so much—better than any editor to date," Cecil Goldbeck.[56] Mr. Goldbeck, a vice president at the Coward-McCann publishing company, had already published one of Pat's novels in paperback, The Price of Salt, and would go on to edit The Blunderer (for which her current relationship with Ellen Hill provided two characters and a situation) and The Talented Mr. Ripley. Now, he wanted to give her a thousand dollars "sight unseen" for her next "suspense" novel. Cecil Goldbeck's enthusiasm for fiction like Pat's seems to have run in his family. His brother, Willis Goldbeck, was the uncredited coauthor of a work whose themes—sexual humiliation and horrible revenge—were also Highsmith favorites: Tod Browning's 1932 classic cult film Freaks.[57]

The nominal purpose of Pat's second visit to Mr. Goldbeck on 28 June was to "consult" him about her hardworking agent Margot Johnson's "value" to her. Throughout her travels in Europe, Pat had been blaming Margot for her long run of bad publication luck. When Pat met the brilliant Proust scholar Mina Kirstein Curtiss (ballet patron Lincoln Kirstein's sister) at a cocktail party at the literary agent Mme Jenny Bradley's house in Paris at the end of 1952—Curtiss had been Margot Johnson's teacher at Smith College—she queried Curtiss sharply about Margot. "There is no better agent," Curtiss replied.[58] Ten days before that, Pat had written to Kingsley from Europe, asking her, too, to assess Margot's reputation in publishing circles: "Margot hasn't sold anything for me in ages. . . . I'd love to know just how her standing is at present."[59]

This time, however, Pat was angling to bypass Margot completely and deal directly with Cecil Goldbeck herself so that she could cut out Margot's commission—a little bait-and-switch maneuver she would try, with variations, eight years later on her French publishers Calmann-Lévy (she ditched them, briefly, for Robert Laffont), and then again in 1979 on her next American literary agent, Patricia Schartle (whom she attempted to shortchange on European commissions).[60] But Mr. Goldbeck honorably assured Pat that "Margot [was] the best agent" she could have. The others were like "factories," he told her, "you produce or are thrown out."[61]

The Mother of Them All: the indomitable Willie Mae Stewart Coates and her husband, Daniel. The hand on the wall belongs to Daniel and Willie Mae's granddaughter, Patricia Highsmith. *(Swiss Literary Archives)*

Little Patsy all dolled up by Mother Mary and expressing herself in the yard of her grandmother's boardinghouse in Fort Worth, Texas. *(Swiss Literary Archives)*

Mary Coates Plangman Highsmith. "I too am an extrovert and never met a stranger," Mary wrote to one of Pat's lovers. *(Swiss Literary Archives)*

Jay Bernard Plangman. Before his mustache, his marriage, and his disappearance from the life of his only child. *(Swiss Literary Archives)*

Mary and Stanley Highsmith, on their honeymoon in Galveston, Texas, in 1924. *(Swiss Literary Archives)*

Mary and Patsy in Galveston. Pat dated this photo "1925," but other photographs and other evidence—including Little Patsy's uncustomary dress and downcast demeanor—indicate that it was taken at the time of Mary and Stanley Highsmith's honeymoon in 1924. *(Swiss Literary Archives)*

Pat, dressed more or less like Jackie Coogan in *The Kid*. From an early age, Pat felt she was a boy in the body of a girl. *(Swiss Literary Archives)*

Handsome Dan Coates, Pat's "Brother Dan," famous in Texas as a rodeo announcer for his "golden voice." He was posthumously elected to the Texas Rodeo Cowboy Hall of Fame. *(Swiss Literary Archives)*

Pat as a teenager, impeccably dressed for mounting an English saddle. *(Collection Annebelle Potin)*

Pat in her early twenties: lovely, secretive, desired by many. *(Swiss Literary Archives)*

Patricia Highsmith, editor of the *Barnard Quarterly*, surrounded by her staff in 1942. On Pat's left is Kate Kingsley (later Skattebol). *(Barnard College Archives, published in* The Mortarboard, *1943.)*

Rolf Tietgens, the German photographer who wanted to marry Pat.

Pat at 21, photographed by her new friend Rolf Tietgens.

Judy Holliday. Pat and Judy were close friends at Julia Richman High School; Pat kept a copy of this photograph.

The witty, wealthy, well-connected painter Buffie Johnson in a characteristic pose by Edward Weston. She and Pat met when Pat was a junior at Barnard College. *(Collection Buffie Johnson)*

Rosalind Constable, a well-known arts journalist, the eyes and ears of the Luce magazine empire, and Pat's idol for a decade. *(Menil Collection)*

Lil Picard, the dress and hat designer, painter, journalist, and performance artist who was Pat's "most inspiring" friend for thirty years. *(Collection University of Iowa Libraries)*

The 1943 Alex Schomburg cover for the Superhero comic *The Black Terror* #2. Pat wrote extensively for Black Terror and his "mild-mannered" Alter Ego, Bob Benton. The Superhero and his Alter Ego first appeared in a Nedor comic in January 1941—and their resemblance to Superman and Clark Kent was entirely intentional.

The splash page for "The Fighting Yank" in the October 1945 issue of *America's Best Comics*. The Yank, who debuted in a Standard comic in September 1941, was another of the second-string comic book Superheroes Pat wrote for.

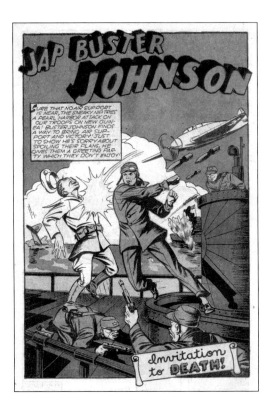

Jap Buster Johnson defeats the Japanese army in New Guinea with extreme prejudice. Pat and Mickey Spillane both wrote for this wartime human killing machine, first published in a Timely comic in December 1942.

The Destroyer, another of the wartime Superheroes-with-double-identities for whom Pat wrote. The first Destroyer story was written by Stan Lee for a Timely comic published in October 1941.

Pat's two meetings with Goldbeck were the bookends to her disastrous re-union with Ellen Hill, who had just returned to New York on 25 June from a trip to Santa Fe. Pat ducked the first evening with Ellen, spending it instead with Jean P., a new attraction. By 28 June, Ellen and Pat's relations were "strained and insane." Ellen wanted Pat to return with her at once to Santa Fe "in the new car. I am saying, due to her foul temper, I will not." Pat was hav-ing "secret talks, all comforting" with Jean.

By the time Pat and Ellen had arrived back in the States on 13 May 1953, and by the time Ellen had returned to New York from her solitary trip to Santa Fe to see her mother at the end of June, Pat was ready to have a little fun with someone else. In fact, she had already been having quite a bit of fun with sev-eral other women in Ellen's absence.

On 1 July, after arguing with Ellen for hours, Pat slipped out at three o'clock in the afternoon for a drink with Ann Smith, the lover with whom she'd intermitted her affair with Marc Brandel. (In a fit of writer's revenge, Marc turned Ann, who was a very pretty blonde, into the caricatural "ugly lesbian" in his novel *The Choice*.) Pat then "arranged with a friend to bring Jean P. out to her place in Fire Island next weekend. By that time I thought to have Ellen en route for Santa Fe or Europe. Ann was wonderful,"[62] Pat confided to her diary, excited, as always, to be juggling three women at once.

After the drink with Ann, Pat returned to the apartment she and Ellen were sharing. She had another "violent" argument with Ellen that lasted two and a half hours, from five to seven-thirty in the evening, and threw a glass on the floor to "emphasize I *did* mean it when I said I wanted to separate."[63] Ellen "has tried everything from sex to liquor to tears to wild promises of giv-ing me my way in everything."[64] Pat's account of this evening is as numb to remorse as any scene Mickey Spillane, the scriptwriter for *Jap Buster Johnson* at Timely comics just before Pat took up Jap Buster's story line, might have slipped into one of his Mike Hammer novels:

"She threatened veronal & insisted on having two martinis with me which she tossed down like water. I said go ahead with the veronal. She was poking 8 pills in her mouth as I left the house. I love you very much were the last words I heard as I closed the door. She was sitting naked on the bed. Had just written her will giving me all her money, & saying give Jo [a woman who had been a lover of both Pat and Ellen] $5,000 when I got around to it. And called me the nicest person in the world for having stayed with her as long as I did this evening."

Ellen had threatened suicide once before, in 1952, when, after browsing Pat's diaries without permission, she got the shock awaiting anyone foolish enough to break into a writer's private thoughts: an uncomplimentary assessment of her own character. The diary shock was mutual and it was repeated: in the summer of 1954, Ellen peeked again at another of Pat's diaries—and was caught again. Her "honest diary," Pat wrote, was what had helped "to keep [her] on the right moral track. . . . Her "purging effect of putting things down in words" had been interrupted and it was all Ellen's fault.[65] Naturally, Pat punished herself: she stopped writing her diaries for the next seven years.[66]

Still, Ellen was neither the first nor the last loved one to read Pat's private writings without permission. Nor was Ellen the last woman to whom Pat would recommend suicide. When the roommate of another friend threatened to jump off a balcony in the 1980s, Pat was quick with her support. "Let her jump!" wrote Pat feelingly, and then followed this up with a gentler suggestion. "I've been in, and also witnessed, such drama, therefore I felt inspired tonight to state: get away from it, no matter what it costs in time and money."[67]

The bonds of love—never mind how eagerly she slipped into them—always eventually felt like iron chains to Pat Highsmith. Emotional blackmail of any kind, one of the many twisted strands by which she was still connected to Mother Mary, brought out Pat's inner executioner and her outer escape artist.

And escape from Ellen Hill she certainly did.

After leaving Ellen in the act of swallowing those Veronal pills (and helpfully cancelling the evening appointment Ellen had made with the Czech painter Jim Dobrochek), Pat went straight to her friend Kingsley's apartment on West Eleventh Street. Pat didn't mention the scene she had just been a part of; she seemed, in fact, to be much more interested in what Kingsley and her beau, Lars Skattebol, were going to say about her latest novel. "They ripped me mercilessly (& stupidly) re my third novel [*The Traffic of Jacob's Ladder*, now lost, which Pat was writing at the same time she was taking notes for *The Blunderer*]: a prerogative, and [said] I'd never write another decent novel having spat out such infantilism."

Then, her usually uncertain appetite stimulated by the evening's excitements, Pat went on to Jean P.'s apartment, where she ate two hamburgers and alarmed Jean with "the sad story of tonight & Ellen." When Pat finally made her way home at two o'clock in the morning (and she took her time about it), she found Ellen in "a coma—out, anyway, beyond coffee & cold towels. . . . A doctor . . . arrived, pumped her stomach to no avail [then] the police, then Bellevue [Hospital] where I delivered her at 4:30 AM.

"There was a note on typewriter which the cops took": 'Dear Pat I should have done this 20 years ago. This is no reflection on you or anyone—' "

Pat spent the night with Jean P., then went in the early morning to Bellevue Hospital, where she answered questions about Ellen's health. The "doctor gives [Ellen] an even chance," Pat noted without comment, and went on to her agent Margot Johnson's apartment. Margot provided "general comfort" and martinis ("unfelt"). Rosalind Constable's lover Claude offered her apartment to Pat for the weekend, but Pat said she was driving Ellen's Morris Minor out to Fire Island—"the first of the black eyes I give myself through apparently crude behavior where Ellen is concerned."

The next morning, 3 July, Pat met Jim Dobrochek, Ellen's artist friend, at the hospital. She told him the whole story and gave him Ellen's "effects." Ellen was still in a coma.

"Jim had been walking streets all night. Told me over AM coffee Ellen mistreated him on his arrival here . . . buttonholed him at the pier & said: Don't ever tell a *soul* that I am Jewish! I had not known before she was totally Jewish, from that tight, sophisticated, brittle German Jewish intellectual set of pre-Hitler Berlin."*

After meeting Jim, Pat made her getaway to Fire Island with Jean P. in Ellen's car. This, she wrote, "is a major strike against me, with Ellen's mother. Ideal weather & connection & its heaven to be out here. I am escaping from hell."68

By the following morning, 4 July, Independence Day, Pat was forcing herself to "work, half believing Ellen dead." At six in the evening, she called Jim from the legendary Fire Island hotel, Duffy's (burned to the ground in 1956), and learned that Ellen "came to yesterday—early this morning. The strain is over." At one thirty that morning, Pat, skunk drunk, "picked [a] fight with some late girl callers." It was a physical fight and she was "sadly beaten," ending up with a chest so bruised that she had to have it X-rayed when she got back to Manhattan. It was Jean P. who broke up the fight and pulled Pat away.

Pat was already planning to take an apartment with Jean, "a major decision . . . that cannot possibly last"; and that evening she drove back to Manhattan with Jean and another friend from New York, Betty—"one of few confidants—in Ellen's car." Betty may have been Pat's confidante, but Pat was confidently double-crossing her: Betty's lover was Ann Smith, Pat had been seeing Ann secretly again, and Betty didn't know a thing about it.

---

* This wouldn't be the only time Pat fell in love with a Jew who was concealing her origins. Daisy Winston, the headstrong, witty little firebrand with the irreproachably anglicized name and the "Righter-than-Right" political attitudes and social prejudices (including anti-Semitism), who was Pat's lover in New Hope in 1961–62, shocked all her friends in Pennsylvania after her death. When Daisy's friends saw her birth certificate, they discovered a secret she'd managed to keep from everyone. Daisy Winston, too, was a Jew.

By 7 July, Pat was installed on Twenty-fifth Street in the apartment of a friend of Jean, cat-sitting, entertaining "T.V. speculations," and feeling "[t]he old ambiguous pull—toward safety & toward destruction." After trying to get away from Ellen, she was now afraid that Ellen was trying to get away from her—and she was dining out or having people in every night and carefully monitoring her "bruised chest," "mental strain," and low red blood cell count: "I am in the 60s in blood."[69]

On the fourteenth of July—a Tuesday—a "Notice arrives *Neue Zuricher* [*sic*] pays me $18.70 [for an article]. Am extremely proud!" Ellen was already receding from her thoughts.

Pat and Ellen had been tempestuously together and rumbustiously apart—it's often hard to tell which was which—since September of 1951, when they were introduced to each other in Munich by a classmate of Pat's from New York, Jo, who had been Ellen's lover and was, secretly, a lover of Pat as well. Pat failed to mention to Ellen that she had been sleeping with Jo, but, pleased as always to be part of a triangle *and* part of its destruction, Pat wrote in her diary that "Jo has suddenly lost me and Ellen as well."[70]

Pat fell hard for Ellen and quickly elevated her to her currently vacant (but always fully endowed) Muses' Chair: that gilded hot seat in her Heaven of Love reserved for women who could inspire her writing. Pat's delight in Ellen produced some superb literary results—as well as an occasional writing voice no one would *ever* associate with Patricia Highsmith.[71]

> *Ellen! Helen! Helena! Hellenes!*
> *Tambourine and sunflower,*
> *Parasol and pumpkin,*
> *Veins of Venus*
> *And Ariadne, spinning her unexpected fruit,*
> *Mother, madonna, womb and matrix,*
> *Placenta, placid, plaisant!*[72]

In July of 1951, a month and a half before meeting Ellen Hill, Pat had been alone in Munich, lamenting the lack of inspiration in her life. "The danger of the celibate. The danger of disaster. He lives for himself alone, must be his own spur, his own inspiration, even his own goal. It's so difficult, and so inhuman. It's so easy to work for someone one loves."[73]

Pat would later write ingenuously to Kingsley that although she couldn't really say why she'd gone to Europe in early February of 1951, she thought it might have something to do with "my very queer life in N.Y., which led to dismal similar cycles by no means normal or usual even in New York, I think. My family had left the state. I had broken with Rosalind."[74]

What Pat didn't mention to Kingsley was that the violent spiral of alcoholism, sexual promiscuity, and psychological destructiveness she was demurely calling "my very queer life in N.Y." had been caused by her desperate feelings about publishing her lesbian novel, *The Price of Salt*: the work that came most directly out of her own history. The real reason Pat went to Europe was to escape herself.

While she may not have fallen in love in Munich in July of 1951, Pat's celibacy didn't last long either. In August, she ran into her old Barnard classmate Jo at the American consulate, and soon invited her to bed. Pat was also returning to "the voluptuous shoulder" of a German woman, Tessa, with whom she had already spent some exciting nights.[75] In late August, Pat "[v]isited Schleissheim DP [Displaced Persons] Camp. . . . There must be something masochistic in my nature." But she didn't describe the camp, just as she hadn't described the postwar, bombed-out or otherwise battle-scarred conditions of the cities she'd been touring: London, Paris, and Munich. In Europe, the scenery Pat chose to write about was usually aglow with her long-term goal: "All I want is to be rich & famous! Not much, eh?"[76]

Cheering up fast (but in her own special way), Pat went to the theater with Jo to see Jean Cocteau's play *The Typewriter*.

"This is the kind of evening (and life) of which I dreamed in college—in a very Scott Fitzgerald way: Europe, a girl, money, leisure, a car. [Pat had a secondhand BMW but no driver's license.] Now I've had *one* night of it, after twelve years."[77]

Pat had been in Europe since "5:15 AM Paris time" of 5 February 1951. She had flown from New York to Paris with "a slight hangover," obsessively marking the height the airplane attained (nineteen thousand feet), the length of the flight (eleven hours), and the price of her one-way ticket (four hundred dollars). She'd had a "hectic departure" at Idlewild International Airport, seen off by Mary and Stanley, Rosalind Constable, Ann Smith, and her agent Margot Johnson, who, after observing Mother Mary and Pat together, remarked in apparent bemusement: "There must be some mistake."

Pat went a little too early in the morning from Le Bourget Airport to Elizabeth Lyne's apartment on the rue de Lille, where she was to stay with Mme Lyne in a nearly empty house of great and dilapidated beauty. She met Janet Flanner and her lover Natalia Danesi Murray immediately for cocktails at the Hotel Continental ("Poor Natalia, a slave for 11 years to Janet"); looked for and then wrote to Ruth Landshoff-Yorck, the writer, refugee, and patron of avant-garde arts she'd known from Leo Lerman's salon; and went to lunch with Lucien Vogel, founder of *VU,* the first journal in France to expose the existence of Nazi concentration camps, and his wife, Cosette, sister of Jean de Brunhoff, creator of the Babar books. Vogel spoke French too rapidly for Pat's comprehension, and André Gide, the Frenchman Pat most wanted to meet, would die later that month, before, as Mme Lyne said to Pat pointedly, Pat could "improve her French so she wouldn't sound like an idiot when she met him." Pat went to "a phony lesbian night club off the Champs-Elysées [which was] a favorite haunt of Peggy Fears"; she met Tom and Theodora Keogh (to whose highly original first novel, *Meg,* she had given such a good review a year ago—the best review she was ever to give a woman writer) at Deux-Magots;[78] saw Esther Murphy Arthur and Paul Monash; and visited her European literary agent, Mme Jenny Bradley, on the Quai Bethune. Mme Bradley, the perfect agent, gave her washcloths and Ivory soap. All this, and much more, Pat did in the first week of her arrival in Paris.

Late in February, Pat flew to London and was met by two reporters who "took a few snaps" and talked about *Strangers on a Train.* She stayed, once again in opulent surroundings on Old Church Street, with her Cresset publisher-to-be, Dennis Cohen, and his wife, Kathryn, for whose signs of love she had waited so anxiously in New York. Pat now took unsympathetic notes on Kathryn's depression (Kathryn committed suicide in 1960), her "cheerlessness," and her obvious lack of response to Pat and to the manuscript Pat would soon be calling *The Price of Salt.* Pat feared Kathryn didn't like the book and wouldn't want to recommend it to her husband to publish. Kathryn didn't and wouldn't. Pat wrote: "I failed with K—as a person, as a writer." Pat's best feelings about *The Price of Salt* dissolved immediately: she suddenly couldn't understand "how Ann Smith could have liked it so unreservedly."

Pat lunched with Rosalind Constable's former lover Maria (with whom Pat had also slept on her last trip to London) and renewed their affair to cheer herself up. She got the idea for her "third decadent novel," called *The Sleepless Night* (*The Traffic of Jacob's Ladder* in its final form), and after her night with Maria, the new book "broke its embryonic waters," and her writing began to go well for the first time. Pat and Maria went constantly to the Pheasantry, a private eating club in Chelsea. "That is bringing the night into the day. That is bringing paradise into the prosaic," Pat wrote about Maria, wondering, however, if she had "lost the giving power of falling in love. . . . Lately it is entirely bound up with whether the person is accessible or not." Pat would have agreed with Ivy Compton-Burnett that the most important aspect of friendship was "availability."

In London, Pat saw a lot of the handsome Austrian writer Raimund von

Hofmannsthal, son of Richard Strauss's librettist Hugo von Hofmannsthal. They discussed, censoriously, the effect comic books had on his children, without Pat saying anything about her long employment in the comics trade. Through Dennis and Kathryn Hamill Cohen, Pat was interviewed regularly by the press and met many people: Alan Pryce-Jones, the John Canters, the actress Constance Cummings (who lived next door to the Cohens). And everywhere Pat went, everywhere she was invited, she saw in bombed-out, still-rationed London only what she had always "dreamt of having": a "[c]harming 2 story house, good martinis and a good dinner with French wine . . . a wife, and books and a Siamese cat."

Pat flew back to Paris on the ides of March, fearing that she had overstayed her welcome at Dennis and Kathryn's (she had), and took a room at the Hôtel des Saints-Pères in St-Germain-des-Pres. She had her usual trouble getting her typewriter out of customs—it took several days and a good lie—and she had to go to Le Bourget Airport for it. She resumed her regular dinners with Janet Flanner and Natalia Danesi Murray. Natalia was trying to engineer a contract with the Bompiani publishing company in Rome (where her mother was an editor) for *Strangers on a Train*.

On her way to Rome, in April, Pat once again visited Jeannot and his mother, Lily, in Marseille. This time it wasn't Jeannot who pressed his attentions upon Pat; it was Jeannot's gorgeous girlfriend who made the "violent pass." "I was cold," Pat wrote, and then "I thought, I am making an awful mistake." As usual, Pat felt she was overeating and overweight. Also as usual, she was thin as a rail, but this feeling of being fat would persist for months. She took a train—she was thrilled to be on a train again—on her way to the isle of Capri to visit Natalia Danesi Murray and her mother, Ester Danesi, who had a "charming apartment next to the Quisisana Hotel. Her mother, formerly a journalist, very calm & slow, working diligently now on p. 67 of [the translation of] 'Strangers.' Very touching & heartwarming."[79]

Pat was plagued by both constipation and also, good Freudian that she was, by deep fears of being entirely without money. She was depending on Natalia Murray for too much, including meals and introductions to many people (the composer Lukas Foss was among them), and she was wrestling with her dependence.

Janet Flanner said to everyone about Pat: "She has talent." But Pat felt inadequate and resentful around Janet: "typical frustrating afternoon which so exposes my own miserable psychological contitution. . . . I am unable to speak, to participate on my own level, but must remain tongue-tied, stupid, dull. Janet F. often affects me like this."[80] When Janet finally left for the United States, "flat broke, homeless in Paris," on 3 May, "everyone [was] chagrined" except Pat, who wrote in her diary: "Very lovely tonight without Janet."[81] (Given Pat's crabbed handwriting, the phrase could have been "very lonely"; certainly, both phrases were true.) A few days earlier, Pat had written about herself and Janet: "How like a schmuck I feel in comparison to her—and in accordance with my perverse nature, I am immediately better (more open in every way) as soon as she is gone, while all I should have liked to do was please her."[82]

In Paris, Pat managed to run into her old lover Natica Waterbury and Natica's lover Maria—leaping across the Boulevard St-Germain when she recognized Natica—and they enjoyed themselves separately and together in a succession of lesbian bars, notably Le Monocle in Montparnasse. But Pat was rarely interested in the women she found in bars. She made an appointment to meet "Sybille Bedford and her smooth-faced friend, Evelyn Keyes," but something interrupted it. Pat went many places in every city she visited, met many people on whom she took extensive notes, but nowhere in her diary notes on Paris, London, or Munich is there any sense that these cities might still be suffering the effects of one of the most devastating conflicts in human history, the Second World War. As she would make Tom Ripley do, Pat continued to see in Europe mostly what she wanted to possess: *"Il meglio."* The best.

On the seventh of May she heard that Ester Danesi, Natalia's mother, had at last secured the Bompiani contract for *Strangers on a Train*, and as she finished the story she was working on, Pat thought: "Christ, I can write, but when I am done I need an editor! God, if it were only easier for me to make decisions."

That evening, she did make a decision. Instead of taking home one of her two dinner companions, "the beautiful Deirdre," she took the other one, "Grant," the man, home with her. "Better than I expected, but in the morning I am uncomfortable and ashamed & feel unnatural."[83]

On 9 May Pat was in Florence, and by the twelfth she was in Venice staying with Ruth Landshoff-Yorck, who, she wrote, was ordering her around the way Rosalind Constable used to. She went to cocktails with Peggy Guggenheim, "Somerset Maugham attending. Short, stutters, extremely polite. We did not talk about writing." It was decades later that Pat thought she remembered Maugham telling her that in mixing martinis, he merely "showed the cork" of the vermouth to the gin. But Maugham said this to everyone.[84]

On 6 June, Pat heard from Margot Johnson that Harper had rejected *The Price of Salt*. "Harper's reports not enough enthusiasm from the editorial board, that I probably can't do the book because I am too close to the subject, haven't the 'mature approach.'" Margot immediately submitted the manuscript to Coward-McCann. (Pat was still "going over my [manuscript] with a fine tooth comb.") Pat sounded relieved about the rejection: "It doesn't depress me in the least." But by 24 June, Coward-McCann had taken it "with compliments" and the promise of "$500 to come."[85]

As usual, Pat's affinities for women waxed, waned, and flared up as unexpectedly as Saint Anthony's fire. Amongst her serious crushes at this time was Ursula—"with whom I am half in love"—a German princess and a friend of Ruth Yorck. Pat was impressed by her title and inclined to listen to her. "Ursula says I write so well but am full of tricks which the reader doesn't quite swallow. A depressing judgement, with perhaps some truth in it."[86] She saw a lot of Ursula and went with her and the writer Wolfgang Hildesheimer—another of the talented Jewish refugees Pat had met and magnetized on her last trip to Europe—to a poetry reading in Munich.

Eight years later in New York, on New Year's Day of 1959, Pat would use the name of Wolfgang Hildesheimer, who was by then translating Djuna Barnes's novel *Nightwood* into German, to try to strike up an acquaintance with the reclusive Miss Barnes. Pat wrote transparently and awkwardly to Barnes at her apartment on Patchen Place to say that Wolfgang Hildesheimer was a "great friend" of hers who might require some help in his translation of *Nightwood* and that she hoped to meet Miss Barnes for a "cup of coffee together or a drink some time, so I can tell him what you are like."[87] Djuna Barnes, far too canny to be so easily trapped, riposted in a letter to Pat five days later that she herself had just written to Hildesheimer to offer him assistance with his translation and, as for the matter of what she was "like," "if [Hildesheimer] wishes a photograph of me he may obtain one from my publisher, Faber & Faber."[88] Pat never met Djuna Barnes.

Now, in 1951, in Munich, Pat was having equally bad luck with her German princess. Pat questioned a translation the princess was doing—it's not clear if it was a translation of one of Pat's stories—and "[t]he Princess blew up and said I was exactly what R. Yorke had said I was, etc."[89] Pat had already acquired a reputation.

Early in July, Pat was in Salzburg buying "a beautiful hunting knife for Shillings 53. About $2.50. I hope I shall have it for many years." (She does still have it; it's in her archives.) In Salzburg, she felt "fat, old" again. "I heard my heart and felt mortal as mortal can be. . . . Thirty—what a turning point. I remember Natalia saying, in Capri: 'Thirty? You don't begin to live until you are 30.' Tonight. My movie opened, I believe."[90] She meant *Strangers on a Train*. It was the first time Pat had claimed any relationship to this other version of her first published work—and the very idea ("my movie") seems to have reminded her that she was going to die.

Late in July she was in Ambach, just outside of Munich, taking driving lessons and coming to the end of "my typing over" of *The Price of Salt*. "Have integrated Richard much more with the action, and also included that element of morbid curiousity [*sic*] and self participation I remarked in Marc [Brandel]." The book was still coming directly out of her life.[91] Pat was also keeping up her usual pace of correspondence, with letters to and from friends, to and from old lovers, and to and from prospective lovers, new acquaintances, and business contacts in the book world. It was the habit she had begun with her first foreign outposting, to Taxco, Mexico, in 1944–45, and chronic correspondence would become her version of fidelity. On paper, Pat was able to keep her affections focused and her loyalties alive. Aside from the colloquies she conducted with herself in her diaries and cahiers, letter writing would serve as her main form of conversation.

By the end of July Pat was back in Munich, thinking that the pseudonymous authorship she'd decided on for *The Price of Salt* was a handicap, that the whole book was a handicap, and, almost as bad, that it was also responsible for her two abscessed teeth. "I know instinctively that anxiety and mental tension can cause this. . . . I live under the threat of having half my remaining teeth removed (tomorrow) and the resulting ignominy and disfigurement."[92] She had seen a "torturing" dentist in Venice and hunted up an American one in Germany, and was working away on short stories, radio pieces, and an article for the *New Orleans Times-Picayune* (it was turned down). Her energy was enormous; her social networking, plans for future work, and persistent physical complaints (and complaints about those physical complaints) never stopped.

On 11 August, she "ended my book [another version of *The Price of Salt*] and it's ready to pack." It was, she felt, time for an accounting and so she did one: counting up her lovers on a little strip of paper she entitled "whole show." She printed their initials out in ink, and the paper is stained with what appears to be beer.

Twenty-one of them! I count—
V-C – B M.S. B.B. *C.S.* R.B. – J.S. *N.W.* – V.C.K. – *J.P.* – J.C. *J.I.* – J.T. –
A.S. – P.F. – S.D. – B.C. – K.G. – M.E. – T.R. K.C.

But Pat was only counting the lovers that still counted for her. There was no Rolf Tietgens (he hadn't, technically, been able to make love with her in their short month of trying years ago, anyway), no Marc Brandel, no male initials discernible, in fact. And she was certainly not counting the dozens, the hundreds, of short flings she'd had with women and a comparatively small number of men, nor the many longer relations she'd had with the women for whom she'd felt more than a passing fancy. This was Pat remembering her memories in the moment and then ranking them, not Pat telling her history on a witness stand. Her diary entries—this can't be stressed too often—were regularly written long after the dates she put on them, and her opinions were always subject to change. ("J.T." is not Judy Tuvim; it is her lover Jeanne, whom Pat continued to try to lure to Europe, and who married shortly after Pat made this diary entry.)

In August in Munich, three weeks after marking and then relinquishing her celibacy to Jo and Tessa, Pat failed a typing test (three times in a row) at the Peterson *Caserne*, the American army base in Munich, where she was trying to get a little work as an army typist in the Criminal Investigation Commission. Pat's interest in the criminal mind and her talent for flunking job interviews never left her. Thirty-seven years later, on Don Swaim's radio program in New York City in 1987, Pat said that she'd "wanted to avoid learning anything useful [so she] never learned to type." She "didn't," she repeated, "want to get stuck with a secretarial job."[93]

By 29 August, in Munich with Jo, Pat found herself staring "at a woman who was staring at me, not knowing it was Ellen Hill. I stared because she was the only attractive woman I had seen in days, and the staring is inevitable in this town."[94] Six days before this sighting, Pat had been prompting Jo to see "if she liked sleeping with me [and] she said 'I suppose basically I'll always want to sleep with you.'" But Jo's opportunity was short-lived; within a week, Pat was madly in love with Ellen Hill.[95]

LES GIRLS

PART 3

Pat's tendency to make marble monuments of her lovers and then to discover, painfully, that their pedestals were made of clay found a perfect match in the array of dominations, virtues, and failures in human tolerance that made up the character of Ellen Blumenthal Hill. Ellen and Pat's long love affair repeated the *Alice in Wonderland* plot of all Pat's major love affairs: first it made her feel larger and then it made her feel smaller.

"O the benevolence! O the beautiful world! O the generosity of the heart as I go walking down the street . . . today, I am vaster. . . .

"How could it be? Isn't she like Titania charmed into loving the donkey?"[1]

Pat followed her usual bliss with Ellen, and had her usual trouble describing her lover. Pat was always at a loss when summing up the good qualities of the women she loved; her natural talent was for describing their bad qualities. But the adjectives she used for Ellen—"small, quite chic, good-looking," "very intelligent and efficient," as well as "possessive," "dominating," and "very feminine"—were the traits before which she always felt most inadequate.[2] And Pat's feelings of inadequacy affected her like potent injections of a love drug.

"Darling, come to me in a silver dress with dragonflies' wings, come to me on a column of smoke, come into my room though a keyhole, and through the crack of the door and the floor. . . . I turn like an idiot in quest of you."[3]

But Pat was never happy to be "an idiot" for long.

The small, neat, elegant, "rather humorless woman" who inspired these effusions was a serious European intellectual with a solid academic background and a German Jewish refugee heritage she was determined to conceal. Ellen's colleague and friend in Munich after the war, the philosophically minded

H. M. Qualunque,* who sensed Ellen's distress on the subject of her ethnicity, says that Ellen "was in charge of the United States resettlement desk at the Munich IRO, the international agency set up by the United Nations to research all Displaced Persons after the war."[4]

Mr. Qualunque was introduced to Pat by Ellen Hill in 1971—he retained an impression of Pat's "aggression" and her physical decay—and he asked Pat a question which Pat thought important enough to note down in her cahier: "a question that I can't answer: if life has no meaning, why has morality?"[5] Mr. Qualunque had spotted Pat's moral contradiction. She was a woman who wrote about the "meaninglessness" of life while still being seriously worried about right and wrong.[6] Pat agreed with him.

"Why my constant preoccupation with morality? It has been the theme of almost all I write, from my first story, 'Crime Begins,' at sixteen, until now, when I write a book about murder."[7]

Ellen Hill, says Mr. Qualunque, was a born moralist with a "cutting-edge" intelligence and "no time for fools." This left her with no time for anyone because "she considered almost everyone else a moron." Still, Ellen was "absolutely devoted to the idea of rational social justice and systems for living [and] was very much respected at the IRO. . . . She was a very difficult person, a rough character, but who isn't? I knew her, so her character didn't bother me and I admired her intellect. . . . It was easy for the average person to describe Ellen Hill because she could be extremely abrasive and competitive. I couldn't care less. I knew how and what she was and I was interested in those aspects of her that were interesting."[8]

During the Second World War Ellen "taught 'Area Studies'—the mores and political makeup of various countries"—at Stanford University in California to diplomats and career officers, and "married Mr. Hill for a British passport, then disposed of him." After her stint with the IRO in Munich, she moved to Rome, where she affiliated herself with a "social research institute and published highly specialized articles in Italian sociological reviews." Later on, she had an office at the University of Zurich. Ellen spoke several languages and managed to produce merciless judgments in every one of them.[9]

Christa Maerker, the Berlin filmmaker and writer, remembers Ellen Hill as "the dragonic General . . . but with a sweet face" whose stentorian voice boomed out over the railway station café in Locarno when she spotted Pat there with Maerker sipping a morning beer: "Pat! Not in the morning!" Kingsley saw Ellen as a "governess" and says that Pat behaved like "an Oriental servant" with her. Daniel Keel describes a luncheon in Zurich during which

---

* H. M. Qualunque is a pseudonym.

Pat did everything Ellen told her to do, exactly—and how Ellen tried, unsuccessfully, to make him do the same thing. And Peter Huber recollects a 6:30 A.M. call in Tegna ("We are late risers," says Huber) from Ellen, who telephoned Huber and his wife to see if they'd taken the advice she had given during dinner the night before about driving to Zurich very early in the morning, "saying how shocked she was that we hadn't left yet and that we really ought to get ready."[10]

But in the sole official record of Ellen's relationship with Patricia—a German television documentary shot at Pat's house in Moncourt at the end of October 1978 in which Ellen interviews Pat in German for the camera—some charitableness of manner is evident. Pat's visual grammar in this documentary is, once again, that of a captive forced to give false testimony in a hostage video. But her awkward, choppy German (a Swiss neighbor says that "German was Pat's best foreign language—and it was bad")[11] is much assisted by the elegant Ellen's gently phrased questions and bridgings of conversational gaps. And in an unguarded moment Pat, suddenly remembering the richly Balzacian possibilities in the old French custom of selling an apartment *en viager* (i.e., an apartment sale that leaves the apartment's elderly former owner in place, while the new buyer pays a regular stipend to the former owner for life, betting that the life will be a short one), forgets the camera for a moment and unleashes a chortle of pure pleasure.

Before Pat and Ellen's first date—it turned out to be a well-wined lunch at a lake restaurant outside of Munich—Ellen had inquired of Pat if she preferred Baroque castles to Rococo castles. This taste for precise distinctions would later grate like sandpaper on Pat's nerves. The two women embraced for the first time two days later on Ellen's sofa—the invitation to do so was Pat's—after primly listening to poetry and classical music on Ellen's radio in her apartment on Karl Theodorstrasse. It was on that day when Pat wrote in her diary that Ellen reminded her physically of Ginnie Catherwood and that the experience of sleeping with Ellen blotted "out everyone who's been between Ginnie and her."[12]

Only Pat, with her rigid categorization of experience and her Procrustean drive to force each new woman into a previous prototype, could ever think that this highly strung, intellectually disdainful European Jew—whose habits were as prim as a paper cutter's—could ever resemble the rich, spoiled, socially registered, alcoholic divorcée, Virginia Kent Catherwood, for whom Pat had fallen so hard in 1946.

It was a matter of weeks before Ellen's precisions were grinding Pat's feelings into a resentful powder; a fortnight before the sound of Pat's typewriter was murdering Ellen's sleep and driving her mad; and just a few days before

Ellen's behavior with her dog was pushing Pat to thoughts of canicide. To be sure, Ellen made Pat order the kind of food in restaurants which her beloved dachshund, Henry, could eat, knowing that Pat's lackluster appetite would guarantee plenty of leftovers. Pat, who rarely forgot anything that happened around a dinner table, gave the character of Clara Stackhouse this same relationship with a dog in *The Blunderer,* the novel into which she wove her complicated and violent feelings for Ellen.

She also gave Clara's husband her feelings for Henry: "Walter restrained an impulse to crush the dog in his hands."[13]

Still, Henry the dachshund gave as good he got. As sensitive to insult and sexual jealousy as Pat was, he tore up the bedroom, brought clothes racks down to the floor, flattened a Christmas package Pat had made for Ellen, and defecated on the parquet. A year into the relationship, when Henry began "attacking [Pat] without provocation" (without *overt* provocation, that is; Pat's thinking about Henry was now running heavily to strangulation fantasies), Ellen, in what even Pat had to admit was a noble gesture, gave the dog away uncomplainingly.

Pat was sufficiently inspired by Henry to make certain that terrible things happened to dogs whenever they appeared in her novels.* (It probably didn't help that Mother Mary had always kept small dogs with names like Wing Wang and Zsa Zsa.) But *The Blunderer* was only just finding its form, and Pat, needing immediate relief, put some of her feelings about Ellen and Henry into a short story "aimed at *The New Yorker*" (it missed the target). She mailed the story off to Margot Johnson in New York, calling it "Man's Best Friend." The story is about Baldur, a German shepherd who is so superior to his dentist master that the dentist tries to kill himself—twice—in order to escape the dog's unbearably severe judgments.[14]

In life, dogs didn't fare any better with Pat than they did in fiction. During one of her many separations from Ellen, while staying briefly with her friend Tity in Florence, Pat made the mistake of taking Tity's dog Mala for a walk. Mala, Pat was moved to write, was "abominable to walk with. Like having an octopus with suction pads below the leash."[15] Pat's description of her lover Jacqui's dog in Paris in 1969 could only have been the product of a long-cultivated disgust: "Her dog sucks his penis all day, and has his ears in my canapes at the

---

* See the painful injuries, maimings, kidnappings, and sudden deaths of dogs in *This Sweet Sickness, The Glass Cell, The Tremor of Forgery, The Cry of the Owl, Deep Water,* and *A Dog's Ransom.* Only in *The Blunderer* does the dog survive unscathed; still, the animal remains in perpetual mourning, and Pat had the satisfaction of killing off Ellen herself in that book. And only in her last novel, *Small g,* does the dog prosper, but by the time Pat wrote *Small g* all her deep feelings had begun to relax—to the detriment of her writing.

cocktail hour."[16] Pat's disapproval of the sexual habits of Pif, the ancient bird
dog living with her next-door neighbors in Moncourt, Desmond and Mary
Ryan, caused her to deliver a swift, secret kick to poor Pif's derrière. Pif, Pat
wrote to Barbara Ker-Seymer, was "sexually obsessed," a condition she could
sympathize with only in herself.[17] And Pat's empathy for her other Moncourt
neighbor's dog—the dachshund living with Hedli MacNeice, ex-wife of the
poet Louis MacNeice—had to do with the dog's superb bloodlines, the knowledge that it had been killed on the road, and the fact that Pat could comfortably blame Hedli for its death.

Even at the end of her life in Tegna, Pat was still having trouble with dogs.
A neighbor's two "huge" dogs continued to romp regularly through her back
garden. Her letters about these canine interlopers are radiant with the urge to
kill.

Nonetheless, Pat would go on to make use of food with her cats in much
the same way that Ellen had done with her dog Henry. The scholar Bettina
Berch noticed it during a visit to Pat's house in Aurigeno in 1984: "I knew very
well that we were eating food that was basically intended for the cats. We sat
down to eat food that was chosen with the cats' palette in mind; herring,
dairy products.

"What do these foods have in common, I thought? That when we're finished with them, the cats will enjoy them. Except, of course, for the beer and
the scotch."[18]

And Christa Maerker was quite certain that at Pat's last house in Tegna she
had been given food the cats had *already* sampled.[19]

Pat's relations with Ellen Hill began as they were to continue for the next
four decades: "Ellen and I argue or misunderstand in all of our conversations."
Still, Pat felt that falling in love with Ellen "was Europe as Europe is supposed
to be, and so few individuals find."[20] And she even "got the curse in the morning [of 8 September]." It was the first time she'd menstruated in seven months,
and she understood immediately that there was "[no] better indication of my
emotional . . . awakening."[21] Pat would get her period more regularly throughout this turbulent affair—as often as "every 35 days"—than at any other time
in her life, except for the years that she was with Caroline Besterman. She almost never menstruated during the months of her ambivalent relations with
Marc Brandel in 1948–49, and ordinarily her periods were so infrequent that
she noted them in her diaries, while continuing to get estrogen shots for
what she called "the usual hormone deficiencies."

By 14 September, Pat and Ellen were on their way in Ellen's car—Ellen at
the wheel, Pat still without a driver's license—to Venice. It was an axiom by
now: the first thing to do after falling in love was take a trip. Jo had been left

to deal with Pat's clothes and car, just as Ann Smith had been left to deal with the possessions in Pat's New York apartment. Margot Johnson sold the rights to *Strangers on a Train* for two hundred dollars to Sweden, so Pat, "terribly happy," bought candy for Ellen and began to drink more. Prostrate before her new queen, she was feeling "like a coolie the gods have suddenly snatched up and made a prince, with ring, a halo, and immortality."[22]

In Venice, "after a long splendid ride in the sun," Ellen insisted on changing their "darkish rooms" for hotel rooms on the Grand Canal. For the rest of their two-week journey, Pat and Ellen would rarely travel less than "first class." The writer Alan Campbell, a friend of Ellen (and twice married to Dorothy Parker, so he was used to difficult women), telephoned immediately from his room in Venice, and Pat thought he was playing "Dan Cupid": he approved highly of Pat. "Who doesn't," Pat wrote with an uncharacteristic flourish, but she was also asking herself a characteristic question: "[W]hat can break this up? And it's so sweet to be able to think of nothing that can." By 16 September, the worm was in the apple and Pat was writing in her diary: "I must watch Ellen from moment to moment to judge her temper. She is *not* easy to get on with."

The next day Pat and Ellen had cocktails with Peggy Guggenheim. Pat thought that Sinbad, Peggy's son by the painter Lawrence Vail, was "looking sickish," and that "Peggy [was] jaded" and that she "barely took in the fact of my movie." The movie again—and Pat was irritated because Guggenheim had ignored it. Without any publication for months now, Pat was beginning to think of the Hitchcock movie of *Strangers on a Train* as her calling card.

Ellen, after entertaining Pat with "wonderfully" silly stories, "tells me I have a new mood every 20 minutes." It was the kind of remark Mother Mary used to make to Pat—and it was the kind of remark Pat used to frighten herself. While she was still with Ginnie Catherwood, Pat had written in a notebook: "I am troubled by a sense of being several people (nobody you know). Should not be at all surprised if I become a dangerous schizophrene in my middle years." And then she'd added: "I write this very seriously."[23]

By 20 September, Pat was still feeling like the "Prince Consort" and Ellen was still on a "spree," signing them into the most palatial establishment (the "swankiest hotel" is what Pat called it) on Lake Como. "I care nothing about money these days, not that I have any," Pat wrote in a moment of *pauvresse oblige*. Ellen was paying for everything. "But it is this . . . unknown side of me that Ellen finds so attractive: impracticality, generosity, imagination, the poet, the dreamer, the child. And I am too inclined to act a part, in all of it." And, because Pat was making her diary entries retrospectively, she added: "This fact is to make the next few weeks difficult."

The difficulty was easy to identify: Ellen had already tired of playing the role of Maecenas, and Pat was bored with playing the role of fey, artistic dependent. Both women were miscast in the melodrama they continued to improvise for each other. It was going to make their next few *years* difficult, not just their next few weeks.

On 22 September, they were in Ascona, Switzerland, with Ellen's stomach upset and Pat in a jealous fit over Ellen's past lovers. (Usually it was the reverse: Ellen was jealous and Pat was in gastric distress.) They both got over their maladies, with Pat deciding that Ellen's past lovers were "*faute de mieux,* as was Jeanne and Ann S[mith] for me. . . . Ellen & I are both extravagantly happy just now." And so they stayed on in Ascona—as Pat wrote in a reference to Henry James's *The Ambassadors*—"like Chad and his European mistress. So seldom do I really live." "Live all you can" is the advice Lambert Strether offers to Little Bilham in that marvellous novel, which was soon to provide both a structure and a story for *The Talented Mr. Ripley.*

On their way to Zurich, Pat was impressed by the St. Gotthard Pass: "most exciting and thrilling to me. As much as the Endless Caverns when I was a child." With Ellen driving and directing, Pat, with her clear understanding of the balance of power, felt as she had on a cross-country car trip to Texas with her parents two decades before when she was nine: "[S]he has the car, therefore all the authority somehow, and I am a child whose nose has to be wiped."[24] The detour Pat's family had made to the Endless Caverns in Virginia on that trip in 1930 was what Pat would later call her "first push in the direction of writing": the otherworldly beauty of the caverns and their *Alice in Wonderland* history (the Endless Caverns were found by two boys going down a rabbit hole) moved Pat to give her first "entertaining" speech in front of her fourth-grade class.[25] Travelling with Ellen Hill would continue to provide Pat with many more of these "pushes" towards creativity—and most of them would be as unwillingly bestowed as they were ungratefully received.

Zurich, Pat found, was "very prim and bourgeois and opulent. I am a bit sated on luxury." A honeymoon with no writing attached to it was making her restless. "I am not really content unless I am pulled at like something on a rubber band—elasticity, limitations, a time schedule, etc. Only with more social graces can I obviate this American bad habit of having to be *doing* something."[26]

Back in Munich in early October she at last saw "the movie," Hitchcock's version of *Strangers on a Train.* "I am pleased in general. Especially with Bruno, who held the movie together as he did the book." By 1988, Pat had changed her mind—by then, she had changed her mind about nearly everything—complaining to a journalist that the changing of Guy's profession had ruined the film; that Guy didn't carry out the murder; and that he was in love with that "stone angel," actress Ruth Roman.[27] (Hitchcock wanted Grace Kelly for the role but couldn't get her released from another contract.) When Pat saw "her movie" for the first time, she didn't seem to know that Robert Walker, the actor who played Bruno with such demonic flair, had died tragically a few weeks after the film opened in the United States, driven by his own particular demons.

Pat and Ellen were late to the Munich showing of *Strangers on a Train,* and Pat's friend from Brooklyn, Jack Matcha, who years later would publish her favorite snail story, "The Snail-Watcher," in *Gamma,* his short-lived American magazine, was there with his friend Tessa. Ellen refused to dine with them on the grounds that they were beneath her socially. "Ellen," Pat wrote, "can be damned unpleasant, especially her voice—and I am ashamed before Jack, who might be a proletarian, but who is still a real guy."

Ellen was now intensely critical, and Pat was drinking heavily and denying it. " 'The minute something goes wrong, you take to the bottle,' Ellen accuses me unjustly—but if anyone ever did drive me to drink, it's she!" Then Pat read a "splendid translation of 'The Snail-Watcher' by [Jean] Rosenthal," and Ellen remarked that the translation was "better than the original." Pat missed the sting in this remark—or perhaps she didn't, because she said she was feeling "sleepy, overweight, indecisive, and unentertaining" and went on to give her friend Jo the "calculated" impression that "Ellen and I shall not be together very much longer." Her affair with Ellen was not yet one month old.

Still, Pat and Ellen had their intensely loving moments—and they both continued to play their roles, with Pat revelling in being the trusting, dependent child. "[Ellen] says she wonders how I survive, in the world, all alone. She means, I suppose, I can't remember figures, and I seem to trust everyone. . . . I've never been so in love with anyone, not even, I think, Ginnie. (At last!)"[28] And Ellen, the authoritarian parent, went right on (between scarring arguments) telling Pat what Pat loved to hear: " 'You're the best lover I've ever seen—heard of—read about. . . . I absolutely adore you. You're exactly what I want.' "[29] But Ellen also remarked that Pat was "the only person she'd ever met who could be in love & critical at once."[30]

By the end of October Pat had a menstrual period so copious that it was "coming on like a faucet" and "terrifying" her. She was making notes for *The Sleepless Night* [later *The Traffic of Jacob's Ladder*] and working on "a great sheet of yellow paper, with the characters and general outlines of chapters. But there will be no chapters. There will be no quotation marks, no prose description or background work. Each person will be the style of it, and that will probably take experiment."[31]

This tantalizing description—was she remembering her enthusiastic response to Virginia Woolf's *The Waves*?—has nothing to do with the ten very ordinary pages of *The Traffic of Jacob's Ladder* left in Pat's archives. Pat began writing the book on 30 October and was immediately depressed: "Every book is perfect until one begins to write it." In early November she got a letter from Margot saying that Alfred Hitchcock was interested in "new material" and would pay Pat's way to London if she had any "new ideas" to tell him. Pat began to "dope out" a "passport idea."[32] It came to nothing.

By New Year's Eve, Pat and Ellen were fighting over every inch of territory in Ellen's Munich apartment and over Pat's "sloppy" habits, as well. Rebellious feelings against an older woman had always made Pat messy, and the more humiliated she felt, the more enthusiastically she described her sexual life with Ellen—or lack thereof. Still, she wrote that "Ellen does me favors, gives me more than I can give her."[33] Again, this imbalance was to prove productive for Pat, and on 11 January she sat down to write a "synopsis of crime by imitation, an idea which currently fascinates me." Two of that developing idea's discarded titles would be "A Man Provoked" and "A Deadly Innocence," but the brilliant novel that eventually issued from her discomfort was published as *The Blunderer*.[34] On 27 January, Pat was finishing a version of *The Sleepless Night* in Ellen's apartment. She was working resentfully in the living room—"I feel I must clear out before she returns from the office"—and was reduced to sullennness, obduracy, and the bottle. She found Ellen's presence "cramping, censorious." She began to stay in Salzburg whenever she could.

When Pat and Ellen drove to Paris, Nice, Cannes, Montpellier, and Barcelona in February and March of 1952 (they always travelled as though pursued by Furies, taking rooms and houses for short periods and leaving them quickly, moving almost as aimlessly as the "beatniks" Pat would later react to with such disgust), their trip was one long quarrel intermitted by the occasional night of passion and long, freezing periods of sexual abstention. In Paris, Pat was "reprimanded" by Janet Flanner for asking favors of others (yet another of Pat's mishaps with objects: this one involved a trunk belonging to Pat which Pat had casually left Flanner to deal with), and Pat admitted that she wasn't doing her "share" in her relationship with Ellen. They saw Mme Lyne: Ellen hated her, pointing to her "Jewishness." They visited Esther Murphy Arthur and her lover in their "palatial apartment" on the rue de Lille. They had a bitter fight in the telephone booth of the Café de Flore and Pat pushed Ellen unceremoniously out of the booth. They saw Robert Calmann-Lévy, director of the Calmann-Lévy publishing house, fighting right up to the door of the restaurant where they were to meet him.

By 7 March Pat was writing "Hell on Wheels," a satirical account of their drive from Paris to Cannes, and was reading, "enthusiastically" and with obvious identification, Saul Bellow's novel *The Victim*. One night, apparently drunk, Pat tried to crawl into bed with Ellen very late and Ellen said: "This or us must stop." Later on—another middle of another bad night—Ellen tried to approach Pat sexually and Pat struck her. Their pattern was set in stone: the relationship would be over a thousand times before it was "over."

By June of 1952, Pat was in Rome, seeing Jim Merrill and his boyfriend Bobby Isaacson and inquiring after, but not meeting, Marguerite Young, one of her recommenders for Yaddo, who was also in Rome expanding the "Miss Mackintosh thing [Young's celebrated novel, *Miss Macintosh, My Darling*] to a 900 page book." Pat read Carson McCullers's *The Heart Is a Lonely Hunter* and McCullers's short stories and found them all "[b]eautiful—a discovery." By 4 July, she was thinking again about *The Blunderer,* a "4th novel . . . which will be about the man who murders by imitation. A model of verity . . . and tragedy in the hopelessness of his unhappy marriage which I shall create from the worst aspects of mine."

In a deadly depression, she went with Ellen to Ischia, Positano, and Naples. At the end of July, Pat travelled alone to Forio to see W. H. Auden for a meeting which disappointed her. She found Auden barefoot and accompanied by a boy. "I wanted to talk of poetry," she wrote, still alive with resentment fifteen years later, "and all he spoke of were the cheaper prices of things here."[35] People would say the same thing about Pat's own conversational gambits in the future. She mailed Auden a copy of *Strangers on a Train,* and he eventually wrote back from his apartment on Cornelia Street in Greenwich Village a letter praising her depiction of Bruno but questioning her portrayal of Guy.[36]

Although Pat and Ellen would quarrel from Anacapri to Ischia, from Florence to Trieste to Rome (there was, in fact, no European city through which they passed in which they *didn't* stage a pitched battle), it was on this trip that Pat, leaving Ellen in bed early one morning, went to stand on the balcony of their shared room in the Albergo Miramare in Positano. The two women were still travelling de luxe: their balcony overlooked the beach. And that's what Pat was doing at six o'clock that morning—looking over the beach and having a quiet smoke—when she "noticed a solitary young man in shorts and sandals with a towel flung over his shoulder, making his way along the beach from right to left. . . . There was an air of pensiveness about him, maybe unease. Had he quarrelled with someone? What was on his mind? I never saw him again."[37]

The solitary young man making a "right to left" cross on the stage of Pat's imagination was one of the "germs" from which Tom Ripley would grow. Whatever the nature of her exchanges with Ellen Hill, however high the volume of Pat's complaints, Patricia Highsmith turned this long, painful relationship with Ellen Blumenthal Hill to extraordinary artistic profit, yeast for the rising loaf of her work. From their union came some of the most crucial elements (or "germs") for *The Blunderer, Deep Water, The Sleepless Night* (aka *The Traffic of Jacob's Ladder*), *The Talented Mr. Ripley,* and *Found in the Street,* and for Pat's unfinished epistolary work, *First Person Novel.* Pat, who phrased so many of her love relationships in terms of "winning" and "losing," liked to think of herself as the "victim" in this affair. But she was never just a victim. As in the dream she had in New York a year later, Pat would always have "two identities: the victim and the murderer."

In September, Ellen was offered employment with the Tolstoy Foundation in Paris, and Pat and Ellen found an apartment at 84 rue de l'Université. It was in this apartment where Pat struck Ellen in bed "to ward her off. Christ, I do believe that she is insane." As in a Highsmith fiction (or in a Freudian interpretation), every gesture between the two women was now subject to reversion, to interpretation as not only itself but its opposite. In late November, Ellen went on a business trip to Geneva, and Pat, refusing to accompany her, bought a plane ticket to Florence, where she checked into a cheap student pensione, the Bartolini. After the upscale comforts of living with Ellen, the contrast seemed awful, but discomfort would always sharpen Pat's perceptions. "Dismal corridors," Pat wrote of the Bartolini, "where you can break your neck after sundown."[38]

It was at this pensione where Pat made the acquaintance of the decade-younger English novelist and journalist Brian Glanville, whose work she would later promote to agents in America and France. They read each other's writing, and Glanville later said that the early extracts he saw of *The Blunderer* were "clumsy and naïve" but that Pat was "charming."[39] Pat thought Glanville's novel *The Reluctant Dictator* was "well constructed, but the facile English style does not build the climaxes sufficiently."[40] It was a classic meeting of young writers.

At her friend Don Porter's cocktail party, Pat met the Columbia University professor Mark Schorer, who was writing about D. H. Lawrence; she liked Schorer well enough to make sure she saw him again. But all the while, Pat was thinking about *The Blunderer*: "It resembles *Strangers* perhaps too much in structure but not in story."[41] "As with *Strangers,* I know *what* will happen but not in detail *how* it will happen. I get my characters and let them go along."[42]

Pat was also thinking about Ellen, and after a few days, racked with the peculiar combination of needs and attractions which bound her so tightly to this relationship, she phoned Ellen in the middle of the night, took a train from Florence to Geneva, disembarked into Ellen's arms, and set out with her on another of their erratic progresses: from Geneva to Paris, thence to Basel,

St. Moritz, Venice, and "gloomy, functional, masculine" Trieste, where they took an apartment at 22 Via Stupavich at the beginning of 1953. Trieste, a port city on the Adriatic coast whose annexation to Italy was not settled until 1954, was polyglot and divided, having been "liberated" by two different countries and balkanized by several languages and dialects. It was still governed by British and American military forces when Pat and Ellen went there to live: a no-man's-land providing the perfect backdrop for their perpetually decomposing affair. In her diary entry of 5 December, Pat wrote forlornly: "I am a cork on her stormy sea, drifting where she goes."[43]

On their stop in Paris in December, Pat had written "a synopsis of the gay book—about character[s] like Pat & Jo"—another commercial idea, using yet another ex-lover—and then she dropped it. She went to Calmann-Lévy and had a private meeting with Manès Sperber, the noted Jewish refugee writer and senior editor at Calmann-Lévy, "who ripped my book (*The Price of Salt*) apart."[44] Sperber said: "[Y]our men are ridiculous . . . they operate by tics instead of character."[45] Pat proudly told him she hadn't intially gotten an advance for the book, that "if any book was written by me because I wanted to, this was it." And in her cahier, stung by Sperber's criticism, she left a sour description of him, a description that was obviously shadowed by her feelings for Ellen: "The mind of a middle European Jew, systematized, formularized, dogmatic, arrogant, superior and closed."[46]

In Venice, Pat once again telephoned Peggy Guggenheim to meet for cocktails at the inevitable Harry's Bar. "With 3 dogs and a fairy is how she appeared," said Pat. Peggy was "amicable" but nervous, and Pat noticed that her dogs were receiving injections for distemper and that Ellen was "very popular due to her international work." At Harry's Bar, Pat started talking to the English writer Mary Oliver and her friend Jody, "Jane Bowles' friends' types. Both queer, in pants." She heard that Jane Bowles was back in New York. "I wish I were," Pat wrote feelingly.

On her thirty-second birthday—"who cares," Pat thought—she wrote in her diary that she was restless and unhappy, "not knowing yet what Harper's has said, nor what has happened to my pictures in my [New York] apartment, the remainder of my books." When Ellen was too tired to make love, Pat became "enraged. Unfortunately, it lasts."[47] Inexpressive in other ways, Pat made many pen and ink drawings. Ellen brought her back a "big gold ring" from Rome to wear on her little finger. Pat kept it all her life.

From Trieste, in January of 1953, at the apartment she shared with Ellen (who was still working to settle Displaced Persons), Pat received a long, depressed letter from Mother Mary, who was shuttling back and forth with Stanley between Miami and Orlando, Florida, facing joblessness and contemplating a trip to Texas for "emotional help." Pat wrote back to Mary what she thought was a "heartening yet still honest letter, in which I reminded her she had a habit of not facing facts until too late."[48] It was the kind of letter Mary was always sending to Pat.

But Pat identified so strongly with Mary that she was actually feeling her pain, understanding "too well" what Mary and Stanley were going through. Both mother and daughter were desperate for money and barely afloat in leaking artistic boats and unsatisfying relationships—and at the same time, too.[49]

In debt to Ellen, with no story sold for a year, Pat was complaining that her "work [was] at a stand-still because Ellen cannot bear the typing." But Pat worked on as she had always worked on, taking copious notes for dozens of stories: the story of a "selfish bachelor" in Trieste, the story of two friends charged with spying on each other for political reasons, the story of a man "who unconsciously seeks failure all his life, and finds himself happiest when he has attained it."[50]

Insisting that she was paralyzed, Pat was never without creative ideas or schemes for advancement. She wrote to the *Fort Worth Star-Telegram,* asking if the paper wanted a piece on the "D.P. Camps which I visited today. . . . I saw the mess."[51] Pat had gone to "San Sabba" and to the "Opicina Camp" for Displaced Persons just outside Trieste with an eye to selling articles about them. Her description of the people interred at San Sabba—mostly Russians and Serbs imprisoned by the Germans who had been displaced by the war and who were now desperately trying to get visas to more salubrious locations—was confined to the observation that they were "shabby, half dirty," "dressed in rags," "a bit anxious." And of the people passing her, all she had to say was: "most of them are old." The weight she gives these refugees is exactly the weight she gave to the camp's "two storied buildings with good roofing" and their contents.[52] And nowhere does Pat note (perhaps she did not wish to notice) that the Displaced Persons camp she had just visited—it was actually called Campo Profughi; she gave it its wartime name, San Sabba—had all too recently been the San Sabba concentration camp: the only extermination camp in Italy during the Second World War.

On 27 January an unwelcome letter from Harper & Brothers arrived—and Pat found herself in a familiar position: arrayed against "the whole world."

"[T]o my rather great disappointment they don't like the book [apparently a version of *The Sleepless Night*]—evidently not at all. . . . They say too much ground covered. . . . Joan Kahn writes it is "not worthy of Pat." [Kahn was to say the same thing of *The Glass Cell* in 1963.] Apparently I am wrong—if the whole world is in accord against me."[53]

Pat did find one pleasure in Trieste: a lecture by James Joyce's brother Stanislaus, who was teaching at Trieste University. It was a lecture on *Dubliners,* and she thought Stanislaus "very entertaining, as different from James as night from day." But she felt lost and "stagnant," could no longer give her relationship with Ellen a name, "not even an adjective." She thought of herself as "a 3rd rate writer" and kept wishing she were in New Orleans, in New York, in Texas—anywhere she had ever enjoyed herself in the United States. And she wished she were back in time, too—for preference, 1946.[54] Perhaps because 1946 was the year she fell in love with Ginnie Catherwood and the year her short story "The Heroine" was published in *Harper's Bazaar.*

Pat blamed Ellen for everything—except when she could bear to acknowledge a more fundamental source: "Most of my depression is caused by overweening ambition," she wrote before the end of 1952.[55] On Valentine's Day of 1953, she went a little further: "My Epitaph '53. Here lies one who always continually muffed his chance."[56]

The two women were supposed to stay a year in Trieste, but stayed only four months: Ellen kept leaving jobs, apparently hoping that a new city would bring new attitudes to their love affair. It never did. They continued to quarrel and harry each other from pillar to post in what Pat was calling "this little private hell of marriage." From Trieste they went to Genoa, took the boat to Gibraltar, and then rattled around in the south of Spain.

It wasn't until May that they finally sailed for New York, and their long hot summer of 1953 began.

Many years later, Pat made an addition to her diary of July 1953, marked with a vertical line to emphasize its importance. She dated it 15–16 July, ten days after Ellen Hill tried to kill herself with Veronal in Lil Picard's apartment: "This evening I met Lynn Roth—267½ W. 11th St Thurs 16 July Ex–girl friend of Ann Smith's—& roommate Doris."[57]

Pat was preparing to fall in love again, the kind of falling in love that usually worked best for her: a few weeks' contact with the woman in question and years and years of yearning fantasies. It is a condition most writers would guiltily admit to finding productive.

· 20 ·

LES GIRLS

PART 4

> A family tree, a diagrammatic view of affairs and duration among les girls. From one individual radiate twenty lines, crossing those of their other partners, coming full circle again. . . . Everybody has been with everybody else.
> —**Patricia Highsmith**, 1947

Although Pat's affair with Lynn Roth in the summer of 1953 would pass as quickly as a fever in a Russian novel, she loved to dwell on Roth's image or, rather, on Roth's "type": a lovely, slim, stylish, inconstant blond girl who wanted to be an actress.

Commendably thorough, Pat was still sleeping with her other lovely blonde, Roth's ex-lover Ann Smith, when she took up with Lynn. And she would in future live with Doris, the blond woman Roth was currently living with and "cheating on" with Pat. Pat herself was now sharing an apartment and a bed with Jean P., and she had also resumed seeing Ellen Hill secretly. In this period of her life, Pat seems to have taken Henry James's dictum that a writer should be someone on whom "nothing is lost" a little *too* seriously.

Pat and Lynn Roth got together quickly. Desperate for places in which to make love (i.e., places where they could avoid their various lovers), and well supplied with keys to other people's doors, they snuck into their friends' apartments without permission—including Ellen Hill's new digs at One Fifth Avenue. Then Ellen surreptitiously visited Pat in the apartment Pat was sharing with Jean. Then Lynn dropped in on that apartment "by accident" when

Ellen was there. Then they all ran into each other, in various combinations, on the streets of Greenwich Village. It was a busy July and August.[1]

Pat's behavior during the summer of 1953 looks like the material for bedroom farce. But it was also guilt-making, manipulative, thrilling for Pat, and criminal in the way that her imagination liked things to be criminal. The remark she would later make to a lover about life having no meaning "unless there was a crime in it" was the word made flesh just now. *The Price of Salt* had been cut to this same cloth: the story of a love affair conducted "on the run," perceived as a crime by the society in which it was set, with the lovers pursued and threatened with prosecution. Pat was reliving this scenario in multiple variations in her novel. She even sounded like a criminal to herself as she failed to unpick her skein of deception.

"Must soon confess or lay cards on the table or whatever. I have ambiguous feelings about Ellen, which hopelessly thwart me: to take her for what I enjoy about her . . . or to be strong & fend for myself?

"If I do decide, I should make a move. I cannot. So I drink. Like any American."[2]

Pat's generous third cousin on the Coates side, Millie Alford, visiting New York this summer, offered her house in Fort Worth to Pat as a refuge. Pat, ashamed of her poverty before a family member just as Mother Mary was always ashamed before "the Texas family" for being poor, suddenly wondered what Millie knew "of my sex life. Because she seems wildly interested."[3]

When Millie left town in August, Pat noted, with something like awakening interest, that Millie had embraced her "for long moments on parting."[4]

By 26 August, Pat, writing furiously, was up to page 110 on *The Blunderer*— "visit of Walter to Kimmel." But, she thought, "my life is so much more important now than the book." Her life was certainly *busier* than her book: her "hero," the "blunderer" Walter Stackhouse, didn't much care for sex with the opposite sex ("Walter could feel her desire like a pull, a drain on him"),[5] and he imitated Pat in other ways, too: he liked to clip out and save articles from newspapers which he used for making lists of "unworthy friendships" (i.e., unequal power relationships) between superior men and their inferior friends. Walter thought such friendships were "maintained . . . because of certain needs and deficiencies that were either mirrored or complemented by the inferior friend."

Pat was still creating Clara, the desperately neurotic wife of Walter Stackhouse, out of her relations with Ellen Hill. (Walter, with his architectural surname, and Clara, with her job as a real estate agent, should have been a perfect pair.) Like Ellen, Clara provides "that old pattern of punishment after favors granted,"[6] and prefers her dog to her husband, her job to her marriage, and the negation of pleasure to the celebration of life. Clara—as Ellen had done with Pat, as *every* lover had done with Pat—constantly accuses Walter of drinking too much. And Walter expresses the violent oppositions love always encouraged in his creator:

> A strange sensation ran through him at the touch of her fingers. A start of pleasure, of hatred, of a kind of hopeless tenderness that Walter crushed as soon as his mind recognized it. He had a sudden desire to embrace her hard at this last minute, then to fling her away from him.[7]

Melchior Kimmel, *The Blunderer*'s "foreign" wife-murderer, whose gross enjoyment of delicatessen food is part of his vivid repulsiveness, commits the murder which first inspires Walter (who, with his "Anglo-Saxon good looks" is the exact opposite of Kimmel) to think about killing Clara. After seeing the actor Gert Fröbe in Claude Autant-Lara's 1965 film *Enough Rope,* Pat said that Fröbe—later to play Auric Goldfinger in the eponymous James Bond movie—was "exactly as I pictured Kimmel."[8]

Because of the way Walter blunders into Kimmel's plans, Kimmel becomes Walter's own "unworthy" Alter Ego, with the usual accompanying sexual undertones. ("Kimmel's fat mouth with the heavy seam along the heart-shaped upper lip seemed to Walter the most vulgar thing he had ever looked at.")[9] As always in a Highsmith novel (and in a Highsmith life, too), everyone is pursuing everyone: Corby (the sadistic cop), Kimmel, and Walter all swerve, dip, and wheel like rapacious birds of prey in confused flight. ("Corbie," the cop's name, is Scots border dialect for blackbird.) The pursuer becomes the pursued—and then turns back again. The characters are always changing places—"Suddenly . . . Kimmel appeared as a shining angel in contrast to a diabolic Corby"[10]—and the violence is both sexualized and gendered: "Kimmel was aware that he felt intensely feminine. . . . it gave him pleasure of a kind he had not felt in years. He waited for the next blow, which he anticipated would strike his ear."[11]

Pat would always have the adept's feel for sadomasochistic relations.

As in her earliest story in this genre, "Uncertain Treasure," it is the chase that matters most, not its nominal motive. "The old favorite sport of the human race, hunting down their fellows" is how Pat phrases it in *The Blunderer.*"[12] Pat's overheated *vie d'amour*—love as a criminal pursuit—was made of the same material. "Cops and robbers. It must take a mind that's nasty or twisted somewhere [Walter] thought, to devote itself exclusively to homicide."[13] But Pat herself was never exclusively devoted to homicide: love and murder would regularly substitute for each other in her works and in her dreams.

Pat was guiltily finding "the suicide & Ellen's character in the book . . . very disturbing & too personal of course." (The suicide disturbed her more when she *wrote* about it than when Ellen had actually tried to commit it.) In Walter's passivity and ineptitude (he implicates himself in a crime he hasn't committed, kills the wrong man, and is murdered himself), it is possible to see Pat's flagellation of herself as a person who always did the wrong thing. German literary critic Paul Ingendaay noticed a curious linguistic tic in Pat's cahiers: "It is striking," he wrote in the Afterword to her short story collection *Nothing That Meets the Eye*, "how often the word 'failure' occurs in the notes and plot sketches."[14]

Next to madness, failure was what Pat feared most, and for a long time she'd been conscious of a cloak of failure settling over her family like a tragic pall. *Death of a Salesman*—the play with whose central character she said she had no sympathy—kept recurring to her as a model for this enveloping doom. Two years later, in the summer of 1955, she would consider making *Salesman* the foundation of an autobiographical novel.

"I revert more and more to the projected novel of my parents and myself. The Death of a Salesman theme in another profession, another period—and to me far more tragic because the aspirations were higher. In this book my parents will be writers, becoming increasingly hack, and I shall become a painter."[15]

But now, at the end of August 1953, Pat suddenly performed one of her lightning substitutions: she went to Provincetown with Ellen Hill, with whom she'd broken up six weeks before. "I do not forget Lynn, yet am content temporarily with Ellen."[16] By the end of September, Ellen and Pat had broken up again; Ellen had decamped for Europe and Pat was in Fort Worth, at the Coates Hotel, her uncle Claude's apartment hotel, for which, to her quiet irritation, Uncle Claude was charging her rent. Before she left New York she saw a doctor for her blood; her weight was 117. She changed the language in which she was writing her diary—as she usually did when she had something to hide—from awkward German to bad Italian.

In Texas, Pat was drinking even more heavily than she had in New York. And she was writing ever more obsessively, transferring the focus from her life's complications with Ellen et al. to the complications posed by *The Blunderer*. She gave an interview to the *Fort Worth Star-Telegram* in which she mentioned "afternoon beer" as an inspiration (but it was the hard liquor she was hitting the hardest), and she moved, briefly, to her cousin Millie's house. It was during this time that Pat had a short sexual relationship with Millie of which "the family" was perfectly aware. Millie Alford would be a supportive friend to Pat for the rest of her life, doing everything she could in later years to persuade Pat to accept her mother Mary's foibles and to get on with her life. But Pat was unresponsive to any pleas that had to do with letting Mary Highsmith off any of the hooks she'd hung her on.

Conscious that her apparent inability to settle anywhere for long made her look bad, Pat wrote to Kingsley: "And by now, I am sure, I shall be permanently placed in your mind as eccentric, or what was it—the most unstable character of your acquaintance." She began to attribute the "chaos" inside her to the country and the system she had spent the last year in Europe yearning to get back to: "America" and "democracy." She wrote a bit of bad verse: "Despite the poverty and destruction [in Europe] / There is order. / It does not exist in America."[17] In her indirect way, Pat—her life in disorder—was identifying herself with her native country.

Ellen Hill was in Mallorca and on her way to Rome, and, in a letter to Kingsley linking Ellen to the character of Clara in *The Blunderer,* Pat was feeling "sorry for her, as she's a tragic character." Feeling sorry for Ellen was the next step to feeling guilty about her, and guilt, once again, would move Pat closer to Ellen. But now, in need of reassurance from Kingsley and having decided on *The Blunderer* as a title for her manuscript at last, Pat was asking: "What do you think of this title, my literary Nestor?" On Christmas Eve, Pat sent a copy of the last page of the finshed manuscript of *The Blunderer* to Kingsley "to prove . . . that it can be done . . . despite discouragement, poverty, and mediocre health."[18]

Meanwhile, Pat continued to drink her way through visits to Dallas, through long drawing sessions, through meetings with family members, and through a reanimation of her friendship with a horseback-riding friend, Florence Brillheart. Pat, who loved to ride, also liked to get herself up in English riding gear when she was in Texas. The number of photographs taken of her over the years wearing jodhpurs, hacking jackets, and gleaming English riding boots and mounted on a horse or posed against a fence in Texas—land of chaps, six-gallon hats, and the Judson (cowboy) Boot Factory (just across the street from Willie Mae's Fort Worth house)—are legion. Pat presents herself in these pictures as a girl boarder at an English prep school—Roedean, perhaps, or the Cheltenham Ladies College—momentarily detained by the camera, but almost certainly on her way to a point-to-point. It was all part of the theatrical oppositions by which this daughter of another kind of boardinghouse operated, oppositions which were deeply rooted in her fidelity to the American Dream.

Still, Dan Walton Coates did remember one glorious day in the 1940s (Pat's diary fixes it as Christmas Day, 1949) when Pat, visiting his father Dan Coates's Box Canyon Ranch in Wetherford, Texas, on a cross-country drive with Elizabeth Lyne, was especially radiant and wearing what he remembered as "her standard wardrobe":

> A starched white shirt, her Levi's, a black wristband on her watch, it looked like one of those Cartier tank watches, and she had on a pair of black loafers and white socks and had a little cuff rolled on her Levi's. We were raising horses and we had a stallion and Pat wanted to ride him. And I said, "Sure." And we went out there and put a bridle on him, and I said, "I'll put a saddle on him." "Oh no," Pat said, "I'll just ride him bareback."
>
> And by golly, she swung up on that son of a gun and loped him down the front of the property and rode him around quite a little while. And then she came back and slid off and she was just exhilarated. I mean it was just one of the best things going for her.[19]

With admirable contrariness, Pat mostly wore her western shirts, her belts from Texas, and her bolo ties with the fancy slides when she was living in France and Switzerland. And it was only to Paris and Marseille that she brought, as presents for her friend Jeannot's young stepdaughter, boy's cowboy shirts from Texas with snap fasteners and pairs of boy's jeans with fly fronts. This was Pat's idea of what a twelve-year-old French girl should wear in the conservative South of France. Jeannot's stepdaughter remembered Pat's beauty, her mysterious "presence," and the very "masculine" and "sexist" conversations Pat was always having with Jeannot; and she also recalled the kindness Pat showed her as a child of a difficult marriage. But then she recollected how much she was teased in Marseille by the other children for wearing those "boy's pants with the zipper in front" that Pat Highsmith had brought her all the way from America's Wild West.[20]

On this particular trip to Texas in 1953, Pat took special care to criticize the "commercialism" of the country music she was hearing on every radio station. She had a point, but her point was personal and contrarian. She was trying hard to reverse the old adage, trying to "take the Texas out of the girl" (herself)—something she was especially prone to doing when the girl herself was actually *in* Texas.

Back in New York in January and still drinking like a sailor on leave, Pat waited until March to haul herself up before the court of her conscience, ensuring the severity of her sentence by making her self-indictment the only entry in English amid all the bad Italian at the end of her diary. Like the American Calvinist she continued to be, Pat thought that being poor was her punishment for bad morals and too much drinking. "The last year . . . nothing made sense. My attitude was have another drink. Nothing makes sense now either (March 16 1954) but as long as one has decided to live, one must always try to 'do the right thing.' I did not try last year. I spent my money like a drunken sailor. And the worst was, I knew what I was doing. It serves me jolly well right if I am broke, or if I land in debtor's prison even. . . . It does not matter that I have worked pretty hard. . . . I have been imprudent, irreverent, false to myself, in fact."[21]

Another interpretation might be: Pat was being true to the only "self" she couldn't bear to acknowledge.

In New York, Pat's despair seemed to increase. Lynn Roth, she thought, was tantalizing her, going back to Doris, moving in and out of her life, only to vanish by spring. Pat thought about making a story out of Lynn: a girl who can associate love only with people she sees secretly, "away from her regular girl friend. She is incapable of forming an orthodox relationship with anyone with whom she enjoys going to bed."[22] Instead of writing this story, Pat wrote several long, tortuous, and abstract disquisitions on the impossibility of homosexual love, once again making the personal into something "political." And Lynn Roth, faithful at least to the complications of homosexual life in mid-century Manhattan, spent the last forty years of her life living with a woman who had been married to one of James Merrill's lovers. Lynn's stable relationship never ceased to irritate Pat, who, in a 1967 letter to Lil Picard, was still calling Lynn "the love of my life"—and referring to her lover as "a quiet bore." By that time, Pat hadn't been in touch with Lynn Roth for years.[23]

In the extremity of her feelings for Lynn, it began to cross Pat's mind again that she might be going "actually insane," so she gave herself another of those little quizzes with which she liked to test her sanity. Could she follow "attentively and with interest" a news broadcast on the radio? She could. But she was still "homeless, miserable, where I am, my possessions—scattered, my love gone and yet worse, not entirely gone: she tantalizes me." She was also suffering with another infected tooth and afflicted—as only an experienced hypochondriac can be—with "the many, many other bodily ailments that remind of Death, the final conqueror." She compared herself to all the "concentration camp victims" she'd failed to describe on all her visits to DP camps in Europe.[24]

It was now that someone told her—she recorded the information with obvious self-reference—that "the manic-depressive affliction is one of the few psychoses that are . . . nearly impossible to cure." And it was now that she composed her clear identification with the "other" side of life.

"Whatever pity I have for the human race is a pity for the mentally deranged, and for the criminals. (That is why they will always be the best characters in whatever I write.)" Normal people "do not need help. They bore me."[25]

Jack Kerouac, one year younger than Pat Highsmith and crisscrossing the United States at about the same time that she was, had already typed out his own identification with the "mad" in 1951: the long, formless, culture-changing riff which would be published as *On the Road* in 1957. He wrote:

> The only people for me are the mad ones, the ones who are mad to live, mad to talk, mad to be saved, desirous of everything at the same time, the ones who never yawn or say a commonplace thing, but burn, burn, burn, like fabulous Roman candles exploding like spiders across the stars.[26]

Kerouac, like many of the Beats, was infinitely more expansive about his experience of life than Pat had ever wanted to be. (Until he, too, aging prematurely and bloated with alcohol, turned to obsessions and anti-Semitism.) It was only William S. Burroughs—older and colder than the other Beats—whose misogyny, repelled examinations of homosexuality, and personal acts of criminality might have resonated with the disaffected Miss Highsmith. Pat and Burroughs could easily have crossed each other's paths in Texas and Mexico City, where Burroughs "accidentally" blew his wife Joan Vollmer's head off in 1951.

It was in this "criminal" mood (but when was Pat *not* in this mood) that the idea of writing a novel about the "pursuit of evil" (*The Pursuit of Evil* would be one of her discarded titles for this novel and *The Thrill Boys*, another one) began to attract her.

LES GIRLS

Pat once said that Ripley was a name she saw on a sign advertising men's apparel on the Henry Hudson Parkway. And this is true: in the 1940s and 1950s, Ripley's was a men's clothing store in Manhattan on Fifth Avenue. But it is also false: a convenient billboard wasn't the only origin of Tom Ripley's name.

"Comics," Pat wrote to Kingsley in March of 1953, one year before she started imagining Tom Ripley, "I was determined when I started, were not going to influence my writing. I still believe they haven't. On the contrary, I might have benefitted more than I did from their stupid but tight plotting."[1] Unwilling to acknowledge influences from popular culture, but always ready to confess to anything that ruffled the surface of her intentions, Pat hid the origin of Ripley's name in one of her favorite places—her work. She put it into *The Talented Mr. Ripley* and allowed Ripley himself to give the secret away, casually, as a play on a phrase that every newspaper reader in America would know.*

Tom Ripley has already murdered Dickie Greenleaf and slipped providentially into Dickie's name and identity. He is in Rome and is on the verge of being prosecuted for having murdered "himself": i.e., the Italian police are now looking for the "missing" Tom Ripley, and they suspect "Dickie Greenleaf" of being his possible murderer. Dickie's "girlfriend" Marge has come to Rome from their village of Mongibello to look for Dickie, and she accosts Tom (who, actor that he is, has to switch back to impersonating his own character

---

* She did the same thing with the name of the writer/killer in her Suffolk novel, *A Suspension of Mercy* (1965), Sydney Smith Bartleby. The narrator tells us that Sydney is named after the English writer and clergyman Sydney Smith, but Sydney himself makes the "Bartleby the Scrivener" joke about his last name.

of "Tom Ripley") just as Tom, in his role of "Dickie Greenleaf," is trying to leave for Sicily. Tom tries to put Marge off with a quickly improvised lie.

"He laughed, his own unmistakable laugh that Marge knew well. 'The thing is, I'm expecting somebody any minute. It's a business interview. About a job. Believe it or not, old believe-it-or-not Ripley's trying to put himself to work.'"[2]

Ripley's Believe It or Not was (and still is) a renowned cartoon, a comics panel, created by Robert Ripley—an incredible figure himself: part commercial artist, part anthropologist, part real-life Superhero—for the *New York Globe* newspaper in 1918. Each illustrated panel of *Ripley's Believe It or Not* tells in a dramatic sentence or two the story of a fantastic but true oddity, culled from a faraway place (or from the New York Public Library on Forty-second Street, where Robert Ripley had a researcher working full-time); and the cartoon itself was eventually syndicated to many American newspapers. By 1936, Robert Ripley was voted the most popular figure in the United States, eighty million Americans a year were reading *Ripley's Believe It or Not,* and the phrase "believe it or not" had embedded itself in American household vernacular where it stayed right up through the 1960s. For a country still powered by the American Dream, Robert Ripley's illustrated course in miracles was virtually required reading.

In 1931 *Ripley's Believe It or Not* was syndicated in its "comics panel" form to the *Fort Worth Star-Telegram,* the newspaper Pat's grandfather, father, and stepfather had all worked for, the paper Pat herself starting reading when she was still a four-year-old in drop-seat overalls in Fort Worth. An avid newspaper reader all her life, not to mention a dedicated clipper of articles, Pat would have seen the *Ripley* cartoon on her many trips back to Fort Worth.[3] During the four months she spent in Fort Worth just before she began to write *The Talented Mr. Ripley,* she was reading the *Fort Worth Star-Telegram* every day, complaining about its "biased" news coverage, and giving an interview to one of its reporters.[4]

Although the Republican-leaning newspaper Pat read in New York, the *New York Herald Tribune,* didn't run the *Ripley* cartoon, it did make its own contribution to *The Talented Mr. Ripley.* In the middle of April 1953, Pat cut out an article from the *Herald Tribune* about a "substitute" murder and pasted it in her cahier. A man from St. Louis, the article said, was presumed dead when "his" burned body was found—and then promptly arrested for murder when someone saw him downing a beer after his own "funeral."[5]

"Believe it . . . or not" is how Americans would have introduced this story of corpse-substitution to each other in conversation, inflecting the phrase ironically, like a quotation. Which, of course, is what it was: a quotation from a popular phrase in common parlance and countrywide distribution.

Pat invoked this phrase when, joining it with the memory of a big billboard on the Henry Hudson Parkway and the love for newspapers which she associated with her earliest attempts to read, she took her favorite character's surname from a source that had already provided her with so much unacknowledged inspiration: the comics.

Thomas Phelps Ripley, alive and kicking, would have made a fine subject for a Robert Ripley cartoon himself. "Believe it or not," a petty grifter with homosexual "attachments" (Ripley is taken up in New York by a man who likes to "sponsor" young men, a character modeled on Myron Sanft, the man at whose Manhattan house Pat had her one and only meeting with Gore Vidal in the 1940s) and a latent talent for impersonation is chosen by a rich man to be the "ambassador" who will bring his prodigal son, Dickie Greenleaf, back from Europe. Instead of discharging his commission, Ripley, disappointed in his Alter Ego–like feelings for Dickie Greenleaf, murders Dickie and Dickie's best friend, assumes Dickie's identity and characteristics (and in the process forgets how to "play" himself), and then forges his way into inheriting both Dickie's trust fund and Dickie's superior attitude.

It's a large part of Ripley's indistinct charm and unadmitted sexuality that he begins his career by preferring to *imitate* the boy rather than being, in Noël Coward's phrase, "mad about the boy"—and Ripley's is the response of an actor preparing for his most rewarding role. The miraculous American "best" would only be just good enough for Tom Ripley from now on. And it's an appropriate goal, too, for the American antihero whose name found its way into Pat Highsmith's most American novel by the most American of means: advertising and a comic strip.

The American novel itself—apostrophized during this time as "the Great American Novel"—was a renewed subject for discussion in mid-twentieth-century American literary life. Many American writers were thinking about expressing the "soul" of their country in a, or in *the*, "Great American Novel." (Although it would be a synaesthetic Russian aristocrat, Vladimir Nabokov, who did it most brilliantly in 1955 in his succès de scandale, *Lolita*.) Pat Highsmith, whose conversations about art were usually with herself, was no exception: she talked the subject over quite a bit in her notebooks for many years.

> Leviathan! I should like to call my first book. It should be long and deep and wide and high. Thick and rich, too, like America. . . .
>
> I should have that peculiar early twentieth century spirit that moved our politicians and our people strangely. . . . I should have the dignity below all of us we never find ourselves. I should answer the question why America chooses to dwell on the surface [and] leave[s] the depths

unexplored and vacant, stately chambers and halls of America, await-ing occupancy.[6]

Pat told Rosalind Constable, who approved her idea, that "the protagonist of the great American novel might not be on American soil."[7] Rosalind's response was: "Do you want to write it?"[8] But by the time she had this exchange with Rosalind in 1968, Pat had long since finished her version of the Great American Novel.

Like Henry James, whose *The Ambassadors* she was partly spoofing, Pat took her best thematic shot—it was an inadvertent one—at a great American novel by setting *The Talented Mr. Ripley* mostly in Europe. And she seemed to think better of Ripley the character than she did of *Ripley* the novel. "Good books write themselves, and this can be said from a small but successful book like *Ripley* to longer and greater works of literature," she wrote modestly.[9] *Ripley,* she thought, was popular because of the "insolence and audacity" of Ripley himself.[10] She gave Ripley all the credit for the book's success.[11]

Pat was often modest, utilitarian, and bluntly practical in discussing her writing, e.g.: "I always say to . . . publishers who contemplate a reprint [of *A Game for the Living*], 'This is my worst book, so please think twice before you buy it.' "[12] But for all her carpenter's explanations in *Plotting and Writing Suspense Fiction* of the practical ways to put a suspense novel together—the careful consulting of "germs," the diagrams of falling and rising actions, the economical use of leftover scraps of emotional memory, the constant employment of builder's tropes ("one has often to dovetail the difficulties so they fit and lock")[13]—she was never able to judge her own writing very well. Thus, after 1970, *The Talented Mr. Ripley* does not usually appear on the short roster of works she tentatively ranked as her best.* That roster, anyway, was composed of novels and short stories which couldn't be cramped into the "suspense" category, and her changeable choices for favorites—like *Edith's Diary* or *The Tremor of Forgery*—were often dictated by how the books had been reviewed or talked about in the press.

Pat's often rough and unadorned prose (never more baldly so than in her little handbook on writing, *Plotting and Writing Suspense Fiction*) has not made it easy for her to be recognized outside the broadly based "suspense" or "crime writers" genre. In much of her work, the sentences plod along with the dull insistence of a headache. At her best, the metaphors incandesce with her

---

* On 4 November 1970, in a cautious interview by mail, Pat wrote: "Tom Ripley is my favorite character in my books . . . because he is easy, for me, to write about. Therefore I could say that *The Talented Mr. Ripley,* my first novel about him, is my favorite novel."

obsessions, but at her worst she has to be read in what Roland Barthes called (in a discussion of the differences in reading nineteenth-century novels and "modern" novels) "two times," two tempos, two separate reading speeds: one for her flat-footed prose style and the other for the wholly unsettling ground those flat feet are covering. The Austrian writer Peter Handke, a serious Highsmith fan, wrote that when reading Highsmith he felt himself to be "under the protection of a great writer"; but he also felt that her "handicraft" was "a means of draining all attention away from the sentences and towards the odd and yet . . . unstylish . . . actions of the characters."[14]

Still, a claim to one of the small allotments in the real estate of the Great American Novel must be made for *The Talented Mr. Ripley*—and it rests on the instability of Tom Ripley's character (so like his creator's) as well as on the Darwinian cruelty (so like his native country's economic system) with which his narrative unfolds. Thomas P. Ripley has been observed by an author who is as ruthless—and as ruthlessly attached to the American Dream—as he is. When Pat Highsmith gave life to Ripley, she was exposing the black backside of her country's Zeitgeist.

Pat always thought a lot about what it meant to be an American (and had just finished reading Tocqueville on the subject when she began to write *Ripley*). And she thought even more about what it meant to be an American in exile. But she had something less theoretical in mind than investigating the meanings of either of these categories while she was writing *The Talented Mr. Ripley*. "I did not turn loose of my main idea, which was of two young men with a certain resemblance—not much—one of whom kills the other and assumes his identity." Once she'd settled on Tom's traits, she found that his story unrolled in front of her like a well-paved road.

Pat began taking notes for *Ripley* (she was calling it "the Third Suspense Novel") at the end of March 1954. She was making up a "young American, half homosexual, an indifferent painter" with a little income and the kind of innocuous look that would make him a good front for a smuggling gang. "At first, a harmless attractive-to-some, repellent-to-others kind of young man, he becomes a murderer, a killer for pleasure. . . . Like Bruno, he must never be quite queer—merely capable of playing the part. . . . His name should be Clifford, or David, Or Matthew. . . . Or Richard Greenleaf—the boy in the beach in Positano." Appropriately, Pat began by conflating the identities of Tom and Dickie, starting with a description of both of them and attaching Dickie's name to it.

And then, suddenly, her notes take off. She finds the name "Tom," and the first thing she does is to dress Tom up in careful clothes—"costuming" would always be a crucial element for this daughter of a fashion illustrator—and then

slip him into the grifting business: "bulldozing American tax payers into paying extra money for 'miscalculations.'" All at once, Dickie Greenleaf's Alter
Ego clicks into place in two paragraphs of notes.

> Tom . . . is the other, a perpetually frightened looking, vaguely hand-
> some young man, who at the same time has the most ordinary forget-
> table face in the world. He resembles a well brought up, mediocre
> young man, who had received a number of sound whippings in his
> youth and had decided long ago that it would be better to conform.
>
> But the exterior . . . was quite misleading. With the same half terri-
> fied, polite expression, he could swindle a thousand dollars out of his
> old Aunt Martha, who badly needed her capital, sitting there all alone
> in her house up in Massachusetts.

But it was Pat who was sitting all alone in a house "up in Massachusetts."
The Talented Mr. Ripley began—as Pat always put it—to "write itself" after she
left Manhattan. Homeless now, and for the moment between all her messy,
simultaneous, collusive, and faintly criminal relationships, Pat had plenty of
interior material with which to occupy herself. In Manhattan, she had already begun to work on her novel *Deep Water*—those last battles with Ellen
Hill had been as inspiring as ever—and she was liberally distributing her
tastes and tendencies over its resident psychopath, Vic Van Allen.

Still, this "Third Suspense Novel" about Ripley was pressing on her imagination. As though in preparation for launching something unusual she
decided to spend the summer where so many of America's classic authors—
Hawthorne, Melville, Thoreau, Dickinson, Edith Wharton—had lived and
worked: western Massachusetts.* Pat's chief reason for moving to the township
of Lenox was probably the same one that led her to New York's Upper East
Side: snobbery. Lenox, Massachusetts, was a very good summer address.

The old Tappan estate in Lenox where Nathaniel Hawthorne wrote his
Tanglewood Tales had been donated for public use by the Tappan family; the
site was then named after Hawthorne's "Tanglewood," and the Boston Sym-
phony Orchestra made Tanglewood its summer home from 1937 onwards,
attracting to its concerts the old-money families and the theater people who
had always summered in the beautiful Berkshire Hills. Tom Ripley, like Pat

---

* The Berkshire Hills in western Massachusetts are also home to Austen Riggs, one of the
most respected and expensive private mental institutions in the United States. Pat had
some exchanges with a psychiatrist there—although it is no longer possible to determine if
the exchanges were personal or professional. But the local librarian, Judith Conklin Peters,
had the impression that Pat was an outpatient at Austen Riggs.

Highsmith, was an ardent pursuer of the dream of success, and Lenox, with its long literary history, its large summer estates, its familiarity with society, celebrities, and royalty (at one point three princesses lived in Lenox, two of them at the old Curtiss Hotel), was an appropriate place to embody that dream—reversed, of course—in a novel.[15]

Judith Conklin Peters, an eighty-eight-year-old retired librarian when I met her in 2002, was one of Lenox's unofficial historians. Legally blind, she knew Lenox so well that she was able to give me an extended physical tour of the village, liberally illustrated with lively local anecdotes. For forty years, Mrs. Peters had been the assistant librarian at the Lenox Municipal Library. The library, in the former courthouse, had been bought and donated to the village of Lenox by one of the Schermerhorn women who summered in western Massachusetts. There were fifty thousand to seventy thousand books in the building by mid-century, and it was maintained by wealthy summer people "like a private home with beautiful furniture and an adjacent reading garden." And that was how Pat Highsmith had been able to borrow the uncommon works she'd wanted to read when she was beginning to write *Ripley*—an 1835 edition of Alexis de Tocqueville's *Democracy in America* and an Italian grammar book amongst them—from a library in a country village whose population was no more than five thousand people.[16]

Judy Peters was the assistant librarian at in the Lenox Library in the summer of 1954, the summer Pat lived in Lenox. She "remembered distinctly" the "businesslike" thirty-three-year-old writer coming in to borrow books. "A woman of medium height, rather slight with dark hair. Very much on her own, not interested in consulting with the librarians and very businesslike about what she wanted. She came in, got what she wanted and left. She didn't socialize, unlike the other visitors to the library."[17]

Mrs. Peters thought Pat must have begun her stay in Lenox at a boardinghouse called Garden Gables because that's where all the "interesting people" stayed. Garden Gables was owned by a brilliant, cultured woman from Czechoslovakia who also ran a gift shop. All her boarders, said Mrs. Peters, were just like her. The other guesthouse in town was run by a demanding German woman; and all her boarders were just like her, too. But Pat, depleted in everything but the resolve to write, seems to have started out in a boardinghouse in Stockbridge, Massachusetts, close to Lenox, briefly renting a tiny, cheap room from a nice woman who made her "uncomfortable, through pity" and whose house boasted "the worst coffee in the entire town."[18]

One day, Pat apparently dropped by Ed Roche's funeral parlor in Lenox, which was just across the street from Garden Gables. Mr. Roche, like all the other undertakers in the area, lived near his work and dabbled in real estate both above and below ground.[19] He had a cottage for rent—it was probably "the Beachwood cottage" says his son—just outside Lenox. Pat struck a deal with Ed Roche for a summer rental.

"I began," Pat wrote in *Plotting and Writing Suspense Fiction*, "*The Talented Mr. Ripley* in what I thought was a splendid mood, a perfect pace. I had taken a cottage in Massachusetts in the country near Lenox, and I spent the first three weeks there reading books from the excellent privately maintained library in Lenox. . . . My landlord, who lived not far away, was an undertaker, very voluble about his profession."

Pat had been "toying with" having Ripley escort a corpse filled with opium from Trieste to Rome. At one point, the corpse was to be Herbert Green-leaf, Dickie's father, murdered by Tom. This elaborate nonsense was reduced to an awkward suggestion for a corpse-smuggling caper by Tom to Dickie—scornfully rejected by Dickie—in the final version of *The Talented Mr. Ripley*. In another set of notes, Pat has Tom push Herbert Greenleaf over a cliff in Positano with Dickie's consent, and then Dickie, unwittingly, pushes Tom over the same cliff during a fight. Tom, of course, survives. Pat thriftily re-created her cliff idea twenty-five years later for *The Boy Who Followed Ripley*, when "the boy," young Frank, pushes his father's wheelchair over a cliff in Maine into the sea. Pat's concentrated interests and rigid conservations en-sured that she made use of every fertile idea, while her compulsion to com-mit fictional murder allowed her to change her victim, her murderer, and her plot in any novel without the slightest sense of artistic self-betrayal. (She would do the same thing in *The Glass Cell* and *A Game for the Living*.) It was the murder, and its attendant psychological disturbances, that mattered most to her. Still, she would always disapprove of crimes that weren't passionate: you could never accuse Pat Highsmith of being a *cold*hearted killer.

"One crime I consider so despicable, I should never write about it, and that is robbery. To me, it is worse than murder, and for this irrational opinion I have a rational explanation: robbery is passionless and motiveless, except for the motive of greed."[20]

While she was still "toying with" the idea of using an opium-filled corpse in her novel, Pat queried her landlord about the hidden details of his trade. He used to stuff his corpses with "sawdust" is what she said the undertaker told her, "bluntly and matter-of-factly." You cut a "tree-shaped" incision in the chest, you prepare the body, and then you fill it with sawdust. Sawdust made sense in New England, where old forests and old mills were still plenti-ful. But Pat, always fascinated by the precisions of every profession, wanted to see that tree-shaped incision for herself. Mr. Roche "drew the line" at that.[21]

Ned Roche, now the director of his father's funeral business in Lenox, was troubled about these supposed revelations by his father. "My father was very protective about the business. He wouldn't have talked to anyone from outside." But on reflection he thought his father might have been as frank as that with Patricia: "He didn't mince words."[22] However it happened, Pat got the information and then didn't use it. Instead, she began "thinking myself inside the skin of such a character [Ripley]," and so, she said, her "prose became more self-assured than it logically should have been." She had already decided that her "relaxed mood was not the one for Mr. Ripley" and had promptly scrapped her first seventy-five pages. She was now "mentally as well as physically sitting on the edge of my chair, because that is the kind of young man Ripley is—a young man on the edge of his chair, if he is sitting down at all."[23]

Here was a writer using something like an actor's exercise to enter the mind and body of a character. Pat prepared herself for Ripley by assuming Ripley's attitudes and positions—they were never very far from her own—and she started Ripley off as a failed actor who couldn't bear rejection and whose best performance piece was a reenactment of Eleanor Roosevelt doing her "My Day" column for the newspapers. So when Tom began playing the role of Dickie Greenleaf, the first thing he reached for was stage makeup.

"Tom had at first amused himself with an eyebrow pencil . . . and a little touch of putty at the end of his nose . . . but he abandoned these as too likely to be noticed. The main thing about impersonation, Tom thought, was to maintain the mood and temperament of the person . . . and to assume the facial expressions that went with them. The rest just fell into place."[24]

Tom had "an audience made up of the entire world. . . . he was himself and yet not himself. He felt blameless and free, despite the fact that he consciously controlled every move he made. . . . He had even produced a painting in Dickie's manner."[25] Tom also found that writing letters in Dickie's "dull" style was easier than writing letters in his own. His approach to life would always be that of an actor playing a role.

And there it is—the other reason Pat was always falling in love with actresses and models like Lynn Roth, Kathryn Hamill Cohen, Chloe Sprague, Anne Meacham, Tabea Blumenschein, et al. Impersonation, the substitution of one identity for another, the forgery of personality and the fluidity of character, were all native states for Patricia Highsmith. She used them over and over in her work, and she was alive and flutteringly responsive to their presence in other people. (But one reason Ellen Hill was able to "anchor" Pat for so long was her absolute immobility of character.)

As a youthful reader of Oscar Wilde, Pat had long since absorbed Oscar's first published notice of his fascination with crime and the counterfeiting of identity: the essay "Pen, Pencil and Poison" (1889) about the forger Wainewright who poisoned others, and about the "marvellous boy" Chatterton, who forged medieval poetry and drama and poisoned himself. Moreover, much of what Pat thought and felt about the volatility of identity is what she would have been hearing from the young actors she knew—all of them studying "the creation of character" on Bank Street in Greenwich Village at HB Studios or farther uptown with the great star of the Yiddish and American theaters Stella Adler, who brought the only *real* news back from Stanislavsky and whom Pat continued to meet at cocktail parties and find "most beautiful and charming."[26]

And so Pat, who had imagined Ripley as a failed actor, gave him some very actorly exercises.

"It was a good idea to practice jumping into his own character again, because the time might come when he would need to in a matter of seconds, and it was strangely easy to forget the exact timbre of Ripley's voice."

Life for Pat was always a matter of entering into another character: "Happiness," she wrote, "is a matter of imagination. . . . We are all suicides under the skin."[27] And much as she jibed at Mother Mary for the "positive thinking" and jibbed at practicing her Christian Science faith, she adopted something very like it when, writing *Ripley,* she tried to project herself into a more uplifted condition. "Existence," she thought, "is a matter of unconscious elimination of negative and pessimistic thinking."

Continuing to fantasize about her thwarted love for Lynn Roth, Pat kept herself going in Lenox "with various kinds of dope: books, written and read, dreams, hopes, crossword puzzles . . . and simply routine. If I were to relax and become human, I should not be able to bear my life."[28]

Pat's inner theater, those intense personal dramas she was always staging for herself, was much more interesting to her than the world around her. "While you are writing a book," she noted, "you must carry around your own stage full of characters with their emotional changes. You have no room for another stage."[29] Pat was almost *always* writing a book, and, like the cast lists of Jacobean tragedies, her inner dramas contained too many characters. " 'You have no idea,' " she wrote in *Plotting and Writing Suspense Fiction,* " 'how many characters ring my doorbell and come to me every day, and I absolutely need them for my existence.' "[30]

In her cottage in the woods in Lenox, Massachusetts, Pat, like her protagonist Ripley, was both giving a performance and watching the show; turning herself into a theater of one. In 1960, Pat would make a little theory about the only depression for a writer being in a "return to the Self."[31] Now, she was making up a Ripley who "hated going back to himself as he would have hated putting on a shabby suit of clothes, a grease-spotted, unpressed suit of clothes that had not been very good even when new." Clothes would always make the man for Pat Highsmith. "No book," she said, "was easier for me to write, and I often had the feeling Ripley was writing it and I was merely typing."[32]

But Pat wasn't the only woman writer at work on psychopathic males. Long before she was revising *Strangers on a Train* at Yaddo and carefully clipping from a newspaper the photograph of the sneering young Ohio murderer Robert Murl Daniels (one of her prototypes for the psychopathic Charles Bruno), other American women "suspense" novelists had already created compellingly psychopathic males in their own novels. Amongst them was the Yale Younger Poet for 1931, Dorothy B. Hughes (1904–93), with her serial rapist and literal lady-killer Dix Steele in *In a Lonely Place* (1947); and Elizabeth Sanxay Holding (1889–1955) with her woman-hating, self-deceiving, alcoholic murderer, Jacob Duff, in *The Innocent Mrs. Duff* (1946).

Dorothy Hughes was regularly touted as a "latter-day Dostoyevsky"—the same compliment the same critics would pay to Pat's work.[33] And the celebrated English biographer and Highsmith fan Antonia Fraser has marked a Highsmith connection to Elizabeth Sanxay Holding's novel *The Blank Wall* (1947): "[I]t is a brilliant psychological thriller with twists and turns, both morally and amorally, worthy of the great Patricia Highsmith herself."[34] But because Pat's "popular" reading went mostly unmentioned in her cahiers, it is impossible to know if she ever read Dorothy Hughes and Elizabeth Sanxay Holding, or if, having read them, she paid any attention to them. Patricia Schartle Myer, Pat's agent for twenty years, says that Pat never showed interest in other writers unless they were hugely famous or conveniently dead.[35]

Still, Pat never forgot a grudge, and so she had good reason to remember Dorothy Hughes. In 1958, Dorothy Hughes wrote a polite reponse to a request from Joan Kahn to furnish a jacket quote for the Harper & Brothers publication of Pat's much-reworked Mexican novel, *A Game for the Living:* "I shall have to confess abjectly that I have an enormous blind spot where Patricia Highsmith is concerned. I don't like her writings, and I particularly did not like what (to me) was her lack of empathy to the Mexican nationals in this [novel]."[36]

The novels of both Hughes and Sanxay Holding contain strongly feminist critiques of the violent behavior of their male murderers, but Pat, always a contrarian when it came to being a "woman" writer, had different sympathies: "I go along, usually, with the [male] murderer. . . . I can't identify with anyone else."[37]

While she was staying in Positano in 1963, Pat hung her "slightly mildewed" Edgar Allan Poe Scroll—it was the Mystery Writers of America Award conferred upon *The Talented Mr. Ripley* in April of 1956—in her bathroom because she thought all her awards looked "less pompous" there. When she took it out of its frame to scrape away the mildew, she added three words to it. Those words turned her award into a declaration of partnership.

"When I removed the glass to clean and dry it, I lettered 'Mr. Ripley and' before my own name since I think Ripley himself should have received the award."[38]

Pat couldn't bear any tampering with Tom Ripley's "image," and she was pained by Wim Wenders's choice of Dennis Hopper to play Ripley in his loose film adaptation of *Ripley's Game, The American Friend*. On rare occasions, she would add Ripley's name to the valedictory of her letters or the dedications of her books, a tip of the Highsmith hat to her partnership with her own particular devil.[39] And although Ripley was always her favorite "character," her French editor Alain Oulman was disturbed by the fact that she occasionally spoke of Ripley as though he were "real," or at least susceptible to insult. But Pat could usually be counted upon to unsettle her friends.

At summer's end, in the beginning of September 1954, Pat, ready for another round in the love ring, got back together again with Ellen Hill, who had returned from her travels abroad. Pat had a novel to finish, and Ellen's goading presence was just the inspiration she needed. She had already provided the reason why: "[T]he functioning, positive artist wants to live with a 'bad influence,' that is a negative, critical, bourgeois, uncreative, cramping woman, for the plain purpose of fighting against her. She represents, and right across the breakfast table, all the artist is fighting against anyway, plus what the homosexual is—of course fighting against—unartistic personalities and the narrow view of life."[40]

Now, in one of her quirkier descriptions, Pat made another attempt to explain what Ellen really meant to her. It was anything but a direct compliment, but it was a compliment all the same. And it was the compliment Pat would continue to pay to Ellen for the next thirty-five years.

"If I shall ever pay tribute to Ellen Hill in words, the most important thing I shall say is that with her, I often had fascinating and valuable conversations between the breaking of a dinner plate and the bathing of a dog. . . . Of no other woman can I say this. . . . It was her challenging mind often irritating, her point not always justified, that inspired the conversations generally, however."[41]

And so Pat and Ellen set out again on one of their long, quarrelsome journeys by car, this time to Santa Fe, New Mexico. Ellen had by now replaced Henry the dachshund with Tina the French poodle, but Pat had stopped keeping her diaries (Ellen had peeked at them again), and there is no evidence that Pat got on any better with Tina than she did with the clever, vengeful Henry. Three years later, Pat amiably included Tina in her dedication of *Deep Water* to Ellen. But in 1970, when Pat was feeling particularly alienated from her home country (she hated Nixon, loathed the civil rights movement, and, although against the war in Vietnam, she was agitated by the protests the war had engendered), she started to write *A Dog's Ransom*, a shambolic novel which begins with a poison pen letter and ends with the thorough corruption of Clarence Duhamel, a New York policeman of high morals, good education, and Pat's own reading habits.[42] But Pat had never met a New York cop, knew nothing about the workings of a police precinct, and had to ask Kingsley, long distance, to do the police research for her.[43] And in this new novel, Pat couldn't resist kidnapping and murdering a poodle, a poodle she couldn't help naming after Ellen's poodle, Tina.

The day after they arrived in Santa Fe, Pat, possessed by her book and without bothering to fully unpack her suitcase, began to write. *Ripley* was to take her only six months, and she finished the manuscript before the end of the year. She sent the original copy (the original is missing from her archives, as are original manuscripts for *The Blunderer, The Cry of the Owl, This Sweet Sickness, The Two Faces of January,* and *A Game for the Living*) to her grandmother in Fort Worth. But two weeks after Pat's thirty-fourth birthday, on 5 February 1955, Willie Mae Stewart Coates, eighty-eight years old and still in possession of the manuscript of *The Talented Mr. Ripley*, fell dead of an aneurysm while working in her garden. Pat, travelling in Mexico with Ellen at the time, was near enough to Texas to go to Willie Mae's funeral. But she didn't go, just as she didn't go to her father's, her stepfather's, or her mother's funeral. Perhaps the news didn't reach her in Mexico in time; perhaps she simply couldn't face a family funeral.

Willie Mae died as she had lived—busy and productive in her own house. A few months before her death, she was up on a ladder painting a twelve-foot-high ceiling. She fell from the ladder, breaking some ribs, and made her lodgers swear not to tell her family what had happened. Even before he learned the truth, her great-grandson Don remembers thinking that Willie Mae—despite the fact that she had always maintained a severely upright Victorian posture—was looking *especially* erect with her secretly taped-up ribs.[44]

Pat's initial mourning for Willie Mae quickly combusted into rage. She decided to blame Mary for the loss of the manuscript of *The Talented Mr. Ripley*, which had disappeared in the confusion following Willie Mae's death. Willie Mae's boardinghouse and its contents were sold to the owners of the Judson Boot Factory, who tore it down to build a parking lot, and Mary told Pat that "the Negroes" (presumably the people living in the boardinghouse's back-shacks) had done the packing up of the house and somehow her manuscript had been lost. Dan Walton Coates bought back his great-grandparents' "bedroom suite" from Judson Boots, but didn't come in time to save from the wrecker's ball those vividly decorated closet panels Pat had painted for Willie Mae in the mid-1940s.[45]

Pat's secondary mourning for Willie Mae—the kind that produces tears—didn't come until years later, but it, too, was triggered by an object. When Pat glanced down at one of her own worn-out shoes—it had taken the shape of her foot—she suddenly saw "the shape, or expression, of my grandmother's foot [and] I shed the first real tears for my grandmother."[46]

Ellen and Pat's car trip from New York to Santa Fe, where they spent three months, along with their travels through Mexico were as unstructured as all their wanderings through Europe; but the movement was productive for Pat. Her notes for *Deep Water* proliferated, and whole passages in her cahier became part of the finished novel. The more intolerable her personal experiences with Ellen were (she called Santa Fe *"l'enfer"* in her notebook—and leaves us to imagine why), the more elevated her creative life. Mexico, too, was inspiring to her—although without the intense enthusiasms produced by her first trip there in 1944. But Pat's higher body temperatures had always favorably affected her writing, and perhaps the extremes of climate and society in Mexico, with the natural colors of the mountain villages and plateaus haloed by the feverish yellow light, affected her imagination as creatively as illness did.

As Pat and Ellen drove from Ciudad Juarez to Mexico City and all the way down to Acapulco, Pat kept a continuous chronicle of their travels—written, with her usual thriftiness, to be reshaped into an article for a magazine like the one which continued to reject her, *The New Yorker.* (Pat calls Ellen "my companion" in her notes, and excludes all sexual and most emotional commentary.) Some of her liveliest descriptions are the result of this running reportage, and the disparity between her situation and that of the Mexican locals was continually on her mind. Unlike her *haute bourgeois* view of Europe, however, all she saw in Mexico was "unjust poverty." But poverty never evoked much of a sympathetic reaction from Pat, and in Hidalgo del Parral, she found "[t]he populace is shockingly poverty-stricken" and wrote that their "frank rags" could "produce fear in the onlooker."[47]

In Mexico City, Pat and Ellen checked into the Majestic Hotel, the only hotel that would take a dog. The bellboys were drunk by 8:00 P.M. on New Year's Eve, and the two women were taken to see the house of the former mayor of New York William O'Dwyer. O'Dwyer was a man who intermittently interested Pat as a subject: she was certainly interested in his beautiful second wife, Sloan Simpson, a John Powers model from Texas, a darling of jet-set society, and a close friend of Pat's future lover Daisy Winston. (Claustrophobia would be a reasonable response to lesbian circles on the eastern seaboard of the United States in the 1950s.) O'Dwyer was more or less an un-indicted criminal, residing (after some putatively shady doings in New York) in Mexican exile or, as Pat put it, "in plain hiding," in the "plush San Angel residential section," which Pat and Ellen entered through an iron gate "like those of Sing Sing Prison (where O'Dwyer ought to be)."[48]

In 1961, Pat finally managed to meet Mayor O'Dwyer in his apartment on the Upper East Side of New York. And the first thing she noticed about him were his shoes: "Short, common feet in common black shoes suggest the feet of an ordinary policeman, walking his beat." Pat was remembering, rather scornfully, that William O'Dwyer had started his political career as a cop walking the beat in Brooklyn.[49]

In Taxco with Ellen, Pat remarked that the Santa Prisca bells were "never accurate," and then, with particular precision, described the braying of a donkey: "It starts out with a honking, squeaking sound, like a bucket being hauled up by a rusty crank, progresses to the agonized E-E-E-aw—*E-E-E*-aw! which winds down to a very melancholy, sobbing line of onck-onck-onck—as if that donkey's world had come to an end."[50]

To Puebla and Oaxaca and Acapulco and Cuernavaca the two women went, with Pat continuing to keep her amusing, impersonal travel diary, just as she had in Switzerland in 1953. In June of 1955, somewhere on their journey—perhaps they were in Santa Fe again, because two days later they were back on the road between Santa Fe and Tulsa, Oklahoma, on their way to New York—Pat made this note under the *Keime* category in her twenty-third cahier. It was the first of her several expressions of interest over the years in the subject of returning a wallet. "A man (or a girl) who finds a wallet in New York with con-siderable money in it, plus the address. He has lost so many wallets of his own, he takes pleasure in returning this with every stamp intact. An adventure begins. . . . The hero or heroine thus walks into a murder story."[51]

And so, Pat's long and troubled association with Ellen Blumenthal Hill produced yet another inspiration. From this *keime*, thirty years later, would come *Found in the Street,* Pat's Manhattan novel of a found wallet and the fatal consequences attending its discovery.

By the end of 1955, Pat and Ellen had finally gone their not-entirely-separate ways. "I am always in love," Pat had written in July of 1954, from the safety of her solitary cabin in Massachusetts, "with the worthy and the unworthy . . . and I wonder now is it a giving or a taking? Before, it was obvi-ously a taking, because I needed merely the emotion, if nothing else."[52] Pat's lover in France twenty-five years later, the novelist and translator Marion Aboudaram, said nearly the same thing, and she said it without rancor: Pat made ruthless use of the women she loved and of the emotions generated by her tangled relationships with them. Without a woman lover, as Pat wrote in her diary shortly after meeting Ellen Hill, "I cannot even develop as a writer any farther, or sometimes, even exist."[53]

Pat managed to keep her affair with Ellen Hill going for more than four years, thereby keeping her all-important Muse's Chair occupied—even if uncomfortably so. Her attachment to this special piece of furniture in her Romance Room would go right on creating art and trouble for her for much of the rest of her life.

· 22 ·

LES GIRLS

PART 6

After separating from Ellen, Pat went back to her flat on East Fifty-sixth Street in Manhattan, the apartment she'd first rented in 1942, with the fire escape and the ladder down to the courtyard that gave easy access to her living quarters. Too easy, it turned out. One day, she returned to the apartment to find five or six boys "hunched over my books and paint boxes": they had already daubed one of her suitcases with paint. She carefully erased their presence by removing the markings from her suitcase with turpentine. On another day, the boys returned and were having a free-for-all on the fire escape "only two yards from where I sat." Pat "backed into the far corner of the room like a scared rat," still frowning with concentration and composing in her mind the sentence she'd left unfinished in her typewriter. She stayed there until the boys clattered down the cast-iron stairs.[1]

It was what Pat called the "vicious emotional cycle" of the boys' noise, and the fear and hatred that were her response to it, that gave her the *keime* for the beginning of a short story, "The Barbarians," about a man "who paints on weekends," is tortured by the sound of handball players just under his window, and takes violent—and ineffectual—action to stop them. Pat called it a story about "the hell of metropolitan society."[2] She was keenly feeling that an apartment menaced by rowdy neighborhood boys was *not* the gracious Manhattan living she had been yearning for in Europe.

Coinciding with the breakup of her four-year relationship with Ellen, and just after the publication of *The Talented Mr. Ripley* in December of 1955, Pat dropped into another of her seasonal depressions. "My life, my activities seem to have no meaning, no goal, at least no attainable goal. . . . I can feel my grip loosening on myself."[3] "One wants to die, simply. Not to die, but not to exist, simply, until this is over."[4]

It was her usual Christmas/New Year/birthday dip into unworthiness, colored by yet another quarrel with Ellen Hill and accompanied by a deep sense of failure. Despite the good reviews *The Talented Mr. Ripley* had just received—her bête noire, *The New Yorker,* found it a "remarkably immoral story very engagingly" written,[5] and *The New York Times Book Review* had praised "her unusual insight into a particular type of criminal"[6]—Pat was plunged into an "undefined, unreconciled self." And that self, if not expressed by daily writing and enhanced by the presence of an attractive woman, was never a self Pat liked to be alone with for very long.[7]

And then, suddenly, in the middle of April, Pat had a new complaint: "What a strenuous thing it is to be in love."[8]

When Pat fell in love with Doris, a midwesterner working in advertising in Manhattan, it was more than a familiar feeling, it was a familial one. Doris had been living with Lynn Roth when Pat had fallen in love with Lynn, and Lynn had been the ex-girlfriend of Pat's lover, Ann Smith. The closeted nature of lesbian life—especially closeted in the 1950s—has always made for imbricated relations, but Pat's relations were more plaited than most. Women were her muses, and she could never quite let go of one woman before reaching for the next one.

But all this was in the past and in the future. Pat, in love with Doris now, was as lyrical as a summer sonnet. She looked into Doris's eyes and thought or at least wrote: "The trust in the eyes of a girl who loves you. It is the most beautiful thing in the world."[9] And she went on to praise the "insuppressibly, incorrigibly, happy and optimistic" *Agnus Dei* of Mozart—as opposed to gloomy old Bach's *B Minor Mass,* "oppressed with the hopelessness of the world's sin."[10]

Falling in love always put Pat in a good mood—at first anyway—and it often increased the number of her petitions to God. So when she fell in love with Doris, Pat made up a little prayer. The prayer shows that love had come again to Pat Highsmith as it always came: violently, subversively, and in the expectation of "pain and disappointment":

My dear God, who is nothing but Truth and Honesty, teach me forbearance, patience, courage in the face of pain and disappointment.

Teach me hard, because I am stubborn and desperate, and one day I shall take you by the throat and tear the wind pipe and the arteries out, though I go to hell for it. I have known Heaven. Have you the courage to show me hell?[11]

Pat was beginning to feel more like her "self."

Doris, a year younger than Pat—Pat generally preferred older women until she became one herself—was a copywriter at the McCann-Erickson Agency in New York. She was also, as Pat wrote to Kingsley, "perhaps overserious, a perfectionist, doesn't like to go out much (socially)—and [is] very pretty."[12] Doris was someone, in short, with whom Pat could imagine living. But Doris did not share Pat's taste for "hell," "pain," and "disappointment," and this was to be a major disappointment for Pat. The crucial consonances as well as the critical oppositions were missing.

Pat and Doris, who had the social connections of Pat's new agent, Patricia Schartle, to thank for their country retreat, moved from New York to what Pat called "Sneden's Landing" in the southernmost part of Rockland County. Snedens Landing (Pat the Grammarian always added an unnecessary apostrophe before the final *s*) was (and is) an exclusive enclave on the Hudson River, part of the hamlet of Palisades, New York. It has always been a haven for people in the arts and show business. Together Pat and Doris bought "a brand new Ford convertible, black, though," said Pat, "with more chrome than I like. I like none,"[13] and shared the rental of a converted barn in whose garden Pat grew radishes, string beans, cantaloupes, and sweet peas. But four months after Pat fell in love with Doris, and a little more than a month after they'd moved to Snedens Landing, Pat was writing about "the danger of living without one's normal diet of passion. Things are so readily equalized, soothed, forgotten with a laugh, with perspective. I don't really want perspective, except my own."[14]

Faced with domestic tranquility, Pat was itching for a good fight.

During the summer of 1956, Pat began to take notes for what she considered one of her least successful works, her "Mexican" novel, *A Game for the Living* (she was calling it, typically, "6th Book" in her cahier). She was also finishing the final revisions on *Deep Water,* the destabilizingly brilliant novel she'd begun as *Dog in the Manger,* when she and Ellen Hill were quarrelling steadily and productively across Europe. Pat had expanded the book as they continued their fruitful squabbling in the Southwest and down into Mexico, and in the character of *Deep Water*'s resident psychopath, Vic Van Allen, Pat created a "hero-criminal" who directly challenges gender categories: he refuses sex, cooks and cleans his house with an apron on, takes care of his child, murders two of his wife Melinda's lovers, and—he's a completist—murders Melinda as well. Vic also upsets all ideas of sexual proclivity: his major excitements seem to be observing the slow copulations of his companion snails and encouraging his pet bedbugs to draw blood from his arm. And he extends the uses of ingenuity by fostering the rumor that he is a murderer before he has actually knocked anyone off. His blackly blooming imagination permeates the book and delivers him to a state beyond morality. *Deep Water* is a deeply uncomfortable novel.

Always the good Freudian, Pat wrote that in Vic's character she was interested in exploring the "evil things," the "peculiar vermin" that arise from "unnatural [sexual] abstinence." Vic, she insisted, was "a paranoiac," a "megalomaniac," a "fascist, a sadist and a masochist," and even "insaner than his wife."[15] Vic is also Pat's only witty psychopath. When his compulsively unfaithful wife, Melinda (a caricature of predatory female sexuality: even her necklace looks like it's made of tiger's teeth), wants to dress herself up as an historical character for a costume party, Vic suggests that she try Madame Bovary. Independently wealthy, Vic's métier is to design and print exquisite, limited-edition books on his hand-operated press. The suspicions of a distinctly lower-class detective novelist—an unattractive author of bad works who is Vic's neighbor and Melinda's ally—lead to the capture of this quietly mad publisher of superior taste and means. *Deep Water*'s class-conscious author slipped her own social resentments into Vic Van Allen: he yearns for a better class of lover for Melinda, whose taste runs, lamentably, to lounge lizards (Vic wants someone for Melinda *he* can live with). Pat also saddled Vic with quite a few of her reimagined traits, talents, and leftover feelings for Ellen Blumenthal Hill. But she didn't acknowledge the resemblances between the author and her psychopathic character when she was ticking off her list of Vic's psychoses, perhaps because they were the kind of maladies that could only be accommodated at institutions like Austen Riggs or Broadmoor.

By the fall of 1956, Pat was worried both *for* her work and *about* it: she was making caustic comments about meticulously editing this manuscript (*Deep Water*) that wasn't going to sell, and then identifying, in another quickly extinguished flare of illumination, the ragged hole in her design for living:

"My continuing troubles about my work. My writing, the themes I write on, do not permit me to express love, and it is necessary for me to express love. I can do this only in drawing, it seems."[16]

Pat made a sexual overture to Ellen Hill during this period—and then had a dream in which she was "reminded" of it. In an entry in (bad) French in her notebook, she wrote that the dream began with her making up a couch-bed in the Highsmith family house, reminiscent, no doubt, of all those couch-beds she'd slept on as a girl. Magically infused with the knowledge that she didn't *have* to sleep on the couch, she suddenly found herself in bed with her mother, Mary, and her stepfather, Stanley. Mother Mary said clearly: " 'I have news for you. I'm going to throw you out of the house.' "

"She gave me the idea," Pat wrote aggrievedly, "that I interfered between the two of them." The idea was not exactly a new one.

The dream came out of Pat's recent late night in Manhattan. She had stayed over at Ellen Hill's apartment and made a pass at Ellen; wordlessly, Ellen let her know that she didn't want to take her back as a lover. "She accepted me, but she rejected me too," Pat wrote. On waking from this dream in Snedens Landing, Pat reached over and touched Doris, and "was very happy to have her."[17] Four days later, recovering from one of her innumerable dental procedures and trying to put herself in the "bored with day-to-day, under-my-nose existence, which is what prompts me to write (work) at all," Pat attacked Ellen Hill bitterly in her notebook.[18]

In the same month, November of 1956, in which she stage-managed this dream, Pat started work on what she later described to the fiction writer, journalist, and critic Francis Wyndham as a "political satire in the manner of Voltaire": a long, labored picaresque she called *The Straightforward Lie*. Over the years, the manuscript was promptly returned by every publisher she sent it to. Joan Kahn at Harper & Brothers returned it in 1959, after reading both the manuscript and Pat's naïve comment that it would be "ideal for a hot summer weekend!"[19]

The Straightforward Lie is more like the crude scenario for a graphic novel than it is like Voltaire's *Candide,* Swift's *Gulliver's Travels,* or Samuel Johnson's *Rasselas.* Still, like Pat's later, equally primitive political satires, it was proleptic: American foreign policy is what she was getting at, and her tendency to see things in black and white, *cru et cuit,* serves the piece all too well.

In *The Straightforward Lie,* a young man, George Stephanost, of dubious sexuality and odd appearance (something about shoes again), wins a trip around the world as a propaganda agent charged with presenting his imperialistic government in the best possible light. George is loathed wherever he goes, beginning his travels by precipitating the suicide of a journalist whose alcoholism he has reported (there's usually a drinker in anything Highsmith writes, and she made a note saying she was going to dedicate this manuscript "to alcohol"). George is propelled through a series of incidents which show him to be a pompous representative of an overbearing government, jibed at by the fools and knaves of other countries.

As though her imagination had rifled the canon of German folk poetry and come up with the old figure of the *bucklicht Männlein*—the little hunchback who causes so much trouble for German children in *Des Knaben Wunderhorn*—Pat provided a small black dancing figure of a man to haunt and harry George. The little man repeats the words "Trouble" and "Evil," and taunts George with: *"They hate you! Ha! HA! Ha!"* George, entirely confused, ends up in "a really attractive summerlike place in the country . . . [t]he Happy Day Asylum," still haunted by the little black man.

Voltaire, it's not—but it *is* Patricia Highsmith. Entirely impaired by her clubbed thumb for satire (her "satire" operates on a level lower than sarcasm) and her less-than-nuanced understanding of global politics, the work still manages to reverse the values other people live by. *The Straightforward Lie* left a ghostly trace in the other novel Pat was working on at the same time: *A Game for the Living.* She slipped it into that book as the title of an "illustrated novel . . . a satire of modern life," which one of the characters is working on.

In Snedens Landing, Pat had her two cats and a growing family of snails, and Doris had a dog. (Doris's dog was probably the model for the bulldog puppy with the mutilated ears in *Deep Water.* Pat wasn't half done with dogs yet.) They took their Ford convertible to Mexico in January of 1957, apparently to allow Pat to absorb the mise-en-scène for her "6th Book" (*A Game for the Living*) and to work off her restlessness, and they drove the length of Mexico, staying on well into March. Pat was transfixed by the Mardi Gras in Vera Cruz. "I can set stories here. I can make it better than it is," she wrote after watching a "Carnavale" parade. In Mexico, it was the transvestites who riveted her: "Gay boys unmasked . . . One in drag, black short dress, pink cheeks, and a bawdy 'I dare you' impudent stare, pursed mouth, and then the tongue stuck out."[20] She didn't forget them. Pat's French lover Marion Aboudaram says that in Paris, twenty years later, Pat was always much more amorous when transvestite prostitutes were working the street outside Marion's apartment in Montmartre.

But Pat's excitements in Mexico failed to transfer to *A Game for the Living.* The book gave her trouble in its initial composition and then troubled everyone else when she finished it. Unhappy with the "first sketch of 58 pages," she wrote: "Don't know where I'm going, resulting in static effect."[21] The book continued to irritate Pat during the several careful revisions her editor, Joan Kahn, requested. This was one of those novels whose murderers Pat changed at an editor's request; Kahn thought, quite correctly, that it made no sense to have an unknown street boy do the murder. So Pat, who was much more attached to the idea of beginning her novel with the murder of a beautiful woman than she was to the inconsequential murderer she'd chosen, put up no resistance at all and switched her killer to "Carlos." It didn't help the story.

No one—including Pat's agent, Margot Johnson, who found the novel verbose and said so—ever liked it much. And Pat's attempt to inflict her external reading on what she was writing—she was using a little Kierkegaard for illumination and finding in the gloomy Dane exactly what she had found in Proust, i.e., a recognition of the compulsion to love[22]—was just as unsuccessful as her later attempts to impress her superficial understanding of American politics on her novel *Edith's Diary* (1977). The real problem was that Pat was uninspired.

Even though Doris left every day for her advertising job in Manhattan, Pat began to complain that she was spending "less time alone" than ever. In January of 1957, she felt crowded enough to invoke her harsh personal rating system again: "In view of the fact that I surround myself with numbskulls now, I shall die among numbskulls, and on my deathbed shall be surrounded by numbskulls who will not understand what I am saying. . . .

"Whom am I sleeping with these days? Franz Kafka."[23]

And on the front of her cahier from this period, in the place where she always put the countries and cities she travelled to, she printed: "New York, Sneden's [sic] Landing, Santa Fe, Mexico, And Greater Inner and Outer *Mediocrity*."[24]

Happiness never made Pat happy for very long.

Pat began to read more, draw more, and think much more about the delights of moving to another country again. Alone, for preference. She was remembering how well she'd worked on *The Price of Salt* when she was sailing back alone from her first trip to Europe in 1949, inspired by her long-distance love for Kathryn Hamill Cohen and shut up in a hot little cabin on an Italian freighter where no one spoke any English.[25] "This recalls my sensation, when in a non-English speaking country, of being more than usually eloquent. The words come from a fresh and purer spring. Their full measure is recovered.

". . . I haven't the precision of intellect that a good writer needs, nor the sense of dignity when I want to call it up. But in drawing or painting I can always achieve this, if I want to, from a source uncorrupted, uncorrupted by pressure and other people's opinions."[26]

Still, by September of 1957, Pat was making notes for an article she eventually published in *The Writer* magazine, an article she would expand in a single month in 1965 in Suffolk into *Plotting and Writing Suspense Fiction*. And she was unusually pleased to project herself into the distinguished company in Colin Wilson's serious study of alienation and creation, *The Outsider*. "The book stirs my mind to the murky depths (emotional depths) in which I lived my adolescence like Van Gogh and T. E. Lawrence trying 'to gain control' by fasting, exercise, routines for doing everything."[27]

But nothing helped her relations with Doris.

By January of 1958 Pat was complaining about feeling physically crowded:

"My present house is not big enough for two people." She began to snipe indirectly at Doris's dog, comparing the "false" loyalty of dogs to the comforting "selfishness" of cats.[28] She was missing the exquisite discomforts of her relationship with Ellen Blumenthal Hill: the constant seesaw of emotion from "elation to depression" which had always inspired her best work.[29] Without this irritation, the oyster couldn't produce the pearl.

A poem—it's an incantation, really—written by Pat in September of 1955, some months before she took up with Doris, makes it plain that her relationship with Doris was doomed before it began.

Her chaste kisses cannot hold me.
Oh! Oh! Oh! Oh!
Nor the way her arms enfold me.
Oh! Oh! Oh! Oh!
Though I know that she has told me
She would love me all my life,
She would always be my wife.
Oh! Oh! Oh! Oh!
I want stronger arms around me,
Insane arms and devils' kisses,
Teeth that bite my lips and wound me,
Girls whose love will never last.
Oh! Oh! Oh! Oh![30]

Trouble, in the form of a secret affair with an attractive older woman (a decade older than Doris), was only six months away.

When Pat and Doris returned from their trip to Mexico in March of 1956, Pat, still feeling the pull of "going to God" on Sunday, joined the choir of the small Presbyterian church in Palisades and continued or tried to continue her peaceful domestic life. Doris worked on a TV script from an idea by Pat, while Pat worked on everything else and made some social gestures. One of her gestures resulted in a meeting with the great choreographer Martha Graham, a neighbor in Snedens Landing; and a photograph of Graham with one of Pat's Siamese cats lives on in her archives. Pat also met another neighbor, Gertrude Macy, the Broadway producer and Katharine Cornell's lover, manager, and biographer, who became a lifelong correspondent. Meanwhile, Pat was still making sporadic efforts to integrate her hopes for the world with her continued acceptance of Jesus Christ: "It is conceivable that mankind, with the guidance of a dominant faith in God, can work a system out for their own good, which will be closer to Communism and the word of Jesus Christ than any form of government yet seen on earth."[31]

Like many Americans in the 1950s, Pat was also thinking about just how the atomic and hydrogen bombs would change the things she cared most about: "the perishability of books . . . due to H-bombs" was preoccupying her. "This total extinction could not have occurred to the mind of Dickens, for instance. . . . Now every writer may see himself and his readers quite wiped out." But she added to her thoughts the inevitable Highsmith detail: "The book may exist, but it's radioactive. Don't touch it."[32] She would use that same caveat about a knife—"Don't touch it"—to end *The Cry of the Owl* in 1962.

Still, nothing could stop the engine of Pat's writing for long, and Pat and Doris even made a book together, a book of cartoons and accompanying rhymes called *Miranda the Panda Is on the Veranda* (Coward-McCann, 1958). Doris made up the rhymes and Pat provided the cartoons, and, even in this sweet, sticky, inconsequential work, Pat refused to allow anything of her seven years' connection to the comics to appear. The jacket copy simply states: "Her one other occupation involved a short term as a salesgirl in the toy section of a large department store." Pat, who had loathed all the other salesgirls at Bloomingdale's, except for one Greenwich Village resident, Rachel Kipness (another of those "good eggs" whose shells she liked to crack), actually preferred to be identified as a "salesgirl" rather than as a writer of comic books.

A book made by two people living together (as Doris and Pat were) suggests a certain degree of emotional stability. Pat couldn't wait to disrupt it. Her domestic relationship with Doris didn't offer the painful oppositions she craved, and she knew that the work she was doing now was far from her best. And so Pat—it was no effort at all—fell deeply in love with Mary Ronin.

Aside from her symbolic first name, there were other ways in which Mary Ronin reminded Pat of Mother Mary. She was a commercial artist in a long-term relationship (a relationship Pat did her best to break up) with a wealthy woman who owned a brownstone on New York's Upper East Side. Charming, from the vivid photograph that remains in Pat's archives, Mary was also creative and witty. When Pat was living with Marijane Meaker in New Hope in 1961, Ronin sent Pat a birthday card with not a single word on it, just a drawing of herself, nude, in front of a calendar opened to Pat's birthdate, 19 January. Mary Ronin was sufficiently older than Pat, and sufficiently unavailable to her, to become the kind of tantalizing inspiration Pat could work with. And so, from this mostly denied relationship came one of

Pat's best novels. It's the story of a pyschopath with a double identity and two names to match it. He creates a house for (and an imaginary relation-ship with) the woman he loves. And he murders her husband. Pat called her book *This Sweet Sickness* (1960), and she dedicated it to the other crucial Mary in her life, her mother.*

---

* In *Plotting and Writing Suspense Fiction,* Pat wrote that she started *This Sweet Sickness* as the story of an insurance fraud.

"I wanted to have my criminal-hero set himself up in a different house with a different name, a house into which he could move when his real self was presumably dead and gone. But the idea did not come to life. One day the second one appeared—in this case a far better motive than I had thought of until then, a love motive."

For Pat, love trumped criminal fraud, but love was also inextricable from the ultimate act of defrauding another human: murder.

23

LES GIRLS

PART 7

In the spring of 1959, Pat, still obsessed with Mary Ronin, had "just that after-noon come back from a trip to Mexico" when a young paperback writer, Mari-jane Meaker, "starstruck" at spotting the author of *The Price of Salt,* introduced herself to Pat in a lesbian bar on MacDougal Street in Greenwich Village.[1] Pat's authorship of *The Price of Salt* was an open secret in New York lesbian circles, and the whisper had gone round the bar: "Claire Morgan is here."

In the 1950s, says Marijane Meaker, "most lesbian bars were Mafia bars, with people watching the ladies' room, letting the women in one at a time and handing them one piece of toilet paper, and a low-level Mafia guy with a pinkie-ring at the door vetting the entrants."[2] Pat, who both liked and de-plored lesbian bars (she hated the overpriced drinks, disparaged the down-market "dikes," and found the casual encounters exciting), was something of a fixture in bars like Three Steps Down and Provincetown Landing, two of the several bars on West Third Street.[3] And she liked (but was less comfortable at) Johnny Nicholson's High Bohemian Café Nicholson on East Fifty-eighth Street, whose garden was the site of Karl Bissinger's iconic 1948 photograph (see "Social Studies: Part 1").

Pat also frequented Spivy's, Jane Bowles's favorite Upper East Side night-club; Romeo Salta's on East Fifty-sixth Street (where, in a wonderful scene in her novel *This Sweet Sickness,* Pat sends her psychopathic hero David Kelsey/ William Neumeister to order two Italian dinners and two cocktails: one for himself and one for his imaginary girlfriend); the bar at the St. Regis Hotel; and the mostly gay male restaurants in Greenwich Village like Aldo's, the Fi-nale, and Fedora (still in business on West Fourth Street), as well as more mixed-gathering establishments like the Pony Stable, Mona's, Show Spot, and the Jumble Shop.[4] These last were places where women could drink and eat, sometimes dance and hold hands, and meet each other for professional and personal reasons.

Liz Smith, America's preeminent show-business gossip columnist, was introduced to Pat "in Greenwich Village in the mid-Fifties . . . by a successful TV producer named Jacqueline Babbin." Fifty years after their meeting, Smith remembered the explanation for Pat's "aloof and forbidding" behavior. "Highsmith was a very odd bird, even in her youth. She took to me because we had both been born in Fort Worth. But it wasn't possible to really know her. Once we had exhausted Texas memories, she was off again into her own odd world. . . . Like many people, she had a serious 'mother has rejected me' problem."[5]

Megan Terry, the feminist playwright whose experimental work put her in the center of 1960s avant-garde theater in Manhattan, met Pat after she'd broken up with Doris and moved to an apartment at 76 Irving Place. Terry, eleven years younger, saw the sweet side of Pat.

"She was wonderful to be with, so beautiful, so much fun. And she was very romantic, always projecting her hopes on her lovers. When I knew her she was very sweet, a lot like a naïve teenage boy. But when you get up to a quart of gin a day, something else happens. I couldn't believe how much [alcohol] she could put away. She needed the alcohol because she was so vulnerable."

Terry remembered a dramatic feature of Pat's Irving Place apartment (yet another Highsmith apartment in the vicinity of an elegant neighborhood, Gramercy Park).* "I used to babysit Pat's cats, stay in her apartment in Irving Place when she was gone. She had a big built-up platform bed there, very theatrical. It was a great apartment."[6]

Pat's first French translator, Jean Rosenthal (he and his wife, Renée, translated many Highsmith novels for Laffont and Calmann-Lévy, including *The Blunderer, The Talented Mr. Ripley, Strangers on a Train, Deep Water, Those Who Walk Away,* and *The Two Faces of January*), remembered a well-watered dinner Pat gave for him in her Irving Place apartment. It was his first trip to the United States, there were ten people invited, he was unused to cocktails before dinner, and Pat, "still very beautiful," was serving copious "dry martinis. I had to aim myself to get to the table." Rosenthal also remembered travelling on a plane from Paris to New York with Pat, who was smuggling "a green

---

* Pat was once again walking in the footsteps of the legendary literary agent Bessie Marbury and her decorator lover Elsie de Wolfe. Before making Sutton Place fashionable, Bessie Marbury and Elsie de Wolfe lived in a town house at 56 Irving Place.

plant" for her mother hidden in her valise. Plants, he said, were like "drugs" to American customs officials, but Mary had asked for it, so Pat was sneaking it into the country.[7]

Long after Pat had left Irving Place, Megan Terry came across a photograph of her aging friend in a book. Like Pat's Barnard College classmates, she was so shocked by the change in appearance that she "just had to close the book. . . . I couldn't believe the way she looked. . . . She was so lovely when she was young. And so much fun . . . She and Marijane Meaker really weren't good for each other at all . . . A real folie à deux and a weird mutual projection."[8]

El's (or L's), the MacDougal Street bar where Marijane Meaker had introduced herself to Pat, was different from most Greenwich Village women's bars. It was the "beginning," says Meaker, "of graciousness in the lesbian bar world." There was no Mafia ownership in evidence and most of the clientele were as well dressed as "young college girls."[9]

Pat—tall, thin, dark, and handsome in a trench coat—was drinking gin and standing up at the bar. She looked to Marijane like "a combination of Prince Valiant and Rudolf Nureyev" and was more than receptive to Meaker's attempt to introduce herself.[10] It was, says Meaker, "a fast take" (although Pat's first question to Marijane was to ask if she liked to travel, so Pat was interested in a fast getaway as well), and they both told lies about their current situations. Marijane, living comfortably with a lover, told Pat she was at the "end" of a relationship, and Pat, still obsessed by Mary Ronin, said that she was entirely unattached.

Pat fell for Marijane deeply enough to cancel one tramp steamer trip to Europe, duffel bag and Olympia typewriter in hand. Then she did leave for Europe on a publication trip to Paris for Calmann-Lévy with Mother Mary in tow—during which she arranged for Mary Ronin to join her in Greece. But Ronin didn't oblige, and Pat spent a month with her increasingly eccentric mother in Paris—seeing the poisoned future that awaited her in the resemblances between herself, her grandmother, and her mother. "It's inevitable, too, to think that there go I in another twenty-five years."[11]

After bundling Mary off to Rome, Pat went to visit the cartoonist Jeannot in Marseille, then travelled to Salzburg, Athens, and Crete with her former lover Doris. But Pat didn't tell Marijane Meaker of her foiled plan to meet Mary Ronin in Greece, and Meaker remained obsessed with Pat the whole time Pat was in Europe. Moving around Europe with Doris, Pat never referred to Marijane in her notebooks and occupied herself with other women *en voyage*.

But when she returned to New York, Pat and Marijane resumed their relations and decided to move together to Pennsylvania, to a farmhouse on Old

Ferry Road seven miles outside of New Hope. Pat's first choice had been posh Snedens Landing, where she'd lived with Doris and where she still had women friends like Polly Cameron, who would design the Harper & Row book jackets for *Deep Water* and *The Cry of the Owl*. "We called [Snedens Landing] the Lesbian Graveyard," says Marijane Meaker.[12] But rents in Snedens Landing and the surrounding Palisades were too high, so the two women moved to New Hope, where Pat also had friends: Al and Betty Ferres in Tinicum, and in New Hope, Peggy Lewis, whom Pat knew from the art gallery Peggy and her husband, Michael, had operated in Greenwich Village and reopened in New Hope.

Peggy Lewis, from a Baltimore Orthodox Jewish family, was liberated from religion, say her daughters, and attracted to "anything artistic." She was a cultural and social force in New Hope, spoke her "very critical" mind, and kept open house for all manner of people. Peggy spent quite a bit of time helping Pat: housing her on trips back from Europe, visiting Meyer's garage in New Hope to check up on Pat's stored car, paying a fraught visit to Pat and Ellen Hill during their drive through Mexico in 1955 (long before Pat moved to New Hope), and reviewing every single Highsmith book for the *Bucks County Life* journal in Doylestown, Pennsylvania. Peggy had started the "Books" column in *Bucks County Life* and enticed Pat to both write and draw for the journal.

Bucks County, where New Hope is located, has always been a gathering place for what used to be called "creative types": homosexuals, bohemians, theater folk, film people, well-to-do commercial artists, and even rural illiterates like Dorothy Parker and her husband Alan Campbell, who in 1936, with many of their friends living in or moving to every hamlet along the Delaware River (amongst them Bella and Samuel Spewack, Ruth and Augustus Goetz, S. J. and Laura Perelman, George S. Kaufman, Moss Hart, Jean Garrigue, Josephine Herbst, Glenway Wescott, and Arthur Koestler), purchased a farm in Pipersville and promptly mowed down a forest of beautiful old trees that was obstructing their "view." All of Bucks Country recoiled in convulsive horror.[13]

Marijane Meaker's romantic memoir of her meeting with Pat in Manhattan and their attempt to live together in Bucks County, *Highsmith: A Romance of the 1950s* (although, says Meaker, it was often "far from a love story"),[14] with its vivid portrayal of the deeply closeted lesbian life in 1950s New York, highlights Pat's sweetnesses and eccentricities: her insistence on dressing for dinner even in the country (shoes shined, a freshly ironed white shirt, a blazer and an ascot); her gentlemanly manners (always standing up for a woman and pulling out her chair); her habit of proffering small presents (a flower on the table, a book of Renée Vivien's poems with a page marked by an autumn leaf, love notes on any old piece of paper that came to hand); her attachment to bad puns and worse jokes; and her instinctively guilty response to any situation for which she might be held vaguely responsible.

But under the romantic vignettes lurk other stories: troubling stories about what happens when two obsessive women writers, each at a different stage in her career and each writing a book whose organizing principle is murder, try to live together for six months in a rural idyll with their cats.*[15] One of the stories has a switchblade in it.

Pat had always carried a knife in her pocket—pointed instruments occupied a practical and fantastical place in the Highsmith imagination for decades (see "The Real Romance of Objects, Parts 1 and 3")—and even her written approaches to love were armed with blades. At eighteen, she'd inserted a couple of cutting edges into a jaunty little sea shanty she called "High Romance." "I happen to like this," she wrote pugnaciously beside the first verse.[16]

> If I were a sailor
> You'd be my wife
> I'd carry a cutlass
> And a big clasp knife.[17]

In New Hope, Pat used her pocketknife for grooming plants, and during one of many arguments with Marijane, she stuck it roughly and repeatedly into a wooden tabletop, let the handle quiver, and pulled it out again, casting menacing looks at her lover all the while.

Meaker was worried enough about the knife to write to Mary Highsmith. Mary wrote back, trying to convince her that fainthearted Pat wasn't capable of slipping a shiv into a lover.

"Never would she have harmed you with that knife deal tho an unspeakable thing to do. She is too much a coward at the sight of blood. She would have been the first to keel over. She faints at the prick of a finger."[18]

In the same letter Mary treated herself to a long, hot, maternal denunciation of all Pat's previous female friends, especially the older ones (see "The Real Romance of Objects: Part 1").[19] It couldn't have been a comfortable letter to receive, and it wasn't a comfortable relationship for either Pat *or* Marijane Meaker by now. Meaker says that one thing kept the two writers together: "By then, we didn't like each other, we didn't want to be around each other, but in bed it was fire."[20]

---

* It was here in Pennsylvania that Spider Highsmith, the "serious" black cat to whom Pat would dedicate *The Glass Cell,* started the travels which eventually landed him with Muriel Spark in Italy.

Pat and Marijane broke up quickly (and then continued to break up slowly) during their six months of cohabitation. And all through 1961 and part of 1962, Pat stayed on in New Hope, meeting attractive women. She met so many women that she felt compelled to lie to Caroline Besterman (whom she'd recently met in London), telling her that there were no lesbians in New Hope at all. But Pat was thinking about her "Ever Present Subject"—and about how to write lesbian stories under her pseudonym of Claire Morgan. Ellen Hill—Pat and Ellen, quarreling as they always did, shared a house in Positano and a trip to Rome in the summer of 1962—figured prominently in Pat's plans for lesbian fiction. At the end of 1961, after discarding the idea of writing a sequel to *The Price of Salt,* Pat added vengeful thoughts about Ellen to her hateful feelings about Marijane and arrived at a sum: another "girls' book" which she thought she might call *The Inhuman Ones.* It would be a book "about the types of female homosexuals who have something missing from their hearts, who really hate their own sex, who must have visible, palpable strife in order to keep going. . . . Remember: E.B.H. [Ellen Blumenthal Hill]—and M.J.M. [Marijane Meaker]"[21]

Marijane, meanwhile, was even more suspicious than Pat. Pat noted grimly that "M.J." caught her with a hammer in her hand and asked if she was thinking of hitting her with it.[22]

The notes Pat took on her affair with Marijane Meaker are free of romanticism. They provide sketches of violent arguments, defensive analyses of motives, and deadpan descriptions of short-term reconciliations enhanced by lovemaking and disabled by recrimination. As usual, Pat chose to record what was wrong and not what was right in her life. Also as usual, she set down her thoughts according to her lights: the lights of someone defending herself against what she felt was an assault.

Desperate to return to Europe, as desperate as she was to return to the United States the last time she was *in* Europe ("I admire the common virtues of the Europeans more than I admire the common virtues of the Americans"), and focused on her perpetually unsuccessful revision of the Mexican novel she'd begun while living with Doris, *A Game for the Living,* Pat was hiding her morning drinking and a few other clandestine activities from Meaker. Since coming back from Europe in February of 1960, Pat had also been working on *The Two Faces of January,* a novel with a trio of dubious characters set in Greece. Two of those characters were a murkily attached male duo: Rydal, a "footloose" young American whom Pat described emphatically as "not a beatnik," and Chester, a middle-aged con man who reminds Rydal of his father. Chester's wife, Olga/Colette, is more or less there to be killed—and she is: by accident and by her husband, who is trying to kill Rydal.

Pat conjured up *The Two Faces of January* out of her feeling of being "slightly rooked by a middle-aged man" with "a highly aristocratic but weak face" when she was in Europe with Doris. A visit to the Palace of Knossos and a "musty old hotel" in Athens were further inspirations.[23] The first title she gave to *The Two Faces of January* was *The Power of Negative Thinking*—a title she thriftily bestowed on the fictional work of her fictional author, Howard Ingham, in her novel *The Tremor of Forgery*. The title was a clue to her mood.

Her editor Joan Kahn's response to the first completed version of *The Two Faces of January* wouldn't have lightened Pat's mood. Kahn called Pat's bluff. "The book," Kahn wrote to Pat's agent, Patricia Schartle, "makes sense only if there is a homosexual relationship between Rydal and Chester. . . . We cannot like any of the characters, but more difficult, we cannot believe in them."[24] A couple of days after she received Kahn's letter, Pat made a note in her cahier: "The ultra-neurotic, which is myself. The Underground Man. To hell with reader identification in the usual sense, or a sympathetic character."[25] Pat was taking Kahn's rejection like a real writer—which is to say she was taking it personally—and Kahn would reject, in all, three revisions of *The Two Faces of January*. The novel was finally published by Doubleday in New York and Heinemann in London, where it won the Crime Writers' Association Silver Dagger for 1965, thus providing Pat with yet another knife: the silver dagger that came with the award. Pat said, no doubt with the sour smile the French call *un sourire jaune,* that she used the dagger to open all her letters.

As was her habit, Pat described herself as the "victim" in her love affair with Marijane Meaker. She couldn't understand why Marijane "attempted to . . . punish me";[26] she was "terrified of [Marijane's] temper"; she felt that "the insults from her have gone beyond bounds."[27] "The morning was the worst. The worst of any verbal conflict to date. M.J. keeps me on the defensive, by wild attacks . . . e.g. accusing me the night before of having whined, of having said that I have the worst of it, in regard to housing."[28]

Pat and Marijane broke up so often, and Pat moved in and out of the house so many times, that they had to change moving companies a couple of times to avoid embarrassment. Pat finally rented—and kept—an apartment and then another house on South Sugan Road in New Hope. And she and Marijane continued to see each other and continued to argue.[29] It was an old pattern by now for Pat, and even the mutual accusations were getting old. Pat wrote down the most familiar of them.

" 'You're trying to defend yourself with what's left of your logical mind, because gin has got it [said Marijane]. You can't make it with Marijane Meaker. I threw you out, Pat, because you're a common drunk.' "

"I said, 'Hang on to it. It's all you've got.' "[30]

Pat's drinking *was* heavy. So heavy that her friend Polly Cameron said her drinks were named for the activities they fueled: "Walking Drinks," "Talking Drinks," "Cooking Drinks," "Dressing Drinks," "Argument Drinks," "Sleepless Night Drinks," "Planting Drinks," etc.[31] And just as she used to complain to other people about Mother Mary, Pat now complained constantly to Al and Betty Ferres about Marijane Meaker. Her theme was that "the mainspring of our difficulties is M.J.'s jealousy of me."[32]

Meaker says that Pat provided "the great epiphany in my work because I was always worried about [repeating the theme of] folie à deux . . . and Pat said: 'That's your bone; sharpen it. That's your bone, make it better.' "[33] When they fell in love, Marijane Meaker, six years younger than Pat, was writing crime novels and lesbian reportage for pulp publishers under a flock of pseudonyms (Vin Packer and Ann Aldrich were two of them). Meaker wanted to break into the prestigious "hardback" market, while Pat was already a "hardback" writer with a fancy French award (the 1957 *Roman policier* for *The Talented Mr. Ripley*), two American distinctions (the Crime Writers of America designations for both *Strangers on a Train* and *Ripley*), and a Hollywood film (Hitchcock's *Strangers on a Train*) under her writer's belt.

Pat slipped something else under that belt, too, when she helped herself to a writer's revenge on Marijane Meaker—by no means her last literary revenge on a woman. "[R]esentment was my second emotion," Pat would later write in response to Caroline Besterman's analysis of her problems with women.

Now you say I hate as well as love
Women and you are quite right.
They have the power to hurt me,
To play with, then run away from me,
Laughing, or at least smug and unhurt.
They have not suffered privation as I have.
Tantalization, as I have.[34]

And in *The Cry of The Owl* (1962), the novel Pat wrote after she and Meaker broke up, Pat managed to murder Marijane "accidentally" with a knife in the character of Nickie: the scheming, taunting, lying painter of many pseudonyms and psychotically jealous ex-wife of the novel's unlucky hero, Robert Forester.

Marijane Meaker's own fictional revenge was as direct as Pat's. In her post-Pat novel, *Intimate Victims* (1962), she had the character she called Harvey Plangman, an obsessively self-improving, list-making, small-time grifter, battered to death with his own hammer.

"Harvey," Meaker wrote forty years later, "was in no way like Pat. I probably just wanted to kill her off, too, so I chose Plangman for the victim's
name."[35] But Harvey Plangman is *very* like Pat: he's a catalogue of her most
Balzacian qualities. He slips German words into his sentences, just as Pat did,
and he imitates her compulsive list making, her obsession with dress, and the
deep social insecurities which ran under her attraction to "quality."

In fact, the abject Harvey Plangman is as clear a portrayal of certain "male"
aspects of Patricia Highsmith as Jill Hillside is of her "female" aspects. Jill Hillside is the ambivalent, sweetly depressed, sexually absent lesbian character in
Marc Brandel's own post-Pat novel, *The Choice* (1950).

Of *The Choice,* Pat had written in her diary: "I am Jill Hillside, & there down
to the last detail of cigarette holder, hands, levis etc. & a screamingly funny
breakfast scene: identical with our own. . . . I suppose it's all over town. I am
called a dike."[36]

Pat, who was as versatile in her self-presentations (when she wanted to
be) as her hero-criminal Tom Ripley, contained many characters. Jill Hillside
and Harvey Plangman were only two of them. As one of her late-life Swiss
neighbors observed with some surprise: "Whenever I talk about Pat, I never
say the same thing twice."[37]

24

LES GIRLS

PART 8

Because New Hope was a charming little country town of artisans and crafts-people, endowed with a "magical aura" and its own mythologies, Pat stayed on in New Hope after she and Marijane had called their very last moving company. "New Hope was fabulous from the Thirties to the Sixties," said longtime resident furniture maker and designer Phillip Lloyd Powell, "and then it went the way of all tourist places."[1] And New Hope was a relaxed place for women to meet and match: Odette's (still in existence) was the restaurant/bar/nightclub where Pat was to pick up at least one lover after she and Marijane Meaker split up. Expedient as always, Pat made advances to the waitress, Daisy Winston.

Phillip Lloyd Powell was Daisy's best friend in New Hope.

"Daisy was so much fun when she was young, big as a minute, four foot something; such a cute little thing, very witty . . . and she'd sing at the Canal House, imitating Ella Logan and Marlene Dietrich. Daisy had a thing called nystigma, it was an eye-movement problem, and she couldn't drive, she couldn't type. . . . I think Pat would be attracted to people who had something abnormal about them. . . . Daisy [was a] go-between between Pat and her mother, a gofer . . . but bitching all the way."[2]

Daisy joined the long line of small, ferocious women (the approximate size and temperament of Willie Mae Stewart Coates) who crowd the lists of Pat's friends and lovers. Peggy Lewis, who thought Pat had a "brilliant future" in front of her, had a hard time imagining what Pat saw in Daisy. But Peggy's eldest daughter remembered Daisy's protective nature: how she'd fished her out of a canal once when she'd fallen in, and escorted her from her school bus past a threatening snake.[3] Daisy's custodial qualities alone would have recommended her to Pat.

Three months into her affair with Daisy, Pat went with Peggy Lewis to meet one of Bucks County's homosexual gentry, the novelist Glenway Wescott, whose elegant and disturbing novella, *The Pilgrim Hawk* (1940), is one of the jewels of American expatriate fiction. Peggy and Pat went to Wescott's younger brother's house first by mistake, and Pat was impressed by Lloyd Wescott's wife, the philanthropist and publisher Barbara Harrison.

Taking advantage of their error, Peggy and Pat looked at the "marvellous paintings collected by . . . Barbara to whom K[atherine Anne] Porter dedicated *A Ship of Fools*." And then the two women went to Glenway Wescott's house, on the grounds of the same estate, and Pat talked to Wescott for "perhaps 45 minutes." What they discussed was the journals of Virginia Woolf.[4] Three years later, Pat wrote a letter to Wescott from her cottage in Suffolk. But by then, Pat was writing to everyone.

Like any artist in conflict with her blood relatives, Pat was always happy to be an *ami de maison*, able, to the end of her life, to enjoy other families more than her own. The list of her adopted families and the ways she joined herself to them is as various as are their opinions of her. In New Hope, it was the Lewises and the Ferreses who were her sounding boards. In Montmachoux, she depended upon Agnes and Georges Barylski, the Polish gleaners who brought her eggs and did her favors. In Moncourt she had her next-door neighbors Desmond and Mary Ryan, and in Paris, she got on so well with Marion Aboudaram's mother, Mme Aboudaram, that Marion used to wonder if perhaps Pat didn't prefer her mother to her.[5] In Aurigeno, Pat had her neighbor Ingeborg Moelich to shop for her, and she eagerly followed the letters coming from her friend Charles Latimer about his intricate family problems, waiting breathlessly for "the big showdown with his greedy sister."[6]

In 1968, living miserably alongside Elizabeth Lyne in their house of double trouble in Samois-sur-Seine, Pat immersed herself in the life drama of a relative who had spent some years in an orphanage as a child (adoption, false or real, was a serious theme in the Coates family). The relative told Pat how she had to travel to New York to retrieve her runaway daughter from the protective care "of a Negro waiter named Ron" on the Lower East Side. ("Maybe you even know him!" Pat wrote a little nuttily to Lil Picard in New York.)[7]

Pat was delighted by her relative's nine-page letter ("not a line of which is boring"), she was fascinated to see how the "plot" of this actual family drama would work out, and she was anxious to commend the woman's young daughter, who was being heckled by her stepfather, into Lil Picard's care. "If you can find someone old enough to be your grandmother *also* on your side—that's something!"[8] It was the old Coates/Highsmith family soap opera all over again (Pat, meanwhile, was following English radio's longest-running soap opera, *The Archers,* with strict attention),[9] and she was doing her best to bring this version of it to the old conclusion.[10]

None of her pleasure in her acquaintance with cousin Ruby, however, stopped Pat from submitting Ruby's name along with the names of eight of her other cousins to her French lawyer in 1976 to ensure that if any of them dared to contest her latest will, they would already be on a list "eliminating" them from inheriting anything at all.[11]

Pat's friend and neighbor in France in the 1970s, Frédérique Chambrelent, had worked in haute couture for Molyneux (where she had watched Natalie Barney, Romaine Brooks, and Janet Flanner come in for fittings), and was, when she met Pat, a publicity representative, a journalist, and a friend of the great French actresses Arletty and Edwige Feuillère. Pat used to enjoy coming to tea with Chambrelent's mother at her country house in Vaudoué, twenty kilometers from Pat's house in Moncourt. Pat came "every weekend for two or three years" and would query Frédérique Chambrelent closely about her niece, Bénédicte, who was attending Columbia University, Pat's alma mater. "She was very interested in Bénédicte's news"—and also very kind to Bénédicte. Pat helped Chambrelent in her garden, and, with a friend, Frédérique Chambrelent painted Pat's workroom in Moncourt for her and visited Pat there regularly. Chambrelent remembers that there was something very wrong with Pat's chocolate point Siamese cat: "The cat chased its tail all the time. It went in circles."[12]

Although Pat drank enough to horrify both Frédérique Chambrelent and Serge Matta (brother of the painter Roberto Matta and a friend of Pat's translator neighbor, Janine Hérisson), she was always perfectly behaved with Chambrelent's mother, imbibing only tea with Mme Chambrelent and comporting herself properly. But when there wasn't a tea party, Pat would stay the whole day in Vaudoué, drinking whiskey (Frédérique Chambrelent says that Pat kept a bottle in her purse "like a sailor": Pat reminded *everyone* of a sailor), and then she would drive herself back home drunk, although she always "held on to her dignity. Pat had her rules, her rigidities, she could be very *bourgeoise,*" as well as having "a really charming side." But she was "like a prehistoric animal." And Chambrelent refused to listen to Pat's disquisitions on "the blacks and the Jews." "Enough is enough," she would say to Pat.[13]

Frédérique Chambrelent wanted to introduce Pat to her friend the renowned French film and theater actress Edwige Feuillère. "I thought Edwige could make a scenario from one of Pat's works, the short story of the two sisters who lived together ["Quiet Night"], and Patricia said: *'Elle est trop snob pour moi.'* She refused to meet her because she was too shy. . . . Pat was very timid, very shy, it was pathological." But in every other way—except in speaking about her own family or her lovers (Chambrelent met Pat's young lover Monique Buffet, but Pat introduced Monique as one of her "agents")—Pat became an *ami de maison*: with regular visits, frequent notes, and interested enquiries about Chambrelent's family.[14]

"I found her very intelligent," says Frédérique Chambrelent. "But how strange she was. How strange she was."[15]

Desmond Ryan,[16] the Anglo-Irish journalist who was Pat's neighbor in Moncourt throughout the 1970s, brought the translators Henri Robillot (translator of Philip Roth and Saul Bellow) and Janine Hérisson, who would translate Pat's novels *A Dog's Ransom* and *Ripley's Game* for Calmann-Lévy, to meet Pat in the house in Montmachoux, where her Portuguese neighbors gave her "the occasion to make many racist remarks." Robillot and Hérisson lived nearby in the Forest of Fontainebleau and knew, through their translations, something about the United States. Pat envied their house, a bohemian dwelling of considerable charm, which she compared unfavorably to her own faux-bourgeois style.

Pat was charmed by Janine Hérisson (Henri Robillot offered the opinion that Pat was perhaps a little *too* charmed), and sent her some very amiable letters, but Mlle Hérisson resisted the kind of "adoption" Pat sought. She found Pat's "racist remarks" uncomfortable to be around.

"When I first met Patricia and I asked her why she left the United States she said it was because of the Negro Problem. And I understood her to mean that it was because of the way Negroes were treated in the United States. But that's not what she meant at all. She meant it was because of the way Negroes were demanding their rights."[17]

One afternoon, Pat, the noise of her Portuguese neighbors nagging at her nerves, drove over from Montmachoux to visit Hérisson and Robillot. They got to talking about the American Civil War—one of Pat's "subjects"—and M. Robillot told Pat that he had a Spencer automatic rifle from 1865, the kind that helped secure the North's victory at Gettysburg. Pat wanted to see and hold the gun. She took it in her hands, raised it, assumed the posture of a shooter, and, pretending to pull the trigger and reload between hits, began to shout: "Fire one Portuguese! Fire two Portuguese!"

At the "third 'Portuguese,'" says M. Robillot, "we stopped her, astonished at her homicidal furor."[18]

All of Pat's house moves and most of her travels—to New Hope, to Suffolk, to Samois-sur-Seine, to Moncourt, to Aurigeno, and finally to Tegna, as well as her visits to Positano, to Marseille, to Tunis, and to Tangier—were assisted by helpful people she'd known for some time. Mary Highsmith's friend, the cartoonist Jeannot (Jean David), housed Pat in Marseille; Caroline Besterman helped her in Aldeburgh and Earl Soham; Elizabeth Lyne found her houses in Bois Fontaine and Samois-sur-Seine and accompanied her to Tunis; Pat's lover at the time "negotiated the Montmachoux house";[19] Desmond and Mary Ryan were responsible for directing her to the house next door to them in Moncourt; and Ellen Blumenthal Hill persuaded Pat to move to Switzerland, picked out the house in Aurigeno for her, and supervised its renovation. And it was Peter Huber who alerted Pat to the property adjoining his wife's family house in Tegna on which Pat constructed her final home. Pat's social "isolation" had distinctly social limits; despite her protestations, she always had a kind of "family" nearby.

And so it was Peggy Lewis's bohemian mother-in-law, Edna Lewis, with whom Pat had attended some Ethical Culture meetings in New York, whose art school in Positano was a base for Pat's passages through Positano. Pat had first gone to Positano during her twenty-day idyll with Kathryn Hamill Cohen in September of 1949, and she returned there with Ellen Hill in 1952 and 1962. But whenever she was alone in Positano, she knew that Edna Lewis's art school was a ready-made social frame. And in that lovely hill village, says Edna's granddaughter, "Any attractive man—never mind his sexual proclivities—would be let into [Edna's] art school for free. She loved attractive men."[20] Much of the company Edna Lewis had around her was male and homosexual—just the kind of company Pat liked.

Larry Kramer, the playwright, novelist, and AIDS activist, remembers meeting Pat in Positano in 1963, just after she'd left New Hope, and the United States for good. Pat, in love "as never before" with Caroline Besterman, was on her roundabout way to join Caroline in England, and Kramer was a young man working for Columbia Pictures in London and staying, by chance, at the good hotel in Positano from whose balcony early one morning in 1952 Pat had first conjured up the idea of Tom Ripley.

"Well, I didn't know much about anything then," says Larry Kramer.

I was sent to Columbia [Pictures] UK from Columbia America to be a story editor, to find stories for the movies we were making. The UK was the biggest company going. Hollywood was dead, Roma had been the fifties, this was the sixties and it belonged to England. I don't know why I went to a travel agent but for some reason he said go to Positano. It's on the Amalfi Coast; you fly to Rome or Naples and then you take a very winding drive along the Amalfi Coast. It's all built on the side of a hill, and it's beautiful. It had a very lively bunch of people too. . . .

There was one great hotel: it was called the Miramare, and I stayed there. It was bliss. You look out over the bay all the time. You sit on the toilet and look out over the bay. You take a bath and look out over the bay. Beautiful.

There was a woman there called Edna Lewis. . . . She was an American who ran an art school there. She must have had a little money and she gave parties and she heard about everyone in town who was vaguely interesting and I guess somehow I met her and, you know, I was in the movie business so she invited me to a party. I guess that's how I met Pat. . . . Pat was lively and we had nice conversations. I was in awe of her because I knew who she was. . . .

I knew she was obviously a lesbian, but we didn't talk about that. We didn't talk about my being gay. Everybody was nervous about being gay then. I suspect I liked her because I respected her writing. . . . I was under thirty and sorta shy still, and not connected to any bigger time that she belonged to.[21]

In early 1971, when Pat was living in her house on the Loing Canal (the Impressionist painter Alfred Sisley's favorite subject) in Moncourt, Larry Kramer, back in America and "not liking it much" (although he told Pat that the United States was "exciting creatively" and that she "might find a lot to write about" there), wrote an admiring letter to Pat:

"I finally obtained a copy of your book on *Plotting & Writing Suspense Fiction* etc. and wanted to write and tell you how excellent I thought it was. It may be one of the very best books I've ever read on writing—how about that? It's just filled with tremendous insights backed up with good common sense. . . . Congratulations—and I shall tout it."[22]

Pat, Larry Kramer says, initiated their correspondence. "She was intimidating, so I wouldn't have made the attempt to be the aggressor."[23] And it's true that Pat was keenly interested in pursuing "movie money" for her novels and that Columbia owned a Highsmith "property" or two. In early August of 1963 Pat went to a party and met again, as she put it in her diary, "Larry Kramer of Columbia in London," who "discussed the difficulties of *Deep Water* script."[24] Six months later, she wrote to Kramer about *Deep Water* and made a note of what he said: "my characters were increasingly psychopath & difficult for movies."[25]

It was Pat's Venice novel, though, *Those Who Walk Away,* which finally got her the kind of money from Columbia Pictures that would make a difference in her life. (Columbia never filmed the novel, and Pat wrote that the novel was "not even a very good book . . . dammit"; she thought *Frankfurter Allgemeine Zeitung* and *Neue Zürcher Zeitung* serialized it "because the Germans love to read about Venice.")[26] In June of 1967 Pat, newly separated from Caroline Besterman, had just rented the house Elizabeth Lyne picked out for her near the Forest of Fontainbleau in Bois Fontaine at 57 rue St. Merry, when Columbia paid Pat twenty-eight thousand dollars for *Those Who Walk Away*. (Seven years later, Pat had Jonathan Trevanny, the "pawn" in her 1974 novel *Ripley's Game*, murdered on the rue St. Merry.)

So only three months after moving to Bois Fontaine, Pat decided to buy the ill-fated stone farmhouse (the shape of the garden was already reminding her of a "tombstone") at 20 rue de Courbuisson in Samois-sur-Seine with her old friend Mme Lyne—and to use her Columbia movie money to pay her share. By 1969, after she and Mme Lyne managed to re-create the very worst of Pat's needs for domination, submission, and conflict—irretrievably ruining their friendship and producing more disobliging comments about Jews from Pat—Pat moved herself from Samois-sur-Seine to a house in Montmachoux, where she was, if possible, even more uncomfortable. Montmachoux was the place where the ten children of her flanking Portuguese neighbors were quickly driving her mad: "I have never understood Catholics and never will."[27] On the other hand, she was writing to Lil Picard that she'd "sold two films last month: *Deep Water* and *The Story-Teller*. . . . it gives me a score of 8 out of 12 books sold to films."[28] Pat was keeping herself sane in the way she knew how: by keeping another list.

In April of 1961, Pat, raking the ashes of her now-dead romance with Marijane Meaker with the idea of turning them into a novel, revealed just why she tended to avoid writers as lovers: "The story of M.J. [Marijane] and myself. Off to a crippled start. The brain washing. The rivalry between two in the same profession. The desperate efforts of one to best the other; and the other's efforts to preserve the relationship, at any cost."[29]

As her ideas for this novel developed, Pat saw herself as "the heroine," whose "charm" is "her naivete and good will. . . . She might be tempted by a younger person to leave . . . her vicious friend. But she cannot even see it for a time." But then, Pat thought: "There is not much use in going on with details until I have a strong story on which to hang this."[30]

Two months later, Pat broke out in German measles, spending her nights scratching twice as much as she was sleeping. But, as always, she "found the fever beneficial to the imagination" and arrived at an ending for the novel she was writing about the unlucky Peeping Tom. It was the ending in which, with obvious satisfaction and Grand Guignol splashings of gore, she stabbed Marijane Meaker's fictional double to death. Pat had been calling her book *The Fruit Tramp* until her editor, Joan Kahn, wisely changed its title to *The Cry of the Owl* (1962).[31] Harking back to her trip to New Jersey in 1950 to spy on the real-life heroine of *The Price of Salt,* Pat gave Robert Forester, the reluctant, gentle stalker who brings catastrophe to everyone, both her habits of surveillance and a vengeful pursuer. She also gave him some of her ambivalent sexual feelings (he's just as hesitant to sleep with the opposite sex as Walter Stackhouse in *The Blunderer,* David Neumeister in *This Sweet Sickness,* and Vic Van Allen in *Deep Water*), more than a few of her talents, her embarrassments and her depressions, and at least one of her physical traits: a growth on his cheek. (Pat had a small sebaceous cyst on her left cheek, visible in some photographs.) She made the girl in the novel a little like one of her early loves, Joan S., who had married and was still the source of some wishful thinking on Pat's part. Pat called the character Louise at first, changed her name to Jenny Thierolf, and had her commit a dreamy kind of suicide for love of Robert Forester.

Like Pat herself—who would come to prefer the photographs of women she desired to the women themselves—Robert Forester prefers to spy on Jenny Thierolf through a window that frames her like a picture. When Forester sees her outside the frame, his "pleasure or satisfaction in seeing her more closely now was no greater than when he had looked at her through the window, and he foresaw that getting to know her even slightly would be to diminish her and what she stood for to him—happiness and calmness and the absence of any kind of strain."[32]

The Cry of the Owl is Pat's most spectral novel, perhaps because Robert Forester is a man who wishes harm to no one, but whose "innocent" act of voyeurism brings death and misfortune to everyone—even, of course, to a dog. (Pat shot the dog in this book.) Pat told Kingsley: "I am writing something out of my system."[33]

Pat also told Kingsley of a misfortune averted: twenty-four of her writer's cahiers—Pat thought they'd been "lost round about the time of my grandmother's death in 1955"—were found in storage in Long Island with a friend of her ex-lover Maggie, just before Pat set sail in the spring of 1963 on her way out of the United States and into Caroline Besterman's arms.[34] Before she embarked, she gave her desk to Alex Szogyi in Manhattan (who kept it lovingly all his life). She also left Alex with the task of disposing of her piano.

In Positano, Pat, vibrant with love and galvanized with purpose, continued to work on *The Glass Cell,* the novel of unjust imprisonment (the crime comes *after* the punishment in this complicated pavane of odd pairs of Alter Egos and yet another orphaned criminal-hero) that she'd begun in New Hope after fruitfully corresponding with an imprisoned convict. She worked six days a week and wrote eight pages a day. Without a radio or a record player, she provided her own entertainment: whittling things from wood in the evenings and painting pictures on Sundays. She also made another will (falling in love made her think of death again), writing to Kingsley that she'd left "half my worldly estate, what it will be at my demise to my mother, half to an English friend."[35] A codicil to this will made Kingsley her official "Literary Executor."[36]

The "English friend" to whom Pat had left half her estate was Caroline Besterman. In the three decades left of her life, Pat was to make many more wills. But she never again mentioned a lover in any of them.

25

LES GIRLS

PART 9

Before Pat and Elizabeth Lyne's twenty-year friendship foundered and broke apart on the house with the double doors and separate wings they bought together in Samois-sur-Seine in 1968 (most of the houses Pat bought or wrote about were divided like the two halves of a brain: *her* brain), they took a trip to Tunisia in 1966 that was to prove an inspiration for Pat's work. Pat began the cahier in which she wrote about this trip on a familiar note.

"My self-esteem has a duration of not more than twenty-four hours."[1]

Restive and angry in the Suffolk countryside in her double cottage at Earl Soham, Pat was also bored and in her usual state of aggravated ambivalence. She was smoking cigarette after cigarette, irrigating herself with coffee, and reaching too often and too early for the alcohol. She had been taking notes on "The English Social Situation," which she decided was comprised of warfare ("'the classes' all pulling against each other"),[2] niggardliness ("Nothing lavish here, keep it miserly. It's no more than you deserve"),[3] and the deliberate intent to deprive her of pleasure ("Any pleasures, rewards, minor vices? Just name it. England will scotch it").[4]

But she avoided addressing by name what was *really* blighting her mind: the dissolution of her relationship with Caroline Besterman in the bitter solvent of her jealousy. She could only limn the matter in a neutral writing voice: "The affair with the married woman [in which] one is not satisfied with taking second place emotionally or even sharing equally, or even being preferred emotionally to the other person."[5]

Naturally drawn to the triangle in relationships, Pat was once again caught up in a geometry she couldn't tolerate.

If only she'd gone to London more often.

After the 1940s in Manhattan, the decade in which Pat had coincided tangentially, but not unsuccessfully, with her epoch (i.e., her work in the new medium of the comics, her story "The Heroine" published in *Harper's Bazaar,* her novel *Strangers on a Train* bought by Alfred Hitchcock), she seems to have operated outside the defining characteristics of any era. Just as she always lived in and wrote about Highsmith Country, her times and her customs were also always her own. Part of this had to do with her intractable and unclubbable nature, and part of it had to do with her refusal to live in cities—the places where "epochs" and "eras" are invented, manufactured, and marketed. During the 1950s, for instance, the Beat writers, all of whom were her contemporaries (and each one of whom was a superb self-publicist), escaped her notice entirely. But she had been "on the road" as often and at the same time as they had—and she had taken far more coherent notes on her experiences than any of them.

In the 1960s, the Beatles and "Swinging London" get no mention in any Highsmith cahier. She never paid attention to rock 'n' roll until her attraction for much younger women took her into the bars where, late in life, she was forced to dance a little and to make other touching forays into "having fun." Even then, her appreciation for the contemporary music she heard went only as far as a single song from a Lou Reed album—and only because it reminded her of her German girfriend. Aside from classical music—"Bach for minor crises. Mozart for major ones" is how she put it in 1966—Pat loved best to listen to songs from the musical comedies created in the era she understood best: the era of the great Broadway musicals of the 1940s and early 1950s.

Pat wasn't too old to ride the crest of any decade's wave; she was simply too odd, too censorious, and too much herself, or, as she might have put it, too much "her selves." She had her own fish to fry and her own snails to tend, and she was still keeping three hundred of the little molluscs in glass terraria at Bridge Cottage in Earl Soham.

Although London went on swinging without Pat, her heavy drinking and fellow feeling for homosexual males might have found her a seat on a barstool in many of the boîtes of Fitzrovia or the public houses of Soho. In Soho, the Coach and Horses, the French, or, best of all, the Colony Room at 41 Dean Street, with its permanent stench and poisonous green walls, would have been a fine place for Pat to drink in public, if, that is, she hadn't disapproved so much of alcoholics. The Colony welcomed a nonpareil collection of truly armigerous drunken writers—the spectacular drunk Daniel Farson, the dressed-like-a-lady drunk Sandy Fawkes, the suited, caned, and supplied-with-dark-glasses drunk Julian Maclaren-Ross, *et al.*—with whom she might have found some rough comfort. If, that is, she hadn't disapproved as much of other writers as she did of alcoholics. The Colony's owner, Muriel Belcher, a foul-mouthed lesbian and brilliant mixologist of artistic and social misfits, had adopted the painter Francis Bacon as a "daughter," paying him a stipend and allowing him to drink for free so long as he hauled in rich customers. Michael Andrews's famous 1962 painting, *The Colony Room,* painted the year before Pat moved to Suffolk, features eight of Muriel Belcher's Colony Room regulars, including the painters Francis Bacon and Lucian Freud, their muse and model Henrietta Moraes (later Maggi Hambling's muse and model), and Muriel Belcher herself with her Cuban lover Carmel.

Francis Bacon was the painter Pat would come to admire most. She loved the tryptich of Bacon's heroin-addicted lover throwing up in a toilet (so true to life, she thought), and in Tegna she kept a postcard reproduction of Bacon's *Study Number 6* propped up on her desk. (This is Bacon's brilliant and horrifying reworking of Velázquez's painting of Pope Innocent X: in Bacon's version, the pope is screaming.) She both wanted and feared to meet Bacon, but never did; she thought the experience would be "shattering." Unfashionably, it was Pat's editor and publishing director from Heinemann who had to guide her towards Muriel Belcher's Colony Room—and Pat went there just the once. Janice Robertson, Pat's editor at Heinemann, recalled the occasion.

"I was out with [Pat and with] Roland Gant, who was a quite lovely editorial director and a friend and an admirer of Pat's. And we had had quite a drunken lunch. And we went into Muriel's. And Muriel's was open in the afternoon which was very racy to me. And when we came out, there was an injured pigeon in the gutter and Pat was totally concerned about this pigeon and couldn't be dragged away."

Pat, who didn't want to leave the curb until something could be done for the dying pigeon, was more interested in the bird than in the bar patrons at Muriel's. The society of the Colony Room would be one of the many roads Pat didn't take.

In the spring of 1965, Pat travelled with Caroline Besterman to Venice for a few days. It was Pat's first vacation in nineteen months, but it wasn't her best one. And it was far from satisfactory for Caroline, who, with obvious restraint, summarized it thusly: "Venice could have been better." When the two women had gone to Rome together, Pat had ignored Caroline's sensitivities; it made for bad feelings all around. On this trip, Pat brought with her to Venice a portable typewriter (supplied by the BBC) along with a BBC deadline for a television script, *The Cellar.* The work and the deadline must have added to Caroline's sense that Venice could indeed have been "better."

Pat's notes on Venice are marbled with her horror at the cost of everything (she wrote down all the prices) and at the presumption of waiters and bag carriers who actually expected to be tipped. As usual, she described the trip as though she'd taken it alone, which may have been how she felt. Attempting to renew her acquaintance with the woman the Venetians had dubbed "the Last Duchess," Pat called Peggy Guggenheim, who was "cool by telephone." Guggenheim didn't invite Pat for a drink at her palazzo on the Grand Canal, and she dismissed Pat's invitation for a drink at Harry's Bar.[6]

Pat—"on duty" as always during her ten days in Venice—made good use of her vigilance. From October 1965 to March 1966, she wrote a draft of *Those Who Walk Away,* her Venetian novel of incessant and often pointless pursuit, and of real and counterfeit attempts at murder and self-erasure. Her first narrative intention for it sounds like something from *Sunset Blvd.*—"A suspense novel from the point of view of the corpse"[7]—and she did begin it with a corpse of sorts. Never one to forget a slight, Pat gave Peggy Guggenheim's first name to the young wife whose suicide, predating the book's action, supplies the motive for murder for the pair of Highsmith males who run from—and after—each other in *Those Who Walk Away.*[8]

The dead woman's husband, Ray Garrett, is pursued by Ed Coleman, the vengeful painter who was her father.[9] Ray starts a game of hide-and-seek with his potential murderer, pursuing his own death by following Ed to Venice after Ed tries to shoot him in Rome. In prose as flat as a roller-rink floor, Ray seems to seek what Gerald, the "hero" of Pat's disappeared manuscript *The Traffic of Jacob's Ladder,* was looking for; what, in fact, all Highsmith hero-criminals are looking for: oblivion through the dissolution of their burden of identity.

Just like wrestlers unable to leave the mat, Ray Garrett and his father-in-law try out different holds and postures on each other, different ways of winning and losing, different means of being brutal and being passive. But there is no death in Venice, and Ray and Ed are both caught in the mantrap Highsmith's imagination first sprang in *Strangers on a Train*: the mantrap that comes alive in Guy Haines's most "horrible" idea:

> Guy had a horrible, an utterly horrible thought all at once, that he might ensnare Owen in the same trap that Bruno had used for him, that Owen in turn would capture another stranger who would capture another, and so on in infinite progression of the trapped and the hunted.[10]

Guy's image of an infinity of entrapments is like Jean Genet's definition of "reality": two mirrors facing each other. But Patricia Highsmith, always a little more frightening than any of her characters, imagined a "reality" that was built around the *whole* of the hunt: the trapped, the trapper, and the terrible necessity of the pursuit itself. Someone as caught up as Pat was with pursuit, someone as much in thrall to the chase, could never settle her feelings on one side of the "hunt" or the other, could never finally choose the hunter over the hunted. Hence the perpetual ambivalence that allowed her to course with the hounds *and* run with the hares. That is why the "hunt" in her work so often turns on a dime—as it did in her first commercially published story, "Uncertain Treasure," when the pursuer becomes the pursued, and vice versa. The constant shifting of roles was a compellingly disruptive premise for her fictions—and a cruelly exhausting one in her life.

Those Who Walk Away was Daniel Keel's introduction to publishing the work of Patricia Highsmith. Rowohlt had been Pat's German-language publisher, but Keel was willing to bring out *Those Who Walk Away* in hardback in 1967 and, later on, to add Pat's work to his prestigious "yellow and black" series. So her German agent, Rainer Heumann, gave Keel the rights to *Those Who Walk Away,* and Pat, who had been in a paperback "ghetto" and had no serious reputation in Germany, was launched in the more respectable hardback form in both Switzerland and Germany by Diogenes Verlag. Keel's only previous association with Pat had been sitting in a movie theater in Zurich when he was twenty-two years old, anxiously waiting for the credits of *Strangers on a Train* to roll so he could see the name of the "genius" who had written the novel from which this "masterpiece" was made. When he saw the name Patricia Highsmith it stuck with him. "I met her in the cinema," he says. And that, in the middle of Pat's present misery, was a piece of good luck.

Although her love affair was going badly, and, as a consequence, she was loathing England, Pat had the support of her enthusiastic editor at William Heinemann in London. Janice Robertson, who left Heinemann in 1972 "after losing the battle for Angela Carter," found Pat "very easy to work with."

"I think everybody at Heinemann found Pat easy. She was very liked, almost loved at Heinemann. I was with Heinemann for thirteen years; I think I worked with Pat, at a guess, between eight and ten years.

"We always worked from typescript, hand-typed by Pat on a not very good typewriter. She never cleaned the keys. She was meticulous, so one didn't edit with Pat as with others. One didn't move the chapter, or cut this paragraph or alter this character. Because she was meticulous, she welcomed little things: you can't catch a train from that station to that place, etc. And she was always extremely good; even if she rejected what you said, there was never any aggravation about it.

". . . There wasn't an occasion to disagree. We all admired her very much and we were all very pleased to publish her."[11]

Because the "years [were] beginning to swim into each other" and because she was no longer keeping a diary, Pat, in 1967, the year *Those Who Walk Away* was published, used her cahier to tot up her growing "case" against Caroline Besterman: "During the entire first draft of [*Those Who Walk Away*] I barely saw [Caroline] once, certainly did not sleep with her." And she helpfully added directions for future judges of her case: "But—as the reader will see . . ."[12] She wrote that Caroline was "continually harping on drinking"—Pat's drinking—especially after Pat "fell down some narrow stairs en route to the bathroom in the dark." When Pat remembered that Caroline had also fallen down some stairs, she stooped to infantile malice: "Ha ha!" she wrote triumphantly. At the time, Pat had just received a lunchtime lecture from Caroline on the "instability of my character." She was able to discount this talking-to because Caroline had "polished off every morsel on her plate." Eating was still high on Pat's list of avoidable sins.

Although she desperately wished otherwise, Pat's troubles with Caroline Besterman were as much a result of the condition she'd noted in her cahier (six months before meeting Caroline) as all her other troubles were: "Until around thirty I was essentially like a glacier or like stone. I suppose I was 'protecting' myself. It was certainly tied up with the fact I had to conceal the most important emotional drives of myself completely.

"This is the tragedy of the conscience-stricken young homosexual, that he not only conceals his sex objectives, but conceals his humanity and natural warmth of heart as well."[13]

Meanwhile, at Bridge Cottage (or "back at the ranch," the phrase which Pat, a mock Texan in her locutions, invariably used about any house she owned, just as she used "turning loose," a term taken from calf roping, for letting go of her emotional ties), Pat kept herself busy in the ways she knew how: writing, first and foremost. Having hired a television set, she began what she called "a religious television play, based on the effect of a friend (Jesus) upon a group of people."[14] The script would eventually turn into her novel *Ripley Under Ground*, with Derwatt the suicided artist, like Pat's dead former lover Allela Cornell, sacrosanct and alive in the memory of his friends—but turned to a perverse use by Tom Ripley.* She conceived and wrote her "second snail story," "The Quest for Blank Claveringi" (published in *Eleven* by Heinemann in 1970 and in altered form as "The Snails" in the *Saturday Evening Post*).[15] She drew and sketched as she had always done, and thought up little inventions: "The

---

* In the early 1970s, Nicole Stéphane, daughter of a Rothschild, magical actress in *Les Enfants Terribles,* and a film producer herself, telephoned Pat's Paris agent, Jenny Bradley, to say she was "really interested" in producing *Ripley Under Ground* but wanted to see a French translation before committing herself. Nothing came of her interest.

Gallery of Bad Art," "a sweating thermometer," and some odd new shapes for "lampshades." The inspiration for her pièce de résistance—a "strychnined lipstick"—must have been a real thrill for a writer to whom the impulse to murder women came so naturally.

Still brooding, Pat returned to some favorite subjects. She pondered the education of children (this was the moment when she decided that American orphanages should be emptied in order to supply the Peace Corps with eight-year-old ambassadors)[16] and philosophized endlessly and lugubriously about love. When she'd had enough of this, she turned to her old panacea—travel—and went to North Africa with Elizabeth Lyne.

Pat travelled to Paris in June of 1966 to pick up Mme Lyne, now retired from designing for Hattie Carnegie to an apartment in the Boulevard Raspail in Paris's Sixth Arrondissement. The two women drove to Marseille, stopping on the way to visit one of Pat's odd, obsessive French fans: a married man who had Pat sign eight of her books and gave her a rare chance to observe French family life. From Marseille, the two women took a boat to Tunis.

Pat's first impression of North Africa was simpler and nobler than the one she finally settled on. "Africa—A splendid place for thinking. One feels naked, standing alone against a white wall. Problems become simplified, one's directions clear. Is this because the land is so different from Europe, the people so different from one's own. . . . Africa does not even turn over in her sleep by way of entertaining tourists. It is like a great, fat, half asleep woman in a comfortable bed—naked herself, indifferent to any approach."[17]

Pat soon changed her mind about Africa's "simplicity." Everywhere she looked she began to notice something familiar: the sight of people trying to cheat her. On Mme Lyne and Pat's arrival in Tunis, Pat had an "altercation" with a porter and an argument about the bill at the hotel desk where the two women were booked. Pat's luggage was confiscated until the bill was settled. In Hammamet, the town in which she and Mme Lyne moved into a bungalow hotel, Pat began to compile complaints against the locals: "Hammamet—of five people of whom we expected slight help—all have let us down here. They take names and telephone numbers, make promises, and do not follow through. This is a mysterious form of ego-building in the East. . . . tomorrow doesn't matter, and out of sight is out of mind. It must be a curious god they have."[18]

In Sidi Bou Said, at a "bar-restaurant" to which she applied the term "clip-joint," Pat noticed "a curious Freudian item": male employess who left their unflushed excrement in the women's bathroom. "A curious card to leave," she thought, keeping one eye peeled for other desecrations. Back in her bungalow hotel in Hammamet, she had plenty of violations to report: the plumbing and the filthy quarters in which the unsatisfactory boy servants were housed were some of them.

She started to compare Arabs, unfavorably, to the entire "peasant" population of Mexico, finding what she'd been looking for all along: deceit and chicanery. "The Mexican peasant is naïve compared to the Arab. The Mexicans have had tourism about fifty or forty years, the Arab for hundreds. The Arab is a trader, essentially, a crook."[19]

The conditions at her bungalow hotel—one large room shared with Mme Lyne in which Pat also had to write, the bad hotel repair service, and the uncertain mail delivery—were destabilizing her. Unable to shelter herself from upsetting circumstances, she found a tortoiseshell kitten and tried to protect it from the feet of careless workers. "At noon I could be a nervous wreck if I were self-indulgent. (A beetle just fell from the ceiling onto my notebook.)"[20]

Pat was finally disturbed enough to begin taking notes for the novel that would become *The Tremor of Forgery:* her attempt to envisage what could happen to a writer, Howard Ingham, when he finds himself in unfamiliar climes, without the support of his customs or his language. This had been Pat's own situation from the moment she left the New World for good, moved to Suffolk, and took Highsmith Country with her. It is the situation of many creative expatriates: strangers in a strange land, living in the museum of their imaginations. In *The Tremor of Forgery,* Pat made Africa a province of Highsmith Country. "The element of terror—anxiety—is important. Perhaps *overconsciousness of details*—by which an individual tries to fix his place, from which he tries to gain security and confidence, but without success. It is the element of security, that is forever missing; the meaning and importance of life that is missing."[21]

Pat took many of the details of her daily life and irritations in Hammamet—the American-made cash register in a restaurant, the filth and evasiveness of the boy servants in her bungalow hotel, the fish *complet* she was always eating for dinner, her growing contempt for Arabs—and put them into the notes for her novel. The borders between the novel's life and her own stayed porous even after she had returned from North Africa and started travelling again. In her cahier notes she sent Howard Ingham to Denmark, and in the novel she created Ingham's friend Jensen, the homosexual painter, as a Dane chiefly because three months after she'd returned from Tunisia she had to travel to Copenhagen on book business.

Pat's notes and her novel continued to bear the weight of her special experiences as an exile from America: the divisions and confusions of her political understanding drained into characters who represented a vaguely muddled

Left (Howard Ingham) and a seriously proselytizing Right (Francis Adams). Howard Ingham's probable return to his former wife at the end of the novel ("never had any woman had such a physical hold over him")[22] was Pat's own wish: she linked the absent, idealized character of Howard's divorced wife Lotte to Ginnie Catherwood—although it was Lynn Roth of whom she'd been dreaming. As late as 1967 Pat was having deep dreams of union, of "fathering" a child with Lynn—"I so often think of Lynn, the joy of my life, and for a time I was the joy of hers"—and she was reprising in imagination the brief, secret *rencontre* she'd had with Roth in New Hope six years ago: "How beautiful when she came for her birthday November 23, 1961, invited herself for two nights (of joy for me), and on the third—by gentle persuasion."

When Howard Ingham commits what is undoubtedly murder by throwing his typewriter at the head of a "thieving Arab" (it is Pat's Olympia Deluxe typewriter, right down to its distinctive brown color), his creator's pleasure in the act is all too palpable: her concern is for the damaged typewriter and not for the dead Arab. Although Pat wished to write Ingham as "a decent (that is, honest) writer . . . [s]o the psychopathic is quite out," she also wanted to allow him freedom from the problem of "self-esteem" that plagued her daily: "A period comes when H. stops trying to maintain identity or morale. Then his 'animal' or primitive side frightens him. But he senses the freedom of having no self-respect to worry about."[23]

The Tremor of Forgery, by a writer most critics were discussing as godless and gripless when it came to morality, is a profoundly American (and therefore inescapably moral) consideration of those cultural crossings at which ethics start to founder and violent acts, such as murder, become meaningless. Pat's Methodist grandmother would have understood very well the motive for her metaphors.

When Pat and Elizabeth Lyne left Tunisia, they sailed to Naples, went on to Austria, and then, in August, Pat returned by herself to Suffolk. In September Pat was on the road again—to Nice, this time, to meet with the film director Raoul Lévy, who wanted to collaborate with her on a script for her novel *Deep Water*. When she returned to Earl Soham, there was a final, painful scene with Caroline Besterman in mid-October. Pat heaved Caroline's valise at the second bedroom, into which Caroline had withdrawn in a "huff" at Pat's lateness in coming to bed. (Pat doesn't say why she was late.) Caroline went back to London the next afternoon with Pat's imprecation that she was "finished with her" echoing throughout Bridge Cottage—and Pat was left shaken to her shoes, the golden bowl of her hopes for love with a married woman in pieces around her. It had been her longest continuous relationship.

Pat's first reaction was desperation: "The very worst time of my entire life."[24]

Then she had the sebaceous cyst which had been on her cheek for the last ten years surgically removed—as though cutting out this growth might rid her of other things, too. Her second reaction was to work more, and she started to write the film script for *Deep Water*. She wrote it between waves of panic and insomnia—she knew that dialogue and dramaturgy weren't her forte—and finished it in a month. Then she wrote a condensation of *Those Who Walk Away* for *Cosmopolitan* magazine, a task she also completed in a month.[25]

Her third and fourth reactions to her devastation were to invite an ex-lover to visit her and to plan for more travel. Daisy Winston came over from New Hope to Earl Soham for a welcome two weeks in December, although practical Pat was sorry to find that Daisy no longer attracted her sexually. It would have been a solution of sorts. After Daisy left, Pat went to Copenhagen for the Danish publication of *The Glass Cell* by Grafisk Ferlag. The trip plunged her into gloom—she gave a bad speech during it—but the crush she later developed on a woman she met in Copenhagen was a pleasant distraction. Gudrun reminded Pat of her old friend Betty, from her Fire Island days.[26]

On New Year's Eve of 1966, Raoul Lévy, the erstwhile film director of *Deep Water,* shot himself dead in St-Tropez. He still owed Pat money for the script she'd written for him in October and November, and her gelid commentary on his death reflects her feelings about his debt: "Alas I never liked him, and obviously he did not like himself." Still, murder worked its usual magic on her, and she couldn't help speculating about where Lévy might have killed himself, although his demise did not ameliorate for one moment the fact that he still owed her twelve thousand dollars. "He never signed the contract nor paid me anything, and all I know is he was very pleased with the first 44 pages."[27] Seeing Lévy in September of 1966 in Nice, where he'd intended to set *Deep Water,* did bring Pat one lasting benefit. She'd gone from Nice to Cagnes-sur-Mer to visit Annie Duveen, and it was at Duveen's house where she met Barbara Ker-Seymer and Barbara Roett for the first time.

In January of 1967 Pat, still looking for escape, accepted an invitation to sit on a jury judging short films at an international film festival in Montbazon, in the Touraine region of France. She drove from Paris to Tours, accompanied once again by Elizabeth Lyne—her need of old friends was obvious—and then she went on alone to Montbazon, where, amongst the French-Canadian, Japanese, Russian, Hungarian, and French panellists, the only member of the film jury she took a shine to was Slawomir Mrożek, the Polish playwright. He was as "surprised as I am at being here"—and he was "shy" and "silent." Pat couldn't bear the intellectual talk, the pretentious theorizing about film, or the competition. "What a lot of nonsense, all this communicating!" she wrote in her cahier, adding, "The atmosphere reminds me of Yaddo, but the ice will not be broken in the same way (and perhaps I am to blame, as much, too) because we are mostly older, more suspicious, more jealous of our (already gained) reputations."[28]

Pat had nothing to say about the festival films themselves, but the trip to France prepared her for her next big mistake: her three-month stay in the rented house on the estate in Fontainebleau—found for her by Elizabeth Lyne—and then her fatal move to Samois-sur-Seine in yet another double house which she and Mme Lyne would purchase together. But France was looking so much better to Pat than a loverless England, and the lack of self-esteem with which she began her twenty-eighth cahier was assuaged by the idea that someone actually wanted to share a home with her.

For the present, though, back at Bridge Cottage in Earl Soham in March of 1967, Pat was writing an article with a title that perfectly expressed her mood: "Writer's Block, Failure, and Depression."[29]

· 26 ·

LES GIRLS

PART 10

In her late forties, Pat began to rehearse the idea that photographs of women might be less damaging to her fantasies than the women themselves, and that her fantasies were more satisfying to her than any actual love life.

By November of 1969, Pat had a long list of personal failures to add up. There was her awful, protracted battle with Elizabeth Lyne in Samois-sur-Seine over their common house and property, and the bitter end of their twenty-year friendship. There was her "betrayal" by her inconstant French lover, Jacqui—the finish of her hopes for love with yet another woman who was "bad for her." There was the fact that her new neighbors on either side of her new house in Montmachoux were exuberant Portuguese Catholic families who made her want to kill. ("It gives me more terror, really, than any crime story ever did, to know that I have people left and right of me who believe in hell.")[1]

From the middle of her personal chaos, Pat wrote to Alex Szogyi in New York:

I am in love with the girl called Anne Meacham, whose picture appeared in MD magazine, as she is an actress in T[ennessee] Williams play IN THE BAR OF A TOKYO HOTEL. I have not seen such a face since I fell in love with Lynn Roth. . . . Do you know her? I would love to see her, just to say 'You look wonderful,' and then faint, or disappear. . . . If you know Miss Meacham, will you say I have lost my heart to her.[2]

Pat kept the torn-out photograph of Anne Meacham*—whom she never met, *refused* to meet by Alex Szogyi's account—for the rest of her life.[3] It is in her archives now, along with another arresting image clipped from a periodical: a photograph of Judy Holliday, looking entirely at ease in male attire and a stylish boy's haircut. The Holliday photograph is a still from *Adam's Rib* (George Cukor's brilliant comic film about the war between the sexes) depicting a scene in which a lawyer (played by Katharine Hepburn), trying to make a feminist point, asks a jury to look at the accused (played by Judy Holliday) as though she were a man. And briefly, before the jury's eyes, Judy Holliday turns into a man: haircut, suit, and attitude. Pat saw *Adam's Rib* in New York at the end of January 1950, with Elizabeth Lyne. Judy was "excellent" in the film, Pat thought.[4] She was right.

When Pat was sickening with love (literally) for the young German actress Tabea Blumenschein at the Berlin Film Festival in 1978, she made a little verse about her rules of attraction. It was more an admission about her feeling for photographs and disguise than about her feelings for the girl:

> *I fell in love not with flesh and blood,*
> *But with a picture:*
> *The sailor cap*
> *The crazy moustache . . .*[5]

Two weeks later, in a letter to Alex Szogyi, she explained how she'd met Tabea both in person and in the film made by Tabea's lover, Ulrike Ottinger, which starred Tabea.

"I fell in love with their film called 'The Infatuation of the Blue Sailors,' in which everyone's sex was reversed. T. played a sailor. . . . I have never even shaken hands with Tabea, I think. I look at her as a kind of 'picture.' It is very strange. I have the feeling that if I ever embraced her, she would fall to pieces. . . . I am afraid of getting a heart attack."[6]

By 1980, Pat was writing in her cahier: "It seems truly best to be in love with someone we cannot touch and do not profoundly know. One is always in love with an idea or an ideal."[7] And for the rest of that decade and into the early 1990s, Pat, says a friend, "carried around an accordion-pleated photo folder—many men have them—of young blond German girls dressed à la *The Night Porter*. [She told her amused friend]: "I send them books, I try to improve their minds."[8]

---

* Anne Meacham (1926–2006), was a friend of Tennessee Williams and a notable interpreter of his work on stage. She also appeared in Eva Le Gallienne's 1964 production of *The Seagull*.

Like Isabel Crane, the young woman in her short story "The Romantic," the death of whose invalid mother should have freed her to pursue her dreams of "real love," Pat chose to cling more and more to her fantasy life, preferring, as Isabel Crane finally did, her fantasies to whatever her "real" life could offer. Pat wrote "The Romantic" in 1984—or more likely she rewrote it then, because it has the mark of her 1940s Manhattan style. She completed the story by shutting the door on Isabel's Crane's sexual life, shortly after the door had been shut on her own.

Pat showed her photos of girls to everyone—even, in one unsettling instance (and between swigs of gin), to a journalist she didn't know during the course of an interview for a London paper.[9] Francis Wyndham remembers Pat displaying pictures of a "German girlfriend" (it was Tabea, but this was long after Pat's relations with Tabea had ceased) to him and Julian Jebb in London, "and she rather sort of boasted. It was so sweet, it was like a sailor on leave with a girlfriend back home. It was endearing in her."[10]

Julian Jebb, journalist, television producer, and the grandson of Hilaire Belloc, made friends with Pat when he went to film her during her unfortunate performance as president of the film jury at the Berlin Film Festival in 1978. (See "A Simple Act of Forgery: Part 1." Six years later, Pat and Francis Wyndham were exchanging letters about Jebb's suicide.)[11] In Berlin, Jebb had been as interested in the heavily made-up Turkish child prostitutes of Kreuzberg as Pat was, and he photographed her amongst the fish tanks in the basement aquarium at the Tiergarten for a BBC documentary that was never completed. Jebb's next-best-known work—perhaps not unrelated to his interest in Pat—was a spoof-documentary about Dame Edna Everage, featuring Barry Humphries dressed up in his elaborate drag as Dame Edna. It was Julian Jebb who loaned Pat his apartment in Chelsea for a London tryst with Tabea Blumenschein.

While Tabea and Pat were staying in Jebb's flat, they went out one night drinking at the Gateways. There, Pat was approached by a young Austrian woman, Linda, who had recognized Pat's face from publicity photographs. Linda and Pat struck up a conversation, and Linda drove Pat and Tabea back to Jebb's apartment. They invited her in for a drink. Tabea, she thought, was "rather beautiful"; she had "some grace to her," and Pat wanted Linda to speak German with Tabea because Pat's own German was so awkward. Linda noticed a film poster with Tabea's picture on it and a whole sketchbook full of Pat's drawings of Tabea in the flat.

As Linda and Tabea were chatting in German, Pat kept making more fast sketches of Tabea, trying to get her down on paper. When Pat went to the bathroom, Linda asked Tabea: "But what do you see in her, she's so much older?"

Linda "found it rather strange because Tabea was so very young. . . . [Still, I had the sense that] Tabea was somehow attracted by Patricia, though what she said to me was: 'You know, Patricia is buying me clothes, she's inviting me, and I let her.' The impression she wanted to give me, and she was without shame about it, was that she was in it for what she could get." Later, Pat told Linda that "Tabea was a fan and had written to her first."[12] (Tabea herself thinks Pat first took an interest in her because Pat wanted to sell her books to film and Tabea was in film.)[13] Perhaps Tabea and Pat were both playing a little with the truth. And perhaps Pat was remembering the furious remark Lil Picard had "bitterly hurled" at her in 1949: that she'd better get someone to keep her in Europe (she did: Ellen Hill) because, after fifty, she would have "to buy" her lovers.[14] In any event, Tabea was Pat's last real erotic obsession—and her last experience of the kind of misery her interpretation of Courtly Love required.

If it did nothing else, Pat's short, fantastical affair with Tabea Blumenschein seems to have persuaded her sophisticated friend Barbara Ker-Seymer of something. Ker-Seymer wrote to her own long-term lover Barbara Roett about it.

"I have been inundated with letters from Pat. She seems to feel I am the only person who truly 'understands' Tabea and her feelings for her. What interests me is that Pat does seem to have a heart after all. I always thought she was completely without one."[15]

In October of 1992, Pat, on a trip to North America that included a stay with Dan and Florine Coates at Box Canyon Ranch in Weatherford, Texas, a reading at the Harbourfront festival in Toronto, and some appearances in Manhattan for *Ripley Under Water,* made a three-day visit to Marijane Meaker in East Hampton, New York. It was the first time the two women had seen each other in twenty-seven years, although they had begun to correspond two or three years before. Pat initiated this exchange, even as she was telling other people that Marijane had written to her first. To Marijane's house in East Hampton, Pat brought pictures of her own "very severe-appearing, fort-like house" in Tegna and of a "smiling, pretty" German girl (Tabea again), which she seemed anxious to show off.

"'If I had to choose between the girl and the house, I'd choose the house,' Pat said," after passing the photos to a roomful of Marijane's friends and colleagues. The women laughed along with her.[16] By now, Pat had travelled a long way from her youthful dreams of romantic love. Real estate and the pressing question of what she should do with her money were to be the major excitements and irritations of her last years.

According to Marijane Meaker, their three-day visit was marked by Pat's constant drinking and what was, by now, her stock parade of prejudices. Like a vaudeville Nazi, Pat reacted to every ethnic minority she saw. The sight of black people eating in a local restaurant—something she said she wasn't accustomed to in her small Swiss village—set her off on a series of remarks about blacks: how they were incapable of figuring out that sexual intercourse leads to pregnancy; how improvident they were with money; how black men got physically ill if they didn't have intercourse "many times a month." Jews brought on a stronger reaction, and with a compulsion that continued to be personal and uncontrollable rather than political and rational, she inveighed constantly against the State of Israel and against the "Jews," never referring to the citizens of Israel as "Israelis."

"The yids," Pat told Marijane, were responsible for banning the ham sandwiches she used to enjoy so much on first-class airplane flights. She inquired of her hostess if "your Jewish friends dance the holly, holly cost?" The picture she painted of racial attitudes in the Ticino, the canton of Switzerland she'd lived in since she moved to Switzerland in the early 1980s, was so extreme that Meaker just had to ask: "Do you live in some little Nazi coven?"[17]

Two years before Pat's visit to Meaker, in August of 1990, a similar outburst from Pat had occurred. Only this time, uncharacteristically, Pat tried to publish her prejudices. Christa Maerker, the German writer and filmmaker who had suggested Pat for the jury of the Berlin Film Festival in 1978, tells the story:

"There was a series on German radio called *Impossible Interviews,* which the German station [Südwestrundfunk] had taken from an original Italian idea, where very famous writers did twenty-minute radio plays. You were allowed to interview in imagination anyone who is dead. I think Pat was declaring poverty at the time so I suggested she write one. 'It's not much money,' I said, 'but it's very fast. You can write it in no time. A person you think you know very well.'

"Pat interviewed [in imagination] somebody in Israel who was still alive at the time. [It was Yitzhak Shamir.] Out of her came something so ghastly that it could be a Nazi text."

What Pat wrote was an eleven-page "radio play" with two characters and one line of action: Patricia Highsmith interrogating a highly caricatured Yitzhak Shamir—at that time prime minister of Israel—about the future of his country. Even allowing for Pat's loathing of Shamir's policies and militant Zionist background, it is an irrational work, poisoned by ethnic prejudices. It reads like a lost chapter from that toxic anthology of anti-Semitic canards, *The Protocols of the Elders of Zion,* and the fact that Pat thought that the Germans—the only people in Europe who have grappled seriously with the ethical history of their country—would be receptive to broadcasting her "interview" is another example of how disconnected she was from anything except the ends of her own nerves.

Pat's unwavering line throughout her script is that the "Jews"—she makes an exception for Amos Oz, whom she suggests will soon be murdered by Shamir's government—are desperate to provoke another Holocaust because of the Holocaust's invaluable fund-raising properties for Israel. Pat's last comments to Shamir, in her role of Interviewer, are: "You seem to be courting another Holocaust. . . . as *you* might say, we'll hold back Holocaust Number Two out of sheer anti-semitism."[18]

The commissioning editor at the radio station was horrified by what Pat had produced, and Christa Maerker—still, she says, unable to accept the fact that Pat could actually *mean* this "disgusting text"—went to talk to the radio station about it. "And the head of the radio station said, 'Good grief! What did you do to me!' It was like [Wolf] Donner and the [Berlin] Film Festival. 'If I publish this, Patricia Highsmith will be dead in Europe.'

"And I said, 'She must have misunderstood me. If I talk to her she could rewrite it.' And he said: 'Do what you please.' So I called Pat and said, 'Would you like me to come and help you retype it?' Lying, instead of saying, 'How dare you write something like this!' I think I always lied to her; I didn't want to disturb her by such primitive notions as my offended sensibility. It's a motherly instinct."

Pat thought Christa's coming to help "type" the document would be a "wonderful idea," so Christa went to Pat's new house in Tegna a week before the opening of the Locarno Film Festival, which, anyway, she always attended in her capacity as a film journalist. When Christa rang the bell, Pat "opened the door and walked away without a word," vanishing into her bedroom to putter around. Christa stood "like a good girl with my suitcase" until Pat came out again and showed her to her room in the guest wing, which, because the house, with its inevitable double wings, was shaped like a U, was as far as possible from Pat's own bedroom.

"While I was looking at cassettes [French telefilms of Pat's short stories] I put some lotion on my arm because I sunburned it hanging out the window while I was driving to Tegna, and, out of the blue—she was able to do this without you hearing her—Pat was standing next to me. You didn't hear her coming. And she said: 'My cat hates your perfume!'

"So I thought, poor Charlotte. And THEN I thought, wait a minute, that cat can't talk. WHO hates my perfume? Pat does. So I said, 'I'm terribly sorry' and went into the guest room and took a shower. And then, suddenly, she's outside the shower door, saying sternly: 'We have to save water.'

"I should have left the next minute.

"Whenever I said, 'Let's talk about the radio play,' she'd say,'Where's Charlotte, where's Charlotte?' The cat had something evil, I thought. If the Hubers had not been there, I would not have been able to bear it. I had promised to come and help her and I insisted on doing it. Of course, we never ever touched the radio play, we never talked about it."

But Pat, in her own provocative way, had already tried to raise one of the subjects of this "interview" with Christa Maerker—from an opposite angle, some years before she wrote the radio version. When Maerker visited Pat in her Aurigeno house in the mid-1980s, she discovered that sometime during their first evening Pat had taken a ballpoint pen and printed a line of numbers on her arm, numbers that were meant to suggest something obvious to a citizen of Germany who had lived through the Second World War.

"I was too shocked to talk about it. Why the numbers on her arm? She wanted to see how a 'Nazi' descendant would respond to [a concentration camp number]. . . . I always thought she was testing me, not just me, but anybody to find out how they react to extreme situations."

When Christa Maerker finally left Pat's house in Tegna she "sang all the way to Locarno. It was as though I left a jail. . . . When I went to my hotel, there was a hand-delivered letter from Pat. . . . She'd written to thank me for being such a good guest. . . . She was aware of how horribly she behaved. . . . In the end . . . I couldn't honestly understand; I'd started to read her short stories and got into the emotions in them and I was unable to judge anything anymore."[19]

A late-life friend of Pat, a young writer in New York at the time she first met Pat, described another unforgettable encounter, as funny as it was awful, during which Pat's ethnic views were once again on parade. On one of Pat's trips to New York from Switzerland—Pat's friend thinks it was in 1990*—Pat asked if they could meet at the lesbian bar Pat had liked to go to when she was younger. The bar was the Duchess, a decades-old lesbian establishment in Sheridan Square, in the heart of Greenwich Village, which had just reopened as the Duchess 2. It was now, unbeknownst to Pat, "basically a black butch bar."

Pat wanted to bring "an old college chum" with her (it turned out to be Kingsley).

"So I said, 'Fine, I'd like to bring my friend Barbara.' Who was a poet and an admirer of some of Pat's work. And Pat said that was fine."

---

* Nineteen ninety was also the year Pat received a letter from a man in Bradford, England, enclosing a picture of his paternal grandfather, Henry Highsmith, a black man born in South Carolina. The Bradford man wondered whether he and Pat were related. Pat's answer made it clear that Stanley Highsmith was not only not her blood relative but that he had no black or "Red Indian" blood.

"And I said to Barbara, who was a Jew, 'Now look, I've told you about Pat, about how she talks.' And she said, 'That's all right, you don't have to mention that I'm Jewish.' But I warned her that there was hardly a conversation that went by without Pat mentioning Jews; it was an obsession. Pat took the subway to Sheridan Square—I didn't know at that time that Pat was too cheap to take a cab—and I thought the friend would be some lesbian friend from college and there was Kingsley! This elderly heterosexual lady with a purse. And I thought, 'Good Lord, what a strange pair to take into the Duchess 2!' But go we did.

"You have to fight though this long narrow bar, a crowd of mostly black women, to get to the postage-stamp-sized tables in the rear. And we finally make it and Pat is very silent and she's arranging herself, and she says, 'Well at least we made it through *THAT*!' And I thought I'm not even going to *TRY* to imagine what she means by that. And there's Kingsley sort of looking around, and we ordered some drinks.

"And Pat said, 'Well yes, this is quite a *BIT* different from when I used to go here.' And there are these big musclely black girls bumping and grinding on the tiny dance floor.

"And Kingsley says, 'I've never been to a place quite like this.' And then Pat said, sipping at her drink, 'Well, there certainly are a lot of blacks in here.' And I said, 'Yes, it tends to be frequented by mostly black women.' 'Well,' she said, 'at least there are not a lot of Jews around.' With that Barbara looked at her and said: 'Excuse me, but I'm a Jew.' And Pat, not missing a beat, shot back, 'Well, you don't *LOOK* like one.'

"I don't know how we made it through the evening. Barbara just went back to her drink. Kingsley was completely out of it. . . .

"For someone who was very perceptive, Pat misread an awful lot of signs. And so she'd test the waters a great deal, 'Well, you know the Holocaust' . . .

"I was convinced it was personal, I thought her father might be a Jew. I wondered who the Jew was, who set her off."[20]

Thirty years before, in 1957, Pat had been thinking quite different thoughts about the Jews: "This afternoon I awakened from a nap, thought suddenly of the German atrocities against the Jewish people, and had a strange feeling that it hadn't happened, that it was impossible—and then—knowing it had happened—that it was more horrible, more bestial than the most eloquent describer has yet said."[21]

And in 1959, during the year she was singing in the Presbyterian church choir in Palisades, New York, Pat's understanding of what good relations on Earth required was still intact. "All the misery on the earth is caused by the indifference of the better off toward those with less. Not only in economics, but in personal misfortunes—so much easier to bear, if there are friends or strangers who show that they care what happens. With this, there is no bitter-ness, no cursing against God, no resentful attacks against one's fellowman. No revolutions."[22]

But by the 1980s, Pat had moved as far from her early ideals of World Peace as she had from her youthful dreams of Courtly Love. The hopes she'd been giving voice to in her thirties came from a—by now—mostly unrecognizable Patricia Highsmith.

27

LES GIRLS

PART II

Pat's nights were often more emotionally telling than her days, and many of the love-dreams she recorded were deep fantasies of killing or being murdered or maimed by Mother Mary, or committing unspeakable acts in Mary's presence, in Mary's stead, or in Mary's bed. Occasionally, Mary did the dream murders *for* Pat, as in a night dream of 1984 in which Mary, "in Lady Macbeth murderous mood," beheaded Pat's young German lover, Tabea Blumenschein, and then "coated the head with transparent wax, thoroughly."[1] (Even asleep, Pat could produce devilish details; that "thoroughly" is masterful.)

At night—*especially* at night—Pat had trouble separating her psyche from her mother's. And sometimes she thickened the nocturnal brew with a grandmother figure and a plot point borrowed from her favorite Dostoyevsky novel, *Crime and Punishment*—as she did in this winter dream of 1961:

> A dream: that I murdered an old lady with an axe, this was just before Christmas. The murder was motiveless. The police went directly to me and charged me. . . . the bulk of it was my imagining my friends . . . thinking P.H.! Could it be! How shocking and horrible!! Because the very next day, before Christmas, the story was in all the newspapers. It was . . . a deep fear that I might some day do this. In a fit of drunkenness or anger. But the victim in my dream was unknown to me.[2]

Many of Pat's dreams were infused with guilt, shame, fear of exposure, and feelings at war with each other. "Just as there is no jealousy without love, there is no hate without fear and mistrust," Pat had written in college. "Emotions run in pairs—like smoke and fire."[3] But her own emotions ran in pairs that contradicted each other.

In most Highsmith fictions, the attractions and repulsions of love—the moment when an urgent embrace becomes an overwhelming desire to strangle—are twisted up in the braid of character. Love and hatred pull together, pull each other apart, and share the same nervous system. This crosscutting of love and hatred—the critic Susannah Clapp calls it "an extraordinary loop of abhorrence and attraction"[4]—which kept the young Pat so busy recording her high school crushes and aversions, wreaked a predictable havoc on her love life. Most of her adult sexual affairs, in flesh or in fantasy, were electrified by violent and contradictory feelings: their landscapes look like war zones. Many of her lovers emerged from these couplings telling tales more closely associated with bombed-out buildings than with burning desires.

Pat herself felt blasted by love, annihilated by it—"It is just like firing a pistol in my face," she said of her love for Caroline Besterman[5]—and the higher she built her love castles, the harder they fell on her, always.

In 1963, newly in love with Caroline, Pat, tempting the Fates (who must have licked their lips in awful anticipation), set down in her cahier these ecstatic phrases: "Up, pipers! I am in love with a most wonderful woman. I am saved. Look me up in ten or twenty years, and see."[6]

I did look her up.

Ten years later, alone in her house by the Loing Canal in Moncourt, Pat was making it her painful duty to add to the list of Major Flaws she had uncovered in the character of that "most wonderful woman," the former love of her life, Caroline Besterman. And she was taking notes for a collection of stories whose bitter inspiration was her separation from Caroline. Pat gave the collection a provisional title: *Further Tales of Misogyny* (with stories named "The Fully-Licensed Whore, or the Wife," "The Prude," "The Gossip," "The Mother-in-Law," "The Breeder," "The Middle-Class Housewife").[7] It was a continuation of a series of stories about women she'd begun in 1969 after she and Caroline had broken up. In 1977, the entire collection was published as *Little Tales of Misogyny.*

Each "tale" in *Misogyny* indulges Pat's mania for classification by exploring the horrors of a certain "type" of woman. Together, these poisonous little pills constitute as enraged an assault on the female gender as the one launched in 1558 by the Scots Calvinist preacher John Knox in his jeremiad *The First Blast of the Trumpet Against the Monstrous Regiment of Women.*[8]

Little Tales of Misogyny was first brought out—this was no coincidence; Pat was exercised on the subject—during the decade in which the Second Wave of

Feminism, the International Women's Movement, had begun its attack on the world's patriarchal structures. *Misogyny's* reviews were mixed, to put it mildly. But it was praised in England, and in France it won Pat and her inspired illustrator, Roland Topor, an important award in 1977: Le Grand Prix de l'Humeur Noir.

When she was twenty-two, Pat had written this in her cahier: "Basically, the reason I don't like men homosexuals is because we . . . disagree. *Women,* not men, are the most exciting and wonderful creations on the earth—and masculine homosexuals are mistaken and wrong!"[9]

Three decades and many painfully ended love affairs with women later, Pat seems to have changed her mind.

In a long article in *The New York Review of Books* on Highsmith in 2001, Joyce Carol Oates detected a "gleeful" tone in a posthumous publication of the stories in *Little Tales of Misogyny* "which Highsmith may have intended as satires of female types, savage in the way of Rabelais or Swift." But, continued Ms. Oates, "these sadistic sketches [are] heavy-handed in sarcasm and virtually devoid of literary significance. . . .

"Highsmith seems to have had little patience, had perhaps little natural skill, for the short story. . . . there is no subtext, only surface; it's as if she conceived of the form as basically a gimmick . . . set to explode in the reader's face in its final lines."[10]

Like some of her more gruesome tales—"Woodrow Wilson's Necktie" and the genuinely terrifying "The Yuma Baby," aka "The Empty Birdhouse"*— the stories in *Little Tales of Misogyny* kept Pat in fits of helpless laughter as she was writing and reading them. "I laugh myself onto the floor. . . . Thus I approach the real joy of a writer . . . amusing other people," she wrote happily to Alex Szogyi in 1969 about "Woodrow Wilson's Necktie,"[11] a story in which an assistant in a wax museum busies himself with murdering the customers and then arranges them in waxy poses on the museum premises. "Woodrow Wilson's Necktie" has many implications—but none of them are funny.†

Still, with *Little Tales of Misogyny,* it was herself Pat was amusing first—and for strictly private reasons.

---

* Pat said she had to rewrite "The Yuma Baby" because the first version was depressing her. The second version—a horror story for any other reader—kept Pat laughing happily as she wrote.
† By contrast, Pat's reading and writing of "Chorus Girl's Absolutely Final Performance" in 1973, a short fiction in *The Animal-Lover's Book of Beastly Murder,* her book of stories about the suffering (and revenge) of animals, provoked an opposite response: "I wrote . . . Chorus Girl's Absolutely Final Performance, which is my elephant story [and] I had to read the thing five times, 5th time being proof-reading, and everytime tears were coming down my cheeks, so I hope it does not affect every reader like this" (PH letter to Barbara Ker-Seymer, 3 June 1973).

Daniel Keel, who first published *Little Tales of Misogyny* in German with Roland Topor's expressive illustrations (Pat had suggested Edward Gorey or David Hockney as illustrators), says that Pat had *"galgen* [gallows] humor and it's the humor of someone who is going to be hanged.

"It comes to my mind that she didn't understand irony—and I like irony like pepper and salt in a conversation. She was too literal for irony. She was too mistrustful for irony—she was irritated at ironic comments and she would say: 'Do you really mean that? What do you mean?' . . . There are several floors you have to be on for irony."[12]

One of the *Misogyny* stories, Keel says, presented a "recognizable" portrait of a woman who was "a very good friend of [Keel and his wife, Anna].

"I told Pat: 'Do you know [this woman] so well that you can portray her in these details?' Pat didn't care; she wanted it published. She could have said if it's a friend of yours, I'll cut it out, but she didn't."[13]

Even Kingsley Skattebol says that "broad and crude" is as "good a characterization as any" of Pat's sense of humor.[14]

Marion Aboudaram thought that Pat did have "a sense of humor, she could be funny"; but her humor was colloquial. It was like some of Pat's fictional work, pitched rather lower than it should have been. "She had no class, but she had distinction," says Marion, making an interesting distinction herself.[15]

There had always been something strange about Pat Highsmith's sense of humor. Its physical expression—her laughter—escaped from her like a rough beast bursting the bars of its cage. Friends and acquaintances have to search their vocabularies to find terms extreme enough to describe the sound of Pat's laughter: it was a "hoot," a "chortle," a "guffaw," "thigh-slapping," "a scream," "loud and uncontrolled," "reckless"[16]—and, as in the novels of Dostoyevsky (and as in Pat's own fictions), it often came in situations in which other people would have recoiled in horror or collapsed in tears.

Her agent for almost two decades, Patricia Schartle Myer, writes:

> The only time I ever heard Highsmith laugh was when we were passing one of those huge posters by subway stations: this one of a couple of children out of a concentration camp. Some creep had even further degraded the children by gouging their eyes out. Highsmith burst into laughter. There was a very dark side that undoubtedly gave an edge to her writing but it lacked humanity.[17]

Jonathan Kent, the British actor and director who says he was "formed" in childhood by seeing Alain Delon in *Purple Noon* (the French film version of *The Talented Mr. Ripley*) and then by reading everything Highsmith ever wrote, visited Pat at her house in Aurigeno in December of 1982, three months after he appeared as Ripley on the British television program *The South Bank Show.* He and Pat had done the show together—it was devoted to Pat's work—and Pat was so pleased by his performance that she wrote to her French editor, Alain Oulman, that Jonathan Kent was "the best Ripley I have seen since Alain Delon."[18]

Kent, who was especially sensitive to Pat's own sensitivities, says that the story of their meeting published in a previous biography—that before Kent had been introduced to Pat she had caught him secretly "stalking" her on their director's orders, backed him angrily up against a wall, and put her hands around his throat—is "not at all the way it occurred. The real, plain truth is that we met first and we set up the shots and she knew I would be trailing her. She didn't back me up against a wall; she would *never* have done that."[19]

Pat and Jonathan Kent occupied adjoining suites at the Savoy Hotel during the filming of *The South Bank Show,* and Kent says that he "could have gone on *Mastermind,* on *The $64,000 Question,* about her; I could have majored in her." And Pat "loved" Jonathan's encyclopedic knowledge of her work, "as much," he says, "as you could ever tell if Pat loved anything. You know, she'd sneak sly looks at you out of the corner of her eye and she would laugh."[20]

For the benefit of such a guest—a handsome young male actor who had just played Ripley to her great satisfaction and who told her he was "formed" by her work—Pat was unusually accommodating. (Perhaps the fact that his surname—Kent—echoed the maiden name of her one of her muses, Virginia Kent Catherwood, had something to do with Pat's reception.) She picked up some chicken nuggets for lunch at the local Kentucky Fried Chicken equivalent—her idea of a feast—and jacked the house heat up so high that one of her cats "sucked all the fur off its tail." Kent's room was so hot that he had to sleep with his windows wide open to the Swiss winter, and he could hear the BBC World Service playing in Pat's room—she slept, as always when without a lover, in her workroom—in the early hours of the morning.

Undisturbed by her habits and feeling quite close to Pat—"I found her completely restful to be with," he says—Kent wanted to offer her something from his own history: a family story, "something I was rather saddened by." So he told her something about his maternal grandmother, who had Alzheimer's "and didn't know who anybody was." One day, his mother took a bunch of daffodils to the old lady. She thought they "were an army coming to get her" and promptly ate their heads off. When Kent related the story to Pat, "she screamed with laughter.

"She made me tell it twice more. And then we went out to lunch with Ellen Hill and she made me tell it again. And every time I told it she screamed with laughter. She had a very odd sense of humor. But I didn't mind because I liked her so much."[21]

Peter Huber, Pat's next-door neighbor in Tegna and the friend who was initially responsible for her move there, repeated the little joke that was Pat's favorite when she was living in her last house in Switzerland. It is called "The Japanese Wife Joke." Pat told it over and over, Huber says, and it sent her into gales of "helpless laughter." It goes like this:

"A Japanese gentleman invited his boss to his home. He instructed his wife exactly how to conduct the evening. And it was a lovely evening, the food was good, the conversation interesting, all went well. When the boss left, the wife made a deep bow before him and at that moment, her self-control escaped her: she broke wind. And everyone went on smiling and ignored the accident.

"When the husband came back into the house after seeing the boss off, he smiled at his wife, took out a sword, and cut her head off.

"She liked that joke so much," said Peter Huber. "That's why I'm telling it to you."[22]

Caroline Besterman loathed *Little Tales of Misogyny* and said plainly to Pat that publishing the stories would be a mistake. Pat noted coolly that Caroline had always found "my misogyny . . . one of my less endearing qualities."[23] Like Djuna Barnes, Pat was capable of writing both "for" and "against" women; but unlike Barnes, who started out with the physical revulsions of *The Book of Repulsive Women* (1915) and then went on to publish her own harrowing lesbian love story in *Nightwood* (1936), Pat began with the more or less romantically balanced power plays of *The Price of Salt* (1952) and went on to the corrosive loathings of *Little Tales of Misogyny* (1977).

Eight years before she'd met Caroline, in her amorous spring and summer of 1954 in New York City, Pat had been in a more accepting mood: "The three women I have loved most intensely in my life have been the only ones of all my amours who were definitely 'bad for me.' J[oan] S[,] G[inny] C[atherwood], E[llen] H[ill]."[24]

The reason these women were "bad" for Pat—it is plain to see in what she wrote in her diary after falling in love with Ellen Hill—was also the reason they were "good" for her: her love for them continued to be partnered by murderous rage and ideas of death. "This ferocious strife between people in love, this clash of arms between the placing of a clock upon the bed-table . . . two people in love . . . bewildered as modern armies fighting with each other."[25]

In Barbara Ker-Seymer's house in Islington in 1968, to which, says Barbara Roett, Pat had brought Madeleine Harmsworth, the young journalist who had come to interview Pat in Montmachoux and stayed on to become a lover,

"Pat would come in, dial something on the phone, and we'd hear the answer-phone saying, 'So and so isn't in, would you please leave a message,' and she'd have a long, made-up conversation with the person and then she'd close the door. And then she'd open it and suddenly say, 'You can stuff it!' . . . Madeleine was there as her guest, [and] Pat's idea of interesting her was to be as dismissive as possible and to . . . telephone supposed lovers which she didn't have."[26]

Ker-Seymer remained "amused" by Pat, perhaps because most of her friends from the 1920s—friends like Nancy Cunard, Brian Howard, and Dolly Wilde (with whom Ker-Seymer used to waltz around Dolly's parlor flat to the strains of a gramophone)—could have matched Pat's eccentric behavior with no effort at all.[27] But even those notorious hell-raisers would never have thought to do what Pat did when the two Barbaras arrived in Moncourt for a visit in the early 1970s.

"We were given a lovely bedroom and we opened some French windows to the garden and Barbara [Ker-Seymer] gave out a piercing scream. And when I ran in there was a dead rat that had been thrown in the window. This was Pat's idea of a joke. So I threw it back out, narrowly missing her. That's how strange she was."[28]

Pat's frequent greeting to the novelist Marion Aboudaram (Marion's two novels were written under her two first names, Dominique Marion), her lover after Madeleine Harmsworth, would be judged an unusual welcome from anyone. Marion was the woman to whom Pat had dedicated *Edith's Diary* ("Pat," says Marion, "couldn't think of anyone to dedicate *Edith* to and so I said why don't you dedicate it to me?"),[29] and she took the suburban train from Paris to Moncourt every weekend to be with Pat from 1976 to 1978. Pat used to meet Marion at the door and then brusquely strip her of her clothes. Not for sexual purposes, Marion says, but for a kind of complicated, cleansing-by-hand ritual that seemed to be wreathed in anger, guilt, and expiation.

"She washed my clothes all the time. When I came in she took off my rain-coat, my trousers, I found myself in a bathing suit and she put the clothes in the bathtub and washed them. She did not even have a washing machine. And she washed her hands all the time and she took two showers a day."[30]

"I should have just stayed one month with Pat. We were together three years—it's ridiculous—but just on weekends. But she phoned me every day, she wrote to me every day, very boring letters. . . . The price of the char, the price of carrots, that's all she ever talked about."[31]

For presents, Pat gave Marion a broom and a vacuum cleaner, but not the radiator Marion had hoped to get for her unheated studio in Montmartre. " 'Put a hot water bottle between your legs,' Pat said. 'That's what I used to do in New York.'" But Marion also remembered how relaxed Pat could be, drinking and smoking and lounging in her garden shed, and how Pat made a tiny wooden boat for the little frog in her backyard to sail on. "Dorothy," Pat called the frog charmingly as she set the amphibian asail on its new craft—although Dorothy's response to suddenly becoming the pilot of a small boat remains unrecorded.

"We laughed a lot," Marion says, "but underneath it, I was anxious because she was such an alcoholic. She used to say to me, 'Poor dear, you're married to an alcoholic.'"[32] And while Pat's written invitations to Marion were humorous, they were also as literal as her other letters. Pat wrote: "Bring your ass and your typewriter but especially your ass."[33]

Marion is still laughing about one invitation she received from Pat. "I'm Jewish and you know I hate Germany because of that. [Pat knew this.] And the only place Pat ever invited me to go was Germany! Her translator in Hamburg, a nice old lady [Anne Uhde], invited Pat, and Pat invited me.

"Germany! The *only* place in three years Pat ever suggested we go together! And Pat cried and cried but of course I wouldn't go."[34]

Francis Wyndham, himself a writer of perceptive fiction, whose brilliant review of *The Cry of the Owl* in the *New Statesman* in 1963 included the first serious analysis of Highsmith's work in the United Kingdom* (he dispensed with the idea that Highsmith was a crime writer; "[g]uilt is her theme," he wrote),[35] says he always found Pat "companionable" and "comfortable" to be with, "without a writer's ego and without a writer's front."[36] But he remembered an anomalous evening when he and Pat went to dinner with one of his colleagues at the *Sunday Times,* a "totally heterosexual" woman, and "Pat did something I've seen sometimes with male gays, a kind of aggression towards the woman. And M. didn't care, but in the end I was rather embarrassed. . . . And then I suddenly realized it was an attraction on Pat's part. It wasn't obvious. It was some kind of aggression towards somebody she'd quite like to get off with. Maybe she'd tried and M. hadn't responded and I hadn't noticed."[37]

Even Pat's love for her cats—often counted as her longest and most successful emotional connection—could bristle with aggression.

At twenty-four, alone in her East Fifty-sixth Street Manhattan studio in September of 1945 with a cat in full estrus, Pat coolly set down in her cahier her violent response to living with an animal in heat.

The contortions themselves, the rolling on the floor, the oddly arched
back while the legs are gathered tautly beneath, are enough to make the

---

* Maurice Richardson wrote first about Pat's work in *The Observer* in 1957.

owner gape, not recognizing her at all . . . wails, bellows, growls . . . The writer cannot concentrate in daytime. . . .

One is reminded of the aggression of the female but this is so obvious it need not be dwelt on. . . .

Interesting to see how soon masochism sets in. In a fit of temper, one may throw her half across a room, slam her on the floor, half throttle her, and she maintains the same expression of stolid, uncomprehending blind obedience to nature's will.[38]

And Peter Huber remembers that in the late 1980s and 1990s in Tegna "Pat's routine way of showing affection to her cats was holding the back of her fist in front of the animals' noses (at a distance of about ten inches)."[39]

A visit to Moncourt in 1974 by the German filmmaker Wim Wenders and the Austrian writer Peter Handke resulted in a penetrating article by Handke about Pat. It ends with this vignette:

A picture of her: One dismal afternoon ("dusk came quickly" is a recurrent phrase in almost all her novels), detained too long, hunched in her large, very cold Moncourt living-room, she starts to walk up and down, hands clasped behind her, stretching only when she has to sneeze occasionally, and at one point she grabs the whining cat by the neck and (as if suffocated by the presence of a stranger) almost wringing it, only to carefully set the creature down somewhere else.[40]

And in Moncourt in the summer of 1971, the two Barbaras from Islington watched in disbelief as Pat, who, as Barbara Roett says, "was really concerned about her cat," picked up her chocolate point Siamese Semyon (the same cat Frédérique Chambrelent saw obsessively chasing its tail whenever she came to visit), and "put it in a tea cloth, this poor crazed, terrified animal. And she swung it round and round the room. And I said: 'Pat, put that cat down!' And she said, 'Na-ow, he loves it.'

"That was her way, her hack-handed way, like a small boy, of showing notice to an animal. . . . She was isolated to a really appalling degree."[41]

In a letter written to Kingsley in October of 1953 when she was still trailing Ellen Hill around Europe, Pat provided a rationale for her *douleurs d'amour.* It is only a rationale (and not a reason), but it shows how historically and psychologically alert Pat could be to the collisions caused by her criss-crossed desires—and how fatalistically she always gave in to them. (*Criss Cross* was one of her first titles for *Strangers on a Train*.)

"The horrible flaw in my make-up is that I never cared for the artistic type like myself, so that sooner or later . . . there is a shipwreck. A fundamental incompatibility."[42]

Pat Highsmith really did live her love life—and most of the rest of her life as well—upside down ("sideways" was another explanation she offered in 1947 in her perfectly pitched "Dialogue Between My Mother and Myself": "sideways is the only way the world can be looked at in true perspective")[43] and doubled over with ambivalence. She was usually unhappier about being happy than she was about being unhappy.

Put it another way: even when Highsmith was desperately unhappy, she wasn't all that unhappy about *being* unhappy—as long as she could write about it.

28

LES GIRLS

In the fall of 1973, a month before she turned her mind to listing those small crimes for "Little Tots" (see "How to Begin: Part 1"), Pat was in London visiting Caroline Besterman, about whom she was still entertaining some rather complicated fantasies and resentments. She distracted herself with alternate futures: the hope that "one can be happy (and happier) alone" and the illusion that "I would be a fool not to be patient for another year in view of the fact that I've sunk eleven years into this."[1]

Once again Pat was keeping another list (and checking it twice) of Caroline's imagined "campaign" against her of more than a decade ago (when they were still lovers) and she noted, matter-of-factly, that Caroline was "now without a buffer state"; her borders were undefended. And Pat was enlisting support from old friends like Arthur Koestler in this long-past love affair's long-lost battles. For Pat, Mars would *always* be in bed with Venus—and making war was the natural concomitant to making love.

When she wrote out her list for "Little Tots" in the middle of November 1973, Pat had just returned from a four-day sojourn at the Hotel Europa in Zurich (the hotel matchbooks are in her desk drawer), making publicity appearances for her Swiss publisher, Diogenes Verlag. In Zurich, she signed books; read from her newly published collection of short stories, *The Snail-Watcher*, in English and German; and lunched several times at the Kronenhalle, where James Joyce used to eat—noting with characteristic precision that Joyce's personal waitress, Emma, was still there, but was now "on part-time duty."

It always takes her "3 or 4 days to quiet down" from a publicity tour—about as long as it takes her to quiet down from receiving a letter from Mother Mary. And she's nervous, too, because she expects to go back to London in

December for a medical test. One of the reasons she made that little list of unobtrusive ways in which children could murder their parents was because it helped to settle her nerves.

Here in Moncourt, in the *hameau*, her isolation is feverishly populated: filled with the writing of gossipy letters, the unexpected ringing of the telephone, the ultimately unwelcome (though usually invited) visitors, and the society of her next-door neighbors, the Anglo-Irish writer-translator couple Desmond and Mary Ryan, with whom she spends so much time socializing— and about whom she will later spend so much time complaining. The Ryans' daughter Juliette, who grew up with Pat next door, still lives in her parents' house. Juliette Ryan always found Pat "very intelligent . . . a great woman." Pat, she said, finally got "fed up" with keeping snails as pets (she'd been travelling with her snails since the 1940s) and "let them loose in the garden, and somehow, many ended in our garden."

And so, to this day, descendants of Patricia Highsmith's original snails are busily reproducing themselves in a *hameau* in suburban France. And whenever Juliette Ryan finds a "Highsmith snail" in her garden she throws it back over the wall onto "Pat's property."[2] But Pat would probably have told her not to bother. In one of the tenderest fictional evocations of lovemaking Pat Highsmith ever wrote (characteristically, the scene takes place between the two snails in *Deep Water,* a novel of extreme psychological violence), the book's central psychopath, Vic Van Allen, hovering over his mating snails Edgar and Hortense, remembers "the sentence in one of Henri Fabre's books about snails crossing garden walls to find their mates, and though Vic had never verified it by his own experiment, he felt it must be so."[3]

The legend, much circulated by French, English, and German journalists (with serious support from Pat), that Pat is a "recluse" in Moncourt because she lives privately, is nonsense. Juliette Ryan remembers:

"Pat would come over just about every night to drink when she finished her workday and she'd stay and stay and stay. And since she wasn't interested in eating, it was difficult [to] get rid of her. . . . I remember the ballet that would ensue when my father would try to escort her to the door. If he got too close, she'd lag back, and he'd have to go a bit forward. It took them quite a bit of time to get Pat to the door every evening."[4]

It was in her upstairs workroom in Moncourt where Pat wrote a revealing essay about another novelist, a novelist who moved house even more than she did (thirty-five times in the Los Angeles area alone)[5] and who was, for a few well-paid weeks, part of the intricate Hitchcock machine that produced the brilliant film of *Strangers on a Train.* Pat's essay on Raymond Chandler—"A Galahad in L.A." (published as the introduction to *The World of Raymond*

Chandler)[6]—was written in the year *Edith's Diary* appeared, 1977. Pat had just read Frank MacShane's biography of Chandler, and it focused her mind on Chandler's life and on what, as a home-schooled Freudian, she did and did not share with him by way of artistic impulse. It was Chandler's childhood in a matriarchal household, his sense of dislocation, his addiction to alcohol, and his chivalrous, intense, and nonmonogamous marriage to an older woman that gave Pat the helping hand she needed to clamber up over the slippery subject Raymond Chandler proved himself to be. "*Strangers on a Train* gave Chandler fits during his Hollywood script writing period," Pat wrote, "and from his grave Chandler has given me tit for tat."[7]

Pat's own obsessive mining of her childhood left her surprised that Chandler didn't "make use of the formidable emotional material at his disposal. But just how formidable or important real events are is a matter of how important a writer cares to make them." Pat wrote as though writers had a choice in the matter of calling up "real emotional events." She herself had very little.

Despite her professed lack of interest in style, Pat revelled in Chandler's. His often lyrical, always outré similes delighted her into repeating one: "He reeled back as if I had hung a week-old mackerel under his nose."[8] It was the compromise he had to strike on style that made Chandler so miserable while he was working on the script for *Strangers on a Train*—work from which Alfred Hitchcock fired him, replacing him with Czenzi Ormonde. Chandler wrote to his agent, Carl Brandt, that any "positive style" in a Hitchcock script "must be obliterated or changed until it is quite innocuous."[9] By which he meant that Alfred Hitchcock's was the only style allowed in a Hitchcock film.

Although Pat acknowledged that Chandler "found his first success in writing tough, popular pulp magazine stories, and his books were outgrowths of this formula fiction," she neglected to mention that she, too, had been published in the very same "best of the pulps," *Ellery Queen's Mystery Magazine*.[10] As always, she buried her biographical references deep in her prose, comparing Chandler's writing with the flat, vivid paintings of Edward Burra, the eccentric, wonderfully talented watercolorist she'd met at Barbara Ker-Seymer's house in London. (Burra seems to have done his best to avoid Ker-Seymer's house when Pat was there; a drinker himself, he was ruffled by her extravagant imbibing.)[11] And comparing it again to the uncompromising black lines of the paintings of Fernand Léger, whose cocktail party she'd been so thrilled to attend with Buffie Johnson in the summer of 1941, Pat slyly inserted her life in her writing in ways that Chandler never did.

In June of 1979, a year after Pat had finished her article on Chandler (and had had her delicate balance overturned by Tabea Blumenschein—and then partially restored by Monique Buffet), a fifteen-page article featuring Highsmith in her Moncourt house was published in a major French magazine, *L'Express*. The article, "Three Days with Patricia Highsmith" by the French novelist and journalist Noëlle Loriot, was advertised rather grandly: "For three days Patricia Highsmith renounced her solitude to receive Noëlle Loriot at her home." The piece is a nuanced and perceptive portrait of Pat in her favorite house, necessarily concealing more than it reveals. The three-day stay with Pat Highsmith proved to be very heavy going for Mlle Loriot.

"To discuss Patricia Highsmith," Noëlle Loriot said to me, "it is necessary to talk about her alcoholism and her lesbianism. The two go together. . . . I think she drank because she could not fully express her lesbianism and was ashamed of it." Loriot, who had been introduced to Pat by a mutual friend some years before she wrote her article, had watched Pat, on the first weekend she'd moved to Moncourt, stare with incomprehension at a bidet. Although Pat had been visiting France since 1949 and had already lived in three houses near Fontainebleau and Nemours, she seemed to have no idea what a bidet was for. Because of this, Loriot concluded privately—it was a very French deduction—that Pat had never slept with a man. Loriot also had the impression that Pat had been a lover of Judy Holliday. Of her three days in Moncourt with Pat, Loriot says:

> She was incredibly difficult to interview; she didn't want to be taped, she didn't want me to take notes. I used to take notes after I'd gone to my room at night. I tried to get her to talk about her work, but she was only interested in talking about lesbians and homosexuals and she showed me a picture of a very young German lover [Tabea again] *en travéstie*.

Noëlle Loriot, like so many other Highsmith guests, spent most of her time in Pat's house going hungry. But because she had come to stay in February, she froze to death as well as starved. Pat kept the house at 16 degrees centigrade (60.8 degrees Fahrenheit) and served one light meal a day. "I kept taking her to bistros and restaurants [to get food and keep warm, Loriot said.] Her physique was frightening; she never ate." Loriot attributed, as any French person might, Pat's lack of humor to her *"côté allemagne,"* her German blood. "At the end of three days, I couldn't stand it anymore—and neither could she!" But, says Loriot, Pat had "a physical dignity" which she kept even when *"morte-ivrogne,"* dead drunk. And she thought Pat had very successfully "pulled the wool" over the eyes of the French and the Germans, because so much of her writing was flat. The French verb for "pulling the wool" over people's eyes is *bluffer*, to bluff. "Pat bluffed everyone," Loriot said.[12]

In a more truthful world, a "reclusive" author who allows a journalist to stay at her house for three whole days probing her life and work for a national magazine might, for starters, have her status as a "recluse" reassessed. Recluses don't open their homes to members of the press—nor do they wish to see their names in national magazines. But such is the world of publicity that this long, illustrated piece in a popular French magazine about the solitary Patricia Highsmith (all too ready to talk about the unpublishable parts of her private life, it turned out, but very reluctant to talk about her writing) only enhanced Pat's reputation for solitude and privacy. Pat's usual economies with the truth and sly withholdings of information didn't help.

Pat refused to admit that she ever saw or corresponded with Mary McCarthy in Paris (she was doing both); she said she knew nothing of Arthur Conan Doyle (Sherlock Holmes was one of the inspirations of her youth, she was rereading Holmes stories in Moncourt, and she'd gone to London in April of 1969 to do a feature piece for *Queen* magazine on Billy Wilder's film *The Private Life of Sherlock Holmes*); she said that suspense didn't interest her (she'd written a book on the subject—admittedly, never really explaining it). Her characters had nothing to do with her, she insisted; she merely observed them "as if they were snails." (This was Pat's biggest bluff.)[13]

She invented nothing, she told Noëlle Loriot. "I read newspapers"—here she was telling the truth—"from the first to the last line: they are what inspire me. A newspaper is an anthology of cruel stories." And then she repeated her usual explanation for her characters. She preferred men for their actions. "Women always return to the house." Just as Pat herself always did.

"Believe me," Pat said, unbelievably, after a long list of the usual complaints about Mother Mary, "I am completely objective concerning my mother."

She had chosen France, she went on, because "the French are less boring than the English and more serious than the Italians. . . . I tried the English countryside: deadly." And she insisted that she visited her neighbors the Ryans only once a week. *Very* briefly. And sometimes the Ryan daughter, back from Oxford, would visit her. "We speak often," Pat said grandly and vaguely of her conversations with Juliette Ryan, "of my childhood."

Noëlle Loriot could not print Pat's revelations about her lovers nor what she herself was feeling: that Pat was not a "sympathetic woman," that "she was not natural with women, for her it was a punishment to make love," that she was "a sick woman." Loriot had already written in a review in *L'Express* that the style of *Edith's Diary* was not commensurate with its insights. "*Edith's Diary*, for me, was her chef d'oeuvre but [Pat] knew that it was badly written." After Jean-François Joselin (another French journalist Pat knew) had contradicted, in *Le Nouvel Observateur,* Loriot's opinion about the awkward style of *Edith's Diary,* Pat had said to Noëlle Loriot: "You were right."[14]

Loriot was reduced to telling Pat that if *Edith's Diary* had been written by a man, "one couldn't have failed to reproach him with misogyny." "What contempt for women!" she said about other women characters in Pat's work. Pat preferred to define her motives to Loriot vis-à-vis her women characters as an inability to respect them because they were dependent on men. That was accurate enough.

Loriot's editor at *L'Express* chose to publish old film stills and old photographs of Truman Capote and Carson McCullers to accompany the article—Pat hadn't seen or corresponded with either Capote or McCullers since the 1940s—and a very old photo of Mary McCarthy (whom Pat didn't admit to knowing in France). Pat, herself, didn't offer up any present-day colleagues to eke out her commentary, and she really didn't want to be photographed. She wanted to use photographs of herself at twenty—photographs so beautiful, said Mlle Loriot, that they reminded her of Simone Signoret, who was born in the same year as Pat and who displayed, Loriot thought, "the same fatalism when it came to the damage that tobacco and drink could wreak upon her."

Pat, says Loriot, "knew she was no longer photogenic," and so Loriot "had an idea, a good idea, which was to photograph the photo of Pat at twenty and use that." But the editor of *L'Express* looked at the photographs of the twenty-year-old Pat and said: "We can't do this, absolutely not. She's unrecognizable. It's another woman entirely."[15]

And Pat, who took many showers a day while Noëlle Loriot was there, said one more thing to her journalist guest, something she had never said publicly before. Sigmund Freud would have been thrilled by Pat's remark—but it was really just another instance of the old Highsmith sleight of hand.

What Pat said was this:

"Whenever I touch paper money or coins before sitting down to write, I have to wash my hands in order not to 'contaminate' my work."[16]

29

LES GIRLS

Exceptional in so many ways, Pat added one more exception to her list. She preferred to surround her writing with a cordon sanitaire of light negativity. Many of her friends didn't care for her work—and if they did, she made it clear that she was uncomfortable with their approval. Of the admiration of her young lover Madeleine Harmsworth, who "refused to call me Pat—saying it would be like calling Dickens Charlie, or Shakespeare Willie," Pat wrote: "I do not wish to be so celebrated."[1]

Some of Pat's more literary friends are still divided between the two classic ways of not liking her writing: one is to admire *Strangers on a Train* and *The Talented Mr. Ripley* and nothing else; the other is to prefer her short stories to her novels.

When Ellen Hill, whose disapprobation undoubtedly added an extra frisson to her relationship with Pat, met Peter Huber for the first time, she took him aside and asked him seriously: "What do you see in Pat's books?" When he told her, she gave him her first-edition copy of *The Tremor of Forgery,* the one Pat had wistfully inscribed: "For Ellen / Maybe you will like this one better than most. / Love, Pat."[2] When DéDé Moser, a painter friend of Ellen in the Ticino, read *This Sweet Sickness,* she thought it was a "wonderful" novel, but "[w]hen I praised it to Ellen, she said: 'I told Patricia when this book came out: You rewrote this thing so many times! I could have finished it in one night!' She did not have a high opinion of Patricia's books."[3]

Some of Pat's lovers and many of her friends, including Kingsley Skattebol (who saves her admiration for Pat's short stories), say they either did not read Pat's books or did not care for the books they had read.[4] Barbara Skelton, memoirist, novelist, and Cyril Connolly's ex-wife, confirmed this interesting attitude in an article in the *London Magazine*: "The odd thing was that most of Pat's friends never read her books."[5]

Vivien De Bernardi, another late-life friend who didn't care for Pat's work, lived near Pat in the Ticino. An American-born children's educational therapist working with Down syndrome children, Vivien was the wife of a Swiss banker when Pat wrote to her with typical modesty (and at Ellen Hill's behest) in 1981 that she, Pat, was a "free-lance writer," "almost always at home,"[6] and looking for comments on the child in her story "The Button." "The Button" portrays a father's horror at having a "handicapped" child, the murder he commits to relieve his feelings, and the button trophy he takes away from that murder. Unaware of Pat's work or reputation when she received her letter, De Bernardi told Pat forthrightly that she thought the child in "The Button" "was presented totally unrealistically . . . but the anguish of the father was incredibly real and powerful, so something in the story rang true."[7]

Pat and Vivien became neighborly friends—perhaps because of Vivien's soothing demeanor and well-ordered household, but perhaps, too, given Pat's turn of mind, because of Vivien's initial critique of "The Button" and disinterest in Pat's novels. Pat's own "buttons" in Switzerland, the ones De Bernardi says she did not "dare to press" for fear of setting off long "rants," were: "sex, Jews, blacks, and money."

Although Vivien De Bernardi was one of those friends who thought Pat "honest and direct," Pat never said a word to her neighbor about her love affairs or sexual preferences. Certainly all Pat's Swiss neighbors knew she was lesbian—those trim oxford shirts and pressed boy's jeans were a dead giveaway in suburban Switzerland—but they never broached the subject unless, like Bee Loggenberg, the wealthy South African who accompanied Pat on her last publicity trip to Paris in the fall of 1994, they, themselves, were gay. Pat was aware of what her neighbors assumed, but she ignored it. Hiding in plain sight had always been her style.

Switzerland, anyway, had become the elephants' graveyard of Pat's amatory hopes, barring the odd attempt to beguile an ex-lover into bed by letter or a half-acknowledged crush on a local pizzeria owner. And Pat's work suffered as only work inspired by love or love's fantasies could do. Still, there had never been room in Highsmith Country for love amongst the middle-aged—or even for love affairs which could be extended into a believable future. No Highsmith novel imagines a sexual affair as anything but a union of people in their teens, twenties, or thirties. Even the "lift" ending, as Pat called it, of *The Price of Salt* cannot get Therese Belivet and Carol Aird beyond an "excited wave" and across the crowded hotel barroom into each other's arms.

By the end of 1989, it was not only love that was missing from Pat's life. She was having to remind herself to do the other things that used to come naturally to her: "I must put more variation in my life, such as drawing & carpentering," she wrote in her diary.[8] Drawing and carpentering had always been part of her creative day—but her days were no longer so creative. By the end of 1991, she was writing: "Typical of this year that there has been no time for anything like a diary."[9] Nineteen ninety-one was the year Mary Highsmith died.

The twenty-third of May 1992 was "[a]nother non-workday (2nd) as I rethink my book *Small g*. It's an interesting plot." *Small g* (1995), the posthumously published novel that was another kind of exception, allows a forty-five-year-old man (an obvious stand-in for the aging Pat) to have limitless sexual connections with teenage boys as well as a possible affair with a thirty-eight-year-old married policeman. But after this short entry there is no more about *Small g* in Pat's diary, just the constant brain chatter of her responsibilities, her "current problem[s]": "3 legal things—my will, my house—have to be arranged, lest I die in my sleep with unfinished matter still unfinished. . . . I tell myself I do ever better keeping the questions, the unresolved at bay, while I summon the creative part of my brain. Would it were so."[10]

Pat was ill (see "The Cake That Was Shaped Like a Coffin, Parts 3, 5, 6, and 7"), she was aging fast, and "the creative part of her brain" was caught up in a very uncreative conversation with the details of sustaining her busy career. The "success" she yearned for had overtaken the solid daily pleasures of making art. And love was no longer the subject of her conversations with herself.

By the time Pat had moved herself to Switzerland, she scarcely resembled the sexual adventurer she had been in youth or the improbable domestic partner she tried to be in middle age. Years of alcoholism, inadequate nourishment, and emotional turmoil had eroded much that would have been recognizable about her to her early companions. (The stomach is now understood by gastroneurologists to be a "second brain"—it uses some of the same neurotransmitters as the "first brain" and has its own controlling "enteric nervous system"—and Pat's stomach had been badly unsettled for decades.)[11] Pat's neighbor Vivien says that she "loved sharing books with [Pat]. We exchanged books all the time and I valued her opinion."[12] But it was not *Pat's* books they exchanged, nor was it Pat's writing they spoke about directly. It was always someone else's.

In a way, in Switzerland, Pat had *become* someone else. Many of her least attractive qualities were intensified in the high-security cell of her Swiss solitudes. Abdication from a love life and long separation from her mother—first by distance, then by the deliberate tamping down of her emotions, and then by Mary's death on 12 March 1991—finished the job. When Pat wasn't vilifying Mary in letters (and even when she was), she was continuing to make anxious enquiries about the "restraining chair" to which Mary was tied in her nursing home, about Mary's behavior in the halls, her fits of cursing, her state of mind. In her own way, Pat stayed attached to this central piece of furniture in her Romance Room, but the boiling hatred and burning love that had characterized their relations were things of the past. So, too, was Pat's best work.

Although she was surrounded by helpful neighbors in Switzerland and backed by a publisher most American writers could only dream about, Pat's separation from the kind of people who knew her history—the kind of people who had *shared* her history—was almost complete. Alone in a crowd of concerned Swiss friends with whom she could never discuss her personal life, Pat Highsmith presents a painful picture of emotional isolation. She had, in the most reduced sense of the word, made herself peerless.

Without the pleasures and pains of her love affairs with women—not to mention the absence of the central drama of her relationship with her mother—Pat had nothing to push against except her own psychological borders, which continued to harden in self-defense. Never one to move towards people in the first place (Pat is often characterized as "taking a step back" when meeting anyone, although her cousins say she never shrank from kissing them, and several living lovers attest to the warmth of her physical demonstrations), she avoided physical contact with people in Switzerland, as she had only sometimes done in Moncourt. Bert Diener and Julia Diener-Diethelm, her attentive next-door neighbors in Tegna, say they had to be careful not to offer their hands to her when they saw her.[13]

Although Pat claimed she preferred to lead a "boring life," her friend Kingsley described just how "boring" Pat herself had become in her last few years in Switzerland and how "disloyal," she, Kingsley, felt to be thinking such a thing about her oldest friend.[14]

If Pat could do without the literary approval of friends, she needed and wanted praise from established sources. She was so anxious about an article about her that was to appear in *The New York Times* in June of 1988 that a young friend working at the *Times* sneaked out an advance copy to her in Switzerland. But Pat wrote to Kingsley that she hadn't "the guts to face it."[15]

Further evidence of how much her work's reception meant to her is in Marion Aboudaram's account of Pat's terrible distress after a party at Mary McCarthy's apartment on the rue de Rennes in Paris. McCarthy, queen of American expatriate literary society in Paris, accidentally let Pat know that she had never heard of Pat's adored Tom Ripley—or of his adventures. "Is he a pop singer?" McCarthy inquired innocently of Pat. "Pat," says Marion Aboudaram, "was very hurt and humiliated. And when she came home [to my apartment] she was absolutely drunk. She banged her head on the wall like mad. I had to give her warm milk with bread inside it and still she banged and banged and banged her head. She had a great complex about Mary McCarthy."[16]

In 1953, Pat had written to Kingsley about Mary McCarthy: "In a coolly intellectual way, I like her, and in her way, she is unrivaled."[17] For years, while she was living in France, Pat kept up a correspondence with Mary McCarthy, seeing McCarthy and her fourth husband, James, more frequently than she ever admitted. As usual, it was Pat who initiated the correspondence, writing to McCarthy in the fall of 1972 from Moncourt to remind her that they'd met at Rosalind Constable's years ago, that she hoped they could meet "again," and that if McCarthy didn't "like the company of other writers, I understand."[18]

The correspondence—about twenty letters from each woman—is marked on McCarthy's side by unfailing graciousness and on Pat's by a certain professional truckling, by polite requests for information, and by long rants about what was becoming her obsession with the taxes levied on Americans living abroad. Pat tried to interest McCarthy in joining tax pressure groups (McCarthy was already far more politically engaged than Pat, writing in Paris in favor of the work of the radical lesbian feminist novelist Monique Wittig and supporting many international causes; and, unlike Pat, McCarthy did her own taxes); and Pat brought Ellen Hill to meet her. McCarthy had worked with Ellen's best friend, Lily Marx, Karl Marx's niece.

Mary McCarthy and Pat wrote to each other about Janet Flanner's memorial service in Paris; McCarthy recommended her new French agent, Mary Kling, to Pat[19] (Pat, in one of her agent-changing fits in the 1970s, had already met with Kling, who gave Pat the impression that she was "swamped with clients");[20] and then she tried to bring Pat together with the other person whose friendship they shared, Ernst Hauser, the journalist Pat had met on her boat trip to Texas when she was seventeen. But when Pat moved to Switzerland, the correspondence with Mary McCarthy thinned, then petered out in 1984.

There is nothing in Pat's letters to McCarthy to indicate anything but polite pleasure in her company ("Really, your apartment was an oasis—of civilisation, after the Salon du Livre") and professional interest in her work ("I thought your article on the novel excellent, in NY Review of Books").[21] And there is nothing to reveal Pat's terrible despair on that October evening in 1977 when Mary McCarthy, with the best of intentions, had confused the talented Mr. Ripley with a rock 'n' roll star.[22]

A year later, Pat sent Mary McCarthy a copy of Edith's Diary. McCarthy included something about the novel in an article she was writing for The Observer in London. The Observer editor cut the reference, and McCarthy, very nicely, sent Pat her apologies and a copy of her original article. Pat didn't keep it. In fact Pat, who continued to archive everything (except her comics work and the cartoons she sent to *The New Yorker*) kept only one of McCarthy's letters—so perhaps Marion Aboudaram was right about Pat's "Mary McCarthy complex."[23]

Marion and Pat never discussed serious subjects, and "certainly," says Marion, they never discussed books or authors. "She never told me what she thought about my two novels; we never had literary conversations; she never discussed any writer.

"I think I was very good company for her. But there was no poetry between us, there was no romance. I had a lot of beautiful girls in my life but Pat was more fascinating than the beauties. . . .

"I had a kind of paranoia after her, I wanted to kill myself. And yet, I have nothing to reproach her with. She was just herself, but I was too sensitive for her. And the effect was terrible. Thank God I got away."[24]

Pat also took a recessive literary line with her very last girlfriend, Monique Buffet. Monique was a shy, blond, attractive twenty-seven-year-old French teacher of English who arrived at Pat's house in Moncourt in the summer of 1977, in the company of one of Pat's English fans, Val. Although Pat's relations with Tabea Blumenschein make a more dramatic story (that of an aging writer reenacting a lesbian version of *The Blue Angel*), and Marion Aboudaram's accounts of Pat are more revealing, it was in this last love affair with Monique Buffet that Pat finally allowed herself to enjoy the comforts of easy loving.

Of her first visit to Pat, Monique says: "I was petrified. . . . I didn't say one word. Pat was doing most of the speaking. She kept getting up and going to the kitchen and coming back. After that I knew why (to drink alcohol), but I didn't know then. . . . And she went in the kitchen and came back, went in the kitchen, came back, it was a bit of a tennis match.

". . . The first time, I don't even know if Pat saw me, but the second time [we saw Pat, in July of 1978] she was very attentive to me and left Val alone . . . and when we left, she asked for my address and phone number and the day after, she called me.

"And the day after that, I had a letter. That's how it started. Pat wanted to go to Paris and to the Katmandou. . . . Pat said, 'Why not give the old clip joint [Katmandou] another try.' "[25]

In the 1970s, Katmandou was Paris's legendary, luxury lesbian bar, operating on the rue du Vieux Columbier near the Place St-Sulpice. It was run, improbably, by a former teacher of high school history from the provinces: the very theatrical Elula Perrin, who was assisted by her business partner and ex-lover, a levelheaded Corsican named Aimée. One of the coat-check girls at Katmandou was more or less for sale; a single drink cost an astounding ninety francs (the price of dinner in a good restaurant in Paris in the 1970s); the bar and the dance floor were frequented by well-known female movie stars, top models, and successful women writers; and the "royal seats" up front were often filled with the Arab princesses who made Katmandou a necessary stop on their way back to the Emirates.*

Pat and Monique arrived at Katmandou at about one o'clock on the morning of 19 August—this was early evening for a lesbian bar in Paris—and Maryem, the regular doorperson, stopped them at the threshold, saying that the downstairs *salle* was packed; there were no places left. They thanked her, told each other, "Never mind, we'll go to Le Jeu de Dames" (a lesbian bar on the rue Montpensier), and turned away into the street. Suddenly, Elula Perrin, Katmandou's *patronne*, came dashing out of the bar, calling loudly out to them in the night: "No no no, WE'VE GOT PLACES!"

Elula had recognized Pat from all the way at the back of her long, narrow establishment—celebrity spotting was one of Elula's talents—and she personally conducted Pat and Monique back inside and sat them down right in the middle of the (empty-at-the-early-hour-of-1:00 A.M.) *"royale"* section.

About twenty minutes after they'd ordered their first drinks, Elula came over, "all smiles," and seated herself next to Pat, asking her politely if she was, indeed, who she seemed to be. Pat ignored the question, so Monique replied to it. Pat was using Monique as an interpreter, and Elula's next remark, *"C'est dans ces moments-là que l'on regrette de ne pas avoir toujours avec soi son livre de chevet'"* ["It's in moments like this that one regrets not always having with one one's favorite book"]—implying that she wished she had one of her favorite Highsmith books with her to be autographed—didn't go down well. "Eventually, Pat replied by a vague smile and something like: 'UGH.'" Elula, who had recently published a book herself, was not yet discouraged: *"Vous savez que nous sommes presque—à mon humble niveau—devenues collègues."* ["You know that we have almost—at my humble level—become colleagues."] . . . And Pat grumbled: "So I've heard."

Finally Elula gave up, and Pat and Monique went on to Le Jeu de Dames, a far more proletarian establishment.

"And, THERE [says Monique] it was a completely different Pat (probably a bit drunker too, but not only that). She was all over the place . . . coming back every 5 or 10 minutes with 'a new girl for me.' We ended with about 10 or 15 girls at our table AND SHE PAID THE DRINKS FOR ALL OF THEM. . . . She was recognized too, but she was having a great time, laughing, joking, and even dancing. At one point, she went up to the DJ's cabin to ask for 'slows.'"[26]

---

* The site of the fabled Katmandou is now the home of another luxury operation for women: the French handbag store Longchamp.

Shipwrecked by the rupture of her mostly fantasy affair with twenty-five-year-old Tabea Blumenschein in the summer of 1978, Pat recognized in twenty-seven-year-old Monique Buffet a lifeline and grabbed it, determined, as always, to get on with her work. As she had done with Tabea in Berlin, Pat plunged with Monique into the lesbian bar culture in Paris. Her habit of bringing back "girls" to the table echoes Barbara Roett's description of her behavior in London.

"Pat was a real innocent with women, the way men can be taken in by a waitress or a starlet. . . . She used to bring [these girls] round . . . like Tabea Blumenschein, just so dying to be a starlet. . . . And then she'd sit like an animal who had brought its prey back to Ba and me and laid it at our feet."[27]

Monique ended by "rescuing" the fifty-seven-year-old Pat from her long dry spell (long for Pat; it was two or three months) of being unable to work on her "4th Ripley novel," *The Boy Who Followed Ripley*. Pat's *coup de foudre* for Tabea Blumenschein in Berlin had opened up a grand canyon of need, and the kindness and calmness and casualness of Monique Buffet helped hoist Pat back up over the edge of the abyss. In July of 1978, two weeks before she began to see Monique, Pat was still writing to Ellen Hill to emphasize how "[m]y depression continues." Pat wrote this phrase twice after explaining how *Edith's Diary* had been optioned by a German film company, how Simone de Beauvoir wanted to meet her, how a Russian actress wanted to do a film on "my way of looking at life," etc. etc.[28]

Nothing made any difference to Pat's blasted sensibilities until the relationship with Monique began to take hold and stabilize her work. Pat's gratitude to Monique for this lifesaving service was repeated like a mantra in almost every letter she wrote, along with her fears that the young woman would cease to be "kind" (i.e., sexual) with her.

Pat's vulnerability in the initial flare of this correspondence was seconded only by her ruthlessness. She was still a writer stuck on "p. 56" of a book she desperately wanted to finish. Her feelings for Monique Buffet—like the photos of Monique which she fetishized, blowing them up, commenting on their detail, and pinning them to her desk—were arranged in ways to stimulate her imagination.

"You are a girl who allows me to dream," Pat wrote to Monique. She meant, of course, that Monique was a girl who allowed her to write. And the rather practical fantasies she wove around this kind young blond woman—already in the first blush of a relationship with another woman and still trying to handle the onslaught that was Pat Highsmith with delicacy and courtesy— allowed her to continue her work.

That work—the manuscript of *The Boy Who Followed Ripley*—shows ample evidence of Pat's terrible state of mind while she was writing it. It is scribbled over, crossed out, interleaved, and stuffed with substitute pages like no other manuscript in her archives. The completed novel forks off in several directions, betraying the anxiety of a writer who knows she has made a false start—several false starts, in fact—and can't find her way home.[29]

Perhaps some of Pat's confusion rested on the fact that she had two muses for young Frank Pierson, the boy who follows Tom Ripley. She began by bringing Frank to many of the *milieux* she'd visited with Tabea Blumenschein in Berlin, meanwhile giving Ripley her Socratic (and other) feelings about Tabea and, later on, about Monique. But she ended by bestowing on Frank some of Monique's moral scruples and at least one of her tastes—a Lou Reed record that Monique had loaned to Pat.

It was typical of Pat's cross-referencing (and of her ability to superimpose the image of one woman on another, to *replace* one woman with another) that the song she particularly relished on the Lou Reed record she borrowed from Monique was the one called "Make Up." Makeup, *maquillage,* was Tabea Blumenschein's speciality. Pat used some of Lou Reed's lyrics from "Make Up" in *The Boy Who Followed Ripley.*

With the inspiration of Monique Buffet's company, Pat managed to finish *The Boy Who Followed Ripley.* Along with it, she fashioned what was probably her most unambiguous relationship. The more than three hundred letters she wrote to Monique over the course of their friendship are phrased with as much generosity as Pat could summon. Perhaps that is why, alone of all Pat's living lovers, Monique Buffet's memories of Pat are unmixed. Pat, she says, was always "an angel" to her, "patient," "generous," and infinitely "kind." Pat even *cooked* for Monique regularly—a fact that would come as a stunning surprise to any of the hapless guests who had visited Patricia Highsmith in the freezing, unprovendered, uncomfortable houses of her older age.

And it was real French lunches Pat cooked, too. Every time Monique visited Moncourt, Pat made a *côte de boeuf* or a *lapin* and a *salade,* and she had a fresh bottle of good wine waiting. And although she wouldn't eat a bite herself, Pat always set the table nicely for two.[30] When she felt like it—which was almost never—Patricia Highsmith could perfectly well play the solicitous hostess.

Pat's younger lovers and her younger late-life acquaintances portray a very different person from the semidisoriented and manipulatively helpless woman who emerges from the descriptions of her older French and Swiss neighbors. Pat reminded Tabea Blumenschein of "Gertrude Stein": she says Pat was a very capable "millionaire businesswoman."[31] Pat's early adventurous lover, Natica Waterbury, felt the same way, and Pat wrote in her diary for 1944 that Natica "often says I am a businessman."[32] Phyllis Nagy says of Pat: "She never

ever ever projected an air of helplessness with me. She projected an air of complete control."[33]

Over and over, Pat implied in her letters to Monique that she didn't want the young woman to take her seriously as a writer, and that she was hoping to blunt the complicated instruments of self-torture by which she had always harrowed up her own feelings: terminal seriousness, murderous jealousy, a compulsive focus on time, and a need for love that was so intense that it consumed itself and destroyed its object. Like paranoia and like her writing, too, love was an organizing principle for Patricia.

So it was a sweet, if somewhat manic, re-creation of herself that Pat rehearsed in these letters to Monique. She invented a writing voice (much edited) which was adolescent in its expression and which, in the end, provided a rather threadbare concealment of her needs. Although Monique came to love Pat, Monique was in love with another woman and not "in love" with Pat. And Pat herself wasn't "in love" with Monique either—at least, not in the old, destructive way. Pat had her triangle again, but this time it didn't destroy her.

And so Pat began to imitate in life the self she was inventing in these letters—they were her most benign forgery—just as Oscar Wilde always said life should do with art.

She wrote to Monique in this (unrecognizable) way:

I am also too serious, but am really trying hard to correct it![34]

If you happen to be late, I shall not mind waiting for you.[35]

Please don't be alarmed by my (perhaps) numerous letters. . . . Please take it easy—and realize I am not putting pressure (I trust!) and I am not the jealous, neurotic type. . . . I really think life should be enjoyed.[36]

Pat's letter to Monique asking permission to dedicate to her *The Boy Who Followed Ripley*—the book whose life she felt Monique had saved—is entirely charming, with its characteristic modesties, its nutty numeric precisions, and its protective retreats into multiple choices.

19 Nov. 1978
Dearest Monique,
    I enclose a little book you will not have to read. I got it because the colours remind me of you. You see I am not always thinking about bed. . . .

I would like to dedicate my new Ripley to you, and offer the following suggestions. Please check one, as they say on exams:

☐   To M.
☐   To M.B.
☐   To Monique (lots of Moniques in the world)
☐   To M?B (I do not know your middle name)
☐   To Monique Buffet (I anticipate a no on this already.)
☐   I don't want or like dedications in principle.
☐   No.

This is because you were such an inspiration on—literally 5/6ths, or last 250 pages of this 300 page book.[37]

Pat took her book dedications seriously. Her books—perhaps more than the books of many other authors—were her life. Her dedications often coincided with a high point in her relations with (or her feelings of nostalgia for) her dedicatees. Not all her books are dedicated, but their dedicatees include five men (two of whom were related to her), one married couple, twenty-one women (and the companion dog of one of them), a political movement, and her cat Spider. *The Animal-Lover's Book of Beastly Murder* was inscribed to her cousin Dan Coates. Pat mentions his home, Box Canyon Ranch, and his home state and hers, Texas, in the dedication. Dan, of course, was the most present male figure of her childhood, just as her father, Jay B Plangman, to whom *A Dog's Ransom* is dedicated, was the most absent. The collection of short stories originally published as *The Snail-Watcher* was consigned to Alex Szogyi, with whom she had a long, warm friendship and a frank correspondence. *The Two Faces of January* was inscribed to Rolf Tietgens, who sometimes seems to be Pat's male homosexual twin—the twin who *didn't,* as Pat and Ripley did, "get away with it." The collection of stories called *The Black House* is dedicated to Charles Latimer, the transplanted Canadian she'd met in the 1960s when he worked for her London publisher, Heinemann. He "thought she was a genius";[38] she responded by temporarily making him one of her executors.

But the preponderance of Pat's books are dedicated to women. Aside from the "false" dedication of *The Price of Salt*—a book full of misdirections (including the pseudonym it was written under), designed to hide the emotional biography Pat had buried in it, and dedicated to three people Pat said she'd made up, "Edna, Jordy, and Jeff"—her book dedications constitute an index to the life of her heart.

Two books were dedicated to Mary Highsmith, and she is the only dedicatee to receive this distinction. *This Sweet Sickness,* written with another Mary in mind—Mary Ronin—was still assigned to the original Mary, and *Miranda the Panda Is on the Veranda*, the book of nonsense rhymes and illustrations Pat and Doris concocted in 1958 (a book which made Janet Flanner "wince" with aesthetic disgust as she thumbed through it),[39] is also dedicated to Mary. It is Pat's silliest book, and she was responsible only for the artwork. The inscription on *Edith's Diary*—requested by Marion Aboudaram—simply reads "Marion."

Strangers on a Train, although dedicated in manuscript to "all the Virginias" and slyly changed to "all the Virginians" in the first paperbook version (a recent paperback edition has restored "the Virginias"), went undedicated in its hardcover publication—as did *The Talented Mr. Ripley*, the book Pat certainly thought of as dedicated to herself. After all, when she gave Ripley a middle initial, it was her own. Tom signs himself in three different novels as "Thomas P. Ripley." *P* was for Phelps—but it was also for Patricia and undoubtedly for Plangman, too.

A Game for the Living (1958) was principally dedicated to Ethel Sturtevant, "my friend and teacher," although Pat thriftily threw in another set of nurturers (Dorothy Hargreaves and Mary McCurdy), whom she cited "for their empathy and for their house." Ethel Sturtevant was Pat's unfailing source of praise and succor—she compared Pat mistily to Edith Wharton in a letter—when she was her literature professor at Barnard College, and she continued to champion Pat until she died. *The Cry of the Owl* went to "D.W.," Daisy Winston, Pat's outspoken ex-lover and friend from New Hope, Pennsylvania, one of the few people to whom Pat gave a sizeable sum of money—a five-thousand-dollar check—when it was most needed.

The Glass Cell (1964) was assigned to Pat's beloved cat Spider, who, three years after the book was published, was conveyed into the hands of the British novelist Muriel Spark—with a little help from Pat's cat-loving Southern friend, Eugene Walter, and some serial obstructions from a Roman landlady. In 1970, Pat listed Muriel Spark along with Iris Murdoch, Kingsley Amis, and Graham Greene as the four British writers she liked "although," she added candidly, "I am not a great reader of anything."[40] In 1971, Pat wrote to her friend Kingsley that "reading Muriel Spark's brilliant *Memento Mori* [made me feel inadequate:] I am appalled at my obtuseness in grubbing over my novel for seven months."[41]

Dame Muriel Spark explained to me how Spider Highsmith had come to live with her:

> I got the cat from mutual friends in Rome. I'm a fan of Patricia Highsmith—those unexpected reversals, that anti-hero. We never met, unfortunately. She couldn't take Spider with her to England. Someone

was supposed to care for him and found she couldn't, and it was supposed to be a temporary arrangement. But after I got to know him I couldn't let him go.

Spider, whom Pat had left in Positano when she went to live in Suffolk, made the train trip from Positano to Rome all by himself. In 1968, Muriel Spark sent Pat a telegram which Pat kept all her life: "Spider is safe with me forever. He is greatly loved. Healthy and youthful. All best."[42]

"[Patricia and I] had a correspondence," said Muriel Spark, "and I wrote to her when he died, of course. We were *devastated* when he died.

"He was the most *wonderful* cat: black—perhaps partly Siamese—with enormous green eyes. And very intelligent. You could tell he had been a writer's cat. He would sit by me, seriously, as I wrote, while all my other cats filtered away.

"He brought," Dame Muriel said, "a bit of Patricia Highsmith with him."[43]

In her 1988 novel, *A Far Cry from Kensington,* Muriel Spark has the narrator explain the importance of a companion cat to a writer. The passage sounds very much like the description she provided of the cat she'd inherited from Patricia Highsmith. "For concentration you need a cat. . . . And the tranquility of the cat will gradually come to affect you, sitting there at your desk, so that all the excitable qualities that impede your concentration compose themselves and give you back the self-command it has lost. You need not watch the cat all the time. Its presence is enough."[44]

Pat dedicated *Deep Water* to "E.B.H. and Tina"—Ellen Blumenthal Hill and Ellen's poodle, Tina. *The Blunderer* was inscribed "For L."—a reference to Lynn Roth, whose short, sharp love affair with Pat had left a lasting impression of "type." The hardback edition of another work went, under disguised initials, to Caroline Besterman, and a paperback edition of *A Suspension of Mercy* was inscribed in the early 1990s to "Betty, Margot, Ann and all the old gang"—the lesbian friends she used to consort with on Fire Island and with whom she'd once again begun corresponding. *Those Who Walk Away* was dedicated to Lil Picard, "one of my more inspiring friends," and *The Tremor of Forgery* was offered to Rosalind Constable. *Ripley Under Ground* (1970) was dedicated to Agnes and Georges Barylski, the Polish gleaners who lived in a trailer 150 yards from Pat's house in Montmachoux. Although Pat privately referred to the Barylskis as "peasants" (and preferred countries "in which there is an acknowledged peasant class"),[45] she thought they were "the only "honest people" she'd met in France. They cared for her cats whenever she travelled and had once paid her "in advance" for a kerosene heater she'd sold to them—an act of faith which thoroughly impressed her.

Found in the Street was dedicated to faithful Kingsley Skattebol, who had lived for years in the mise-en-scène of that novel, Greenwich Village: first on West Eleventh Street and then at One Christopher Street. *Small g,* Pat's posthumous novel, was inscribed to "my friend Frieda Sommer"—another of Pat's "good eggs": a woman from Zurich prone to crushes on prominent women, who did Pat many favors and who was responsible for much of the Zurich research for *Small g.* Pat eventually made Frieda Sommer one of the trustees of her final will. Only *Ripley Under Water* (1991) was not inscribed to an individual but to the "dead and dying among the Intifadeh and the Kurds." It was a dedication with which Pat hoped to make a point and raise some hackles. In the end, the hackles she raised were mostly her own.

Meanwhile, at the end of the 1970s, sweetness, a little light, and fun fun fun were the themes of Pat's letters to Monique Buffet. But because this was, after all, Patricia Highsmith writing letters to a young lover, some imp of the perverse was bound to make a cameo appearance, and occasionally, through Pat's shiny filter of "fun," the little imp showed up. "Just so you will destroy this letter, I shall add, that I love lying on top of you (if I do not weigh too much) and kissing your neck. Don't you think your father would enjoy this letter?"[46]

In the meantime, Monique, struggling with two relationships, did not emerge unscathed. She thinks that the seven cysts she had to have removed from her eyes during the time she was intimate with Pat (Pat, typically, did a drawing of her treating one) were a *"somatisation"* of her feelings about their situation. Pat, she said, never forced her to make love although she could be tacitly very insistent—and Monique made love with Pat because she wanted to. Still, every time she did so she "felt bad." Monique was newly in love with another woman, and seeing Pat was like "walking a tightrope" for her.[47]

For Monique, Pat "had the stigmata of alcoholism," but she also "had a great charm, incredibly piercing eyes like an Indian, her voice was lovely, she had a very soft voice. . . . She looked directly at me . . . up through her hair with her head down. [And] she was so tender and so attentive and so affectionate that you forgot that she looked butch."[48]

Pat could still attract, could still, in the late 1970s and early 1980s, act out of a softer part of herself and try to re-create some of the fun she'd had when she was Monique's age. In this affair she was playing down both her feelings and her reputation.

"PLEASE do not consider me a heavyweight, or an intellectual, or a good writer, or anything serious like that. With you it is nice to have fun, and I want you to have fun also, with me or anyone else."[49]

And so Pat's relations with Monique Buffet provided a partial resolution of the perpetual "romantic" problem she had described clearly, clausally, and with a great deal of psychological sourcing to Alex Szogyi in 1969:

> I may not be capable of [love]. . . . I want something romantic, perhaps not definite. If I have the steady thing, I reject it; this has happened over and over—rather I made it happen. I repeat the pattern of mother's semi-rejection of me. Her "abandonment" of me to my grandmother, when I was aged 12, when my mother took me to Texas, with a promise she would divorce my stepfather . . . but within a couple of weeks, my stepfather came from New York and took her away, back to New York, and I was left for a dismal year—going to school with kids two and three years older than I—in Texas. . . . I never got over it. Thus I seek out women who will hurt me in a similar manner, and avoid the women who are—good eggs.[50]

Allela Cornell drawing for dollars near her studio in Greenwich Village. During their short affair, Allela painted a prophetic portrait of Pat. *(Swiss Literary Archives)*

Pat on the Circle Line, the boat that goes around Manhattan, in the 1940s. Shipping out to anywhere was what she loved best. *(Swiss Literary Archives)*

THE "JEANNOT" ALBUM: Jean David ("Jeannot"), a French cartoonist from Marseille who was a friend of Mary and Pat Highsmith since the 1930s, kept these unique photographs—never before published—of Pat and Mary on album pages, which he decorated to represent their lives. The pen notes on the photographs are by Pat, suggesting that it was she who sent them to Jeannot. *(Collection Annebelle Potin)*

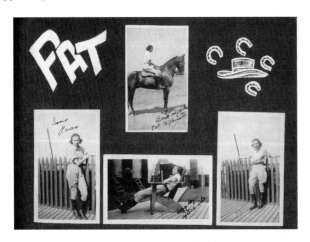

LA PECHE À "JE NE SAIS PAS QUOI"...

AU TEXAS   DANS "LE NEW HAMPSHIRE"

MARY C. HIGHSMITH.

CHRISTOPHE COLOMB..   _YES JE SAIS NAGER..!!

..DÉCOUVRIT L'AMÉRIQUE..

..ET MISS HIGHSMITH   ROBINSON CRUSOE
SES JAMBES...   et sa maman
dans l'île déserte..

West House at Yaddo. It was on the floorboards of West House porch that Flannery O'Connor, to Pat's everlasting disgust, said she saw an image of the radiant face of Jesus. *(Collection the Corporation of Yaddo; photographer Joseph Levy)*

Marc Brandel, Pat's "fiancé" of the late 1940s, on the beach in Provincetown in 1955, the year before he adapted *The Talented Mr. Ripley* for American television's *Studio One*. *(Collection Ruta Brandel Dauphin)*

Kathleen Wiggins Senn, the married woman whose two-minute meeting with Pat in Bloomingdale's department store in 1948 sparked Pat's most personal novel, *The Price of Salt*. *(Collection Priscilla Senn Kennedy)*

Kathleen Wiggins, unmarried and flying a plane. *(Collection Priscilla Senn Kennedy)*

Pat in France with Sylvia David and her husband, the political cartoonist Jean David (Jeannot). Pat's desire to be an *"ami de maison"* wasn't always an innocent one. *(Collection Annebelle Potin)*

Pat and her favorite cat, Spider Highsmith, the dedicatee of *The Glass Cell*. Muriel Spark, who adopted Spider, remarked: "He brought a bit of Patricia Highsmith with him." *(Collection Ogden Kruger)*

Ellen Blumenthal Hill in the bed Pat has just left to take this photograph. Ellen's four-year affair and thirty-odd-year friendship with Pat added new terrors to the word relationship—and brought new inspiration to Pat's work. *(Swiss Literary Archives)*

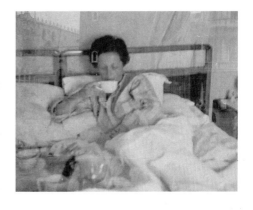

Dame Sybil Thorndike and Heather Chasen in *Call Me Jacky*, Enid Bagnold's play about a homicidal alcoholic lesbian. Chasen, who played the title role, based her costume and some of her characterization on her friend Patricia Highsmith. *(Collection Heather Chasen)*

Pat and Arthur Koestler in Alpnach on her visit to the Koestlers in the summer of 1969. Pat and Koestler had an interesting history. *(Swiss Literary Archives)*

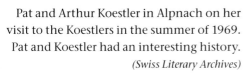

Pat, wearing her trademark Levi 501 jeans, in Montmachoux in 1973 with George and Agnes Baryliski, the gleaners to whom she dedicated *Ripley Under Ground*. *(Swiss Literary Archives)*

Pat at her rolltop desk in Moncourt with some creative aids: a cigarette, an ashtray, and her coffee-colored 1956 Olympia Deluxe typewriter.

Novelist Marion Aboudaram, Pat's lover in France from 1975 to 1978. Pat made suggestions for Marion's translation of Rita May Brown's *Rubyfruit Jungle,* then left her for Tabea Blumenschein. *(Collection Marion Aboudaram)*

Tabea Blumenschein disguised as a girl. *(Swiss Literary Archives)*

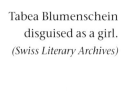

Tabea Blumenschein disguised as a boy. *(Swiss Literary Archives)*

Pat and Monique Buffet in Pat's garden in Moncourt. Monique "saved" Pat's novel *The Boy Who Followed Ripley*; it is dedicated to her. *(Collection Monique Buffet)*

Pat, Monique Buffet, and Frédérique Chambrelent at a fashion event at Maxim's organized by Chambrelent. At Pat's request, Monique is pretending to be her agent. *(Collection Monique Buffet)*

Pat happily tranquillized by Francis Wyndham's cat. Wyndham's 1963 article in *New Statesman* gave her work its first and best introduction in England. *(Collection Francis Wyndham)*

Pat in 1980 at Diogenes Verlag in Zurich, conferring with Daniel Keel (center) and Gerd Haffmans. *(Collection Diogenes Archive)*

Ruda Brandel Dauphin introduces Douglas Fairbanks Jr. to Pat at the American Film Festival in Deauville in September 1987. Pat spent two evenings there draped over the piano in the bar of the Normandy Hotel, singing Cole Porter songs.
(Collection Ruda Brandel Dauphin)

Pat—who gleefully suggested this ominous pose in front of her sharpened instruments—photographed by Richard Schroeder in Tegna, Switzerland, in 1990.
(Collection Richard Schroeder)

Pat and her friend Jeanne Moreau, on Pat's last publicity trip to Paris in 1994. *(Swiss Literary Archives)*

The Fortress of Solitude. Pat standing guard over the back side of Casa Highsmith/ Highsmith Haus in Tegna, during its construction in 1988–89. *(Swiss Literary Archives)*

30

LES GIRLS

PART 14

As late as the fall of 1992—Pat's brief sexual relationship with Monique Buffet had been over for eleven or twelve years by then—Pat was still writing to Monique self-deprecatingly about her work. Concerning *Ripley Under Water,* she cautioned: "Never mind my new book, the Ripley. It is all right, but nothing great."[1] The fact that Pat was correct in her appraisal is almost beside the point.

Francis Wyndham, who remarks that almost every story he tells about Pat "has a cat in it," recalled one story that didn't. He had said to Pat about a book of hers, "'That belongs on my Highsmith shelf.' And she was very annoyed: 'I haven't GOT a shelf,' she said. She didn't like me treating her with that sort of reverence, putting all her books together. She sent out a signal: treat me as an artisan."[2]

Pat's intellectual uncertainties were such that she liked to cite "authorities" to back up her assertions, and for much of the rest of her life the irrefutable Ellen Hill was one of her "most referenced authorities."[3] Joan Juliet Buck noted in a 1977 article for *The Observer Magazine* that Pat was constantly quoting Hill's opinions to give substance to her own.[4] Pat's ambivalences required an anchor to steady them—and Ellen's anchor was made of the heaviest metal.

To be sure, Ellen's overbearing behavior at dinner parties, restaurants, and private homes was matched—overmatched, in fact—by Pat's own comportment at the table. On a too-quiet evening, Pat was perfectly capable of leaning over a candle to set her hair on fire[5] or of hauling a clutch of snails out of her handbag and encouraging them to "leave silvery trails on the mahogany."[6] The smell of burning hair and the sight of snails were just the things to put her tablemates off their food.

Caroline Besterman remembers an evening when she and Pat were both guests at a gracious dinner party given by a married couple, one of whom was Jewish. During a lull in the conversation, Pat looked up from her plate and suddenly erupted with a line from the awful internal drama she had been rehearsing: " 'I'm sick of the Jews!'

"It just came straight out of her mouth," said Caroline Besterman, "and there was a silence, and then people went on talking as though it never happened. They ignored it."[7]

Christa Maerker, who felt "protective and motherly of Pat," recalls a painful luncheon in the 1980s at the Locarno Film Festival when Pat "attacked a cigarette machine in a restaurant. . . . She jumped up from the table, very aggressively, and went over to it and started hitting it and kicking it with her feet and yelling. And everybody was highly embarrassed. There was music downstairs in a disco and she thought the cigarette machine was making it; she thought it was a jukebox."[8]

And Philip Thompson, Alex Szogyi's longtime partner, had a disquieting experience at a dinner party in Pat's house in Moncourt in the 1970s. Alex and Philip were visiting Pat in France, and Pat, unusually, was cooking a real home-style Southern meal for them with chicken and biscuits, gravy, and mashed potatoes. She hated cooking, said Alex, and when she did cook it was "sort of"—he paused politely to find the right term; he was a food writer—"Texan." The other guests at Pat's house, all women, were speaking French with Alex. Philip, who didn't speak French and who, anyway, had a rather tetchy relationship with Pat, was listening uncomfortably to the conversation, trying to catch a word here and there. Finally, Philip went into the kitchen and said to Pat, "Gee I wish they would speak English, I can't understand a word." And Pat turned on him immediately. "What a pity," she retorted coldly.

That, Philip thought, was when the trouble began.

Also present at the dinner party was a "charming young journalist from London"—Madeleine Harmsworth—and Philip and Madeleine began talking and getting along wonderfully, and Pat didn't much like that, Philip felt. At some point during the evening, Pat's "Confederate" swords were taken down from the wall, and Philip and Pat posed for a picture *"en garde,"* which, Philip thought, was quite symbolic of their relationship.

At the end of the evening, and after eating the dinner Pat had prepared, Philip Thompson became violently ill. He was the only person at the dinner party who did so, and it's a measure of the uneasy possibilities Pat's character could evoke for her friends that it crossed the minds of both Alex and Philip that Pat might have had something to do with Philip's illness, that she might have "poisoned" Philip: put something in the food on his plate to make him sick. Alex, enormously sympathetic to Pat in every respect and unreservedly complimentary of her work, said he was worried about this. Alex and Philip laughed about it, but ever after they continued to refer to that dinner party in Moncourt as "the night of the poisoning."[9]

While Pat's social depredations continued to be suppressed by embarrassed friends or ignored by shell-shocked hosts, Ellen Hill's rudenesses were remarked upon and tallied up: mostly by Pat's friends and principally in the context of her bullying relationship with Pat.

But what Pat's friends always failed to understand was that Ellen was providing Pat with the painful contradictions she craved: sexual admiration (when Ellen learned that Kingsley Skattebol was not a lesbian and had never had an affair with Pat, she said to Kingsley: "Too bad, she was a wonderful lover");[10] sexual rejection (in Mallorca, six months into their relationship, Pat and Ellen were sleeping in separate beds and avoiding kissing each other good night); and the psychological domination Pat had identified as so essential to her psyche at the age of twenty: "I cannot imagine a domination without love, nor a love without domination."[11]

Of *course*, Ellen's behavior infuriated Pat. Humiliation as a technique has a very short shelf life even in the best circumstances (i.e., when it is welcomed by its object). Granted that Pat was excited by the idea of being humiliated, she could have done with a great deal less of it from Ellen Blumenthal Hill.

Monique Buffet, watching Pat and Ellen together in Moncourt twenty-five years after their affair was over, found their relationship hilarious. "The sight of Pat and Ellen together, Pat complaining about Ellen all the time, was enough to make you die laughing. Pat was like a little sullen girl with Ellen but she did what Ellen said. Ellen was very nice to me, she was funny, a great woman, but the way she ordered Pat around was extraordinary."[12]

Five years after that, Bettina Berch saw Pat and Ellen together in Aurigeno in a more subdued dialogue. "They were pretending that they were very neutral acquaintances, like this is my best friend here, or something. You could tell in some sort of subliminal way that they had been lovers; every now and then there was the little nickname—Ellen called Pat 'Teacup' . . . and the formality slipped."[13]

"Teacup" suggests that Ellen understood something about Pat's fragilities. But Pat's jabs at Ellen's nagging and her compulsive cataloguing of Ellen's faults (there are long, long lists devoted to Ellen Hill's Serious Flaws in Pat's notebooks) continued for decades after the end of their affair. In the end, Pat's friendship with Ellen Hill provided her with the kind of emotional contact she could best sustain with an ex-lover: intense irritation.

Only one of Pat's short relationships in Europe had anything like the kind of creative consequences that Ellen Hill's rough loving had provided. Pat and "Jacqui" had an intermittent affair in Montmachoux and Paris in 1968 and 1969. It was punctuated by some exciting physical fights brought on by Pat's increasingly obsessional behavior: "I pulled down a very tall curtain of the kitchen [in Jacqui's apartment], because it was utterly, unspeakably filthy, stuck it in the tub and washed it. Jacky was so furious, she pulled my hair and slapped my face."[14]

Pat liked to think of herself as singed by Jacqui (or Jacky, as the woman herself sometimes liked to spell her name), and noted that Jacqui had cancelled seven dates with her in a row—always a shortcut to Pat's heart. "Jacky is a fire I walk into,"[15] she wrote to Alex Szogyi proudly. And Pat told Alex that she had borrowed Jacqui's "foul tempers (but nothing else) for Heloise [Plisson]," Tom Ripley's richly inattentive, spoiled French wife.[16] But Pat was being coy; she would borrow quite a bit more from Jacqui than her "foul tempers" for Heloise. She imported Jacqui's *désinvolture*, her blond beauty (the "gold" lights in Heloise's hair remind Tom of money), her love of long absences on cruise ships with female companions, and her amorality. But Pat gave Tom and Heloise a much cooler relationship than she'd had with Jacqui, a relationship that, despite its improbability, would *last*.

After the shock of her parting with Tabea Blumenschein in 1978, Pat continued, with long intermittences on Tabea's part, to correspond with Tabea, whose chaotic further adventures are told in a number of the charmingly illustrated letters she sent to Pat. (Pat had most of Tabea's letters thrown into the garbage when she was preparing her archives for eternity.) In her cahiers, uncharitably, Pat went on criticizing Tabea's housing and money troubles; "failure" was still a sin for Pat, and Tabea hadn't fulfilled her expectations of becoming a movie star or a famous costume designer.

Early in 1988 Pat started to think about writing a story called "The Suicide of the Moth"—"Further adventures of T.B. whose balloon ruptured somehow around 1984. Prior to then she was going upward. . . . 'Was she too mighty?' Yes, sure of herself, of the red carpet, of admirers, lovers. When she wrote me after 2½ yr. lapse, she had lost apartment. Was living on Gov't. charity, alone, jobless."[17]

Still, Pat continued to pull out her accordion-pleated billfold of photos of Tabea and Monique Buffet and to flash it around to friends, like an aging Edwardian gentleman showing naughty postcards of his chorus girl favorites. Pat and Tabea didn't meet, but Pat saw Monique for the last time when she went to Paris on book business in 1988. Pat was staying at the Hotel Edward VII, and she and Monique went out to dinner at a nearby Chinese restaurant. No doubt it was the same Chinese restaurant at which Pat, on future visits, dined with the French writer and literary critic Josyane Savigneau and, later still, met with her new accountant, Marylin Scowden. Pat never did like to change venues once she'd gotten used to them. The night they met, Pat proudly showed off the plans for her "Casa Highsmith," her last house in Tegna, to Monique—something she did with everyone now. And she claimed responsibility for the house's double-pronged design, too, never mentioning that she had an architect, Tobias Amman.

At dinner that night was the first time Monique had ever seen Pat obviously drunk. It was also the first time, says Monique, that she had ever felt "ashamed" of her. Pat was "making a fool of herself" in the restaurant, behaving badly to the waitstaff, but not to Monique. Pat asked Monique to spend the night. Monique refused. They continued to write to each other. And Monique, like Buffie Johnson and so many of the old friends Pat was inviting to Switzerland, found excuses for not visiting Pat in her forbidding new house.[18] The day after it happened, Monique heard the news of Pat's death, casually, between courses and cigarettes, in a bistro in the Boulevard St-Germain. She was dumbstruck.

In early 1989, Pat had written to Kingsley: "I am sick of [Ellen's] scolding and all around domineering, and have bid a polite adieu."[19] But even at the very end of their friendship, Ellen Hill's authority was still looming large enough for Pat to have a "vivid dream in which Ellen Hill had been elected president of the United States." Ellen's dream-elevation to America's highest office produced in Pat "an atmosphere of hope and change," and her immediate response to it was typical—and it was funny, too, given her auslander prejudices, although Pat herself didn't see the humor in it. But when Pat woke up with the image of the newly presidential Ellen in her head, her most pressing thought was that Ellen Hill must be "the first person not born in USA to be elected President."[20]

In Pat's short story "Two Disagreeable Pigeons" (published posthumously in 2002, but outlined in 1973 after she'd settled into Moncourt), an eponymous pair of London pigeons, Maud and Claud[21]—observed humorously and maliciously—are "simply mates, for two or three years now, loyal in a way, though at the bottom of their little pigeon hearts they detested each other." Their regular Highsmith-colored day features persistent bird battering by vicious humans and the pigeons' own coordinated attack on a baby in a pram. Maud and Claud peck the infant's eye out and flutter away unrepentant and unpunished.

At day's end, Maud, the female pigeon, remembers how her mate Claud snatched half a peanut out of her beak and cheated her out of a meal, and how "she couldn't count on him for anything, not even to guard the nest where there was an egg." She wonders: "Why did she live with him? Why did she, or they, live *here* . . . Why?" And then she settles down to sleep next to Claud in their nook in a wall in Trafalgar Square, "exhausted by her discontent."[22]

Aside from Tom Ripley's unconvincing marriage to Heloise Plisson (Heloise is often absent enjoying herself on a cruise ship with a female friend; Tom is usually out having flirtatious fun with the boys); or Edgar and Hortense, the "truly in love" snails of *Deep Water* whose lengthy copulations are observed so tenderly by the psychopath-in-residence, Vic Van Allen; or Jack and Natalia Sutherland, the young couple in *Found in the Street* whose marriage is frankly enlivened by their mutual attraction to the same underage girl, the history of Maud and Claud, the two disagreeable pigeons united by hard living and even harder feelings, is the sole portrait of lasting conjugal relations to appear in any Highsmith fiction. And it's an accurate portrait, too, of the only union imaginable in Highsmith Country: bleak, untrusting, and undependable.

We might say, as Richard Ellmann said of Oscar Wilde, that Highsmith's fiction is a record of her feelings of love in that it excludes them so thoroughly. But it would be closer to the experience of Highsmith Country to acknowledge that Pat's work records her feelings of love by reversing them as faithfully as she did in life. Love, like no other emotion, brought out her ambivalence—and with it the awful rage that glares out so painfully from some of her later photographs.

Many of the murders in her novels can usefully be thought of as counters on her abacus of love. They substitute for love, they are instigated by love, they replace or react or add up to love. The murderers may change from draft to draft in her manuscripts, and so may the victims, but murder itself continues to be the categorical imperative, the one act which must take place in her work. And murder, in a Highsmith fiction, is almost always love's partner—while love itself is usually murder's victim. Only in *The Price of Salt*—a novel where the murder is confined to the metaphors—is love allowed to live on.

Pat's own defeats in the Love Wars were mostly self-defeats. Her doubts about her gender couldn't have helped. At the age of twelve she was already assessing herself: "I am a walking perpetual example of . . . a boy in a girl's body."[23] In her twenties, she was haunted by what a New Orleans fortune-teller had said to Mother Mary: "You have a boy," the fortune-teller began and then stopped. "No, you have a girl—but she was meant to be a boy." After Elizabeth Lyne had teased Pat about having her period, Pat wrote in her diary: "I can't help my other hormones, can I?"[24] And, having used the word "woman" about herself in a letter to her friend Ronald Blythe, she quickly corrected herself: "if I can call myself that."[25]

Although she took all the women whose names appear in the crowded diaries of her long, hot summers of 1944 and 1953 as lovers, Pat found it impossible to stay with any of them. Nor did she stay with any of the Virginias, the Jeans, the Jeannes, the Joans, the Anns, the Annes, the Ellens, the Katherines, Kathryns, Catherines or Carolines, the Diones, the Sheilas, the Helens, the Marions, the Lynns, the Moniques, the Marias, the Mickeys, the Billies or the Marys, *et al.*, who had, at one time or another, been so achingly available to her.

But even if she was unable to sustain her long relationship with Ellen Hill (so good for her work, so bad for her living) or her equally long relationship with the married Caroline Besterman (the last "adult love" of her life), Pat did manage to keep the resentments and furies of these failed love affairs alive and well for decades, as hot and bright—almost—as love itself.

31

THE REAL ROMANCE OF OBJECTS

PART I

> Possessions are nine tenths of my life.
> —**Patricia Highsmith**, 1945

> Finally she said, "Do you want to see my cellar?" And there were three of them. One for cheese—there was no cheese. And one for *jambon*—no *jambon*. It was a Highsmith cellar—probably *cadavres*.
> —**Josyane Savigneau**, in conversation with the author

> And then she wanted me to see her cellar which went on forever. It was a Hitchcock cellar.
>   "Can't we go upstairs?" I said.
> —**Daniel Keel**, in conversation with the author

> At midnight she said, "Come on, let's go down to the cellar" . . . and it was terrifying. And you knew if you screamed, no one in the world would hear you, just the rats.
> —**Christa Maerker**, in conversation with the author

In the three levels of dark cellars under her high, narrow stone house in Aurigeno, the light-deprived seventeenth-century Swiss village to which she moved after the French fiscal authority, the *douane,* raided her house in Moncourt, France, Pat Highsmith kept, to borrow a phrase from one of her short stories, "nothing that meets the eye."

Strictly speaking, however, there *were* a few objects tucked away in the first of her cellars, objects no Highsmith house was ever without: "a long trestle table . . . brown paper and string . . . saws, nails, screwdrivers, chisels, sandpaper," as well as hammers, rasps and awls[1]—the whole panoply of pointed, edged, angled, blunted, and sharpened instruments Pat used for the precise brutalities of her furniture making. Since 1933, when she was twelve and the only girl in the woodworking class at her junior high school in Fort Worth, Pat had been ripping raw materials apart and putting them back together again to make something new. It wasn't, she thought, all that different from what she did every day at her desk.

But in the penumbral cellars beneath her workroom, just where you might expect a writer obsessed by secrets, lies, and the rusty hinges of guilt to hide some of her best evidence, Pat stored nothing that belonged to her. Only a "neighbor's bicycle" (spotted by a sharp-eyed French journalist), leaned against a cellar wall, declining in the Stygian gloom.[2]

Still, like a magician who makes a great show of pulling something out of a top hat and then suddenly displays the hat's empty crown, Pat liked the drama of flaunting these hollow, shadowy, scary spaces before her guests. Many a nervous visitor followed her past her worktable and down into the dark.

Was there, Highsmith's guests couldn't help but wonder, something those bare spaces might be concealing? Something like the corpse of the American art collector Tom Ripley had so casually dispatched (with a bottle of vintage Bordeaux) in his *own* black cellar at Belle Ombre in *Ripley Under Ground*?[3] Pat must have known how uneasy she was making her visitors—and still she continued to lead them down those cellar stairs and into the gloom.

Cellars, anyway, were never really where she stored the things in which she invested her feelings. She preferred to keep her meaningful objects under her eyes or close at hand, hiding their significance (as she hid so much else) in plain sight.

"I am superstitious about the influence of mental attitudes," Pat wrote. "Therefore I am superstitious about the objects . . . with which I surround myself which in turn create my mental attitude. It is, in terms of actions, if one acts upon it, a really strong superstition."[4]

And she was very particular about the placement of her things. Kingsley, who was one of Pat's major sources of mailed objects and materials for nearly half a century,[5] recalls that "Pat was a bit like . . . do you remember a play called *Craig's Wife*?* About a woman who, if you removed a matchbox an inch

* *Craig's Wife*, by George Kelly, Grace Kelly's uncle. When it was made into a film in 1936 by Hollywood's only openly lesbian director, Dorothy Arzner, it became a protofeminist drama.

away from where she had left it, she would go berserk. Pat had a kind of fetish about placing things. When she couldn't locate something, she'd get quite upset. I moved an ashtray once on her table in Tegna, and she very rapidly swept it back into its proper position. She didn't say anything, but she glowered."[6]

Something similar happened shortly after Pat moved to Bucks County with Marijane Meaker—"probably the fall of '60," says Meaker. Pat, who had been "complaining [that] her desk was so small," was soon the recipient of a surprise gift: Marijane's own large desk, which Pat had "always envied." Pat "clapped her hands with delight" and then, at dinner "she began to cry. She said it was so sweet of me but she could not give up writing at her small desk. She hadn't known how to tell me."[7]

Meaker wrote about the desk incident to Mary Highsmith (who had her own, well-bevelled reasons for keeping in touch with Pat's girlfriends), using it "to explain how [Pat] often was mysterious to me . . . [and making it an] example of the varied signals she sent out."[8]

Pat's behavior with the objects she owned continued to puzzle friends and lovers for decades; her "varied signals" seemed to be part of her own special binary code. Like a transmitting device left behind on the (bi)polar permafrost, she went on emitting contradictory messages for decades. Not until the very end of her life—when she had aged and iced and set herself down in Switzerland, a terrain as unfamiliar to her as real permafrost might have been (but she loved the "order" and "cleanliness" of it)—did she relax what Julian Symons called her "anacondan grip" and "turn loose of" some of her deep psychological divisions. Along with them went the distinctive doublemindedness that had always marked her writing. It was a serious artistic loss.

Josyane Savigneau, the French critic, writer, and eventual editor of *Le Monde des livres* in Paris, first went to interview Pat in her house in Aurigeno with a photographer early in 1987. Pat, Savigneau noticed, spoke a pure, old-fashioned American, "completely preserved by her exile." She was "like a cat who might reach out and suddenly scratch," and she "was terrified we would break something or move something; we were like barbarians to her." Savigneau, "already paralyzed with respect for her," was trying to be as delicate as possible with Pat, but "when the photographer started shooting, Pat became terrified; her sense of space was entirely invaded. . . . 'Be careful,' she kept saying.'Be careful. BE CAREFUL!!' "[9]

Phyllis Nagy, who met Pat in late 1987 in New York (see "The Cake That Was Shaped Like a Coffin: Part 5"), visited her in the spring of 1989 soon after Pat moved from Aurigeno to Tegna. Phyllis noticed that Pat's bookcases were filled with all the editions of her own published works and with nothing else.

"Not another book by another writer was on display," says Nagy, and Pat was in no hurry to unpack the rest of her library.[10]

"Pat," says Nagy, "was very capricious, easily offended, very touchy about all the things in her house. If you didn't compliment something she liked, she'd hold it against you."[11] Nagy found this attitude surprisingly "feminine." Pat stopped corresponding with Nagy for "almost a year" when Phyllis failed to praise some of her paintings (and wrote to Kingsley that "Phyllis is without a doubt the most un-visual person I've ever encountered").[12] When they resumed corresponding, Pat was as forthcoming as ever.

Because Pat never strayed far from her own psyche in creating, destroying, or accumulating—"My stories are another form of telling what I wish to do," she remarked genially to an interviewer (who failed to flee the room, proving he didn't understand her meaning)[13]—she invested all her possessions with her long history of emotional advance and violent retreat, and with her deepest spiritual yearnings. With a brutality that cut through her natural reticence, Pat was perfectly capable of taking back certain objects she had given away, especially if she thought she might regret her "loss" later on.

In the heady New York summer of 1941 (Pat was twenty; the world and the relationship were new), her friend-and-something-more, the talented, well-connected, generous painter Buffie Johnson, "gave me a small green polo belt last night from Paris. . . . I started to give her my bracelet. I put it on her. But thinking about it . . . I made her give it back."[14]

But this is mild. A livelier attempt at repossession began soon after Stanley Highsmith's death in 1972, when Pat, newly settled in her Moncourt house, waged a fiercely fought four-year struggle in letters with her mother for custody of the "Hamilton Watch" and "watch chain" which she, Pat, had inexplicably given to Stanley Highsmith at the ages of twelve (watch) and twenty-one (chain). Or perhaps—Pat varied her stories—she was thirteen and twenty-two when she gave these gifts to Stanley.

In lengthy letters to Mary Highsmith, to her cousin, Dan; to her father, Jay B Plangman; and to Nini Wills, a friend of Mary, about the Hamilton watch and chain—objects whose long absence from Pat's sight had endowed with vibrant emotional drama—Pat wrote fetishistically graphic descriptions of both objects. She detailed their every scratch, curve, and surface, and her letters show how deeply and poignantly she invested her "earned objects" with her history and her desire, her sorrow and her rage, and her brokenhearted and perpetual sense of loss.

In an attempt to win Mary's friend Nini Wills over to *her* side of the Hamilton watch story—Pat still loved to tattle on Mary—Pat allowed herself to exercise a few of the compulsions with which she usually responded to any disturbance: numeration, classification, and substitution. Writing to Nini Wills on 9 March 1972, Pat mixed up her money and her memory, put a number to every single thing she did, and—unsuccessfully—tried to replace her mother with a pocket watch:

> And if you will forgive me for saying so, I am sorry to part with the watch and chain, which I chose for aesthetic value . . . when I had more taste than money. . . . I cut the grass for my Grampa Daniel Coates 24 times at 50 cents a whack, and so I arrived at $12.00 which bought the watch back in 1933. The watch cheered me up during a miserable year, when I missed my mother. . . . I had thought to remain with my mother, aged 12, when we had just come from New York to Texas, to be free, alone, happy with my Grandmother Coates. . . . I was in a very depressed state, but the watch was something to work for, something to achieve. . . .
>
> . . . I think even [my mother] has a dim idea of what spiritual sustenance this small object of beauty gave me, during the saddest year of my life.[15]

Nini Wills said to Mary Highsmith about the letter: "My God, no wonder she has that grim tight mouth in that newspaper picture. Boy, she went back to the embryo and scraped the womb, wouldn't you say?"[16]

And Pat—fifteen years later, still brooding over the Hamilton watch but now hoping to turn the incident into a fiction about "the sick and cruel types who prey upon the elderly and the feeble-minded"—decided on no evidence at all that it was "[l]ikely [Nini Wills's] son got the famous pocket watch."[17]

Countering Pat's watch-and-chain sallies from France with a few forays of her own from Texas, Mary Highsmith, whose sense-memory for objects was exactly like her daughter's, began to agitate for the return of Pat's "teething ring." Pat fended her mother off with a storm of logic, a tidal wave of accusation, and a Baedeker of the teething ring's travels since Mary had deposited it in London with Pat's ex-lover Kathryn Hamill Cohen "in Sept. 1959."[18] And then Pat added another skirmish to the watch-and-chain war: now, she wrote, she also wanted "Stanley's cufflinks," which had been "promised" to her. (This was a splendid but entirely futile diversionary tactic on Pat's part.)

Mary eventually won the watch-and-chain battle—that is, she didn't give them back to Pat—but it is difficult to say whether she prevailed through native cunning or whether the matter had merely slipped her failing mind.

Far more than cuff links, watches, and teething rings were involved in this last struggle for love and possession between the two Highsmith women. Like the emotional sleight-of-hand artists and serious drama queens they both were, Pat and Mary managed to substitute small items for large emotions, and to replace their disappointed love for each other with titanic quarrels. They went right on doing so for the rest of their lives.

During the same school year in which Pat acquired the Hamilton watch (1933–34)—the year Mary had gone back to Stanley in New York and Pat took up working with wood and sharpened instruments—the twelve-year-old Pat made another purchase. Somewhere in Fort Worth, Pat said, she picked up two "Confederate swords" (that's how she always described them)—and they are still in her archives: large, heavy, and absolutely lethal looking. The swords were an unusual acquisition for a twelve-year-old girl—but Pat was an unusual twelve-year-old.

Pat's swords might have been brandished south of the Mason-Dixon Line during the Civil War (still enshrined in memory by the Coates family who lost sons, brothers, and slaves to it), but they were certainly forged in Massachusetts: in Chicopee and Springfield, according to the inscriptions on their blades. Pat kept them in the classic crossed, duelling position on the walls of every house she ever occupied. It was not until the end of Mary Highsmith's life—but without mentioning Mary's decline and death as a motive—that Pat at last uncrossed her swords and displayed them, aligned and pointing in the same direction, on her wall in Tegna.

Kingsley Skattebol remembers that Pat told her more than one story about how she got the swords. One time, Pat said they belonged to one of her "Confederate uncles"; another time, she said she bought them in an antiques store. And on a trip to New Hampshire with Mary and Stanley in July of 1937 when she was sixteen, a trip on which she managed to lose the "garnet ring which I chose & paid for myself" (Pat always had bad luck with rings), Pat wrote in her high school journal: "I buy second sword."[19]

No matter where Pat got her swords (or what stories she told about how she got them), she preferred to believe that she brought them back with her as souvenirs of her miserable year in Texas in 1933–34—the year she *never* forgave her mother for. Reading between her lines, Pat returned to her parents' cobbled-together marriage and cramped apartment in New York as double-minded as she was ever to be, with an offering of peace in one hand (the Hamilton watch for Stanley) and an instrument of war (a duelling sword or two) in the other. The other thing she brought with her to New York was less tangible, although her feeling for it lasted just as long as her feeling for her swords. It was her grandmother's good-bye kiss "wet on my upper lip, and I let it stay, dreading the inevitable time when the wind would dry it, and the coolness would be gone."[20]

If Pat's arrival in New York from Texas in 1934 had occurred six or seven decades later, the unhappy preteen might have found herself enshrined in the collective family nightmare that is American social history. The profile Pat created of herself as a miserable child in Fort Worth in 1933–34 is very close to the tabloid image of terror that haunts America now: an adolescent misfit, depressed, enraged, seething with images of destruction, and armed to the teeth. But Pat was a born writer; she waited. And so she was able to take her most efficient revenge in fiction.

In 1980, as a token of her warm feelings for her editor at Calmann-Lévy in Paris, Alain Oulman, Pat gave him a small table she had made out of wood. M. Oulman, nephew of Calmann-Lévy founder Robert Calmann and the "Pitou" of his long, affectionate correspondence with Pat, was the person who had done more for Pat's reputation, career, and domestic comfort in France than anyone else. He dealt with the notoriously slow French telephone company for her, he helped her with her more difficult houseguests, and he counselled her through her long, "tough" negotiations with Diogenes for world representation.[21] And it was Alain Oulman who introduced Pat to her neighbor in the country, Colette de Jouvenel, daughter of Colette. De Jouvenel appeared with her Siamese cat at a dinner party to which Oulman had invited Pat, she became Pat's friendly neighbor and warm correspondent, and she had the good sense to bring her own lunch in a basket whenever she visited Pat in Moncourt.

At this same dinner party, Oulman also introduced Pat to James Baldwin. "Baldwin was an interesting pain in the ass, much as I had expected," Pat complained to Alex Szogyi[22]—and wrote that she didn't need to be told by Jimmy Baldwin, although she *was* told, that "all us whiteys . . . shall soon be murdered."[23]

Alain Oulman patiently shepherded Pat's visiting ex-lovers to and fro, and gave her, according to Calmann-Lévy's publicity representative Claire Cauvin, the most extraordinary support at book festivals and on book tours. He was, says Cauvin, "always by her side."[24] Pat herself wrote regularly of the many times she went to Oulman for advice and consent. A Jew like so many of her honorary counsellors, Oulman continued to serve as Pat's sounding board.

Nonetheless, Pat—who said she didn't know how she managed this, but seemed to manage it anyway—found the "courage" to ask Alain Oulman to return the small handmade table she'd given to him. She was justified in doing so, she wrote guiltily, because she felt she had merely "lent" him the table.[25] In fact, she'd given the table as a gift to Oulman and then just couldn't bear to be parted from it. Oulman returned the "loan" graciously.

Pat felt even more intensely about a drawing she'd given to Caroline Besterman during their long affair. "If I'd come to London now, I'd have asked for that drawing back. I mean it."[26]

Pat's relationship to one of the most important "objects" in her life is best expressed in her response to the first love letter she got from Caroline. She wrote that it made her feel like a "millionaire." Pat's friends, lovers, and associates rock with laughter (when they're not writhing with less comfortable reactions) when they describe the role money played in her life. Stories of Pat pocketing tips left by other people at restaurant tables, refusing loans to starving friends (but giving money to more affluent ones), shortchanging an impoverished neighbor in Aurigeno, and driving sixty miles for a cheaper plate of spaghetti are set pieces in the oral histories of most of the people who knew her.

Even Pat's very last will (she drafted too many wills for an accurate count) was delayed because she didn't want to pay a lawyer to copy it over.[27] It was the will in which she effectively disinherited her oldest friend, Kingsley Skattebol, who, for fifty years and through many testaments, had been promised the executorship of Pat's literary estate. Pat replaced Kingsley with Daniel Keel, of Diogenes Verlag, her *"vermittler,"* as she called him. It was a sensible decision: Keel is a great figure in European publishing, and Pat's estate was going to be administered from Switzerland, while Kingsley lived in New York. But Pat, as usual, had another motive in mind. For years, she had expressed increasing disapproval of her own goddaughter, Kingsley's daughter, and she told several people that she didn't want the girl to get her hands on the money.

Although the thought of dispensing cold cash could sometimes drive Pat to Olympian acts of avoidance, check writing was another matter.

Marion Aboudaram's three-year affair with Pat in Moncourt (see "A Simple Act of Forgery: Part 1" and "Les Girls: Part 2") depended on her willingness to travel from Paris, because Pat rarely came into the city. Marion was working in an art gallery in Paris for low wages at the time she was seeing Pat, living on lentils and pasta in an unheated flat on the rue Germain Pillon, then one of the seediest streets in Montmartre, now as chic as the rest of that mythic quartier. Pat had already let Marion know that she wasn't going to be suckered into buying her a radiator for her unheated apartment. At this time, says Marion, "Pat's will [Pat was on about her fifteenth version of it] and her taxes ate her mind. That's all she would talk about."[28]

One middle of the night, when Pat and Marion were in bed together, Pat, undoubtedly under duress, finally cracked.

"I'm fed up [with your poverty]!" she said to Marion. "I'm going to give you ten thousand francs!" Despite the lateness of the hour, Marion responded with great presence of mind. "Get up immediately and sign that check!" she told Pat. And Pat did it. She got up out of bed and made out a check to Marion Aboudaram at two o'clock in the morning for ten thousand francs. And then Pat did something even stranger: instead of handing the check to Marion, she put it in Marion's purse.

Pat knew perfectly well she'd hate herself in the morning for having given Marion money. (Another woman might have prided herself on assisting a lover.) Still, Pat liked to think of herself as an honorable woman (she continued to have recurring daydreams of returning a found wallet—an act whose awful implications she would explore in *Found in the Street*), which was why she put the ten-thousand-franc check into Marion's purse instead of leaving it on the bedside stand. It was like a deposit in Marion's bank account: a gift Pat wouldn't be able to take back after she'd changed her mind.

Pat's respect for private property amounted to a principle, and her special feeling for purses and wallets keeps cropping up on her gift lists—a gift-wrapped handbag for Mary Highsmith was in the boot of her English Volkswagen when the car was stolen from the Montereau train station—and in her accusations: she liked to insinuate that lovers were rifling her purse. Pat did a little purse rifling herself, apologizing to Monique Buffet *in writing* for going through her book bag when she was absent. "If it had contained (what????) something more personal, I'd never have done it," Pat wrote nervously to Monique.[29] And Pat had once looked into Mary Ronin's purse, when Mary went out of a room, to see if the new wallet she'd just given to Mary was "thin enough for her handbag." That was her excuse, anyway, and, just like the lovers who read her cahiers or diaries without permission and were horrified at what they'd read, Pat saw something she didn't want to see when she opened Mary's wallet.

Tabea Blumenschein's lightning, then lingering, tour through Pat's emotional and imaginative life (see "A Simple Act of Forgery: Part 1")—Pat left Marion Aboudaram for Blumenschein, and the "aftershocks" of Blumenschein's dropping *her* after four weeks went on for "about four years"—inspired the stricken Pat to an eruption of mostly bad love poetry. One rueful little stanza, more shapely than anything that preceded or followed it, expresses just what Pat's "objects" might be substituting for and why those substitutions were so necessary.

If I were only a good poet
Able to distill all this into

A clear and beautiful little sphere
Like a gem one could see through, polished,
Something to keep, small in my pocket,
Something to look at
That wouldn't hurt.[30]

It was only at the very end of her life that Patricia Highsmith began to let go of some of the things that meant something to her. A friend says: "In the year before she died—she described all her treatments in detail so she knew she was dying [but would never admit it]—she would send me bits of her life, objects: an ashtray from the famous lesbian bar in Paris in the twenties . . . a little brick from Tennessee Williams's house in Key West that she had [Charles] Latimer steal, and she sent me a little silver locket that one of her girls had given her. And then she started sending me her books in early signed editions. . . . When she started sending these gifts, that's when I knew that she was going to go."[31]

And, in July of 1994, seven months before she died—again without ever saying she was mortally ill—Pat wrote to her "brother Dan's" wife, Florine, offering her and her son Don the most precious of her family possessions: "a quilt made by Grandma. . . . I like to see these things passed on. . . . the four nearly life-sized photographs of Gideon Coates and his wife, a Penn. And of Dr. Oscar Wilkinson Stewart and wife, a Deckard or Deckerd . . . the only things I asked Grandma for as inheritance."[32] (It was Pat's great-great-grandmother who was a Deckerd; Oscar's wife, Pat's great-grandmother, was a Pope.)

For someone so conscious of objects, so careful with money, so good with her hands, and so given to listing her assets, Pat had unusual problems with her possessions. The physical world seemed to retreat before her efforts to stage-manage it. Too many times, she arrived at destinations ahead of her luggage or her typewriter—as she did on her first foreign trip, to Taxco, Mexico, in 1943 and on several different visits to Europe. Or she found herself departing before expected items arrived, as she did in Paris, in 1951. In Switzerland, something as simple as shopping for grocery items seemed to a neighbor to be beyond Pat's capacities.[33] But some of Pat's "helplessness" was cultivated—and she always managed to surround herself with people who were quick to offer assistance.

The accordion Pat bought from her first trip to Italy in 1948 (entrepreneurial as ever, she hoped to resell it in New York) stuck to her like glue for months and months; even with paid advertisements in the papers she couldn't get rid of it. And despite her obsessive attention to her cahiers, she left them with friends during one of her travels, then forgot where they were for a while. They eventually turned up in a house on Long Island, but the original manuscript of *The Talented Mr. Ripley* disappeared into the aether in Fort Worth after grandmother Willie Mae died, and almost all traces of her unpublished manuscript, *The Traffic of Jacob's Ladder,* are gone as well.

Of that lost manuscript, Kingsley Skattebol, the last person alive who read and still remembers it, writes: "if *Mrs. Dalloway* can be called a meditation on past intentions and what time has and has not done to the people who cherished them: this was the crux of Pat's lost novel *The Traffic of Jacob's Ladder,* unlike anything else in her oeuvre before or since."[34]

But when Kingsley and her then-beau Lars Skattebol first read the work in 1953—Pat was calling it "Book #3" then or *The Sleepless Night*—they attacked it (see "Les Girls: Part 2"), irritating Pat no end. And the last ten pages of *The Traffic of Jacob's Ladder*—all that remain of the novel in Pat's archives—support the critique: they are awkwardly written in the standard Highsmith formula of two men, Gerald and Oscar, obsessed with each other, latently homosexual, etc., etc. At the end, Oscar is dead in a hotel room, and Gerald, like all Highsmith characters, wants only to get lost: "like Oscar he could vanish into nowhere in Paris, too, if he chose, and no one could find him, if he only threw his passport and his papers into the Seine, the envelope Oscar had addressed to him, and the money."[35] The manuscript of *Jacob's Ladder* was roundly criticized and then rejected by the publishers who saw it, and perhaps that was why it, too, got "lost." Perhaps, also, these remaining ten pages are from an early draft and the book was better than this remnant.

Pat's beloved 1956 Olympia typewriter had its wear-and-tear problems (six to eight pages of fiction and five furiously typed letters a day took their toll) although she was to tell an interviewer—stressing the typewriter's German origins and her identification with it—that it "never needed a repair."[36] When she found an abandoned typewriter by her "garbage bins" in Aurigeno, she stalked the typewriter case for several days—circling it in indecision, unable to believe that she could get something that meant so much to her for nothing—before swooping guiltily down on it. "I expect a mysterious knock on the door: Have you taken the typewriter left below?, etc? but so far no one has knocked."[37] Pat could never accept anything without having first earned it, *worked* for it—this was part of her Calvinist ethic—but she also enjoyed the complicated, criminal feelings that getting something for nothing afforded her.

On a publicity trip to receive the Prix Littéraire at the American Film Festival in Deauville in September of 1987, Pat thought she had left the only ring she ever wore (it was also the only ring she ever kept)—the circle of gold given to her by Ellen Hill in 1953 when their relations were at a nadir—on top of a piano in the bar at the Normandy Hotel and was "depressed for four days." When her part-time *femme de ménage* found the ring on the rug beside her bed in Aurigeno, Pat's spirits soared. She was also cheered by the thought that the housekeeper was actually earning her salary.

"People don't like losing things—of sentimental value," she wrote about the ring in an odd, alcohol-wreathed letter to the piano player of her Normandy Hotel weekend, a Mr. Abe Janssens, on whose piano she thought she'd left the ring. Unbidden, Pat decided to confide this feeling (and quite a few other sentiments) to what must have been a very surprised Mr. Janssens a couple of weeks after returning to Aurigeno from the film festival at Deauville. Happily lit up with drink during the two-day cocktail hour that she'd made of her short residency at the festival, Pat had draped herself over Janssens's piano in the hotel bar for two nostalgic September evenings of Cole Porter sing-alongs.* This cavalcade of the classic American songbook would have reminded her of one of the happier aspects of her parents' apartment on Grove Street in Greenwich Village, that it was on a street of famous piano bars. Pat loved piano bars.

Pat's acquaintance with the piano player Janssens was limited to the length of the sets he played—he kept calling her by the wrong name—and, in a phrase only she could have used, Pat wrote to him that she "couldn't pick him out of a line-up" if she had to.[38] A man who didn't know her name, someone she couldn't have recognized under police lights, was the perfect repository for her inebriated, confessional, and very nostalgic letter. But Pat needed to use the subject of her ring to launch the communication. It was something like the way her fictional killers use "trophies" from their victims to keep the connections alive.

Pat's car troubles were of a simpler nature. Because of her many travels, and because her houses were always rural or suburban, she had to drive to train stations and airports to get to where she wanted to go. Once there, she tended to leave her vehicles parked, and those vehicles—worse luck—tended to get stolen. One of her cars was taken in New Hope in 1962, and two of them were taken in France. She said that the theft of her English Volkswagen in

---

* She also wrote a wistful letter to Monique Buffet when she arrived on 7 September saying that Deauville looked "charming" and "romantic." "I've never been in love here. Bette Davis is at Hotel Royale and I hope I meet her, even if briefly, I have the highest respect for her." Pat did meet Davis, briefly, and Douglas Fairbanks Jr. was introduced to her by Marc Brandel's second wife, who was one of the festival organizers (see illustration).

1969 from the parking lot "near the Montereau railway station" hastened "my rapid progress toward persecution complex," although "[t]his somewhat risky theft is a pleasure to me compared to sneaky, cowardly thefts."[39] She was thinking of the two lovers she suspected of rifling her purse.

In Switzerland, Pat's luck with automobiles didn't much change. There was a bad accident in her Aurigeno neighbor Ingeborg Moelich's car on the way back from their visit to the Bayreuth Festival—for which her friend Charles Latimer (who insisted on being driven out of the way) bore some moral responsibility. It provoked an ungenerous response from Pat, who was not going to be cheated out of her feeling of total innocence in the matter—even though her map reading had probably contributed to the accident. Finally Pat, whose own driving was distracted when sober and deeply inattentive when drinking (she flunked her English driving test twice in Suffolk and then flunked the French driving test three times after she'd moved to Moncourt in 1969),[40] managed an unusual way to reenact the title of her first novel, *Strangers on a Train*. At a small railway crossing near her home, she ran straight into a locomotive with her car.[41]

In November of 1952, after a year of trailing Ellen Hill around Europe— their wearisome cycle of fighting, separating, loving, and separating again was well established by then—Pat wrote in her twenty-first cahier:

> "Care of Mrs. Somebody." I am always "Care of Mrs. Somebody." Or "Mr. Somebody." I have never a home. I wander from New York, to Paris, to London, to Venice, Munich, Salzburg, and Rome, without a real address. My letters arrive by the grace of God and Mr. or Mrs. Somebody.
>
> Someday, perhaps, I shall have a house built of rock, a house with a *name*—Hanley-on-the-Lake, Bedford on the River, West Hills, or plain Sunny Vale. Something. So even without my own name on the envelope letters will reach me, because I and only I shall be living there. But that can never make up for these years of standing in line at American Express offices from Opera to Haymarket, Naples to Munich. Can never make up for the tragic, melancholic, humiliating mornings when one has gone with hope for a letter, and turned away empty handed, empty hearted.[42]

Pat spent her adult life the way all wandering expatriates do: leaving things here, storing them there, asking people to look after what she left behind. She added her own twist to the tale, however, often accusing the unhappy caretakers of her goods and chattels of cheating her of her possessions—or of using them without permission. She abandoned her possessions and then she felt abandoned by them, making use of her retreats from them to produce or to justify certain emotions which were necessary to her writing. Her policy with women was much the same.

Pat's complaint that it was Mary Highsmith who lost the manuscript of *The Talented Mr. Ripley* was a useful one for a writer who wanted to contrast her mother unfavorably with her grandmother. Pat also complained that she had been cheated out of Willie Mae's house by Mother Mary—when Willie Mae's will clearly left the house to Mary and her brother Claude. Pat accused her ex-lover Tex of driving her car without permission in New Hope (she'd left the car in Tex's care), and then worried that the local mechanic was also making free with it (she demanded an odometer reading) and that the sublettor of her house in Pennsylvania was unreliable ("everything is out of hand, my car, my house)." And she hated everyone who ever sublet her East Fifty-sixth Street apartment (and touched her possessions), except for Truman Capote.

The mostly imagined chaos in Pat's arrangements in New Hope in 1963 made the idea of remaining in Suffolk—where she had gone to be near Caroline Besterman—easier for her. Her unvoiced accusations against two of her lovers for rifling her purse for money when she wasn't looking were also put to practical use: they allowed her to distance herself from unfulfilling relations with women she had fetishized and objectified, just as she fetishized and objectified her favorite possessions. Her despairing responses to these women had the effect of casting Pat as a kind of object herself: the bucket in the well of loneliness.

Late one night in June of 1984, Pat, so depressed in her sunless stone farmhouse in Aurigeno, Switzerland, that she hadn't been able to read a book for the last "two and ¼ years,"[43] opened a bottle of cheap beer, lit up a Gauloise *jaune,* and sat down to give her hopeful houseguest, a young social scientist teaching at Barnard College named Bettina Berch, an unusually direct piece of her mind on the subject of women.

Bettina Berch and Pat, who had been corresponding for a while, had already missed a couple of opportunities to meet each other in New York. At the last missed meeting place—a bookstore reading Pat was doing in Manhattan—Bettina had left for Pat "a small bottle of the best scotch I could find. The pint size, because part of the beauty of the present was the bottle." Pat was delighted with her gift: "I shall keep refilling it," she wrote. "And," says Bettina, "she did keep refilling it." Bettina's visit to Aurigeno was their first face-to-face encounter, and it lasted for several days.[44]

Pat was well-disposed towards Bettina Berch ("sawed-off Russian-Jewish name," Pat wrote to Kingsley, noting, as she always did, if a person she liked was a Jew; "quite decent, left-wing")[45] despite the fact that Bettina had expressed the desire to write Pat's biography and was, as Ellen Hill darkly suspected, "an ardent feminist."[46] Ellen Hill, says Bettina, was still quite "territorial" about Pat, thirty years after their love affair had ended.

Always hungry for news of the States, Pat began by pumping Bettina Berch for the kinds of facts she could use in her fictions. Although she continued to set many of her novels in the United States, Pat was by now woefully out of touch with the textures, tastes, locutions, and even the products of her native country. Don Swaim, her perceptive radio interviewer in New York at WCBS in 1987, noted that Pat was giving the word "story"—i.e., the floor of a building— its English spelling and had referred to shopping carts as "trolleys." Pat admitted to him that she was confusing the English term "coffee white" with the American term "coffee regular."[47]

It was in the 1970s—the first full decade she'd spent outside the United States—when Pat began to make errors of American fact and understanding in her novels, errors like having Edith Howland of *Edith's Diary* bring a bottle of rye, one of Pat's favorite bottle drinks of the 1940s, to a neighbor's dinner party. (By 1977, when *Edith's Diary* was published, rye had not been produced in the United States for at least twenty years.) Pat had to write to her still-radical friend Lil Picard to ask her for names of the leftish magazines Edith Howland would be reading and sending articles to; in Indiana, she watched American television for a week to pick up pointers about religious extremists for *People Who Knock on the Door*; and she wrote to ask Kingsley to do crucial research on New York police procedures for *A Dog's Ransom*.

Pat always knew what she needed for her work, but because her experience of America was now that of an expatriate—and more or less limited to the *International Herald Tribune*, the occasional *Time* and *Newsweek* magazine, and the *National Lampoon* (she was a subscriber for a while, she told Lil Picard)—she was out of touch with the large and small shifts of custom and conversation which make all the difference in fiction. Her short story "I Despise Your Life" (first published in her collection *The Black House* in 1981) is an attempt to dramatize embattled father-son relations in the context of hip young wasters who are drugging, dancing, and living in a loft in SoHo; and whatever measures she took to ensure its accuracy were a terrible failure. The slang is decades out of date, the dialogue is unrecognizable, and not one element, including the money-based relations between the father and son, carries any more authenticity than a superficial article criticizing "the youth of today" in a supermarket tabloid. Bettina Berch, who had lengthy conversations with

Pat, says: "*Newsweek* is what she based her opinion on and that's not what I consider political analysis."[48]

During Bettina's visit, Pat was trying to work up a mid-1980s Manhattan atmosphere for her novel *Found in the Street,* but she had lost Manhattan as a subject. She lost it, imaginatively, in the way that Raymond Chandler said he'd "lost Los Angeles" when he moved to La Jolla. By now, her personal experiences of American places and times, the impressions and details and behaviors she'd gathered on her nighttime prowlings of Manhattan and on her lengthy boat, train, and car journeys to Texas, New Orleans, Mexico, and Maine in the 1940s and 1950s, were no longer alive enough in her mind to be made into fiction. Sunk in depression in her rock-rimmed canton in Switzerland and too far—temporally and physically—from what she was writing about, Pat was reduced to asking Bettina Berch for the *Village Voice* newspaper and a map of New York.[49] But Pat always asked everybody for maps.

Bettina and Pat had already discussed in their letters some of the themes Pat liked to walk her wits around, and Pat, straining for a topic that might appeal to a feminist guest, searched her memory to produce some slight evidence of the social injustices suffered by women. She herself had suffered none, she said firmly, and expressed a special disgust for feminists. On her part, Bettina patiently tried to explain to the long-exiled Pat some of the mysteries of the New America—like how to use a bank card to get money out of a wall. Pat, says Bettina, was "very funny about it. That was one of those moments of displaced humor, sitting at the other end of the world, explaining how to put in a PIN code in an ATM machine in Manhattan. What Pat eventually described doesn't do anything wrong although it doesn't incorporate any of these details."[50]

Pat's secondhand research usually managed to produce a halo of strangeness around her already strange fictions, an atmospheric dislocation which a writer who gets her experience firsthand would find almost impossible to achieve. But further strangeness in her work wasn't what Pat was after. She was just, as Bettina Berch says, "doing her research" *her* way, long distance. Her imagination simply couldn't leave America alone.

As she sometimes did when she thought she'd been remiss as a hostess (by the 1970s and 1980s, Pat was quite lax in the hostess department, and worse was to follow), Pat wrote to Bettina Berch in New York when the visit was over to apologize for her "nervousness."[51] And—a sure proof of Pat's affection—on the big, square, gilt-edged mirror in her last house in Tegna, Pat actually stuck up a snapshot of Bettina Berch cradling her infant daughter. It's the only picture of a mother and daughter ever to grace a house inhabited by Patricia Highsmith.

In the lengthy, taped conversation which unrolled that June night in Aurigeno between the two Barnard graduates, Pat, touchy about being questioned, tired because the conversation went on until one in the morning, and worried about her sick cat who "wasn't getting any better,"[52] allowed herself to be drawn into a few clarifying statements about women, statements which recall her work in the comics as well as her serious fictional work.

> It's hard for me to see women (as a whole) standing on their own feet. I still see them as sort of in relationship to a man. . . . Which is very curious because my mother was very (as women go even now), she was definitely rather brave. She had a career since the age of twenty, and when . . . she wanted to divorce my father she did. And my father offered money and so on, you know, for the doctor when I was born, at least. [There was no doctor; Mary Coates was "midwived" by an upstairs neighbor.] My mother said "no thanks." So I had in my childhood the image of a rather strong independent woman—and yet I don't see them that way. I see them as a bunch of pushovers, for the most part. I see them as whining, to tell you the truth. Especially this feminist thing—whining, always *complaining* about something. Instead of doing something. . . .
>
> Men can leave the house. Ripley leaves his house. He's got a wife there, plus a servant. I don't see women leaving the house.* Maybe it's just a quirk of mine, or something wrong in me.[53]

Whatever objections Pat had to her comic book writing in the 1940s, the fact that comic books concentrated on the feats of male heroes wasn't one of them.[54]

After twenty-seven years of silence, Pat initiated a correspondence with Marijane Meaker (telling everyone that Meaker had written to her first) in October of 1988 by writing to ask if "you might have a missing 3 pages from my family papers, which you were interested in. . . . they were of Civil War years . . . so you can imagine how I miss these."[55] It was an odd way to approach a former lover—especially because Meaker says she had no memory of the papers and no memory whatsoever of being interested in them. Pat

---

* As a woman who wrote in her own bedroom, gardened in her own yard, and made furniture in her own workroom, Pat, by this time, was quite reticent about "leaving the house" herself. In late middle age she did so only for reasons of professional, medical, or sexual urgency.

seemed to be more comfortable reaching out to Marijane through feelings she could attach to objects or activities.

Josyane Savigneau had a similar experience with Pat at their first meeting in Aurigeno. Pat kept offering her things: "'Do you want something to drink . . . do you want something to eat?'" Savigneau says. "She couldn't just say, do you want to stay a little longer. . . . She couldn't say just sit down and stay—because it was clear that she liked me—and so she always had to propose an activity."[56]

Fear of loss, instigated by a world of people and objects out of her control, was a constant theme in Pat's life. It put its unmistakable patina on much of her work—that long, slow crawl over the surface of things that can be counted, described, and handled—and it underscored all her professional transactions. The letters in which her prevailing sense of loss attaches itself to the details of contracts and business proposals would run to several stupefying volumes. The files of her literary agents—particularly Patricia Schartle Myer of McIntosh & Otis in New York, and Mme Jenny Bradley of the William Bradley Agency in Paris—show that they bore up as graciously as they could under the constant epistolary batteries launched by their profit-and-loss-minded client.

Pat's relentless demands on Patricia Schartle Myer to reduce commissions for negotiating European sales of her work were reluctantly agreed to by Mrs. Myer. But when Pat unilaterally decided in 1979 to deal with all her agents separately and to confine McIntosh & Otis to her American sales rather than having them take care of her international business as per contract, Mrs. Myer, after "twenty years" of representing Pat, had had enough. "Since you clearly feel that you have been cheated on commissions by two of the world's most reputable agents, I am not willing to continue to represent your work," Mrs. Myer wrote to Pat in August of 1979. "It has, of course, come to my attention from many sources that you have reported the downright libel that McIntosh & Otis and Heath [A. M. Heath, Pat's London agents] charge you an unfair commission."[57]

Pat made equally extravagant claims (and cast equal blame) on almost every other literary agent who ever worked with her. Eventually she left them all (or, as in the case of Mrs. Myer, they left her) for her supportive and highly profitable arrangement with Daniel Keel and Diogenes Verlag. But not without seven months of fully armed negotiations by Pat with Diogenes for the terms she wanted.

Pat's intense focus on money and objects—like her conviction that every love affair was doomed to go down in flames—became a self-fulfilling prophecy. What she feared most was what she most attracted. In two or three novels—one of them is *The Talented Mr. Ripley*—Pat describes the power of one pair of eyes to attract another, and she makes Tom look away so as not to pull towards him the gaze of the person he is covertly watching. By the terms of her own belief, with her mind so obsessively fixed on money and taxes, she could hardly avoid attracting the unwelcome attentions of the two French government services devoted to finance: the dreaded *fisc* and the French customs office, the *douane*. And in March of 1980, in Moncourt, France, that is exactly what happened.

32

THE REAL ROMANCE OF OBJECTS

PART 2

The sudden intrusion of the French customs office, the *douane,* into the occasional peace and relative calm of Pat Highsmith's workroom in Moncourt, France, on the twenty-sixth of March 1980 was both a long-awaited and an already-imagined nightmare.

Pat had always railed against her taxes in England, France, and the United States, and she had a long history of sheltered taxes (Tomes Ltd., the company she formed in London, protected her earnings there); financial redistributions (some untraceable doings in Puerto Rico and the Bahamas,[1] a proliferation of bank accounts and investments in several countries, as well as some casual currency smuggling: "Have just last week discovered an outlet for the barred franc—via Canada through a friend");[2] and royalty checks arriving in business envelopes from foreign sources. Any one of these activities would have caught the attention of French tax officials; keeping foreign bank accounts, for instance, was illegal for foreign residents like Pat. All of them together were like a cluster of signposts pointing the authorities in the direction of an investigation.

Samuel Okoshken, Pat's tax lawyer and accountant in Paris in the 1970s and 1980s, explained what he knew of her tax situation. "She received envelopes from [Diogenes Verlag in] Switzerland and [the *douane*] thought anything with a Swiss address was proof positive of some malfeasance. . . . Maybe there were things she didn't tell me. [Author's note: there were.] If she had secret stuff, I obviously didn't know about it. But I had no reason to believe that she was not up-front. I felt she was completely okay, and she felt that too. But she was so offended by the French government and what they had done to her that she decided to leave."[3]

The official French inquiries into her finances were enough to give Pat—so prone, herself, to feeling guilty and to making accusations—an excuse for the drastic act of moving to Switzerland. Pat took the investigation as an accusation, just as any French citizen would. But the *douane*'s raid was only an excuse for her to move and not a reason. The reasons for her removal were two (mistaken) assumptions: first, that she could save tax money by living in Switzerland for six months of the year, and second, that she didn't want to live in a country which suspected everyone of being "a slight crook." (This, of course, was Pat's own view of most of the people she met.) A fortnight before the *douane* raided her house, Pat, under Ellen Hill's direction, had *already* picked out another house for herself to buy in Aurigeno, Switzerland.

Since 1979 and before, Pat had been given large and small warning signs of tax troubles in France. For years, she'd been complaining of spending too much of her time filling out tax forms. Two months before the raid, she'd written to Monique Buffet: "I think I told you the French *fisc* is desperate to get their hands on 60% of my global income for past many years, and are asking me where I was physically when I wrote this and that."[4]

Her attempts to lighten her French taxes ran the usual expatriate's gamut ("My accountant has 3 ideas, all of which I can do from home, by way of my NOT having to go to Switzerland"),[5] but an escape to Switzerland was still very much on her mind. Ellen Hill, to whom Pat continued to turn for opinions and ideas, lived in Cavigliano. And Pat, having quarrelled with her other literary representatives, was in the middle of six or seven months of what she called her "tough" negotiations with Diogenes Verlag in Zurich to be her world representatives. Still, she had the satisfaction of beating the *douane* to the punch; they knocked on her door five days after she'd come back from her house-buying expedition to Switzerland.

Of the taxes Pat complained of so persistently—"most people would smile at the news of [103,000 francs in royalties], but I hit my head and say 'Oh Jesus!' . . . it all goes for taxes"[6]—Samuel Okoshken says: "She paid a good bit, but she had a lot of American income that was treated favorably under the treaty. I think she got a pretty fair deal."[7] Pat felt differently. Cursing her tax bracket and lamenting the loss of "the fruits of her labor"—while never failing to brag about her large income to her young lover Monique Buffet—Pat wrote: "Sat. I signed a check for $31,302 (dollars) to USA tax people. . . . It's the second-biggest check I ever signed in my life."[8]

In January of 1980, three months before the Moncourt raid, Pat had written proudly to Monique: "the French taxman was amazed that I have declared all my earnings, and no doubt about that. This means I am not considered a 'tax fraud.'" Whatever her inner feelings were (and her insistence that she wasn't "considered a 'tax fraud'" probably meant she felt like one), innocence in the eyes of others, a sense of her moral uprightness acknowledged, meant a great deal to her. Samuel Okoshken thought she was "trying to undo what [the *douane*] had done" by moving to Switzerland.[9] In this, Pat resembles the Coateses of her mother's family, whose sense of propriety was so great that they added that extra *e* to their surname—changing it from Coats to Coates—so that no one would ever confuse them with their orthographical doubles, the other Alabama Coats family: that low-down bunch of horse thieves who went out and got themselves hanged. Pat was always ready to add a metaphorical *e* to whatever name she was giving to her activities.

Pat's often-quoted remark that she was so "honest" that she "trembled before customs inspectors" was made some time before the French customs inspectors (the *douane*) actually came to *her*. Like almost everything else she fed to the press, this remark was a misdirection. People who bear what she once called "a lighter burden of guilt" (her idea of innocence) don't tremble before customs inspectors. No one understood this better than Pat, who deliberately titled her 1969 novel *The Tremor of Forgery* (about the man who is writing a Highsmith-like novel on a Highsmith-like typewriter in the same hotel where Highsmith actually stayed in Tunisia) because "forgers' hands usually trembled very slightly at the beginning and end of their false signatures."[10]

If Pat trembled before customs inspectors, it was probably because of the objects she was trying to slip, untaxed and/or unconfiscated, across French, English, Italian, and Swiss borders. Live snails lugged across borders were only the most exotic in her long history of transporting undetected and/or undertaxed chattel.

Like all expatriates, Pat had only to leave her native country to begin to crave its goods and services. The post offices in every hamlet, mountain village, and rural retreat Pat had ever lived in were besieged with the Levi's and western belts Pat requested from her cousin Dan in Texas ("The size is fine. . . . But I still would not mind some time a plain dark brown, no colors, no colors on the buckle. . . . I do not like color decorations.")[11] and the jackets, vests, and pants she mail-ordered herself from Brooks Brothers in New York. Homemade cookies, favorite shirts, and slightly too small shoes (Pat's feet were getting larger)—all respectively baked, bought, boxed, and shipped by Mary Highsmith from New York, from Florida, and from Texas for her daughter—followed Pat all over Europe. Daisy Winston sent Campbell's soups and chili peppers and more shoes from New Hope; while cat doors, Fritos for Pat's cat Semyon, diligent background research on Manhattan police procedure, crucial books like Menninger's *The Human Mind,* and the special, "dirtcheap"

Columbia University notebooks Pat used as cahiers, were faithfully posted from New York by Kingsley Skattebol for forty years.

A sample order from Pat to Kingsley on 9 July 1973: "The point is, I need three more cahiers, these spiral notebooks—which measure 7 inches by 8¼— have faintly greenish paper, emblazoned with Columbia on the front cover, stating that they contain 80 sheets also. . . . Price 33c [that was the 1942 price], but I am sure those days are gone forever, and they are now 75c."[12]

The lavender floor wax to which Tom Ripley and his creator were so attached was mailed to Pat by the two Barbaras from Islington. But her peanut butter (at the end of her life, she lived mostly on beer and peanut butter),[13] also ordered from England because it was cheaper, was an American brand. (Alabama, Pat's ancestral state, is one of the United States' largest producers of peanuts.) She counselled everyone to mark each parcel sent to her as being worth "under $10" to avoid customs taxes. If she was paying the postage herself, cash on delivery, she insisted that the packages be sent to her by the cheapest possible surface mail.

In the harsh glow of hindsight, the *douane*'s descent upon the House of Highsmith in March of 1980 looks less like a personally directed tax raid and more like yet another expression of Pat's lifelong struggles with income streams, owned objects, and demanding governments. It was also, of course, something more than a metaphor. It was an assault on her property and her privacy—and the stuff of her very worst nightmare.

On the morning of 26 March 1980,* the French *douane* staged a quiet "invasion" of the house on the rue de la Boissière. Two "lurking" French tax officers and one policeman "knocked on my door, proceeded to rifle my papers, and went off with USA bankbook, all current business papers (letters which I need). These creeps are after foreign bank accounts which of course I have declared."[14]

"The French are preying on me, because I am an easy mark, a soldier standing up in the field, not protected by a trench. . . . Ellen Hill . . . asked me if the douane had seized my passport, and I ran upstairs to see, and told her that they had not. . . . She has been through the Hitler period. . . . she knows what this is, so I really do listen to what she says."[15]

It was a clarifying moment for a writer whose worldview could charitably be described as paranoid. The raid brought together most of Pat's fears and many of her intolerances, and it proved to her, once again, that she was correct in her inclinations, justified in her prejudices, and arrayed alone against the world: that little island of virtue floating in a sea of swindlers we saw in "A

---

* Pat misdated the raid in her cahier as "10 March 1980," a sure sign of distress.

Simple Act of Forgery." Two days after the raid, Pat was thinking that "[m]y phone is probably now tapped" and was watching her language in telephone conversations.[16]

Ellen Hill's analysis of the raid made Pat think of the "Hitler period," which, naturally, made her think of the Jews—never far from her thoughts by now. She managed, indirectly, to implicate two Jews in the raid in her letters: her amiable accountant, Samuel Okoshken ("my accountant is really to blame for this")[17] and the only French inspector whose name she mentioned: a Monsieur "Roger Cohen," who reminded her "twice . . . that it was not allowed to have a foreign bank account." Her response to the French government was more general: an execration of all things French and, again indirectly, a phrasing of her problem with the government in terms of the Israeli-Arab situation. She was, she said when the French government wanted to honor her, "not accepting the Crystal Stopper" [symbol of the award the French government wanted to give her] . . . just like Sadat refused to appear with Begin."[18] Whenever Pat was feeling threatened, her mind fell naturally into this comparison.

Whatever she was thinking privately, Pat continued to consult with Samuel Okoshken for years, even encouraging him in his own hopes to become a writer and providing a jacket quote for one of his novelist friends. He has fond memories of her: "I could see," he says, "the young girl she had been."[19] She made her complaints to everyone but Okoshken himself about the way her tax matters were handled. As luck would have it, her last lover in France, Monique Buffet, was acquainted with Okoshken's then-secretary—and Pat was "terrified" that "information" (of what kind, she never told Monique) would make its way to Okoshken via the secretary gossip circuit.[20]

Despite the depopulating nature of the curses Pat called down upon the French government, there seemed to be enough officials left in high places in France to nominate Patricia Highsmith for several honors. Characteristically, she accepted every distinction the French had to offer, including, in 1990, the Officier des arts et des lettres. Paul Bowles, in quite a characteristic mood himself, wrote to Pat wondering if it really would be "fun to receive the order of *Officier des Arts et Lettres?*" It was a rhetorical question, and naturally, he answered it himself. He didn't think it would, he wrote.[21]

The tax inspectors remained in Pat's study for several hours that March day in 1980. They seemed to her to be uncommonly thorough, staying on until one o'clock.[22] They opened her desk drawers, they fingered her possessions, and they laid their hands on her Olympia typewriter. Horrified at this breaching of her boundaries, Pat felt—*any* writer would feel—that her writing room was being violated by the *douane*'s presence and polluted by its searches. The place where she worked was sacred to her, and nearly twenty years before she had written about "the strange power that work has to transform a room, any room, into something very special for a writer who has worked there, sweated and cursed and maybe known a few minutes of triumph and satisfaction there."[23]

Pat always preferred to carry out the physical exertions of the writing room in secret. "It is the lonely nature of writing that these strong memories and emotions cannot be shared with anyone," she advised the readers of *Plotting and Writing Suspense Fiction*.[24] Pat's bed was in her writing room, and its exposure to the eyes of the tax inspectors would have been especially painful to her. Her feeling for privacy, her horror at being revealed in ways she couldn't control, went right down to her cells.

Oddly, or not so oddly, since novelists often write their lives before living them, Pat had already imagined something like this invasion in *Edith's Diary*, written in the very house, in the very *room*, which the *douane* had just defiled. In the novel, Edith's ex-husband, Brett, has brought in a psychiatrist to evaluate Edith, whose irregular behavior has attracted the attention of everyone around her. The two men walk, uninvited, into Edith's workroom, where her diary lies open on a table. " 'Get out! *Both* of you!' . . . She realized that her teeth were bared, that she was panting. 'You might have given me some notice! I think this is simply awful!' She heard her own voice shrieking, as if the voice belonged to someone else."[25]

After the French inspectors left her bedroom, Pat, "still in shock,"[26] telephoned to Ellen Hill in Cavigliano for help. In her most martial mode, Ellen told Pat to pack her bags immediately and get out of the country right away. That's when Pat remembered that Ellen Hill had been through the "Hitler period" and must know what she was talking about.[27]

And then, with another of those ritualized actions with which she met life's daily disorders, Pat started right in to wash her troubles away. What she was accustomed to doing twenty times a day to her hands, and twice a day to her body, she now did to everything the tax inspectors had touched.[28] She cleaned and recleaned her typewriter and she washed and wiped down her desk, trying to dissolve in water and cleaning solution her profound sense of violation. And it was not only the violation she was removing. She was scrubbing away at that soiling feeling of guilt—as palpable to her as spilled ink on her desk or the heavy hands of the intruders on her papers—which overcame her every single time she was accused of something.

In her obsessive and prophetic way, Pat had always tended to see the world in terms of dirt and detritus. "We throw out as much as we take in," she wrote irritatedly in 1971.[29] To her love of bathroom humor and toilet jokes, she added a fixation with recycling "the eternal waste products of existence."[30]

Kingsley remarks that this fixation extended to Pat's "compost pile," for which she would "save everything" and which she would "visit" all the time.[31] Pat liked the look of decomposition. In her second summer in Moncourt, the summer of 1971, Pat had been pondering the possibility of writing a novel called *Garbage*. It would have to do, she reckoned, with "the human concern from birth until death with washing diapers, flushing toilets, bedpans, and then what to do with the corpse. Not to mention all the orange peels and whiskey bottles . . . the dust, the emptying of Hoover bags, the blowing of snot and soot into Kleenexes, the abortions, the hysterectomies."

But how should she begin a novel with such an unpromising subject? Pat didn't have to look beyond her mirror. "I need a character obsessed with all this. I've got one, myself."[32]

And now, as in some awful fairy tale in reverse, the *douane*'s mephitic touch had turned the golden tools of her "workroom" into "garbage."

Pat wouldn't go near the office of the *douane* to retrieve her confiscated goods, but she had, as usual, an obliging neighbor to do the necessary. "Mary Ryan fetched my xeroxed papers for my accountant from the *Douane*. I consider them filthy."[33] Pat was now "writing 3 pages a day instead of 5 or 8 [of *The Boy Who Followed Ripley*], but if I didn't make this effort, I'd be down the drain. Finished."[34] Profoundly upset, Pat knew what she needed. She needed to work. And so she marshalled her forces and soldiered on.

Until the last possible moment, Pat Highsmith held off making her final will. She had, however, made quite a few penultimate testaments over the years, whose revoked clauses at the end of her life left her friends with many an unpleasant surprise. Marylin Scowden, Pat's last accountant, felt so protective of her that she worked for Pat outside her own firm so she wouldn't have to charge her. "I knew she needed more than tax service; she needed someone to talk to, and . . . I couldn't charge her for all that," Scowden says. But in December of 1995, two months before Pat died, Scowden put her professional foot down. "I said we have to put things in order and I knew she was very reluctant to tell one person everything. I knew I had some pieces [of the puzzle of Pat's estate] but not everything. I had even advised her to give away everything beforehand to avoid taxes. . . .

" 'I'm sorry,' " she said to me, you may think I'm very stingy but I'm just too afraid to do that.

"It was really heart-wrenching to hear that admission from her, that fear of not having money. She was ashamed to admit it to me. Both of us were surprised that she admitted it. . . . She *never* made comments like that."[35]

As soon as Pat started making good money—much earlier than she tended to let on to friends and interviewers ("oddly, I keep earning quite sufficient money [and] am now cynical, fairly rich . . . lonely, depressed, and totally pessimistic," she wrote in her diary of January of 1970)[36]—her "house fever" kicked in. She began to burden herself with more houses than she could ever live in, in more countries than she could ever like. In 1969, she wrote her "Brother Dan" from Montmachoux that she was "house-poor . . . a condition you're doubtless familiar with, as it turns up in the South.

"I have neither sold nor rented my house in Suffolk (England), still own half a house in Samois-sur-Seine, 20 miles from here; plus owning this house."[37]

Rosalind Constable, resuming relations with Pat by letter in 1967, suggested none too delicately that Pat's problems with houses and co-owners were self-inflicted: "It does make me furious however to see you so successful and so miserable. . . . [L]ife is too short . . . to be spent in terror and tears."[38]

While living in Montmachoux in 1968, Pat was struggling with three unwieldy properties: Bridge Cottage in Sussex (she had more bills than she was willing to pay), her half share of the house in Samois-sur-Seine (where she was in serious litigation with Elizabeth Lyne over charges), and the house in Montmachoux, where, eventually, she found herself flanked by two large Portuguese families, one of whom shared a "common wall" with her. Pat, whose extreme sensitivities converted all sound into "noise" and for whom the word "family" would have been enough to spoil *any* house purchase, was driven to her usual assessment of family life and those who partake of it. "The Portuguese—it is like a pot of boiling soup next door, every vegetable leaping out of the pot and screaming—probably for privacy. Sometimes it sounds like a pigpen with boiling water being poured over it, scalding off the skins."[39]

By July of 1969, she was entertaining, not for the first time, pleasant thoughts of infanticide. They were curbed only by her respect for "personal property."

"I can easily bear cold, loneliness, hunger and toothache, but I cannot bear noise, heat, interruptions, or other people.

"Some people who actually own the babies kill them because of their noise. How much harder it is for people who do not own the babies."[40]

"I am really very sorry you are so unhappy," wrote Rosalind Constable again, and wondered why Pat didn't just check into the Chelsea Hotel in New York for the winter.[41] "You seem to have plenty of money," Rosalind wrote.[42] Indeed, as Pat's finances swelled, her problems seemed to multiply. The number of her bank accounts, lawyers, *notaires,* accountants, literary agents, limited companies, and offshore investments (that shadowy attempt to put money in Puerto Rico, a secret scheme to invest in railroad cars in the United States, etc.)[43] were legion, and it is unlikely that the full extent of their complications will ever be known. (See "The Cake That Was Shaped Like a Coffin: Part 7.")

Through it all, Pat managed to find fault with most of the arrangements made to handle her growing fortunes (sometimes with good reason)—and with most of the people attached to those arrangements. And her constant complaint, broadcast hundreds of times in hundreds of letters and conversations, was that she had no time left to work.

In truth, in one way or the other, Patricia Highsmith managed to foul every nest she ever occupied and curse every country she ever inhabited. She was comfortable only when she was *un*comfortable. Discomfort—the condition with which she was most at home and least at ease—was a productive state for her; it usually kept her writing. And Pat's most serious criticisms were reserved for the United States, the country she had abandoned *before* it could reject her, and the country which—abandoned by her—then did reject her. (Her relations with the United States were always those of a disappointed lover—or, more accurately, those of an enraged daughter.)

Late and painful proofs of this rejection arrived in terms she understood too well. In 1983, *People Who Knock on the Door,* her disjointed novel about the depredations of the Christian Right (it contains a precise portrait of the making of a fascist in the character of the younger son) was turned down by three American publishers, leaving her without an editor in the United States. "It is a flat book," she wrote modestly and accurately to Bettina Berch, "but popular in France, Germany and E. Germany."[44] At the end of her life, her last novel, *Small g,* was regretfully rejected by her editor, friend, and admirer at Knopf, Gary Fisketjon, and she was left without an American publisher at her death. And when she offered her archives to the Harry Ransom Center at the University of Texas at Austin, she received a letter (opened in the presence of her publisher Daniel Keel and his wife, Anna) suggesting the sum of twenty-five thousand dollars for her papers.

"The price of a used car," Pat said bitterly, and refused to let Texas have her literary bones.[45]

Still, Pat continued her forays to the United States, scouting material for her novels. The Greenwich Village of her youth was her literary stalking ground, just as it had been her sexual stalking ground all those years ago, and she was still taking notes on the streets she had roamed as a young woman. Alex Szogyi and Philip Thompson, who lived in Greenwich Village, remembered how Pat used to call them from Europe and ask about the features of certain buildings and the addresses of favorite places in the West Village and if this building was still there and what the name of that restaurant was.[46] Pat kept her imagination of the Village as alive as she could, and she also kept a fertile eye on the rest of the United States. A visit to Michel Block and Charles Latimer in Bloomington, Indiana, in January of 1981, shortly before she moved into her stone house in Aurigeno, produced a "germ" and a character—a sweetly alcoholic next-door neighbor—for *People Who Knock on the Door.*

Tentatively and rather covertly—never saying that this was what she was doing—Pat used these trips to the United States to survey the American countryside for possible places to live—California, New Mexico, Long Island, and Pennsylvania were places she considered—in terrains where she had previously stayed or worked or more or less enjoyed herself. But she could never make up her mind to actually settle on a property and acquire it. Michel Block, Charles Latimer's lover for many years, told his last companion, Robert Lumpkin, that Pat, sitting in the back of his car, had wept silent, bitter tears at the beauty of the Pennsylvania countryside they were driving through—a beauty which, practically speaking, was denied her only because she continued to refuse it, continued to choose to exile herself.[47] In Europe, Pat was a bona fide literary star; in the United States, she was a blur on the book horizon, an oddity, a cult favorite. Superman in Europe, Clark Kent at home, is how her old comics colleagues might have put it.

"The reason she lived [in Europe was because] she was admired and respected as a writer in Europe," Block told a previous biographer after Pat's death.[48] "I really think Pat sacrificed her everyday life to her reputation as an artist. . . . she would have been much happier living in the United States."[49] Michel Block was a reliable witness, a man who was sensitive to the nuances of other artists' feelings. A consummately talented concert pianist whose own concert career never measured up to his gifts, he was another one of those Jewish expatriates to whom Pat seemed to be drawn. Block took his unusual piano phrasing from the rhythmic flexibilities of the great French chanteuse Barbara—and his rubatos are like no one else's: as moody and cloudy as an April in Paris. Pat, who used to visit Michel Block and Charles Latimer in their country house in the Lot region of France during the 1970s, gave to Ripley her preference for Block's version of the "Rondeña" from *The Iberia Suite* by Isaac Albéniz (great-grandfather of Cécilia Sarkozy, former wife of the current president of France). And Block's version of the "Rondeña" was one of the special records Pat chose as a favorite for her appearance in April of 1979 on BBC Radio's prestigious interview program *Desert Island Discs.*

When it came to countries, Switzerland alone seems to have escaped Pat's maledictions—although it did not come in for a great deal of praise. In a paragraph in which she had already equated "seriousness" with "depression" Pat wrote: "Above all, I like the seriousness of the people. . . . Didn't Nietzsche like *die Schweiz* after all?"[50] She seems, partly, to have been curbing her tongue in favor of her ambivalent application for Swiss citizenship. She was nervous about a planned interview with the magazine *Linea d'ombra*: "for something too extreme the Swiss could oust me. This could go for extreme left or extreme right, and maybe I'm guilty of both."[51] (She was *always* guilty of both.) Four years later, a visit from two former neighbors in France pushed her to another kind of extremity.

In 1990, Barbara Skelton, Pat's new friend from the Île-de-France, and Mary Ryan, Pat's longtime next-door neighbor in Moncourt, made the long drive to Tegna to see the Casa Highsmith. Mary, who had been "hugging a bottle of gin" all the way to Switzerland, landed on her back in Pat's driveway when she tried to get out of Skelton's car.

"Whereupon Pat's pent-up years of scorn poured out in venomous abuse while standing over Mary like a gauleiter with a whip. 'What will the neighbors think! People just don't behave like that here. This is a very puritanical country. Suppose one of the neighbors saw you lying in my drive drunk! I risk having my Swiss citizenship annulled.' It was all said with sadistic contempt, and set the tone of the visit."[52]

Withal, Pat's attempts to keep her cash and possessions under her control and out of the hands of native and foreign tax officials by moving to Switzerland backfired in large and small ways. Although Yaddo, the artists' colony in Saratoga Springs, New York, where Pat spent eight crucial weeks nearly fifty years before her death, finally did inherit about three million dollars and her literary royalties, Swiss and American taxes got the lion's share of her holdings. (See "The Cake That Was Shaped Like a Coffin: Part 7.") Still, a few weeks before her death, at the instigation of Daisy Winston, Pat sent a check for either one thousand or two thousand dollars (there are two accounts of this) to the New Hope–Solebury Library, in New Hope, Pennsylvania, where Daisy still lived. The librarian's first gesture was a graceful one: Highsmith novels were bought with the money. But Pat's closest friends, many of whom were in financial trouble, got just what Pat put in her cellars in Aurigeno: nothing at all.

And Pat, whether she wanted to or not, also effectively disinherited Charlotte, her last cat. Charlotte was another of Pat's "barn" cats—the cats who always gave her opportunities to make derogatory references to their breeding. There were no provisions made for Charlotte in Pat's last will (or outside the will, either) and after Pat died, Charlotte spent some time with Marylin Scowden in Geneva (under the bed, says Scowden; Charlotte was terrified of Scowden's cat and of everything else), and then went on to the De Bernardis in Tegna, where she lived, cosseted and loved, to the great age of nineteen—longer than any of Pat's other cats. But Charlotte never became a sociable cat. Perhaps that was because Charlotte, like her longtime human companion Patricia Highsmith, had never really been socialized.

Many of the remaining objects Pat kept in her house are small enough to hold in the hand. They radiate significance; they are the *lares* and *penates* of a writer whose walled-up emotional life found much of its meaning in things. As an artist who harvested her final, practical style from the details of daily living, every single object Pat possessed meant the world to her; meant *a* world to her—and they meant just as much as she aged and her work began to thin down to what was more or less in front of her.

In most of her mid- and late-life novels, Highsmith treats people and their possessions in the same deadeningly objective way. Her often unlovely prose puts one flat foot in front of the other, levelling every action with the same even tread, dumping her burden of observations and/or her aggressions directly onto the page. The result is a mass of seemingly commonplace material, each individual item of which is stripped of the adjectives and images which graced such works as *The Price of Salt, This Sweet Sickness, The Blunderer, The Talented Mr. Ripley,* and *The Cry of the Owl.* She gives as much attention to the things in her later fictions as she gives to the characters who handle them or look at them or think about them.

In her earlier works, her objects are merely fetishized, like the glass of milk in *The Price of Salt* or like Dickie Greenleaf's two rings, which Tom rips from Dickie's murdered fingers and keeps as trophies. One of these rings is a "large rectangular green stone set in gold,"[53] and it is also an insider joke. Pat knew, from reading Frank Harris's scurrilous and entertaining books about Oscar Wilde, that Oscar always wore a "great green scarab ring."

In her later works, the push broom of Pat's paragraphs sweeps the detritus of daily life before it, stopping, from time to time, to pick up the odd, controlling comma, then advances relentlessly onwards, trailing strings of objects or mundane actions or simple thoughts in an accumulation of detail as dispassionate as that found in most pornographies.

The novel Pat was writing when the *douane* swooped down on her in Moncourt, *The Boy Who Followed Ripley,* offers salient examples of the author at work with her push broom. In this book, she allows Ripley, in his Balzacian way, to handle the abstract details and practical calculations of the problem that harried her all the way to Switzerland: income tax preparation. (Tom started his crime career by impersonating an income tax official who extorts checks—he doesn't cash them—from his terrified "clients.") The following passage, inconceivable in anything other than a fiction written by Pat Highsmith, sounds like a business letter from a tax consultant whose fantasy life has been made conspicuous by dreams of larceny. Excruciating to read, it was doubtless a joy for her to write.

> Tom went back to his room, where he had set himself the boring task of spending one hour, by the clock, on his monthly income and expenses for his accountant. . . . Heloise's income or allowance from her father was given her in cash, so was not liable for income tax on the Ripley bill. Tom's Derwatt company income—maybe ten thousand francs a month or close to two thousand dollars if the dollar was strong enough—came also under the table in the form of Swiss franc cheques, this money being filtered almost entirely through Perugia where the Derwatt Art Academy was, though some came from the Buckmaster Gallery sales too. Tom's ten per cent of Derwatt profits derived also from Derwatt-labelled art supplies, from easels to erasers, but it was easier to smuggle money from northern Italy into Switzerland than to get it from London to Villeperce. Then there was the income from Dickie Greenleaf's bequest to Tom, which had risen to about eighteen hundred dollars a month from the original three or four hundred years ago. On this, curiously enough, Tom did pay full USA income tax, considerable because it was capital gains.[54]

And the passage goes on, with riveting dullness, for much, much longer, bringing in stocks, U.S. Treasury bonds, the differences in declaring income for the French and American governments, the separate worksheets required, etc., etc., as Tom calculates his ill-gotten gains on his "efficient-looking pale green graph paper, income above, output below."[55]

Who else but Pat Highsmith would insert an instructional manual for income tax evasion into a novel? But this kind of brain chatter was a large part of her life, and by now she couldn't be much bothered to transform it. So she put her financial anxieties, uncooked, into her fiction—and she let Tom Ripley deal with them.

"Possessions are nine tenths of my life," Pat had written in 1945.[56] The difference, now, was that she had so many more possessions to deal with.

· 33 ·

THE REAL ROMANCE OF OBJECTS

PART 3

As is the way of the world, every remaining object Pat Highsmith kept under her eyes and out of her cellars is now kept entirely out of sight in someone else's cellar: the enormous, climatically controlled cellar of the Swiss Literary Archives in Bern, Switzerland. The Highsmith Archives are on the lowest of the seven custodial levels in the national archives' large white Bauhaus building, and they belong to the people of Switzerland.

The building housing the Swiss Literary Archives looks like the original structure from which Pat's white block of a house in Tegna might be an abbreviated quotation. There is something official about both structures: they resemble large and small editions of municipal monuments, although the archive building is beautiful in its severity, and Pat's house in Tegna is merely . . . severe. But the apparently windowless Casa Highsmith is more fortified, even, than the large, light, extravagantly windowed literary archives. And like its first owner, the Tegna house has no obvious windows, is divided into two sections, and looks inward upon itself. But from above, light streams into the Casa Highsmith, and out in back—where no public eyes can pry—it overlooks a garden and sky and trees.

"Hitler's bunker," said a friend at first sight of the Casa Highsmith's blind front. Pat laughed grimly.[1]

Like all of Pat's houses, the cellars of the Swiss Literary Archives are fiendishly cold, kept at temperatures which prolong the life of acid-impregnated papers. Every single thing Pat had in her house at the time of her death—barring the special trinkets distributed to friends and neighbors after her death and the furniture she bought or made—is there, boxed and catalogued, for as long as the world lasts. An enthusiastic archivist of her own effects, Pat would have appreciated the archives' filing system.

In carefully numbered acid-free boxes, long flat drawers, and library shelves, all of Pat's earthly remains—except what she sometimes seemed to value the most, her money—sit in that cold cellar in Bern. Bern is the capital of Switzerland, a verdant, fragrant mountain city of breathtaking views and shadowy arcades which Pat seems to have visited only by letter. The city is encircled by an azure blue, ice-cold, glacier-fed river, the River Aare. It is as dangerous as it is beautiful, with a current so swift that every five meters a handrail is riveted into its banks so that swimmers in trouble can hold on and try to catch their breath. Many swimmers do indeed plunge into the Aare—but not all of them come out alive. And that is another detail about the Swiss capital of Bern that Pat Highsmith would have appreciated.

The Highsmith possessions in the Swiss Literary Archives have all survived their owner's turbulent life, transiting tastes, and long expatriation. They contain, as nothing else does, what Janet Flanner once called "the specific invisible remains" of Pat's long relationship with them.

So here they are for you to see. Or rather, here *it* is: a sizeable sampling of Patricia Highsmith's goods and chattels in the form of a list, Pat's preferred method of organizing her life. The order of the list is simply the order in which the objects came before my eyes. Wherever necessary, I've added interpretative notes, but for the most part the list is descriptive: a catalogue raisonné of Patricia Highsmith's hidden history of possessions.

By now, you will be able to work out for yourself most of the meanings contained in her things.

OBJECTS

A coffee-colored **Olympia De Luxe portable typewriter,** manufactured in 1956, with a standard QUERTYUIOP American keyboard, an easy action (I tried it, repeatedly), and an E key whose identifying letter has been worn away long ago by heavy use. Four little rubber feet. Its hardshell, whale gray case has the curves and swells of a Slipstream trailer and has travelled everywhere: it is covered with stickers from airlines and foreign countries. Two addresses are affixed: 77 Moncourt and Tegna. The name Patricia Highsmith is attached to both addresses. This is the typewriter Pat used for most of her work from 1956 onwards.

A box of **Caran d'Ache pencils.**

Assorted **pens.** An **eraser.**

A **Swiss Army knife.** With attachments.

A **dagger.**

Some straight **pins.**

Food **tins** and jam **jars,** rinsed and cleaned, for pencils and pens.

A very sharp **letter opener,** bladed.

A **Wite-Out** pencil.

A **recorder.** (She used to play this, delicately wiping off the mouthpiece when she handed it to guests to try, and wiping the mouthpiece again when she took it back.)

The **prescription for her regular glasses:** +3 (right eye), +2½ (left eye).

A **pair of reading glasses:** yellow with black tops or "eyebrows." Quite dandyish.

A medallion from the French government: **Ordre des arts et des lettres.**

The **1964 Critics Award from the Crimewriters' Association.**

Another **recorder.**

Trivets of straw that hold little seashells.

A **wooden head,** whose face is frozen in an expression of horror and sorrow. Approximately ten inches high with a wooden base. It seems to be the head of a male, but it looks uncannily like the long-faced portrait Allela Cornell painted of the twenty-three-year-old Pat Highsmith. Pat gave this little wood sculpture to Rosalind Constable, and Rosalind, at the end of her life, sent it back to Pat so that, as Rosalind wrote in her letter, prospective biographers "can see what you do with your left hand."

Little **decorated boxes.**

A **paperweight:** the small, very heavy **head of a longhorn cow skull,** cast in bronze by her second cousin, Dan Walton Coates, a western artist of note, in his spare time, in 1991.

A papier-mâché **cat's-head box** (the head lifts off) which holds Swiss coins. Inscribed: "The Cat Who Followed Pat by J & L." Given by Linda and her friend Joëlle, the same set of friends who gave Pat a fancy address book and painted her kitchen in Moncourt.

Two large, old, heavy **house keys** from her Aurigeno house, marked "Ornamental, lock now changed. Main Back Door."

Many odd little **animal totems.**

A **goat's bell.**

A very large pair of **binoculars.**

A large gilt-edged **mirror,** with photos and postcards Scotch-taped to the sides of the glass; amongst them, a postcard of Colette in drag, a postcard of a panel from the Bayeux Unicorn Tapestry, and a photo of Bettina Berch with her newborn daughter.

A double **magnifying glass.**

A cheap **pencil sharpener.**

Another **knife.**

Two long, very heavy **swords.** These are the **"Confederate swords"** Pat said she bought in Texas during the year she was left with her grandmother in Fort Worth while Mary went back with Stanley to New York. She kept them in the crossed, dueling position on the walls of each of her houses. As Mary Highsmith was dying—and without mentioning Mary's death as a motive—Pat finally uncrossed them. The swords were forged in Massachusetts: one in Chicopee and the other in Springfield.

A lethal-looking carving **knife and fork set,** large enough to dismember a buffalo.

An **empty bullet casing made into a pen.**

Many little **cat figurines and toys.**

Inkwells.

Coupons for **stamps** and **mixed change** from many European countries in another inkwell.

A **box of buttons and stones.**

A gigantic nineteenth-century **stereograph,** carved, detailed, and very difficult to use. It is accompanied by dozens of stiff cardboards imprinted with the double photographic images which convert into three dimensions when viewed through the stereograph.

A **cork bulletin board.**

Reproductions of **David Hockney drawings.**

An **Al Fatah pin.**

A **blackboard** with the names "B. Skelton" [Barbara Skelton, her neighbor in France] and "Millie"[Millie Alford, the cousin with whom she had a short involvement and a long friendship] printed in chalk. At one point in her life, Pat kept blackboards in both her kitchen and her workroom, so she could make lists of what she had to do on them.

A laser copy, framed in plastic, of a photograph of her former lover **Natica Waterbury,** grinning and alone in a boat on a lake.

The **painting of the twenty-three-year-old Pat Highsmith by Allela Cornell.** Pat's huge hands are wrapped around her body and she has the look of a woman already weighted down by her future. Pat hung this painting in every house she ever lived in.

Two objects which Pat's Swiss neighbors the Dieners took as mementos:

A **lace snail** encased in fiberglass and given to Pat on her sixty-sixth birthday.

An **artistic deck of cards** which can be arranged into a complete visual landscape. The landscape can be changed by moving the cards. Printed in Leipzig.

And one object that was given to me: A bleached and mended pair of Pat's iconic **Levi-Strauss 501 jeans.** She wore them all through the 1970s in Moncourt, and they still hold the shape of her body.

LIBRARY

Pat's library is another matter. The books that remain suggest the collection of a woman whose serious reading stopped at the college literature level. It is the library of someone who had a good classical education—and decided not to pursue it. Not much seems to have been added since her days as a student at Barnard, and many of the newer volumes are works by friends and colleagues (sent by publishers), copies of books she had been asked to review (also sent by publishers), or books by Pat herself in various languages and editions. The range of books attests to her insularity: she lived much of her adult life in Europe, but there are almost no books in any of the several continental European languages she practiced in her cahiers and diaries.

Here are some of the books left in her personal library, in some cases listed by title, in others by author.

The Personality of Cats
Erich Fromm
History of the Arabs
Grimm's Fairy Tales
Edward Said
Colin Wilson
Snobbery with Violence
Bob Son of Battle, 1901 edition (a heroic dog story)
G. K. Chesterton
Daylight and Nightmare
Brigid Brophy
Rubyfruit Jungle by Rita Mae Brown (Pat had this book in English because

Marion Aboudaram was its French translator and Pat helped her a bit with the translation; it's a picaresque lesbian novel.)

Paul Bowles

Bitter Fame: a biography of Sylvia Plath, with crucial points bracketed by Pat; e.g., the fact that Plath used to leave the house without money in her pocket is marked with a word that expressed Pat's feelings on the subject: "Horrors!" She also marked approvingly anything that favored Ted Hughes.

André Gide

Glenway Wescott

Fred McDarrah's photographic study of Greenwich Village

Kay Boyle's reedition of Robert McAlmon's *Being Geniuses Together*

George Orwell

Chester Himes

Edith Sitwell

William Hazlitt

Merck Manual

Gray's Anatomy

Latin Grammar

Plotinus

Domestic Manners of Americans by Frances Trollope

The Savage God: A Study of Suicide by A. Alvarez

Le Spiel, a novel by Dominique Marion (Marion Aboudaram, Pat's former lover)

Many books about cats

Rider Haggard

Raymond Carver

Ian Rankin (*Knots & Crosses*); she had many more suspense and detective books than she ever admitted to reading.

The Minerva Collection of Twentieth-Century Women's Fiction

Other Authors and Titles

Wolfgang Hildesheimer

Peter Ustinov

Dominique Marion

Carl Laszlo

Graham Greene

Brian Glanville

Arthur Koestler

Grimm's Fairy Tales, given to her in 1944 by Rosalind Constable and dedicated "And this is the way it was Xmas, 1944 RC"

Heinemann edition of all five Ripley novels bound in red calf with gilt letters

Various dictionaries

Colorful French

Latin Grammar (she bought it in 1938)

Latin & English Dictionary

Spanish-English Dictionary

The Clans, Sects, and Regiments of the Scottish Highlands

A number of the McGraw-Hill Compendia from the 1950s on France, Germany, Great Britain, the Provinces of France, the Netherlands, Greece, Portugal, The Paris We Love, etc.

Gone with the Wind by Margaret Mitchell

Some early Chekhov plays given to her by Alex Szogyi in 1965

The Age of Reason by Thomas Paine

J. S. Mill

Canterbury Tales (bought when she lived at 48 Grove)

Books in the Guest Wing

1990s editions of the *Criminologist's Journal*

1960 edition of Yarmolinsky's biography of Dostoyevsky

A biography of Graham Greene which she reviewed, giving offense to Greene's son when she suggested he hadn't been close to his father.

Main Room Library

Remembrance of Things Past given to her in 1944 by Natica Waterbury (a four-leaf clover is pressed in it)

Intentions—essays by Oscar Wilde bought by Pat in 1938

A little Henry James, very little Hemingway, and no Fitzgerald; a little Auden and less Poe

A 1950 edition of Djuna Barnes's novel *Nightwood,* with a clipping about Barnes from the *International Herald Tribune* inserted

Webster's Ninth Collegiate Dictionary

Biographies of Paul Bowles, Truman Capote, Simenon, Edgar Allan Poe, Marlene Dietrich (Pat wrote Dietrich a fan letter when she didn't show up at the 1978 Berlin Film Festival), Sylvia Plath

Books of essays by Gore Vidal, Mary McCarthy, William Hazlitt, Thomas
   Mann
Twenty-nine tattered volumes of the eleventh edition of the *Encyclopaedia
   Britannica* with update volume for twelfth edition

Salon Room (Chimney Room)

Only books by Patricia Highsmith

Bedroom

Controversy of Zion by Douglas Read: in it, Pat inserted a clipped-out article
   from the *International Herald Tribune* about how a director at Oberam-
   mergau failed to make the Passion Play less anti-Semitic because its very
   nature was anti-Semitic
Roget's Thesaurus
The Loom of Language
Oxford Dictionary of English Etymology
Large picture books in German sent by Diogenes
The Basic Book of Cats
Gray's Anatomy
Merck Manual
German-English Dictionary
Complete Shakespeare
The Holy Bible in a box: in it she has placed another clipped-out article:
   "Archeologist finds the tomb of Caiphus, the Jewish High Priest who
   handed Jesus Christ over to the Jews"
Chambers Twentieth-Century Dictionaries
Greek-English lexicon
Harrap's Shorter French-English Dictionary
Book on Italy
Gay & Lesbian Literary Companion with the section on Highsmith marked
   with a piece of paper. There is a picture of Pat at twenty-seven slipped
   into it. She wears an ornamental robe, and for once, her huge hands are
   wholly visible. Her hands look much older than she does.
A half dozen art books: Henry Moore, Rodin, Edvard Munch, Egon Schiele,
   Salvador Dalí
Many travel books from many countries

Desk Drawers

Dozens of maps from every city and country Pat ever visited or wanted to visit, from a beautifully produced 1946 map of Charleston, South Carolina, to 1988 maps of Hamburg, Germany, and a 1991 map of the Fort Worth–Dallas area—some of them notated, colored, and drawn upon by Pat. All of them are much more worn than her books.

Many little receipt books and notebooks and drawing pads filled with Highsmith sketches of the myriad places she travelled to. And there are fourteen pressbooks, carefully kept up to date—and with covers designed by Pat.

Finally, there are the things which mattered most to her, discovered in her linen closet after her death:
Thirty-eight cahiers
Eighteen diaries

34

THE CAKE THAT WAS SHAPED

LIKE A COFFIN

PART I

It must be strange to enter a house and begin living there, and fix it up, know-ing it is the last house you will ever live in and fix up, and that you will die there.

—**Patricia Highsmith**, 1961

Switzerland is a country where very few things begin, but many things end.

—**F. Scott Fitzgerald**

A few months before Patricia Highsmith's death in early February of 1995, Daniel Keel, knowing that Pat was ill and fading fast, decided to make the long railway journey from Zurich to Pat's house in Tegna to talk to her about preparations for the publication of one of her books.

While Pat was still living in Aurigeno, she had admired the sheepskin and leather coat Keel was wearing, and in a gallant gesture, he offered it to her on the spot. She tried it on, and "strangely enough," says Keel, "it fit her: we were the same size." Although "flustered," Pat took the coat. Perhaps the gift ap-pealed to something deep and doubled in her nature: Keel had kept an exact copy of the garment himself and continued to wear it, so whenever it was cold Pat and her publisher were twins. It was this same attention to his author's needs that prompted Daniel Keel to ask Pat if he could bring her something from Zurich when he came to visit.

"Flowers?" he offered. "No, no flowers," she said. Good, he thought, be-cause his wife, the painter Anna Keel, told him that Pat had thrown out the last bouquet of flowers they'd brought her—and it had cost a small fortune. Pat, anyway, had expressed herself fully on the subject of flowers in another telephone call: "Your wife Anna always brings me bunches of wonderful roses. But I don't like flowers. Do you mind not bringing them anymore?"

Daniel Keel couldn't have known this, but Pat had already left a trail of broken blossoms behind her in New York. Her next-to-last American publisher, Otto Penzler of the Mysterious Press, brought Pat to New York from Switzerland in the mid-1980s to do a little publicity—"not," he says, "realizing the idiocy of what I was doing"—for his specially designed, limited editions of *People Who Knock on the Door* and five collections of Highsmith short stories:[1] slipcovered volumes with the copies numbered and signed, all issued between 1985 and 1988.* On her first night in New York, Penzler took Pat out to dinner at his favorite Italian restaurant, Giordano's at Thirty-ninth Street and Ninth Avenue, and watched in disbelief at what she did when his publicity representative handed her a single perfect rose at the restaurant table. "Pat took the rose and dropped it on the floor. Didn't acknowledge it, didn't say thank you, just took the rose and dropped it on the floor."[2]

And then Penzler watched again—this time in rigid silence—while Pat "ranted" and "yelled" at Roberto, the restaurant's popular maître d', because the veal chop he'd gone to the kitchen to personally select for Pat—"He made every effort," says Penzler; "he couldn't do enough for her"—was too large for her liking.[3]

Pat's performances at dinner tables—by now, they were site-specific and designed to give maximum offense to whomever she was sitting next to—still retained their power to shipwreck an evening and shape an opinion. Before that restaurant party and the subsequent days he spent escorting her on publicity junkets, Otto Penzler had been thinking of Pat Highsmith as "one of my heroines because I loved her fiction." He ended by describing her as "the most unloving and unlovable person I've ever known . . . a really terrible human being. . . . I never heard her say a positive thing. Except once. She said: 'I like beer.'"[4]

A year later, waiters in the United States had apparently wised up to Patricia's ways—David Streitfeld, book columnist for *The Washington Post,* says the serving staff at the hotel restaurant where he was interviewing Pat in November of 1988 "was giving us a wide berth"—but she was still able to create havoc at a table. Pat's plane had just spent three hours stalled on a runway ("I'm a very lousy Christian, but I don't believe in revenge," was how she dis-

---

* Penzler had Pat's novel *Found in the Street* already in type with a dust jacket designed when Pat refused to allow him to publish the book.

missed the disruption), she was at her most gnomic, and David Streitfeld thought she "seemed a little batty." He had planned to do a feature article on her, but their conversation was so scattered that he couldn't make his piece "cohere."

Pat was "cackling"—often—and she brought to the luncheon table a book of medical symptoms which she said she found more interesting than any novel.[5] She "betray[ed] no interest in the food," but she did favor Streitfeld with some readings aloud from her medical book. And she seemed happy to examine the long list of all her published titles her interviewer brought with him. "'This looks good,'" she said. "'It always makes me feel strong. Either strong, or exhausted.'"[6]

It was during this luncheon that Pat, eating nothing herself but providing some food for thought, told David Streitfeld why she'd parted company with Otto Penzler as a publisher. Penzler, she said, had "deliberately" suppressed her dedication to the Intifada in his edition of *People Who Knock on the Door,* and she told Streitfeld exactly why: "'Do you know why he did that?' Highsmith hissed to me. 'Because he's a Jew.'" ("I don't," says David Streitfeld, "as a reporter, use the word 'hissed' very often. But in this case, it's a literal description.")[7] As it happened, Pat was wrong in both her assumptions: Otto Penzler, like Pat's father J. B. Plangman, is a German Protestant. And Penzler had asked permission from the Diogenes representative in New York to delete Pat's dedication because he felt it would create trouble for the book with local reviewers.[8]

So Daniel Keel, on the telephone to Pat in Tegna, asked her again: "'What can I bring you, what can I bring you that you would like?'

"And she said, instantly, 'Chocolate cake.'" Keel was quite surprised to hear this because, as he says, he had "never seen her eating cake, or anything else" for that matter. When she'd come to dinner at his house in Zurich she had two large whiskies before dinner and then asked if she could bring her glass to the table, sipping the whiskey instead of eating. Anna Keel had especially prepared the classic Swiss dish *roesti* for Pat, and Pat had pushed the food around and around on her plate with her fork, redesigning it the way a child of two with a shovel might reconfigure a sand castle. She'd scraped the meat into the vegetables, the vegetables into the meat, and the whole into an "unrecognizable mess." Anna Keel, worried that she'd cooked a dish which didn't please her guest, asked Pat if perhaps the *roesti* wasn't too dry for her. Yes, Pat said baldly, the *roesti was* too dry.

Keel's publisher's lunches and dinners with Pat over the years had yielded the same arid conversational results. "For the first twenty years we would meet and she would say yes and no, and sometimes ask something. Nothing unnecessary, she was very spare. As though you had to put in a franc to get even a word." Everything he learned about her "came through her books." And when the Keels visited Pat in Tegna "towards the end," Pat, doing her part, had made an attempt to serve them an unidentifiable mass that was in her refrigerator, a kind of "pudding," which she announced was "a chicken without legs." (She was being allowed alcohol again by her doctors—who obviously figured it no longer mattered.) "I hope you don't mind," Pat said as they ate; "I gave the chicken legs to the cats." She had also been cooking something to serve with the chicken—something that had celery in it—but forgot to serve it. She announced this in the middle of the meal as well.

That was why Daniel Keel was so surprised to hear his author requesting something as edible as a chocolate cake from Zurich.

"It was on a Sunday that I next went to the Ticino," Keel says, "and I went alone." He'd called the famous sweet shop, Sprüngli in the Main Station in Zurich, told them he was taking an afternoon train "at the last minute, I'm always late," and asked them to prepare a medium-sized chocolate cake ("Pat had said 'not a small one and not a big one'") and to put it in a box for transport. At the last possible moment, Keel picked up the cake from Sprüngli, paid for it, and "ran to the train."

Dense, rich, and deeply delicious, Sprüngli chocolate cakes are famous all over Switzerland. One of the great pleasures of arriving at the Main Station in Zurich by train is that the Sprüngli store is located right there in the station. The Sprüngli chocolate cakes—usually a few of the cakes are displayed in the shop window—are oddly shaped: geometrically angled at one end and rectangular at the other. Like the cases for miniature musical intruments, I thought when I first saw them—until Daniel Keel's story clarified for me what those cakes *really* looked like.

When Keel arrived at Pat's house in the Ticino, he gave her the box with the chocolate cake in it, told her it was from Sprüngli, and then they sat down to work on the manuscript. After a few hours, Pat—no doubt reluctantly—mentioned that she thought perhaps they should eat something. And Keel said: "Dessert. We can have a piece of your chocolate cake."

And so Pat put the cake box on the table, opened it, and Daniel Keel and Patricia Highsmith had a shared and immediate shock. Both of them realized at the same moment that the Sprüngli chocolate cake Keel had brought from Zurich (he was unfamiliar with this particular cake and saw it only after it had been boxed) "had the shape of a coffin." An "elegant and expensive coffin." At the time, of course, Pat was seriously ill, she was obviously dying, and Keel was beside himself at the implications of the gift he'd carried into her house: "I was so shocked, I was speechless. I didn't know what to say."

What finally slipped out of his mouth was a horrified acknowledgment: "I didn't know," he said to Pat.

"I have friends," says Keel, "who, in that situation, would laugh and say: 'Look, I'm dying, and you bring me a chocolate cake in the shape of a coffin!' But Pat wouldn't laugh. She didn't say anything. But I saw her eyes, and I know she realized that the cake had the shape of a coffin.

"We ate a piece and she put it back in the kitchen." And nothing more was said about the cake.

When Daniel Keel returned to Zurich, he had his secretary call up the Sprüngli shop to suggest that because "other old and sick people were receiving these cakes that were in the shapes of coffins," perhaps Sprüngli would care to reconsider the kinds of cake pans they were using. And the lady on the telephone line from Sprüngli was astonished. This chocolate cake was a *famous* cake and *no one,* until now, had *ever* remarked on its shape; there was certainly no reason to change it.

"It's strange," Keel says about Patricia Highsmith and the cake that was shaped like a coffin, "that it happened with her and to her."[9]

35

THE CAKE THAT WAS SHAPED

LIKE A COFFIN

PART 2

Pat's move to what would be her last house in Switzerland—the fortress-like Casa Highsmith, whose planning and design made her so happy and whose building and expense caused her so many nervous moments—took a long time and went through many stages. "I can't stand any more strain from Tegna house. . . . The land itself is tough to deal with, all sandy & stony,"[1] she wrote, and sent her architect, Tobias Amman, questions, complaints, and demands for repairs for at least two years after the house was completed.[2] Like much else that happened to Pat in the second part of her life, the impetus to go to Switzerland seems to have come from Ellen Blumenthal Hill.

In early January of 1953, Pat and Ellen, rolling through Switzerland on their automobile trip from Paris to Trieste, stopped over in Zurich. They were on the first leg of the journey whose domestic horrors Pat would satirize in the short story she called "Hell on Wheels." As usual, the notes Pat was taking in her cahier were doing double duty: she was shaping them into a sunny little tourist article aimed at the newspaper market (her notes are marked "*Neue Zürcher Zeitung,* 'Magnet Zurich'") about the glories of "fair Helvetia." She portrayed herself as travelling alone and very cheerful about it.

Oddly for Pat's later reputation as a woman who ate practically nothing, her initial notes on Switzerland are all about food: the "huge portions in restaurants . . . enough liver and onions . . . to feed a couple of husky men"; the "hot rich milk" of Zurich; the "best coffee" she'd had since Italy; a lunch at Möven Pick during which "I nearly killed myself sampling about five items" and where "I can imagine I'm right back in America [because] the waitress even speaks English with an American accent." She praised the rich provender in the "Self-Service Market" by the Storchen Hotel: "All those endless shelves of cans & cellophane wrapped cookies, breakfast foods, cheeses, delicatessen, meats, fresh vegetables, cigarettes and candy, are not only like America but—(I whisper it gently)—even better."[3]

Food and also clothes were Pat's focus because this was the trip in which Switzerland revealed itself to be the only country in Europe that could fit Highsmith's big feet with the right-sized shoes. As for the other clothes, she wrote, the clothes she was buying in Zurich in January of 1953, they were not only cheaper than clothes in Paris but they, too, "fit my American figure."[4]

The ways in which Pat, in 1953, lingered over her fulsome accounts of what seems to have been just ordinary good Zurich food are like the semi-erotic fantasies of a woman who has been starving for a long time. And her descriptions of the countryside between Basel and Zurich—"delightful farm villages, happy, healthy looking children, stronger bigger horses than those of Eastern France . . . the vine-like trees that are trained to grow horizontally, supporting the house corners like living arms"—made a paradise of what she later complained was a car trip that drove her crazy.[5] This trip did something other than drive her crazy, however. It gave her a line of travel into her future.

Here is how Pat began her Swiss notes in 1953: "Whenever I get desperately homesick, but still not desperately enough to spend several hundred dollars getting back to America, I go to Switzerland. . . . And in fact it was that astonishingly self-confident statement in the Swiss tourist bureau ad in the Paris *Herald Tribune*—'The only country in Europe where all your hosts speak English'—that gave me the final push to come."[6]

And here is how she ended her notes: "As long as there's a Switzerland, I don't know when I'll get around to going home again."[7]

Switzerland reminded Pat Highsmith of the United States. Principally, it was the fact that she could find English speakers there: Pat resolutely refrained, as much as possible, from speaking the language of any country she lived in if that language wasn't English. Wherever she lived, she remained oblivious to local holidays, customs, and newspapers, reserving her reading for the *International Herald Tribune* and her understanding for the fluctuations of currency exchange and the prices of goods and postal services. But it was also the abundance of produce (Switzerland, ostensibly "neutral" during the Second World War, was not subject to the vastations visited on the other countries Pat had passed through), the plenitude, the richness of the countryside, and the cleanliness of the cities that attracted her. Throughout the 1980s Pat would continue to contrast Zurich with the filthy and crime-ridden Manhattan.

Above all, there was the famous orderliness of Switzerland, and order was a necessity for an author whose first written lines of fiction, set down when she was fourteen, began with two shoes neatly aligned beside a bed. Certainly, the idea of a country outside the battle lines drawn by the rest of the world, a country in a state of so-called neutrality, had the greatest appeal for a woman who said she couldn't bear conflict, who yearned for world peace, and who was so often painfully and chaotically at war, divided against herself.

Although it was her love affairs which drove her from pillar to post and from the United States to Europe, the main reason Pat went to Switzerland was because of the emotion that was slowly replacing love in her life: the desire to hang on to her money. The French law forbidding foreign residents in France from keeping their money in other countries—Pat left France because of it—was rescinded just after Pat moved herself to Aurigeno. She wrote to Monique Buffet that she wouldn't have gone if she'd known about it.[8] But the fact that her literary affairs were concentrated in Switzerland—Daniel Keel and his publishing company, Diogenes, were now her world representatives and were making a great deal of money for her—was crucial to her move.

Daniel Keel doesn't think he "ever quarrelled with Pat," and he came to understand and appreciate her in a humorous and balanced way. (When I told him that the most frequent sentence I heard about Pat was "She wasn't nice," he replied: "That's quite an understatement." When I mentioned that Pat had written three hundred unusually kind letters to her last lover, he responded: "They'll ruin her reputation.") "She could be very hard," he says, "with her voice, or with an answer or a question. 'Don't sit there!' she would say. . . . She could be nervous and unpleasant . . . but only in a quite superficial way, just about a certain deal or event, or a check she didn't like, or a title [of a book]." When Keel published *Found in the Street* in German, he called it, in German, *Elsie's Love of Life*. It was a phrase he'd found in the book. Pat didn't like the title change, but she accepted it. And a book which had sold sparsely in the United States became a bestseller in Switzerland.

In fact, Pat never complained in writing or in conversation about Daniel Keel. When she was cavilling about the details of some transaction—and there were serious confusions in the selling and reselling of the Ripley film rights that went on and on and cost Diogenes, Pat, and the producer Robert Hakim time and money and angst—she always displaced her anger onto the company or the company's lawyer. Given her tendency for finding fault, her complaints about Diogenes were remarkably controlled. Keel, in his turn, treated her like royalty.

It was during a visit to Moncourt by Wim Wenders and Peter Handke in 1974* that Pat was first introduced to the picturesque European custom of

---

* Handke brought her a present from Jeanne Moreau: an igneous ball on a pedestal, "black and clear."

authors being represented by their publishers, a custom as unthinkable in the United States as appearing in court without a lawyer. Wim Wenders had come to negotiate for a Highsmith novel to adapt to film—and, as he describes it, he arrived at her house with an already well-developed obsession for her work.

I read one book by Patricia Highsmith, and that was *The Tremor of Forgery,* and I liked it so much that I read the next, and the next, greedily, until there was none left that I could have read. I was completely preoccupied by her writing. The sharpness of the observation! The immense knowledge of MEN and how their subconscious worked, but not written by a fellow man, but by a woman! . . .

And I became obsessed with the idea of turning one of her books into a film. And of course, I started with my favorite and you remember right, that was *Cry of the Owl.* . . . I slowly worked my way through her entire bibliography. EVERYTHING was sold, that was the sad truth. Mostly bought up by American studios who weren't doing anything with the properties. And then I finally summed up my courage and wrote to her. I wrote how appalling I felt that "hoarding" of her books was, and that I figured the studios had bought up all her books so nobody else could use them. I also wrote to her WHY I wanted to shoot a film based on a work of hers. My friend Peter Handke had given me her address. Soon afterwards, I got a letter by Patricia Highsmith in return. She had somehow already heard of this German director determined to turn a novel of hers into a film and she was curious what was behind it. . . .

And we talked for a while. I guess she wanted to find out for herself, if I was somehow "trustworthy." And then she pulled this fat typewritten manuscript out of the drawer of her writing table and gave it to me. (Well, it must have been a copy.) And she said: "Even my agent hasn't read this one yet. So I'm certain the rights are not sold yet. Maybe you want to read it." Did I want to read it!? The title said: *Ripley's Game.* I had finished it before I was home in Munich on the train. And I wrote to her: "Yes, absolutely. I want to acquire the rights to make a film after this novel!" And it became *The American Friend.* My first working title was: *Framed.* Did I know that she was Texan? Sure. I knew she was from Fort Worth. I had come through there once, so I knew HOW TEXAN that was!

. . . After that initial meeting I only saw her again when I showed her the film. I was really happy with the picture and couldn't wait to have Patricia see it. But then, to my great disappointment, she was quite disturbed by it, didn't conceal that either and didn't have anything good to say about it after the screening. I left utterly frustrated.

Months later, I got a letter from her. She said she had seen the film a second time, this time in a public screening on the Champs-Elysées, during a visit in Paris. And she had much better feelings about it now. . . . And she was full of praise for Dennis Hopper, too, whom she had flat-out rejected the first time. She now wrote that my film had captured the essence of that Ripley character better than any other films. You can guess how relieved I was![9]

During her meeting with Peter Handke and Wenders, Pat had been fascinated when Handke explained the European practice of editors representing authors. The idea might have been at the back of her mind one late evening in the summer of 1979 as she sat on a stool in Daniel Keel's living room in Zurich, finding bitter fault with her sales, with her American agent (Patricia Schartle Myrer had just dropped Pat for her behind-the-scenes machinations over international commissions), and with most of her publishers. She was, says Keel, "very unhappy," and so he suggested that he should telephone her current German-language representative in Zurich, Rainer Heumann, while she was still sitting there and talk to him about representing her more fully.

"He's already your German agent," Keel said; "he handles things beautifully. . . . He'll be transported with joy [or words to that effect] if he can manage your world rights."

So Daniel Keel picked up the telephone and called Mr. Heumann—now it was almost midnight and Pat was sitting at his elbow—and Heumann "shouted" back at him: "Are you mad?! I don't want her *or* her world rights! She's much too difficult and don't you ever wake me up at midnight again!"

Heumann, Keel says, "was afraid of her difficult nature," and Keel had to struggle to keep the agent's response from leaking out of the telephone. And so Daniel Keel offered to take over the world agenting for Pat, and the whole business of Diogenes becoming Pat's world representative was the result of "an accident," an accident whose final terms Pat negotiated for just as toughly as Diogenes over the next seven months. She sought constant counsel from Alain Oulman, and, anxious to preserve her ability to deal directly with Calmann-Lévy, she sent back at least one contract to Diogenes unsigned. Finally, the papers were signed in March of 1980, the month the *douane* invaded her house in Moncourt.[10]

Marianne Liggenstorfer met Pat when she came to work in the foreign rights department at Diogenes in 1981. Pat took a distinct shine to her new rights representative, and although Marianne says she was unaware of any special feeling from her author, Pat was soon asking for Marianne Liggenstor-fer whenever she telephoned Diogenes from Aurigeno. Liggenstorfer was trying to reorganize the complicated Highsmith backlist, centralizing and reselling her works to only one publisher in each country. "We always tried to get the best offers for her and then she'd say how expensive the house was, and would it be possible to get more money."[11]

An exceptionally patient woman, Marianne Liggenstorfer says she always took her cues from Pat's own behavior: "It was very indirect; she didn't ex-actly give me orders. . . . It was very important when dealing with Pat that you were not too fast with her. She needed a lot of time to get used to you and be comfortable."[12]

Marianne accompanied Pat on two separate publicity junkets to Spain, at the behest of Pat's Spanish publisher: once they went to Barcelona, and then they travelled to the film festival at San Sebastian, where Pat was the guest of honor in an homage to *Plein Soleil*, René Clément's film version of *The Tal-ented Mr. Ripley*. They stayed for about ten days each time, and although Pat "could blow up and calm down twenty times a day," they enjoyed them-selves. Pat drew all the time on both trips: "She'd go into her room, sit at the window, and she'd sketch." She drank beer continually, and, says Marianne carefully, "when she drank a little more than usual, she was sometimes laugh-ing very strangely, a stifled laugh, not very loud." That was Pat having her own special kind of fun. At the festival, Pat answered a lot of questions amia-bly, and then, fascinated as always by a group of transvestites in the hotel hall, sat in the bar watching, and drinking, and talking about them.[13]

When Liggenstorfer married a director at Diogenes, Pat came to her wed-ding party, and to everyone's astonishment, she danced with both Daniel Keel and Liggenstorfer's father. (There is a photograph of Pat on the dance floor, one enormous hand lightly bunched at the knuckles and resting on the shoul-der of the smiling father of the bride.) And when Pat gave a housewarming party for the Casa Highsmith in Tegna in 1989 ("The house was HER," says Marianne), Marianne Liggenstorfer (now Fritsch) came with her husband and stayed the night, suffering agonies because she'd forgotten her cat-allergy medicine and Pat's cats were everywhere. It was part of the special care with which Pat was treated at Diogenes that Marianne never said a word about the "nightmare" of suffering caused by her allergies that night: she wanted to spare Pat's feelings in her new house.[14] Pat's contract with Diogenes would make her a multimillionaire at a time when a million dollars was still a good definition of the American Dream.

But becoming a Swiss citizen—a long and arduous process of certification which can last for fourteen years—was another matter, and Pat seems to have alternated her desire for it (she thought it would help her tax bill in America) with her fear of losing her American citizenship, one of her crucial identities. America was still the country which commanded her imagination, still the country with which she had the strongest emotional ties. As late as the end of 1991, she was writing to one of her legal advisors that "for sentimental reasons I may not wish to renounce USA citizenship."[15] And the depth of her feeling for her native land could always be measured by the agitated abuse she continued to heap on it. When she wrote to Kingsley about her campaign to become a Swiss citizen, it was in terms which reflected her ambivalence: "I am seriously considering switching to Swiss citizenship. . . . If I switch I'll probably have to stay in bed 2 days, because of emotional shock."*[16]

If America remained the focal point of many of Pat's feelings, her house in Moncourt, France, continued to be the locus of her dreams and her regrets.

In 1988, after seven gardenless years in Aurigeno, Pat looked at "20 envelopes of photos from my desk cubbyholes"[17]—they were photographs of her Moncourt garden—and allowed them to put a halo of nostalgia around her feelings for the house. She wrote to Monique Buffet about it.

"I must say I was touched by the sight of that garden in colour. Nothing can substitute for a happy garden (walled to boot), and nice friends around. I did not dwell on the photos; I am just serious on the subject; not the same kind of seriousness that brings tears, not at all."[18]

Perhaps Pat, a nightly reader of dictionaries, knew that the word "paradise" is derived from the Persian word for "walled garden."

In 1992, the house in Moncourt was very much on her mind when she sent a letter to Barbara Skelton in the Seine-et-Marne:

"As I look back, as they say—I think I should have tried for compromise in 1980 with the frogs. 1971–80 was the happiest time of my life to work, garden, cats, friends. What else is life all about?"[19]

But Pat's Moncourt house was long since sold, and death would take the thorny question of citizenship out of her hands. She died an American citizen, with her American-born, Geneva-residing accountant, Marylin Scowden, as her very last houseguest. Pat had first met Marylin Scowden in Geneva on the evening of the April day in 1992 when she'd been chauffeured to Peter Ustinov's house in Rolle for a double interview by German *Vogue*.[20] Ustinov had

---

* Despite her fierce desire to hang on to her money (and all those "political" letters sent pseudonymously to newspapers so she wouldn't attract the Swiss government's attention), it would not have been "out of character" for Pat to pull out of her application for Swiss citizenship at the last possible moment. She had already tried to reverse the sale of her Moncourt house; ambivalent behavior was a Highsmith way of life.

requested Pat as his lunch partner for the interview, and she was quite taken with both Peter Ustinov *and* the paintings he had hanging in his house.[21]

Although Pat was fond of Marylin Scowden and had gone some distance in the direction of trusting her (not, to be sure, with any personal information), and although Scowden had come to Tegna to settle some important financial matters with her client (Pat made her last will just three days before she died), Pat probably preferred the way in which this final guest availed herself of the hospitality of the Casa Highsmith, arriving, as Scowden did, at the white block of a house a little *after* Pat had been taken to the hospital in Locarno. Of previous visits to Pat in Tegna, Scowden says: "I think she was happy I came and *very* happy when I left."[22] This time—the very last time she had company—Pat was not obliged to share her house with her visitor.

And there are strong indications that she didn't want to share her hospital room, either. When Scowden arrived in Tegna, she had a necessary meeting with Pat's banker at Pat's house, and then went straight to the hospital in Locarno with papers for Pat to sign.

"I said to Pat: 'This can wait till tomorrow,' and Pat said: 'No no, I want to sign them now.' Her intuition made her feel that it was necessary to sign those papers: it was done at her insistence. . . . She was on morphine, very uncomfortable, and she kept saying 'My legs are hurting, my legs are hurting,' and I tried to massage them, and there was no muscle left."[23]

But Pat couldn't bear the personal attention. "You should go, you should go, don't stay, don't stay," she repeated several times to her deeply concerned visitor.[24]

And so Marylin Scowden, with no indication from the doctors that this was to be Patricia Highsmith's last night on earth, left the room.

In January of 1980, on the third or fourth day after she had been hospitalized in Nemours, France, for a catastrophically gushing nosebleed, Pat asked a nurse to leave the door of her hospital room open. She was afraid of dying alone, and the prospect felt very near: she was "losing" more blood than she was "gaining." She thought then that it was "maybe . . . a sign of vitality or brotherliness to want to speak to someone at the last and say, 'Stay with me a minute, please—I'm going.'" The nurse refused her request to open the door because the children on the ward were "very *impressionnant* about blood," and Pat, bleeding copiously every two hours, was covered with it. Pat was angry at the nurse, but she was also "ashamed of my fear of dying alone, since I've always known death is an individual act anyway. I swear to myself next time I'll be better prepared."[25]

Perhaps her insistence in Switzerland, a decade and a half later when she really *was* dying, on sending her final visitor out of her hospital room—it is

Pat Highsmith's last reported act—was what she had meant by being "better prepared." But as the longtime companion and close observer of many felines, Pat would also have known that when a country cat is mortally ill, it begins its instinctive transit out of life by going off into the woods to die alone.

The contrast between the happy little Swiss travel piece Pat was working on in her notebook in 1953—overflowing with praise and pleasure and local color— and the glum, grim, grayed-out notes she took when she actually *moved* to Switzerland in the early 1980s (to the house in Aurigeno which Ellen Hill, with the assistance of architect Tobias Amman, had picked out for her) is marked. Pat hadn't had so much peace and quiet since she'd left her double cottage in Earl Soham in 1968—and its effect on her was that her inspirational flame burned low and her depression was awful. She experienced "some of the blackest moments of my life, when for fifteen minutes at a time, I would feel that I'd got myself into a trap, and an unhappy one."

Part of the problem was the lack of light. The seventeenth-century stone summerhouse Ellen had chosen for Pat sat in the Maggia Valley in the deep shadow of the Dunzio Mountain; in the winter the house got sunlight for perhaps two hours a day. The windows of the house were small (and some of them were barred), and the walls were a good half meter thick, so that even when the sun was out the house was dark and cool.

Daniel Keel says: "People come to the Ticino for the light, and she put herself into the darkest, most cramped house, no room, no quality of life; she didn't give her guests anything, but she didn't give herself anything either. It was the most uncomfortable house in the world with the mountains right up against it, which cut out even the two hours of sunlight a day the town got."[26]

"This is where I write," Pat told Keel, showing him her desk corner. Her desk, as usual, faced the wall and was accompanied by the "most uncomfortable chair" in the house.[27]

In an odd—a *very* odd—article entitled "Winter in the Ticino" (the canton in which both Aurigeno and Tegna are located), Pat wrote that in Aurigeno she chose to fraternize only with Germans or Swiss Germans, even though she was living in the Italian-speaking part of Switzerland. She described her house as a "submarine"—but a submarine set in stone and not in water—and evoked the peculiar mineral emanations from the heavy concentrations of granite in the mountains, concentrations which produced a "magnetic effect" said to drain you of your life's energy. Pat seemed to like this idea and to accept it fatalistically: "How can one escape the density of rock?"[28]

Although Pat began her residency in Aurigeno by giving a cocktail party on her terrace on the day before the opening of the Locarno Film Festival (one guest's report on the hors d'oeuvres: "Boiled eggs, cut in half, mayonnaise out of the tube, the food was quite terrible and unattractive; whoever did it was not exactly an aesthete in food matters"),[29] her description of her social life was bleak. "There is only one American, a retired widow, in the region and she lives in Ascona." (That was Ellen Blumenthal Hill.) "I recently met an Englishman," she continued, as though she'd been bird-watching and had spotted a rare specimen. She "happen[ed] to like the quiet," she wrote, but the village appeared to be "without inhabitants." (Counting Highsmith, the population was 106.) She was a submariner living in a ghost town.[30]

There was a weekly "or so" dinner party in Aurigeno in which wine and food seemed to play a central role. "Food is important here," a friend said to her, "because there's nothing else that's very amusing." These weekly dinners engendered heated political arguments until "2 in the morning," conducted by guests "made happy on wine."[31] (Were they unhappy without it?) Once again, Pat found someone to do favors and errands for her—a kind and considerably overburdened neighbor in the village, Ingeborg Moelich, a former opera singer, who had a car but very little money, and who was not, say neighbors, adequately recompensed for her efforts. She shopped for Pat, she did some sewing and some laundry, as well as many driving errands. And she continued, faithfully, to stop by Pat's house in Tegna during Pat's last illness. It was Ingeborg Moelich who drove Pat, leaning heavily on Julia Diener-Diethelm in the backseat of Moelich's car, on her very last ride to the hospital in Locarno in early February of 1995.

Pat also befriended the one man in the village who had fought for Germany during the Second World War, a grouchy old gentleman to whom no one else spoke. She found the elderly soldier from Hitler's army quite interesting. But when the man died, Pat, like any good New Yorker, immediately began to speculate on the possibilities of buying his house, situated on the steep stone grade just above hers.[32]

Someone said to her: "Nothing's alive. Have you noticed that?" She had.[33]

And so, in the way of a woman with a turbulent imagination who spends time alone in a dark house talking to herself, Pat, once again, began to dream up little inventions to lighten her days. She thought about a "Minivac—small hand-held vacuum cleaner . . . to dust the tops of books in bookcase."[34] But this was nine years after her native land had produced the ubiquitous Dust-Buster hand vacuum with its myriad irritating attachments: Pat was out of touch with the material facts of her home country. Ditto for her idea for the "small wringer . . . for kitchen, in order to extract liver paste from tube which has been in fridge"—a device she felt would be a welcome addition to any home.[35] Her thumbs, arthritic by now, couldn't squeeze the paste out of chilled food tubes, and she was putting the tubes on the floor and using her feet on them. But once again Pat had been preempted in her invention: it was already being manufactured in America to extract the very last drops out of stubborn toothpaste tubes.

On 1 March 1983, shortly after Pat made her initial move to Aurigeno, Arthur Koestler, whom Pat had known for thirty-five years and who was by now dying of leukemia and disabled by Parkinson's disease, killed himself in his London home. His wife, Cynthia, joined him in what was apparently a suicide pact. Pat hadn't seen Koestler since 2 May 1978 when she'd brought Tabea Blumenschein over to the Koestlers' London town house to show her off. Tabea had been worried because she hadn't read any of Koestler's work, but Pat quickly relieved her of her doubts: "Never mind, my dear, the last thing writers want to talk about is their work."[36] Pat was at Peter Huber's house in Zurich when she got the news about Koestler, and she was alone a day later when she found out that Koestler's wife was also dead. Pat was furious: "My first thought was that he had gently persuaded her; my emotion plain anger."[37]

Pat wrote to everyone about the Koestlers' suicides, but she wrote most fully to her sympathetic German translator, Anne Uhde. Murder—self-murder in this case—always fired up Pat's imagination, and as she was writing her description to Uhde she couldn't help re-creating the scene of the "crime," altering it rather prudishly to suit her taste and echoing in a backhanded way her own short tale of horror and gore, "Woodrow Wilson's Necktie."

Yes, the news about Koestler knocked me for a loop, I must say. . . . I felt upset, angry. . . . I am sorry mainly about Cynthia.

I know their sitting room very well indeed, and know the armchairs they always took, so I can imagine the scene. They probably took the pills after a pleasant dinner together. I know exactly where they had to leave the note to the maid, saying, "Don't go upstairs. Call the police at . . ." So I keep thinking about that living room, and—absurdly—thinking they should have done it lying on two different beds, dressed of course, as if they had fallen asleep reading a newspaper. I feel that some waxworks is going to show them exactly in that room (this is the first time such an idea crossed my mind), and it will be Mme Tussaud's, London, and I do not not wish to see it. I see, frankly, no reason for Cynthia to have died, and I've the feeling, maybe wrong, that K. persuaded her.[38]

A year later the Koestlers' suicides were still on Pat's mind, and now she was blaming both of them: "Cynthia was a willing, clinging vine. . . . Arthur would never have tied himself up with a woman who had any ambition, will, even strong personality of her own."[39]

The lack of light in Aurigeno was draining Pat; the jagged mountain—the mountain view from her Aurigeno house is so exaggerated as to almost induce vertigo—was minatory. Worse, all the stone houses in Aurigeno have roofs which are sharply peaked, so the village itself looks like a miniature mountain range. Even in summer the steep walk to Pat's house up the solid stone walk was slippery, and the house's barred windows were forbidding. Pat wrote that the mountain produced "a depressing effect, a feeling of being closed in, with consequent emphasis on self-sufficiency, tendency to smugness, maybe alcoholism in the types prone to it. . . . I notice among outsiders like me who live here, that a great deal of time is spent in relating real or imaginary slights, insults, neglects, attitudes, to any friend or ally that will listen. Maybe it is because the community is small and little new blood comes in. Or does Ticino make people nervous?"

"Nothing's alive"? Self-sufficient characters drinking alone in dark houses and brooding over "imaginary slights, insults, neglects"? A "depressing effect, a feeling of being closed in," a terrain that makes people "nervous"? We are in Highsmith Country again, the only country on earth with a permanent population of one. But for its sole begetter, living in Highsmith Country was less comfortable than imagining it. In the shadows, immured in granite, Pat was beginning to let go of much of what had defined her in the past. The woman who in her teens and twenties had insisted that reading was her major "drug" stopped reading in Aurigeno for more than two years. She continued to saw and hammer away in her workroom, but for the first time she had no garden, and nothing bloomed for her but the sprouts from an occasional avocado pit skewered by a toothpick and suspended over a glass of water. The house itself was not—as almost every one of her other dwellings had been—anywhere near the sight or the sound of water. She had, in every sense, set herself in stone.

Every few days Pat turned on her portable Grundig radio to "restore her sanity" with a little classical music. "I realise that I may be reaching the point at which I think everyone is a bit cracked but me. What are people saying about me behind my back? Could I face it if I knew?"[40]

She began to give herself little sanity tests again. Could she follow the sense of this World Service broadcast? She could. But her mood lightened only with travel or with new acquaintances—and then not for very long.

One of Pat's new acquaintances was David Streiff, who had recently taken over the directorship of the Locarno Film Festival and was busily raising its profile. Streiff wrote to Pat, offering her an "Honor Card"—a free pass to the festival, which he also offered to other notables in the area like Luise Rainer, the film actress Pat had met in New York in 1948 at Leo Lerman's Sunday salon. Pat was "proud to have the Honor Card," pleased to be singled out, and, of course, delighted not to have to pay for her tickets.[41] She never much liked the films.

In the blistering August heat of 1983, during the running of the Locarno Film Festival, David Streiff invited Pat to the Grand Hotel in Locarno. "She didn't want the menu, but she wanted a pizza," he says, "which they had to bring back from some other place, and even then, she only ate the tomatoes." Whenever they dined together after that, they went mostly to Tegna to Pat's favorite little restaurant next to the cemetery, and Pat would always order spaghetti. And Streiff always paid for the meals.

"The ritual was I came to her house, we drank something there, I beer, she whiskey, we went by car, her broken-down car, to the restaurant. I accepted the fact that she only took a few spoonfuls and the rest went into this famous plastic bag [for] the cats . . . and then she took me back to Locarno. . . . She was not a very good driver, absentminded, not practical [but] she always found her way back and she sent a postcard or a call so I knew she got back alive. . . . She'd drive back with [a bottle of scotch] in her car."[42]

She remained, he says, consistent in "character"—that is, dominating—but revealed more of herself to him as their relations progressed. They always spoke in "American," and Pat, never happy to come to a settled opinion about anything by herself, made use of Streiff's expertise in film, sending him the Diogenes film contracts for her books to look over. From her comments on the films she saw, Streiff doesn't think Pat knew what was "good or bad vis-à-vis her own work in films." They had "an easy contact" because he, too, is gay, and she seemed, he says, "kind of proud" that she'd made some sort of "contribution" with *The Price of Salt,* but she never discussed her relations or her fantasies—all she had left, by then, of her love life—with him. Except, of course, for the obligatory complaints about Ellen Hill.[43]

"I felt enriched, I was proud to be in touch with such a famous writer and to be close to her," says David Streiff. And Pat, too, was proud: she used to tell people that Streiff took the trouble to visit her when she moved to Tegna. A few weeks before her death, Pat, prompted by Daniel Keel, telephoned Streiff, who was by then the director of the Swiss Federal Office of Culture, to ask about placing her manuscripts and personal papers at the Swiss Literary Archives. The day Streiff sat down to discuss the terms of acceptance with Daniel Keel was the day Pat died, 4 February 1995.[44]

In 1991, when Streiff retired from the Locarno Film Festival, a television documentary was made about him. Pat was asked to appear in it, and, judging from the film outtakes, she gave her usual performance before a camera as the mute and rebellious heroine of a hostage video. She managed to indicate that she "didn't know David Streiff very well" and then, taking offence at a question, abruptly refused to go on being filmed.[45]

In her thirtieth cahier, shortly after separating from Caroline Besterman in 1968, Pat had written: "To live alone, to feel occasional depression. Much of the difficulty is from *not* having another person around for whom one puts on a slight show—dressing nicely, presenting a pleasant expression. The trick, the sometimes difficult trick is to maintain one's morale without the other person, the mirror."[46]

In Switzerland, Pat had found a supportive publisher and world representative in Daniel Keel and Diogenes, a German-speaking public eager for her work, and not one single person, really, for whom she could perform her "self." The "difficult trick" she spoke of—that of maintaining her morale without the presence of another like-minded person (well, perhaps not exactly "another person"; Pat's definition of "the other" is also Narcissus's, i.e., a "mirror")—was something she never mastered.

Settled in her stone house in Aurigeno in the world's most pristine country (and continuing to remark on how "clean" Switzerland was), Pat just naturally found her mind turning to images of cancer, toxic waste, the effects of radiation, poison, rape, torture, and the horrors of nuclear war.

Not that her imagination hadn't turned to these entertainments before. Even in her first novel, *Strangers on a Train,* the architect Guy Haines, in a series of thoughts that leads to the inevitable conclusion ("There's also a person exactly the opposite of you, like the unseen part of you, somewhere in the world, and he waits in ambush"),[47] starts with the notion that the "splitting of the atom was the only true destruction, the breaking of the universal law of oneness. . . . Perhaps God and the Devil danced hand in hand around every single electron!"[48] And *The Price of Salt,* with its references to bomb shelters and young physicists, is as casually shadowed by the atom bomb as any American novel of the 1950s: an era when all North American schoolchildren were subject to special drills during which (to the sound of a buzzer/bell like the alarm in Samuel Beckett's play *Happy Days*) they learned to dive under their desks to take shelter from the shower of splitting atoms that—any minute now—would be coming their way from Moscow.

Pat's notebooks in France throughout the 1970s wince at the world's wastage, and are punctuated by her eccentric plans for improving life on earth. The story collections which resulted from her comparatively happy occupancy of the house by the Loing Canal at 22 rue de la Boissière in Moncourt

(*Little Tales of Misogyny* [1974], *The Animal-Lover's Book of Beastly Murder* [1975], *Slowly, Slowly in the Wind* [1979], *The Black House* [1981 in England, 1988 in the United States]) had already begun to throb with both a personal, character-based malice and with the kind of disasters that destroy small ecologies and little institutions: a vengeful pond, killer ferrets, abusive parents, a subtly toxic network of liberal friends, and a skyscraper permanently infested with pests.

"The Terrors of Basket-Weaving," the best story in *The Black House* and one of Pat's more evocative tales, extends the situation of a middle-class, well-employed, childless-by-choice press relations officer into something larger: a study of the dangers of creation itself. Diane Clarke, with puzzling precision and inexplicable historical accuracy, repairs a damaged basket she finds on a beach with an ability she didn't know she had. She is increasingly frightened by this "hidden talent" which she cannot explain. "What she felt was most certainly not guilt, though it was similarly troubling and unpleasant. . . . Diane felt she had lost herself."[49] Soon, she asks for a leave of absence from work, and is feeling "as if a lot of other people were inside me besides myself."[50] She ends by destroying the basket, and is "no happier" after doing so. "For a week, she realized, she had grasped something, and then she had deliberately thrown it away."[51] The act of creation has permanently disturbed her life, just as "The Terrors of Basket-Weaving" permanently disturbs our idea of what "making something" means to an artist.

"Please Don't Shoot the Trees," a story written in 1976–77 and included in *Slowly, Slowly in the Wind,* is another example of the way Pat's mind was beginning to turn from the cracks in character to the crises in the cosmos. It is marked by its sneering tone, its prairie-flat prose, its comic book science—but also by its deeply discomfiting prescience. Nature, Pat imagined in her notes, "revolts—at its rape, at its reversed rivers and cut down trees—and erupts in volcanoes, collapses in earthquakes, everywhere gobbling, burning, crushing people."[52] The United States has been partitioned into "big fortresses," the great cities are "unsupervised prisons of the poor and the black. . . . New York and San Francisco [are] dirty words," and all the trees are shooting out inflammable sap—something like napalm—at the human inhabitants of earth.

The trees end by destabilizing the world, and a "land mass, big as a continent" (it's the continent of North America) drops "into the dark blue waters."

A vein of pure, vengeful nastiness—an underappreciated literary quality, but a literary quality nonetheless—runs through much of the work Pat did in Europe. By the end of 1976 in Moncourt, when she had begun to take notes on her "4th Ripley" (*The Boy Who Followed Ripley*), her confidence was "flitting sideways, like a bird, out of sight now." She was finding concentration difficult, she had started too many projects, and her life was "but a kind of darkness full of dark and empty shadows." She couldn't wait for clarity of mind because "to have patience [would be] to erase all pride, satisfaction in a day's work." And the fair manuscript copy of *The Boy Who Followed Ripley* bears witness to her near-crippling indecisiveness: interleaved, crossed out, and overwritten, it is her most anxious manuscript.

In the first difficult phase of writing the novel (before the spring of 1978 provided her with the other difficulty of Tabea Blumenschein), it was money, again, and taxes, again, that were making her feel futile—once again. She kept on working because she *had* to, stabilizing herself with a plot for her novel that was concerned with money and vengeance. (Her other title for the book was *Ripley and the Money Boy*.) It was another prescient work: in *The Boy Who Followed Ripley* Pat imagined a relationship for Tom Ripley with a very young admirer. Within the next year and a half, she would have two such relationships herself. The first, with Tabea Blumenschein, prevented her from working on the novel, while the second, with Monique Buffet, allowed her to finish it. Highsmith's life and work would always give the appearance of a balancing act.

Pat's initial notes for *The Boy Who Followed Ripley* center on young Frank, who, attracted by Ripley's dubious reputation, has run away from his family to see Ripley after pushing his "great uncle over a terrace wall" in America. (Pat later changed the victim to Frank's grandfather, then to his father.) "Tom smells out the boy's terror of possessing money, also fascination." Frank—and he is anything *but* frank at first—is the heir to a great food fortune (there's a whiff of Pat's discomfort with food in this), and "so strong" is Frank's "adherence to Tom" (the Whitmanic adjective is Pat's) that Tom's wife, Heloise, suspects young Frank of being a *"tapette,"* a "fairy." Ripley, Pat noted from bitter personal experience, "cannot really win with H[eloise] because if he intrudes on her privacy it is too much, & if he doesn't, it is a sign of indifference."[53]

In the early days of 1977, Pat was also brooding about (but not reading) Dostoyevsky's efforts to "reconcile God's will with God's indifference" and calling it "rubbish." Money and taxes were now at the center of her thoughts. "Artists, writers and some filmmakers," she wrote with asperity, "like Ingmar Bergman—end up as they started . . . writing for love, working for love, not money because taxes take almost all the money. A strange cycle."[54] By the end of 1977, she was writing that Christ (still a touchstone for her and the only divinity with whom she never argued) was lucky "not to be able to see this unchristian, uncharitable and dishonest Catholic community in which I live."

Once again, Pat had decided that she was surrounded by thieving enemies and—a slight variation—that her friends were crooks as well. She described her next-door neighbor Desmond Ryan as a petty criminal—"an alcoholic adulterer, now pilfering firewood bought by me to give to the poor"—and she would later curse him roundly to Barbara Skelton, one of whose husbands, the millionaire physicist Derek Jackson, had been "an old school chum" of Ryan.[55] Everyone, she thought with the kind of satisfaction that familiarity brings, was cheating her. Pat was settling comfortably into one of her oldest themes.

Expatriatism and the loverless wilderness into which she finally wandered in Switzerland did nothing to alter this view, and napalm-shooting trees, murderous ferrets, and killer ponds were not the only vengeful organisms in the Highsmith stories to come: the author, too, was beginning to wreak a near-biblical vengeance on all the *milieux* she'd abandoned (and by which she felt abandoned) in America. By 1977, Pat had chronicled the very American Edith Howland's slow slippage into insanity in *Edith's Diary,* accompanying it with Edith's confused but condign jeremiads about America and the war in Vietnam. (Edith's political "thinking" is that of a thinly sourced article; her ideas are mostly superficial summaries.) Pat was entering a long period of focusing her talents on broader targets than those which lurked in the hearts of men.

36

THE CAKE THAT WAS SHAPED

LIKE A COFFIN

PART 3

Before she moved to peaceful, pristine, orderly Switzerland, Pat had never been tempted to make the decline and fall of the earth a focus of her artistic attention. Nor had she summoned up the world's decay in anything more substantial than a halo of implication around the protagonists of her novels (like Edith Howland's poisoned suburban family in *Edith's Diary* or the brutal effects of Howard Ingham's identity-dissolving holiday in Hammamet in *The Tremor of Forgery)*, or explored it in anything more serious than a few caricatural short stories. But Pat's thirty-sixth notebook, which bridges her life in Aurigeno, Switzerland, from August of 1983 to August of 1988, explodes in a series of apocalyptic horrors. Most of the *keime* in this journal—those creative "germs" which inspired and infected her work—are viral, carcinogenic, and irradiated.

She imagined (and then crossed the notebook entry out) a "small country in East Africa, composed of blacks and Spanish mixed," where "[c]ruelty to the elderly provokes laughter" and [n]urses, p[hilanthropists]—all murdered and raped."[1] Another crossed-out entry: "Begin story with stuck elevator which has 20 corpses in it, putrefying."[2] Another idea: "A contagious E. Coli germ gets loose. Devastating diarrhea . . . abandonment of beaches, hotels, resorts . . . Eels triumph on the beaches, eating even the corpses of . . . swimmers. Mercury poisoning . . . a pretty girl swimmer swallows a morsel of human excrement."[3] Another entry: a story called "Mass Unemployment," which details a series of disasters in which the "survivors of the human race have fled to Switzerland," where they hope to live in unpolluted air. "But even Switzerland has been bombed."[4]

At the end of 1984, two years after Michael Jackson's revolutionary album

Thriller appeared, Pat beamed her laser briefly on the idea of writing Michael Jackson into a short story. She saw something metastasizing in Jackson, something she recognized and understood and was drawn to. She began—shrewdly, for the limited amount of information she had about him—to parse Jackson's character. Like so many other of her subjects now, her brief re-creation of Michael Jackson returned her to the motive of money.

"A type like Michael Jackson, [ambiguously gendered,] in love with himself. Sterling image to the public. Schizo finally. He talks to himself as he dresses. He becomes two persons within himself. Friends are aware of this—but the boy is a money-maker."[5]

Along with the odd note for a novel about murder-minded protagonists who kill, steal, and/or exchange guilts for love, and the occasional plot summary about toxic relations in a small circle of people, Pat, from her rocky perch in Switzerland, continued to widen her scope at the expense of its depth: her imagination was indicting worldwide institutions (like the Catholic Church) in her short story "Pope Sixtus VI—about which the Catholic convert Graham Greene (who, according to Muriel Spark, "wasn't happy if he wasn't sinning")[6] wrote Pat an approving letter. In other short stories such as "Nabuti: Warm Welcome to a UN Committee," or her crude parody of Ronald Reagan's presidency, "President Buck Jones Rallies and Waves the Flag," she was destroying whole civilizations.

Pat had already published the rancorous results of her move to Switzerland in *Found in the Street* (1985), a novel which upsets the premises of her other inverted Manhattan fairy tale, *The Price of Salt*. This time, the lovely young ingenue to whom everyone is attracted (and who spices up the marriage of Jack and Natalia, the young couple living in Highsmith's old apartment building in Grove Street) comes to Manhattan to "try her luck" and is brutally murdered in front of what appears to be Buffie Johnson's loft building on Greene Street. (See "Patricia Highsmith's New York.") And the net in which every character is ambiguously snared is the paranoid consciousness of the crank and failure, Ralph Linderman: very much a product of the same Pat Highsmith who, forty-odd years before, had created the single-room occupant with the withered ear, Archie, in her first published story, "Uncertain Treasure." (The novelist Anita Brookner, in a *Spectator* review of *Found in the Street,* called Linderman "a nuisance and a bore. In the country of the laid-back he is an intruder.")[7] Single men in single rooms would always be a Highsmith speciality.

Ralph's honorable return of a wallet (as we have seen, Pat yearned to return a wallet herself; it was the ultimate proof of honesty required by her criminal mind) and his judgement of Manhattan as a sinful city plagued by irritating minorities and sexual deviants enjoying themselves, is the ostinato of *Found in the Street*. Pat left out of the novel the ugly little ethnic dictionary she'd made up for Ralph, but she still allowed him to use a repugnant epithet for Jews and to imagine black Americans as apes swinging from trees.

But the fact that Ralph Linderman is both the "moral center" of the book (all his puritanical predictions of disaster come true) *and* an obsessive nut-case who misinterprets things attests strongly to his creator's still-active, still-generative, still-productive ambivalence. Amongst the other things this novel "finds in the street" is a female murderer who is also a "butch dyke" and a far more caricatural depiction of lesbianism than the one which irritated Pat so much in Marc Brandel's 1950 novel, *The Choice*. Sisterhood had never been a Highsmith theme.

Like all of Pat's writings set in America in the 1970s and 1980s, *Found in the Street* was subject to her misunderstandings of the culture she'd left behind. The food and drink in the novel are from 1960s New York, not 1980s Manhattan; her re-creation of the habits of hip young couples in Greenwich Village is unrecognizable; and the social scenes into which she inserts her characters seem to be dramatized by someone who has been observing Manhattan from another galaxy, not to mention another epoch. Pat's French editor, Alain Oulman, politely found the relationship between the young couple, Jack and Natalia, unbelievable—"they don't speak or act as if they were husband and wife," he wrote Pat—and he was correct: they are difficult to believe in.[8]

Still, Pat divided some of her own personal quirks between Jack and Natalia: Jack, who is working on something like a graphic novel, has, like Pat, a tendency to prefer pictures of women to the women themselves, while Natalia has secret affairs with women and loves to mark passages in books the way Pat marked them, with little brackets. And Pat gave to the crackpot Ralph Linderman more than a few of her own ethnic prejudices: proof, perhaps, that her artistic self was more "advanced" than the self which harbored the prejudices. Oddly—this would always be a Highsmith trademark—the novel's social disjunctures and cross-cultural misunderstandings add another layer of creepy fascination to what is already a decidedly creepy work.

It was the American publication of *Found in the Street* in January of 1988 that prompted Terrence Rafferty's lucid, praiseful consideration of Patricia Highsmith's work (he called it "peerlessly disturbing—not great cathartic nightmares but banal bad dreams that keep us restless and thrashing for the rest of the night[,]" and characterized her prose as "blunt and straightforward as a strip search") in *The New Yorker* that same month.[9] The article seems to have given Pat, who as late as 1969 was still having her stories and poems and cartoons rejected from *The New Yorker,* the most pleasure she'd gotten out of a piece of journalism since Francis Wyndham's unparalleled survey of her work (part of his long review of *The Cry of the Owl*) for English readers in 1963. Wyndham had written:

> Her peculiar brand of horror comes less from the inevitability of disaster, than from the ease with which it might have been avoided. The evil of her agents is answered by the impotence of her patients— this is not the attraction of opposites, but in some subtle way the call of like to like. When they finally clash in climactic catastrophe, the reader's sense of satisfaction may derive from sources as dark as those which motivate Patricia Highsmith's destroyers and their fascinated victims.[10]

Nine years after Wyndham's piece appeared, Julian Symons, doyen of British crime writers, biographer of his interesting older brother A. J. A. Symons (Pat liked and, of course, identified with the subject of A. J. A. Symons's innovative biography, the effortlessly eccentric Baron Corvo), and a critic who regularly championed and occasionally chastised Pat's novels in print, extended the public awareness of her duality.

"There are no more genuine agonies in modern literature than those endured by the couples in her books who are locked together in a dislike and even hatred that often strangely contains love."[11]

Symons understood how necessary "violence" was to Pat: "the threat or actuality of it produces her best writing."[12]

Two months after Terrence Rafferty's piece was published, the American journalist Joan Dupont travelled from Paris to Aurigeno to interview Pat, sympathetically, for *The New York Times*—editing out Pat's more intemperate comments about Israel, to Pat's irritation. But neither Rafferty's essay nor Dupont's article helped Pat's new novel in the United States: *Found in the Street* sold fewer than five thousand copies.

After *Found in the Street,* Pat's next letter to the world from Switzerland was a collection of short stories written in the cartoonish spirit of her early comics work: *Tales of Natural and Unnatural Catastrophes* (1987). Pat never lost her interest in cartoons and even sent some cartoon ideas to Gary Trudeau for his nationally syndicated *Doonesbury* strip while she was living in Aurigeno. She also sent Trudeau a copy of *Tales of Natural and Unnatural Catastrophes,* thinking that these stories would be prime material for a political cartoonist.[13] And they would have been: each story in *Catastrophes* is as distorted by repulsion as an expressionist caricature.

Most of the *Catastrophes* collection could also have found its way into that strangest of American pulp magazines, *Weird Tales* (see "Alter Ego, Part 1")—especially the oddest story, "The Mysterious Cemetery." Inspired by Pat's friend Anne Morneweg's bout with breast cancer and the blackly humorous way Morneweg recounted her experience to Pat,[14] "The Mysterious Cemetery" tells the story of a secret cemetery near a hospital which is infected with metastasizing growths, growths which come from the bodies of the hospital's illegally experimented-on cancer patients, who are buried in the cemetery grounds. The growths propagate and burgeon, and Pat likens them to "a man-made wreckage of his own soul, to an insane tinkering with nature, such as that which had resulted in the accursed atomic bomb."[15] She imagines that the strange blooms will become cult objects, revered artifacts—enlivening the work of artists, scientists, and writers.

"The Mysterious Cemetery" could have been the Highsmith version of a bitter "environmental" dialectic, but the contrapuntal voice, the antiphon of the dialectic, is missing. And so the tale, like all the tales in *Catastrophes*, remains another exhibit in the Highsmith Museum of Contemporary Maladies. The same impulse—the impulse to attack—had inspired *Little Tales of Misogyny*, but the *Misogyny* tales (although Pat cast the women in them as "types") are more bitter and more personal: they are directed against women, in some cases against specific, living women. The *Catastrophes* tales are directed against the entire world.

After a publicity trip to Manhattan in late October of 1987 (see "The Cake That Was Shaped Like a Coffin: Part 5"), Pat flew from New York to London to promote *Tales of Natural and Unnatural Catastrophes*. Aside from the usual round of interviews and meetings with friends and colleagues (she invited a young writer, who had just accompanied her on a publicity junket to Green-Wood Cemetery in Brooklyn and was flying to London herself, to a luncheon "at which Patricia Losey arrived with her husband's ashes [film director Joseph Losey] in an urn"),[16] Pat made an unusual appearance on the BBC2 television program *Cover to Cover*, presented by the Australian poet and novelist Jill Neville. Other *Cover to Cover* panellists included the biographer Victoria Glendinning, the young actor Jack Klaff, and Kenneth Williams, farceur, review artist, and caustic star of the *Carry On* films. Kenneth Williams's mordant diaries make Pat's own complaint-filled journals seem like chronicles of unrestrained joy.

Three books were on *Cover to Cover*'s agenda for the evening, and Pat's collection of short stories came second, to be followed by Richard Ellmann's biography of Oscar Wilde, a work which later appeared on Tom Ripley's own reading list. Pat didn't get around to reading the Ellmann book until April of 1990; she really wasn't reading anything in Aurigeno. But when she finally did read it, she joined Oscar in her mind with her favorite spiritual hero— "Oscar's story reminds me of that of Christ"—and then coerced his destructive relationship with Bosie into a parable about her own life: "Art is not always healthy," she wrote, "and why should it be?"[17]

Panellist Jack Klaff's memory of the taping of *Cover to Cover* was "very strong."

There was this legendary writer, not only having a book up for review, *Tales of Natural and Unnatural Catastrophes,* but she was actually going to *be* there. . . . I suppose we were all expecting crime stories and stuff like that and then we got these rather socially conscious stories. When a writer of that stature writes something like that, you pay attention, even if the stories are slightly confused.

My impression [of Patricia] was, well, she was quite sunken into herself. . . . She had a sort of molelike or badgerlike aspect. She was perched at the end of the table, she was hunched over, her eyes were sad, even before she started. . . . She looked like a person who spent her life just writing.

Kenneth Williams, at the far end of the on-set table, was

sitting ramrod straight, arms folded, legs crossed, couldn't wait for the Ellmann bio of Wilde. . . . I think he had two months to go before he died. He was not in a good mood, not feeling well, and he went into makeup not in a good state. And [Pat] had made this huge fuss over Kenneth Williams in makeup; everyone got the impression that she adored the films, the stage work; there was this huge buildup for him to return the compliment. And he just carpetbombed her. He said what a load of crap the book was. . . . I'm not sure if he actually said the book should be chucked on the rubbish bin, but he did say how much he'd enjoyed *The Talented Mr.* "this" and *Strangers on the* "that," and it was clear that he absolutely loathed this book. . . .*

* Both Kenneth Williams's and Pat's diaries confirm the fact that Pat was thrilled to meet Williams and took no umbrage at his criticism: "screaming gay, but v. pleasant" is how she described him later, and Williams wrote that she strode across the greenroom and "greeted me with outstretched hand" and that he couldn't believe she actually knew his acting work.

But with enormous respect for her dignity, and in the most polite way possible, she didn't really betray any reactions. . . . She simply responded to what he had to say. . . . She said perhaps Mr. Williams means this and means that. . . . If the author is present, they usually defend themselves. She didn't do that, she simply took it on the chin. Perhaps she was awed by this man. . . . We'd all been polite about the book, in some cases enthusiastic, but Kenneth Williams felt it was up to him to say what he said. It was hugely uncomfortable. . . .

Well, they edited the show very, very strongly; they cut out a lot of Williams's stronger comments.[18]

In fact, Victoria Glendinning's praise of *Tales of Natural and Unnatural Catastrophes* is what comes through most prominently in the edited version of the broadcast. Glendinning compared it to *Animal Farm* and described it, accurately, as dealing with "the psychopathology of the entire world." But Pat's personal dignity comes through just as forcefully. Even her embarrassed demeanor couldn't hide the quiet distinction of her responses.

Thus, it was from Switzerland where Pat launched her last creative reversal of values. She began, unconsciously as always, to rechannel the Calvinist-influenced, world-correcting thinking of her grandmother Willie Mae (as well as those cranky little human-improvement theories she'd begun to confect in Moncourt in the 1970s, like the course designed for "ten year olds" to be given "on life's problems," a course she felt sure "would be very popular among children")[19] into an imagined destruction of the planet Earth, a planet she now saw as poisoned and choking on its own refuse.

There are no suggestions for world betterment in *Tales of Natural and Unnatural Catastrophes*—this was, after all, a chronicle of decay—but Pat's writing, both good and bad (and in its final phases unhelpfully sourced by the exhaustion of her inner resources and her second- and thirdhand knowledge of social conditions) was still marked by an eerie ability to predict the future. The instability, the fractured consciousness, the murderously repressed rages she was accustomed to detailing in relationships and psychologies, she now projected onto whole societies and grand institutions. In her own way, and in her own voice, Pat was abandoning the particular for the general, "turning loose" of psychology in favor of cosmology. It had interesting consequences for her work.

One of those consequences seems to be the growing social "relevance" of Pat's later and less satisfactory writings. Amongst the reasons this late work continues to signify is that the "facts" of contemporary life have now begun to imitate her "fictions." The planet, in its rapid decay, is finally catching up with Patricia Highsmith's imagination.

In 1987, in a notebook entry she never developed into a story, Pat returned for a moment to a double view of Mother Mary, rewriting her early relationship with her mother into something resolute, and casting herself, as she did in another story she wrote about her mother, "No End in Sight," in the role of a son. Picking up the stitch of her suspicions that Mary's friend and former neighbor in Fort Worth had a son who was pilfering things from Mary (see "The Real Romance of Objects: Part 1"), Pat imagined a teenage homosexual, a thief, whose mother "mocks him for effeminacy." The mother negotiates the will of their "dotty female neighbor," then tries to get her son to murder the old woman, to push her down the stairs. The boy rebels and murders his mother instead because in a "brief moment of confidence, spontaneity, [the dotty neighbor who] has spoken to the boy as if she has known all along that he was homosexual, asks him about a young man with whom the boy is in love. This opens the gates of love, of humanity, for the boy."[20] Splitting Mother Mary into two characters—both the evil mother and the dotty neighbor—was a momentary relief from Pat's usual characterization of Mary as the Bitch from Hell's Inner Precincts. But Pat never wrote these notes into a story.

Instead—increasingly irritated at having to contribute $1,100 a month towards Mary's care at the Fireside Lodge in Fort Worth—Pat moved Mary into the entirely unforgiving neigborhood of "No End in Sight," a story she included in *Tales of Natural and Unnatural Catastrophes.*

In *Gulliver's Travels,* Lemuel Gulliver is thrilled to hear of a race of humans, the Struldbruggs, who cannot die. He is less thrilled when he learns that they continue to age and to live "without relish or appetite." ("At 90 they lose their teeth and hair. . . . In talking they forget the common appellation of their nearest friends and relations.") Naomi Barton Markham, the main character of "No End in Sight" ("a hundred and ninety, some say two hundred and ten, with no end in sight"), whose faithful son Stevey died "a hundred and ten years ago" is a Struldbrugg to the life. A Struldbrugg in a rest home in Oklahoma.

Although Pat wasn't reading Jonathan Swift, her inner Swift could always be ignited by thoughts of Mother Mary and the money that she, Pat, was "wasting" on her, and this story is vibrant with a daughter's resentments and repulsions, disguised as those of a son's. Pat is the self-acknowledged "son" of "No End in Sight," just as she was the "son" in the story she called "Under a

Dark Angel's Eye" (published in *The Black House*) about the nefarious dealings of the rest home and the community to which an unloved mother has been consigned. In "No End in Sight," Pat focused her resentments on her current obsession, repeating ad infinitum that Naomi Barton Markham was a lifeless "tube" into which money was being ceaselessly funnelled at the Old Home-stead Nursing and Rest Home.*

Into the story Pat also slipped a sly reference to an Atwater-Kent radio—the company owned by her old lover Ginnie Kent Catherwood's father—and added a little true-life crime vignette taken from Mary's increasingly grim days at the Fireside Lodge. To curb her wandering, Mary was often strapped into an adult high chair at the lodge. When she wasn't strapped down, she used to creep into the rooms of other residents, remove their sets of false teeth, and hide them in blankets in her room.[21] Naomi Barton Markham does the same thing.

Pat makes a great deal of Naomi's bodily functions and dysfunctions and how costly they are: "Those wet, nasty, stinking diapers!" Although practi-cally insensate, Naomi is characterized as sly and cunning, and the atten-dants at the rest home hate her ("She's a horror!"). Pat gives to Naomi Mary Highsmith's pregnancy history with a malicious twist: in "No End in Sight," it is Naomi who wants a miscarriage more than her first husband does. (The opposite was true in the Plangman marriage.) Naomi divorces her first hus-band, gives birth to her son, leaves him with her mother, and goes off to Chi-cago to pursue a vaudeville career. And then she lives on forever in the rest home, "insane," writes Pat, and disturbing the staff by talking "in a some-what Southern accent." "You'll finish us all, Naomi," Pat ends the story, "you'll bury us all. . . . How does this incubus feel, lying on its back with a rubber ring under the rump to avoid bedsores?"[22]

"No End in Sight" is entirely fueled by physical disgust (the opposite of physical passion) and by hatred (the opposite of love). And Pat wrote it in the single-sided, artistically "unbalanced" state to which she'd reverted in her own "black house" in Aurigeno.

Whatever she told herself about it, Mary's long-livedness, the wandering of her wits, her sinking into near speechlessness and, finally, into immobility,

---

* Every single person conversant with Pat in the last part of her life recounts her constant complaints about having to pay to "keep her mother alive." In fact, with Mary's and Stan-ley's government pensions, Pat was responsible for only half the bill at the Fireside Lodge, the private nursing home in Fort Worth to which Mary had been consigned. Pat's "share" began at about $7,800 a year—more, she said, than she spent on herself—and went up to about $13,000 a year. But Pat's "brother Dan" admitted to his sons at the end of his life that Pat had been irregular in her payments for Mary's care; Dan himself was sometimes left to pay some of the bills.

were a constant source of pain and rage to Pat. That same sense of confusion of "selves" between the mother and daughter—the psychological twinning of Pat and Mary which breached the borders of their bodies and their desires and led Mary to impersonate Pat for some French journalists in a hotel lobby in Paris in 1959 and rendered Pat unable to work when her mother was angry or ill or poor—lived on in Pat, in an exhausted state, long after Mary had lost most of her memory. In 1985, Pat wrote to Kingsley that Mary was "worse" since her hip operation last March and that "[a]ll this simply depresses me . . . and it plays havoc with one's concentration."[23]

The last time Pat had seen her mother in Texas (it was at the end of September 1974), Mary had been having one of her "bad" days and hadn't, Pat said aggrievedly, "looked" at her own daughter; she'd watched television instead. Pat, on this visit, was still intent on getting that "Hamilton watch" from Mary (see "The Real Romance of Objects: Part 1"), and she was deeply distressed at the "total disorder" in which she'd found Mary's house: "dishes from days back in the kitchen sink, old newspapers, letters, envelopes on the living-room floor, the fat dog full of fleas, the oven full of half-finished plates of food." Back in Manhattan, where Pat stopped on her way to Moncourt, her cousin Millie Alford had given her a letter from Mary, a letter with which Mary ended the lifelong volley of love and damage she and her daughter had continued for so long. Mary's letter scumbles the line between mother and daughter, lays claim to the same feelings Pat had about her, and reads like a message from a heartbroken lover, full of the dashes Mary always used to catch her breath between emotions.

"Well, you've done it—broken my heart—yet gave me a freedom I've not felt in years. . . . That you could use the word to me that you used in describing the man you asked to adopt you . . . It's good you never had children—they'd be forever criticized and then never come up to your demands. You can think of no one but yourself. . . . Don't write—I shan't."[24]

Pat's identification with Mary's mental state was serious enough to push her into writing letters blaming Mary for her own dementia. She was so exercised on the subject that she lashed out at friends who were advising "kindness" to the afflicted or the ill.

When Caroline Besterman expressed the thought that comatose people should be kept alive because their dreams might be so pleasant, Pat got angry all over again. When Christa Maerker wrote to tell Pat that she had moved in with her own much-loved, very ill mother in order to care for her, Pat wrote back "an incredibly nasty letter . . . about how crazy it is to take care of your mother." The letter was so belligerent that Christa didn't communicate with Pat for "several years" after she received it.[25]

In March of 1987, Jeva Cralick, the lively, levelheaded fashion illustrator who had been Mary Highsmith's closest friend in New York and "a full-fledged member of the Highsmith clan . . . since Pat was 5 or 6,"[26] and who had kept up an affectionate correspondence with Pat for decades, wrote to Dan and Florine Coates in Weatherford, Texas, from her apartment in Brooklyn about Mary's deteriorating condition—and about what it might mean for Pat.

"We know what a vibrant, gifted, articulate person Mary was. And how proud she was of Pat and how much she loved Pat—Pat will never know or choose to remember—but she must sense how much she has inherited from Mary. Well Pat is Pat."[27]

And that's how the laissez-faire Coates family says they used to explain Pat's increasingly armigerous letters about her mother. "Well, that's Pat" became their standard response to nearly everything Pat said or did.

· 37 ·

THE CAKE THAT WAS SHAPED

LIKE A COFFIN

PART 4

By January of 1988, after five years in Aurigeno, Pat was once again handing her problems over to Thomas Ripley in the notes she was taking for Ripley's final appearance in a novel. (Perhaps Terrence Rafferty's favorable *New Yorker* article had something to do with Ripley's reappearance.) Tom Ripley—that master of escape—was now beginning to escape "into another person. A form of schizophrenia . . . Tom feel[s] that he is . . . touching madness, experiencing it, as he could not do in the presence of Mme Annette [his devoted housekeeper] and Heloise." Like Pat, Ripley was turning outwards, brooding on the "variety of horror that man has invented for himself, *against* himself: Chains, whips, sadism—yes, in marriages, the nagging defiling wives, the wife-beaters. The animal torturers. Tom felt that this destructive rage in man . . . seemed to equal the beauty of architecture, painting, music. . . . It was like a dramatic balance," Pat wrote. The balance she had been able to maintain in her work (and, more precariously, in her life) was now, without love to counter it, heavily weighted in favor of decay and destruction. Tom was merely keeping pace with his creator's feelings.

Certainly a spur to finishing *Ripley Under Water*—she'd put the manuscript aside for a while—was the journey Pat finally decided to take to visit Buffie Johnson in Morocco in mid-August of 1988. Pat, who had long since started a correspondence with Buffie and had visited her in her East Forty-third Street apartment and again in her Greene Street loft in New York, knew that Buffie had inherited the lease of Jane Bowles's apartment in the Immeuble Itesa in Tangier (on the floor beneath Paul Bowles's apartment) from Maurice Grosser, the lover of the composer Virgil Thompson. The idea of remeeting Paul Bowles figured into Pat's travel plans, and Buffie had initially suspected that

Bowles was Pat's chief reason for coming. He wasn't. But Bowles did become her chief reason for enjoying the trip.

Paul Bowles was just the man to interest Pat: a homosexual widower from a milieu she'd known in Manhattan whose exquisitely glacial style and continuing expatriatism had given him a kind of international cachet—although style was never the royal road to Pat's affections. Pat had been in light correspondence (twenty letters) with Bowles's friend Gore Vidal since 1978, making her first note to Vidal a modest request to send "a comment" for the Lippincott publication of *The Boy Who Followed Ripley* in New York. ("If you say a flat no, I shall understand. . . . But you might even like the book," she'd written shyly and boldly to Vidal.)[1]

When Pat returned to Switzerland from her trip to Tangier, she and Paul Bowles developed a gossipy, mutually admiring habit of writing letters to each other (Pat had thirty-six letters from Bowles), much focused on Buffie Johnson, but also dragging in the usual writers' complaints about translations, money, expatriatism, the selling of archives, and the total treachery of publishers. The correspondence was sparked by Pat's sending two of her books to Paul when she got back to Aurigeno and by an article she wrote about meeting him. And Bowles admired Pat's writing: he told her that even on the third reading of *Strangers on a Train* he'd forgotten and was again "shocked and disappointed" by the fact that the hero was apprehended. "It's such a good novel," he wrote.[2]

It is worth noting that Pat's collection of affirming quotes from well-known male writers did her a power of good. The quotation Gore Vidal sent to the Atlantic Monthly Press in 1988, ten years after she'd first written him[3] ("One of our greatest modernist writers," he'd written)—a quotation for which she'd asked Vidal—and the quotation from Graham Greene's introduction to a collection of her short stories ("the poet of apprehension" was Greene's phrase)—an introduction for which she'd paid Greene—are reproduced more frequently than anything else that has been written about her work.

But no one quotes the entirely spontaneous comment made by Arthur Koestler to Cyril Connolly in a 1965 interview in the London *Sunday Times* on the occasion of Koestler's sixtieth birthday. Koestler said: "Patricia Highsmith is in a very high class." And Connolly responded: "I don't know about her." "Don't you?" said Koestler. "There is a joy waiting for you."[4]

Practical as always, Pat got a commission from the *Sunday Times* to write an article about Tangier before she left Aurigeno (the article was rejected, but from it she salvaged the much shorter piece about Bowles which she finally published in *Le Monde*), and full of enthusiasm, she flew to the exotic North

African port "where," as Buffie Johnson later said, "intrigue was a way of life," and Pat "wanted to see everything in Morocco." Buffie wasn't in her fifth-floor flat when Pat arrived—she'd gone out for a yoga class—so Pat ascertained from the concierge the number of Paul Bowles's apartment and went up to the sixth floor to knock on his door. She found Paul in bed, eating and tended to by his protégé Mohammed Mrabet. When Buffie returned, Pat was "ensconced in Paul's apartment drinking scotch."

Buffie and Pat were at odds about what to see and do in Tangier. Buffie said that all "that was normal" for her was "new" to Pat; Pat was interested in everything in Tangier except the prehistoric ruins—the only thing Buffie hadn't explored in her five summers in Tangier. Buffie's flat, in a building solidly constructed by the French, had a large living room and two bedrooms, one of which, the room Pat was sleeping in, Buffie had turned into a painting studio. Buffie was not happy to give up her work as Pat lingered for almost two weeks in the bedroom. Pat, unbothered, was amusing herself by using her window like the frame of a painting: "The view of the Medina, or Old City from my breezy window would be a joy for Bracque—and it looks already like a horizontal Klee composition—chalky-white squares of houses of varying sizes with tiny dark squares of windows in them, the scene topped by what looks like a water tower."[5]

Buffie dutifully took Pat sightseeing, and on the third day after Pat's arrival, Pat and Buffie were chauffeured to Woolworth heiress Barbara Hutton's palatial house for a private tour. Pat, whose observation was sharpened by the foreignness of Tangier (and by the parts of it that reminded her of Hammamet), recorded that the walls of the Hutton house were composed of "squares of white stone, about 6×6 inches, hand-carved with filigree, all identical. It is said that 1,000 workmen worked here at the same time." She noted that Miss Hutton had her initials—"B.H."—tiled into the bottom of the swimming pool; then they went on to visit financier Malcolm Forbes's Museum of Toy Soldiers. Pat drank cocktails at the El Minzah Hotel (and spent a lot of time looking for places where she could drink beer), and noted that the water supply in Tangier was cut off at 3:00 P.M. every day and that the city and its services had decayed considerably "since the French left"—all observations that would turn up in *Ripley Under Water,* along with the Bay of Tangier, the weather, and bits of local color like this description of a café that Pat tucked into her cahier: "Home notes: La Haffa, the Hole, on the ocean, a tea-café, arcades, where one can smoke kif, recline on mats, be semi-private. Stone steps downward, and mind how you go."[6]

Pat couldn't look at a flight of stairs without imagining someone falling down them.

During the time Pat was staying with Buffie, Paul Bowles, whose apartment was a favorite stop for writers passing through Tangier, was visited by the novelist and critic Edmund White, who had come to interview Paul for *Vogue* magazine and to gather information for his acclaimed biography of Jean Genet. White carried away with him a fleeting impression of Pat.

Patricia, Edmund White remembered, "was perfectly pleasant, although bloated, naturally," from what he assumed to be "alcohol"—and she was "not entirely sober." Paul Bowles was as "elegant" as always, but "out of it" because he smoked kif from morning till night.[7] Withdrawal had always been Bowles's style, and in his essay about Bowles, White quoted Jane Bowles's description of her husband: "There's a disconnection. Even if he's on the same floor, he's in a different room."[8] Gavin Lambert, the British-born screenwriter, novelist, and biographer, a close friend of Bowles who was then living in Tangier, was much in evidence: he dropped in on Buffie and Pat, and went to dinner with them. And he told Paul Bowles some stories about Buffie's second husband which Bowles relayed to a very interested Pat.

Buffie, nervously preparing for the publication of her book about goddess history, thought Pat "had by then the look of someone no longer enjoying life." She said she'd never accepted Pat's invitations to visit her in Moncourt (she'd known Pat's next-door neighbor Desmond Ryan from London) or in Switzerland (where she'd lived while meeting with Carl Jung) because "over the years I felt Pat had grown increasingly detached and though I did not understand why, I began to feel uncomfortable in her company." "Pat," she also said, "tried very hard to be a good houseguest," but the gift of good guesthood just wasn't in her personality.

Meanwhile Pat, fixing on Buffie's apparent self-absorption, had a few complaints of her own. When she got back to Aurigeno, she wrote in her notebook: "What am I to make of B.J.? . . . I was slowly but surely disturbed by her. She is slow in reacting, speaking, obsessed by pill-taking; walk-taking, self . . . But she is not over the self absorption; what Merck [the *Merck Manual*] mentions as syndrome of Alzheimer's."[9]

The trip to Tangier—one of many escapes she was to make from Aurigeno—did its job, and in the two weeks before she went off to Hamburg, Pat took copious notes which she used in her "5th [and final] Ripley": *Ripley Under Water*. Later, her notes would include, as they often did for other Ripley novels,[10] the kind of music that might inspire Ripley in his crimes: "Rachmaninof's 3rd Piano Concerto. Exuberantly beautiful and strong. Not so sad as #2. Tom would like the 3rd."[11] She also wrote to Kingsley, asking her to find another copy of Karl Menninger's book *The Human Mind,* with its case histories of deviation. She could use it, she thought, for *Ripley Under Water,* and she told Kingsley that she still found Menninger, the Freudian popularizer of her youth, "more inspiring to me than Jung." Pat had just had an earful of Carl Jung from Buffie Johnson.[12]

Shortly after she returned from Tangier, Pat was visited by a young German filmmaker, Peter Goedel, who wanted to make a film of *The Tremor of Forgery.* Goedel had the usual years-long, complicated correspondence with both Pat and Diogenes about acquiring the rights to make a feature film of the novel. He got something less than he bargained for—and something more, too.

When Goedel first called Diogenes about *The Tremor of Forgery,* he was instructed to send a précis of his intentions and told that the important thing was what Highsmith would think of his proposal. After his proposal was submitted, he was informed that Patricia wanted to meet him personally, and he was given the means to contact her. He dialed her number in Aurigeno nervously and Pat gave him directions to her house. "She never gave an address but just said things like: there's an old fountain in the center of town and to the left of it is an old farmhouse and there's a little green door in the farmhouse and if you knock I'll open it."[13]

"It was like a fairy tale," says Goedel, and, like a character in a fairy tale, he was to have three meetings with Patricia Highsmith. This first meeting, at her house in Aurigeno, was the longest one. Her green door was very small indeed, and when Pat opened it Goedel saw a woman dressed in dark clothes, with a little osteoporotic hump on her back, and a cat threading the space between her feet. The house was very dark with small windows, "kind of a mess, really," with her sculptures and work tools scattered hither and yon. Goedel felt as though he were entering "the house of a witch."

It was ten o'clock in the morning when he arrived, and there were many empty beer bottles around, big ones—bottles that had once contained the cheap Swiss beer Kalenda. (Whichever state, province, or country Pat lived in, she always managed to find and consume its cheapest native beer.) Pat asked Goedel what he wanted to drink. "Coffee," he said, and thought right away that he'd made a mistake. So he finished the coffee quickly and asked for a beer and she was *very* happy to drink beer with him at ten in the morning. It seemed to "put her at her ease."

They had a "great conversation," Goedel says, although Pat never spoke about herself but rather about the trip she'd taken to Tangier "to see Paul Bowles [she didn't mention Buffie Johnson]," by whom she was "very impressed." She had photos of the trip and of Paul Bowles and showed them proudly. In 1990, she would take them out again, along with Paul's letters, to show to Richard

Schroeder, the French photographer who managed to capture Pat in a pose of terrifying hostility in front of a wall hung with her saws and hammers. But it was Pat herself who had gleefully suggested the setting.[14]

Pat's force field of self-protection was very strong, says Peter Goedel. She was interested only in the matter before them: what he intended to do with her novel. She sat hunched over, balled up, with one leg crossed over the other, her body in a defensive position, looking up at him from her lowered head through her hair and eyebrows. "She absolutely fixed you with her gaze, you couldn't avoid it, you were trapped in it," says Goeddel.

After three hours of Pat wanting to know his ideas of how he would write and film *The Tremor of Forgery,* Goedel was exhausted. He'd had too many un-accustomed morning beers; he was drunk, and he was happy to leave. It was, he says, "too much."

When Goedel had finished his script and sent it to Pat, a letter came from Pat saying it was fine, she liked it; then three days later, another letter came saying she had showed it to a friend of hers, the woman thought the script was horrible, and Pat was withdrawing permission. They went back and forth for two years, and he thinks she was waiting for a more famous director to make the film. She was: at the end of 1988, the Spanish director Pedro Al-modóvar had expressed interest in buying the book for a feature film.[15] Pat, who had to be told who Almodóvar was, quickly decided that she liked him.

Goedel, still anxious to make his film, tracked Pat down at the Bayreuth Festival in the summer of 1989. He met her in her hotel for a quarter of an hour. It was an old, small, dark hotel, they met in the lobby, and this second meeting was a repetition of the first meeting. Pat was dressed appropriately but in somber colors, the room was dark, and she was again evasive: "Oh, I don't know, something to think about, I'm thinking about it . . .", etc., etc. The script in its current form was making her angry, she wrote to Monique Buffet; she didn't really want to give the film rights to him.

While he waited out several months without any news, Goedel got a Ger-man producer involved, they had a meeting with Daniel Keel, and Goedel was advanced on to his third and final meeting with Patricia, who had by now moved into her house in Tegna.

The house appeared to Goedel as it appeared to everyone: windowless. But then he saw that the windows were high up between the walls and the ceiling so that light could come in but no gaze could intrude. The feeling of the house was very different from their last two meeting places—white walls and ceilings and a much lighter atmosphere. Pat herself, however, was the same, her manner unchanged. They were there for an hour or so and Pat kept say-ing: "I have to speak to Daniel about this." And Daniel Keel had said: "I have to speak to Patricia about this." The German producer didn't do well with Pat because he refused to drink beer in the morning.

Finally, Goedel got a call from Diogenes saying that Pat had agreed to his film, but only for the TV rights, not as a feature film. (In fact, it was Daniel Keel's idea.) Goedel was unhappy at the evaporation of his hopes for a feature film but decided to go ahead with a television film anyway. Pat had many suggestions for his new teleplay and she presented them in her typical list form: 1, 2, 3, 4. "They were very detailed and they were good," he says.

When Goedel went to Tunis to film his script, he kept looking for a bungalow hotel in which to set the action, and in Hammamet he finally found one that was closed. When he contacted the owners, it turned out that he had found the very place where Patricia had stayed with Elizabeth Lyne in the summer of 1966 when she was taking her notes for *The Tremor of Forgery*. Goedel was amazed: Pat's descriptions in the book had been so accurate that he'd been able, unconsciously, to select the exact place she had described. The owners remembered Pat, as did the owner of the restaurant in Hammamet—Ashua (Melik's in *The Tremor of Forgery*)—where she and Mme Lyne as well as the protagonist of *The Tremor of Forgery,* Howard Ingham, had gone every night for dinner during their stay in Hammamet.

When Pat finally saw Goedel's television film in the summer of 1993, she sent him a perfectly characteristic postcard. She objected, she wrote, to Howard Ingham's belt and shoes.[16] They were wrong for him. But she had never liked Goedel's decision to change Ingham's profession from writer to archaeologist, and—a recurrent theme in her letters to other people—she hated the fact that Goedel was using her title, *The Tremor of Forgery* (his final title was *Trip to Tunis*), for the film after she had asked him not to.

38

THE CAKE THAT WAS SHAPED

LIKE A COFFIN

PART 5

Although Pat was revisiting all her old themes in Switzerland, her notes and her published fictions continued to favor only half of her customary double obsession with love and murder. (It wasn't the love half.) Now her notes were without many of the references she had used to anchor herself to her American past. And her "nightlife" was confined to the theater of dreams she was staging for herself as she slept. Many of these dreams, fueled by fears for her health and apprehensions about the medical operations she was beginning to have, were taking place on or near railway stations. They had more violence and less sex in them than ever. Here are a few of them:

Pat is with two women on a train, and she's suddenly stabbed by an attacker. She rushes to board a boat. She recites to her two women companions the statistics of how much deeper the stab wound would have had to be to penetrate her lung, and says she feels no pain.[1]

She's dining in a restaurant with Tanja Howarth, her Diogenes agent in London, and Howarth returns from the ladies' room with one of her wrists slashed and bleeding.[2]

Pat sees a "Spanish type young man" who stares her straight in the face and says: "I have no heart." She looks hard at his chest and sees that in place of his heart is only "an X-form of crossing blood vessels." His heart has been crossed out.[3]

Pat runs into Tabea Blumenschein on a railway train "disguised as an 18 yr. old male tough" who is "fond" of a very young male urchin. The urchin confronts Pat holding a shield "in a hostile manner." Pat has to "hit at the fingers of his right hand several times, till they are bleeding, and he is staggering, before he drops the shield and is defeated. It is a close thing." She exits this dream down a jagged metal staircase which has a section missing.[4]

Pat is in a "busy hotel" and wants to ring up a girl whose name she can't remember, a most attractive girl who has invited her to lie down with her on a bed and rest. But Pat has to "take care" of some journalists first and watches a clock creeping towards some sort of deadline with the girl. She misses the deadline, she misses the girl, and she still can't remember the girl's name: "I feel a loss and am unhappy."[5]

And it is here in Switzerland where Pat had her graphic dream about Mother Mary "in Lady Macbeth murderous mood," cutting off Tabea Blumenschein's head and coating it "thoroughly" with transparent wax.[6]

The double identity—so crucial to all Pat's work and to all the characters who inhabited her—was collapsing into a single self. Sex and love, God and the Devil dancing hand and hand around that electron in *Strangers on a Train,* were no longer present to balance out her inclination to violence. She began, visibly, to shrink; the hunch in her shoulders and the dowager's hump on her back were remarked on by many people. Her references to the sex lives of others coarsened: she seemed furious that her attentive friend Ingeborg Moelich's "artistic, angelic-looking" daughter had a long-term boyfriend, referring to the man vulgarly and often as the young woman's "latest lay."[7] Her "5th Ripley" book, the final Ripley, *Ripley Under Water,* finished in 1990—a sour, thin, but still recognizably Ripleyan effort—was focused, she hoped, more graphically on the power relations that had always fascinated her. "Ripley Under Water is my S&M novel," she wrote to Kingsley in September of 1990.

In her letter to Kingsley, Pat also included some unconsciously funny advice to her goddaughter, Kingsley's daughter, gleaned from Pat's own, more or less S&M history of pursuing women: "Tell her: 'Men like to do their own chasing. Not only like it, they do it—or else!' "[8] "It's okay to give them the eye, slightly, but due to Elby's genuine interest in Their Work, her interest becomes too heavy."[9] Pat's advice to the lovelorn was usually offered from the male chauvinist's point of view. By now, it was a view many male chauvinists would have been embarrassed to own up to.

Despite what Pat wrote to Kingsley (and said to Peter Huber, who says she queried him as a literature professor and a Freudian about sadomasochism), *Ripley Under Water* makes only the vaguest intimations of marital abuse between the Pritchards, the two unappealing married strangers who shadow Ripley with the intent of exposing him. Pat was still moving sideways, allusively, and with evident embarrassment. Although she was under the impression that she had directly taken on the fetish of sadomasochism in the novel, *Ripley Under Water* is more (and more characteristically) a matter of the class challenge that the ill-dressed, badly equipped, and unattractive David Pritchard flings at Thomas Ripley's assumed identity as a gentleman of the manor.

Pritchard, rather like Don Wilson, the bad crime novelist in *Deep Water* who enviously dogs the trust-funded Vic Van Allen, takes an instant dislike to Ripley in an airport because of Ripley's beautiful clothes. He determines to expose him as the murderer of Murchison (the art collector Ripley murdered with a bottle of vintage Bordeaux in *Ripley Under Ground*) and calls Ripley a "snob crook" to his face. Ripley, who kicks Pritchard in the crotch (Pat demurely referred to it as Pritchard's "middle"), despises Pritchard's crass self-presentation, his clothes, and his furniture. In an ending which reads like an unintentional parody, Pritchard and his wife drown in the shallow pond behind their house after being interrupted in an S&M romp. Ripley laughs happily as he listens to their cries for help.

From Aurigeno in 1987, Pat, never comfortable with the way her work was treated on film, had written about her initial displeasure with Wim Wenders's Ripley film, *The American Friend*: "I was so-so happy with the Wenders film, and I did not like the ending with Ripley laughing at a burning car. Wenders quite changed Ripley into a modern no-boundary pot-smoking type as you saw."[10]

Now, in 1990, Pat's "own" Ripley was laughing uncontrollably as he listened to his enemies drown noisily in their pond. But Pat had been a fan of inappropriate laughter ever since she'd written "Quiet Night" at Barnard, and then, in the summer of 1948 while working on *Strangers on a Train* at Yaddo, had pasted a newspaper picture of the grinning young killer Robert Murl Daniels in her seventeenth cahier and written the name "Bruno" beneath it. Like their author, many of Pat's protagonists were guilty of a grin in the wrong place or a giggle at a bad moment. "Hurrah for maniacal laughter," Pat had written in 1970. "People who don't like it label it empty. *Tant pis*."[11] Tom Ripley's intense absorption of whatever was obsessing Pat would always make him something of a cracked mirror for his creator's urges. As Pat's own inner wars began to exhaust her, as she was drawn more and more to the surface of her psychology, Ripley, too, began to dwindle to a kind of shorthand notation for the complex and fascinating character she had launched in *The Talented Mr. Ripley*. But Ripley manages to remain Ripleyan still. Even in his feeblest and most uncongenial appearance, *Ripley Under Water*, he compels us to prefer him to the unstylish forces of justice.

The book did give Pat an excuse to make her trip to Tangier to see Buffie Johnson. She needed the Tangier location for her novel, and by then she probably needed the contact with an old friend. Pat had alienated so many people that the two Barbaras in Islington were worried, telling Heather Chasen to start writing to Pat again because they thought she had pushed everyone away.[12] Alex Szogyi, the (gay, Jewish) college professor in New York with whom Pat had one of her longest, happiest friendships and frankest correspondences, was cut out of her life in what Alex said was Pat's irritation at his blossoming friendship with Jeanne Moreau—to whom Pat had introduced him.[13] Szogyi, who had nothing but admiration for Pat, thought because she complained to him so much about her girlfriends that she was "a failed heterosexual."[14] But Pat was also, in her own way, a "failed homosexual"—except in her fiction, where she was anything she wanted to be.

Pat had confided her "dear desk" to Alex when she'd left the United States in 1963; she'd allowed him to work up her horoscope in 1973 (see illustration), "referring to [the] horoscope with increasing interest" in several letters as its predictions seemed to her to come true; and, in the dazed aftermath of her first tryst with Tabea Blumenschein in London in 1978, she'd asked Alex to analyze Tabea's handwriting for her.[15] Alex provided the kind of handwriting analysis that also flattered Pat for her choice: Tabea, he wrote, was "a big personality. I imagine she doesn't suffer fools gladly. . . . A superior lady, indeed."[16] Pat cared for Alex so much that she wrote to Lil Picard: "[E]veryone adores him. . . . I am so fond of him, it is almost worth moving to NY for, just to see him once a week!"[17] (Meeting once a week was Pat's idea of intimate friendship.) Now, Pat had cut both Alex Szogyi *and* Lil Picard out of her life.

The people Pat spent time with in Switzerland, aside from Ellen Hill and her publisher Daniel Keel, were new acquaintances. They were kind, cultured, unbelievably helpful, and very fond of Pat, but there was nothing to tie them to the rich set of associations governing her past—the *fons et origo* of her writing—and she never invited them into the secrets of her life. Her move to Tegna, in December of 1988, even though it suffused her life with some badly needed light, did not settle her restless spirit. After thinking about it for five or six months, she purchased a raw piece of meadowland in Tegna in April of 1987, paying too much for it, everyone said, at a price of 490,000 Swiss francs. The land overlooked the beautiful Centrovalli, and there was a little river just beyond the bottom of the property. She'd heard about the property from Peter Huber,[18] who, with his wife's sister's family, the Dieners, alternated the occupancy of an adjoining vacation house.

"I just told her [about the land]," Huber says, "because I thought it was so outrageously expensive. We were offered it ten or fifteen years [before] for thirty thousand Swiss francs and then we were offered it for five hundred thousand. And do you know what Pat said? I'll take it. Just like that. She was desperate."[19]

Even as her house was being constructed, Pat was worrying about the "numerous Huber family" next door, but she consoled herself that her neighbors would use the house only seventy days a year.[20] But when the Hubers were there, Pat drifted over every night just as she had done with the Ryans in Moncourt: "The moment," says Huber, "we switched on our lights in the evening."

Along with everything else Pat took from Aurigeno to Tegna was a pile of firewood she'd already carted from Moncourt to Aurigeno. "But," says Peter Huber, "it wasn't even firewood, it was construction-site wood, covered with plaster, scrapwood with rusty nails. . . . I made a fire with a lot of newspapers. [Pat had invited him to do so.] There were a few little flames coming up from it and she took the big [piece of wood] she'd decided to sacrifice for this occasion and she knocked it on the stone. And I said, 'Pat, don't, you're extinguishing it!' And she gave me a very pained look."[21]

After that, there were very few fires in the fireplace at Casa Highsmith; Pat had, after all, paid "good money" for the wood and she wasn't going to "waste" it. Fire, like food, was one of the life-affirming comforts Pat spent her later years rejecting. The impoverished young writer who wanted a fireplace so badly in 1943 that she'd painted a perfect trompe l'oeil fireplace on the wall of her cheap studio apartment on East Fifty-sixth Street was now a well-known author in possession of a real fireplace in an expensively designed house—and she simply couldn't allow herself to enjoy it. The counterfeit fireplace of her tiny Manhattan flat would have suited her better.

By spring of 1991, Pat was already looking for an escape from her new house, writing to Kingsley in New York to ask if she wanted to join forces and buy a flat in London. "My house here is pleasant, but also boring at times, only socially, but that's bad enough. . . . So to have a flat big enough in London, to be able to go there—it is a nice pipedream. . . . But I thought I'd sound you out."[22]

It was Kingsley's dream to live in London too; she had worked there as a television producer for CBS News and she was yearning to return. But she was out of a job now, and out of funds, and she wrote to Pat that she could only afford to be a tenant. Pat said she didn't want to be a landlord—and that was the end of the matter.

A month later, Pat's ideas for a novel included one about a man who "wishes he could take a pill to stop falling in love."[23] After another year in Tegna, Pat, expanding a little in this brighter, lighter house (its back, as opposed to its forbidding front, was open to the light), returned superficially to love and death and sketched an idea for a young person "in extremis of love affair plus job crisis [who] thinks of suicide by stepping out window onto a ledge." Then she began her initial framing of *Small g: A Summer Idyll*, her last novel, set in the "gay-friendly" Jakob's Bierstube-Restaurant bar in Zurich (the small *g* is the designation gay guidebooks use to indicate that the clientele is "mixed" gay and straight) and based partially on a forty-five-year-old man she'd met in Zurich, "R," a friend of Frieda Sommer. In Pat's first version of the plot, "R" likes to fake robbery/murder for his teenage lover by "being bloody-faced in bed when the boy comes in with his key." When he enters the teenager's flat and "finds him bloody-faced, in bed," he thinks the boy is pretending and then there's a "[h]orrible scene" when he realizes his lover is actually dead.[24]

The light flooding into the back of Casa Highsmith and slipping in through its high window slits was apparently doing something for Pat; she was feeling her way back to impersonation again, to imagining the counterfeiting of a crime. For Pat Highsmith, still looking at the world upside down, being able to counterfeit meant something like being able to be authentic. "Faking it" was how she approached being "herself." The rapprochement didn't last.

In November of 1985, Pat had sent her old fiancé, Marc Brandel, now living in Santa Monica, California, a check for eight thousand dollars to encourage him in his development of a film script of her novel *The Blunderer*. In one of the many tangled exchanges Pat had with agents, studios, producers, and her publisher, Diogenes, about the film rights for her novels, she'd put Brandel's name forward for the film adaptation of *The Blunderer* after she'd signed a film contract for the book with an English producer in New York at the end of 1983. In 1956, Brandel had adapted *The Talented Mr. Ripley* for a one-hour television broadcast by *Studio One* (the longest-running—from 1948 to 1958—and most significant anthology drama series in U.S. television history), and Marc and Pat began a correspondence after seeing each other "for a day" in Moncourt in 1979. Marc had nothing but fond words for Pat, and when the deal with the film producer collapsed, Pat sent Marc her personal check so he could continue to work on the script. They had a strict understanding that she would be paid back if a film deal didn't materialize or if Marc got money directly from another interested producer.

The "charming, young, polite, talented" film director Kathryn Bigelow (Pat's description), whom Pat had met at the Locarno Film Festival in 1981 (Bigelow lived on Grove Street in Greenwich Village, which added to Pat's interest) and who was "mad" about *The Blunderer,* had also written a script from the novel, entirely on speculation. Bigelow's script came to "naught," Pat wrote, but in April of 1990, Pat, who had also been corresponding with Joseph Losey's widow, Patricia, about producing *The Blunderer,* was so interested in Bigelow's "success" with the film *Blue Steel* that she was pressing Kingsley to find Bigelow's current address.[25]

Contrary to her reputation, Pat often tried to involve herself in both the publicity and the behind-the-scenes-maneuvering for her work's promotion and production. ("Would you like to review *A Dog's Ransom* for the NY Times Book Review?" she'd written to Alex Szogyi in one of many suggestions she would make. "I could put in a word with my editor Bob Gottlieb.")[26] Her early and enthusiastic endorsement of the ways in which authors can promote their own careers (the cultivation of translators, the regular writing of letters, etc.) had been published for all the world to see in her covert artistic autobiography, *Plotting and Writing Suspense Fiction.*

Not unexpectedly, the check for eight thousand dollars Pat sent to Marc Brandel caused some trouble. Pat was unhappy that Marc's agent cashed it (he wanted his 10 percent right away), and by January of 1987 Marc was apologizing for their "misunderstanding" over her advance and promising to return the money if anyone bought the screenplay.[27]

The Brandel screenplay was never produced, but a candid passage in a letter Marc wrote in response to something Pat asked about his children (Pat queried everyone about their offspring) shows that her attraction to Marc Brandel at Yaddo in 1948 was probably more appropriate than it seemed. He'd never wanted a son, he wrote, and was greatly relieved to have produced only girls. He almost believed that if he *had* produced a son he would have "liked him to be gay."[28]

When Pat went back to Moncourt to look for another property to buy in the summer of 1986—Aurigeno was already wearing on her badly—she failed to find anything she liked as much as the house she had finally sold in a flurry of agonized ambivalence. While in the Île-de-France, she managed to offend her former neighbor, the temperamental Barbara Skelton, with a question about the French language. Skelton snapped back that Pat's French was "abominable." Pat reflected bitterly (and enviously) on Skelton's ability to "prove that she's living in England when she's in France, and vice versa, thus avoiding any income tax whatsoever." And then Pat added the category of "tax cheat" to a list of things she didn't like, making the personal political once again.[29]

In early April of 1986, Pat had an appointment in London with a physician on Harley Street, John Batten, for an X-ray and an opinion. The appointment had been secured on very short notice by Caroline Besterman after a desperate call from Pat. Pat's faithful neighbor in Aurigeno, Ingeborg Moelich, drove her all the way to the Zurich airport from Aurigeno, and Pat was admitted to the Brompton Hospital for a biopsy of her right lung: a cancerous tumor was suspected.

Pat spent the night in the hospital, and just as she was leaving, her doctor hurried up to her, said he'd had the tumor biopsy "rushed through," and asked Pat to sit down. She noticed—Pat never stopped noticing—that he glanced away for an instant before speaking to her: "We think it should be taken out and we hope you'll agree." "This sounds like a death sentence to me," Pat wrote, "as I've never heard of anyone surviving such, or anyway, not for long." She agreed to the operation, was taken into a room with five men, one of whom was Mr. Paveth, "who operated on Princess Margaret for (nearly) the same thing." He "sank strong finger ends" into the base of her neck. Roland Gant, her publisher from Heinemann, came from the office to fetch her. They went straight out to his car and drank boilermakers.

Pat had been "feeling awful" in Aurigeno since December of 1985. She'd suffered through a perpetual round of colds and intestinal flu, while a struggle between Diogenes and Heinemann over *Found in the Street* (Diogenes wanted more advance money "and threatened to break the contract," while Heinemann was "hiring lawyers") had forced her to go to London for "business" and upset her nerves. When she got back to Switzerland, in the dead of winter, "without heavy underwear" and wearing her usual jeans, she shoveled snow off her car and saddled herself with a heavy case of bronchitis. During her second checkup for it, her doctor in Locarno suggested a lung X-ray "because you smoke." A spot on her right lung was detected, a needle biopsy was done, and before the results were obtained, Pat went off to Paris for six days to do publicity for the Calmann-Lévy publication of *Found in the Street*. Oddly enough, considering her ingrained habit of complaining, Pat never mentioned a word of her medical "troubles and *Angst*" to her friends and colleagues in Paris. The matter was so serious that she kept it to herself.

On her return to the Ticino, the doctor in Locarno told Pat that the biopsy results were "inconclusive" and that "something else would have to be done." Ellen Hill, still firmly ensconced as Inspector General of Pat's life, gave Pat her marching orders: "Don't waste time with Locarno; go to London."

And that's when Pat called Caroline Besterman for help.

And so, as Pat wrote in her thirty-seventh cahier long after the fact, she had her operation in London on 10 April 1986 and was released the next week, with the doctors saying—"maybe genuinely," she noted suspiciously—that she had made "fast progress." She came away with a fourteen-inch-long scar along her fifth rib, and after "31 days in London," she went back home to Aurigeno. She made a little list of the friends who sent things to her hospital room, and after the operation "the months [were] somewhat *Angst*-filled also, as I did not know whether or not the cancer would recur." She'd stopped smoking while waiting for the other shoe to drop, and that didn't help her angst. And she was resting, dutifully, an hour after lunch. But she was "quite unable to do any creative work, though in my house there is always quite enough else to do. The mental fear needs a thousand words to describe. [But Pat did not provide them.] It is as though death is right there—suddenly—and yet one feels no pain, one is talking in a calm voice to friends & doctors."

By 12 July, three months after her operation, Pat was back in London, and accompanied by Caroline Besterman, she went to Brompton Hospital to be X-rayed again by Mr. Paveth and Dr. Batten. They kept her waiting as they examined the film for ten anxious minutes during which she "nearly" finished the contents of the little glass flask—her present from Bettina Berch—in her handbag. She could hear Caroline Besterman's voice calling for her; she answered Caroline, and, like the ghost she must have felt herself to be by now, she was not heard. The nurse finally told her to come out of the dressing room, and she and Caroline crossed the road to Mr. Paveth's consulting rooms, where the X-ray was hanging high on the wall with a light behind it.

"Paveth says, Perfect, in a calm voice, a word I never expected to hear. It is like a reprieve from death."

And then Mr. Paveth told her that her tumor was glandular and could have occurred whether she smoked or not. Pat was so happy that when she spotted Dr. Batten's registrar (he was from Australia, so naturally she called him Sydney) she said "Hello Sydney," and extended her hand to this stranger in "good cheer."[30]

Under circumstances that would have surprised her Swiss neighbors—life and death was one of them—Pat Highsmith was still happy to shake someone's hand.

The year after her operation, in the autumn of 1987, Pat's enthusiastic editor Gary Fisketjon, who had published or republished nine of Pat's books at Atlantic Monthly Press,[31] helped to arrange a jaunt for her to New York for Atlantic's publication of *Found in the Street*. "I was putting out whatever Highsmith novels were available and trying to get something going for her in the U.S.," he says. "It worked marginally well, not as well as I had hoped."

Fisketjon and Pat had a jocular relationship, brokered by Anne-Elizabeth Suter, Diogenes's representative in New York, who was "terrific to deal with and very fond of Pat," says Fisketjon. (Suter, like so many of Pat's agents, tried to protect Pat from the rejections she was receiving for her short stories and succeeded only in making Pat angry.)[32] Pat and Gary Fisketjon were both Civil War buffs, they liked to raise a glass together, and Pat, still fascinated by the relations between parents and children, continued to inquire after Fisketjon's infant son and to send cards and drawings for the child's birthday, which almost always arrived, says Fisketjon, "exactly on the day and she never missed a lick." (Meanwhile, her birthday greetings to her own goddaughter usually consisted in apologies from her "evil fairy godmother" for having forgotten her birthday.) Gary Fisketjon and Pat met very rarely.

"I was very fond of her," says Fisketjon. "It was very easy; there was never any kind of difficulty. . . . We spent a lot of time in restaurants, but drinking and smoking was the main event, not eating." He took her to the restaurant Odeon in SoHo in New York, when it was still "of the moment" and she was "very interested to register downtown bohemia. It sort of lit her up." Pat, in return, favored Fisketjon with one of her intricate little plans for social improvement. She had been insisting that the "homeless" in New York "weren't homeless" at all, they were "living in hotels." And Fisketjon was trying to explain to Pat the horrors of the single-room occupancy hotels the city used to warehouse its homeless. "And she had this peculiar concept whereby you could solve the homeless situation because, she figured, most of these people come from Africa where you can have many wives. So if bigamy were legalized, people wouldn't run off all the time leaving these women and children bereft and homeless."[33]

Along with her appearances in New York for *Found in the Street,* Pat, who had avoided going to the funerals of her entire family, got a little cemetery experience. A supplement of *The New York Times,* "The World of New York," wanted to commission a walking tour of the famous old Green-Wood Cemetery in Brooklyn. Ruth Rendell had been the editor's first choice to write the article (Pat didn't know this), but Rendell wasn't in New York, and Pat was. Pat said she'd love to do it, and asked to have someone accompany her. The editors thought it would be nice to send someone who knew her work, and so Phyllis Nagy, a fledgling playwright working as a researcher for the *Times,* went along for the ride. Pat had been living outside the United States for more than twenty-five years by now, and this is how she struck the young researcher.

> I had never seen a picture of her so I didn't know what I was looking for except a woman in her sixties. When I finally realized who I was looking for I saw she was wearing her favorite rumpled mac, with her head

bowed, and she had enormously large hands and feet. That was what I recall. I don't know what I expected, but it wasn't that. She was maybe slightly taller than I, but she was rather bowed, and she was wearing these white boat shoes which made her feet look larger, white canvas deck shoes. Nothing about her suggested woman's dress. She was wearing a tweed jacket. And her hair was the way it appeared to be for forty-three thousand years. The head ducked, a deep voice. It was alluring and completely without a hint of any European accent. But she had a very odd unplaceable American accent. She was not placeable. And she was pretty gruff, it was like meeting a famous old guy. "Hello." Handshake. Extremely quiet. Said very little. I felt why does she want to speak to some kid.

The *Times* hired a huge black limo to take us to Green-Wood [it looked like a hearse] and it was raining, drizzly, and I think the limo made her uncomfortable. It was very inappropriate. And she said not one word. She was on one side and I was on the other and she was staring out the window and I really didn't know what to say. . . . Finally she turned to me and said "They"—and who knows who the "they" were—"they tell me you want to be a playwright." "Yes, that's true," I said. "Hmmm," she said. "Hmmm." *Silence*. More staring out the window, passing cars. "What do you think of Eugene O'Neill?" I thought, I don't know what she wants to hear here, so I guess I just better say what I think. And I said. "Not much." And she said. "Umm. Good." More window. Ten minutes elapsed between her utterances. And then she said: "Tennessee Williams. What do you make of him?" And so I said, "I like him." "Hmmm. Good," said Pat. As we were driving into the cemetery she said, "Now, I saw a play called *Fool for Love* by a chap called Sam Shepard. Now, what do you make of that?" And I said: "Well, that's a very interesting play." And she said: "Yes, I thought so too."

With that, we take our tour of Green-Wood. Completely and utterly silent, she said not one word. We must have been there for ninety minutes poking around. She did make some vague exclamation when she came on Lola Montez's grave and then there was a Steinway vault in the shape of a keyboard and she thought and said, "That was terrible." That was it. And then we went to the crematorium, where we were subjected to a number of ghastly little pranks, like sticking your hand into still warm ashes, and she seemed to quite like that. And we finally got outside and it was late morning. And she took out this hip flask from her mac, and she said: "I don't know about you, but I need a drink." She carried around a flask and she held it out to me and I knew it was a challenge, though I didn't know what she was offering, and so I took a slug and it was scotch.

And I got back into the limo and she said:

"I don't suppose you'd be free for lunch."

So I said, "Oh sure," and we went back to her hotel room and the booze was lined meticulously up on the bureau. "Do you want a scotch or do you prefer beer?" "Beer," I said, and Pat opened the little hotel fridge and it was full of beer. Budweiser, I think.

And that was lunch.[34]

39

THE CAKE THAT WAS SHAPED

LIKE A COFFIN

PART 6

One of the many ways Pat kept herself company in both France and Switzerland was by animating her old relationships in America. She did this by restarting correspondences with old friends, *very* old friends in fact; the women she'd known from all those places in the 1940s and 1950s where women went to seek each other's company: Manhattan, Fire Island, New Hope, Provincetown, Santa Fe, Snedens Landing, the Isle of Capri. This circle of women—most of whom were lesbians and many of whom had been each other's lovers, friends, and/or rivals—were now, like Pat, getting old and getting ill. Most of them still kept cats; some of them had lost their lovers through death or misadventure; some of them were drinking heavily and feeling left behind by life. But all of them were quick to say how much they admired Pat for her accomplishments and how they were looking forward to her next book. Whatever else had happened (or hadn't happened) between these women and Pat, they all possessed, in ways that Pat's current neighbors never could, an important piece of her past.

As Rosalind Constable wrote to Pat when explaining why she found it hard to make real friends in her new house in New Mexico: "Friendships simply have to have roots. Our roots, my dear, go down to China."[1]

And so Pat, without anything resembling a parking place in Switzerland for what was left of her deepest feelings, turned to this correspondence with her past. Perhaps it was to remind herself of days and loves and lives gone by, but it was also, almost certainly, to keep up with the gossip. With these old lesbian friends whose love affairs, given the times and the customs, had to be kept well under the social radar, it was the gossip which took the place of any recorded history. Gossip was both the most trivial and the most important record these women would ever leave of their lives. And Pat, harking back to her younger self, was avid for it. Closemouthed, opaque, and censorious about other people's sex lives in older age in Switzerland, Pat had been, in her Manhattan youth and to the consternation of many, a pot-stirring tattletale and, in the right circumstances, quite the chatty Patty.

Thus, in the Highsmith Archives there is a series of letters by women Pat had known for decades, written in answer to letters sent out by Pat; letters which on both sides evoke the good old days and the wild old times and provide descriptions of the smaller satisfactions these women were living with now. Rather like Proust and his Last Round-Up in the Guermantes' salon in the final volume of *In Search of Lost Time,* Pat, by writing to her old friends and lovers in America, summoned up her heady affectional past and invited it to tread the thin emotional ground of her present. Her history began to parade before her in the form of nostalgic and touching news from women whose names had had vivid meaning for her when her future was still in front of her.

Betty, Pat's confidante from Fire Island during the days after Ellen Hill's suicide attempt in 1953, wrote that she was living next door to her own old lover, Margot; she wrote that Lynn Roth, the sulphurous love of Pat's most complicated Manhattan summer, was retiring from work with emphysema and living on Long Island with her longtime companion; she wrote that she, Betty, recalled how she and Pat had "got overly pickled at our reunion, and the next time we're going to have to go more slowly," and that "poor old Ellen Hill" had just invited her to her apartment in New York, and then tried, forcibly, to sell her an old coat that was much too large for her. (Pat tried the very same maneuver on Peter Huber, her neighbor in Tegna, and succeeded in making him pay for a pair of shoes that were too small for him. "I never argued with Pat," Huber says, adding: "Of course, that was a kind of despising of her as well.")[2] Betty offered the opinion that Ellen Hill must be "missing some marbles somewhere" and provided several even more amusing examples of Ellen's costiveness.

Out of a job after being insulted by her "26 year old boss," Betty had just discovered the singing voice of Patsy Cline and was struck to the soul by three viewings of the romantic lesbian film *Desert Hearts.* ("Like maybe some old bell rang in me," she wrote.) She announced her shock at the death of the photographer Berenice Abbott—that great figure from Pat's youth and her own—and giggled over the fact that at the New York Public Library exhibition of Abbott's work, Berenice, in her nineties and "looking like a million . . . hugged Margot . . . and whispered in her ear, 'Hi baby, how ya' doing?' . . . All these people looking on and not knowing!"[3]

"Dear Lord," Betty wrote in her last letter to Pat in 1993, "just don't take away my cocktail hour!"[4]

Gert Macy, the theatrical producer and lover of famed actress Katharine Cornell, wrote from Snedens Landing to say that she heard "from Doris occasionally" (the Doris who had been Pat's lover), that she was just getting around to "corresponding about Kit's death," and that she was collaborating (with Tad Mosel) on a biography of Cornell.[5]

Lynn Roth wrote to decline Pat's invitation to Switzerland (Pat was inviting everyone she could think of to Aurigeno), and to say that although she wasn't much of a letter writer, she would be glad to see Pat if Pat ever came back to Long Island.[6]

Natalia Danesi Murray, Janet Flanner's widow, said it was an "unexpected pleasant surprise" to hear from Pat, that she'd seen her name in *Publishers Weekly* and wondered where she was living, and that the publication of her own book, *Darlinghissima: Letters to a Friend* (1985), a collection of Janet Flanner's letters to her since 1944, "was a tough decision to make, but after all why not? I wonder what you'd think of it?"[7] (What Pat thought was that Natalia should have sent her a free copy.)

Gina, a photo editor who had lived with Natica Waterbury (Pat's ex-lover) and had taken some of Pat's book jacket photos, responded that she was in an old people's home in the "hick town" of Ithaca, New York, and that, "unfortunately," her brain surgeon had been very good. ("I had a serious operation on my head & I'm on pills til I kick the bucket.") She reported that "Emmanuelle" (a woman they both knew) had been hospitalized for alcoholism, and that Annie Duveen, who had introduced Pat to the Barbaras of Islington, was dying of cancer. Annie's lover had had a stroke. Gina wondered why Pat hadn't sent her Annie Duveen's address ("She's #1 for me"), adding that she and Mary Ronin (Pat's old lover) "are corresponding all the time" and that Mary would like to hear from Pat. Mary, she said, was living on the money Natica Waterbury had left her, and Mary's longtime lover—the woman whom Mary had chosen over Pat all those years ago (thus inspiring Pat's novel *This Sweet Sickness*)—was dead.[8]

Polly Cameron, the designer friend responsible for two of Pat's early book covers, who had been living in the renovated barn Pat first rented with Doris in Palisades, New York, more than three decades ago, sent Pat a photo of her 1990 Christmas tree, perched on "The Highsmith Bench"—"a wonderful crude redwood bench" Pat had made for the garden of the barn in the late 1950s. Polly moved it to her new house in Snedens Landing. "I said to myself 'Highsmith lives along the Hudson' as indeed you do." There were mostly deaths to report now: Polly said she missed Gert Macy the most, but that Doris was comfortably ensconced with "a rich attractive painter, ably managing her affairs & money I'm sure."[9]

Betty Curry, a cousin of the artist Jean Tinguely, who had her own travel agency in New York, wrote back to say that she did indeed "remember that weekend in New Hope very well. It was somewhat like the twilight zone . . . an elysian setting with hell going on inside. Natica [Waterbury] making like she was Toad of Toad Hall. . . . And I recall Pat Highsmith drifting dark and concerned from one room to another." Natica was staying with Betty Curry now, and Betty was caring for her as she died slowly of the throat cancer provoked, Betty thought, by "excessive smoking and long years of alcoholism."[10]

Perhaps it was this decade and more of news from friends and ex-lovers looking after each other in old age that prompted Pat to send the impecunious Daisy Winston in New Hope that unexpected check for five thousand dollars in April of 1992.[11] Daisy wrote back that she felt like she'd won the Irish Sweepstakes.

Daisy, in any case, had always had plenty to say and plenty to do for Pat, who asked many favors of her. But Daisy never did those favors quietly, and, unlike nearly everyone else, she never had any trouble speaking her mind to her exigent old friend: "I read your 'First Love' article in London Times—after it had made the rounds of New Hope. . . . in my opinion—it sounded rather stilted."[12] "It amused me when you spoke of your social security as though it was a pittance—my problems would be minimal if I drew that amount rather than *my* pittance of $384."[13]

When Daisy had shipped out yet another pair of American shoes for Pat's big feet, she added her comments to the package: "In that size they should come with oars!" When Pat sent her a nasty letter, Daisy retorted immediately: "Your snide and insulting letter could not have come at a worse time. . . . I may run your errands but I'm not an underling & I never expect another letter as degrading as the last."[14] In January of 1985 Daisy was busy investigating the "Hood" house in New Hope for Pat—it was yet another of Pat's desperate and unachieved ideas for escaping the stones of Aurigeno and moving back to America. And Daisy reproved Pat for the inhuman temperature at which she kept her houses: "Now why are you freezing to death? You seem to go from one cold house to another. . . . I really don't understand you—don't you know that 58 degrees is cold???"[15]

At the end of 1991, Daisy, going through mounds of papers and letters, found the remnants, as she wrote to Pat, of their yearlong affair: "an envelope with a number of short notes—dated 1961—some very dear, some humorous, but all brought back very good memories. But you never brought me flowers—oh well, I won't hold that against you. But fear not—it all went up in smoke."[16]

Buffie Johnson, who had responded to Pat's queries about selling the several houses Pat had on her hands in the 1970s, continued to answer Pat's questions about old friends after Pat moved to Switzerland. Yes, Buffie said, she *had* known Jane Bowles, but her relationship with Jane had been a short one. Jane liked to be "taken care of," Paul Bowles knew how to do it, and besides, Jane liked older women. And, by the way, it was probably Jane's enthusiastic consumption of gin that killed her—not the ministrations of the Arab woman who was Jane's last lover.[17]

Buffie only knew "of [Natica] Waterbury," but Buffie had befriended the feminist writer Kate Millett and other, younger women writers. Buffie sympathized with Pat's lack of sunlight in Aurigeno and invited her to Tangier, an invitation Pat finally took up in 1988. She kept Pat up to date with her art exhibitions, and told her that she found Janet Flanner "a pleasure," and that she thought she might send Pat a xerox of Karl Bissinger's photograph of her, Gore Vidal, Tennessee Williams, Donald Windham, and Tanaquil LeClercq "all lunching in a garden when we were young and lovely." She asked Pat for a book jacket quote for her goddess book (and Pat sent a review of the book to *Le Monde*), and she confided to Pat the terrible troubles she was having with the property she owned in Manhattan.[18]

When Pat became convinced that the journalist Joan Dupont was going to write a biography of her or do a picture book about her or use some of the interviews she'd done with her in an unauthorized way (Pat, after being interviewed for television by Dupont in October of 1989, began to suspect Dupont of being a "circling vulture"),[19] she spent an evening at the end of 1989 making a list of people close to her whom she was "warning against [speaking to] Dupont."[20] Buffie, along with the French journalist Noëlle Loriot, Alain Oulman, Gary Fisketjon, and Tanja Howarth, was on the list.[21]

Buffie and Pat's correspondence survived Pat's visit to Buffie in Tangier in 1988, and when Buffie finally gave up Jane Bowles's apartment in Tangier ("The Arabs [are becoming] so hostile that it is far from pleasant"), she continued, from her loft in New York, to write to Pat—whose chief interest in answering from Switzerland was to reengage with her past.

Ellen Hill, of course, had no need to write to Pat. She spent most of her time in Europe (between 1975 and 1985, Hill did not return to the United States), and, with apartments in both the Ticino and Zurich, she lived near enough to Pat to see her regularly. Until late in 1988, Pat and Ellen continued their quarrelsome friendship, meeting and telephoning and irritating each other as often as their mutual miserliness would permit. But in 1978, shortly after Pat had stopped speaking to Lil Picard, Ellen wrote consolingly to Lil and with surprising sympathy for Pat: "Don't worry about Pat, she was mad at me for years and has now forgotten it. She does have a hard life, I am sure she will mellow finally."[22]

Lil Picard's long friendship with Pat produced loving letters ("Dearest Lil," Pat always wrote, and her valedictory was almost always "much love"), full of Pat's acknowledgment of Lil's work as an artist. In response to a request Lil made for a publicity quote at the end of 1975, Pat wrote: "Lil Picard is fun. I have known her and her work for twenty-eight years and she is still fun. She is incapable of creating a boring drawing or painting."[23] Pat and Lil had numerous European and New York meetings (and quarrels) and then a full stop, caused, without a doubt, by one of their rampageous political arguments.

In 1976, Pat was on her second trip to Berlin. There she would hear (without much comprehension) Allen Ginsberg declaim his poems and Susan Sontag wade through a thirty-page paper about her recent trip to China. Out of this evening, Pat carried away with approval only Sontag's firm declaration that she didn't and wouldn't belong to any writers' group.[24] (Sontag later succeeded Hortense Calisher as president of PEN American Center, the most influential "writers' group" in the United States: so much for promises.) Pat and Lil Picard were staying in the same Berlin hotel and this gave them the opportunity to irritate each other. Pat kept calling the Communists "bastards" and Lil kept calling Pat a "racist" and a "fascist." They even managed to argue over Wim Wenders's script for *The American Friend*: Pat thought he'd created Ripley as a "hoodlum"; Lil dutifully reminded Pat that "hoodlums [are made] by society."[25] The next year, 1977, the year Pat broke off with Lil, was the year Pat's interest in the Middle East began to assume an attitude best characterized as obsessive. But Lil was still on Pat's mind after she had moved to Tegna.

Pat wrote to Kingsley in March of 1991 describing Lil as "another volcano with which/whom I've parted company." But Pat had been close enough to Lil to respond with surprising warmth and enthusiasm to Lil's idea of having Pat collaborate on a book about Lil's life. Despite the fact that Pat was eager to take the project on and wrote to Lil several times about it, Lil seems never to have sent the autobiographical tapes she said she was making. And so Pat, in 1991, reaching out from her unrooted present in Switzerland, asked Kingsley: "Could you look in phone book and see if Lil Picard is still at 40 W. 10th or maybe 40 E. 10th?" Lil was still residing at 40 East Ninth Street, but Pat's memory was only one block off and she was apparently thinking of writing to Lil again. Lil lived on until 1994, dying, like Mary Highsmith, at the age of ninety-five.

Rosalind Constable tracked Pat down herself in 1967 and restarted their

correspondence. She continued to write to Pat for the next two and a half decades about all the well-travelled, high-living, artistic lesbians whose acquaintance they shared. "You seem to have Natica [Waterbury] on your mind.
[A]ny news of Natica that is more than a week old is probably out of date. . . . I
am totally fascinated by her, but I think she is sheer destruction," Rosalind
wrote in 1968.[26] And Rosalind had much more to say.

"I'm so glad you told Janet [Flanner] about my article, as I'm afraid she'd
given me up as a bad job. I was terribly drunk last time I saw her, and I'm so
sorry, as I admire her more than any other woman in the world. If I ever see
her again I'll probably be drunk again. You know how misfortunes like that
dog one. . . . Mercedes de Acosta, I am very sorry to tell you, died about a year
ago."[27]

"I have a slight hangover from a dinner party I gave last night: Janet [Flan-
ner] and Natalia [Danesi Murray], Sybille Bedford, Eyre de Lanux [artist, writer,
furniture designer, famous beauty, and the reputed model for the eponymous
character in Tennessee Williams's novel *The Roman Spring of Mrs. Stone*], Maria
Vogt, etc. A delicious dinner that took me two days to prepare, and vintage
wine, or rather two wines, for Sybille, who is a *Chevelier du Tastevin*. It was a
good party."[28]

Rosalind continued to advise Pat on the long, winding road of Pat's feelings for Caroline Besterman. Pat was thinking of approaching Caroline again
as a lover, years after their relationship had ended.

> I think you have a problem in your emotional life, and I don't know
> how you are going to solve it. I would say that perhaps you always
> choose the wrong person, but for the life of me I don't know what kind
> of person would be right for you. . . .
>
>   Jo Carstairs [the Standard Oil heiress, champion speedboat racer, and
> ex-lover of Marlene Dietrich, a well-known seducer on the interna-
> tional lesbian circuit whom Pat knew slightly] was out here for a couple
> of days, and whenever I see her I am reminded of her rigid rule: "Never
> get involved with a married woman." (Only in her case, of course, she
> would probably be sued for 10 million by an outraged husband.)[29]

It is worth noting that in the penultimate entry of the last notebook
in which she took any notes—Cahier 37—Pat was still trying to puzzle out
Caroline Besterman's character. On New Year's Eve of 1992, thirty years after
she had fallen violently in love with Caroline, Pat wrote "a final note"—it was a
bitter one—about Caroline Besterman. It was the last extended notebook entry
Pat ever made. And the final entry she made in her last diary—the ultimate

sentence of Diary 18—was also a kind of harking back to an early theme. "The oddball Swiss," Pat wrote, "enamored of locomotives."[30]

Rosalind Constable also wrote to Pat to announce the painter and gallerist Betty Parsons's stroke; she wrote to say that, no, she really didn't think Natica Waterbury looked like Greta Garbo (Pat thought everyone she was attracted to, including Mother Mary, looked like Greta Garbo); she wrote that Natasha von Hoershelman had visited with "her mistress" Eyre de Lanux, and soon after that "her wife," Katherine Hamill, died. (This was a different Katherine Hamill from the Kathryn Hamill Cohen Pat fell in love with in 1949.) Eyre, said Rosalind, was now "88 and pretty frail."[31]

As Pat's political statements got more intemperate and more frequent, Rosalind responded gently: "You seem much more interested in world affairs than I remember you being."[32]

In 1992, from her home in New Mexico, Rosalind finally sent Pat the little wooden sculpture Pat had given her in the 1940s in the first flush of love and heroine worship. (See "The Real Romance of Objects: Part 2.") "In case you wonder why I am parting with it and also, in the foreseeable future, airmailing all my collection of your drawings, it is because I am putting my house in order. I expect one day soon, if not already, somebody is going to write a life of you, and these evidences of what you do with your left hand might come in handy."[33]

This circle of mostly lesbian women—far-flung themselves now, and doing their best to keep in touch and look after each other as they settled into the reduced pleasures and greater indignities of old age—was really the only "club" Patricia Highsmith had ever belonged to. But her ties to it were ambivalent, and she always kept her membership card close to her chest.

40

THE CAKE THAT WAS SHAPED

LIKE A COFFIN

PART 7

People are drawn to closure, and demand it (usually in vain) of both art and life. And so the stories about Pat Highsmith's death, her cremation, and her memorial service in the Catholic church in Tegna—as well as the halo of blurred memories evoked by these events—tend to have an obituarial tinge. They are gentle stories, curtain tales, and they put a softly rendered end to the sundered psychologies and murderous passions, the bad motives and good intentions, and the infernal filiation of paradoxes, hesitations, cruelties, seductions, successes, prejudices, and surprising kindnesses that made up the character of the talented Miss Highsmith. Pat's former publisher Otto Penzler was the exception amongst her editors to give an unambiguously unfavorable opinion of the dead, but there was one other exception as well: the distinguished American editor and man of letters who leaned over me in a Paris bookstore and whispered, feelingly and off the record, "I *loathed* her."

Soon after Pat's death, Barbara Skelton, that tempestuous femme fatale who had been Pat's neighbor in the Île-de-France, "was visited by a small owl of intense beauty, its eyes sparkling with wisdom." The owl came down the chimney of Skelton's stone house in the Seine-et-Marne and perched on her windowsill, staying for two days. Skelton thought the owl had something to do with Pat and that it was bringing a message to her: "Have no fear! This is my afterlife and ergo, it's not so bad, is it!"[1]

Daniel Keel chose a poignant and spare little poem about a flowering tree taken from *Edith's Diary* to print in the program for Pat's memorial service, and he read out another poem written by Pat—somewhat uncharacteristically celebrating the efforts of underdogs (successful underdogs like van Gogh, however)—during the service itself. The critic Peter Ruedi, in his funeral oration, laid to rest the distinction without a difference that had dogged Pat's work since *Strangers on a Train* was published in 1950: "So let us waste not another word on the ridiculous differentiation between the crime-thriller and literature. It is one which never troubled her readers, but merely those people who would try to pull the wool over their eyes and tell them that black was white." And then he quoted the great literary philosopher Walter Benjamin's description of Robert Walser's work as the "most appropriate thing that can be said about the finest of [Highsmith's] characters: 'They emerge, out of the night, where it is at its blackest, a Venetian night if you like, a night lit by feeble lanterns of hope, with something of a festive sparkle in their eyes, but distraught and so sad as to make you weep.'"[2]

Tanja Howarth, Pat's former Diogenes' representative in London, in an attempt to "get close to Pat" after her death, spent a terribly disturbed night at the Storchen Hotel in Zurich where Pat used to stay. Her room—it was the room Pat always took and it was referred to by the hotel staff as belonging to "the lady with the typewriter"—was haunted, Howarth was sure, by the spirit of a disgruntled Highsmith, who was not at all pleased with this postmortem attempt at intimacy. But Howarth also tells a story about how, during the memorial service in Tegna, the little train to Domodosilla passed right alongside the churchyard and all the young "strangers on the train" waved cheerily to all the friends, fans, and dignitaries who were assembled to honor Pat.[3]

The day of Pat's memorial service, 11 March 1995, was "a glorious day, cold and crisp, the sort of day where you wonder: Would I like to be buried on a day like this? Blue skies and crisp weather suited Pat so much better."[4]

The little church in Tegna was filled: local people from the village had gathered, and Daniel Keel made sure that publishers, editors, and journalists flew in from all over Europe. It was, said one mourner, "a big hoopla,"[5] with Pat's publishers from Italy, Switzerland, France, the United Kingdom, and Germany all represented, but not the United States, where Pat's last American editor, Gary Fisketjon, "after tearing my hair out about it," had finally rejected *Small g: A Summer Idyll* in July of 1994. "It was a trifle of a trifle," he says regretfully. "[C]areless and left-handed . . . to publish [it] would be to set us back years."[6] Pat wrote him back, saying that she didn't take the rejection "personally." But she reminded him—since Fisketjon was now at Knopf and Pat was still counting—that this was, by the way, her "second rejection" by Knopf.[7]

Peter Huber—it was his memorial tribute—sported the red vest Pat had bought him from L.L. Bean to wear on 1 August, the Swiss national day—

"Very red," he says, "the national color of Switzerland."[8] Pat had also bought a twin of the vest for herself, just as she had kept her double of Daniel Keel's coat. Doubling was the theme of her life, as it had been the theme of her work.

The only ex-lover who might have come to Pat's memorial service—the only one who had been invited—was Ellen Blumenthal Hill, and she had refused to come, telling the journalist Joan Dupont that she'd had "trouble with Miss Highsmith" in the last years. Daniel Keel, who organized the service, and Pat's local friends in the Ticino who had done some of the inviting, knew next to nothing of Pat's past life. Kingsley Skattebol, Pat's last connection with her American past and her oldest friend, had also been kept out of many of Pat's affairs and affections: she had never met most of the women friends and ex-lovers Pat was corresponding with now, and she knew only the pieces of Pat's life which touched upon her own—and even some aspects of these came as a surprise to her after Pat's death. The biggest surprise, says Kingsley, was that Pat had been a member of the Young Communists when they were at Barnard College together. Kingsley had never suspected it.

"Pat and I were on the same wavelength but not in the same orbit," says Kingsley. A starry-eyed sixteen-year-old freshman when she met the rather superior nineteen-year-old upperclasswoman that was Pat Highsmith at Barnard College in 1940, Kingsley "knew right away Pat was brilliant." Sixty-odd years later, she was still counting Pat as "the most important relationship of my life."[9]

The results of Pat's silence about her past were all too visible at her memorial: the writer who had spent so much of her life dying for love (metaphorically) and also killing for it (symbolically) had neither family members nor old lovers at her memorial service in Tegna. None of the women Pat had loved and hated in the United States, in France, in England, or in Germany were there to remember her. It was Kingsley, Pat's platonic friend for fifty-five years, who carried the urn with Pat's ashes in a processional to the columbarium. It seemed to Bert Diener a "breathtaking [act], the maximum you could experience as a human being. She was walking in a trance, sort of floating." Tanja Howarth thought Kingsley looked like a "Greenham Common woman," wrapped up in her big anorak, and watched her "put the urn in the anorak and zip it up. It was like carrying a baby and she was sobbing as she carried it to the cemetery and put it in the little niche." Kingsley, who says that with Pat as her friend she "needed no other," thinks that she was perhaps weeping silently, but not openly, as she took up the urn for the solemn procession and that her walk to the columbarium "was, in any case, one of the worst moments of my life."[10]

There *was* someone at the church who was weeping openly for Pat, however, and that person was an alien in the crowd, a stranger. Uninvited, he had placed a framed photograph of Pat cradling one of her cats into the niche where her urn was being sealed up. When asked, he said no, he'd never met Patricia Highsmith, but he had "read all her books." *That's* why he was weeping.[11] Three decades before her death, Pat, an alien and a stranger to almost everything herself, had made a similar pilgrimage. Standing in front of Oscar Wilde's grave in Père Lachaise Cemetery on a bright July day in 1962, her eyes welling with tears, she'd read "those great and most biting lines" inscribed on Oscar's monument: "And alien tears will fill for him / Pity's long-broken urn / For his mourners will be outcast men / And outcasts always mourn."[12] Liz Calder, Pat's publisher from Bloomsbury who had taken the train from Zurich with Tanja Howarth, handed out English-language copies of Pat's last novel, the posthumously published *Small g: A Summer Idyll.* And so everyone went home with a memorial program and "with something that was Pat."

Daniel Keel, with an eye to posterity, had arranged to have the ceremony filmed for German television—just as he had invited a documentary filmmaker, Philippe Kohly, into Pat's house before it was dismantled. There were cables uncoiling everywhere in the small church, and, says one guest, "the television people ran all over everything like rats. The urn stood on a plain refectory table and I was convinced they were going to knock it over with their cables. And I thought that would be just like Pat, her ashes splattered everywhere. But it didn't happen." Frieda Sommer, one of Pat's executors and another of her "good eggs," the woman who had done much of the Zurich research for *Small g,* was the most visibly struck by Pat's death. Tanja Howarth, curious about the burial arrangements, asked some pertinent questions of the local officials about just how you get yourself a niche in a wall in a Swiss columbarium. The responses they gave sound like a paraphrase of Pat's lifelong problems with her possessions.

"You have to be a great member of the community" is what Howarth says she was told, "and you have to pay a lot of money and of course the urn behind yours has to be taken out, so you're displacing someone. They can't drill into the mountain forever."[13]

No information is currently available as to whether or not Patricia Highsmith's urn occupies a space that had previously been the resting place of a good Swiss citizen. But there is something appropriate in raising the possibility of such a substitution. The switching of one urn for another is a *keime* of which Pat would have made gleeful artistic use; urn burial (with a twist) is a fine subject for a Highsmith short story.

Just as good a subject for a Highsmith story would have been the little comedy of official errors that transpired shortly after Pat died. Bert Diener, in the house next door, was the recipient of the 6:30 A.M. telephone call on Saturday, the fourth of February, that announced Pat's death. When the owner of a Swiss house expires, the house's contents must be assessed and certified for tax purposes, and the dwelling is immediately sealed up with sealing wax—like a letter that will never be sent. So Diener-Diethelm called the "Syndical" early in the morning to report Pat's death, thereby provoking an "incident" with the local authorities, who found they couldn't shut up the house with Marylin Scowden, Pat's accountant, staying in it. Two of the three officials wanted to lock Scowden out. "Local politics," says Bert Diener, "they thought in this house was a lot of money and riches beyond imagination."[14]

Pat Highsmith's life was full of repetitions, and this last little contretemps over property and possession seems to be another one, reprising the *douane*'s disturbing raid on her house in Moncourt fifteen years before. But this time, as though to confirm the Marxian formulation, history came back as farce and not as tragedy and the Casa Highsmith resisted the invasion as though it were still inhabited by the spirit of its owner. Wherever the officials tried to put their sealing wax, which was, apparently, the wrong kind of wax—on the walls, on the lintels, on the doors themselves—it wouldn't stick; the substance slid sloppily down towards the floor. In the end, says Diener, they "just gave up." They put the things they judged valuable—eccentric choices including Pat's many-volumed, leather-bound edition of the *Encyclopaedia Britannica*—into one room and hung "some sort of official ribbon on the door handle."[15] And that was that.*

Except, of course, that it wasn't. It took eight long years to settle the estate of Mary Patricia Highsmith, which—with its twists and turns of tax laws and unexpected surcharges, its fiduciary blind alleys, its unknown investments in various countries and odd trusts in several currencies, its "alien" signatory who had simply been unable do the "sensible" thing and give up her estate to Yaddo before she died—turned out to be just as eccentric as its namesake.†

Pat did manage to keep everyone in the dark about how much money she had. When she invited her neighbor Vivien De Bernardi to be a financial

---

* Pat's cahiers and diaries were found neatly stored in her linen closet. Another case of life following art: Pat had made Edith Howland of *Edith's Diary* hide her diary where she kept her linens.
† Even the "last" Highsmith will wasn't going to be the last one. There were further revisions envisaged, but Pat didn't live to make them.

administrator of her estate (Vivien's husband, Renata, was a banker), Vivien had "no idea" what Pat's innocent request would entail.

"'Would you be my executor? I have an account with ten thousand dollars, is this enough?' And then," says Vivien, "later I find out she had six million Swiss francs!* Everyone got just a little glimpse through the window. Pat never gave everyone the full picture."

Donald Rice, the tax attorney and Yaddo board chairman who spent a long time "guiding" Pat on her bequest to Yaddo, says: "I did know how much money Pat had—but what to believe and where it was, was yet another issue."

It was Pat who launched the typically complicated exchanges she would have with Yaddo in the last three years of her life, exchanges which provided her with the kind of fun she liked best, the kind that turns everything upside down. Pat had written to Yaddo's then-director, Myra Sklarew, wondering if Yaddo would accept the testamentary gift of her new house in Tegna as a kind of "Yaddo in Switzerland." Then, "little by little," says Sklarew, "she began to send checks to Yaddo in torn envelopes."[16] Myra Sklarew passed Pat's suggestion on to Don Rice, with whom, by 1992, Pat was having intense conversations about financial matters, and Rice saw that the Tegna house wouldn't do as a colony: it was too small, too eccentric, and there was no money to maintain it. When Mike Sundell took over the Yaddo directorship, he got in touch with Pat in 1993 as a matter of courtesy. On the alert, she told him "curtly that she was 'not going to increase her contribution to Yaddo.'" Sundell responded that "she was being quite generous already," and, by the way, he and his wife, the art historian Nina Sundell, would be in Italy during that summer and could he take her to lunch. Pat was "agreeable" to being taken to lunch.[17]

The year Pat's relations with Yaddo began to thicken, 1992, was also the year in which she began, laboriously, to work on *Small g,* the only long fiction she would set in Switzerland. She'd written, hopefully, to Liz Calder that the city at the center of the novel she was thinking about, Zurich, "can be a violent town,"[18] but before she started the book in March, she was presented with a serious intimation of mortality: another operation. It was the prelude to a long series of hospital stays.

Pat had been having bad pains in her left leg, her "smoker's leg," for some time, and in January of 1992 she finally went to London to get it looked at. Her friend the actress Heather Chasen accompanied her to the Royal Free Hospital for her checkup, and then Pat went on to see a Toulouse-Lautrec exhibition. The only thing Pat noticed about the art was that every single print

---

* More than five million dollars today—but it's quite likely that Pat was worth twice this amount.

had a round or square stamp on it "so that no thief could steal it":[19] she was still on the lookout for life's little felonies. On 19 January, Chasen gave a tea party at her mews house near Harley Street for Pat's seventy-first birthday. Amongst the guests were Heather's son Rupert, with whom Pat had "interesting conversations"; the actor Jonathan Kent, who had taken over the directorship of the Almeida Theatre; the writer Jill Robinson, daughter of former M-G-M studio head Dore Schary; and four or five other people. "It wasn't friends of Pat's," says Heather Chasen; "there weren't many left."[20] Liz Calder picked Pat up from the tea party and took her to dinner at her house. Pat made a note of Calder's "light-green" parrot—"maybe 38," she guessed at his age, still fascinated by numbers—and nothing else.[21]

During the operation on her leg the following day, Pat's left femoral artery was "ballooned" out (Pat wrote down, as always, a minute description of the procedure), the operation was a success, and her surgeon, Mr. Hamilton, told her: "Well, you were lucky." "I *feel* lucky," Pat replied.

Back in Tegna, Pat started writing *Small g* in the spring of 1992, sending letters to her sometime neighbor, Julia Diener-Diethelm, who owned a dressmaking business in Zurich (and who altered Pat's clothes for no charge) about apprenticeships in fashion and about inheritance, since the book turned on the inheritance of a fashion business. Frieda Sommer was Pat's proxy researcher on the Zurich gay scene.

On 10 October 1992, Pat was back in the United States visiting "brother Dan" at Box Canyon Ranch, "now my only family-connected house in Texas,"[22] and, as she usually did in conservative Texas, Pat slipped into her vocal role as a political "liberal." She criticized Dan and his wife Florine's lack of books, their old-fashioned ways, and, most sharply, their conservative politics: the very politics Pat herself would instantly adopt whenever she came face-to-face with anything that resembled a New York "liberal." Pat had expressed great admiration for Margaret Thatcher, and she'd voted for George Bush in his initial presidential run, telling a British journalist that she hoped Bush would "take a more realistic stand about the situation in Palestine."[23] A month after visiting Dan and Florine, still horrified by the violence of the Los Angeles riots in April of 1992 that followed the police beating of Rodney King (King, out on parole for robbery, had a history of spousal abuse and drunk driving), Pat "voted Perot [a Texan, an independent, and a fiscal conservative], feeling sure Clinton would win."[24]

But Pat had already experienced "the glaring truth" of American violence a little closer to home: her "brother Dan," suffering from Parkinson's disease, had been stabbed in Weatherford, Texas, in 1990 "on his own property" for no discernible reason by someone he didn't know. Pat's stay in Texas in 1992 made the incident real for her, and she wrote about it as though it had just happened, "criminalizing" and complicating the behavior of the local police in her own special way. "[T]he local police were (and are) too afraid to bring the culprit to justice, because he is in the drug racket, & either the police are being paid off, or are too afraid for their own lives to tackle the problem."[25]

From Texas, Pat, who had been invited to appear at the Harbourfront festival in Toronto, flew to Canada in the middle of October. There she met Margaret Atwood, one of the handful of women writers whose work she had reviewed. (Pat felt she could forgive the feminism of *The Handmaid's Tale* in light of the novel's undeniable power.) But the focal point of her trip to North America was the nine days she'd spent in New York before she went on to Texas and Canada. Three of those days were passed at Marijane Meaker's house in East Hampton, Long Island, during which Pat soaked herself in alcohol; behaved, according to Meaker, like a social terrorist; and produced a series of remarks that would make her "conservative" Texas relatives sound like committed Trotskyites.

Pat had decided to add New York to her Texas and Toronto itinerary so that she could have more dental work done, and at the last possible moment her editor, Gary Fisketjon, called Bob Lemstrom-Sheedy, the publicist for the Rizzoli Bookstore in SoHo—one of the "hot" places to do readings in Manhattan in the early 1990s—to ask if he could set something up for *Ripley Under Water*. It would be Pat's last professional appearance in the United States.

The ads, says Bob Lemstron-Sheedy, went up on a Tuesday, the reading took place on a Thursday, and the bookstore was completely packed with people. Pat arrived with a woman friend and read sections from each of the four preceeding Ripleys, setting them up in her "marvellous, deep, gravelly voice." She didn't speak extemporaneously, but read from notes typed on a very thin piece of onionskin.[26]

She began by introducing *The Talented Mr. Ripley*.

"I was on my balcony in Positano very early in the morning, and way down below on the beach I saw a young man walking, in Madras shorts with a towel around his neck; it was"—here she paused dramatically, and everyone expected her to say Tom Ripley, because that had always been her shorthand explanation to the press about how she'd conjured up Tom—"Dickie Greenleaf!"[27]

Pat was very professional in her signing, and people waited eagerly in a long line to get her signature. She knew how to handle herself personally. "I don't want to sit down anymore," she said, and went to sign books at the bar, where the bookstore had arranged a little collation. "Too tired," she said.[28]

Then Gary Fisketjon took everyone out to the Odeon for dinner and Pat continued talking in her "marvellous voice." She drank glass after glass of whiskey, ordered a hamburger and mashed potatoes, made her usual fuss over the food because the potatoes were, she said, "cold," and then performed her customary *acte gratuite* at a dinner table: Bob Lemstrom-Sheedy watched her stub out her ever-present Gauloise in the potatoes. Still, he says, "I've seen everything in authors, believe me, from the obsessional to the hysterical—but I thought she was terrific, a real professional."[29]

Pat was also taken to Scribner's bookstore for a shelf signing. Scribner's was run by Lemstrom-Sheedy's wife, Kaarin, who had just read *Edith's Diary* and told Pat what a wonderful book she thought it was. And Pat said immediately: "Yes, I don't know how I did that."[30]

Because Pat was thinking about leaving her house in Tegna to Yaddo as an art colony, she took the opportunity while she was in New York to meet with Don Rice in his law offices. "So," says Rice, "as we talked the thing through—with her smoking Gauloises, in violation of every extant law and some intermittent complaints from people walking down the hall—we talked about the impossibility of this thing and her interest in wanting to be a benefactor."

As Rice got to know Pat, he began to think of her "self-presentation" as someone from "the English moors. The way she was dressed in a heavy tweed something or other, lots of material, lots of layers, strong smell of tobacco and the gravelly voice. I mean I liked her . . . and I think she trusted me."[31]

Pat's sporadic work on *Small g*—the novel she'd hoped would tell a "current" story—was the work of an ill and intermittently exhausted woman; Pat wrote her way through it between hospital diagnoses and the many intrigues she was hatching in life for the disposal of her wordly goods. *Small g* was another Highsmith "fairy tale" whose plot would mutedly summarize (rather than dramatize) all her themes. Viewed in terms of the rest of her work, the novel might be considered—not entirely facetiously—as the "classic comic book" version of a Highsmith novel.

Presenting a cavalcade of recognizably Highsmithian characters, it begins with an incidental murder, ends with an accidental death, and highlights: bisexual relations; a series of forged identities; the sexual idealization of youth; hoaxed and entrapped situations; the specter of AIDS (another hoax); and a clubfooted "witch," Renata Hagnauer, who has a fashion business, a mentally deficient henchman, and a semierotic attachment to Luisa, the "fairy-tale princess" who is also Renata's beautiful young apprentice. It again features what is probably one of Ellen Blumenthal Hill's dogs—the white poodle. It is the same dog for whom Ellen, a few years after Pat's death, would prepare the same killing pills she herself took when she came to the characteristically disciplined decision that she was too old and too ill to go on living.*[32]

But what *Small g* obviously lacks as a novel is what Pat herself had almost given up on by now: the overarching idea of the "double."

Small g has a happier ending than its murderous beginning promises: Rudi Markwalder, the aging gay male protagonist, *doesn't* have AIDS; everyone ends up sleeping with someone; and no one kills the dog. Still, Pat did not hesitate to frighten Renata Hagnauer down the stairs to her death—an accidental murder by the novel's merry band of pranksters—so that her assistant, Luisa, can inherit her fashion business. Murder and malevolence are not entirely erased from this final work, but, like its author's other deep feelings, they are half extinguished by the book's material concerns. Pat was a long way from the summer of 1955, when, "sick" with emotion and alight with inspiration, she wrote Tom Ripley's murder of Dickie Greenleaf as an act that was indistinguishable from love.

Nonetheless, the desire to stalk and keep secrets, the obsession with pursuit and threat, the flirtation with forgery and "getting away with it"—all of which had sustained Pat's fictions for five decades—were still alive in her imagination. And it is with these themes that Pat made her last, truly characteristic work, a creation that was much more representative of Highsmith at the height of her powers than this newer, tamer, timelier novel—*Small g*—whose writing was costing her so much effort. It was a final hurrah for Pat—this flaring up of old obsessions—and she enjoyed it enormously. But instead of consigning her inspiration to the pages of a notebook or a new fiction, she used it to light up her life, acting out, intermittently and in her own character, the transgressive motifs into which she had always poured everything, including her love. And so Pat began to bend the relationship that was blossoming between herself and Yaddo towards all the themes she had left undeveloped in *Small g.*

Just as she'd done when she was writing *The Price of Salt,* Pat started to play stalking games with Donald Rice, turning the magnificent possibility of her bequest to Yaddo (it was finally three million dollars: the largest bequest ever made by a former Yaddo resident, the cornerstone of Yaddo's capital campaign, and an encouragement to other Yaddo colonists to make similar bequests) into

---

* Pat was a card-carrying member of EXIT, the Swiss-based euthanasia society, and a great recommender of euthanasia—for other people. Even in her terminal illness she doesn't seem to have considered for one moment exercising the privileges of her EXIT membership.

an elaborate game of pursuit, escape, and disguise. Coincidentally, Rice, who was looking at Pat's work in an attempt to get to know her better, read *The Price of Salt,* which he "thought was brilliant and very, very touching. It may be my favorite book of hers. That's when I became aware of her sexuality and it was so subtle in that book, so beautifully portrayed."[33]

It was an unlikely pairing, Donald Rice and Patricia Highsmith, and it had the unlikeliest of results: Pat would manage to inspire a prominent lawyer with her most personal and unconventional novel, while Rice would manage to interest an author not known for magnanimity in some very serious philanthropy. By now, Pat didn't want anyone she knew to profit from her death (this was, after all, the woman who had written to her mother's lawyer to get *herself* disinherited), she was anxious not to pay trustee fees, and she wanted free advice from Donald Rice to help coordinate all the other free advice she was soliciting. But she was also, as always, having her own complicated kind of fun. And she was ill and knew it and really did need a place to put her money. And so the slowly growing idea of bestowing her worldly goods on the artists' colony—that "supreme hospital," as she'd once called it—where she had developed her first published novel, would come to seem both a pragmatic solution to her problems and the highest of the high ideals with which she began her life as a writer. Pat Highsmith never did anything for just one reason.

But first, Pat was ready to improve her current financial state by making use of Donald Rice as a sounding board for her intricate schemes. Rice thought that "with me, she was on a mission." In fact, they were both on missions.

"She had the mind of a criminal genius . . . [S]he could perfectly legally have produced more money for herself but she indulged in these fantasies and these phone calls, which I would repeatedly receive after she'd talked to someone about this or about that, seeking my opinion about this or that or the other thing. This was something she immensely enjoyed, I think."

Pat telephoned Don Rice "many many times" from what sounded to him like public telephone booths because "she suspected she was being wiretapped by people who were after her money." And when Rice telephoned back she would tell him she'd have to call him again; she didn't want anyone listening in. "It was all fantasy," he says, "all part of her personality."[34]

Meanwhile, Mike Sundell, Yaddo's current director, made his way in early June of 1993 from the Isola dei Pescatori in Italy by bus, boat, train, and taxi to Pat's house in Tegna to take her to lunch. He found the Casa Highsmith a "terrifying house, it had a kind of majestic purity to it, grotesque, but still . . ." But Pat was "very welcoming," the inside of the house was light and comfortable, and Sundell and Pat spent hours together drinking scotch and talking about Yaddo, about mutual friends like Buffie Johnson, about Pat's work and its reception, and about the United States and Europe.[35] The subject of money was "off the table," says Sundell, "though it was in my mind and may have been in hers."[36] (It was.) Pat told Sundell "with a cackle" that the room she'd occupied at Yaddo was now known as "Sylvia Plath's room."

And she told him how, when she was working there on *Strangers on a Train,* "she'd be typing every night and there was a young woman near enough to hear the typewriter who was having writer's block and said mournfully to Pat how could she go on and on typing like that. And Pat said she'd tried to explain that she was really just typing and revising to make the woman feel better. . . . Finally, Pat put her typewriter on a pillow so that it wouldn't upset the woman in the next room."[37]

Five weeks after Mike Sundell's visit, Pat went to see her local doctor, Dr. Del Notaro. She'd been dogged by a debilitating cold all that spring while finishing the troublesome first draft of *Small g,* she was having nosebleeds again, and she was tired; bone-tired, as it turned out. Tests showed that she was seriously anemic. The disease that had lurked in her blood since adolescence, focusing her attention on blood and breeding, was expressing itself with a vengeance. The doctor hustled her into the hospital within the hour and she was transfused. Her bone marrow was also suspected of being deficient, and tests showed that her blood lacked white platelets.[38] She was ordered to give up drinking, and she did so, cold turkey, for three weeks.

In the middle of September, she went to the hospital in Locarno, where a large, benign polyp was removed from her lower intestine, and then, on 10 October, she was sent to the Kantonspital in Basel for seven days, "a big modern place which has a division specializing in blood matters." She had been losing weight alarmingly—"15 kilos"—during the last year, and at the Kantonspital she was treated with daily injections to counteract what her doctors thought she was suffering from: a deficiency of the special cells that encircle and neutralize bacteria in the body and a lack of thrombocytes. "Thrombocytes," she wrote to Barbara Skelton with her usual clinical interest, "are the clotting factors in blood, and with insufficient, one becomes a bleeder or haemophiliac—that's me. . . . I am said to be stable now. To me that means I may not die in the next months, which I certainly thought I would do last year and most of this year."[39]

Finally—Pat said it took months—a full diagnosis was made, and, metaphorically at least, the results would not have been a surprise to anyone who understood anything at all about the life and work of Patricia Highsmith. Pat was suffering from two malignant and contradictory diseases: treating one of them would mean hastening her death from the other one.

Pat had, first of all, aplastic anemia, which meant that her bone marrow had "gone to sleep"; it wasn't producing the "haemoglobin and thrombocytes" her blood needed to regenerate itself. (She continued to hope her bone marrow would "wake up" and "swing back into action.")[40] Second, a lung and one of her adrenal glands were pocked and pitted with small, presumptively cancerous, tumors, too tiny to be surgically removed. And the modern poisons medical science was prescribing as treatment for the tumors—chemotherapy and radiation—couldn't be used without further endangering her degraded bone marrow. It was the classic Highsmith theme made flesh: the Alter Ego, the Evil Twin, the inner civil war. "There's also a person exactly the opposite of you, like the unseen part of you, somewhere in the world, and he waits in ambush," Patricia had written in *Strangers on a Train*. Suddenly, something very like that ambush had just been sprung on its author.

Pat's work and life had always been the product of an irreconcilably divided mind, and now her dying was to be the result of two incompatibly treatable diseases. It was a finish she could have written for herself, as grotesquely ironic as it was appallingly suitable.

While she was in Basel, Pat had been given a short, intensive course of drugs to prevent her body from attacking its own bone marrow and to stimulate the production of new blood cells. Then she was returned home to Tegna, where her kind neighbors alternated in driving her to Locarno for the transfusions her condition required, and a young nurse came to her house twice a week to test her blood. What she couldn't bear was the wasting of her days, and she wrote to Bettina Berch that she felt leashed to the hospital "as if I were a dog" and that her illness had "cost me more time than I care to think about."[41]

By the spring of 1994, it was obvious that Pat shouldn't continue living alone in the house; she needed regular chauffeuring to her blood treatments and some kind of surveillance at home. Naturally, she wasn't willing to pay for it. Bruno Sager, who had been an orchestra and theater consultant in Zurich but was now between jobs and newly divorced, had a daughter who worked for Diogenes. And so it was through Diogenes that Sager was suggested as a possible companion for Patricia Highsmith as her health declined. Sager came to the Casa Highsmith at the end of May, successfully passed whatever laser, radar, and X-ray tests Pat applied to him—"when she knew I was sent by Diogenes and that I knew Daniel Keel, that was reference enough," he says—and moved into one part of the pitchfork-shaped Casa Highsmith sometime between the seventh and the tenth of June 1994, while Pat went on occupying the other part: her part. Pat paid Sager 400 Swiss francs (less than $225) a month; but he didn't come for the money. After six months with Pat, he left to join a monastery.

"No," said Bruno Sager, smiling, "she didn't drive me into the monastery." He was already a religious man, thinking about joining a monastery before he met Pat; Pat knew this, and the Highsmith house was Sager's preparation for spiritual seclusion. She told him that she wasn't used to living with anyone, that it might be difficult. She had two or three phones in the house, but only one line: "she wouldn't pay for another one." The first night he was there, Pat cooked a "huge piece of roast beef" to "welcome" him, but she left it "two hours too long in the oven," and then, he says, "for the next week, it was my duty to finish that roast beef." After that, Sager, "a passionate cook," did most of the cooking. And Pat ate a little.

Sager also did the shopping for the house as well, and Pat made him advance his own money for all the groceries, scrutinizing every bill carefully to make sure he'd bought the best bargains.

Their conversation was limited to small talk, to music—about which they could agree—and to family matters—*his* family matters, since Pat, as always, was fascinated by other people's families. When his daughter and then his son came to dinner, Pat was "a perfect hostess." She didn't have many visitors: Ingeborg Moelich, a "sunny person," came by often, the Hubers were intermittently next door, the Keels came a couple of times from Zurich, and Vivien De Bernardi was a very occasional visitor. Pat had no guests to stay overnight in the house during the time Sager was there, but she had frequent telephone conversations with Kingsley, whom she described as "my best friend." Sager couldn't discuss politics with Pat because "her politics were very extreme, based on certain prejudices, not on analysis." He found that he couldn't discuss religion either, but from their conversations, he concluded that Pat "was one of these persons searching for some kind of god or soul but she never could stand the cages of Catholicism or any of the other religions. She was not an atheist, not at all."[42]

About all her editors, except for Daniel Keel, "she was vicious. 'Oh, he's a Jew, you know, he's a Jew,' she would say about them." And she put up a huge fence to screen out her dog-owning Italian neighbors on the other side of her house.

Sometimes, Sager says, Pat would walk "around the house with a ferocious look on her face." When he first came to Casa Highsmith, he thought she must always be angry, but later on, he thought simply: "If she's not conscious, this is how her face looks." But there were moments when her "young face came through, when her youth came through. Maybe when she was watching the videos of her novels. Then, like a flower, she could open."[43]

They got on well, Sager says, and he "felt fond of her."

"I didn't want to be her servant. . . . I was living with her, I did more than I had to, but I was enjoying myself, I had my pleasures in doing a good job—and I did it for myself as well."[44]

It was probably the best way to live with Pat.

When Sager arrived in June, "the garden was a terrible mess, it was never mowed, she wouldn't employ a gardener—too expensive." So on the Monday after he settled in, he started to do the gardening. It wasn't part of his job description; he just did it. Eventually he was even able to persuade Pat to allow him to water the dead lawn, brown as a hall carpet by now because she hadn't wanted to pay the water bill. But when she saw the lawn turn green under his care, she agreed to a little lawn care. She still loved the snails in her garden, allowing herself to be photographed with them for a magazine feature one day when Charlotte, the cat, who was supposed to be the companion animal in the article, intuited two hours before the photographers arrived that they were coming—and ran away for four days. And Pat liked the many little spiders crawling about in her house, always asking Sager to carry them outside, rather than kill them.

But she didn't seem to care much for Charlotte, her unpedigreed, orange "barn cat" and last living animal companion. Charlotte continued to remind Pat of a "dog."

"She wasn't affectionate with the cat. But she wanted always to know where she was: 'Did you feed the cat?' She wasn't very nice to Charlotte but the cat was still important to her. Like a family member, I imagine, with whom perhaps she didn't get on very well, but she was still concerned with her welfare."[45]

Sager gave Pat notice that he'd been accepted to a monastery about a month before he left. In the meantime, Anna Keel had found "a young Spanish girl of good family" (the parents were doctors; the girl was twenty) to go and stay with Pat after Sager had gone. It wasn't a happy idea. The girl was in Pat's house for two weeks, from about 6 December to just before Christmas. She told Anna Keel that she was too scared to leave her room—scared, perhaps, that Pat might have had designs on her. The girl left Pat's house before Christmas "for vacation"—and she never came back.[46]

When Bruno Sager had first arrived at Casa Highsmith, Pat didn't tell him what was wrong with her. It seemed to him that she "didn't look sick, she just looked very fragile"; she was "a string bean." By his last month in the house, November 1994, Pat was looking "extremely unwell."[47] When he heard about her death, his first thought was that if he'd stayed a little longer, she might have lived a little longer. He came from his monastery in March to go to her memorial service.

Pat was weak, she was terribly tired, but still she travelled to Paris in November of 1994 for three days (the twenty-third to the twenty-fifth) for a celebration of the thirtieth anniversary of *Le Nouvel Observateur* (she had been one of the authors asked to describe an "ordinary day" in an April 1994 issue devoted to prominent people) and to do some prepublication interviews for *Small g*. She asked a part-time neighbor in Tegna, a wealthy, gay male from South Africa, Bee Loggenberg—a man she enjoyed, "flamboyant" and "funny," says Sager—to accompany her as minder. But when Jean-Étienne Cohen-Séat of Calmann-Lévy invited her to come back to Paris in 1995 for the official publication of *Small g*, she wrote to him regretfully that she hesitated "to make plans" now because she "hadn't the strength I had a year ago."[48] A year ago, she'd only *thought* she was dying.

Pat was put up in comfort at the Paris Ritz, in her favorite room at the back of the hotel. And it was there that her new editor at Calmann-Lévy, Patrice Hoffman, first met her. He was, he says, beyond excitement to be meeting this woman who "was a myth in the company." By late 1993, Hoffman had received the final version of *Small g*, and he and François Rossot—"a great translator"—sat down to read it carefully.

> I was so honored as a young editor to have this manuscript, but then when I saw it . . . To tell you the truth, we were rather disappointed by *Small g*. There was an *ambiance bizarre* like the ambiance in the best Highsmith books. In this she succeeded, but in nothing else. . . . I could sense a number of themes hiding behind this book [but] they just didn't hang together. . . . [S]he kept her troubled characters, all this was interesting, but the dramaturgy was bad and the dialogue was worse. We worked for almost a year on the translation, François has a *très belle plume*, we tried to cut the redundancies and to raise the level of the dialogue. Much was trimmed, much was elevated, [François] did a parallel work. . . . Of course, I wondered if any other of her other [translated] books had been "improved."[49]

But *Small g*, Hoffman felt, was an exception: "She had been sick for so long." When the novel was published in France the month after Pat's death, it sold fifty thousand copies "because," says Hoffman, "it was Highsmith, the myth. She had incredible reviews; there must have been fifty articles and none of them was negative. . . . She benefitted even from her death."

The best part about the novel for Hoffman was that "it brought me the good fortune of meeting Highsmith before she died." He was with Pat "two times at the Ritz bar and then . . . in discussion for an hour or an hour and a half." And he was in her room for half an hour before the journalists came. Pat "was continually spitting into a handkerchief," and he marvelled at her determination.

"Dying, she came for her publicity. . . . She seemed totally exhausted, but she had a way of looking that was very direct, a judging eye, an inquisitor. It was very impressive. . . . [S]he sized me up so acutely. She was a fascinating woman, like a snake fascinating her prey."[50]

It was Pat's last public performance as a writer.

But on the inside back cover of the last notebook in which she made entries, Cahier 37, Pat left the ghost of a hint for a future performance she was thinking about. Still playing with oppositions, still imagining a life for the character who had meant so much to her since he'd walked into her imagination on a beach in Positano all those years ago, Pat wrote down two new titles for a novel about the talented Mr. Ripley. One of those titles was *Ripley's Luck*. The other one was *Ripley and the Voices of the Dead*. It was the second title that Pat crossed out.

41

THE CAKE THAT WAS SHAPED

LIKE A COFFIN

PART 8

The "first mysterious check" from Pat to Yaddo—nearly thirty thousand dollars—arrived from her Swiss bank without her name on it in July of 1994. The letter sent by the bank said simply "on behalf of our client." The client wasn't named. The second one—a check for three hundred thousand dollars—came from the same place five months later with the same message, "on behalf of our client," and Mike Sundell had to look at the number several times to reassure himself that he wasn't adding a few zeros to it in his mind. He and Don Rice figured out that it must have come from Pat and arranged a conference call with her in Tegna as soon as they could. Pat acknowledged the check, but didn't want to talk about it over the phone with Mike Sundell. "She thought she was getting money to Yaddo that she could avoid being taxed on. It was all very mysterious and foolish, really, but she was perfectly happy to talk about it later."[1]

When Sundell consulted with Pat about how to use the money, they decided that half of it should go into an annual fellowship at Yaddo for young novelists, and "she got the idea in her head that her birth name should be used. And so it's called the Patricia Highsmith-Plangman Residency at Yaddo. Pat thought her father would have liked that."[2]

But Pat's machinations in life were rarely as successful as they were in art, and in the past she had often found herself hoist on her own petard. And so it is not surprising that Donald Rice was left with a curious feeling about Pat's estate: a lingering afterimage of other secrets hiding behind the secrets Pat revealed. In one way or another, it is an impression by which everyone who knew Patricia Highsmith is haunted.

Rice's sense was that the people responsible for administering Pat's estate to this day, do not know whether we know all the [bank] accounts she may have had. . . . [M]y friend Mr. Volcker [Paul Volcker, the former chairman of the U.S. Federal Reserve Bank, a law partner of Donald Rice] has been very actively involved in dealing with claims of Holocaust victims and we've learned a tremendous amount about the Swiss banking system. There is no law of escheat in the Swiss provinces. [When account holders die, Swiss banks] just take the unclaimed accounts into their capital. So I have no idea whether we or anyone knows the full extent. I don't think Pat would have dealt with just one bank.*

And the irony to me in all this—and this is a point I made to Pat on many occasions—she was a great shopper for legal and accounting advice. And the various machinations she might have been thinking of when administered by honest people were not going to be able to accomplish the tax avoidance she had hoped for [by moving to Switzerland]. . . . In Switzerland she was subject to substantial estate taxes. Whereas by living in the U.S. and temporarily sojourning in Switzerland, without being domiciled in Switzerland, there would have been no taxes to pay.

None.[3]

Even former friends who were angry with her and current friends who had been sorely tested knew the sack of sorrows Pat woke up to every day. They were as moved by her physical fragility—just skin and bone at the end—as they were pained by the way she'd wrapped up her psychological fragility in anger and glazed it with alcohol. Marylin Scowden says, "The hurt person is what I remember, my heart goes out to her still. I think she must always have been in pain." Anna Keel remembers Pat's *"fou rire,"* her wild laughter, like that of a "twelve-year-old child who couldn't stop giggling," and thinks that although "she could be unjust with people in life, she was never unjust in her books." (I, on the other hand, find Highsmith's pursuit of personal vengeance in her work—a kind of literary vigilantism—one of her more beguiling traits.) Daniel Keel recalls Pat blushing like a child if you intimated she was doing something wrong. She was *pudique,* he says—and firmly believes in her "genius," the kind of genius that coerces her readers into the world of her fictions: "She's one of the rare authors of whom I have read every single word."[4]

---

* As early as 1948, the young Pat was prudently dividing her small cash reserves between two Manhattan banks.

Most of Pat's Swiss neighbors—as long as they didn't get too close (and Bert Diener, who had been in the airlines business, used his knowledge of human spatial limitations on airplanes in his dealings with Pat)—say they found something touching about Patricia, a "sort of yearning for affection even though she wasn't open to it."[5] They were attached to her, they made great exceptions for her, they prized their association with her, and her mysteriousness continued to intrigue as much as it frustrated. "I'm still missing Pat and thinking about her and figuring her out," says her neighbor Vivien De Bernardi; while Bert Diener and Julia Diener-Diethelm, whose discretion Pat appreciated so much that it was to them in Zurich, and not to her much nearer neighbors in the Ticino, that she'd telephoned in distress three days before her death (they packed their bags and drove straight down to help her into the hospital), say simply: "We really loved her."[6]

But the longer Pat is dead, the more her Swiss, French, and German friends reflect on what was going on under the behavior they had observed so silently. Success, of course, provides its own hedge against honest response, and Pat's *réclame* in Europe was as much an element in the way her worst behavior remained unchallenged as it was an alluring "fact" that drew people to her. Anne Morneweg, who first met Pat at the Berlin Film Festival in 1978, who was a guest at her houses in Moncourt, Aurigeno, and Tegna, and for whom Pat "was a very pleasant, very beloved friend," says: "We were all cowards about her anti-Semitism. We didn't speak with her about it [because] we were *sidérés,* flabbergasted, by it. We put it down to the fact that she was older and sick. It didn't show so much earlier."[7] Pat managed to keep most of her later friends (and many of her earlier ones) in separate compartments, as though she'd filed them in the pigeonholes of her big rolltop desk. There would never be any danger of consensus.

Marylin Scowden, left alone in Pat's house just after Pat's death with Pat's cat Charlotte, who wouldn't stop crying—"I felt it was possible the cat knew," Scowden says—was under the impression that Pat had *no* friends. "Hardly any. But I was AMAZED at the number of people who assembled. Within an hour [after her death was announced] there were about eight people [most of whom barely knew each other]. I was amazed at how she had done that, kept everyone apart like that."[8]

But separation had often been Pat's modus operandi with her friends; it was her daisy chain of lovers she used to want to introduce to one another. Like her favorite hero-criminal, Tom Ripley, and like Carol and Therese, the fugitive couple of her only lesbian novel, Patricia Highsmith got away with a hell of a lot.

Still, no one could say Pat hadn't tried to do her best in what mattered to her most. To make sure of it, she put herself on trial at the end of every work-ing day.

"It is impossible for me to live from day to day without putting myself to a judgement—of some kind. How well have I done? What did I mean to accom-plish today?"[9]

She spent her life writing through those "awful dawns," through the bad binges, the "shattering" psychological states, the self-punishing, hope-dashing, heartbreaking love affairs. Her incessant moves from house to house and from country to country and her insistent, restless travels did not stop her; she took what she needed and turned her experience to good use in her work. She kept her central wound—that terrible certainty that she was cursed at birth and was, really, nobody's child—stubbornly intact (she could not have done otherwise), and she found a fountain of inspiration in it, although not beauty or peace, for a very long time. With it, she managed to create a Bizarro World* of inverted values and unstable psychological states which exceeded even her own instabilities. She did her job.

Perhaps, working as doggedly as she had worked all her life, Patricia High-smith did more than her job. She wrote five or six of the more unsettling long fictions of the twentieth century. Anyone who has read even one of these novels with close attention has taken out citizenship papers in Highsmith Country and been provided with a passport that can never be revoked. The works are indelibly odd: *Strangers on a Train, The Price of Salt, The Talented Mr. Ripley, The Blunderer, The Cry of the Owl, Deep Water,* and *This Sweet Sickness* are my own favorites. Pat herself would have added *Edith's Diary* and *The Tremor of Forgery* to the list—and then changed her mind the following week. But in all her long fictions and in her best short works, there is always something wounding, something disorienting, and something that doesn't meet the eye—something deeply damaging to the reader. Few authors have been so willing to bite the hand that buys them.

Even to the very end of her life, Pat was uncertain as to what her own last name really was. Did Stanley Highsmith's illegitimacy entitle him or his adopted daughter to the name Highsmith? Did she legally change her name at twenty-five from the right one—Plangman—to the wrong one, the name she wasn't entitled to but had been using since she was in school in New York City—Highsmith? No one seemed to know, and the Swiss lawyers she wrote

---

* The "Bizarro World" of the Superman comics is a cube-shaped planet called Htrae ("Earth" spelled backwards) where doppelgängers of Superman, Lois Lane, and other characters featured in the Superman stories live lives exactly opposite to the lives of their earthly originals. They hate beauty, love ugliness, and criminalize the desire for perfection. Every-thing is backwards in the Bizarro World, just as it is in Highsmith Country.

to at the end of her life were unable, apparently, to disentangle the matter for her. She'd voiced the hope that Yaddo might use some of her legacy to put up a plaque inscribed with her double surname: Patricia Highsmith-Plangman. But it is not the policy of Yaddo to put up plaques, and her urn burial in Tegna is marked only with the name she made famous: Patricia Highsmith. Is Patricia buried under a pseudonym? Given the body and blood and meaning of her work, it's an idea with definite appeal.

And there is one more thing. In death, Pat Highsmith appears to have been delivered from the slow dissolve of her powers in the last decade of her life and restored once again to her most vibrant state: that volatile ambivalence which allowed all her violent and contradictary emotions to meet and mate and ignite into art.

In the little Catholic church in Tegna, Switzerland, close by the railroad tracks to Domadosilla and festooned with all the colorful symbols of orthodox Catholic faith (faded frescoes, cherubim on the wing, a profusion of flickering candles, and a large statue of the Madonna), the niche in the columbarium where Pat's ashes are walled up is piled high with the *yahrzeit* pebbles left by her Jewish admirers. After half a lifetime of refusing religion (and holding up Jesus Christ as her spiritual and social model), of ranting against "the Jews" (and sleeping with them, too), of bitterly rejecting one country after another (and desperately seeking to make a home in each of them), Pat is suspended once again between the poles of opposite passions: interred in a sanctified Catholic space, visited by the children of Sarah and Abraham, and attached in the most final way to the country of which she had never managed—quite—to become a citizen.

It is possible to imagine (but only in the language spoken in Highsmith Country) that Patricia Highsmith has ended up in a kind of equipoise. *Her* kind of equipoise: the kind that makes for inspired writing.

Any moment now she might hitch up her chair to the big rolltop desk, pluck a smouldering Galoise *jaune* from the edge of an ashtray for one last, inspirational drag, then raise those huge hands over the keyboard of the coffee-colored Olympia typewriter and begin to strike the keys with a sound like little pistol shots; busy, as always, with her daily work—the work of a serious writer about to add a new terror to the world.

When Pat was twenty-six years old and still alight with a hundred new ideas a day, still attracting lovers like a magnet, still writing for the comics, still having the time of her life in a Manhattan where the American Dream was still vibrantly alive, she picked up her pen in the early hours of the last day of December 1947 and condensed her hopes for the coming year into a single sentence. She called this little challenge—for that's what it was, a youthful fist raised in the face of Fortune—"My New Year's Toast." She could as easily have called it "My Epitaph."

> 2:30 A.M. My New Year's Toast: to all the devils, lusts, passions, greeds, envys, loves, hates, strange desires, enemies ghostly and real, the army of memories, with which I do battle—may they never give me peace.

They never did.

ACKNOWLEDGMENTS

To the many people around the world who offered their time, their minds, and their materials, I owe too much to tell here. This book is the down payment on my very great debt to them.

The iridescent conversation and radiant spirit of the late Theodora Keogh, my dearest friend, sustained me through much of this work. Don Coates, Pat's closest living relative and an invaluable resource, opened his archives, his family history, and his Texas connections without reserve. Kate Kingsley Skattebol did the same, placing her considerable intelligence at my service and giving me a clear idea of just how lucky Pat was to have her support during their fifty years of friendship. Jim Amash guided me through the Golden Age of American Comics, introduced me to its living creators, and generously shared his research, his knowledge, and his classic comic books.

Daniel Keel, fonder of Diogenes Verlag and Pat's literary trustee, allowed me to read the Highsmith diaries and notebooks, provided hitherto unknown details of Pat's life, and is publishing this biography in Switzerland. Anna von Planta's experience as Pat's editor at Diogenes and her astute critical suggestions enriched both my writing and my thinking. At St. Martin's Press, Tim Bent gave me the entrée into Highsmith country, and Michael Flamini adopted the manuscript as his own, and allowed me the time I needed to write the book I wanted. Vicki Lame picked up the dropped stitches, Ellis Levine unpicked the legal knots, and John Morrone proffered crucial solutions. Russell Galen's agenting has been, as always, my best support.

The following people opened their private collections to me, greatly enhancing the scope of this work: Jim Amash, the late Jerry Bails, the late Ruth Bernhard, Ronald Blythe, Monique Buffet, Frédérique Chambrelent, Donald

Oscar Coates, Ruda Brandel Dauphin, Peter Goedel, Janine Hérisson and Henri Robillot, the late Buffie Johnson, Priscilla Senn Kennedy, Ogden Kruger and Nora Ellen Lewis, Noëlle Loriot, Marijane Meaker, Christa Maerker, Christopher Petit, Annebelle Potin, Janice Robinson, Francis Wyndham.

For repeated interviews in the United States, Canada, the United Kingdom, France, Germany, and Switzerland, I am deeply grateful to: Marion Aboudaram, Dr. Gerald Albert, Jim Amash, Larry Ashmead, the late Mark Barty-King, the late Sybille Bedford, Daniel Bell, Pearl Kazin Bell, Bettina Berch, the late Ruth Bernhard, Caroline Besterman, the late Ginette Billard, the late Karl Bissinger, Ronald Blythe, Tabea Blumenschein, Monique Buffet, France Burke, Miriam Burstein, Philippa Burton, Camilla Butterfield, Liz Calder, Claire Cauvin, Frédérique Chambrelent, Heather Chasen, Sarah Clapp, the late Dan Walton Coates, Don Coates, Jean-Étienne Cohen-Séat, the late Betty Comden, Betty Curry, Ruda Brandel Dauphin, Vivien De Bernardi, the late David Diamond, Bert Diener, the late Julia Diener-Diethelm, Joan Dupont, Dorothy Wheelock Edson, the late Will Eisner, the late Vince Fago, Michael Feldman, Gary Fisketjon, Peter Goedel, Robert Gottlieb, the late Elizabeth Hardwick, Janine Hérisson, Patrice Hoffman, Tanja Howarth, the late Anita Huber-Speck, Peter Huber, Helen Kandel Hyman, Peter Hyun, Al Jaffee, Marc Jaffee, the late Buffie Johnson, Olivia Kahn, Deborah Burstein Karp, Stanley Kauffmann, Daniel Keel, Priscilla Senn Kennedy, Jonathan Kent, the late Theodora Roosevelt Keogh, Everett Ray Kinstler, Jack Klaff, M. Knet, Ogden Kruger, Linda Ladurner, Marie-Jaqueline Lancaster, Alice Gershon Lassally, Ricky Leacock, Bob Lemstrom-Sheedy, Nora Ellen Lewis, Marianne Liggenstorfer-Fritsch, Noëlle Loriot, Robert Lumpkin, Christa Maerker, Marijane Meaker, Anne Morneweg, DéDé Moser, Patricia Schartle Myrer, Phyllis Nagy, Samuel Okoshken, Otto Penzler, the late Judith Conklin Peters, Patrick Peters, Christopher Petit, the late Phillip Lloyd Powell, H. M. Qualunque, John Rhodes, Donald S. Rice, Henri Robillot, Janice Robinson, Edward J. Roche, Barbara Roett, Florence Rosen, Jean Rosenthal, Juliette Ryan, Bruno Sager, "Sam," Josyane Savigneau, Richard Schroeder, Marylin Scowden, Rita Rohner Semel, Kate Kingsley Skattebol, Myra Sklarew, the late Dame Muriel Spark, David Streiff, Mike Sundell, Anne Elisabeth Suter, the late Alex Szogyi, Philip Thompson, Tereska Torres, Tommy Tune, Anna von Planta, Wim Wenders, Donald Windham, the late William Woolfolk, Francis Wyndham.

For important help from individuals and institutions, I am indebted to: Constance A. Brown, registrar, Barnard College; Donald Glassman and Astrid Cravens, archivists, Barnard College Archives (Patricia Highsmith records et al.), New York, New York; Elisabeth Laye, Calmann-Lévy Archives (dossier Patricia Highsmith), Paris, France; Columbia University Rare Book and Manuscript Library (Harper & Row Archives), New York, New York; Maria Webb and Caitlin James, the Library at Fairleigh Dickinson University, Madison, New Jersey; Donna S. Kruse, Fort Worth Public Library (*Fort Worth Star-Telegram* Archives), Fort Worth, Texas; Gary Fisketjon, Alfred A. Knopf (the Fisketjon publishing files concerning Patricia Highsmith), New York, New York; Tara Wenger, the Harry Ransom Humanities Research Center (Alfred A. Knopf Archives, William Aspenwall Bradley Archives, Jane Bowles Archives), University of Texas, Austin, Texas; Birgitta H. Bond, the James A. Michener Art Museum (Patricia Highsmith records), Doylestown, Pennsylvania; Geraldine Amaranda, archivist, the Menil Collection (Rosalind Constable Archives), Houston, Texas; L'Office National Metéorolgique, Paris, France; New York Public Library (Yaddo Archives, *The New Yorker* Records), New York, New York; Mary Pisido, Public School 122 (Patricia Highsmith Records), Astoria, Queens, New York; Ridgewood Public Library, Ridgewood, New Jersey; Chris Hayes, the Assessor's Office of the Village of Ridgewood, New Jersey; Stéphanie Cudré-Mauroux and Ulrich Weber, archivists, Swiss Literary Archives (Patricia Highsmith Archives), Bern, Switzerland; Julie McLoone, archivist, University of Iowa Libraries Special Collections Department (Papers of Lil Picard, 1915–94), Iowa City, Iowa; Tate Gallery Archives (Barbara Ker-Seymer Papers, 1925–81), London, England; University of Maryland Libraries (Djuna Barnes Collection), College Park, Maryland; The New York Society Library, New York, New York; Dean M. Rogers, Vassar College Library, Special Collection (Mary McCarthy Archives), Poughkeepsie, New York; Lesley Leduc and Candace Wait, Yaddo, Saratoga Springs, New York.

For research, information, visual aid, referrals, quotes, kind letters, and other favors, I thank: Phillippe Apeloig, Wynne Alexander, Deirdre Bair, Stanley Bard of the Chelsea Hotel, the late Ginette Billard, Mary Blume, Edith Brandel, the late Hortense Calisher, Valérie Caillon-Gervier, Teresa Davidson, Marianne de Pury, Joe Goodrich, Madeleine Harmsworth, Sally Higginson Begley, Merlin Holland, Miles Hyman, Dannie Jost, Keith Kahla, Marlies Kornfeld, the late Paula Lawrence, Stan Lee, Robert Lumpkin, the late Norman Mailer, Judy McCombs, Honor Molloy, Michael Neal, Robert Nedelkov, Laurence Parade, Ned Rorem, Steven Rowe, David Scribner, Marian Seldes, Liz Smith, Jane Stevenson, Roy Thomas, Julia Van Haaften, Dr. Michael Vasallo, Gore Vidal, Allen Waddle, Camilla Wespe, The Village Voice Bookstore (Paris), the late INSIDE Restaurant (New York), the Cornelia Street Café (Greenwich Village).

For early readings of the manuscript, I thank: Deirdre Bair, Stéphanie Coudré-Mauroux, and Ulrich Weber.

For the following permissions, I thank: Marion Aboudaram for her photograph; Monique Buffet for photographs of and letters from Patricia Highsmith;

Florence Sultan of Calmann-Lévy for quotations from Calmann-Lévy's "dossier Patricia Highsmith"; Daniel Keel of Diogenes Verlag for quotations from the novels, cahiers, and diaries of Patricia Highsmith; Diogenes Verlag for the photograph of Daniel Keel and Patricia Highsmith; the Barnard College Archives for photographs, college transcripts, and other materials; Olivia Kahn for Joan Kahn's letters; Priscilla Senn Kennedy for photographs of Kathleen Wiggins Senn; Ruda Brandel Dauphin for photographs of Marc Brandel and Patricia Highsmith; the Swiss Literary Archives for photographs relating to Patricia Highsmith; Vassar College Library Special Collections for Mary McCarthy's letters; the late Buffie Johnson for her writings and photographs; the late Ruth Bernhard for her portrait of Patricia Highsmith; the University of Iowa Libraries for letters and photographs of Lil Picard; Bettina Berch for her unpublished interview with Patricia Highsmith; Richard Schroeder for his portrait of Patricia Highsmith; Annebelle Potin for "The Jeannot Album"; the Corporation of Yaddo for Joseph Levy's photograph of West House.

JUST THE FACTS

(with Notes by the Author and Commentary by Patricia Highsmith)

PATRICIA HIGHSMITH: CRADLE TO GRAVE

1921. 19 January: Mary Patricia Highsmith born in Fort Worth, Texas, in the boardinghouse owned by her maternal grandparents, Willie Mae Stewart Coates and Daniel Oscar Coates, at 603 West Daggett Avenue. Pat's mother, Mary Coates Plangman, an artist and fashion illustrator, divorces Pat's father, Jay Bernard Plangman, a graphic artist, nine days before Pat is born. From birth, Mary and the Coates family are the sole support of little "Patsy"; Jay Bernard Plangman disappears from family history until Pat is twelve.

1921–26. Pat spends her first few years under the love and discipline of her Calvinist-inclined, Presbyterian- and Methodist-influenced grandmother Willie Mae, as Mother Mary goes out to work as an illustrator. Pat lives in the family boardinghouse with her mother and her older, orphaned cousin Dan Coates. At the age of three and a half, Pat is introduced to the Fort Worth graphic artist Stanley Highsmith, who is marrying her mother. It is hate at first sight.

1924. 24 June: Mary marries Stanley Highsmith and he joins the household at 603 West Daggett Avenue.

1927–38. The Highsmiths take Pat to New York City, where they have been working as graphic artists. They live first in Manhattan at West 103rd Street, then in Astoria, Queens, at two addresses from 1930 to 1933. Pat reads and is deeply marked by Karl Menninger's *The Human Mind,* Arthur Conan Doyle's Sherlock Holmes stories, and an anatomy book used by her artist parents, *The Human Anatomy.* She never forgets that she shares her 19 January birthday with Edgar Allan Poe. In 1929, the Highsmiths return to Fort Worth, where Pat is enrolled for a year in the old Sixth Ward School (Austin Elementary), the same school her biological father attended as a child.

1930–33. January: The Highsmiths move to 1919 Twenty-first Road in Astoria, at the end of Queens County near Wards Island (where the largest mental hospital in the world is located), Rikers Island (where New York's largest prison facility was being established), and Hell Gate Bridge, the longest railway bridge in the United States. The family moves a few blocks away to Twenty-eighth Street, and Pat becomes a student at P.S. 122 on Ditmars Boulevard in February of 1930. Both Hell Gate and Ditmars Boulevard will later occupy Pat's imagination. At ten years old, she joins a girl gang and refuses to learn French before studying Latin, because, as she says, that is the classical order observed in English schools.

1933. Summer: She is sent for a month to a girls' summer camp near West Point, New York. She writes letters home. Her attention is caught by her female tennis instructor and the camp rituals of girls swimming naked, and counsellors and campers exchanging clothes. Her letters are published in 1935 as an article in *Women's World Magazine.*

1933–34. Mary and Pat return to Fort Worth to Willie Mae's boardinghouse; Mary has promised Pat that she will divorce Stanley. Stanley travels from New York to Fort Worth and persuades Mary to return with him to New York. Pat is left with Willie Mae for a year to go to school in Fort Worth. Pat says she purchased her two "Confederate" swords (they were made in Massachusetts) during her stay in Fort Worth; she probably didn't. She calls this "the saddest year of my life"—and never forgives Mary for "abandoning" her. She meets her father, Jay B Plangman, for the first time during this year and attends the junior high school on South Jennings Avenue in Fort Worth, where she is the only girl in her woodworking class.

1934–38. Pat is retrieved from Texas by Mary and Stanley in 1934 and taken back to New York, where the Highsmith family has moved to Greenwich Village in Manhattan and is living at One Bank Street. Pat attends the all-girl, eight-thousand-pupil Julia Richman High School on East Sixty-seventh Street where she falls in love with various classmates and befriends Judy Tuvim (Judy Holliday).

Like Fiorello La Guardia, the half-Catholic, half-Jewish mayor of New York from 1934 to 1945, and like New York City itself, the majority of the Julia Richman High School population is unevenly divided between Catholics and Jews. Pat's memories of high school are resentful: "There are never enough Protestants to throw a party." She begins making the rounds of Greenwich Village bars and cafés: her favorite is the Jumble Shop on MacDougal Street. She starts to take notes on her surroundings and relations; she transcribes these early notes in her Cahier 9.

1935. Pat begins her first story. It is lost, but in 1968 she still remembers the first sentence: "He prepared to go to sleep, removed his shoes and set them parallel, toe outward, beside his bed." This sentence gave her, she says, "a sense of order, seeing the shoes neatly beside the bed in my imagination."

1937. June: Pat writes her second story, "Crime Begins," done, she said, because she was tempted to steal a book from the Julia Richman High School library, but instead wrote a story about a girl who steals a book. "Crime Begins" and another story, "Primroses Are Pink," are published separately in the *Bluebird,* the Julia Richman High School literary magazine.

1938. Pat begins her first official cahier with these words: "A lazy phantom-white figure of a girl dancing to a Tschaikowski waltz."

1938–42. Pat attends Barnard College, where she serves on the editorial board of the school's literary magazine, the *Barnard Quarterly,* and enters the Barnard Greek Games as a "hurdle-jumper." She studies zoology, English, playwriting, Latin, Greek, German, and logic (in which she receives a D grade) and earns a Bachelor of Arts degree in English. At Barnard she meets Kate Kingsley (later Skattebol), who becomes her lifelong friend and correspondent. Pat joins the Young Communist League, but not for long. During her college years, much of Pat's social life is conducted outside school: she goes to parties at the Commerce Street studio of the photographer Berenice Abbott, meets the wealthy painter Buffie Johnson and the "eyes and ears" of the Luce organization, the English journalist Rosalind Constable. Buffie Johnson, Rosalind Constable, and Constable's lover, the painter and gallerist Betty Parsons, introduce Pat to many well-placed people in New York.

1939. The Highsmiths move briefly from One Bank Street to 35 Morton Street, also in Greenwich Village.

1940. The Highsmiths move to 48 Grove Street, a street of piano bars and historically revolutionary residents. They live directly across the street from the Federal mansion in which John Wilkes Booth is said to have plotted the assassination of Abraham Lincoln.

1940. Pat starts her first diary, "containing the body."

1941. September: Pat writes "The Heroine," rejected everywhere—even by her own college literary magazine, the *Barnard Quarterly*. The story will make its debut in the August 1945 issue of *Harper's Bazaar* and is reprinted in the *O. Henry Prize Stories* volume of 1946. In the spring of 1941, the *Barnard Quarterly* publishes "The Legend of the Convent of St. Fotheringay," a story about a boy raised as a girl in a convent of nuns (Pat gives the boy her own first name, Mary), who engineers a violent escape in order to become a boy again.

1942. Pat graduates, jobless, from Barnard in June.

1942. Summer: She forms an intense friendship with the great émigrée photographer Ruth Bernhard, intersected by a relationship with another émigré photographer Rolf Tietgens. Both Bernhard and Tietgens photograph Pat. Rejected by the major magazines she hoped to work for, Pat is employed by Ben-Zion Goldberg at FFF Publications, writing material for the Jewish press.

1943. December: She answers an ad at the Sangor-Pines Comics Shop at 10 West Forty-fifth Street, a comic book packaging and production company. She is hired by the respected comic book editor Richard E. Hughes, creator of the Superhero Black Terror, and works for a year in the writers' bullpen, scripting comics. She writes Superheroes with Alter Egos, "text stories," "funny animal comics," westerns, war hero comics, "real-life" stories, and "fillers," and then spends the next six years as a freelance comics scripter for many different comics companies. Her favorite company is Timely comics; it later becomes Marvel Comics.

Vince Fago, her editor at Timely, tries to arrange a date for her with another comic book writer, Stan Lee. Neither Lee nor Pat is interested, so Spider-Man (the Superhero Stan Lee cocreated) misses his opportunity to date Tom Ripley (the antihero Pat Highsmith created). Pat and Mickey Spillane both work on the same comic title, *Jap Buster Johnson*, at different times. Pat is one of the few women—perhaps the only consistently employed female scriptwriter—to work regularly in comic books during the Golden Age of American Comics. She begins to extend the notes for her first novel, *The Click of the Shutting*, which, like most of her work, is colored by the world of comic book Alter Egos. She completes a short story, "Uncertain Treasure," also influenced by the comics. She will remove all traces of her comic book work from her archives.

1943. May: Pat falls in love with a young painter, Allela Cornell: "I love Allela and God within her . . . "[S]he is the best!" She also falls in love with Allela's girlfriend, Tex Eversol. Allela paints a prophetic portrait of Pat, which Pat keeps all her life. For most of the 1940s Pat never stops falling in love with women—sometimes for no more than an hour or an evening. She also begins to date a few men.

August: Pat's short story "Uncertain Treasure" is published along with some drawings in *Home and Food;* it is her first work featuring two men in pursuit of each other.

1943–44. Pat travels to Mexico, in the company of the still-married blond model with whom she is temporarily in love. They quickly separate, and from January to May Pat lives in Taxco, working on her never-finished novel *The Click of the Shutting.* This Mexican trip is the first of her many foreign travels, and her behavior in Taxco sets the pattern for all her foreign residencies: intense correspondence, fervid note taking, fiction writing, serious drinking, and a yearning for home.

1944. She makes a synopsis of *The Dove Descending*, one of her three unfinished novels of the 1940s. She stops after seventy-eight pages.

Summer: She writes more comics scripts and has simultaneous affairs, including one with the blond, alcoholic socialite Natica Waterbury, whose daredevil exploits (she flies planes) and literary interests (she assisted Sylvia Beach at Shakespeare & Company in Paris) command Pat's attention. Pat will later dedicate a collection of stories to Natica.

1945. "Movies in America destroy that fine, seldom even perceived sense of the importance and dignity of one's own life," Pat muses on 27 August. Six months later, on 16 December, during a walk in Hastings-on-Hudson, New York, with her parents, the idea for her novel *Strangers on a Train,* which will be made into a classic film by Alfred Hitchcock, comes to her. She goes home and outlines the plot, giving it, amongst other titles, *At the Back of the Mirror.*

1946. Pat notices two snails, locked in hours-long coitus, in a fish market in New York and takes home six of them to keep as pets. She also tells an alternate story about her introduction to snails: In 1949, she writes, she saw a pair of snails "kissing" and rescued them from the cooking pot. She says she finds it "relaxing" to watch snails copulate. "I admire snails for their self-sufficiency. . . . I usually take five or six of my favorites with me when I go on holiday" (*Reveille,* 28 April–4 May 1966). When she lives in Suffolk, in the 60s, she keeps three hundred snails. She gives Vic Van Allen, the psychopath-hero of her novel *Deep Water,* her feeling for snails—and she names his favorite snails Edgar and Hortense after two of her own favorite snails. Pat says, pointedly, in a self-interview about snails: "It is quite impossible to tell which is the male and which is the female."

1946. June: Pat meets again a woman she'd met in 1944 at a party of Rosalind Constable, Virginia Kent Catherwood. Virginia is a divorced, alchoholic, wealthy socialite—she has been presented at the Court of Saint James's—and she occupies a high position in the American Dream Pat has been chasing. Pat falls in love with Virginia and uses Virginia's own marital history in *The Price of Salt.*

    September: Allela Cornell attempts suicide, and suffers a lingering death: her suicide has nothing to do with Pat, but Pat feels guilty. Virginia and Pat separate over infidelities in 1947, but "Ginnie" becomes one of Pat's enduring "types." Two years after Virginia Kent Catherwood's early death in 1966, Pat writes in her 1968 diary: "She is Lotte in *The Tremor of Forgery*—the woman whom my hero will always love."

1946. "The Heroine" is published in the *O. Henry Prize Stories* collection.

1947. Pat meets, in an elevator on the way to a "gay" party, Lil Picard, the refugee arts journalist, milliner, and performance artist from Alsace-Lorraine, who becomes "one of my more amusing friends." (Picard is Jewish and a Marxist; she considers Pat a "fascist." In the 1970s, Lil Picard writes a famous arts column for the *East Village Other* in New York.) Pat begins to write her short story "The Snail-Watcher," in which a man is suffocated by the proliferating snails he keeps as pets.

April: "The World's Champion Ball-Bouncer" is published by *Woman's Home Companion.*

On 23 June she begins to write *Strangers on a Train;* in November she briefly meets the black writer Owen Dodson, who reads the first part of *Strangers,* says it has "good economy" and that it can "be a *terrible* story"; he names a character "Deaconess Highsmith" in his current novel. She also shows the first eighty pages of the book to her old editor at FFF Publications, Ben-Zion Goldberg, who reminds her that she has used this two-man theme before in *The Click of the Shutting,* the novel she failed to finish in Mexico.

1948. Pat meets Truman Capote during one of her visits to Leo Lerman's Sunday evening salons, and Capote recommends her to Yaddo, the artists' colony in Saratoga Springs, New York. Pat spends two months there, drinking heavily, flirting successfully, and doing serious work on *Strangers on a Train.* Chester Himes has the room across the hall, Flannery O'Connor is also in residence, and so is the British novelist Marc Brandel, who becomes Pat's on-again-off-again fiancé.

1948. November: Pat enters psychoanalysis (her friend the composer David Diamond has recommended two analysts) for six months because of her homosexuality and her ambivalance about marrying Marc Brandel. Though Dr. Eva Klein's Freudian therapy presents her with some new perceptions ("I am acting out that with which my mother served me—the loving and leaving pattern, the basic heartlessness & lack of sympathy"), Pat soon rebels against Dr. Klein's conclusions, and when the doctor suggests that she join group therapy with some "married women who are latent homosexuals," the end is near. Pat remarks of the married women: "Perhaps I shall amuse myself by seducing a couple of them."

1948. 8 December: Mrs. E. R. Senn, wife of a wealthy executive from New Jersey, buys a doll from Pat, who is temporarily employed behind the toy counter at Bloomingdale's department store. This "two or three minute" meeting becomes the "germ" for *The Price of Salt.* Pat goes home, love-struck, and writes up the entire plot in one sitting, aided by a high fever and a case of chicken pox. She never meets Mrs. Senn again.

1949. Spring: Pat sails to Europe, her first trip to London, Paris, Marseille, Italy. In London, Pat falls in love with Kathryn Hamill Cohen, the psychiatrist-wife of her London publisher, and manages several other adventures as well. In Marseille, she visits one of Mother Mary's young "protegés," Jean David, called "Jeannot," an aspiring artist-turned-cartoonist. A flirtation ensues. Jeannot had been a guest of the Highsmiths in New York, invited because, after seeing one of Mary's illustrations in a magazine, he wrote to Mary from France. Pat continues to be an *ami de maison* in Jeannot's family.

1950. Pat works on the novel that will become *The Price of Salt* and writes the first of what will be many reviews and articles: a highly favorable critique of Theodora (Roosevelt) Keogh's *Meg,* a New York novel about a preadolescent girl who has many of Pat's own childhood characteristics—including a fascination with knives and a precocious interest in adults. Pat meets and befriends the Austrian Jewish émigré writer and adventurer Arthur Koestler.

15 March: *Strangers on a Train* is published.

1951. *The Price of Salt* is rejected by Harper & Brothers, but published in May of 1952 by Coward-McCann. Pat goes to Paris, London, back to Paris, then Rome, then travels from Rome to Naples with Natalia Danesi Murray, Janet Flanner's lover, then to Florence and Venice—where, at Peggy Guggenheim's palace, Somerset Maugham mixes her a perfect martini. She goes on to Munich, where she polishes *The Price of Salt* for publication and works on her four-hundred-page "lost" novel, now called *The Sleepless Night,* but later titled *The Traffic of Jacob's Ladder.*

Alfred Hitchcock finishes his film of *Strangers on a Train* (he buys the book for $6,800 plus a bonus of $700), starring Farley Granger, Robert Walker, Ruth Roman, and his daughter, Patricia Hitchcock. (In 1958, Pat told her editor Joan Kahn that the Hitchcock contract for *Strangers on a Train* was lost, mistakenly thrown out by a cleaner at the A. S. Lyons office, where her agent Margot Johnson worked.) Hitchcock's version of the transaction: he disguised his name and voice when telephoning Margot Johnson so he could get the book for less money. But Margot Johnson's records indicate that she knew she was dealing with Alfred Hitchcock. Raymond Chandler, then Czenzi Ormonde, are Hitchcock's scriptwriters. Chandler finds the book's plot unworkable and says it drives him crazy. He is fired. Robert Walker, the actor who plays Bruno, dies shortly after the film is released.

1951. Fall: Pat meets Ellen Blumenthal Hill in Munich and falls in love. Their affair lasts four years, and goes through many phases, during which they traverse much of Europe, some of America, and quite a bit of Mexico. Their quarrelling friendship lasts until 1988, and Pat moves to Switzerland in the early 1980s to be near Ellen Hill.

1952. Ellen Hill attempts suicide after reading Pat's diary comments about her. The William Bradley Agency begins to represent Pat in Europe; the legendary Mme Jenny Bradley becomes her agent.

1952. *The Traffic of Jacob's Ladder* is rejected by both Harper & Brothers and Coward-McCann. The manuscript, except for ten final, awkwardly written pages, vanishes later in the 1950s: "Some have said," Pat wrote, [it was rejected because of] the triteness of its ideas."

May. *The Price of Salt* is published by Coward-McCann. Pat insists on publishing it under a pseudonym, Claire Morgan.

Summer: While travelling with Ellen Hill, Pat begins *The Blunderer*, based on her already "poisoned" relations with Ellen Hill. It circles around the theme of one man, Walter Stackhouse, who is inspired by the murderous act of another man. Like Pat, the novel's hero, Walter, takes notes on the unequal relations between pairs of male friends, one strong, one weak. Pat kills Ellen off fictionally—a suicide—in the character of Walter's wife.

From the balcony of her room in the Albergo Mirimare in Positano, Italy, Pat sees, at six o'clock one morning, a young man "in shorts and sandals," with black hair, walking on the beach. His separation from all context intrigues her, and he becomes one of the "germs" for Tom Ripley. She pays an unsatisfactory visit to W. H. Auden, who is staying near Positano, and eventually sends him a copy of *Strangers on a Train*. He writes her a not entirely favorable critique from his apartment on Cornelia Street in New York City.

1953. July: Ellen Hill tries suicide again in Pat's presence, and Pat walks out of the apartment. Ellen survives and they separate. Pat finds several girlfriends in New York, amongst them a twenty-eight-year-old blonde, Lynn Roth, who wants to be an actress and is one of "Pat's types."

By September Pat is in Fort Worth, where she works on *The Blunderer* until January 1954. She stays first at her uncle Claude's apartment-hotel and then at her cousin Millie Alford's, and continues to work on *The Blunderer*. She is still calling the novel *The Man in the Queue* and *A Deadly Innocence* and gives it its final title in November 1953, when she finishes the first draft. She is drinking heavily.

1954–55. Summer 1954: Pat rents a cottage from an undertaker in Lenox, Massachusetts. She begins *The Talented Mr. Ripley*—two of its early titles are *The Pursuit of Evil* and *The Thrill Boys*—reading Tocqueville's *Democracy in America* in preparation.

September: She reunites with Ellen Hill and begins to write the second part of *Ripley* in Santa Fe, New Mexico, where she lives with Ellen.

December: Pat and Ellen and Ellen's French poodle (Pat kills a similarly named poodle in *A Dog's Ransom*) drive down through Mexico, arguing from El Paso to Acapulco and back again. Once again, her quarrelsome relations with Ellen produce the nerves of an excellent novel, *Deep Water* (published in 1958). "I want to explore the diseases produced by sexual repression," Pat writes about *Deep Water*. She does so.

Pat sends a copy of the manuscript version of *The Talented Mr. Ripley* to grandmother Willie Mae; Willie Mae dies on 5 February 1955 and the manuscript is lost. Before the end of 1955, Pat and Ellen separate, and Pat moves back to her apartment on East Fifty-sixth Street in Manhattan.

The Talented Mr. Ripley is published by Coward-McCann in New York in December 1955. Pat will later make many remarks that allow her to be identified with Tom Ripley: "Pat H, alias Ripley," "I often felt that Ripley was writing it," etc.

1955. She begins *The Dog in the Manger,* published as *Deep Water* in 1957. She shares with its pathological hero a fascination with snails.

1956. June: Pat starts to make notes for *A Game for the Living.* She gives up her apartment at 356 East Fifty-sixth Street after thirteen years.

1956–58. She falls in love with an advertising copywriter, Doris, and goes to live with her in Snedens Landing. They write a rhyming book for children, *Miranda the Panda Is on the Veranda,* a book which later makes Janet Flanner "wince." Pat does the illustrations and dedicates the book to Mary Highsmith.

1957. Le Grand Prix de la littérature policière is awarded to Pat for the French edition of *The Talented Mr. Ripley,* published by Calmann-Lévy. Pat publishes her first story in *Ellery Queen's Mystery Magazine,* "The Perfect Alibi."

1958. Pat joins the choir of a small Presbyterian church in Palisades, New York. She has been writing fervently about Jesus Christ for most of her life—and she continues the argument she started with God when she was in her twenties.

Summer: She begins, at Doris's suggestion, to draft a novel about "a man who creates a second character" and lives a second life. It will become *This Sweet Sickness.* While continuing to live with Doris, she begins a clandestine affair with Mary Ronin, a commercial artist who lives on the Upper East Side of Manhattan with another woman. Her fantasies about Mary Ronin pour into her manuscript. Pat and Doris move to Sparkill, New York, in September, but by the end of the year their relationship is over. Pat moves back to New York alone, to 75 Irving Place, in December, just across the street from Pete's Tavern. She continues to see Mary Ronin.

Special Award from the Mystery Writers of America for *The Talented Mr. Ripley.*

1958. *A Game for the Living,* her much revised and awkwardly constructed Mexican novel, is published by Harper & Brothers, In May, she suggests herself as the godmother for her friend Kingsley's daughter: "Let me know how you feel about my presenting the new first born with a Bible. After all, it *is* traditional." Pat leaves Margot Johnson's literary agency (A. S. Lyons) and signs with Patricia Schartle (later Myrer), then a partner in Constance Smith Associates. Schartle represents her for the next twenty years.

1959. Pat writes *This Sweet Sickness,* using her feelings for Mary Ronin as the inspiration for the psychopath David Kelsey's delusions about the married woman he wants to marry, the woman for whom he buys a house and constructs a second identity. Again, Pat dedicates the book to Mary Highsmith.

Mme Jenny Bradley, Pat's European agent, sells the rights to *The Talented Mr. Ripley* to Robert and Raymond Hakim, who produce René Clément's classic film version *Plein Soleil,* starring Alain Delon, Marie Laforêt, and Maurice Ronet.

Pat meets and begins a brief affair with pulp novelist Marijane Meaker, then goes to Europe on a publicity tour at the end of September with Mother Mary, who is recovering from a bad depression. Pat hopes to meet Mary Ronin in Greece, but Mary Ronin doesn't come. Mother Mary and Pat quarrel on the European trip; Mary impersonates Pat for two journalists in their Paris hotel lobby, intimating that her action was a joke. "I think a psychiatrist would put another meaning to it," Pat writes to her cousin Dan. Pat continues her travels with her ex-lover Doris. She goes to Marseille, back to Paris, to Greece, and then to Crete.

1960. February: Pat returns from Europe. *This Sweet Sickness* is published. In May she begins to take notes on the the idea of an American embezzler who travels to Greece, the start of a tortuous series of revisions which result in her novel *The Two Faces of January.* (Other titles for *January*: *The*

Power of Negative Thinking, Rydal's Folly.) She rekindles her romance with Marijane Meaker and moves with her to a house on Old Ferry Road, seven miles outside New Hope, Pennsylvania, for a turbulent six-month relationship. During this time, she reworks *The Two Faces of January* and writes several short stories, amongst them "The Terrapin" (published in *EQMM* in 1961). "The Terrapin" wins the Raven Award from the Mystery Writers of America. She produces many inadequate drafts of *The Two Faces of January.* Her editor at Harper & Brothers, Joan Kahn, reluctantly rejects all of them. In May 1962, the final Harper & Brothers reader's report submitted to Joan Kahn about *The Two Faces of January* contains this sentence: "A very unhealthy air hangs over it . . . and I finished it all with a strong sense of revulsion."

1960. Spring: She meets Alex Szogyi, a professor at Wesleyan University, who admires her work and becomes a close friend. When she leaves permanently for Europe in 1962, she gives him her writing desk. They continue a mostly epistolary friendship until the 1980s, when she becomes "possessive" over his growing friendship with Jeanne Moreau (to whom she introduced him) and their relations break off.

1961. January: Pat begins work on *Girls' Book*, which becomes *First Person Novel*, about a woman recounting her lesbian experiences to her husband by letter. She stops the book after fifty-nine pages.

Spring: Pat and Meaker separate; Pat moves to an apartment and then to a house in New Hope at 113 South Sugan Road. She begins a yearlong affair with Daisy Winston, later a travel agent, now an occasional waitress at Odette's, a nightclub in New Hope. Daisy becomes a lifelong friend.

April: Pat begins *The Cry of the Owl*, set in Lambertville, Pennsylvania, just across the river from New Hope. She writes to Kingsley that with this book, "I am writing something out of my system." In it, she again kills off a girlfriend: Marijane Meaker in the character of Robert Forester's pathological ex-wife. A case of German measles in June helps her work along.

1962. Summer: She travels to Europe, sharing a house in Positano with Ellen Hill; they immediately begin to quarrel again. They go on to Rome and Pat travels to Venice, staying at the Pensione Seguso, which she will make use of in her Venice novel *Those Who Walk Away.* In July, she is in Paris, weeping over Oscar Wilde's grave in Père Lachaise. During this summer in Europe, she meets Caroline Besterman and falls in love "as never before." She returns to Pennsylvania, struck to the heart.

September: Back in New Hope, Pat begins to write *The Glass Cell*, inspired in part by a correspondence with an inmate in a Chicago prison. She visits Doylestown prison for atmosphere (but isn't allowed inside), and takes some details for the novel from a book about an unjustly imprisoned engineer who was strung up by his thumbs in prison and became a morphine addict—details she attaches to *The Glass Cell*'s hero, Philip Carter.

1962. Obsessed by her love for Caroline Besterman and unable to work, she decides to move to England to be near the married Caroline.

1963. February: Pat takes a boat to Lisbon, then to Positano, where Edna Lewis, mother-in-law of her New Hope friend Peggy Lewis, has an art school. She rents the house she had the year before. At Edna Lewis's party she meets the writer Larry Kramer and spends time with some expatriate artists. She makes a quick trip to London to see Caroline, whose husband has been told of their affair. While in London, she does a radio interview with the writer Francis Wyndham, the first person in England to write about her at length as a serious novelist. (Maurice Richardson wrote about her work for *The Observer* in 1957.) Wyndham writes a subsequent article in the *New Statesmen* which effectively introduces her work to Britain. Caroline comes back with her to Positano. Pat is so deeply in love with Caroline that she changes her will, leaving half her estate to Caroline, half to Mary Highsmith, and her manuscripts to her friend from Barnard College, Kate Kingsley Skattebol. She is in the habit of changing her will frequently, but she has never left money to a lover before—nor will she ever do so again. The depth of her feeling for Caroline is contained in this characteristic statement: "I have imagined killing myself, strangely, more strongly now than with anyone else I have ever known" (Diary 15, 3 May 1963).

Pat moves to Aldeburgh, to 27 King Street, in Suffolk. Then she buys Bridge Cottage in Earl Soham, Suffolk. Caroline visits on weekends.

Pat writes *A Suspension of Mercy* (published as *The Story-Teller* in the United States) and makes friends with her neighbor, the writer Ronald Blythe, and his circle, which includes James Hamilton-Paterson, future author of *Cooking with Fernet-Branca*.

1964. *The Two Faces of January* is finally published by Doubleday in the United States and Heinemann in the UK in 1965. *The Two Faces of January* wins the Crime Writers Association of England's Silver Dagger Award for best foreign crime novel of 1964. Julian Symons is president of the awards committee and becomes another of her British champions, as does the novelist and political activist Brigid Brophy. Pat adds the Silver Dagger (it's an actual dagger) to her growing collection of sharpened instruments.

1965. Pat starts to make notes for the novel which becomes *Ripley Under Ground,* published in 1970. The idea for the central figure, the dead artist Derwatt, came to her in 1952 when, sojourning on the Riviera with Ellen Hill, she wrote down a memory of Allela Cornell's studio on Washington Square, with "Allela like Christ, returned to be a painter. Who could be in her presence without being suffused with joy and contentment . . . ? I should at some time like to do a story permeated with this paradisical atmosphere of the life creative and creating in her studio, destroyed in the fleshly suicide (so was X [Christ] a suicide) but living on always in the hearts of people who knew her" (Cahier 21, 4/5/52).

May: Pat goes to Venice with Caroline Besterman: "my first vacation in nineteen months." She does many drawings and is snubbed by Peggy Guggenheim, who refuses her invitation to Harry's Bar. Pat never wastes a trip, and she doesn't waste this one, later telling Mike Sundell, director of Yaddo, that she plotted *Those Who Walk Away* from her Venice maps. From October 1965 to March 1966 she writes *Those Who Walk Away,* her Venice novel of endless, topographically accurate, and paranoid pursuits.

November: She begins to think of *Ripley Under Ground* as a television play: *Derwatt Resurrected.* "A religious television play, based on the effect of a friend (Jesus) upon a group of people. The Jesus figure dies, some what of a suicide, whereupon his influence grows." Her thoughts about Jesus Christ, always present, are finding creative forms.

1966. She writes a "ghost story" at the suggestion of Caroline Besterman, "The Yuma Baby," and one of her snail stories, "The Quest for Blank Claveringi." She makes some tables out of wood.

June: Pat drives to Marseille with her old friend the designer Elizabeth Lyne. They take a boat to Tunis, where they put up at a hotel in Hammamet for a few weeks, then sail to Naples and go overland to Alpnach, Austria. Pat's notes from the Tunisian part of her trip go into *The Tremor of Forgery*—as do her feelings about the Arab population's "petty thieving."

August: Caroline Besterman joins Pat for five days in Paris.

September: At Anne Duveen's house in Cagnes-sur-Mer, Pat meets, for the first time, the former photographer Barbara Ker-Seymer and her companion, Barbara Roett. Pat is in the South of France because the film director Raoul Lévy wants her to collaborate on his screenplay of *Deep Water*. She finishes the script, but Lévy shoots himself dead on New Year's Eve and the film is never made. Pat returns to Earl Soham.

October: Pat and Caroline separate; Pat calls this "the very worst time of my entire life." Pat continues to refer to the relationship in her cahiers (but not in her fiction) for most of the rest of her life.

Pat makes notes about writing a more "intellectual and funnier" Ripley. Claude Autant-Lara makes a film of *The Blunderer, Le Meurtrier. Plotting and Writing Suspense Fiction* is published in the United States.

1967. January: Pat begins the year with an indictment of Caroline Besterman's behavior—and moves to the Île-de-France. Over the next several years, she rents a house near Fontainebleau, then buys a house in Samois-sur-Seine with her old friend from New York the designer and painter Elizabeth Lyne, then rents another house in Montmachoux. Her cotenancy with Mme Lyne is not a success. Pat thought Lyne had "what was known as a Man's Mind." Instead she finds her like "Every Woman." Their arguments about co-ownership end up in a court of law.

Pat begins *The Tremor of Forgery,* based on her trip to Tunisia with Mme Lyne. Originally planning to give her "hero," the divorced writer Howard Ingham (who is writing a book called *The Tremor of Forgery*), an affair with an Arab boy, she is instead content to deracinate him in other ways. He kills an intruding Arab with his typewriter and dissembles the act. Ingham's divorced wife—who never appears in the book—is based on the remnants of Pat's feelings for Ginnie Catherwood and Lynn Roth. The book is finished in February of 1968. Set during the Israeli-Arab Six-Day War, it is pervaded by contradictory political sentiments. Rolf Tietgens tells her that the politics of *Tremor* "is the weakest part of the book."

1967. Daniel Keel, cofounder of Diogenes Verlag in Zurich, takes over from Rowohlt as Pat's principal German publisher with his German-language publication of *Those Who Walk Away*. Keel, who saw Hitchcock's film of *Strangers on a Train* as a young man and stayed in the theater until he could identify the author's name on the credits, will include Pat's work in his renowned "black and yellow" crime series in 1974. After seven months of what Pat called "tough" bargaining between Pat and Keel (1979–80), Daniel Keel becomes Highsmith's world representative as well as her principal publisher. At the end of her life, Pat appoints him as her literary executor. Keel and Diogenes Verlag are responsible for much of Pat's fame and a large part of her fortune.

1968. March: In Paris, Pat dines with Janet Flanner and lunches with Nathalie Sarraute, with whom she debates the "femininity" of Colette. (Pat doesn't think Colette is feminine.) "[Sarraute] was absolutely charming and wrote a wonderful inscription" in the Sarraute novel, which, typically, Pat borrowed from Elizabeth Lyne. Pat begins a yearlong affair with a young journalist, Madeleine Harmsworth, who comes to Samois-sur-Seine to interview her for *Queen* magazine.

April: Pat buys a house in Montmachoux and moves from Samois-sur-Seine. 25 April–6 May: she stays with Barbara Ker-Seymer and Barbara Roett in North London, returning to France in time to be outraged by the student revolution of May 1968.

20 June: She moves to Montmachoux and works on a play for a London producer called *When the Sleep Ends*. She is writing the lead role for her friend the actress Heather Chasen. Chasen later remarks that Pat was unable to write dialogue, and anyway, the character Pat was creating for her was a "perfect bitch." The play is never produced.

1968. October: Pat begins to take notes for the book that will become *Ripley Under Ground,* centering the plot on the "Christ-like" dead painter Derwatt (for whom Allela Cornell provides the inspiration), and the international forgery business that a now-married Ripley (he turns "green" with terror at his wedding) murders to protect. She is also inspired by Hans van Meegeren, the man who fooled Hermann Göring with his forgeries of Vermeer. She falls in love with "Jacqui," a Parisian, who perpetually disappoints her. Pat borrows some of Jacqui's traits for Heloise Plisson, Tom Ripley's wife in *Ripley Under Ground.*

1969. Madeleine Harmsworth breaks off with Pat.

July: Pat visits Arthur and Cynthia Koestler in Alpnach.

1970. February: Thinking of moving back to the States, Pat flies to New York and travels to Fort Worth, where her battles with Mother Mary result in letters like this one from Mary: "My doctors say if you had stayed 3 more days I would be dead."

March: Pat goes to Santa Fe to stay with Rosalind Constable for a couple of weeks, finishing her corrections on the manuscript of *Ripley Under Ground.*

May: She starts to write *A Dog's Ransom,* reviving her interest in poison-pen letters. She gives the dog in question, a poodle, the name of Ellen Hill's poodle (Tina) and kills it off. She gives Greta Reynolds, one of the fictional Tina's owners, some of Lil Picard's traits. *A Dog's Ransom* is her jeremiad against a "corrupt" and "corrupting" New York; its confusions are a result of the fact that her chief contact with the United States is limited to daily readings of the *International Herald Tribune*. She concentrates the story on an idealistic young policeman who becomes infected by the venality he hopes to fight. Pat didn't know any policemen, and she was relying on Kingsley Skattebol's research on New York police procedure. The novel is interpreted in Europe as an expression of Pat's ability to find the surreal in the real and is highly praised.

Summer: Doubleday publishes her story collection *The Snail-Watcher and Other Stories*: she pays four hundred dollars of Graham Greene's five-hundred-dollar fee to write the introduction. She isn't completely pleased with what Greene writes: "A trifle hectic the prose, but not bad, I suppose."

1970. October: Throughout her sojourn in France, Pat has been supported in every way by her editor at Calmann-Lévy, Alain Oulman, with whom she has a warm friendship and an extensive correspondence. He introduces her to both James Baldwin and Colette de Jouvenel, daughter of the writer Colette. Colette de Jouvenel and Pat are neighbors in the Île-de-France and share an interest in cats as well as in Jouvenel's mother.

14 November: She moves to a *hameau* in Moncourt, buying a house at 21 rue de la Boissière, next door to two Anglo-Irish journalists she knows and likes, Desmond and Mary Ryan. As usual, proximity diminishes her liking. She meets many interesting people through the Ryans, including Isabella Rawsthorne, Francis Bacon's muse.

1971. March: Pat's almost thirteen-year-old goddaughter, her college friend Kingsley's daughter, comes for a fortnight to stay with Pat in Moncourt and to travel. Pat takes her to London but does not prove to be a sympathetic hostess, remarking in a letter to Ronald Blythe that her goddaughter is five feet three inches and 138 pounds, and that she fears for the cases in the British Museum when the girl leans on them. Pat regularly refers to herself in letters to the girl as "evil fairy godmother," "old witch," and "delinquent godmother."

June: Barbara Ker-Seymer and Barbara Roett visit Moncourt and have the usual experience of many Highsmith guests: if they want to eat, they have to buy the food. On another visit, Pat throws a dead rat up from the garden through their bedroom window: her idea of a joke.

1971. Fall: Pat leaves Doubleday, publishers of her last five books in the United States, when her editor, Larry Ashmead, turns down *A Dog's*

Ransom—which is then accepted by Knopf. Her editor at Knopf, Bob Gottlieb, suggests revisions, as does her editor at Heinemann, Janice Robertson. Pat is not pleased to make revisions.

November: She is taking notes for the book that will become *Ripley's Game*. One of her early ideas is that Tom should carry out a series of revenge murders for a sixty-year-old writer (Pat is fifty). She calls this idea "A dialogue with myself."

1972. January: She continues developing *Ripley's Game* and begins to note down some ideas for the collection of short stories that will become *The Animal-Lover's Book of Beastly Murder*.

September: Stanley Highsmith dies. Pat asks for—and receives—his autopsy report. Pat and Mary begin their long correspondence about the watch and chain Pat gave to Stanley when she was twelve or thirteen. Pat wants it back. She doesn't get it.

1973. 26 May: "I'd love to meet Francis Bacon some time. I would imagine he is a very 'disturbing' type, in the sense that the mentally deranged can be disturbing. I may be quite wrong. He is probably well organized on the surface. Artists react to such temperaments at once—a sensation I have always described as 'shattering.'"

"Shattering" is the word Pat uses most often to describe the effect Mother Mary has on her. In her house in Tegna, Pat keeps a postcard of Francis Bacon's *Study Number 6*—it is one of his screaming popes—on her desk.

1974. Film director Joseph Losey is interested in adapting Pat's novel *The Tremor of Forgery*. The project comes to nothing, but cordial relations develop between Pat and Losey and his writer-producer wife, Patricia.

28 June: Wim Wenders and Peter Handke come to see Pat in Moncourt. They bring a gift from Jeanne Moreau (whom Pat met when Moreau was starring in a Handke play in Paris): an igneous ball on a pedestal "black and clear." Handke says to Pat: "When I start any of your books, I have the feeling that you love life, that you want to live." Pat's comment in her Cahier 33: "That's very nice!" (Ten years later, in November of 1984, Pat writes to her German translator, Anne Uhde: "By the way, I find Peter Handke's prose writings quite boring much of the time"—and then goes on to say that Ellen Hill thinks his plays are brilliant.) Wim Wenders says that it is Handke who introduced Pat to the European custom of having your publisher for an agent. Pat hands over to Wenders a manuscript of the book she has just finished, *Ripley's Game,* and he is eager to make it into a film.

August: The germ of *Edith's Diary*: Pat plans a book about "a modern intellectual" who is so disappointed in her family and "her beautiful dream of America" that she creates a better world in her diary. (This leaves the "truthfulness" of Pat's own diaries open to some interesting questions.) Edith, undeveloped as an "intellectual" character, goes mad as her diary develops a saner, far more bourgeois world than the one she inhabits. Pat takes the son of a former lover as a model for Cliffie, Edith's criminal and psychologically puzzling son (another of Pat's "literary" revenges), and writes to Lil Picard for political positions for the increasingly crackpot Edith. "Edith's ideas are partly mine," Pat says. Edith is pulled to her death down a flight of stairs (one of Pat's own recurring nightmares) by the weight of the bust of her son she has been sculpting. Pat gives to Edith her preferred quotation from Thomas Paine: a reminder of the plaque featuring Paine on Grove Street, a block from where the Highsmith family lived in Manhattan in 1940–42.

September: Pat goes to Fort Worth, to find Mother Mary's house in terrible disorder and Mary deteriorating. "What terrifies me is the insanity, the knowledge that it will only get worse. She doesn't eat properly. Food is rotting . . . the dog has the mange . . . [the visit] is 'shattering.'"

Pat stops in New York, where she stays with women friends. "Overall impression: extroversion, constant stimulation, causing 'resentment' or 'reaction' such as, 'I'm holing up this weekend,' or 'I'll hang onto my little handful of friends.' Neither of these phrases uttered of course. Variety—no doubt, in New York. One is flung from the best in the arts, to the worst of humanity." As usual she haunts Greenwich Village, finding Jane Street still "quite lovely" and Eighth Street "a dump and a slum. What a shame! I remember it aglow with pretty shops" (Cahier 33). She meets with Robert Gottlieb, who will edit her at Knopf.

December: Marion Aboudaram, a novelist and translator from Paris, contacts Pat for an interview in Moncourt (for which Aboudaram has not been commissioned and which never transpires: Marion just wants to meet Pat).

1975. January: Marion and Pat become lovers. Pat works on *Edith's Diary*.

April: She goes to Stockholm on a publicity tour, noting, as always, the amount of alcohol on offer. Another note in her cahier: "7/27/75—~60 milligrams to 100 milli-litres, permitted alcohol content for drivers of cars. U.K."

"A day to remember—perhaps. On 6 August, my mother accidentally set her Texas house on fire—with a left cigarette." The place is gutted, the dog dies, and Mary is installed in a care facility, the Fireside Lodge, by her helpful nephew Dan Coates. Pat stays away, but pays for part of Mary's care.

September: Pat, along with Michael Frayn and Stanley Middleton, is invited by the Swiss Association of Teachers of English in Hölstein, Switzerland, to speak at a weeklong series of seminars. She discusses *The Glass Cell*—"its origins and difficulties"—and meets Peter Huber and Frieda Sommer. The former will become her neighbor in Tegna; the latter, one of her executors.

Jay Bernard Plangman, Pat's father, who has maintained a friendship with Mary Highsmith, offering to give her driving lessons, dies in Fort Worth, Texas. Pat does not return for her father's funeral.

1976. June. *Edith's Diary* is rejected by Knopf.

1977. Wim Wenders makes a film of *Ripley's Game, Der Amerikanishe freund* (*The American Friend*), scripted by Peter Handke. It stars Dennis Hopper and Bruno Ganz and features seven film directors in minor roles. "What have they done to my Ripley is my wail," Pat writes to Ronald Blythe. Wenders says Pat ultimately told him she liked the film. *Little Tales of Misogyny* wins the Grand Prix de l'Humeur Noir in Paris for Pat and her illustrator, Roland Topor. Hans Geissendörfer makes a film of *The Glass Cell*, *Die gläserne Zelle*. Pat likes it.

May: *Edith's Diary* is published by Heinemann in London and, later in the year, by Simon & Schuster in New York.

Claude Miller makes a film of *This Sweet Sickness, Dites-lui que je l'aime* (with Gérard Depardieu and Miou-Miou). Pat doesn't like it.

Belle Ombre, a play adapted from two Highsmith short stories—"When the Fleet Was In at Mobile" and "The Terrapin"—is produced by Francis Lacombrade at Théâtre de l'Épicerie, in Paris.

1978. Pat is elected president of the jury at the Berlin Film Festival, another unhappy public experience. Committee work is not her forte and she didn't really want the job. She remeets actress and costume designer Tabea Blumenschein and film director Ulrike Ottinger in Berlin.

Spring: Pat falls in love with Tabea Blumenschein. It is a short relationship and Pat is devastated by its end; it is as though she met her own youthful self in a mirror and then lost her. She and Tabea exchange letters for some years, meet infrequently, then fall into silence. The violence of her feelings for Tabea will affect Pat for several years.

August: Begins an affair of a few months with a young French teacher of English, Monique Buffet—it is the last affair of Pat's life. It produces many letters, good relations, and a satisfying friendship, and allows Pat to finish the novel that was interrupted by her breakup with Tabea, *The Boy Who Followed Ripley*. She dedicates the book to Monique.

1979. *Slowly, Slowly in the Wind (Leise, leise im Wind)*, a collection of reliably perverse tales, is published in England by Heinemann and in Zurich by Diogenes.

1980. 26 March: The French fiscal authority, the *douane*, raids Pat's house in Moncourt, looking for evidence of tax evasion. She is profoundly disturbed by the intrusion. Pat gives this raid as her reason for buying a house in Aurigeno, Switzerland, but, at Ellen Hill's direction, she had picked out a house in Aurigeno *before* the *douane* raided her. Pat works on a new edition of *Plotting and Writing Suspense Fiction* for St. Martin's Press and begins some stories that will appear in the collection *The Black House* (published in 1981 in the UK and 1988 in the United States.)

October: She begins to work on *People Who Knock on the Door,* published in 1983 in the UK and in 1985 in the United States.

1981. January: She travels to the United States to look at the question of Christian fundamentalism as a subject for *People Who Knock on the Door*. She goes to New York, where she sees Larry Ashmead, now at Simon & Schuster, and then goes on to Indianapolis, where she stays with her friends the concert pianist Michel Block and Charles Latimer, ex–advertising director at Heinemann. She watches televangelists on their television for a week, researching her novel at one remove. She travels to Fort Worth and Los Angeles. The entire trip takes three weeks.

February: She moves to Aurigeno, Switzerland—but just barely. French tax law requires that she spend six months out of the country and six months in it, and that's what she does, shuttling between Moncourt and Aurigeno for several years, ambivalent as to whether or not she should sell the house in Moncourt. She advertises the Moncourt house in *The New York Review of Books* for one hundred thousand dollars, reduces the price to seventy-five thousand dollars, and receives tentative interest in buying it from Peter Handke, Hedli MacNeice (her neighbor in Moncourt and the ex-wife of poet Louis MacNeice), and a "nice bachelor." In her absences, she doesn't heat the house sufficiently and the radiators burst.

1983. *People Who Knock on the Door* published in the UK. *The Black House*, a collection of short stories, and *People Who Knock on the Door* rejected by Harper & Row. She is without a publisher in the United States for two years.

April: She travels to Paris to publicize *People Who Knock on the Door*. The filmmaker and journalist Christa Maerker visits her in Aurigeno; Pat coolly points out to Maerker the local railway crossing where she has recently driven her car into a train.

June: Pat starts to plot out *Found in the Street,* a novel which takes place in her old Greenwich Village neighborhood. She gives two of her protagonists her old address on Grove Street, and her heroine is murdered at Buffie Johnson's address on Greene Street. The precipitating event in her story is a returned wallet—Pat had always dreamt of returning a wallet—and "Half the characters," she writes to her longtime correspondent Barbara Ker-Seymer, "are gay or half-gay." (Pat never did get the opportunity to return a wallet, but in Paris, in 1952, her own lost wallet was returned. She wasn't particularly grateful.) The heroine is a young girl who inspires dreams of love in all the major characters—but only the male protagonist's wife gets to sleep with her. In this work, Pat's rendering of the Manhattan ambiance of the early 1980s is based on some interesting cross-cultural misunderstandings.

Naiad Press, the lesbian publishing company in Florida founded by Barbara Grier and Donna McBride, buys the rights to reprint *The Price of Salt*. In spring of 1989 Pat writes a new preface for Naiad's edition of *The Price of Salt*.

November: She flies to New York to do more "research" for *Found in the Street,* stays in East Hampton, and sojourns in Greenwich Village at the venerable Hotel Earle (now the Washington Square Hotel). Her stay inspires the cockroach story in *Tales of Natural and Unnatural Catastrophes*. She meets both Otto Penzler, founder of the Mysterious Press, who tells her he wants to publish her books, and Anne-Elizabeth Suter, who represents Diogenes's writers in the United States.

1984. June: Bettina Berch, who teaches at Barnard College, visits Pat in Aurigeno and conducts a revealing interview with her.

October: Pat goes to Istanbul to write a travel piece about the Orient Express; it's another of her pleasurable experiences with trains. She doesn't travel now unless she is paid—or unless she can make use of her travels in a book or an article.

1985. *People Who Knock on the Door* published by Simon & Schuster in the United States. After 1985, Highsmith is without a trade publisher in the

United States. It is Otto Penzler who takes up the publishing burden with his Mysterious Press, and he publishes six Highsmith titles between 1985 and 1988. He admires her work but finds her behavior odious.

May: Marc Brandel visits her in Aurigeno with his third wife to discuss his scripting of her novel *The Blunderer* for an English film company. In 1956, Brandel had adapted *The Talented Mr. Ripley* for New York television's *Studio One*. She advances him eight thousand dollars of her own money to write the script. The film is never made.

In March, she lists "Twenty Things I Like" and "Twenty Things I Do Not Like" for Diogenes Verlag. Amongst the things she doesn't like: "A TV set in my house," "People who believe that some god or other really has control over everything but is not exercising that control just now," "Fascists," and "petty thieves and well-to-do housebreakers who specialize in silverware." Her likes include: "Swiss army knives," "Things made of leather," "Making anything out of wood," "Fountain pens with real points," "Kafka's writing," and "Being alone." In May, she answers the Proust Questionnaire for the *Frankfurter Allgemeine Zeitung* (10 May 1985 *"Fragebogen"*): she says that her best quality is "perseverance," her biggest fault is "indecision," she likes "intelligence" in women, her favorite color is still "yellow," and, at the moment, the painters she likes are "Munch" and "Balthus." (In March, her favorite painter was "Kokoschka.") She quotes Noël Coward: "Work is more fun than play."

"The only thing that makes one feel happy and alive is trying for something that one cannot get" (Cahier 36, 5 August 1985).

September: *Mermaids on the Golf Course* published by Heinemann.

1986. February: *Found in the Street* published by Heinemann and by Calmann-Lévy in Paris.

10 April: She is successfully operated on for a cancerous tumor in her lung at Brompton Hospital in London. "You must not think I had to use any discipline to stop smoking," she writes to Patricia Losey (with whose husband, Joseph Losey, she had been in discussion about a film) on 12 June 1986, "it was fear alone that made me stop."

June: She finally sells the house at 21 rue de la Boissière in Moncourt: she has owned it longer than any other house, sixteen years. The day she sells it, she tries, unsuccessfully, to buy it back for 125,000 francs more than she was paid for it. In August, she goes back to Moncourt to look for another house to buy; she fails to find anything suitable.

She sends the first of many letters to the *International Herald Tribune* criticizing Israel. Most of these letters are written under one of at least forty pseudonyms; this one is signed Edgar S. Sallich and is published on 9 July. She returns to the Brompton Hospital in London for an examination in July and is told that there is no recurrence of her cancer and that her tumor was glandular and unrelated to smoking. She lights up immediately.

1987. *Tales of Natural and Unnatural Catastrophes* is published in the UK. Her most political book. Much of the satire in the stories is awkward (vide: "President Buck Jones Rallies and Waves the Flag"), though prescient in its analysis. One of the stories, "No End in Sight," is a revolted meditation on Mary Highsmith's condition at the Fireside Lodge, her nursing home in Fort Worth. In the story, Pat gives Mary a son, who she says is herself. Pat wants to write an even more revolted sequel to "No End in Sight" called "The Tube." She never gets around to it.

April: Peter Huber tells her of the land for sale adjacent to the house he and his wife share with Bert Diener and Julia Diener-Diethelm. She buys it and works with the architect, Tobias Amman, who renovated her Aurigeno house, to design "Casa Highsmith": a white, seemingly windowless block of a house, divided into two "lobes," whose seclusions and divisions suit her imagination. She calls it "a strong house." It is a variation on the old Coates boardinghouse in Fort Worth, whose design she consults while constructing it. She signs a contract with the Atlantic Monthly Press to publish her books in America. Gary Fisketjon becomes her editor.

Claude Chabrol writes and directs a French film adaption of *The Cry of the Owl, Le Cri du hibou* (starring Christophe Malavoy, Mathilda May, Virginie Thévenet, Jacques Penot).

Pat changes her English publisher from Heinemann to Bloomsbury.

29 October: Pat appears in genial form on *New York Book Beat,* Donald Swaim's CBS radio interview program for authors. She has come to publicize Atlantic Monthly's publication of *Found in the Street,* and she makes some (for her) revealing statements.

1988. January: "Ripley touches madness," Pat writes in a cahier. Pat starts taking notes for her fifth Ripley book, *Ripley Under Water.* It becomes the last and most awkwardly plotted of the Ripleys, drawn from her fascination with sadomasochistic relations, and from her trip to Tangier to visit Buffie Johnson (and Paul Bowles). Ripley again laughs inappropriately at the double death of the "odd couple" who irritate him, and he once again tosses incriminating evidence into the Loing Canal, the canal which bordered Pat's best-loved house in Moncourt.

August: Pat goes to visit Buffie Johnson in Tangier, where Buffie is living and painting in Jane Bowles's apartment at the Immeuble Itesa just beneath Paul Bowles's apartment. Pat takes extensive notes on life in Tangier which she will use for *Ripley Under Water* and befriends Paul, whom she knew slightly from her New York years. Paul Bowles and Pat begin a correspondence. The ideas for story and novel titles at the end of her cahier become more bitter: *Sweet Smell of Death, King of the Garbage, The Bearer of Bad Tidings, Bright Murder, Dull Knife*—and the bilingual jokes get worse: *Creepy School (Crepuscule), A Fete Worse Than Death.*

September: Pat receives the Prix litteraire from the American Film Festival in Deauville, France.

December: Pat moves to her new house in Tegna.

1990. Pat is made an Officier de l'Ordre des Arts et des Lettres of France.

1991. 12 March: Mary Highsmith dies at ninety-five.

1992. January: *Little Tales of Misogyny* performed as a theater piece by the Companya Teatre de Barcelona.

Spring: Pat visits Peter Ustinov's house in Rolle for a double interview with German *Vogue*. She begins to consult with an American accountant in Geneva about a subject never far from her mind: her double taxation problem. She starts to write *Small g: A Summer Idyll.*

October: Pat travels to the United States on a publicity junket for *Ripley Under Water,* published by Knopf. She reads at Rizzoli's bookstore in New York and meets the chairman of the Yaddo board to discuss the possible donation of her house in Tegna as an artists' retreat. She is dissuaded from this idea—it is impractical—and she begins to think of other ways she might endow Yaddo. She goes to Box Canyon Ranch in Weatherford, Texas, to visit Dan and Florine Coates, then travels to Toronto to read at the Harbourfront festival on 18 October. Having initiated a correspondence with Marijane Meaker after twenty-seven years of silence, Pat spends three days at Meaker's house in East Hampton. The visit does not go well.

1993. July: She is diagnosed as seriously anemic and told to stop drinking. She does so—cold turkey—for three weeks.

1994. Fall: She makes a last, promotional trip to Paris accompanied by a Swiss neighbor; there she meets her new editor at Calmann-Lévy, Patrice Hoffman.

1995. 4 February: Pat dies in the hospital at Locarno of two competing diseases, aplastic anemia and cancer, and she dies an American citizen. The last friend she speaks to in the hospital is her American accountant, Marylin Scowden, on the evening of 3 February. Six weeks before her death, Pat changed her will, appointing Daniel Keel, already her publisher and international representative, as her literary executor; he replaces Kingsley Skattebol. Her assets and royalties are left to Yaddo. Her notebooks and diaries are found in a linen closet. 6 February: She is cremated at the cemetery in Bellinzona.

11 March: A memorial service for Pat, organized by Daniel Keel and filmed for German television, is conducted in the Catholic church at Tegna. Highsmith publishers from all over Europe fly in and join her friends in paying their respects. No editor from America comes; she no longer has a publisher in America. Pat's ashes are interred in the church's columbarium.

February: *Small g: A Summer Idyll* is published posthumously. Its most implausible plot point—a gay man is falsely told by his doctor that he has AIDS to frighten him into safe sexual practices—is taken from life: Pat's friend Frieda Sommer, who researched the book's Zurich details, has a friend on whom the character of Rikki Markwalder is vaguely based. The novel is like a classic comic book version of all previous Highsmith themes—but with attempts to be "current"; it strains towards inclusion and modernity. Even the dog in the novel—dogs in Highsmith fictions usually get kidnapped or shot—is a charming poodle who has a happy life. Pat's old friend from Florence in 1952, Brian Glanville, writes in *European Magazine* that he wishes the book "had not appeared." Josyane Savigneau, another friend, is more charitable in *Le Monde*: she says the book might be thought of as a kind of testament, "disturbed however by the evident wish for a happy end" (*Le Monde*, 17 February 1995).

1996. Pat's papers are sold to the Swiss Literary Archives in Bern, Switzerland, where they become one of the library's largest holdings.

The settlement of her estate takes eight years.

PATRICIA HIGHSMITH'S NEW YORK

From 1927 to 1960, with short intermissions, Patricia Highsmith and her parents kept apartments in New York City. Pat was schooled in New York, she started her cahiers and diaries there, and she began both her "secret" career as a scriptwriter for comic books and her public career as a writer of fiction in Manhattan.

Wherever she lived in the world, Pat continued to set many of her novels and stories in New York or in small, imaginary suburban towns—in Massachusetts, Pennsylvania, Connecticut, and New York State—just a railway ride away from the city. New York was a kind of terminal for these fictions, and her imagination went out from it and returned to it again and again.

This map shows some of the "real" addresses in Pat Highsmith's city life and some of the "fictional" addresses that feature in her work. Often enough the two coincide, especially when Pat had murder on her mind.

FACT

1. Manhattan: The Highsmiths' first Manhattan apartment on West 103rd Street.

2. Astoria, Queens: The Highsmith apartments on Twenty-first Road and Twenty-eighth Street.

3. Hell Gate Railway Bridge; Wards Island: the largest mental hospital in the United States; Rikers Island: the largest prison in New York State. These

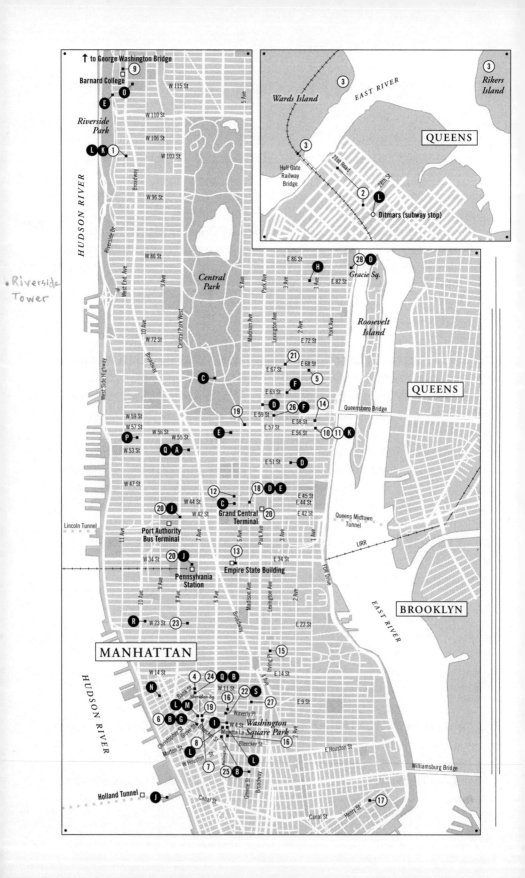

to George Washington Bridge

Barnard College

W 115 St

Riverside Park

W 110 St

W 106 St

W 103 St

Broadway

W 96 St

Riverside Dr

W 86 St

HUDSON RIVER

West End Ave

3 Ave

5 Ave

Central Park

Wards Island

EAST RIVER

Hell Gate Railway Bridge

21st Road

28th St

Ditmars (subway stop)

QUEENS

Rikers Island

Riverside Tower

West Side Highway

Riverside Dr

Broadway

Central Park West

W 72 St

W 59 St

W 57 St

W 56 St

W 55 St

W 53 St

10 Ave

9 Ave

W 47 St

Lincoln Tunnel

11 Ave

Port Authority Bus Terminal

W 44 St

W 42 St

7 Ave

Grand Central Terminal

W 34 St

Pennsylvania Station

8 Ave

Empire State Building

Madison Ave

10 Ave

9 Ave

W 23 St

MANHATTAN

W 14 St

HUDSON RIVER

Bank St

Sheridan Sq.

Christopher St

Grove St

Bleecker St

Waverly Pl

W 4 St

Minetta La

Washington Square Park

Bleecker St

Morton St

W Houston St

Greene St

Canal St

Holland Tunnel

Madison Ave

5 Ave

Park Ave

Lexington Ave

3 Ave

2 Ave

York Ave

1 Ave

E 86 St

Gracie Sq.

E 82 St

E 72 St

E 68 St

E 67 St

E 63 St

E 59 St

E 58 St

E 57 St

E 56 St

E 51 St

E 45 St

E 44 St

E 42 St

E 34 St

E 23 St

E 14 St

E 9 St

E Houston St

Roosevelt Island

Queensboro Bridge

QUEENS

Queens Midtown Tunnel

LIRR

FDR Drive

BROOKLYN

EAST RIVER

Williamsburg Bridge

Canal St

Henry St

two landmarks are in the waters just beyond Pat's first childhood apartments in Astoria.

4. The Highsmith apartment at One Bank Street in Greenwich Village (on the site of an apartment building formerly occupied by Willa Cather).

5. Julia Richman High School at 327 East Sixty-seventh Street.

6. The Highsmith apartment at 48 Grove Street. The radical political philosopher Sidney Hook was a neighbor here; John Wilkes Booth is said to have plotted the assassination of Abraham Lincoln in the Federal mansion across the street.

7. Marie's Crisis Café: The piano bar on Grove Street at whose site Tom Paine died, it is a block from the Highsmith apartment at 48 Grove and next to the building where the murder that inspired the film *On the Waterfront* took place. Pat loved piano bars and musical comedy; she followed the Revuers—Judy Holliday, Betty Comden, and Adolph Green—in all their Greenwich Village venues.

8. Pat's summer sublet on Morton Street in 1940. "I consider my experience in Morton Street, my contact with various people there, quite invaluable."

9. Barnard College, Pat's "ivory tower," 1938–42.

10. Mary and Stanley Highsmith's apartment on East Fifty-seventh Street.

11. Pat's apartment at 353 East Fifty-sixth Street.

12. Sangor-Pines Comics Shop, 10 West Forty-fifth Street.

13. Timely comics (later Marvel Comics), Empire State Building.

14. Café Nicholson on East Fifty-eighth Street.

15. Pat's apartment at 75 Irving Place.

16. Village hangouts: The Jumble Shop, the Prohibition era tearoom at 176 MacDougal Street, and the lesbian bar L's (or El's) at 116 MacDougal Street.

17. Henry Street Settlement House: Where Pat took piano lessons from Judy [Tuvim] Holliday's mother.

18. Brooks Brothers, Madison Avenue at Forty-fourth Street, Pat's preferred place to buy shirts and vests.

19. Art galleries: Christopher Fourth: the Village art gallery belonging to Pat's friends in Manhattan and New Hope, Peggy and Michael Lewis. The Midtown Galleries where Betty Parsons worked; the Betty Parsons Gallery opened in 1946.

20. Train and bus stations: Pennsylvania Station: The old Penn Station, modelled on the Baths of Caraculla; Grand Central Terminal; Port Authority Bus Terminal.

21. Caso's Drugstore: Corner of Third Avenue and Sixty-eighth Street, "where I used to go at sixteen and fifteen, when I went to high school a block from here. . . . And the crises I have known here, the faces I looked for, and saw, or missed, the afternoons metamorphosed by some overwhelming event that happened in school that day, days that twisted one's life around completely and permanently, I remember them."

22. The Hotel Earle: corner of Waverly Place and Washington Square (now the Washington Square Hotel); Pat stayed here and so did Mary Highsmith.

23. The Chelsea Hotel: Pat stayed here several times in the 1960s when she was taking notes on her old Greenwich Village haunts.

24. Kingsley Skattebol, Pat's friend from Barnard, had an apartment on West Eleventh Street.

25. Buffie Johnson, Pat's old friend, owned a loft building at 102 Greene Street.

26. Bloomingdale's department store: Pat, in real life, met Kathleen Senn here while she was working in the toy department and living on East Fifty-sixth Street.

27. The East Village and East Ninth Street: Respectively, the artistic domain and home of writer and performance artist Lil Picard, Pat's longtime friend.

28. Gracie Square: The Upper East Side address where Pat visited the painter Fanny Myers [Brennan], who, like Cleo in *The Talented Mr. Ripley*, painted miniscule landscapes.

FICTION

A. *Strangers on a Train*: Guy Haines's apartment on West Fifty-third Street which Charles Bruno, his Alter Ego, haunts.

B. *Found in the Street*: Ralph Linderman's apartment on Bleecker Street Pat makes two geographical errors in *Found in the Street*: she gives Ralph a job at an arcade on Eighth Avenue in the West Eighties. Eighth Avenue becomes Central Park West at Fifty-ninth Street, and the arcades themselves would have been in the West Forties.

    Found in the Street: Natalia and Jack Sutherland's apartment on Grove Street.

    Found in the Street: Elsie Tyler shares an apartment on Minetta Lane and works in a coffee shop on Seventh Avenue South. She is photographed at the Chelsea Hotel.

    Found in the Street: The Armstrongs' apartment on West Eleventh Street. (Kingsley Skattebol had an apartment at West Eleventh Street.)

    Found in the Street: Elsie Tyler's apartment on Greene Street, where she is murdered. (Buffie Johnson owned a loft building at 102 Greene Street.)

C. *The Blunderer*: West Forty-fourth Street: Walter Stackhouse's law office, around the corner from the Sangor-Pines office.

    The Blunderer: Central Park, where Walter Stackhouse mistakes a stranger for Melchior Kimmel, kills him, and is himself murdered by Kimmel.

D. *The Talented Mr. Ripley*: East Fifty-first Street between Second and Third avenues is where Tom Ripley shares a dingy brownstone apartment with Bob, "a window dresser." He receives extorted checks there under the name George McAlpin. Previously Ripley lived in a brownstone on East Forty-fifth Street with a man who likes to shelter young men.

    The Talented Mr. Ripley: Park Avenue: home of Dickie Greenleaf's parents, Herbert and Emily.

    The Talented Mr. Ripley: Gracie Square: Ripley's friend, Cleo Dobelle, who paints pictures so small they can be viewed only through a magnifying glass, lives at this Upper East Side address.

The Talented Mr. Ripley: Brooks Brothers: Tom Ripley buys clothes for Dickie Greenleaf and himself here.

E. *This Sweet Sickness*: Romeo Salta's Restaurant on West Fifty-sixth Street where David Kelsey, in the character of his Alter Ego, William Neumeister, appears with his imaginary girlfriend Annabelle and insists on "Two orders of everything, please." The owner of Salta's later sent Pat a case of wine in New Hope to thank her.

This Sweet Sickness: 410 Riverside Drive, the apartment from which David Kelsey/William Neumeister jumps to his death (near Barnard College in Morningside Heights).

This Sweet Sickness: Brooks Brothers: Kelsey/Neumeister wants to shop here, but can't.

F. *The Price of Salt*: Frankenberg's department store (Bloomingdale's in real life) at Fifty-ninth Street and Lexington Avenue, where Therese meets Carole, while working in the toy department.

The Price of Salt: East Sixty-third Street is where Therese lives; it is also where Pat rented her first room after graduating from Barnard College.

The Price of Salt: Frankenburg's department store (Bloomingdale's in real life). Pat has a salesgirl steal Therese's steak from the cloakroom—"Wolves, she had thought, wolves, stealing a bloody bag of meat"—just as someone stole her own steak while she was working at Bloomingdale's in December of 1948.

G. *Edith's Diary*: Edith Howland's apartment on Grove Street, where Cliffie tries to suffocate the family cat.

H. *The Cry of the Owl*: The apartment on East Eighty-second Street where Nickie Jurgen, Robert Forester's pathological ex-wife, lives with her new husband. She hides Robert's opponent, Greg Wyncoop, in a shabby hotel "off Fourth Avenue." Fourth Avenue is also where Carol, at the end of *The Price of Salt,* gets a job in a furniture store.

I. *The Tremor of Forgery*: Howard Ingham's apartment on "Fourth Street near Washington Square" where John Castlewood, the director of the film Howard is writing, kills himself.

J. *Strangers on a Train, The Price of Salt, The Cry of the Owl, This Sweet Sickness,*
etc.: all novels in which the Holland Tunnel, the George Washington
Bridge, the Port Authority Bus Station, and New York's two train stations
are featured.

K. "The Terrapin": Victor, who murders his artist mother (and is given Pat's
childhood preferences in books), lives with his mother on Riverside Drive
(on the Upper West Side, where the Highsmiths first lived in Manhattan),
then on Third Avenue, in the vicinity of Mary and Stanley Highsmith's
last New York apartment.

L. *A Dog's Ransom*: Riverside Park, where Tina the poodle is kidnapped and
killed. The dog's owners, Greta and Ed, live nearby on West 106th Street.

    A Dog's Ransom: 103rd Street and West End Avenue, where Kenneth
Rowajinski, the poison-pen writer and dog killer, lives. It is the site of the
Highsmiths' first apartment in New York. York Avenue in the East Sixties:
the ransom dropoff for the dog is near Pat's first rented room in the East
Sixties, and near the Julia Richman High School on East Sixty-seventh
Street.

    A Dog's Ransom: Astoria: Clarence Duhamel, the good cop, is brought up
in Astoria, reading the authors Pat read: Krafft-Ebing, Freud, Dostoyevsky,
and Proust. He also has Pat's home subway stop, Ditmars—which she misspells in the novel. MacDougal Street in Greenwich Village is where he
stays with his girlfriend.

    A Dog's Ransom: Morton Street: the location of the apartment to which
the dognapper Kenneth Rowajinski is released from Bellevue Hospital. He
is killed there.

M. *The Click of the Shutting*: Gregory Bullick lives in a Greenwich Village loft
with his father. His subway stop is Pat's home stop when she was his age
and living on Grove Street: the Christopher Street station at Sheridan
Square.

N. "Blow It" (from *The Black House*): Jane Street, Harry Rowe's apartment in
Greenwich Village where he separately entertains the two women he
can't decide to marry.

O. "The Baby Spoon" (from *Slowly, Slowly in the Wind*): Faculty housing near
Columbia University (Pat's alma mater) where Claude Lamm, the pompous

professor, is murdered by his former student, Winston, who steals his wife's baby spoon. "Claude suspected that Winston had a vaguely homosexual attachment to him, and Claude had heard that homosexuals were apt to take something from someone they cared for." Winston lives in a "genuine garret at the top of a brownstone in the West Seventies."

P. "The Romantic" (from *Mermaids on the Golf Course*): West Fifty-fifth Street: location of the apartment where Isabel Crane takes care of her invalid mother.

Q. "The Network" (from *Slowly, Slowly in the Wind*): "Seventh Avenue and 53rd Street" along with "West 11th Street, Gramercy Park, even Yorkville"—all of them considered "hearts of the city" by a network of friends in Manhattan portrayed by Pat as part of the great scamming racket that is New York. The "East Village" is a place where blacks "cut your fingers off if they can't get the rings off" easily.

R. "The Still Point of the Turning World": Mrs. Robinson lives in the London Terrace Apartments on West Twenty-third Street. Philip and Dickie have their encounter in the little park on the West Side Highway.

S. "Notes from a Respectable Cockroach": The Hotel Earle (Pat calls it the Hotel Duke) inspired this cockroach story.

CHARTS, MAPS, DIAGRAMS, AND PLANS

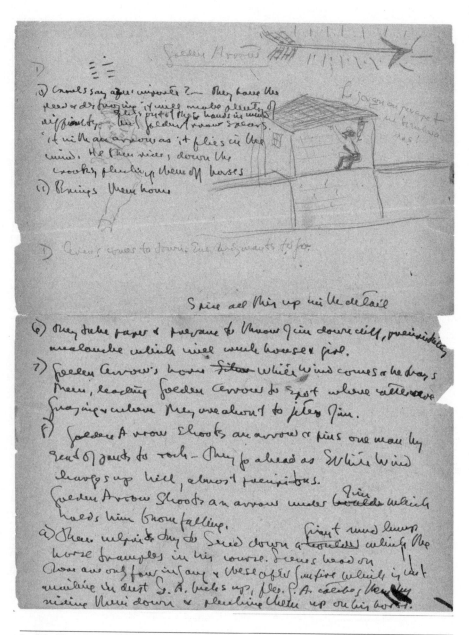

1. "Golden Arrow" Diagram. Drawn by Pat Highsmith to help plot a comic book script.

2. Lover Chart. This is the chart Pat Highsmith created in 1945 to rank and compare her lovers. The initials of the women have been removed to protect their privacy.

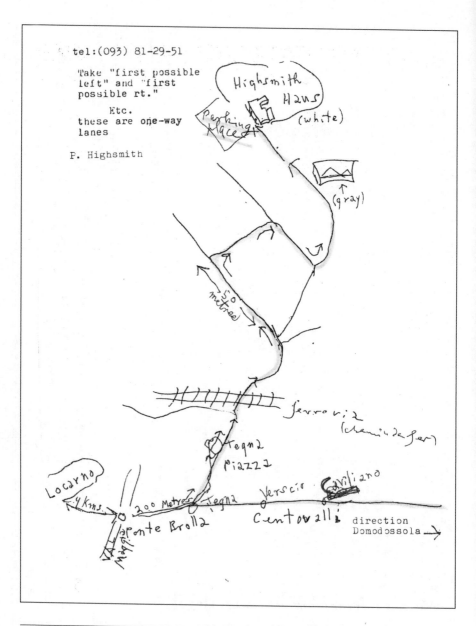

3. Map to Highsmith Haus in Tegna, made by Pat Highsmith for Monique Buffet.

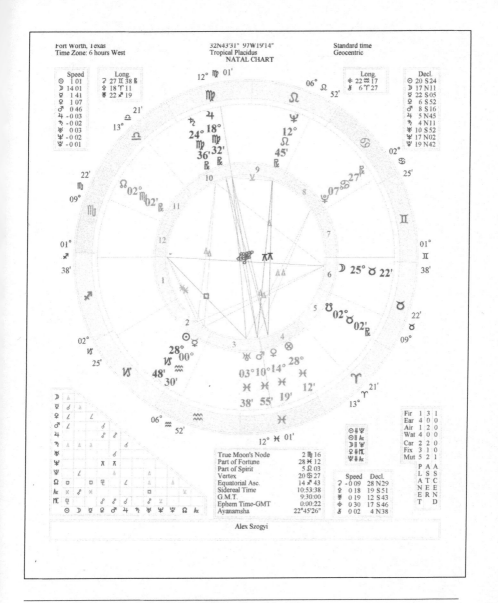

4. Natal Chart of Patricia Highsmith by Alex Szogyi.

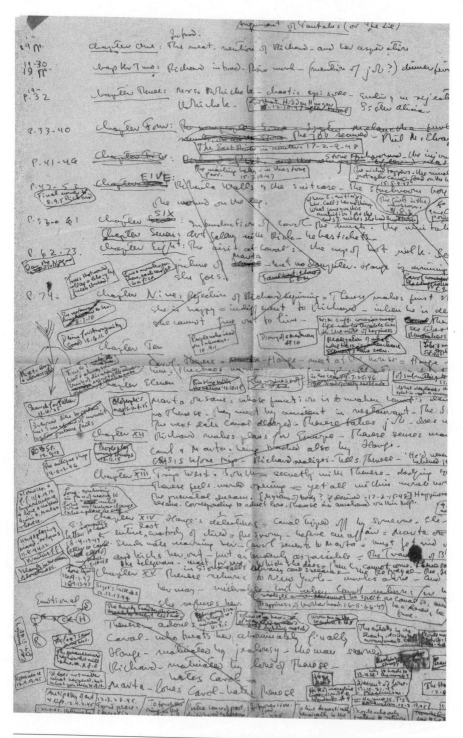

5. Diagram for *The Price of Salt*, called here *Argument of Tantalus* (or The Lie).

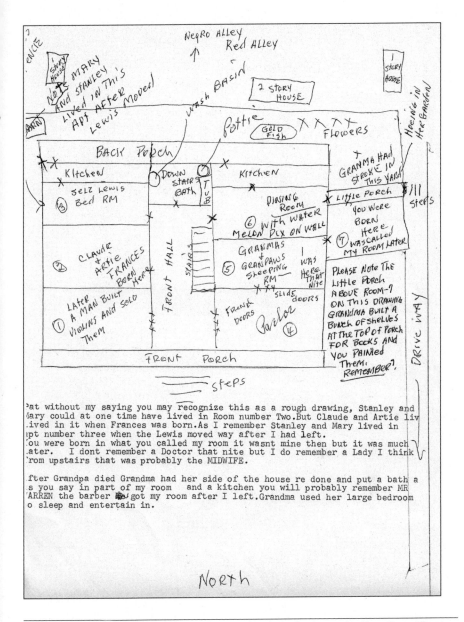

'at without my saying you may recognize this as a rough drawing, Stanley and
Mary could at one time have lived in Room number Two.But Claude and Artie liv
.ived in it when Frances was born.As I remember Stanley and Mary lived in
ipt number three when the Lewis moved way after I had left.
'ou were born in what you called my room it wasnt mine then but it was much
.ater.   I dont remember a Doctor that nite but I do remember a Lady I think
'rom upstairs that was probably the MIDWIFE.

.fter Grandpa died Grandma had her side of the house re done and put a bath a
.s you say in part of my room   and a kitchen you will probably remember MR
'ARREN the barber got my room after I left.Grandma used her large bedroom
o sleep and entertain in.

6. Plan of Willie Mae's boardinghouse in Fort Worth, drawn by Dan Oscar Coates.

NOTES AND SOURCES

Patricia Highsmith used the American dating system in her cahiers and diaries—except, of course, when she didn't. I have kept to her wayward customs as nearly as possible, using the numbers and forward slashes she employed for her diary and cahier entries, and reverting unwaveringly to European dating for interviews, letters, articles, and other written communications. Unless otherwise indicated, all primary (and much secondary) material comes from the Swiss Literary Archives in Bern, Switzerland. Translations from the French and Spanish are my own; German translations are by Ulrich Weber, Anna von Planta, and Ina Lannert.

The following abbreviations have been adopted for some of the institutions and proper names cited in the notes:

BCA—Barnard College Archives (Patricia Highsmith Records: photographs, transcripts, college publications), New York, New York

BKS—Barbara Ker-Seymer

CLA—Calmann-Lévy Archives (dossier Patricia Highsmith), Paris, France

CURB—Columbia University, Rare Book and Manuscript Library (Harper & Row Archives), New York, New York

DOC—Dan Oscar Coates

FWPL—Fort Worth Public Library (*Fort Worth Star-Telegram* Archives), Fort Worth, Texas

GFF—Gary Fisketjon's publishing files concerning Patricia Highsmith; courtesy Gary Fisketjon, New York, New York

HRC—Harry Ransom Humanities Research Center (Alfred A. Knopf Archives,

William Aspenwall Bradley Archives, Jane Bowles Archives), University
of Texas, Austin, Texas

JAMAM—James A. Michener Art Museum (Patricia Highsmith Records), New
Hope, Pennsylvania

JBP—Jay Bernard Plangman

KKS—Kate Kingsley Skattebol

MB—Monique Buffet

MC—Menil Collection (Rosalind Constable Archives), Houston, Texas

MCH—Mary Coates Highsmith

NM—L'Office National Météorologique, Paris, France

NYPL—New York Public Library (Yaddo Archives, *The New Yorker* Records),
New York, New York

PH—Patricia Highsmith

PS 122—Public School 122 (Patricia Highsmith Records), Astoria, Queens,
New York

SH—Stanley Highsmith

SLA—Swiss Literary Archives (Patricia Highsmith Archives), Bern, Switzerland

TGA—Tate Gallery Archives (Barbara Ker-Seymer Papers, 1925–81), London,
England (Courtesy Jane Stevenson)

UIL—University of Iowa Libraries Special Collections Department (Papers of
Lil Picard, 1915–94), Iowa City, Iowa

UML—University of Maryland Libraries (Djuna Barnes Collection), College
Park, Maryland

VCL—Vassar College Library Special Collections (Mary McCarthy Archives),
Poughkeepsie, New York

For simplicity, all written communications are referred to as "letters" and
are followed whenever possible by their dates of composition. All interviews
are indicated by the abbreviation CWA, "conversation with the author." All
interviews are dated except those with Don Coates, Kate Kingsley Skattebol,
and Jim Amash—with whom I conversed so frequently over the years that
dating every one of our communications seemed beside the point.

NOTES

A NOTE ON BIOGRAPHY

1. CWA Marylin Scowden, 1 Sept. 2002.
2. Diary 10, 14 June 1950.
3. "It is curious that in the most interesting periods of one's life, one never writes one's diary. There are some things that even a writer cannot put down in words (at the time). He shrinks from putting them down. And what a loss!" Cahier 22, 8/18/53.
4. "I must remember to use books as books instead of a drug." Cahier 2, 5/27/40.
5. Cahier 22, 9/25/53.
6. Virginia Woolf, Notebooks, Monk's House Papers, University of Sussex, quoted by Hermione Lee in *Virginia Woolf* (New York: Vintage Books, 1999), p. 10.
7. PH letter to Mr. Reichardt, 3 Nov. 1970 (Montmachoux).
8. Cahier 24, 12/15/55.
9. Diary 3, Sept. 17, 1942.
10. PH letter to DOC, 26 Dec. 1968.
11. Diary 8, May 10, 1948.
12. Cahier 28, 8/31/66.
13. PH, *Plotting and Writing Suspense Fiction* (Boston: The Writer, 1966), p. 51.
14. Cahier 26, 10/14/60.
15. Pat scribbled this phrase on a letter from DOC about her mother, Mary, in February 1974, adding: "There is no end and no hope."
16. Pat thought this about herself as well: "Further consolation: my personal maladies and malaises are only those of my own generation and of my time, heightened." Cahier 20, 10/9/50.
17. Cahier 24, 1/3/56: "And then alone, unconsoled, one rejoices suddenly at being able to take part in that purely human sport of thinking. One is at last a member of the human race, in the only way one can be. To think, thinking, is the only passport."

1. HOW TO BEGIN: PART 1

1. CWA Dr. Jerry Bails, 13 Mar. 2002.
2. Cahier 31, 8/15/72.
3. CWA Don Coates, 20 Apr. 2002. PH herself wrote to President Jimmy Carter, senators, and cabinet officials with her own suggestions for improving the country.

4. Cahier 28, 3/30/66. Also PH, *Edith's Diary* (New York: Atlantic Monthly Press 1989), pp. 94–95. Pat had a precedent for her plans to mobilize children: in the early 1940s, when she was writing scripts for comic book publishers, the legendary team of Simon and Kirby created the *Boy Commandos*, a comic strip about a group of children from Allied countries whose covert and patriotic operations often stopped Hitler's worst plans.

5. Cahier 11, 10/14/44.

6. "[A]ny manuscript, even a perfectly typed one, looks absolutely awful. . . . Pages become dog-eared if not grimy, and all in all the manuscript no longer looks like something you want to present with pride to your parents." PH, *Plotting and Writing Suspense Fiction*, p. 101.

7. Cahier 3, 4/27/41.

8. Cahier 31, 1/30/70.

9. Cahier 32, 11/25/73.

10. Cahier 31, endpaper list of titles.

11. In a 1989 letter to Kingsley Skattebol, she was still calling it "my favorite" typewriter.

12. CWA Phyllis Nagy, 26 June 2002.

13. PH, *Plotting and Writing Suspense Fiction,* p. 68.

14. CWA Josyane Savigneau, 1 July 2002.

15. CWA Henri Robillot, 6 Nov. 2002.

16. CWA Linda Ladurner, 10 May 2003.

17. Barbara Skelton, "Patricia Highsmith at Home," *London Magazine,* Aug.–Sept. 1995.

18. Cahier 7, June 12, 1942.

19. Cahier 27, 9/10/62

20. Cahier 5, 12/2/41.

2. HOW TO BEGIN: PART 2

1. CWA Camilla Butterfield, 17 Dec. 2003.

2. Diary 1, Dec. 31, 1941.

3. PH letter to KKS, 8 Jan. 1965.

4. Diary 13, Nov. 16, 1962.

5. Pat may have lost her head over Caroline Besterman, but she never lost her consciousness of details or objects; she noted the loss of that earring very precisely. See "The Real Romance of Objects: Part I."

6. Diary 13, Nov. 12, 1962.

7. The Prix Goncourt for 1962 was won by the novel *Les Bagages des Sables*, written by André Langfus. Pat, nonetheless, notes in her diary that the award was "[w]on by a woman."

8. Diary 13, Nov. 16–20, 1962.

9. Diary 13, Nov. 26, 1962.

10. Cahier 27, Dec. 5, 1962.

11. Ibid.

12. Cahier 27, Dec. 7, 1962.

13. CWA Ronald Blythe, 20 Sept. 2004. He says that both he and Pat had brick-floored studies.

14. Cahier 27, 12/13/64.

15. Ibid., 12/16/64.

16. PH letter to KKS, 8 Jan. 1965.

17. MCH letter to PH, undated.

18. PH letter to KKS, 8 Jan. 1965.

19. CWA KKS.

20. PH letter to Ronald Blythe, 25 July 1972 (Collection Ronald Blythe).

21. Ibid. (Collection Ronald Blythe).

22. CWA Ronald Blythe, 20 Sept. 2004.

23. Ibid.

24. Cahier 5, 4/12/41.

25. CWA Ronald Blythe, 20 Sept. 2004.

26. CWA Barbara Roett, 18 May 2003.

27. Ibid.

28. It was demolished by a friend of Evelyn Waugh who hoped to put up something even better.

29. PH letter to Alex Szogyi, 12 May 1965.

30. CWA Camilla Butterfield, 17 Dec. 2003.

31. Ibid.

32. Ibid.

33. Ibid.

34. Ibid.

35. Ibid.

36. MCH letter to PH, undated.

37. PH letter to DOC, 13 May 1977.

38. PH letter to Alex Szogyi, 10 July 1967.

39. PH letter to Ronald Blythe, 25 July 1972.

40. PH, "No End in Sight"; (*Tales of Natural and Unnatural Catastrophes*, London: Bloomsbury, 2005); numerous letters, remarks.

41. "I have in my possession two large envelopes of letters from my mother, going back as far as 1958. These are labelled FOR DOCTOR OR PSYCHIATRIST ONLY."

42. Cahier 36, 5/28/85.

43. PH letter to KKS, 27 July 1964.

44. PH letter to BKS, 17/2/68.

45. Cahier 2, Dec. 1939. Italics added.

46. MCH letter to Marijane Meaker, "Friday AM 11th" (no other date).

47. Diary 1, Dec. 1941, p. 109.

48. Ibid., p. 112.

49. Cahier 26, 8/4/62.

50. Ibid., 10/7/61.

51. Ginette Billard letter to the author, 23 Mar. 2002.

52. CWA Linda Ladurner, 10 May 2003. Letters to the author 12–16 May 2003.

53. She put this in Cahier 26 in 1960, and ten years later it turned up in slightly altered form in the writings of the dead painter Derwatt in *Ripley Under Ground*.

54. Cahier 12, 4/6/45.

55. Henry James, "Preface to the New York Edition," *Portrait of a Lady* (London: Penguin 2003), pp. 41–55.

56. Chart of Apr. 1945, inserted in Cahier 12.

57. Ibid.

58. CWA Gary Fisketjon, 10 Dec. 2002.

59. CWA Larry Ashmead, 26 Nov. 2002.

60. CWA Otto Penzler, 27 Dec. 2002.

61. Cahier 29, 1/28/67.

62. Cahier 16, 11/20/47.

63. PH, "My First Job," *Oldie*, 1993.

64. PH letter to KKS, 1 Dec. 1986.

65. Cahier 9, PH transcription of high school notebooks, 1938.

66. CWA KKS, 31 Aug. 2005. It was a very late-life tattoo, and how Pat came by it is unknown. Pat's last three lovers, Marion Aboudaram, Tabea Blumenschein, and Monique Buffet, all say she had no tattoo when they knew her. Kingsley Skattebol caught sight of it in Tegna once when Pat's watchband moved to reveal it.

67. Cahier 13, 8/30/45.

68. Ibid.

69. Michael Haederle, interview with PH, *Houston Chronicle*, Feb. 3, 1991.

70. Diary 8, Dec. 22, 1947.

71. Cahier 25, 7/8/58.

72. Cahier 28, 9/12/65.

73. Cahier 5, 4/12/41.

74. Cahier 16, 10/4/47.

75. Cahier 17, 5/14/48.

76. Pat's notation in Cahier 21 on 4/2/52 is one of many examples: "And Ellen telling me gleefully, gleefully, with a smile that spreads over her whole little face, that she likes going to bed with me more than with anyone she has ever known before. . . . Ah women."

77. Cahier 18, 10/21/49.

78. Ibid., 10/24/49.

79. Diary 10, Mar. 15, 1950; Mar. 28, 1949.

80. PH letter to KKS, 5 Mar. 1958: "I have joined the very small Presbyterian choir out here in Palisades. Only trouble is I can be heard when I sing."

81. CWA KKS, 20 May 2002.

82. PH on Don Swaim's radio show, *Book Notes*, 29 Oct. 1987.

83. Diary 8, 22/6/1947.

84. Cahier 17, June 30, 1948.

85. "Between Jane Austen and Philby", PH, typed on ms: "Sept. 1968 written for 'Vogue, London." June 1968. MS.

86. Cahier 15, 3/8/47

87. CWA M. Knet, 6 Nov. 2002.

88. Cahier 27, Dec. 5, 1962.

3. A SIMPLE ACT OF FORGERY: PART 1

1. Pat's London hostess informed her by note that a writer from *Harper's Bazaar* wanted her comments on the man "who has just knifed the Poussin in the National Gallery." In a postscript, the hostess, a worldly woman quoting a former Highsmith comment, recommended that Pat tell the journalist to "stuff it."

2. Cahier 35, 3/18/81.

3. PH, *The Boy Who Followed Ripley* (London: Vintage, 2001), p. 183.

4. PH letter to Alex Szogyi, 15 Mar. 1969.

5. Ibid.

6. Cahier 32, 5/8/72.

7. Diary 4, 7/20/43.

8. Cahier 2, 2/40.

9. "You can easily see / Upon closer enquiry / There are things in this book / That belong in a diary / But there're things in my diary / (Where you'll never look) / That with proper deletions / might go in this book" (Cahier 2, 7/13/40)

10. CWA Dan Walton Coates, 22 Nov. 2003.

11. Gore Vidal, *Palimpsest* (London: Penguin Books, 1995) p. 5.

12. CWA Tabea Blumenschein, 15 June 2003.

13. Diary 16, 20 Aug. 1969.

14. Draft letters, pseudonymous political correspondence of PH.

15. CWA Christa Maerker, 21 July 2004.

16. Ibid.

17. Cahier 34, 3/22/78.

18. CWA David Streiff, 20 Jan. 2001.

19. PH letter to Lil Picard, 20 Aug. 1970 (UIL).

20. CWA Christa Maerker, 21 July 2004.

21. CWA Susannah Clapp, 2 Jan. 2003.

22. CWA Caroline Besterman, 19 Dec. 2003.

23. CWA Marion Aboudaram, 23 Sept. 2002.

24. CWA Linda Ladurner, 10 May 2003.

25. PH letter to Lil Picard, 11 June 1969 (UIL).

26. Ibid.

27. CWA Susannah Clapp, 2 Jan. 2003.

28. Ibid.

29. Gerald Peary, "Patricia Highsmith," *Sight and Sound* 75, no. 2 (Spring 1988): pp.104–5.

30. PH, *Plotting and Writing Suspense Fiction* (New York: St. Martin's Griffin, 1990), p. 57.

31. PH letter to KKS, 14 Mar. 1968. Sarraute, who loved Americans and gave Highsmith a warm welcome, said that Colette was too feminine for her; Highsmith bravely defended Colette's virility.

32. Cahier 34, 12–18 June 1979.

33. CWA Tabea Blumenschein, 15 June 2003.

34. PH, *The Boy Who Followed Ripley* (London: Vintage, 2001), p. 90.

35. PH, *Edith's Diary,* p. 251.

36. Cahier 34, Mar. 22, 1978.

37. Cahier 12, Apr. 4, 1945.

38. Cahier 3, 2/10/41; Cahier, 3, 4/12/41.

39. CWA Tabea Blumenschein, 15 June 2003.

40. CWA Marion Aboudaram, 23 Sept. 2002.

41. Cahier 34, Apr. 11, 1978.

42. Duncan Fallowell, "The Talented Miss Highsmith," *Sunday Times Telegraph Magazine,* 20 Feb. 2000 (interview with PH conducted in 1987).

43. CWA Barbara Roett, 18 May 2003.

44. Alain Oulman letters to PH, 23 May and 25 Sept. 1985 (CLA).

45. CWA Susannah Clapp, 2 Jan. 2003.

46. PH, *The Price of Salt* (Tallahassee, FL: Naiad Press, 1993), p. 21.

47. Ibid., Afterword (no pagination in this edition for the Afterword).

48. Cahier 20, 10/20/50. "Now, now, now, to fall in love with my book—this same day I have decided not to publish it, not for an indefinite length of time. But I shall continue to work on it for some weeks to come, to polish and perfect it. I shall fall in love with it now, in a different way from the way I loved it before. This love is endless, disinterested, unselfish, impersonal even (P. of S.)."

49. Cahier 34, 4/4/78.

50. Ibid.

51. PH letter to Christopher Petit, 19 Apr. 1978 (Collection Christopher Petit).

52. CWA Christopher Petit, 9 Jan. 2004.

53. PH letter to Christopher Petit, 19 Apr. 1978.

54. Christopher Petit letter to the author, 29 Jan. 2004 (Collection Christopher Petit).

55. Pat did this again in March of 1989, when she complained in a letter to the *Washington Post* that the writer David Streitfeld didn't mention her "resentment" against Israel in the interview he did with her.

56. Christopher Petit letter to the author, 29 Jan. 2004.

57. Ibid.

58. PH letter to Christopher Petit, 25 Apr. 1978 (Collection Christopher Petit).

59. PH letter to Christopher Petit, 8 Aug. 1978 (Collection Christopher Petit).

60. PH, *This Sweet Sickness* (New York: Norton, 2002), p. 238.

61. PH, *The Boy Who Followed Ripley* (London: Vintage, 2001), p. 178.

62. PH, *Those Who Walk Away* (London, Hamlyn, 1985), p. 117.

4. A SIMPLE ACT OF FORGERY: PART 2

1. Cahier 28, 12/7/62. Every subsequent quotation in this chapter, unless otherwise noted, comes from Pat's notebook entry of 12 July.

2. Joan Schenkar, *Truly Wilde* (London: Virago, 2000), p. 240.

5. LA MAMMA: PART 1

1. Anna von Planta, "Notes on Stories" in PH, *Nothing That Meets the Eye* (New York: W.W. Norton, 2002), p. 451.

2. Cahier 31, 6/5/71.

3. CWA Janice Robertson, 22 June 2003.

4. PH letter to Curt Johnson, editor of *Who's Who*, undated.

5. PH letter to *EQQM*, Jan. 5, 1962 (CURB).

6. CWA Janice Robertson, 22 June 2003.

7. Barbara Skelton, "Patricia Highsmith at Home," *London Magazine*, 1995.

8. Cahier 18, 6/13/49.

9. CWA Dan Walton Coates, 22 Nov. 2003.

10. MCH letter to PH, Jan. 1965.

11. CWA Tommy Tune, 14 Jan. 2003.

12. Ibid.

13. Ibid.

14. Ibid.

15. JBP letter to PH, undated.

16. JBP letter to PH, undated.

17. CWA Dan Walton Coates, 22 Nov. 2003.

18. JBP letter to PH, undated.

19. On 24 Oct. 1971, in Cahier 31, Pat wrote: "My mother told me she saw my father first in a photograph in a Ft Worth photographer's window and—sought (somehow) his acquaintance. It occurs to me I have preferred people who sought *me* out, essentially, rather than those I had to make an effort for. I mean my emotional fascination lingered . . . far longer for those who made the first advances to me."

20. On 9 Apr. 1978, in Cahier 34, Pat wrote a love poem to her last *coup de coeur,* the twenty-five-year old actress Tabea Blumenschein: "I fell in love not with flesh and blood / But with a picture. . . ."

21. PH letter to JBP, 15 July 1971

22. JBP letter to PH, 30 July 1971.

23. CWA Dan Walton Coates, 22 Nov. 2003. Dan Coates, who said that Coates family members still wear Judson cowboy boots, was wearing a pair of Judson boots himself when he spoke with me.

24. Joan Dupont "The Poet of Apprehension," *Village Voice*, 30 May 1995.

25. CWA Don Coates, 14 Apr. 2002.

26. CWA Dan Walton Coates, 22 Nov. 2003.

27. PH letter to MCH, 12 Apr. 1966.

28. MCH letter to DOC, 1965, undated.

29. PH letter to DOC, 13 May 1977.

30. PH letter to DOC, 12 Dec. 1974.

31. PH letter to JBP, 27 Mar. 1972.

32. MCH letter to PH, undated.

33. CWA Camilla Butterfield, 6 Nov. 2003.

34. CWA Marijane Meaker, 1 Feb. 2004.

35. Cahier 36, 5/28/85.

36. PH letter to DOC, 11 Nov. 1986.

37. MCH letter to PH, "Tuesday AM" (no date).

38. MCH letter to PH, 1 Jan. 1965.

39. Ibid.

40. Ibid.

6. LA MAMMA: PART 2

1. Bettina Berch, unpublished interview with PH, 1984 (Collection Bettina Berch).

2. MCH letter to PH, "Tuesday AM" (no date).

3. Coates and Highsmith family home movies shot in Texas and New York State, 1930s–1950s.

4. In later life, Pat was to become obsessed by the Stewart genealogy although, with all her travelling, she never managed to visit either of the Stewart countries of orgin: Scotland and Ireland. One of the Stewart cousins Pat corresponded with at the end of her life was a state trooper with a passion for the works of Tom Clancy and Len Deighton. "I get the reading from both my Mother and Father," he wrote to Pat, adding that he "was really tired of seeing death." Mary Highsmith, with Pat's same interest in family genealogy, had already corresponded with his parents.

5. Masonic Lodge No. 158, Winchester, Tennessee: entries for William Stewart.

6. Stewart family history compiled by Samuel Smith Stewart, 1935.

7. Marshall Wingfield, *General A. P. Stewart, His Life and Letters* (Memphis, TN: West Tennessee Historical Society, 1954), pp. 204–5.

8. Obituary: "Mrs. D.C. Coates, 88, to Be Buried Today," *Fort Worth Star-Telegram*, 7 Feb. 1955.

9. Wingfield, *General A. P. Stewart*, pp. 204–5.

10. CWA Don Coates, 7 Sept. 2002.

11. CWA Don Coates, 22 Aug. 2003.

12. *Houston Chronicle*, "Fisher Dye Works Owner Does Pictures on Paper by Embroidery," 7 Aug. 1955. "He often watched his mother, the late Mrs. Willie Mae Coates, as she embroidered an old picture of the family homestead in Coates Bend, Alabama. So about six years ago he decided to try the art himself."

13. Joan Dupont, "The Mysterious Patricia Highsmith," *Paris Metro*, 9 Nov. 1977.

14. CWA Don Coates, 22 Aug. 2003.

15. Ibid.

16. CWA Dan Walton Coates, 22 Nov. 2003.

17. Ibid.

18. CWA Don Coates, 22 Aug. 2003.

19. PH letter to SH, 29 Aug. 1970.

20. Eugene Walter letter to PH, 14 Sept. 1992.

21. MCH letter to PH, undated.

22. MCH letter to PH, undated.

23. Diary 12, 23 Jan. 1953.

24. MCH letter to PH, undated.

25. Cahier 36, 28/5/85.

26. Cahier 9, PH transcription of high school notebooks, Apr. 27, 1938. "Mother warns me about letters to Cralick & Marj."

27. CWA Annabelle Potin, 24 Mar. 2007.

28. MCH letter to PH, undated.

29. Cahier 16, 7/5/47.

30. CWA Don Coates, 11 May 2002.

31. CWA Don Coates, 14 Apr. 2002.

32. CWA Dan Walton Coates, 22 Nov. 2003.

33. An "orphan" who still has parents is Judith Thurman's useful description throughout her biography of Colette, *Secrets of the Flesh* (New York: Alfred A. Knopf, 1999).

34. CWA Don Coates, 22 Aug. 2003.

35. PH, *Plotting and Writing Suspense Fiction* (Boston: The Writer, 1966), p. 20.

36. Ibid.

37. CWA Dan Walton Coates, 22 Nov. 2003.

38. PH, "An American Book Bag," circa 1974, 6 carbon pages, publication unknown.
39. MCH letter to PH, undated.

7. LA MAMMA; PART 3

1. Cahier 1, 2/7/39.
2. CWA Dan Walton Coates, 22 Nov. 2003.
3. "Slimming Sickness," *London Sunday Times*, 9 Feb. 1969.
4. Cahier 9, PH transcription of high school notebooks, Dec. 14, 1937.
5. Ibid., Feb. 1938.
6. Cahier 9, PH transcription of high school notebooks, Feb.–Mar. 1938.
7. Ibid.
8. *The Book Programme*, BBC2, 11 Nov. 1976.
9. PH letter to SH, 29 Aug. 1970.
10. Cahier 20, 7/27/51.
11. CWA Dan Walton Coates, 22 Nov. 2003.
12. Ibid.
13. MCH letter to PH, 26 Nov. 1970.
14. Cahier 3, 1/30/41.
15. PH letter to MCH, 9 Apr. 1971.
16. CWA Don Coates, 20 Apr. 2002.
17. MCH letter to PH, May, no year, presumably 1971.
18. MCH letter to PH, undated.
19. Diary 2, 11 June 1942.
20. Cahier 31, 1/12/70.
21. Diary 12, Dec. 25, 1952.
22. Ibid. Jan. 27, 1953.
23. Ibid. Jan-Feb. 1953.
24. Ibid. Jan. 13, 1953.
25. Ibid. Jan. 23, 1953.
26. Ibid.

8. LA MAMMA: PART 4

1. CWA Marijane Meaker, 1 Feb. 2003.
2. Karl Augustus Menninger, *The Human Mind* (New York: Knopf, 1930), p. ix.
3. Ibid., p. 5.
4. PH, "A Try at Freedom," undated, unpublished.
5. Ibid.
6. Pupil's record card for PH, 1930–33, New York State Dept. of Education (P.S. 122, Queens, New York).
7. PH, "A Try at Freedom."
8. Ibid.
9. Ibid.
10. PH letter to Karl Menninger, 8 Apr. 1989.
11. Janet Watts, "Love and Highsmith," *Observer Magazine*, 9 Sept. 1990.
12. CWA Janine Hérisson, 29 Oct. 2002.
13. PH, "Christmases—Mine or Anybody's," marked "sent to *Granta* 23 March 1990."
14. Cahier 13, 3/4/46.
15. Jeva Cralick letter to PH, undated.
16. CWA Vivien De Bernardi, 15 Aug. 2002.
17. CWA Peter Hyun, 26 Apr. 2008.
18. Ned Rorem letter to the author, 10 Jan. 2008.
19. PH, "E. 57th St. Tomboy," *Saturday Review*, 1 Apr. 1950.

20. Karl Menninger letter to PH, 17 Mar. 1989.
21. Cahier 4, 8/29/40.
22. PH, *Plotting and Writing Suspense Fiction*, p. 22.
23. Ibid., p. 16.
24. Cahier 31, 1/2/70.
25. Cahier 10, Jan. 5, 1940.
26. PH, *Plotting and Writing Suspense Fiction*, p. 3.
27. Ibid.
28. PH letter to BKS, 22 Feb. 1972.
29. Paul Ingendaay, Afterword, *Nothing That Meets the Eye* (New York: W. W. Norton, 2002), p. 442.
30. CWA Vivien De Bernardi, 15 Aug. 2002.
31. PH, "Between Jane Austen and Philby," *Vogue,* September 1968.
32. Ibid.
33. Diary 10, May 16, 1950.
34. PH, "Between Jane Austen and Philby."
35. "PH, "Some Christmases—Mine or Anybody's."
36. Ibid.
37. Ibid.
38. Cahier 2, 7/8/40.
39. Ibid.
40. Cahier 17, 3/8/48.
41. Ibid.
42. PH, *The South Bank Show*, Episode 125, 14 Nov. 1982.
43. PH letter to DOC, Montmachoux, 26 Dec. 1968.
44. Cahier 19, 4/2/50.
45. Ibid.
46. Cahier 13, 9/20/45.
47. Cassette tape recorded by DOC and sent to PH in Moncourt, Aug. 1975.
48. PH letter to DOC, 31 Aug. 1976.
49. PH letter to Bettina Berch 2 July, 1983.

9. GREEK GAMES

1. PH, "A Try at Freedom."
2. Cahier 9, PH transcription of high school notebooks, Aug. 1938.
3. Ibid., 1937.
4. Ibid., Aug. 7, 1939.
5. Ibid., 1938.
6. Ibid., Sept. 1937.
7. Ibid., Feb. 2, 1938.
8. Ibid., Feb. 4, 1938.
9. Ibid.
10. Ibid., Sept.–Oct. 1938.
11. Ibid., Sept. 1937.
12. PH, "A Try at Freedom."
13. PH to Joan Dupont, quoted in a letter to KKS, 14 Mar. 1988.
14. Ibid.
15. Programme, Barnard College Greek Games, 1939 (BCA).
16. BCA.
17. Archives, Julia Richman High School.
18. Cahier 36, 29/12/83.
19. Ted Solotaroff, ed., *Alfred Kazin's America* (New York: HarperCollins, 2003), p. 45.
20. Cahier 36, 29/12/83.

21. CWA Alice Gershon Lassally, 22 Feb. 2003.

22. CWA Helen Kandel Hyman, 16 Feb. 2003.

23. CWA Alice Gershon Lassally, 22 Feb. 2003.

24. CWA Helen Kandel Hyman, 16 Feb. 2003.

25. Ibid.

26. CWA Alice Gershon Lassally, 22 Feb. 2003.

27. CWA Rita Rohner Semel, 18 Feb. 2003.

28. "A Minute on the Death of Miss Ethel G. Sturtevant," presented at the Faculty Meeting at Barnard College by Professor Cabell Greet, 28 Oct. 1968.

29. Cahier 6, 4/24/42.

30. Diary 1, Jan. 1–17, 1940.

31. Diary 8, 4/8/47.

32. Cahier 3, 1/6/41.

33. Cahier 24, 24/5/57.

34. CWA KKS.

35. Cahier 5, 9/16/41.

36. Cahier 6, 12/17/41.

37. PH, *The Price of Salt*, p. 221.

38. Cahier 6, 12/17/41.

39. Ibid.

40. Ibid.

41. Cahier 12, 11/12/44.

42. "Thrillers and Crime Fiction," interview with PH, 3 Dec. 1972, BBCTV.

43. Cahier, 1 Feb. 1938.

44. Cahier 24, 2/7/56.

45. Cahier 1, Aug. 1939.

46. Craig Little, "Interview with PH," *Publishers Weekly*, 2 Nov. 1992.

47. Diary 1, 1941.

48. Cahier 18, 8/20/49.

49. Ibid.

50. Cahier 9, PH transcription of high school notebooks, 1935.

51. Cahier 18, 11/5/48.

52. Ibid., 7/29/49.

53. CWA Caroline Besterman, 19 Dec. 2003.

54. Cahier 4, 9/19/40.

55. Cahier 24, 1/5/56.

56. Cahier 5, 9/10/41.

57. Cahier 4, 9/15/40.

58. Diary 3, Feb. 19, 1942.

10. ALTER EGO: PART 1

1. Jim Amash, "I Let People Do Their Job," *Alter Ego,* Nov. 2001.

2. Cahier 2, 5/22/40.

3. Ibid.

4. In her radio interview in New York in 1987 with Don Swaim for the Atlantic Monthly Press publication of *Found in the Street*, Pat referred to the advertisement she'd read as an ad for a "reporter/rewrite" job and said she thought she might be applying to a newspaper, but then saw, in the office, "posters of Black Terror on the walls."

5. Will Murray letter to the author, 6 Aug. 2002.

6. Quoted in Jamie Coville, "The Comic Book Villain, Dr. Frederic Wertham," *Integrative Arts* 10, 2/11/2002.

7. Dawn Powell, *The Locusts Have No King* (South Royalton, VT: Steerforth Press, 1999), p. 279. "He thought suddenly of an ancient Latin fragment called The Pumpkinification of

Claudius. The idea amused him. You might try to get Al Capp or Caniff started on a dumb boy named Claud who has the best of intentions but always takes some wrong step that turns him into a pumpkin, he said, and then noting Miss Jones' blank expression added, 'Never mind.'"

8. CWA Everett Ray Kinstler, 10 July 2004.

9. "The Fighting Yank," *America's Best Comics* 16, Jan. 1946.

10. "One day in 1943," Stanley Kauffmann said to me, "I went back to Cinema Comics to go out to lunch with a friend. He said, 'Would you like to meet your replacement, Pat Highsmith?' We said hello—and that was that" (CWA Stanley Kauffmann, 9 May 2002).

11. CWA Everett Ray Kinstler, 10 July 2004.

12. CWA Everett Ray Kinstler, 1 July 2004.

13. Kahn would later tell fellow editor Keith Kahla that while *Strangers on a Train* was a "good book," its author was a "terrible person."

14. CWA Marc Jaffee, 18 July 2003.

15. In 1958, Cecil Day-Lewis, under his pseudonym of Nicholas Blake, published *A Penknife in My Heart*, a Harper Novel of Suspense with a crime-switching plot similar to *Strangers on a Train*. In an author's note in the paperback edition, he disclaimed all knowledge of *Strangers on a Train*, and apologized to "Miss Highsmith for being so charmingly sympathetic to the predicament in which the long arm of coincidence put me."

16. Quoted in Terry Teachout, *The Skeptic: A life of H. L. Mencken* (New York: Harper-Collins, 2002), p. 125.

17. Patricia Schartle Myrer letter to author, 17 Feb. 2003.

18. *EQMM*, August 1960.

19. Diary 4, 7/8/43.

20. Pat selected Bellow as her favorite writer in an essay entitled "My Favorite Writer(s)," sent to *Konkret Sonderhefte*, Hamburg, Germany, 20 July 1987.

21. Diary 10, Oct. 13, 1950.

22. William Shawn letter to PH with opinion attached, 24 Sept. 1942.

23. PH letter to Joan Kahn, 3 Feb. 1958 (CURB).

24. Diary 3, Dec. 1, 1942.

25. Diary 2, May 28, 1943.

26. Ibid., Saturday, June 6, 1942.

27. PH letter to DOC, 7 Oct. 1976.

28. CWA Caroline Besterman, 6 Nov. 2003.

29. PH letter to Willie Mae Stewart Coates, undated, but probably written when Pat was between eight and ten.

30. PH, "Between Jane Austen and Philby."

31. Cahier 9, 11/23/42, "Sonny—(a real boy of L. Island)."

32. PH, *Strangers on a Train* (New York: W.W. Norton, 2001), p. 12.

33. Ibid., p. 279.

34. PH, *Plotting and Writing Suspense Fiction*, pp. 19–20.

35. Cahier 22, 8/7/51.

36. CWA France Burke and "Sam," 5 Feb. 2003.

37. Cahier 22, 1/3/52.

38. CWA Julia Diener-Diethelm, 1 Apr. 2003.

39. Cahier 26, 12/1/61.

40. Cahier 5, Sept. 23, 1941.

41. Cahier 4, Sept. 1940; this history of Ruthie and Eddy was dropped down in the middle of the cahier without date or further reference, and was marked by PH "Interesting" at a later date.

42. PH, "Venice: The One and Only," 6/7/ 1992 (manuscript).

43. CWA Janice Robertson, 23 June 2003.

44. PH, "Twenty Things I Like," a list made for Diogenes Verlag, 12 March 1983.

45. Cahier 19, 7/22/50.

46. Cahier 17, 6/3/48.

47. Diary 3, Dec. 13, 1942.

48. Marijane Meaker in her memoir, *Highsmith: A Romance of the 1950s* (San Francisco: Cleis Press, 2003), p. 9.

49. CWA Bert Diener, 1 Apr. 2003.

50. CWA Caroline Besterman, 6 Nov. 2003.

51. PH letter to MCH, 1 Nov. 1969, 10:00 P.M.

52. PH, *The Talented Mr. Ripley,* p. 249.

53. SH letter to PH, 3 Mar. 1970.

54. CWA Marijane Meaker, 1 Feb. 2003.

55. CWA Caroline Besterman, 19 Dec. 2003.

56. Diary 2, June 17, 1942.

57. Ibid.

58. Sherill Tippins, *February House* (Boston: Houghton Mifflin, 2005).

59. CWA Daniel Bell, 24 Aug. 2003.

60. Emily M. Morison letter to PH, 8 Aug. 1945, Alfred A. Knopf Archives (HRC).

61. "The Heroine" was also reprinted in *O. Henry Prize Stories,* 1946, and in *Today's Woman,* Mar. 1948.

62. Cahier 11, 8/19/44.

63. CWA Daniel Bell and Pearl Kazin, 24 Aug. 2003.

64. CWA Daniel Bell, 18 Aug. 2003.

65. CWA Robert Gottlieb, 6 Aug. 2003.

66. CWA Gary Fisketjon, 10 Dec. 2002.

67. CWA Norman Mailer, 23 June 2002.

68. Diary 1, 1940.

69. Diary 2, May 31, 1942.

70. Ibid., June 4, 1942.

71. Ibid., June 1, 1942.

72. Ibid., June 6, 1942.

73. Donald Swaim, *Book Beat,* interview with PH, WCBS-Radio, New York, 29 Oct. 1987. Pat said the same thing in print interviews.

74. Cahier 20, 10/23/50.

75. Ibid.

76. Cahier 17, 3/8/48.

77. Cahier 17, 2/23/48.

78. Diary 10, Nov. 17, 1950.

79. Ibid., Jan. 8, 1943.

80. Document of the Jewish Antifascist Committee of the USSR, 21 June 1946, Library of Congress.

81. Diary 2, Dec. 1, 1942.

82. Ibid., June 26, 1942.

83. Ibid., June 24, 1942.

84. Ibid., July 3, 1942.

85. PH, *Plotting and Writing Suspense Fiction,* p. 138.

86. Diary 2, July 31, 1942.

87. Ibid., July 7, 1942.

88. PH, "My First Job," *Oldie,* 26 Mar. 1993.

89. Ibid.

90. Ibid.

91. DOC letter to PH, undated.

92. Pat accused Miss Phimister, her sublettor at 353 East Fifty-sixth Street, of being "a small-time crook" and of "using my stuff"—Pat's usual reaction to anyone she put in charge of anything belonging to her. PH letter to KKS, 17 May 1951.

93. Diary 5, 10/6/43.

94. Diary 5, 12/8/43.
95. CWA KKS, 14 Nov. 2006.
96. CWA Buffie Johnson, 24 Dec. 2002.
97. CWA Vince Fago, 28 Nov. 2001.
98. Cahier 16, 10/24/47.
99. Cahier 8, 9/22/42.
100. CWA Marion Aboudaram, 23 Sept. 2002.
101. PH letter to Elby Skattebol, 9 Jan. 1983.
102. Cahier 11, 10/18/42.
103. Cahier 8, 9/25/42.
104. Cahier 23, 2/14/55.
105. Diary 6, 28 Dec. 1944.
106. Cahier 18, 8/27/49.
107. PH letter to KKS, 14 June 1952.
108. Ibid.
109. PH, *The Talented Mr. Ripley* (New York: Vintage, 1992), p. 290.
110. CWA Everett Ray Kinstler, 10 July 2004.
111. Ibid., 20 Sept. 2004.

11. ALTER EGO: PART 2

1. CWA Marijane Meaker, 5 Dec. 2001.
2. CWA Everett Ray Kinstler, 10 July 2004.
3. PH letter to "Elby," 15 June 1969.
4. Ibid.
5. CWA Barbara Roett, 18 May 2003.
6. PH letter to "Elby," 15 June 1969.
7. Cahier 27, 7/14/63.
8. Jim Amash letter to the author, 4 Dec. 2004.
9. CWA Gerard Albert, 15 Jan. 2005.
10. Diary 4, 24/8/43.
11. CWA Kingsley Skattebol, 20 May 2002.
12. CWA Gerald Albert, 15 Jan. 2002.
13. Ibid.
14. Ibid.
15. Diary entries, June 1949.
16. Diary entries, Oct. 1949.
17. CWA Jim Amash, 25 Feb. 2007.
18. Trina Robbins's influential book, *The Great Women Cartoonists*, traces the women who made a career in the business.
19. Gerard Jones, *Men of Tomorrow: Geeks, Gangsters, and the Birth of the Comic Book* (New York: Basic, Books, 2004), p. 57, and CWA, Michael Feldman, comics historian and a source for *Men of Tomorrow,* 20 Sept. 2004.
20. James R. Mellow, *Charmed Circle: Gertrude Stein and Company* (New York: Praeger Publishers, 1974), p. 393.
21. Arie Kaplan, "How the Jews Created the Comic Book Industry," *Reform Judaism Magazine* 32, no. 1. (Fall 2003).
22. CWA Jim Amash.
23. Gerard Jones, *Men of Tomorrow*, p. 237. Figures provided by Michael Feldman.
24. CWA Jim Amash.
25. Will Murray letter to the author, 6 Aug. 2002.
26. Cahier 30, 12/16/68.
27. CWA Jim Amash, also Steven Rowe, 4 Dec. 2001.
28. Along these same lines is the disappearance of the workbooks of Pat's Sangor-

Pines shop editor, Richard E. Hughes, workbooks whose information would make an important addition to the history of the comics and to this biography. In his workbooks, Hughes meticulously registered both the assignments he gave and the artists and writers who carried them out. On his death, Hughes's widow passed the workbooks on to his alma mater in New Jersey. In an episode Highsmith herself might have imagined, the university library became a "sick building" and the institution "deaccessioned" many of its holdings—including Hughes's workbooks, which were sold to a man who does not live in the United States and did not acknowledge to the author his ownership of the workbooks. The history of the American comic book continues to be plagued by incidents like this one.

29. Comics companies changed their names as frequently as they churned out different Superheroes; thus, Mr. Hughes might be editing comics for Cinema, Better/Standard, or ACG, amongst others, all under the umbrella of the Sangor-Pines shop, which provided the various companies with complete, camera-ready art.

30. Kaplan, "How the Jews Created the Comic Book Industry."

31. Ibid.

32. Don Swaim interviews PH, *Book Notes*, WCBS-Radio, New York, Oct. 1987.

33. Angelo S. Rappoport, *The Folklore of the Jews* (London: Soncino Press, 1937), pp. 195–203.

34. Kaplan, "How the Jews Created the Comic Book Industry."

35. Jules Feiffer, quoted in the exhibition *Masters of American Comics*, at the Jewish Museum, New York City, Sept. 15, 2006–Jan. 28, 2007.

36. Umberto Eco's useful term in his foreword to Will Eisner's last book, *The Plot: the Secret Story of the Protocols of the Elders of Zion* (New York: W. W. Norton, 2005).

37. Diary 10, Friday, 6/16/50.

38. Cahier 23, 10/1/54.

39. Cahier 23, 2/14/55.

40. Ripley's triumph is the opposite of the destiny of Raskolnikov, Dostoyevsky's surly graduate student with a Napoleonic complex, whose *acte gratuite* in *Crime and Punishment* was one of Pat's favorite crimes. But Raskolnikov's murders do not transform him into the superman of his dreams; they lead to the pursuit, the confession, and the Christian redemption which Dostoyevsky insisted was his real point in writing *Crime and Punishment*. Modern readers of *Crime and Punishment* usually overlook the Christian themes in the novel because the suspenseful deployment of Raskolnikov's guilt (Pat thought Dostoyevsky should be considered a suspense writer) is so much more compellingly written than the sullen student's eight-year conversion to Christianity in dreary Siberia by Sonia, the faithful prostitute with the golden heart.

Pat also made Ripley's fate the reverse of Lambert Strether's, the "ambassador" in Henry James's eponymous novel. Strether must take nothing for himself, must "fail" as an ambassador, in order to do the right thing, while Ripley escapes failure by only doing the wrong thing. Ripley's operating principle—winner take all—is Pat's version of Strether's famous advice to Little Bilham: "Live all you can."

41. Diary 4, 6/28/43.

42. Diary, Apr. 14, 1949.

43. All of these, according to her multiple diary entries, were Superhero titles Pat wrote for in the 1940s.

44. Bettina Berch interview with PH, 1984, unpublished.

45. Ibid.

46. Don Swaim interviews PH, *Book Notes*, WCBS-Radio, Oct. 1987.

47. "Uncertain Treasure," *Home and Food* vol. 6, no. 21 (August 1943).

48. Diary 4, 3/25/ 1943.

49. Gerard Jones, *Men of Tomorrow*, p. 237.

50. PH, "Primroses Are Pink" published in the Fall 1937 issue of the Julia Richman High School literary magazine, the *Bluebird*.

51. Cahier 4, 8/25/40.

52. Don Swaim interviews PH, *Book Notes*, WCBS-Radio, New York, Oct. 1987.

53. Cahier 9, 12/19/42.

54. *Real Life Comics* no. 13.

55. *Real Life Comics* no. 18.

56. PH's personal library at SLA; translations from the Russian are by Constance Garnett.

57. Diary 3, 6 Jan. 1943.

58. Note from *Real Life Comics* editor "CSS," 1/2/46, pasted into Diary 6.

59. Letter from "LHS," 5/13/46, pasted into Diary 7.

60. Diary 4, May 14, 1943.

61. Interview with Bob Oksner by Jim Amash, 4 Dec. 2004 (Collection Jim Amash).

62. CWA Gerald Albert, 15 Jan. 2002.

63. Cahier 11, 10/2/44.

64. Cahier 17, 2/17/48.

65. Diary 17, Nov. 25, 1990.

66. CWA KKS, 11 June 2004.

67. CWA KKS, 21 Apr. 2002.

68. Diary 2, Jan.–Aug. 1942.

69. Diary 4, 7/8/43.

70. Diary 3, Jan. 1943.

71. Ibid., Jan. 8, 1943.

72. Numerous diary entries, 1940s.

73. Terry Gross interviews Stan Lee, *Fresh Air,* NPR, 4 June 2002.

74. All these items can be seen in the Highsmith Archives at the Swiss Literary Archives in Bern, Switzerland.

75. Notebook and two lists, undated, private collection.

76. Cahier 1, Aug. 21, 1939.

77. Drawing of "Golden Arrow," private collection.

78. PH letter to Lil Picard, 20 Feb. 1969 (UIL).

79. Andrew Wilson, *Beautiful Shadow* (London: Bloomsbury, 2003), p. 286.

80. CWA Heather Chasen, 22 Sept. 2002.

81. Cahier 14, 12/18/46.

82. Many comics writers had been pulp writers themselves "and liked the comics even less than they liked the pulps, but needed the comics work because pulps were dying" (CWA Jim Amash).

83. Diary 9, Apr. 7, 1948.

12. ALTER EGO: PART 3

1. Westchester County Surrogate Court, adoption papers for Mary Patricia Plangman, filed November 1946.

2. Ibid.

3. CWA Everett Ray Kinstler, 10 July 2004.

4. Diary 2, Jan. 3, 1942.

5. CWA Don Coates, 20 Apr. 2002.

6. MCH letter to PH, undated.

7. Diary 10, Aug. 10, 1950.

8. Ibid.

9. Ibid.

10. Ibid.

1) Constant self-consciousness—visual and mental—"What does the world—my relatives, etc. etc. think of me?"

2) Uncoordinated attitudes—M[ary] B[aker] Eddy and spirituality vs. love of show,

e.g. when she goes to Texas, she intends to "look like the money." Yet she will ridicule anyone who avowedly sets his standards by money.

3) Blank, vague expression when she flatly says something palliative about a situation I know fully—the economic situation at home. *Refusal to face facts*—to speak forthrightly and seriously on matters both of us know about.

4) Wrongly placed consideration for others—carrying dishes 2 ft. further toward kitchen at the Minots.

5) Intellectual laziness. Unwilling to challenge self to utmost for the sheer joy of it on any puzzle or game, though she continually escapes life via games. Veers away from controversial matter once I broach it for mutual discussion.

6) Thought patterns that are rigid—on the Negro question; homosexuality; "respect for elders" people I call dull, etc. etc.

11. CWA Marijane Meaker, 1 Feb. 2003.

12. Diary 4, 7/31/43.

13. Cahier 29, 11/1/67.

14. Rolf Tietgens letter to PH, 7 Aug. 1969. Also see photographs of PH by Rolf Tietgens in illustrations.

15. Diary 4, 6/21/43.

16. Ibid., May 20, 1943.

17. According to Fawcett comics expert Paul Hamerlinck, this dialect was later removed by Fawcett's executive editor, Will Lieberson. The only *Jasper* comic I have seen, a late one published in 1948, was couched in the president's, if not the King's, English.

18. "Invitation to Death," "Jap Buster Johnson," *USA Comics*, no. 14, Fall 1944.

19. "Come Back to the Raft Ag'in, Huck Honey," Leslie Fiedler, *Partisan Review* 15, June 1948.

20. *Desert Island Discs,* BBC4, 21 Apr. 1979.

21. PH letters to Bettina Berch, 7 Jan. and 25 Sept. 1987.

22. Diary 4, 8/19/43. Also 8/22/43.

23. Ibid., 5/30/43.

24. Ibid., 6/21/43.

25. Ibid., 1/7/43.

26. Cahier 9, PH transcription of high school journals.

27. Diary 4, 6/13/43.

28. Diary 5, 10/15/43.

29. Diary 4, 6/6/43.

30. Diary 5, 10/11/43.

31. Ibid., 10/10–11/43.

32. Diary 4, 6/6/43.

33. Diary 5, 9/30/43.

34. Ibid., 10/18/43.

35. Diary 4, 9/19/43.

36. Diary 5, 10/27/43.

37. Ibid., Oct. 29–30, 1943.

38. Ibid., 10/27/43.

39. Ibid., 10/27/43.

40. Diary 5, 10/15/43.

41. Ibid., 10/25/43.

42. Diary 5, various entries, fall 1943.

43. Ibid., Oct. 11–17, 1943.

44. Ibid., 11/13/43.

45. Ibid., Oct. 11–17, 1943.

46. CWA David Diamond, 18 Dec. 2004.

47. Ibid.

48. Ibid.

49. Ethel Sturtevant letter no. 5, undated letters, 1962–68.

50. PH, "My Life with Greta Garbo," 1990.

51. Ibid.

52. Joan Juliet Buck, "A Terrifying Talent," *Observer Magazine*, 20 Nov. 1977.

53. Bettina Berch interview with PH, 1987.

54. Diary 2, Feb. 7, 1942.

55. Ibid., Feb. 17, 1942.

56. Ibid., Apr. 5, 1942.

57. MCH letter to Marijane Meaker, undated (Collection Marijane Meaker).

58. Diary 1, July 23, 1941.

59. Diary 9, July 22, 1948.

60. Diary 8, 27 May 1947.

61. Diary 4, 24/6/43.

62. PH reading list from 1950.

63. Cahier 16, 9/4/47.

64. Cahier 33, 1/12/74.

65. PH personal library. *The Art of Loving* is inscribed from her parents for her birthday, 19 Jan. 1967.

66. PH letter to BKS, 13 Sept. 1983.

67. Cahier 24, 3/25/56.

68. *After Dark*, Channel 4, 18 June 1988.

69. Diary 4, 7/18/43.

70. Ibid., 28/6/43.

71. Ibid.

72. Ibid., 22/8/43

73. Diary 5, 7/11/43.

74. Ibid., Oct. 1943.

75. Ibid., 8/11/43.

13. ALTER EGO: PART 4

1. Diary 5, 8/11/43.

2. Sybille Bedford, *A Visit to Don Otavio* (New York: Counterpoint, 2003), p. 286.

3. "I Got a Scheme," interview of Saul Bellow by Philip Roth, *New Yorker,* 15 Apr. 2005.

4. Bedford, *A Visit to Don Otavio,* p. 286.

5. Ibid., p. 282.

6. Diary 9 (Mexico Diary), Dec. 1943.

7. Ibid., Dec. 1943–9 Mar. 1944.

8. Ibid., p. 27.

9. Ibid., 19 Jan. 1943.

10. Ibid., Dec. 1943–9 March 1944.

11. Ibid., Mar. 11, 1944.

12. PH, "In the Plaza," *Nothing That Meets the Eye.* First draft written in April 1944.

13. PH, "The Car," ibid. First draft written in March 1945, revised in December 1962.

14. Joan Kahn, PH's editor at Harper & Brothers, suggested many such changes to her.

15. Cahier 23, 6/26/54 and 6/30/54.

16. Don Swaim interview of PH, *Book Notes,* CBS-Radio, New York, Oct. 1987.

17. Cahier 11, 3/25/44.

18. Ibid., 4/16/44.

19. Ibid., 4/14/44.

20. Ibid.

21. Cahier 8, 9/25/42.

22. Cahier 11, 4/14/44.

23. Francis Wyndham, "Sick of Psychopaths," *Sunday Times* (London), 4 Nov. 1965.

24. Diary 2, Jan. 1942.

25. Cahier 9, Jan. 1, 1943.

26. Ibid., p. 1.

27. Dickie Greenleaf's signet ring—the ring Tom pulls over his "scuffed knuckle" after he murders him and then wears forever after—is green. Pat knew about Oscar Wilde's "great green scarab ring" from reading Frank Harris's books about Oscar.

28. Cahier 11, 12/24/43.

29. In this extract from *Plotting and Writing Suspense Fiction*, written at exactly the same time she was asserting the contrary to Francis Wyndham, Pat admitted:

The theme I have used over and over again in my novels is the relationship between two men, usually quite different in make-up, sometimes obviously the good and the evil. . . . [I]t was a friend, a newspaperman, who pointed it out to me . . . a man who had seen the manuscript of my first effort at twenty-two [*The Click of the Shutting*], the book that was never finished. This was about a rich, spoiled boy and a poor boy who wanted to be a painter. They were fifteen years old in the book. As if that weren't enough, there were two minor characters, a tough athletic boy who seldom attended school (and then only to shock the school with things like the bloated corpse of a drowned dog . . .) and a puny clever boy who giggled a great deal and adored him and was always in his company. (p. 145)

30. Interview with E. L. Doctorow, *Time*, Feb. 26, 2006.

31. Shirley Jackson, *The Haunting of Hill House* (New York: Viking Press, 1959), p. 1.

32. Cahier 8, 9/25/42.

33. Cahier 9, 12/19/42.

34. Ibid., 11/30/42.

35. Ibid., 12/29/42. "Gregory often amused himself before falling asleep, by finding the brief, fleeting sensations of being another person—someone of course he did not know—a face which was entirely out of his own mind."

36. Margaretta K. Mitchell, *Ruth Bernhard: Between Art & Life* (San Francisco: Chronicle Books, 2000), p. 75.

37. PH, *The Click of the Shutting*, manuscript, p. 138.

38. Ibid., p. 134.

39. Ibid., p. 170.

40. Ibid., p. 5.

41. Ibid., p. 4.

42. Ibid., p. 5.

43. Cahier 34, 12/17/76.

44. Ibid., 7/15/78.

45. Cahier 9, 11/23/42.

46. Ibid., 12/29/42.

47. PH, *The Click of the Shutting*, manuscript, p. 144.

48. Ibid., p. 67.

49. Ibid., p. 70.

50. Ibid., p. 217.

51. Ibid., p. 139.

52. Diary 9 (Mexico Diary), Wednesday, Mar. 15, 1944.

53. Ibid., Mar. 11, 1944.

54. Ibid., Monday, Mar. 13, 1944.

55. Ibid., Monday, Mar. 20, 1944.

56. Ibid.

57. Diary 2, Feb. 23, 1942.

58. PH letter to KKS, 12 May 1944.

59. Ibid.

60. CWA Dan Walton Coates, 22 Nov. 2003.

61. Cahier 1, undated 1938.
62. CWA Dan Walton Coates, 22 Nov. 2003.
63. Cahier 11, Sept. 29, 1944.

14. ALTER EGO: PART 5

1. Jap Buster Johnson appeared in *USA Comics* nos. 6–15; *All Select Comics* nos. 2, 8, and 9; *Complete Comics* no. 2; and *Kid Komics* nos. 6 and 8–10. (Information provided by Dr. Michael J. Vassallo.)
2. CWA Vince Fago, 30 Nov. 2001.
3. Ibid., 28 Nov. 2001.
4. CWA Stan Lee via Roy Thomas, Nov. 29, 2001.
5. Jim Amash letter to the author, 10 April 2009, quoting his 2005 interview with the late Leon Lazarus.
6. CWA Will Eisner, 23 Dec. 2002.
7. The Whip first appeared in *Flash Comics* no. 1, in 1940.
8. CWA William Woolfolk, 15 Dec. 2001.
9. Ibid.
10. Ibid.
11. PH letter to SH, 1 Sept. 1970.
12. CWA Elizabeth Hardwick, 12 Apr. 2002.
13. Roy Thomas, editor of *Alter Ego*, cites this as a letter to the editor by Pierce Rice, appearing in a mid-nineties issue of Robin Snyder's *The Comics*, p. 56.
14. Ibid.
15. A remark made by Mickey Spillane to a British interviewer. When the interviewer asked if that's how Spillane treated his wife, he replied: "We're talking about fiction" ("Obituary, Mickey Spillane," *Guardian,* 18 July 2006).
16. Ibid.
17. Cahier 22, 6/12/53.
18. CWA Vince Fago, 28 Nov. 2001.
19. Ibid., 30 Nov. 2001.
20. Ibid.
21. *Who's Who of American Comic Books*, volume 2 (1974), is the volume that first mentions Patricia Highsmith.
22. PH letter to SH, 1 Sept. 1970.
23. PH letter to Anita Bryant, 13 May 1978.
24. CWA Jerry Bails, 3 Dec. 2002.
25. Ibid.; also see *Who's Who of American Comic Books*.

15. SOCIAL STUDIES: PART 1

1. Cahier 3, 12/23/40. "Unfortunately, [Proust] wrote of an age just past, as an historian rather than a prophet. . . . A writer like Steinbeck . . . can write in the present, of the present, of people's passions."
2. Cahier 12, 4/6/45.
3. Ibid., 3/26/45.
4. Chart made by PH and inserted by her in Cahier 12, Apr. 1945.
5. Cahier 19, 11/23/49.
6. Ibid.
7. Cahier 4, 9/2/40.
8. Cahier 29, 7/17/68.
9. Ibid.
10. MCH telegram to PH (Collection Annebelle Potin).
11. SH letter to PH, 23 Aug. 1970.

12. PH letter to SH, 29 Aug. 1970.
13. Don Swaim interviews PH, *Book Notes.*
14. Cahier 13, 9/8/45.
15. Cahier 3, 10/30/1940.
16. Diary 4, May 31–June 6, 1943.
17. Cahier 9, PH transcription of high school notebooks, Oct. 18, 1937.
18. Diary 2, Wed. Apr. 8, 1942.
19. Eugene Walter, *Milking the Moon* (New York: Three Rivers Press, 2001), p. 86.
20. Francis King, *Oldie,* "Angry Old Woman," Sept. 2003.
21. Betty Curry letter to PH, 5 Nov. 1977.
22. CWA Betty Curry, 26 Aug. 2003.
23. Liz Smith, *Natural Blonde* (New York: Hyperion, 2000), p. 117.
24. Patricia Schartle Myrer letter to the author, 17 Feb. 2003.
25. Ibid.
26. CWA Caroline Besterman, 6 Nov. 2003.
27. Ibid., 19 Dec. 2003.
28. CWA Camilla Butterfield, 17 Dec. 2003.
29. Ibid.
30. Diary 8, Feb. 27, 1949.
31. CWA Karl Bissinger, 3 Dec. 2004.
32. Diary 2: Vendredi le 13 juin, 1941, "Berenice Abbot m'a invité à une soirée chez elle le vendredi prochain."
33. Mitchell, *Ruth Bernhard,* p. 57.
34. Diary 2, Jan. 22, 1942.
35. Diary 1, summer and fall of 1941; diary 2, winter of 1942.
36. PH, *The Talented Mr. Ripley,* pp. 245–47.
37. Cahier 9, PH transcription of high school notebooks, Sept. 1938.
38. Ibid., 21 Dec. 1938.
39. Ibid., Aug. 24, 1939.
40. Anatole Broyard, *Kafka Was the Rage* (New York: Vintage Books, 1997), pp. 7–8.
41. Diary 1, June 13, 1941.
42. Mitchell, *Ruth Bernard,* p. 57.
43. Diary 3, 9 Aug. 1942.
44. Ibid.
45. Cahier 8, 11/11/1942.
46. Diary 5, May 26–27, 1943.
47. Ibid.
48. Ibid., July 28, 1941.
49. Diary 1, July 6, 1941.
50. CWA Ruth Bernhard, 14 Feb. 2003.
51. PH letter to Bettina Berch, 22 Dec. 1991.
52. CWA Donald Windham, 30 June 2004.
53. Buffie Johnson interviewed by Romy Ashby, *Goodie* no. 3.
54. CWA Buffie Johnson, 14–16 Nov., 29 Nov., 1 Dec., 13 Dec. 2001; and 26 Apr., 30 Apr., 24 Dec. 2002; 26 Aug. 2003; and undated memoirs.
55. Diary 1, July 5, 1941.
56. Diary 2, June 30, 1942.
57. Ibid., Feb. 9, 1942.
58. CWA Sybille Bedford, 16 June 2005.
59. Sybille Bedford, *Quicksands: A Memoir* (New York: Counterpoint, 2005), p. 124.
60. CWA Daniel Bell, 18 Aug. 2003.
61. MCH letter to Marijane Meaker, "Friday AM, 11th" (no other date).
62. MCH letter to PH, dated "Tues AM."
63. Diary 4, Aug. 16–22, 1943.

64. Diary 2, Jan. 10, 1942.

65. Ibid., Feb. 3, 1942.

66. PH letter to SH, 1 Sept. 1970.

67. Diary 8, Oct. 1947.

68. Hortense Calisher, 26 Feb. 2003, at the Yaddo benefit honoring PH.

69. Diary 2, Feb. 10, 1942.

70. Ibid.

71. Ibid., June 4, 1942.

72. Ibid., June 6, 1942.

73. CWA Dorothy Wheelock Edson, 7 June 2004.

74. Kay Redfield Jamison, *Touched with Fire* (New York: Free Press, 1993), p. 36.

75. CWA Phillip Lloyd Powell, 8 Feb. 2003.

76. Ibid.

77. CWA Heather Chasen, 22 Sept. 2002.

78. Ibid.

79. Christian Gonzalez, "Jeanne Moreau: La Vie Me Nourris," *Figaro Madame*, July 2004.

80. CWA Phyllis Nagy, 26 June 2002.

81. PH letter to DOC, 14 Oct. 1977.

82. CWA Vivien De Bernardi, 15 Aug. 2002.

83. CWA Don Coates, 9 Dec. 2005.

84. Shirley Jackson, *The Lottery—or, The Adventures of James Harris* (New York: Farrar, Straus, 1949).

85. Diary 4, June 24, 1943.

86. Diary 8, Mar. 17, 1949.

87. Author's note: Before her death in 2001, I saw Fanny Brennan's entire current oeuvre, perhaps sixty or seventy paintings, hanging in her coat closet in New York. The paintings were so small that they fit comfortably in the tiny closet, which had been kitted out as a miniature art gallery.

88. PH letter to Lee Israel, 19 Mar. 1974.

89. Cahier 36, 5/16/88.

90. Ibid.

91. CWA Christa Maerker, 27 July 2004.

92. Ibid.

93. CWA Betty Comden, 25 Aug. 2003.

94. Cahier 16, 12/9/47.

95. Ibid., 12/28/47.

96. Diary 8, May 14, 1947.

97. Diary 10, May 8, 1950.

98. Diary 8, May 27, 1947.

99. PH letter to Millicent Dillon, 5 June 1977 (HRC).

100. Diary 8, 5/27/47.

101. Drawing of Jane Bowles by PH, undated.

102. Diary 10, Wed., Nov. 1950.

103. PH letter to Millicent Dillon, 5 June 1977 (HRC).

104. Ibid.

105. Ibid.

106. Diary 8, May 13, 1947.

107. Diary 10, August 16, 1950.

108. Diary 8, May 15–16, 1947.

109. Nancy Mitford letter to Evelyn Waugh, 3 Dec. 1962. Quoted in *The Letters of Nancy Mitford & Evelyn Waugh*, ed. Charlotte Mosley (London: Sceptre, 1997), p. 469.

110. Leo Lerman, *The Grand Surprise* (New York: Knopf, 2007), pp. 425–6.

111. Ibid., p. 329.

112. Ibid., p. 202.

113. Grey Foy, speaking about Leo Lerman's salon in *Truman Capote*, George Plimpton, ed. (New York: Anchor Books, 1997) p. 44.

114. PH letter to Millicent Dillon, 5 June 1977 (HRC).

115. Diary 10, Mar. 17, 1950.

116. Diary 8, Jan. 25, 1948.

117. Ibid., Feb. 13, 1948.

118. Ibid., Feb. 21, 1948.

119. Ibid., Feb. 26, 1948.

120. Ibid., Feb. 29, 1948.

121. Diary 9, 11/3/48.

122. Gerald Clarke, ed., *Too Brief a Treat: The Letters of Truman Capote* (New York: Random House, 2004), p. 53.

123. CWA Donald Windham, 30 June 2004.

124. Truman Capote letter to Elizabeth Ames, 2 Mar. 1948 (NYPL).

125. Diary 9, 5/2/48.

126. PH, Proposed Snail Interview (with Herself), undated.

127. Diary 8, Mar. 6, 1948.

128. PH letter to KKS, 2 June 1948.

129. PH letter to KKS, 30 June 1964.

16. SOCIAL STUDIES: PART 2

1. MCH letter to Miss Townsend, 27 Apr. 1948.

2. PH letter to KKS, 2 June 1948.

3. Diary 8, May 11–30, 1948.

4. Ibid., May 11, 1948.

5. There is no evidence in Pat's Yaddo file that she applied to Yaddo again, but Pat writes in her diary that both she and Marc Brandel had their applications for another residency rejected. She thought her public use of alcohol and their sleeping together had something to do with the rejections.

6. Cahier 15, 16/6/48.

7. Diary 8, July 5, 1948.

8. Letter PH to KKS, 2 June 1948.

9. CWA Phyllis Nagy, 13 Oct. 2002.

10. Cahier 17, 6/21/48.

11. Cahier 17, 5/19/48.

12. CWA Ruda Brandel Dauphin, 31 Jan. 2009.

13. Cahier 17, 19/5/48.

14. Diary 8, June 17, 1948.

15. Ibid., Dec. 22, 1947.

16. Cahier 17, 7/25/48.

17. PH, *Strangers on a Train*, p. 181.

18. Ibid., p. 180.

19. Ibid., p. 274.

20. Bruno, who reads only comic books and detective stories and is obsessed with creating "perfect crimes," enters Guy Haines's nightmares as a creature who looks a lot like the Superhero Batman. Guy dreams of Bruno as "a tall figure in a great cape like a bat's wing" who climbs up the side of his house and "springs" into his room. Before trying to throttle him, Guy asks, " 'Who are you?' 'You,' Bruno answer[s] finally" (PH, *Strangers on a Train*, p. 181).

And Bruno imagines himself joined to Guy, two heroes flying through the sky: "He longed for Guy to be with him now. He would clasp Guy's hand, and to hell with the rest of the world! Their feats were unparalleled! Like a sweep across the sky! Like two streaks of red fire that came and disappeared so fast, everybody stood wondering if they really had seen them" (ibid., p. 167).

"Is it a bird? Is it a plane? It's Superman" is the catchphrase that Bruno's fantasy would have suggested to many mid-century Americans—no matter how sophisticated their literary tastes. Beginning in 1940, that phrase introduced the radio program taken from the *Superman* comic books (and then was used in the comic books themselves), and it was as widespread and accessible as the phrase "Ripley's Believe It or Not"—another locution from America's popular culture which would find its way into a Highsmith novel.

21. PH, *Strangers on a Train* (New York: Bantam Books, 1951), p. 257.

22. Diary 9, Feb. 21–28, 1949.

23. Ibid., May–June 1948.

24. PH letter to SH, 1 Sept. 1970.

25. Ibid.

26. Diary 9, Sept. 30, 1948.

27. Ibid., Nov. 14–25, 1948.

28. Pat, exercising a bit of poetic license in the Afterword she finally wrote for *The Price of Salt*, telescoped the time frame of the effects of meeting Kathleen Senn, the woman who inspired the plot of *The Price of Salt,* and the outbreak of chicken pox she suffered while making her first notes for that novel. In fact, she met Senn on 8 December and didn't come down with chicken pox until ten or twelve days later. And it's not entirely clear when she actually scribbled the plot of *The Price of Salt* down in her notes; perhaps it wasn't the precise day she met Mrs. Senn. But the high-fever part was true—and her inspiration for the novel came about, metaphorically at least, just as she said.

29. Diary 9, Dec. 22–29, 1948.

30. Edmund Bergler, "The Myth of a New National Disease: Homosexuality and the Kinsey Report," *Psychiatric Quarterly* 22 (January 1948).

31. Diary 9, Dec. 22, 1948.

32. PH letter to SH, 29 Aug. 1970.

33. Diary 9, Jan. 11, 1949.

34. PH letter to SH, 29 Aug. 1970.

35. Diary 9, Jan. 27, 1949 (fourteenth visit to psychoanalyst).

36. Ibid., Mar. 1, 1949.

37. Ibid., Feb. 22 and 24, 1949.

38. Ibid., 1949 (twenty-second, twenty-fourth, twenty-ninth visits).

39. Ibid., May 3, 1949.

40. Ibid.

41. Ibid., May 6, 1949.

42. Ibid.

43. Ibid., May 18, 1949 (forty-fifth visit).

44. Ibid., May 24, 1949 (forty-seventh visit).

17. LES GIRLS: PART 1

1. "A heavy rain dissolved yesterday most of the 4-inch snowfall of Wednesday and left many slushy thoroughfares here and in the suburbs." "The Weather Bureau," *New York Times,* 12–17 Dec. 1948.

2. PH, Afterword, *The Price of Salt.*

3. Ibid.

4. Ibid.

5. Diary 10, June 1950: "Pray God, she never troubled to look up my name. (After the Xmas card.)"

6. Ibid.

7. Ibid.

8. PH, *Carol* (London: Bloomsbury, 1990), p. 260.

9. Ibid.

10. Ibid.

11. Cahier 26, 6/18/61. "As usual, I have found the fever beneficial to the imagination, and found an ending for my book."

12. Diary 10, Dec. 23, 1949.

13. PH, *The Dove Descending*, unpublished manuscript.

14. PH, *The First Person Novel*, unpublished manuscript.

15. PH, *Plotting and Writing Suspense Fiction*, p. 143.

16. Cahier 26, 1/21/61.

17. She also used the first-person narrative in two short stories about animals: "Chorus Girl's Absolutely Final Performance"—the story made her weep—and "Notes from a Respectable Cockroach."

18. PH, *Plotting and Writing Suspense Fiction*, p. 89.

19. Diary 10, Oct. 24, 1950.

20. Ibid., Jan. 19, 1951.

21. And she used the name Senn in her very last novel, *Small g*, the novel that is both a summary and a parody of her career. Senn is, conveniently, a Swiss name, and for *Small g* it was used for Thomas Senn, a sturdy blond Zurich detective. By 1995, Pat had come a long way from obsessive love.

22. Cahier 18, 12/9/48.

23. Ibid., 12/9/48.

24. Ibid., 9/9/48.

25. Priscilla Senn Kennedy letter to the author, quoting Kathleen Senn's deceased cousin, 14 Feb. 2009.

26. "[S]omething of a fairytale, something of a castle" was Pat's comment on Mrs. Senn's Murray Avenue house on her second trip to Ridgewood, New Jersey, to spy on Mrs. Senn.

27. PH, *The Price of Salt* (New York: Bantam Books, 1958), p. 197.

28. Ibid., p. 174.

29. Ibid., p. 136.

30. Cahier 19, June 28, 1950. Written the day before another finishing touch was put on the novel.

31. André Gide, *The Counterfeiters*, trans. Dorothy Bussy (New York: Vintage Books 1973), p. 123.

32. Diary 10, Dec. 10, 1949.

33. Property listings in the Ridgewood, New Jersey, property directory, in 1940: Book: 8052, p. 533. Block: 1811, Lot: 21.02. According to the property directory, the address became North Murray Avenue in 1952 (Ridgewood Public Library).

34. Diary 10, Sunday, Jan. 21, 1951.

35. Ibid., June 5, 1950.

36. Ibid., June 8, 1950.

37. Ibid., June 30, 1950.

38. Ibid.

39. Ibid., June 12, 1950.

40. Ibid., July 1950.

41. Ibid., July 2, 1950.

42. Ibid.

43. Ibid., Oct. 24, 1950.

44. Cahier 19, 6/6/50.

45. Diary 10, May 17, 1950.

46. Ibid., Oct. 17, 1950.

47. Ibid., Oct. 27, 1950.

48. Ibid., Sept. 6, 1950.

49. Cahier 13, 8/27/45.

50. Diary 1952–54, Feb. 25, 1953 (Trieste). Dan Walton Coates, eldest son of Pat's "brother Dan," who spent time as a boy with Pat at Willie Mae's house in Fort Worth whenever Pat passed through Texas, remembered something about Pat's teeth that alarmed him. He thought it was tied in with her "artistic" temperament and how she felt that she had to suppress her good looks. But first he wanted to talk about the fun he'd had with Pat. When Pat was young, Dan said, she was "very upbeat and she'd cuss like a sailor and of course I liked to cuss even as a kid so we'd talk out of Grandma's hearing because she would not have had THAT. We had a lot of fun in the early years."

Both Pat and Mary Highsmith helped young Dan with his artwork—he grew up to be an investment advisor, a rancher, and a painter and sculptor of western subjects—and Mary, Dan said, was "the most patient thing" with him. "A lot of Pat's things were still at Grandma's, her sketchbooks and so forth," and so most of Dan's conversations with Pat centered on art. Pat and Mary would buy him sketchbooks and critique his work seriously, as though he were already an artist, and Dan retained a shining memory of Pat's beauty, which, during "these early years, was drop-dead gorgeous. Dark dark eyes, that raven dark hair in a pageboy and golly she just looked great." It was his memory of Pat's stunning looks in the 1940s that made his next experience of her so shocking.

"Well, she went to Europe and it may have been five years, ten years later—I'm not worth a darn on dates—and I'll swear to God I couldn't believe it. She looked like the wrath of God. . . . Come to find out, for some reason only known to Pat, she had filed her teeth. They were all jagged-looking and from that point on her dental problems got worse" (CWA Dan Walton Coates, 22 Nov. 2003).

51. PH letter to KKS, 25 Jan. 1974.
52. Cahier 19, 12/19/49.
53. PH letter to KKS, 3 Oct. 1988.
54. PH letter to KKS, 20 Aug. 1970.
55. Ibid.
56. CWA Caroline Besterman, 6 Nov. 2003.
57. Cahier 20, 8/13/51.
58. Cahier 19, 12/19/49.
59. CWA Dan Walton Coates, 22 Nov. 2003.
60. Diary 11, Sept. 24, 1951.
61. Diary 10, Aug. 22–Sept. 6, 1950.
62. Ibid., Oct. 29, 1950.
63. CWA Jean-Étienne Cohen-Séat, 26 June 2007.
64. Diary 10, Oct. 29, 1950.
65. Ibid., Oct. 21, 1950.
66. Ibid., Nov., 1950.
67. Ibid., Nov. 1, 1950.
68. Ibid. 10, Nov. 8, 1950.
69. Ibid., Nov. 11, 1950.
70. Ibid., Dec. 1950.
71. Ibid., Dec. 1950.
72. Ibid., Dec. 1950.
73. Ibid., New Year's Eve, 1950.
74. Cahier 19, 7/1/50.
75. Cahier 16, 9/7/47.
76. Diary 10, Oct. 11, 1950.
77. *Time*, 13 Jan. 1941.
78. Ibid.
79. PH letter to KKS, 19 Apr. 1964.
80. Cahier 16, 9/4/47.
81. PH letter to Virginia Kent Catherwood, 6 Sept. 1947.
82. Diary 9, Jan. 4, 1948.

83. PH letter to KKS, 22 Mar. 1952.

84. In her diary for 1968 Pat wrote of Ginnie Catherwood: "She is Lotte in *The Tremor of Forgery*—the woman whom my hero will always love."

85. "The Private Life and Times of Prince David Mdivani," on Glamour Girls of the Silver Screen Web site, www.glamourgirlsofthesilverscreen.com.

18. LES GIRLS: PART 2

1. Cahier 18, 6/19/49.

2. Diary 8, June 26, 1949.

3. Ibid., July 1, 1949.

4. Ibid., July 27, 1950.

5. Cahier 19, 12/12/49.

6. Cahier 19, 2/27/50.

7. Cahier 24, 11/17/57.

8. CWA Caroline Besterman, 19 Dec. 2003.

9. CWA Barbara Roett, 18 May 2003.

10. Diary 11, Oct. 14, 1951.

11. CWA Joan Dupont, 7 Nov. 2002.

12. PH letter to Alex Szogyi, 27 Aug. 1977.

13. CWA Marion Aboudaram, 2 Oct. 2002.

14. PH letter to BKS, 16 Apr. 1968.

15. Ibid., 10 Feb. 1969.

16. PH letter to Alex Szogyi, 18 Feb. 1969.

17. Ibid., 4 Nov. 1968.

18. Ibid.

19. Cahier 17, 2/29/48.

20. Cahier 19, 8/11/50.

21. Diary 10, Oct. 13, 1950.

22. Ibid.

23. Ibid., Oct. 15–16, 1950.

24. Ibid., Oct. 13–14, 1950.

25. PH, *Strangers on a Train,* p. 26.

26. CWA Marijane Meaker, 17 Apr. 2002.

27. Cahier 20, 9/14/51.

28. Cahier 23, 6/13/55.

29. Cahier 23, 11/11/54.

30. Diary 11, Sept. 4, 1951.

31. Diary 12, May 24, 1953.

32. Ibid.

33. Diary 4, Aug. 8, 1943.

34. Rolf Tietgens letter to PH, 7 Aug. 1968.

35. Ibid., 12 Mar. 1969.

36. Ibid., 22 Feb. 1969.

37. Dorothy Wheelock Edson letter to the author, 26 June 2004.

38. Ibid., 14 June 2004.

39. Diary 10, July 17, 1950.

40. Diary 11, June 5, 1951.

41. PH letter to Lil Picard, 2 June 1971 (UIL).

42. PH letter to Ellen Blumenthal Hill, 8 July 1978 (UIL).

43. Lil Picard letter to PH, 21 Oct. 1970.

44. Diary 9, 5/10/47.

45. PH letter to BKS, 12 Apr. 1972.

46. Diary 12, insert, May 29, 1953.

47. Diary 12, June 1, 1953.

48. Ibid., May 23–29, 1953.

49. Ibid., June 1953.

50. Ibid., June 15, 1953.

51. Ibid., May 24, 1953.

52. Ibid., June 17, 1953.

53. PH letter to KKS, 14 June 1952.

54. Ibid.

55. Cahier 22, 6/18/53.

56. Diary 12, June 24, 1953.

57. Willis Goldbeck, entry in Internet Movie Database, www.IMDb.com.

58. Diary 12, Dec. 24, 1952.

59. PH letter to KKS, 15 Dec. 1952.

60. Patricia Schartle had been the first woman editor in chief in American book-publishing history (introduction by Brian Garfield to Second International Congress of Crime Writers, Mar. 15, 1978).

61. Diary 12, June 24–28, 1953.

62. Ibid., July 1, 1953.

63. Ibid.

64. Ibid.

65. Cahier 23, 6/12/55.

66. Ibid. "I stopped writing my diary nearly a year ago—but for the very good reason that I knew somebody was reading it (E.B.H. alas)."

67. PH letter to Monique Buffet, 8 Apr. 1988 (Collection Monique Buffet).

68. Diary 12, July 3, 1953.

69. Ibid., July 4, 1953.

70. Diary 11, Sept. 7, 1951.

71. In the same vein, Pat was indulgent about Buffie Johnson's long-researched book *Lady of the Beasts: The Goddess and Her Sacred Animals* (1988), corresponding with Buffie at length about the work. Keeping whatever private thoughts she had on the subject to herself, Pat loyally sent a review of it to *Le Monde* in Paris.

72. Cahier 20, 10/17/51.

73. Diary 11, 7/19/51.

74. PH letter to KKS, 14 June 1952.

75. Diary 11, Sept. 2, 1951.

76. Ibid., Mar. 3, 1952.

77. Ibid., Aug. 23, 1951. Subsequent quotations by PH about her private life are from Diaries 11 and 12.

78. PH, review of *Meg, Saturday Review*, 1 Apr. 1950.

79. Diary 11, Apr. 23, 1951.

80. Ibid., May 1, 1951.

81. Ibid., May 3, 1951.

82. Ibid., Apr. 28, 1951.

83. Ibid., May 7, 1951.

84. Ibid., May 9–12, 1951.

85. Ibid., June 6–24, 1951.

86. Ibid., June 18, 1951.

87. PH letter to Djuna Barnes, 1 Jan. 1959 (UML).

88. Djuna Barnes letter to PH, 6 Jan. 1959 (UML).

89. Diary 11, Oct. 1, 1951.

90. Ibid., July 3, 1951.

91. Ibid., July 23–27, 1951.

92. Ibid., July 29, 1951.

93. Don Swaim, *Book Notes,* Oct. 1987.

94. Diary 11, Aug. 29, 1951.

95. Ibid., Aug. 23, 1951.

19. LES GIRLS: PART 3

1. Cahier 20, 9/8/51.

2. PH letter to KKS, 13 Aug. 1952.

3. Diary 11, 1/11/51.

4. CWA H. M. Qualunque, 3 Aug. 2004.

5. Cahier 31, 4/18/71.

6. CWA H. M. Qualunque, 3 Aug. 2004.

7. Diary 8, 12/13/47.

8. CWA H. M. Qualunque, 3 Aug. 2004.

9. Ibid.

10. CWA Peter Huber, 20 Apr. 2003.

11. Ibid.

12. Diary 11, Sept. 4, 1951.

13. PH, *The Blunderer*, (New York: W. W. Norton, 2001), p. 23.

14. Diary 12, July 9, 1952. "Man's Best Friend" was published posthumously in a much later version with a different ending.

15. Diary 11, Nov. 16, 1951.

16. PH letter to Alex Szogyi, Sept. 24–25, 1969.

17. PH letter to BKS, 2 June 1972.

18. CWA Bettina Berch, 10 Aug. 2003.

19. CWA Christa Maerker, 3 Aug. 2006.

20. Diary 11, Sept. 4, 1951.

21. Ibid., Sept. 9, 1951.

22. Ibid., Sept. 14, 1951.

23. Cahier 16, 11/13/47.

24. Diary 11, Dec. 3, 1951.

25. PH, *Plotting and Writing Suspense Fiction* (New York: St. Martin's Griffin, 1990), p. 81.

26. Diary 11, Sept. 30, 1951.

27. Gerald Peary, interview in Toronto with PH, www.geraldpeary.com., 1988.

28. Diary 11, Oct. 22, 1951.

29. Ibid.

30. Ibid., Oct. 28, 1951.

31. Ibid., Oct. 25, 1951.

32. Ibid., Nov. 5, 1951.

33. Ibid., Dec. 3, 1951.

34. Ibid., Jan. 11, 1952.

35. PH letter to KKS, 5 Jan. 1967.

36. W. H. Auden letter to PH, dated "Mar 23" and pasted in her Scrapbook no. 1, 1950–61.

37. PH, "Scene of the Crime," *Granta* 29 (Winter 1989). Also published in the *Frankfurter Allgemeine Zeitung*, 24 Aug. 1991.

38. Cahier 21, Dec. 2, 1952.

39. Andrew Wilson, *Beautiful Shadow* (London: Bloomsbury, 2003), p. 182.

40. Diary 12, Dec. 5, 1952.

41. Ibid., Nov. 27, 1952.

42. Ibid., Dec. 1, 1952.

43. Ibid., Dec. 5, 1952.

44. Ibid., Dec. 17, 1952.

45. Cahier 21, 12/2/52.

46. Ibid.

47. Diary 12, Jan. 19, 1953.

48. Ibid., Dec. 25, 1952.
49. Ibid., Jan. 23, 1953.
50. Cahier 22, *Keime*, entries from 1952–53.
51. Diary 12, Feb. 12, 1953.
52. Cahier 22, 2/15/53.
53. Diary 12, Jan. 27, 1953
54. Ibid., Feb., various dates, 1953.
55. Cahier 21, 10/28/52.
56. Cahier 22, 2/14/53.
57. Diary 12, July 15–16, 1953.

20. LES GIRLS: PART 4

1. Diary 12, July and Aug., various dates, 1953.
2. Ibid., Aug. 6–7, 1953.
3. Ibid., June 8, 1953.
4. Ibid., Aug. 20, 1953.
5. PH, *The Blunderer* (New York: W. W. Norton, 2001), p. 189.
6. Ibid., p. 16.
7. Ibid., pp. 99, 93–94.
8. PH letter to Alex Szogyi, 17 Aug. 1965.
9. PH, *The Blunderer,* p. 97.
10. Ibid., p. 167.
11. Ibid., p. 97.
12. Ibid., p. 188.
13. Ibid., p. 148.
14. Paul Ingendaay, Afterword to *Nothing That Meets the Eye* (New York: W. W. Norton, 2002), p. 446.
15. Cahier 23, 8/21/55.
16. Diary 12, Aug. 26 and 31, 1953.
17. Cahier 22, 10/27/53.
18. PH letters to KKS, 27 Oct. and 24 Dec. 1953.
19. CWA Dan Walton Coates, 22 Nov. 2003.
20. CWA Annebelle Potin, 24 Mar. 2007.
21. Diary 12, Mar. 16, 1954.
22. Cahier 23, 4/14/54.
23. PH letter to Lil Picard, 20 Dec. 1967 (UIL).
24. Cahier 23, 4/22/54.
25. Ibid.
26. Jack Kerouac, *On the Road* (New York: Viking Press, 1957).

21. LES GIRLS: PART 5

1. PH letter to KKS, 23 Mar. 1953.
2. PH, *The Talented Mr. Ripley*, p. 174.
3. *Fort Worth Star-Telegram,* archives for 1931 (FWPL).
4. Cahier 23, 4/24/54.
5. "Man 'Buried' as Fire Victim Seized as Murder Suspect," *New York Herald Tribune*, 16 Apr. 1954.
6. Cahier 6, 2/23/42.
7. PH letter to Rosalind Constable, 15 Jan. 1968.
8. Ibid.
9. PH, *Plotting and Writing Suspense Fiction* (New York: St. Martin's Griffin, 1990), p. 76.
10. Ibid., p. 75.

11. No one ever mentions Willa Cather's wonderful short story "Paul's Case" (1906) in connection with *The Talented Mr. Ripley*; it is perhaps time to do so. Pat admired Cather, lived for two years with her parents in a building on the site of Cather's old Greenwich Village residence on Bank Street, and would certainly have known "Paul's Case" as one the few overtly American examples of a doubtfully sexed protagonist. There is something of the stagestruck Paul in Ripley and in his effeminacy, compulsive lying, felonious instincts, love of fine costume, and loathing of the low condition of his family. But Paul finishes, like Anna Kerenina, under the wheels of a train, while Tom Ripley ends up in the best hotel in Athens.

12. PH, *Plotting and Writing Suspense Fiction*, p. 140.

13. Ibid., p. 123.

14. *Patricia Highsmith: Leben und Werk*, eds. Franz Cavigelli, Fritz Senn, and Anna von Planta (Zurich: Diogenes, 1996). Peter Handke: "Die Privaten Weltkriege der Patricia Highsmith," pp. 169–180 (trans. Anna von Planta).

15. CWA Judith Conklin Peters, 1 June 2002.

16. Ibid.

17. Ibid.

18. Cahier 23, 6/13/54.

19. Ibid.

20. Ibid., 5/27/55.

21. PH, *Plotting and Writing Suspense Fiction*, p. 74.

22. CWA Ned Roche, 24 May 2002.

23. PH, *Plotting and Writing Suspense Fiction*, p. 75.

24. PH, *The Talented Mr. Ripley*, p. 131.

25. Ibid., pp. 137–38.

26. Diary 8, May 12, 1947.

27. Cahier 23, 10/1/54.

28. Cahier 23, 3/7/54.

29. Cahier 24, 9/29/57.

30. PH, *Plotting and Writing Suspense Fiction*, p. 50.

31. Cahier 26, 8/19/60.

32. PH, *Plotting and Writing Suspense Fiction*, p. 76.

33. Lisa Maria Hogeland, Afterword to *In a Lonely Place,* by Dorothy B. Hughes (New York: Feminist Press, 2003), p. 240.

34. Antonia Fraser, "The Unsuitable Suitor in the Lake," *Spectator*, June 2003.

35. Patricia Schartle Myrer letter to the author, 17 Feb. 2003.

36. Dorothy B. Hughes letter to Joan Kahn, Dec. 1958 (CURB).

37. Don Swaim, *Book Notes*, Oct. 1987.

38. PH, *Plotting and Writing Suspense Fiction*, p. 75.

39. Pat added Ripley's name to a letter to Barbara Ker-Seymer and did the same in a book dedication to Charles Latimer.

40. Cahier 23, 5/3/54.

41. Ibid., 11/19/54.

42. Duhamel was the name of one of PH's French translators.

43. PH letter to KKS, 6 May 1970.

44. CWA Dan Walton Coates, 11 May 2002.

45. CWA Dan Walton Coates, 22 Nov. 2003.

46. PH, *Plotting and Writing Suspense Fiction*, pp. 23–24.

47. Cahier 23, 12/28/54.

48. Ibid., "New Year's Eve," 1954.

49. Cahier 26, 8/30/61.

50. Cahier 23, 12/6/55.

51. Ibid., 6/26/55.

52. Ibid., 7/3/54.

53. Diary 10, Jan. 6, 1951.

22. LES GIRLS: PART 6

1. PH, *Plotting and Writing Suspense Fiction*, pp. 20–21.
2. Cahier 24, 2/29/56.
3. Ibid., 1/28/56.
4. Ibid., 1/13/56.
5. "Books in Brief," *The New Yorker*, 14 Jan. 1956, p. 100.
6. "Criminals at Large," Anthony Boucher, *New York Times Book Review*, 25 Dec. 1955.
7. Cahier 24, 3/28/56.
8. Ibid., 4/13/56.
9. Ibid., 6/8/56.
10. Ibid., 6/17/56.
11. Ibid., 5/29/56.
12. PH letter to KKS, 23 Sept. 1956.
13. Ibid., 4 June 1956.
14. Cahier 24, 7/31/56.
15. Cahier 23, 6/4/55.
16. Cahier 24, 10/21/56.
17. Ibid., 11/23/56.
18. Ibid., 11/27/56.
19. PH letter to Joan Kahn, 14/9/59 (CURB).
20. Cahier 24, 3/7/57.
21. Ibid., 5/1/57.
22. Ibid., 5/22/57.
23. Ibid., 1/15/57.
24. Ibid., front cover.
25. PH letter to KKS, 24/9/53.
26. Cahier 24, 8/27/57.
27. Ibid., 9/30/57.
28. Ibid., 1/3/58 and 1/16/58.
29. Ibid., 1/3/58.
30. Cahier 23, 9/28/55.
31. Cahier 24, 5/19/57.
32. Ibid.

23. LES GIRLS: PART 7

1. Pat's and Marijane's agent, Patricia Schartle Myrer, described Marijane as "starstruck" by Pat in a letter to the author, 17 Feb. 2003.
2. Marijane Meaker interviewed by Terry Gross, *Fresh Air,* NPR, 12 July 2003.
3. CWA Marijane Meaker, 1 Feb. 2003.
4. Diary 11, July 27, 1951.
5. Liz Smith, *Natural Blonde* (New York: Hyperion, 2000), p. 258.
6. CWA Megan Terry, 29 Oct. 2006.
7. CWA Jean Rosenthal, 30 Oct. 2002.
8. CWA Megan Terry, 29 Oct. 2006.
9. Marijane Meaker, *Highsmith: A Romance of the 1950s*, p. 1.
10. Ibid., p. 2.
11. Cahier 25, 9/28/59.
12. CWA Marijane Meaker, 1 Feb. 2003.
13. Marion Meade, *Dorothy Parker: What Fresh Hell Is This?* (New York: Penguin, 1989), p. 266.
14. CWA Marijane Meaker, 1 Feb. 2003.
15. Ibid., 1 Feb. and 12 Nov. 2003.

16. Cahier 3, 7/7/40.

17. Ibid., 1/10/40.

18. MCH letter to Marijane Meaker, "Friday AM 11th" (Collection Marijane Meaker).

19. Ibid.

20. CWA Marijane Meaker, 1 Feb. 2003.

21. Cahier 26, 12/1/61.

22. Ibid., 3/23/61. "She denied having asked me, when I was replacing a hammer in the rack last night, 'Do you want to hit me, Pat?' I said of course not and hung up the hammer."

23. PH, *Plotting and Writing Suspense Fiction*, pp. 11–12.

24. Joan Kahn letter to Patricia Schartle, 21 Feb. 1961 (CURB).

25. Cahier 26, 3/3/61.

26. Ibid., 3/14/61.

27. Ibid., 3/22/61.

28. Ibid.

29. Meaker, *Highsmith*; a theme of the book.

30. Cahier 26, 3/22/61.

31. Meaker, *Highsmith*, pp. 20, 166. Meaker is quoting Polly Cameron on Pat's drinking.

32. Cahier 26, 3/22/61.

33. CWA Marijane Meaker, 1 Feb. 2003.

34. Cahier 27, 12/28/64.
> It was no doubt a tragedy that I saw
> "Forbidden" written like a word in red paint,
> "Stop," and could read it, when I was six,
> A tragedy that at sixteen and eighteen,
> Love still a new gift to me, ungiven because untaken,
> A tragedy that I would have given this best that I had,
> Better than precious stones I read about in books.
> It's perhaps a tragedy I had to swallow my precious stone
> At sixteen, watching careless boys and girls
> Walking hand in hand down public streets,
> As indifferent to what people thought of them
> As they were to their own sensations,
> walking the next day with someone else.
> MY envy turned to hatred
> And the hatred to contempt. . . .

35. Meaker, *Highsmith*, p. 179.

36. Diary 10, Nov. 24, 1950.

37. CWA Vivien De Bernardi, 15 Aug. 2002.

24. LES GIRLS: PART 8

1. CWA Phillip Lloyd Powell, 13 Feb. 2003.

2. Ibid.

3. CWA Nora Ellen Lewis, 14 Feb. 2006.

4. Diary 13, Sunday, 16 Sept. 1962.

5. CWA Marion Aboudaram, 23 Sept. 2002.

6. PH letter to KKS, 30 Mar. 1988.

7. PH letter to Lil Picard, 23 Jan. 1968 (UIL).

8. Diary 15, Jan. 23., 1968.

9. CWA Linda Ladurner, 10 May 2003.

10. PH letter to Lil Picard, 23 Jan. 1968 (UIL).

11. PH letter to KKS, 11 Feb. 1976.

12. CWA Frédérique Chambrelent, 19 May 2003.

13. Ibid.

14. Ibid.

15. Ibid.

16. Anthony Cronin, one of Samuel Beckett's biographers, writes of a boisterous, bibulous Desmond Ryan, on a night out with Samuel Beckett and Ralph Cusack in 1947, hurling ecclesiastical chair after ecclesiastical chair down the hundreds of steps which descend from the front of Paris's second-best-known church, Sacre Coeur.

17. CWA Janine Hérisson, 29 Oct. 2002.

18. Henri Robillot letter to the author, 29/10/02.

19. PH letter to MCH, 3 May 1968.

20. CWA Nora Ellen Lewis, 14 Feb. 2006.

21. CWA Larry Kramer, 14 June 2006.

22. Larry Kramer letter to PH, 10 Feb. 1971.

23. CWA Larry Kramer, 14 Feb. 2006.

24. Diary 15, Aug. 11, 1963.

25. Ibid., Jan. 31, 1964.

26. PH letter to Lil Picard, 11 June 1969 (UIL).

27. Ibid., 8 July 1969 (UIL).

28. Ibid.

29. Cahier 26, 3/4/61.

30. Ibid., 9/4/61.

31. Ibid., 6/16/61.

32. PH, *The Cry of the Owl* (New York: Atlantic Monthly Press, 1989), p. 27.

33. PH letter to KKS, 6 Feb. 1963.

34. Ibid.

35. Ibid., 3 May 1963.

36. Ibid., 4 June, 1964.

25. LES GIRLS: PART 9

1. Cahier 28, 12/15/64.

2. Ibid., 3/3/65.

3. Ibid., 4/23/65.

4. Ibid., 7/12/65.

5. Ibid., 8/5/65.

6. Ibid., 1/15/67.

7. Ibid., 4/12/65.

8. Ibid., 4/12/67.

9. Most of the character names in *Those Who Walk Away*, like most character names in other Highsmith fictions, are unconvincing as names: they sound like bad aliases. Whether they're the product of an imagination which spent quite a bit of time inventing for the comics, where similarly incredible proper names abound, or whether they are merely the result of Pat's tin ear for intonation, is impossible to determine. If we contrast, for example, the name Odile Masarati, the woman in the Highsmith short story "The Cruellest Month" who is proud to be physically scarred in her pursuit of a Graham Greene–like author, with any of the names on Vladimir Nabokov's pitch-perfect list of Lolita's little classmates in the novel *Lolita*, the difference between a fictional name that sounds real and one that sounds false becomes obvious. Pat did pluck one surname for *Those Who Walk Away* from her grandmother Willie Mae's family history: she made the unseen Mallorcan landlord of Ray and Peggy Garret a Deckkard.

10. PH, *Strangers on a Train,* (New York: W. W. Norton, 2001), p. 270.

11. CWA Janice Robertson, 22 June 2003.

12. Cahier 28, 1/15/67.

13. Cahier 26, 2/3/62.

14. Cahier 28, 7/11/65.

15. Ibid., 2/7/66.

16. Ibid., 3/30/66.
17. Ibid., 7/13/66.
18. Ibid., 7/7/66.
19. Ibid., 7/19/66.
20. Ibid., 7/19/66.
21. Ibid., 7/21/66.
22. PH, *The Tremor of Forgery*, p. 87.
23. Cahier 28, 1/27/67.
24. Ibid., 1/16/67.
25. Ibid.
26. Ibid.
27. Ibid., 1/2/67.
28. Cahier 29, 1/27/67.
29. Cahier 28, 3/28/67.

26. LES GIRLS: PART 10

1. PH letter to Alex Szogyi, 14 Nov. 1969.
2. Ibid.
3. CWA Barbara Roett, 18 May 2003.
4. Diary 10, Jan. 27, 1950.
5. Cahier 34, 4/9/78.
6. PH letter to Alex Szogyi, 24 Apr. 1978.
7. Cahier 35, 8/24/80.
8. CWA Phyllis Nagy, 26 June 2002.
9. Sally Vincent, "Wave from Afar," *Observer*, 27 Apr. 1980.
10. CWA Francis Wyndham, 20 Dec. 2003.
11. Francis Wyndham letter to PH, 4 Nov. 1984.
12. CWA Linda Ladurner, 10 May 2003.
13. CWA Tabea Blumenschein, 15 June 2003.
14. Diary 9, 27 Jan. 1949.
15. BKS letter to Barbara Roett, 8 June 1978 (TGA).
16. Meaker, *Highsmith*, pp. 189, 190.
17. Ibid., pp 183–98.
18. PH, unpublished "Impossible Interview" with Yitzhak Shamir, 1990.
19. CWA Christa Maerker, 21 July 2004.
20. CWA Phyllis Nagy, 26 June 2002.
21. Cahier 24, 9/30/57.
22. Cahier 25, 11/19/59.

27. LES GIRLS: PART 11

1. Cahier 36, 4/3/84.
2. Cahier 26, 12/22/61.
3. Cahier 4, 9/15/40.
4. CWA Susannah Clapp, 2 Jan. 2004.
5. Cahier 26, 8/25/62.
6. Cahier 27, 1/19/63.
7. Cahier 32, 6/17/73.
8. Ibid.
9. Cahier 9, 9/29/43.
10. Joyce Carol Oates, "Dark Laughter," *New York Review of Books*, 15 Nov. 2001; also in Oates, *Uncensored: Views & (Re)views* (New York: Ecco, 2005), p. 44.

Nothing That Meets the Eye, a second posthumous collection of Highsmith stories written between 1938 and 1989, is not a collection Highsmith herself would have approved. The stories appeared in such publications as *Ellery Queen's Mystery Magazine, Alfred Hitchcock's Mystery Magazine, Woman's Home Companion, Cosmopolitan, Today's Woman,* and *Home and Food.* In a letter to Kingsley Skattebol on 27 September 1994, four months before she died, Pat strongly objected to the publication of her early work: "What I am against—since you're my lit. exec.—is publishing inferior products of mine. . . . My point is, it's scraping the bottom of the barrel, just to make a few francs. . . . I decided today to refuse to publish (or work on) such a book, and so wrote to v. Planta."

11. PH letter to Alex Szogyi, 10–11 Mar. 1969.

12. CWA Daniel Keel, 12 Apr. 2003.

13. Ibid.

14. CWA KKS, 12 Sept. 2003.

15. CWA Marion Aboudaram, 21 Sept. 2002.

16. Descriptions of Pat's laughter come from Vivien De Bernardi, Charles Latimer, Joan Dupont.

17. Patricia Schartle Myrer letter to the author, 17 Feb. 2003.

18. PH letter to Alain Oulman, 18 Sept. 1982 (CLA).

19. CWA Jonathan Kent, 18 Nov. 2003.

20. Ibid.

21. Ibid.

22. CWA Peter and Anita Huber-Speck, 18 Apr. 2003.

23. PH letter to BKS, 11 Sept. 1973.

24. Cahier 23, 5/2/54.

25. Cahier 21, 11/30/51.

26. CWA Barbara Roett, 18 May 2003.

27. Ibid.

28. Ibid.

29. CWA Marion Aboudaram, 21 Sept. 2002.

30. Ibid., 23 Sept. 2002.

31. Ibid., 25 Sept. 2002.

32. Ibid., 23 Sept. 2002.

33. Ibid., 25 Sept. 2002.

34. Ibid., 23 Oct. 2002.

35. Francis Wyndham, "Miss Highsmith," *New Statesman,* 30 May 1963.

36. CWA Francis Wyndham, 20 Dec. 2003.

37. Ibid.

38. Cahier 13, 9/6/45.

39. CWA Peter Huber, 22 Apr. 2003.

40. Peter Handke, "Die Privaten Weltkriege der Patricia Highsmith," pp. 169–180.

41. CWA Barbara Roett, 18 May 2003.

42. PH letter to KKS, 26 Oct. 1953.

43. Cahier 15, 4/16/47.

28. LES GIRLS: PART 12

1. Cahier 32, 10/20/73.

2. Juliette Ryan letter to the author, 8 Nov. 2002.

3. PH, *Deep Water* (New York: W. W. Norton, 2003), p. 84.

4. CWA Juliette Ryan, 6 Nov. 2002.

5. Judith Freeman, *The Long Embrace: Raymond Chandler and the Woman He Loved* (New York: Pantheon Books, 2007).

6. PH, Introduction to *The World of Raymond Chandler,* edited by Miriam Gross (London: Weidenfeld and Nicolson, 1977).

7. Ibid., p. 5.

8. Ibid., p. 2.

9. Raymond Chandler letter to Carl Brandt, 11 Dec. 1950, *Selected Letters of Raymond Chandler*, edited by Frank MacShane (London: Jonathan Cape, 1981), p. 247.

10. PH, Introduction to *The World of Raymond Chandler*, p. 3.

11. Edward Burra letter to BKS, autumn 1971 (TGA).

12. CWA Noëlle Loriot, 5 July 2002.

13. All direct quotations, unless otherwise cited, come from Noëlle Loriot, "Trois Jours avec Patricia Highsmith," *L'Express*, 8 June 1979.

14. CWA Noëlle Loriot, 5 July 2002.

15. Ibid.

16. Ibid.

29. LES GIRLS: PART 13

1. PH letter to KKS, 14 Mar. 1968.

2. CWA Peter Huber, 18 Apr. 2003.

3. CWA DéDé Moser, 2 Aug. 2004.

4. A partial list of people close to Pat who fall into one of the several categories of not caring for Pat's work—or not reading it: Kingsley Skattebol, Ellen Hill, Caroline Besterman, Peter Huber and Anita Huber-Speck (with reservations), Vivien De Bernardi, Monique Buffet, Marion Aboudaram (with reservations), Tabea Blumenschein, and Barbara Ker-Seymer.

5. Barbara Skelton, "Patricia Highsmith at Home," *London Magazine*, Aug.–Sept. 1995.

6. CWA Vivien De Bernardi, 15 Aug. 2003.

7. Ibid.

8. Diary 17, Dec. 24, 1989.

9. Ibid., Nov. 15, 1991.

10. Ibid., May 23, 1992.

11. Mary Ford, "This Is Your Second Brain," *Sunday Telegraph,* 4 Sept. 2005.

12. CWA Vivien De Bernardi, 15 Aug. 2003.

13. CWA Bert Diener and Julia Diener-Diethelm, 1 Apr. 2003.

14. CWA KKS, 6 Jan. 2003.

15. PH letter to KKS, 14 June 1988.

16. CWA Marion Aboudaram, 24 Sept. 2002.

17. PH letter to KKS, 23 Mar. 1953.

18. PH letter to Mary McCarthy, 3 Oct. 1972 (VCL).

19. Mary Kling remembers "two or three lunches [with Pat]—and I knew if she wanted to be my client I couldn't refuse her, but . . . she wasn't conversable."

20. PH letter to Mary McCarthy, 9 Sept. 1983 (VCL).

21. Ibid., 16 May 1983 (VCL).

22. Ibid., 10 Oct. 1977 (VCL).

23. Mary McCarthy Archives (VCL).

24. CWA Marion Aboudaram, 23 Sept. 2002.

25. CWA Monique Buffet, 7 Apr. 2003.

26. MB letter to the author, 27 Sept. 2004.

27. CWA Barbara Roett, 18 May 2003.

28. PH letter to Ellen Hill, 10 July 1978.

29. PH, *The Boy Who Followed Ripley*, manuscript.

30. CWA Monique Buffet, 7 Apr. 2003.

31. CWA Tabea Blumenschein, 15 June 2003.

32. Diary 6, 11/14/44.

33. CWA Phyllis Nagy, 13 Oct. 2002.

34. PH letter to Monique Buffet, 13 Aug. 1978 (Collection Monique Buffet).

35. Ibid., 23 Aug. 1978 (Collection Monique Buffet).

36. Ibid., 27 Sept. 1978 (Collection Monique Buffet).
37. PH letter to MB, 19 Nov. 1978.
38. CWA Barbara Roett, 18 May 2003.
39. Meaker, *Highsmith*, p. 48.
40. PH letter to Mr. Reichardt, 4 Nov. 1970.
41. PH letter to KKS, 16 Mar. 1971.
42. Muriel Spark telegram to PH, 1968.
43. CWA Muriel Spark, 24 May 2005.
44. Muriel Spark, *A Far Cry from Kensington* (New York: New Directions, 1988), pp. 93–94.
45. Cahier 26, 7/3/60.
46. PH letter to MB, Sept. 13, 1978 (Collection Monique Buffet).
47. CWA Monique Buffet, 21 June 2003.
48. Ibid., 7 Apr. 2003.
49. PH letter to MB, 6 Sept. 1978 (Collection Monique Buffet).
50. PH letter to Alex Szogyi, 18 Feb. 1969.

30. LES GIRLS: PART 14

1. PH letter to MB, 24 Sept. 1992 (Collection Monique Buffet).
2. CWA Francis Wyndham, 20 Dec. 2003.
3. Meaker, *Highsmith,* p. 60.
4. Joan Juliet Buck, "A Terrifying Talent," *Observer Magazine,* 20 Nov. 1977.
5. Andrew Wilson, *Beautiful Shadow* (New York: Bloomsbury, 2003). p. 286.
6. Francis King, "Angry Old Woman," *Oldie,* 6 Jan. 2004.
7. CWA Caroline Besterman, 6 Nov. 2003.
8. CWA Christa Maerker, 21 July 2004.
9. CWA Alex Szogyi and Philip Thompson, 9 Dec. 2002.
10. CWA KKS, 19 Apr. 2005.
11. Cahier 3, 4/12/41.
12. CWA MB, 7 Apr. 2003.
13. CWA Bettina Berch, 10 Aug. 2003.
14. PH letter to Alex Szogyi, 31 Mar. 1969.
15. Ibid., 4 Nov. 1968.
16. Ibid., 23 Aug. 1970.
17. Cahier 36, 2/8/88.
18. CWA Monique Buffet, 5 Dec. 2003.
19. PH letter to KKS, 6 Feb. 1989.
20. Cahier 36, 18/5/88.
21. One of Pat's uncles, Mother Mary's brother, was named Claude, and he and Mary were coexecutors of Willie Mae Coates's estate, the disposition of which had left Pat feeling cheated. (She hadn't been cheated, but she didn't forget the incident, either.)
22. PH, "Two Disagreeable Pigeons," in *Nothing That Meets the Eye* (New York: W. W. Norton, 2002).
23. Cahier 19, 7/22/50.
24. Diary 10, Jan. 4, 1950.
25. PH letter to Ronald Blythe, 26 Nov. 1966 (Collection Ronald Blythe).

31. THE REAL ROMANCE OF OBJECTS: PART 1

1. PH, "The View from My Window," draft article dated 1980.
2. CWA Josyane Savigneau, 1 July 2002.
3. *Ripley Under Ground* (1970) features a cellar in which one man is murdered and another man mimics suicide. Of the enormous cellar in her house in Tegna, Pat wrote to her

architect: "The guests can go in the cellar." Nothing good happens underground in the Highsmith imagination.

4. Cahier 23, 5/6/55.

5. PH letter to KKS, 27 Oct. 1953.

6. CWA KKS, 12 June 2004.

7. Marijane Meaker letter to the author, 7 Nov. 2003.

8. Ibid. Mary responded to Meaker with a tsunami from Texas: five closely typed single-spaced pages setting out (1) Pat's terrible treatment of Mary on several continents; (2) a long list of the older women Mary held responsible for influencing/corrupting Pat; (3) Mary's own formerly glorified circumstances including her "Filipino house boy ("He was small, slight, attractive and graceful as a ballet dancer and made an effort to please me in every way"); and (4) a self-assessment: "I too am an extrovert and have never met a stranger." Mary—so much like her daughter—had no trouble in emptying the contents of her mind onto a page when she was exercised on a subject:

> First of all and I think you will agree—PAT IS SICK. Somewhere along the line she is insecure, unsure and completely swayed by women older than herself whom I have met and loathe[d] on sight—Rosalind [Constable], [Elizabeth] Lyne, [Lil] Picard and the like. . . . It's the last person Pat is with who has the influence. She is exactly like a chamelian [sic] changing colors and turning on a good friend as tho mesmerized. . . . Can you figure her out. . . . I think Pat is wearing a very uncomfortable hair-shirt of her own designing. . . . I can only wait—I still have faith in Pat, I brought her up and I know her background.

9. CWA Josyane Savigneau, 1 July 2002.

10. CWA Phyllis Nagy, 13 Oct. 2002.

11. Ibid.

12. PH letter to KKS, 31 May 1989.

13. Don Swaim, *Book Notes,* Oct. 1987.

14. Diary 1, July 7, 1941.

15. PH letter to Nini Wills, 9 Mar. 1972.

16. MCH letter to PH, 10 May 1972.

17. Cahier 36, 2/11/87.

18. PH letter to MCH, 9 April 1971.

19. Cahier 9, PH transcription from high school notebooks, July 1937.

20. PH letter to DOC, 26 Dec. 1968.

21. Alain Oulman letters to PH, 3 Dec. 1979 and 8 Feb. 1980. PH letters to Alain Oulman, 21 Aug. 1979 and 10 Feb. 1980 (CLA).

22. PH letter to Alex Szogyi, 23 Aug. 1970.

23. PH letter to BKS, 24–25 Oct. 1970.

24. CWA Claire Cauvin, 4 July 2002.

25. PH letter to BKS, 1 Mar. 1972.

26. PH letter to Alex Szogyi, 10 Sept. 1973.

27. CWA Vivien De Bernardi, 15 Aug. 2003.

28. CWA Marion Aboudaram, 23 Sept. 2002.

29. PH letter to MB, 2 July 1980.

30. Cahier 34, 12 Aug. 1978.

31. CWA Phyllis Nagy, 13 Oct. 2002.

32. PH letter to Florine Coates, 9 July 1994.

33. CWA Vivien De Bernardi, 15 Aug. 2003.

34. KKS letter to the author, 16 Jan. 2003.

35. PH, *The Traffic of Jacob's Ladder,* manuscript fragment.

36. Don Swaim, *Book Notes,* Oct. 1987.

37. PH letter to Bettina Berch, 17 May 1984.

38. PH letter to Abe Janssens, piano player at the Hotel Normandy in Deauville, France, 15 Oct. 1987.

39. Cahier 30, 11/9/69.
40. PH letter to Lil Picard, 11 June 1969 (UIL).
41. CWA Christa Maerker, 21 July 2004.
42. Cahier 21, 11/30/52.
43. PH letter to Ellen Blumenthal Hill, 30–31 Jan. 1982.
44. CWA Bettina Berch, 10 Aug. 2003.
45. PH letter to KKS, 7 May 1989.
46. PH letter to Bettina Berch, 13 Apr. 1984.
47. Donald Swaim, *Book Notes,* Oct. 1987.
48. CWA Bettina Berch, 10 Aug. 2003.
49. Ibid.
50. Ibid.
51. PH letter to Bettina Berch, 21 July 1984.
52. Bettina Berch, introduction to unpublished interview, "A Talk with Patricia Highsmith," 15 June 1984.
53. Bettina Berch, "A Talk with Patricia Highsmith," pp. 10, 17.
54. CWA Vince Fago, 28 Nov. 2001.
55. PH letter to Marijane Meaker, 18 Oct. 1988 (Collection Marijane Meaker).
56. CWA Josyane Savigneau, 1 July 2002.
57. Patricia Schartle Myrer letter to PH, 21 Aug. 1979.

32. THE REAL ROMANCE OF OBJECTS: PART 2

1. On 18 October 1973, Pat's literary agency in Paris, the William Bradley Agency, wrote her: "According to your final instructions, we have just asked Morgan Guaranty Trust Co. here to transfer to your account with S.R.M. Management, E. D. Sassoon, Nassau, Bahamas, the film monies received from Film Number one and Glan Productions for *The Tremor of Forgery.*"
2. PH letter to KKS, 25 Aug. 1969.
3. CWA Samuel Okoshken, 25 June 2003.
4. PH letter to Monique Buffet, 14 Jan. 1980 (Collection Monique Buffet).
5. Ibid., 9 Oct. 1979 (Collection MB).
6. Ibid., 14 Jan. 1980 (Collection MB).
7. CWA Samuel Okoshken, 25 June 2003.
8. PH letter to Monique Buffet, 14 Jan. 1980 (Collection Monique Buffet).
9. CWA Samuel Okoshken, 25 June 2003.
10. PH, *The Tremor of Forgery,* pp. 139–40.
11. PH letter to DOC, 9 Nov. 1969.
12. PH letter to KKS, 9 July 1973.
13. CWA Vivien De Bernardi, 15 Aug. 2003.
14. PH letter to BKS, 31 Mar. 1980.
15. PH letter to MB, 29 Mar. 1980 (Collection Monique Buffet).
16. Ibid.
17. PH letter to BKS, 19 June 1980.
18. Ibid., 31 March 1980.
19. CWA Samuel Okoshken, 25 Aug. 2003.
20. CWA MB, 7 Apr. 2003.
21. Paul Bowles letter to PH, 23 Feb. 1990.
22. PH letter to MB, 28–29 Mar. 1980 (Collection Monique Buffet).
23. PH, *Plotting and Writing Suspense Fiction* (New York: St. Martin's Griffin, 1990), p. 143.
24. Ibid.
25. PH, *Edith's Diary,* p. 296.
26. PH letter to MB, 28–29 Mar. 1980 (Collection Monique Buffet).
27. Ibid.

28. CWA Marion Aboudaram, 21 Sept. 2002. Also CWA Christa Maerker, 27 July 2008.
29. Cahier 31, 8/25/71.
30. Ibid.
31. CWA KKS, 20 Dec. 2002.
32. Cahier 31, 8/25/71.
33. PH letter to MB, 9–10 Apr. 1980 (Collection Monique Buffet).
34. Ibid.
35. CWA Marylin Scowden, 1 Sept. 2002.
36. Diary 16, Jan. 17, 1970.
37. PH letter to DOC, 9 Nov. 1969.
38. Rosalind Constable letter to PH, 15 Jan. 1968.
39. Cahier 30, 8/13/69.
40. Cahier 30, 7/29/68.
41. Rosalind Constable letter to PH, 3 Mar. 1968.
42. Ibid., 14 Nov. 1969.
43. CWA MB, 25 Aug. 2004.
44. PH letter to Bettina Berch, 4 Sept. 1985.
45. CWA Daniel Keel, 20 Mar. 2003.
46. CWA Alex Szogyi, 11 Dec. 2001.
47. CWA Robert Lumpkin, 1 Aug. 2004.
48. Andrew Wilson, *Beautiful Shadow* (London: Bloomsbury, 2003), p. 341.
49. Ibid., p. 388.
50. Cahier 35, 6/1/83.
51. PH letter to Bettina Berch, 14 Feb. 1986.
52. Barbara Skelton, "Patricia Highsmith at Home," *The London Magazine,* Aug.-Sept. 1995.
53. PH, *The Talented Mr. Ripley*, p. 49.
54. PH, *The Boy Who Followed Ripley*, pp. 63–64.
55. Ibid., p. 64.
56. Cahier 13, 8/12/45.

33. THE REAL ROMANCE OF OBJECTS: PART 3

1. CWA Phyllis Nagy, 26 June 2002.

34. THE CAKE THAT WAS SHAPED LIKE A COFFIN: PART I

1. *The Animal-Lovers Book of Beastly Murder, Little Tales of Misogyny, Slowly, Slowly in the Wind, Mermaids on the Golf Course, The Black House.*
2. CWA Otto Penzler, 23 Dec. 2002.
3. Ibid., 27 Dec. 2002.
4. Ibid.
5. David Streitfeld, "Highsmith's Final Twist," *Washington Post*, 8 Mar. 1988.
6. David Streitfeld, *Washington Post*, 29 Jan. 1989.
7. David Streitfeld letter to the author, 2 Jan. 2006.
8. CWA Otto Penzler, 27 Dec. 2002.
9. CWA Daniel Keel, 12 Apr. 2003.

35. THE CAKE THAT WAS SHAPED LIKE A COFFIN: PART 2

1. Diary, 17, 18 Sept. 1988.
2. PH letters to Tobias Amman, 1988–90.
3. Cahier 22, 3/1/52 (misdated in cahier; it's 1953).
4. Ibid.

5. Ibid.

6. Ibid.

7. Ibid.

8. PH letter to MB, 11 Oct. 1982 (Collection Monique Buffet).

9. CWA Wim Wenders, 20 Sept. 2006.

10. CWA Daniel Keel, 20 Mar. and 12 Apr. 2003. It could hardly have escaped Pat's attention that, with Daniel Keel, she added another Daniel to the long line of Daniels that had been her Coates family inheritance.

11. CWA Marianne Liggenstorfer-Fritsch, 20 Mar. 2003.

12. Ibid.

13. Ibid.

14. Ibid.

15. PH letter to Dr. Girsberger, 19 Dec. 1991.

16. PH letter to KKS, 20 Dec. 1987.

17. PH letter to MB, 2 Feb 1988 (Collection Monique Buffet).

18. Ibid.

19. PH letter to Barbara Skelton, quoted in Skelton, "Patricia Highsmith at Home."

20. PH letter to KKS, 25 Apr. 1992.

21. Liz Calder, "Patricia Highsmith," *Oldie*, Mar. 1995.

22. CWA Marylin Scowden, 1 Sept. 2002.

23. Ibid.

24. Ibid.

25. Cahier 35, 1/15/80.

26. CWA Daniel Keel, 20 Mar. 2003.

27. Ibid.

28. PH, "Winter in the Ticino," in *Ticking Along with the Swiss*, edited by Dianne Dicks (Basel: Bergli Books, 1988).

29. CWA David Streiff, 19 Sept. 2002.

30. PH, "Winter in the Ticino."

31. Ibid.

32. PH letter to KKS, 20 Mar. 1984.

33. PH, "Winter in the Ticino."

34. Cahier 37, 6/10/88.

35. Ibid., 12/5/89.

36. PH letter to KKS, 15 May 1978.

37. Ibid., 14 May 1983.

38. PH letter to Anne Uhde, 6 Mar. 1983.

39. PH letter to Patricia Losey, 16 Apr. 1984.

40. PH, "Winter in the Ticino."

41. CWA David Streiff, 30 July 2002.

42. Ibid.

43. Ibid.

44. Ibid.

45. Documentary film, David Streiff, outtakes, Switzerland, 1991.

46. Cahier 30, 12/12/68.

47. PH, *Strangers on a Train*, p. 251.

48. Ibid., pp. 180–81.

49. PH, *The Selected Stories of Patricia Highsmith* (New York: W. W. Norton, 2001), p. 410.

50. Ibid., p. 414.

51. Ibid., p. 416.

52. Cahier 34, 4/30/77.

53. Ibid., 7/25/77.

54. Ibid., 12/10/77.

55. Skelton, "Patricia Highsmith at Home."

36. THE CAKE THAT WAS SHAPED LIKE A COFFIN: PART 3

1. Cahier 36, 10/18/83.
2. Ibid., 3/24/84.
3. Ibid., 4/16/84.
4. Ibid., 4/7/83.
5. Ibid., 10/12/84.
6. CWA Muriel Spark, 24 May 2005.
7. Anita Brookner, "Found in the Street," *Spectator,* 19 Apr. 1986.
8. Alain Oulman letter to PH, 19 Aug. 1985 (CLA).
9. Terrence Rafferty, "Found in the Street," *The New Yorker,* 4 Jan. 1988.
10. Francis Wyndham, "Miss Highsmith," *New Statesman,* 31 May 1963.
11. Julian Symons, *Bloody Murder: From the Detective Story to the Crime Novel: A History* (London: Faber & Faber, 1972), p. 178.
12. Ibid.
13. PH letter to KKS, 8 Mar. 1988.
14. CWA Anne Morneweg, 22 Jan. 2004.
15. PH, *Tales of Natural and Unnatural Catastrophes* (London: Bloomsbury, 2005), p. 19.
16. CWA Phyllis Nagy, 13 Oct. 2002.
17. Cahier 37, 2/21/90 and 5/20/90.
18. CWA Jack Klaff, 14 Jan. 2004.
19. Cahier 35, 11/24/79.
20. Cahier 36, 4/15/87.
21. CWA Dan Walton Coates, 22 Nov. 2003, and Don Coates, 20 Apr. 2002.
22. PH, *Tales of Natural and Unnatural Catastrophes,* p. 139.
23. PH letter to KKS, 9 Sept. 1985.
24. MCH letter to PH, 31 Sept. 1974.
25. CWA Christa Maerker, 21 July 2004.
26. Jeva Cralick letter to Dan and Florine Coates, Christmas, 1978.
27. Ibid., 12 Mar. 1987.

37. THE CAKE THAT WAS SHAPED LIKE A COFFIN: PART 4

1. PH letter to Gore Vidal, 6 July 1979.
2. Paul Bowles letter to PH, 15 Dec. 1991.
3. PH letter to Gore Vidal, 29 Jan. 1988.
4. Cyril Connolly, "Koestler at Sixty," *Sunday Times,* 19 Sept. 1965.
5. Cahier 37, 8/19/88.
6. Ibid., 8/29/88.
7. CWA Edmund White, 19 Aug. 2006.
8. Edmund White, "Paul Bowles," in *Arts and Letters* (San Francisco: Cleis Press, 2004).
9. Cahier 35, 1/9/88.
10. Stéphanie Cudré-Mauroux, "Tom Ripley, collectionneur et psychopathe," *Studer, Bärlach, Ripley, Gunten & Co., Quarto,* revue des Archives littéraires suisses, 21–22, 2006.
11. Cahier 37, 12/5/89.
12. PH letters to KKS, 16 and 28 Oct. 1988.
13. CWA Peter Goedel, 16 June 2002. All subsequent quotations concerning Goedel's dealings with PH are from this 16 June interview, unless otherwise attributed.
14. CWA Richard Schroeder, 19 Jan. 2004.
15. PH letter to Patricia Losey, 7 Jan. 1989.
16. PH postcard to Peter Goedel, undated (Collection Peter Goedel).

38. THE CAKE THAT WAS SHAPED LIKE A COFFIN: PART 5

1. Cahier 36, 26/1/87.
2. Ibid., 29/1/87.
3. Ibid., 25/1/87.
4. Ibid., 20/8/87.
5. Ibid., 25/9/87.
6. Ibid., 4/3/84.
7. CWA Vivien De Bernardi, 15 Aug. 2002.
8. PH letter to KKS, 1 Sept. 1990.
9. Ibid., 25 Apr. 1990.
10. Ibid., 26 Aug. 1987.
11. Cahier 32, 1/26/70.
12. CWA Heather Chasen, 22 Sept. 2002.
13. CWA Alex Szogyi, 11 Dec. 2001.
14. Ibid.
15. PH letter to Alex Szogyi, 22 Mar. 1973.
16. Alex Szogyi letter to PH, 19 June 1978.
17. PH letter to Lil Picard, 23 Oct. 1974 (UIL).
18. PH letter to KKS, 1 Dec. 1986.
19. CWA Peter Huber, 18 Apr. 2003.
20. PH letter to KKS, 30 Dec. 1987.
21. CWA Peter Huber, 18 Apr. 2003.
22. PH letter to KKS, 27 May 1991.
23. Cahier 37, 30/6/91.
24. Cahier 37, 14/3/92.
25. PH letter to KKS, 24 Apr. 1990.
26. PH letter to Alex Szogyi, 22–23 Jan. 1972.
27. Marc Brandel letter to PH, 6 Jan. 1987.
28. Ibid., 17 Nov. 1979.
29. Cahier 36, 27/8/86.
30. Cahier 36, *Brompton Account,* April–July 1986. The entire history of Pat's lung operation is taken from two pages in Cahier 36, labelled *Brompton Account.*
31. *The Cry of the Owl, Edith's Diary, Found in the Street, A Game for the Living, Tales of Natural and Unnatural Catastrophes, Those Who Walk Away, The Tremor of Forgery, The Two Faces of January, Eleven.*
32. CWA Anne Elizabeth Suter, 8 July 2004.
33. CWA Gary Fisketjon, 10 Dec. 2002.
34. CWA Phyllis Nagy, 13 Oct. 2002.

THE CAKE THAT WAS SHAPED LIKE A COFFIN: PART 6

1. Rosalind Constable letter to PH, 21 Feb. 1983.
2. CWA Peter Huber, 18 Apr. 2003.
3. Betty Curry letter to PH, December 19, 1991. Also letters of 21 June 1974, 12 Dec. 1986, 21 May 1989, 18 Dec. 1991.
4. Ibid., 23 May 1993.
5. Gert Macy letter to PH, 22 Nov. 1974.
6. Lynn Roth letter to PH, 20 June 1985.
7. Natalia Danesi Murray letter to PH, 1 Dec. 1985.
8. Gina letters to PH, 24 July 1978–22 Sept. 1989.
9. Polly Cameron letter to PH, 23 Dec. 1990.
10. Betty Curry letter to PH, 5 Nov. 1977.
11. Daisy Winston letter to PH, 20 Apr. 1992.

12. Ibid., Friday, 22 Mar. (no year).
13. Ibid., 1 Nov. 1992.
14. Ibid., undated.
15. Ibid., 16 Jan. 1985.
16. Ibid., 28 Dec. 1991.
17. Buffie Johnson letter to PH, 11 Mar. 1986.
18. CWA Buffie Johnson, 1 Dec. 2001.
19. PH letter to KKS, 20 Oct. 1989.
20. Ibid., 28 Nov. 1989.
21. PH letter to Alain Oulman, 27 Nov. 1989.
22. Ellen Hill letter to Lil Picard, 2 Jan. 1978 (UIL).
23. PH letter to Lil Picard, 28 Dec. 1975 (UIL).
24. Cahier 34, 9/23/76.
25. Ibid.
26. Rosalind Constable letter to PH, 7 Apr. 1968.
27. Ibid., 16 Sept. 1968.
28. Ibid., 3 Sept. 1968.
29. Ibid., 28 Sept. 1973.
30. Cahier 37, 31/12/92.
31. Rosalind Constable letter to PH, 3 May 1982.
32. Ibid., 9 Apr. 1989.
33. Ibid., 17 Nov. 1992.

THE CAKE THAT WAS SHAPED LIKE A COFFIN: PART 7

1. Skelton, "Patricia Highsmith at Home."
2. Peter Ruedi, "For Patricia Highsmith, Tegna 11 March, 1995."
3. CWA Tanja Howarth, 22 Oct. 2002.
4. Ibid.
5. CWA Vivien De Bernardi, 15 Aug. 2003.
6. CWA Gary Fisketon, 10 Dec. 2002.
7. PH letter to Gary Fisketjon, 26 July 1994 (GFF).
8. CWA Peter Huber, 18 Apr. 2003.
9. CWA KKS, 21 Apr. 2002.
10. Ibid., 7 Oct. 2007.
11. CWA Tanja Howarth, 22 Oct. 2002.
12. Cahier 26, 7/12/62.
13. CWA Tanja Howarth, 22 Oct. 2002.
14. CWA Bert Diener, 18 Apr. 2003.
15. Ibid.
16. CWA Myra Sklarew, 1 Mar. 2004.
17. CWA Mike Sundell, 4 Mar. 2004.
18. CWA Liz Calder, 9 May 2003.
19. Cahier 37, 8/2/92.
20. CWA Heather Chasen, 19 Oct. 2002.
21. Cahier 37, 2/8/92.
22. Cahier 37, 10/10–13/92.
23. Lucretia Stewart, "Animal Lover's Beastly Murders," *Sunday Telegraph,* 8 Sept. 1991.
24. Ibid.
25. Cahier 37, 10/10–13/92.
26. CWA Bob Lemstron-Sheedy, 25 July 2003.
27. Ibid.
28. Ibid.
29. Ibid.

30. Ibid.
31. CWA Donald Rice, 25 Feb. 2004.
32. CWA DéDé Moser, 2 Aug. 2004.
33. CWA Donald Rice, 25 Feb. 2004.
34. Ibid.
35. Mike Sundell letter to the author, 29 Nov. 2007.
36. Ibid.
37. CWA Mike Sundell, 4 Mar. 2004.
38. PH letter to Dr. Stewart Clarke, 18 July 1993.
39. Skelton, "Patricia Highsmith at Home."
40. PH letter to Bettina Berch, 19 Mar. 1994; PH letter to Florine Coates, 9 July 1994.
41. PH letter to Bettina Berch, 19 Mar. 1994.
42. CWA Bruno Sager, 7 June 2003.
43. Ibid.
44. Ibid.
45. Ibid.
46. CWA Anna Keel, 20 Mar. 2003.
47. CWA Bruno Sager, 7 June 2003.
48. PH letter to Jean-Étienne Cohen-Séat, 27 Oct. 1994 (CLA).
49. CWA Patrice Hoffman, 26 Aug. 2004.
50. Ibid.

41. THE CAKE THAT WAS SHAPED LIKE A COFFIN: PART 8

1. CWA Mike Sundell, 4 Mar. 2004.
2. Ibid.
3. CWA Don Rice, 25 Feb. 2004.
4. CWA Daniel Keel and Anna Keel, 20 Mar. 2003.
5. CWA Marylin Scowden, 1 Sept. 2002.
6. CWA Bert Diener and Julia Diener-Diethelm, 18 Apr. 2003.
7. CWA Anne Morneweg, 22 Jan. 2004.
8. CWA Marylin Scowden, 1 Sept. 2002.
9. Cahier 35, 5/9/80.

SOURCES FOR *THE TALENTED MISS HIGHSMITH*

PRIMARY SOURCES

A complete bibliography of Patricia Highsmith's work is beyond the scope of this book. The Web site for the Patricia Highsmith Papers at the Swiss Literary Archives in Bern, Switzerland (http://ead.nb.admin.ch/html/highsmith.html), will give interested readers an idea of her ferocious industry. In Bern, I consulted more than two hundred "unknown" Highsmith manuscripts (dozens of which had been published in different versions in *Ellery Queen's Mystery Magazine*), looked hard at her photograph albums and her sketchbooks, and read straight through her thirty-eight cahiers (1937–94), her eighteen diaries (1940–94), her fourteen scrapbooks, her business notebooks, and the many manuscripts of her published works.

The following works—the current Highsmith canon—are amongst the primary sources for this biography. They are listed here along with the details of their first publication in the United States. I have used various editions of Highsmith's works in writing this biography; all of them are cited in the endnotes.

NOVELS

Strangers on a Train (New York: Harper & Brothers, 1950)
The Price of Salt (as Claire Morgan; New York: Coward-McCann, 1952)
The Blunderer (New York: Coward-McCann, 1954)
The Talented Mr. Ripley (New York: Coward-McCann, 1955)
Deep Water (New York: Harper & Brothers, 1957)
A Game for the Living (New York: Harper & Brothers, 1958)
This Sweet Sickness (New York: Harper & Brothers, 1960)
The Cry of the Owl (New York: Harper & Row, 1962)
The Two Faces of January (New York: Doubleday, 1964)
The Glass Cell (New York: Doubleday, 1964)
The Story-Teller (UK title: *A Suspension of Mercy*; New York: Doubleday, 1965)
Those Who Walk Away (New York: Doubleday, 1967)
The Tremor of Forgery (New York: Doubleday, 1969)
Ripley Under Ground (New York: Doubleday, 1970)
A Dog's Ransom (New York: Knopf, 1972)
Ripley's Game (New York: Knopf, 1974)
Edith's Diary (New York: Simon & Schuster, 1977)
The Boy Who Followed Ripley (New York: Lippincott & Crowell, 1980)
People Who Knock on the Door (New York: Otto Penzler Books, 1985)
Found in the Street (New York: Atlantic Monthly Press, 1987)

Ripley Under Water (New York: Knopf, 1992)
Small g: A Summer Idyll (New York: W. W. Norton, 2004)

SHORT STORY COLLECTIONS

The Snail-Watcher and Other Stories (UK title: *Eleven*; New York: Doubleday, 1970)
The Animal-Lover's Book of Beastly Murder (New York: Otto Penzler Books, 1986)
Little Tales of Misogyny (New York: Otto Penzler Books, 1986)
Slowly, Slowly in the Wind (New York: Otto Penzler Books, 1979)
The Black House (New York: Otto Penzler Books, 1988)
Mermaids on the Golf Course (New York: Otto Penzler Books, 1988)
Tales of Natural and Unnatural Catastrophes (New York: Atlantic Monthly Press, 1987)
The Selected Stories of Patricia Highsmith (New York: W. W. Norton, 2001)
Nothing That Meets the Eye: The Uncollected Stories of Patricia Highsmith (New York: W. W. Norton, 2002)

NON-FICTION

Plotting and Writing Suspense Fiction (Boston: The Writer, Inc., 1966)

CHILDREN'S LITERATURE

Miranda the Panda Is on the Veranda (Doris Sanders, illustrations by PH; New York: Coward-McCann, 1958)

SECONDARY SOURCES

All journals, magazines, articles, published and unpublished interviews (by and about Highsmith), comic books, and Web sites are cited in the endnotes.

SELECTED BIBLIOGRAPHY

All books are dated according to the edition used, not the date of first publication.

Baldwin, Neil. *Henry Ford and the Jews: The Mass Production of Hate*. New York: Public Affairs, 2003.

Bardin, John Franklin. *The John Franklin Bardin Omnibus*. Introduction by Julian Symons. London: Penguin, 1976.

Barnes, Djuna. *Nightwood*. New York: New Directions, 1961.

Bedford, Sybille. *A Visit to Don Otavio*. New York: Counterpoint, 2003.

Benjamin, Walter. *Illuminations*. Edited by Hannah Arendt. New York: Schocken, 1969.

Blake, Nicholas. *A Pen Knife in My Heart*. London: Perennial Library, 1980.

Bloom, Harold, ed. *Lesbian and Bisexual Fiction Writers*. Philadelphia: Chelsea House, 1997.

Brandel, Marc. *The Choice*. New York: Dial Press, 1950.

Broyard, Anatole. *Kafka Was the Rage: A Greenwich Village Memoir*. New York: Vintage, 1997.

Chabon, Michael. *The Amazing Adventures of Kavalier & Klay*. New York: Picador, 2000.

Clarke, Gerald. *Capote: A Biography*. New York: Simon & Schuster, 1988.

Connolly, Cyril. *Enemies of Promise*. London: André Deutsch, 1988.

Dillon, Millicent. *A Little Original Sin: The Life & Work of Jane Bowles*. New York: Holt, Rinehart & Winston, 1981.

Dostoyevsky, Fyodor. *Crime and Punishment*. London: Vintage, 1993.

———. *Notes from Underground*. London: Vintage Books, 1993.

Eisner, Will. *The Plot: The Secret Story of the Protocols of the Elders of Zion*. New York: W. W. Norton, 2005.

Flanner, Janet. *Darlinghissima: Letters to a Friend*. Edited by Natalia Danesi Murray. New York: Random House, 1985.

——. *Paris Was Yesterday*. New York: Penguin, 1979.

Foster, Jeanette Howard. *Sex Variant Women in Literature*. Baltimore: Diana Press, 1975.

Freeman, Judith. *The Long Embrace: Raymond Chandler and the Woman He Loved*. New York: Pantheon, 2007.

Garber, Margery. *Vested Interests: Cross-Dressing & Cultural Anxiety*. New York: Routledge, 1992.

Gide, André. *The Counterfeiters*. London: Vintage, 1973.

Ginzburg, Natalia. *A Place to Live*. New York: Seven Stories Press, 2002.

Greene, Graham. *The Quiet American*. London: William Heinemann, 1955.

——. *The Power and the Glory*. London: Penguin, 1962.

——. *The Third Man and The Fallen Idol*. London: Vintage, 2001.

Guggenheim, Peggy. *Out of This Century: Confessions of an Art Addict*. New York: Universe, 1987.

Harrison, Russell. *Patricia Highsmith* (United States Authors Series). New York: Twayne, 1997.

Hughes, Dorothy B. *In a Lonely Place*. New York: Feminist Press, 2003.

James, Henry. *The Ambassadors*. London: Penguin, 1986.

James, M. R. *Collected Ghost Stories*. Hertfordshire, UK: Wordsworth Ed. Ltd., 1992.

Jamison, Kay Redfield. *Touched with Fire: Manic-Depressive Illness and the Artistic Temperament*. New York: Free Press, 1993.

Jones, Gerard. *Men of Tomorrow: Geeks, Gangsters, and the Birth of the Comic Book*. New York, Basic, 2004.

Kafka, Franz. *The Penal Colony*. New York: Schocken, 1972.

Katz, Jonathan Ned. *The Invention of Heterosexuality*. New York: Dutton, 1995.

Kazin, Alfred. *Alfred Kazin's America*. Edited by Ted Solatoroff. New York: HarperCollins, 2003.

Keogh, Theodora. *Meg*. New York: Signet, 1951.

Koestler, Arthur. *Darkness at Noon*. London: Vintage, 1994.

Lee, Hermione. *Virginia Woolf*. New York: Vintage, 1999.

Legman, Gershon. *Love & Death*. New York: Hacker Art Books, 1963.

Lerman, Leo. *The Grand Surprise: The Journals of Leo Lerman*. Edited by Stephen Pascal. New York: Knopf, 2007.

Maclaren-Ross, Julian. *Memoirs of the Forties*. (Harmondsworth, UK: Penguin, 1984.

Meade, Marion. *Dorothy Parker: What Fresh Hell Is This?* New York: Penguin, 1989.

Meaker, Marijane. *Highsmith: A Romance of the 1950s.* San Francisco: Cleis Press, 2003.

Menninger, Karl. *The Human Mind.* Garden City, NY: Garden City Publishing, 1930.

Milford, Nancy. *Zelda.* New York: Harper & Row, 1970.

Mitchell, Margaretta K. *Ruth Bernhard: Between Art & Life.* San Francisco: Chronicle Books, 2000.

Mitford, Nancy. *The Letters of Nancy Mitford & Evelyn Waugh.* Edited by Charlotte Mosley. London: Sceptre, 1997.

———. *Love from Nancy: The Letters of Nancy Mitford.* Edited by Charlotte Mosley. London: Sceptre, 1993.

Nabokov, Vladimir. *Lolita.* New York: Vintage, 1997.

Oates, Joyce Carol. *Uncensored: Views & Reviews.* New York: Ecco, 2005.

Osbourne, Lawrence. *The Poisoned Embrace: A Brief History of Sexual Pessimism.* New York: Vintage, 1994.

Packer, Vin [Marijane Meaker]. *Intimate Victims.* New York: Manor Books, 1963.

Phillips, Adam. *Houdini's Box: The Art of Escape.* New York: Vintage, 2001.

Plimpton, George. *Truman Capote: In Which Various Friends, Enemies, Acquaintances, and Detractors Recall His Turbulent Career.* New York: Nan A. Talese, 1997.

Poe, Edgar Allan. *Complete Stories and Poems.* New York: Doubleday, 1966.

Powell, Dawn. *The Locusts Have No King.* South Royalton, VT: Steerforth Press, 1999.

Proust, Marcel. *The Captive & The Fugitive.* Vol. 5, *In Search of Lost Time.* New York: Modern Library, 2003.

Robb, Graham. *Strangers: Homosexual Love in the Nineteenth Century.* New York: W. W. Norton, 2003.

Sanders, Marion K. *Dorothy Thompson: A Legend in Her Time.* Boston: Houghton Mifflin, 1973.

Sanxay Holding, Elisabeth. *The Blank Wall.* New York: Pocket Books, 1950.

———. *The Innocent Mrs. Duff.* New York: Dell, 1946.

Schenkar, Joan. *Truly Wilde.* London: Virago, 2000.

Shand-Tucci, Douglass. *The Crimson Letter.* New York: St. Martin's Press, 2003.

Smith, Jane S. *Elsie de Wolfe.* New York: Atheneum, 1982.

Solanas, Valerie. *SCUM Manifesto.* New York: Olympia Press, 1970.

Spark, Muriel. *A Far Cry from Kensington.* New York: New Directions, 1988.

Steranko, James. *Steranko History of Comics.* Reading, PA: Supergraphics, 1972.

———. *Steranko History of Comics 2*. Reading, PA: Supergraphics, 1972.

Symons, A. J. A. *The Quest for Corvo: An Experiment in Biography*. (New York: NYRB, 2001.

Teachout, Terry. *The Skeptic: A Life of H. L. Mencken*. New York: HarperCollins, 2002.

Thurman, Judith. *Secrets of the Flesh*. New York: Knopf, 1999.

Torres, Tereska. *Women's Barracks*. New York: Feminist Press, 2005.

Vidal, Gore. *Palimpsest*. London: Penguin, 1995.

———. *United States (Essays 1952-1992)*. London: Abacus, 1993.

Walter, Eugene. *Milking the Moon: A Southerner's Story of Life on This Planet*. As told to Katherine Clark. New York: Three Rivers Press, 2001.

Wertham, Frederic. *Seduction of the Innocent*. New York: Rinehart, 1954.

———. *A Sign for Cain*. London: Robert Hale, 1966.

Wescott, Glenway. *The Pilgrim Hawk*. New York: NYRB, 2001.

Wilde, Oscar. *The Complete Oscar Wilde*. London: Collins, 1990.

Wilson, Andrew. *Beautiful Shadow: A Life of Patricia Highsmith*. London: Bloomsbury, 2003.

Wineapple, Brenda. *Genêt: A Biography of Janet Flanner*. New York: Ticknor & Fields, 1989.

Wingfield, Marshall. *General A. P. Stewart, His Life and Letters*. Memphis, TN: West Tennessee Historical Society, 1954.

Wolff, Charlotte, M.D., *Love Between Women*. New York: St. Martin's Press, 1971.

Woolf, Virginia. *A Room of One's Own*. London: Harvest Book, 1989.

Yronwode, Catherine, and Trina Robbins. *Women and the Comics*. Forestville, CA: Eclipse Books, 1985.

INDEX

Note: PH stands for Patricia Highsmith. Names of characters are uninverted, e.g., Tom Ripley (character) is filed under "T". Foreign articles such as "La" and "Der" are not inverted.